The Three Escapes of
HANNAH ARENDT

The Three Escapes of
HANNAH ARENDT

A Tyranny of Truth

Ken Krimstein

BLOOMSBURY PUBLISHING

NEW YORK . LONDON . OXFORD . NEW DELHI . SYDNEY

BLOOMSBURY PUBLISHING
Bloomsbury Publishing Inc.
1385 Broadway, New York, NY 10018, USA

BLOOMSBURY, BLOOMSBURY PUBLISHING, and the Diana logo
are trademarks of Bloomsbury Publishing Plc

First published in the United States 2018

ISBN: - HB: 978-1-63557-188-2; eBook: 978-1-63557-190-5

Library of Congress Cataloging-in-Publication Data is available

2 4 6 8 10 9 7 5 3 1

Printed and bound in China by RR Donnelley Asia Printing Solutions Limited

To find out more about our authors and books visit
www.bloomsbury.com and sign up for our newsletters.

Bloomsbury books may be purchased for business or promotional use. For
information on bulk purchases please contact Macmillan Corporate and
Premium Sales Department at specialmarkets@macmillan.com.

For my father, Jordan "Jordie" Krimstein

AUTHOR'S NOTE

AS FAR AS I CAN TELL, THE
DATES AND PLACES IN THESE
PAGES CONFORM TO WHAT THE
CHARACTERS WERE DOING AT
THE TIMES I DESCRIBE.

"Don't follow leaders,
  Watch the parking meters"

Bob Dylan
"Subterranean Homesick Blues"

ALL TOO HUMAN:

INTRODUCTION TO A LIFE

TOO SOON. TOO ANGRY.
TOO SMART. TOO STUPID.
TOO HONEST. TOO SNOBBISH.
TOO JEWISH. NOT JEWISH ENOUGH.
TOO LOVING, TOO HATEFUL,
TOO MANLIKE, NOT MANLIKE ENOUGH.

WHAT FOLLOWS IS A STORY
OF A LIFE OF A PERSON CALLED
HANNAH ARENDT. BORN INTO
A LOST WORLD IN A LOST COUNTRY
IN ANOTHER ERA,
A REFUGEE PHILOSOPHER THINKER
WHOSE NAME MAY SOUND FAMILIAR.

IN THE END (AND IN THE BEGINNING)
REMAINS THE QUESTION:
WHY DID THIS PERSON, ARGUABLY
THE GREATEST PHILOSOPHER
OF THE TWENTIETH CENTURY,
RENOUNCE PHILOSOPHY?
AND, DESPITE THAT,
DOES HER THINKING OFFER
A VIABLE WAY FOR HUMANITY
TO MOVE FORWARD?

The Sorrows of Young Hannah

East Prussia

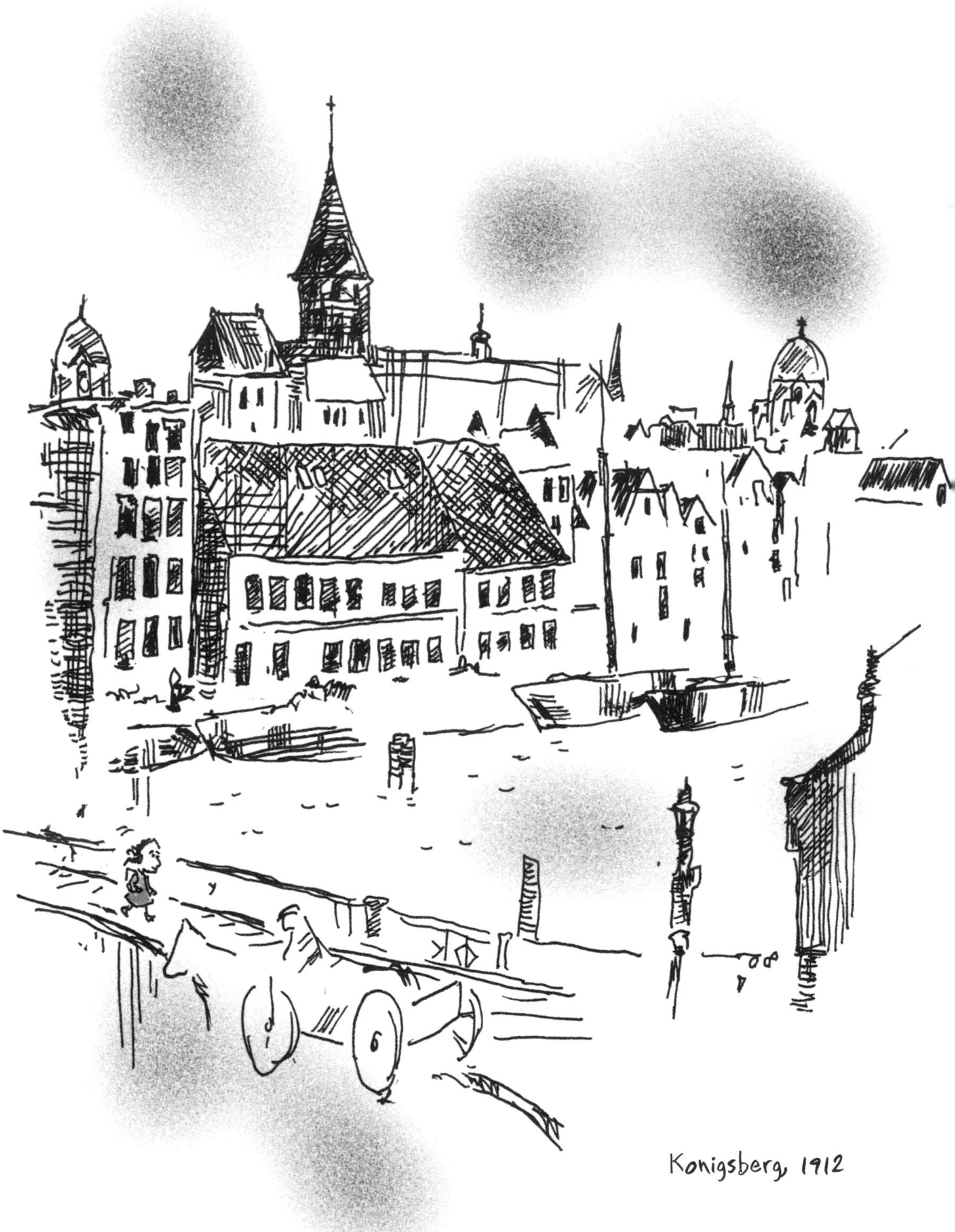

Konigsberg, 1912

THE WHOLE WIDE WORLD: MOMMA, POPPA, GRANDPA, MUSIC, BIRDS, PLAYS, PICTURES, TOYS, COOKIES, COLOR, LIGHT, SOUND, TOUCH, AND BEST OF ALL, DELICIOUS, DELICIOUS STORIES I COULD EAT TILL THEIR JUICE RAN DOWN MY CHEEKS! IF I LOOKED AT SOMETHING, AND I LOVED IT, I COULD FIGURE IT OUT. AND IF I COULDN'T TOTALLY FIGURE IT OUT, THE MORE I FELT IT AND ITS WON ESS AS IT UNFOLDED, IT BECAME EVEN MORE W KE, FOR INSTANCE, THE FIRST TIME M MOZART, IT WAS PRETTY. THEN, THE M THE WALLS IN HIS MUSIC KIND OF RE CONNECTED ONTO EACH OTHER, WAL PERFECTLY ON A BEAUTIFUL WINDOW HOT A RAINBOW TO ANOTHER WALL, A M ANCING GLOW. "AGAIN! AGAIN!," I'D SHOUT, AN IKE MAGIC, MOMMA WOULD REVIVE MOZART. BUT POOR POPPA...HE'S COMING BACK AGAIN FROM THE CLINIC TOMORROW. WHEN HE'S THERE, SOMETIMES HE'S IN THE BRIGHT WHITE ROOM WITH THE ORANGE FLOWERS, BUT SOMETIMES HE'S IN THE DARK GRAY ROOM IN THE OILY CANVAS JACKET WITH CHAINS ON IT, SWEATING. WHY? HOW? WHAT? I KNOW THAT THE ANSWER HAS TO BE SOMEWHERE OUT THERE IN THE WONDERFUL WIDE WORLD. I KNOW IT.

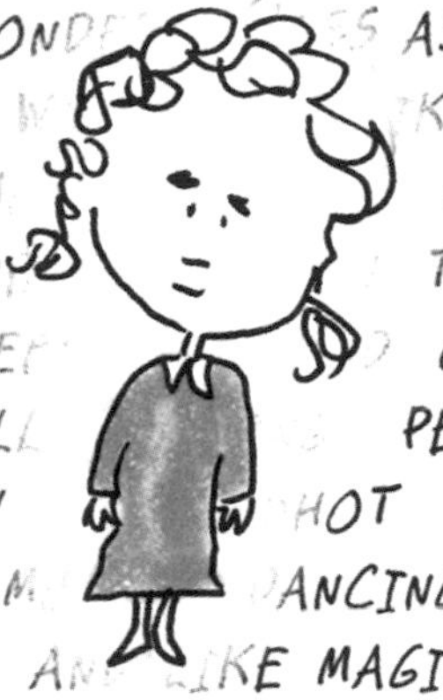

I'M FIVE YEARS OLD. THE STREETS ARE FOUR HUNDRED. I'M SKIPPING HOME FROM SCHOOL AND I'M HAPPY.

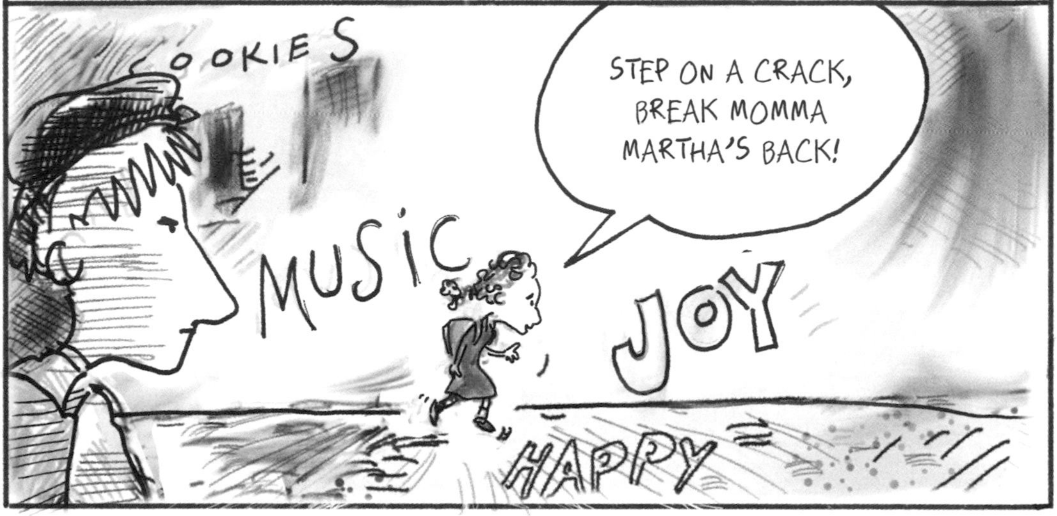
COOKIES
STEP ON A CRACK, BREAK MOMMA MARTHA'S BACK!
MUSIC
JOY
HAPPY

EXCEPT WHEN ONE OF THOSE NEW "AUTOMOBILE MACHINES" STARTS HONKING AT ME.

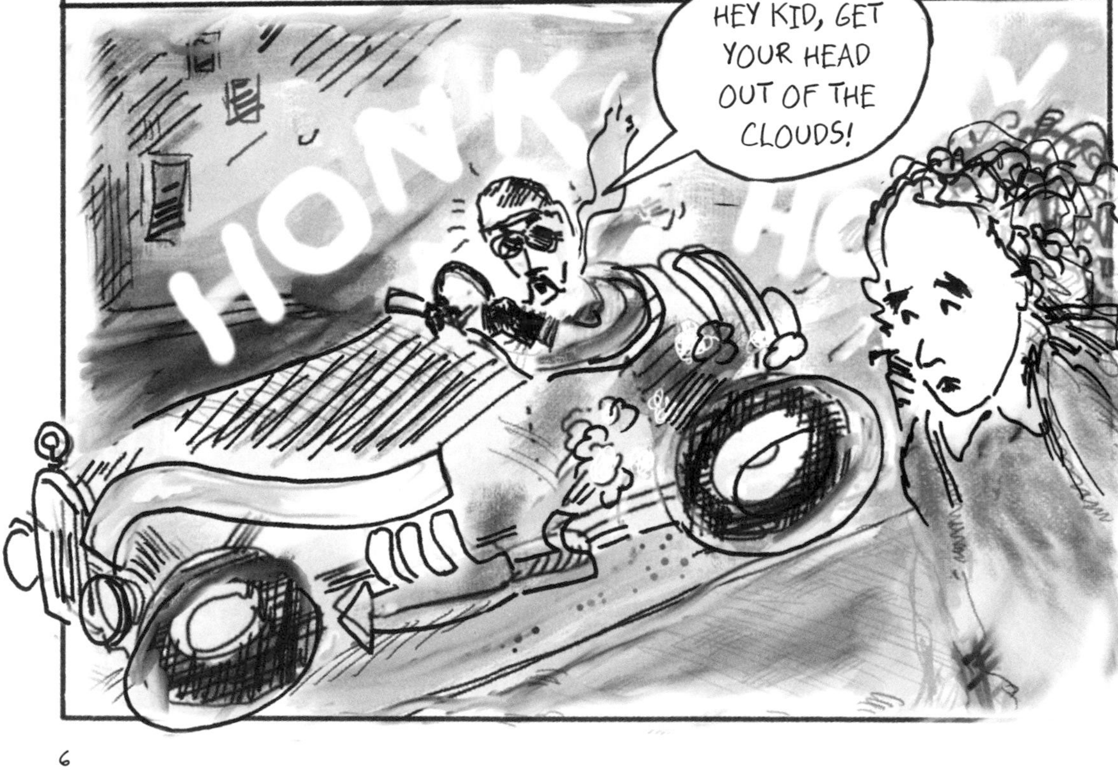
HEY KID, GET YOUR HEAD OUT OF THE CLOUDS!
HONK

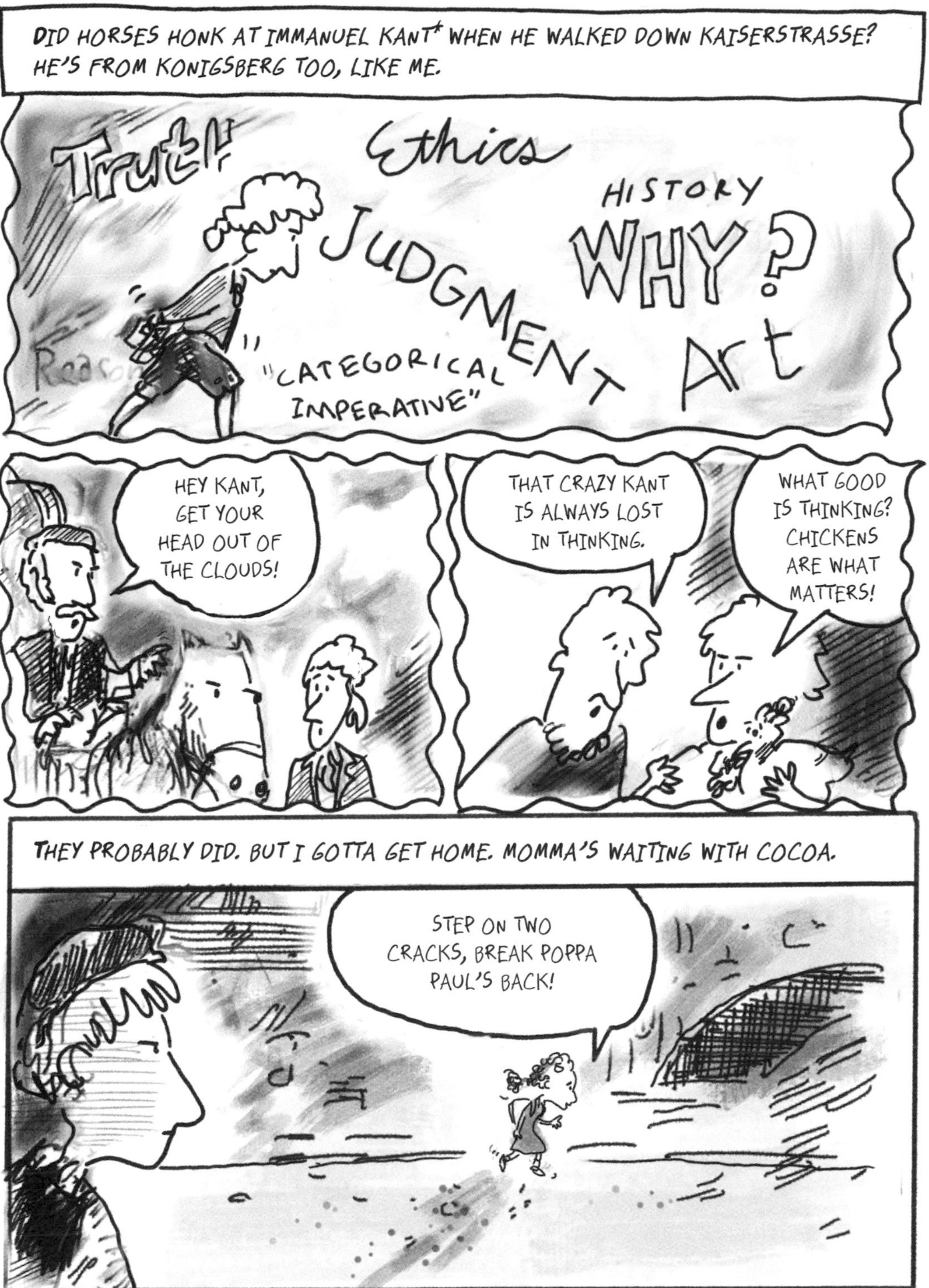
DID HORSES HONK AT IMMANUEL KANT* WHEN HE WALKED DOWN KAISERSTRASSE? HE'S FROM KONIGSBERG TOO, LIKE ME.
Truth!
Ethics
HISTORY
JUDGMENT
WHY?
Art
"CATEGORICAL IMPERATIVE"
HEY KANT, GET YOUR HEAD OUT OF THE CLOUDS!
THAT CRAZY KANT IS ALWAYS LOST IN THINKING.
WHAT GOOD IS THINKING? CHICKENS ARE WHAT MATTERS!
THEY PROBABLY DID. BUT I GOTTA GET HOME. MOMMA'S WAITING WITH COCOA.
STEP ON TWO CRACKS, BREAK POPPA PAUL'S BACK!

* Immanuel Kant (1724–1804). German philosopher from Konigsberg who pretty much wrote the book on modern philosophy. He put the human mind at the center of all experience.

I'M INTERRUPTED BY HANS, FROM SCHOOL. BUT HE'S BEING WEIRD.

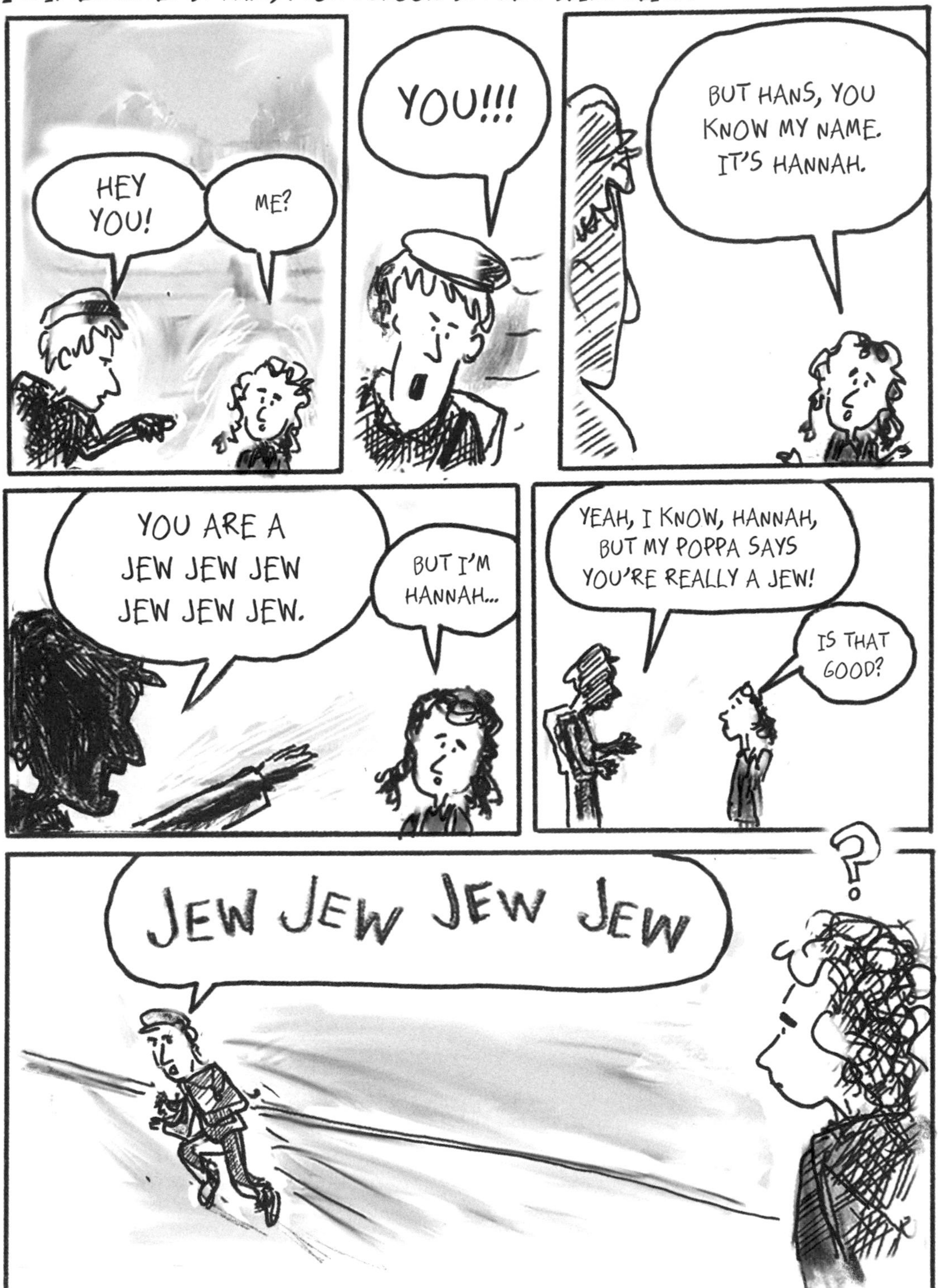
HEY YOU!
ME?
YOU!!!
BUT HANS, YOU KNOW MY NAME. IT'S HANNAH.
YOU ARE A JEW JEW JEW JEW JEW JEW.
BUT I'M HANNAH...
YEAH, I KNOW, HANNAH, BUT MY POPPA SAYS YOU'RE REALLY A JEW!
IS THAT GOOD?
JEW JEW JEW JEW
?

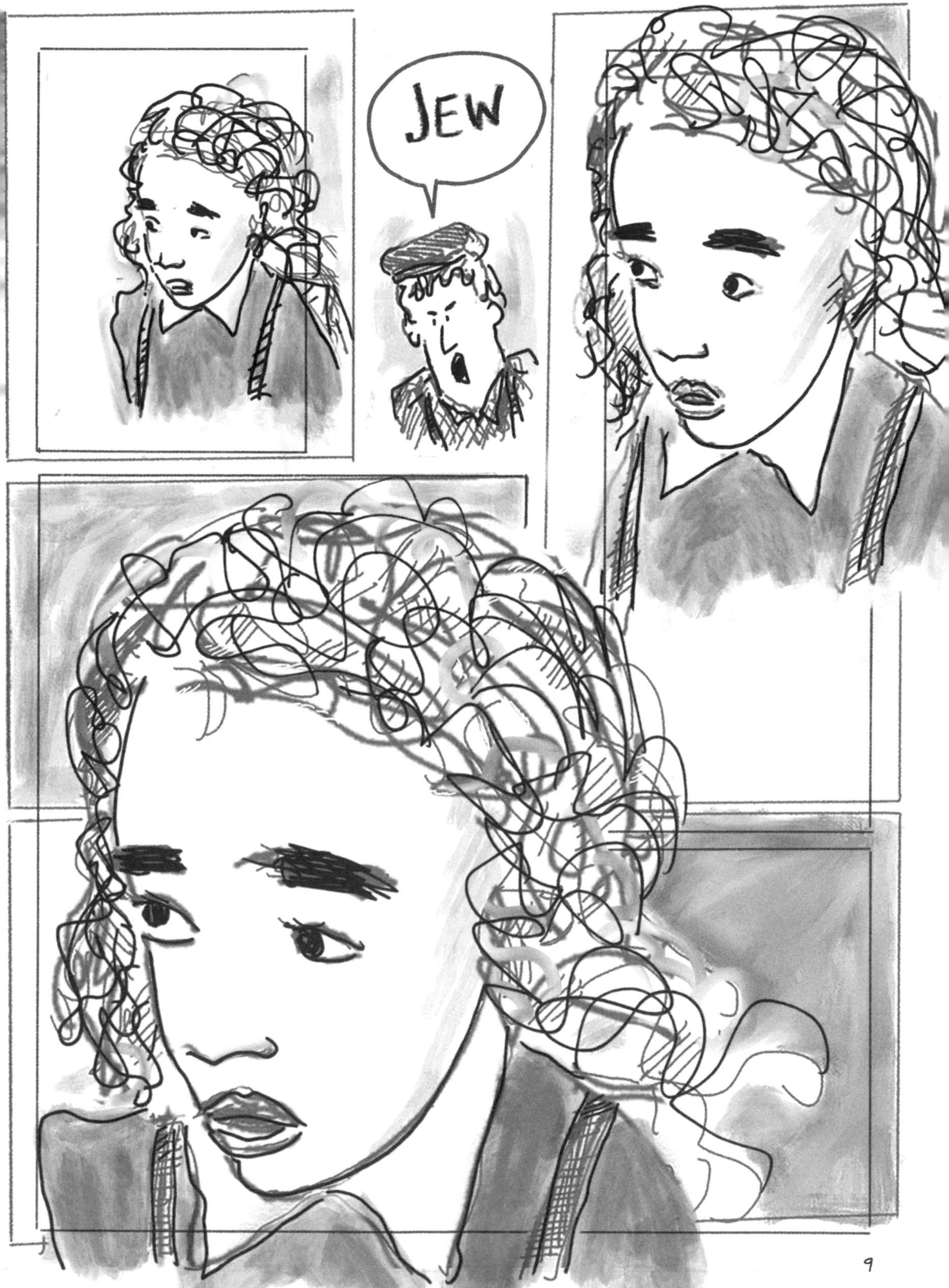
JEW

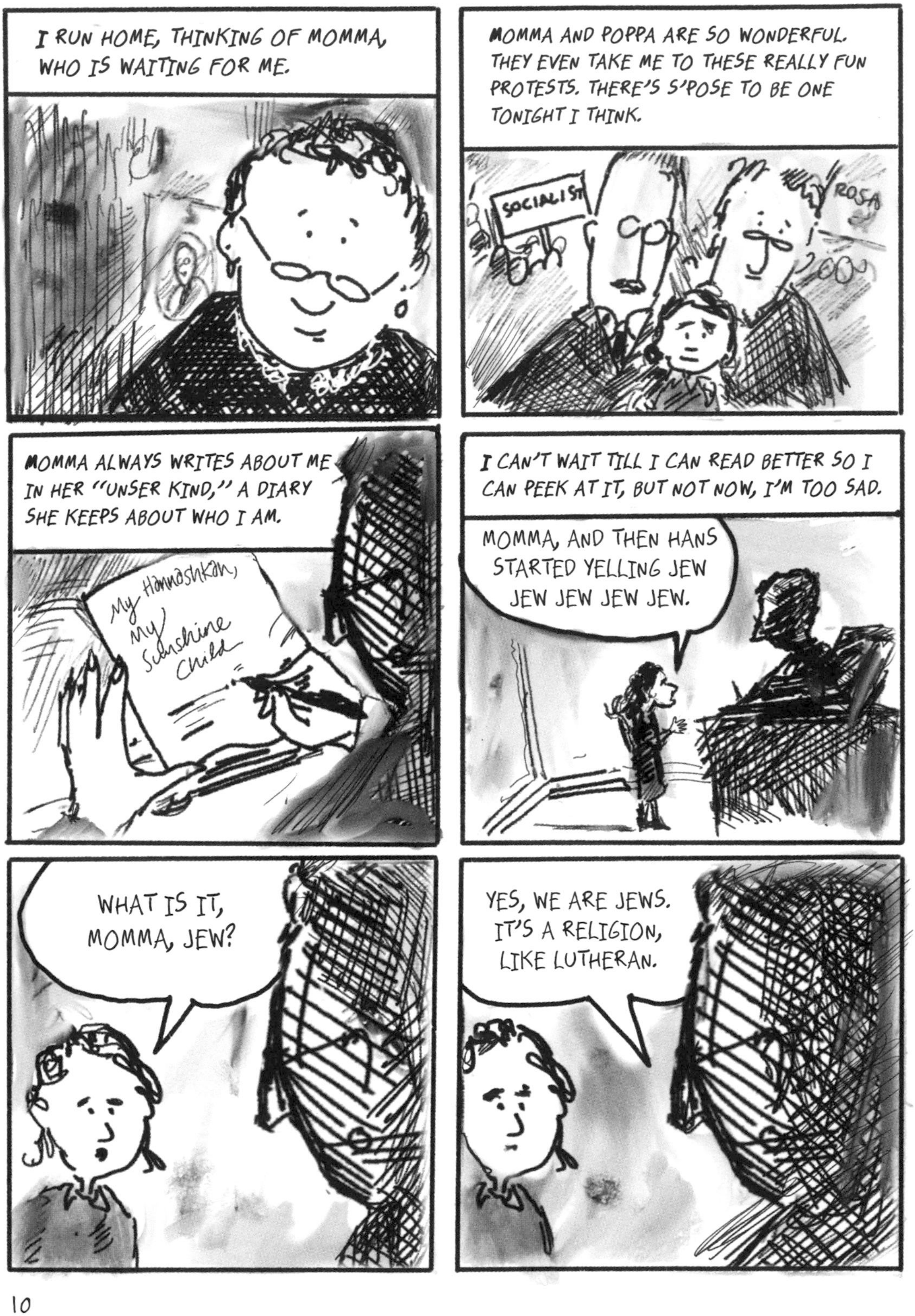
I RUN HOME, THINKING OF MOMMA, WHO IS WAITING FOR ME.
MOMMA AND POPPA ARE SO WONDERFUL. THEY EVEN TAKE ME TO THESE REALLY FUN PROTESTS. THERE'S S'POSE TO BE ONE TONIGHT I THINK.
SOCIALIST
ROSA
MOMMA ALWAYS WRITES ABOUT ME IN HER "UNSER KIND," A DIARY SHE KEEPS ABOUT WHO I AM.
My Hannashkah, My Sunshine Child
I CAN'T WAIT TILL I CAN READ BETTER SO I CAN PEEK AT IT, BUT NOT NOW, I'M TOO SAD.
MOMMA, AND THEN HANS STARTED YELLING JEW JEW JEW JEW JEW.
WHAT IS IT, MOMMA, JEW?
YES, WE ARE JEWS. IT'S A RELIGION, LIKE LUTHERAN.

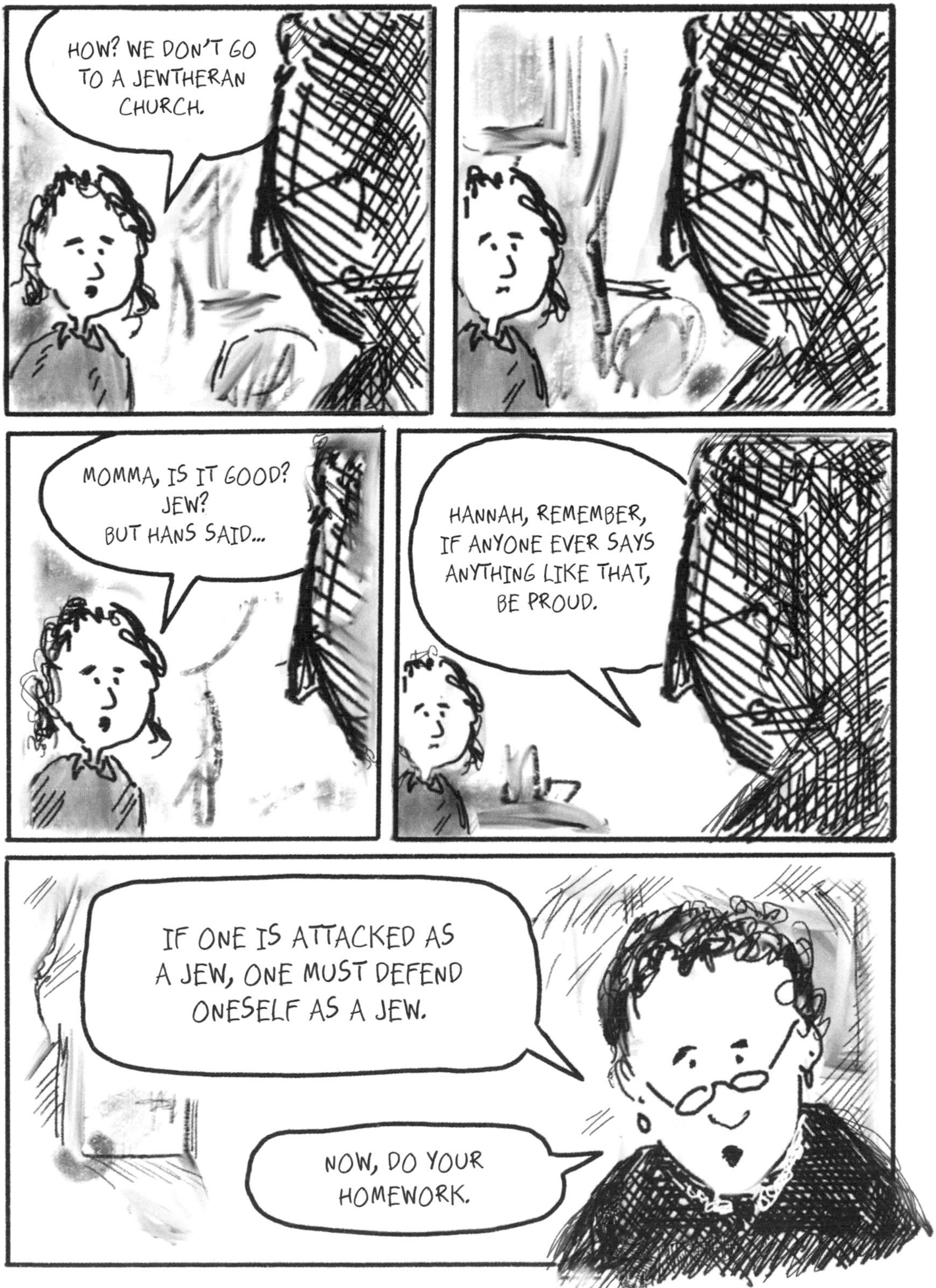
HOW? WE DON'T GO TO A JEWTHERAN CHURCH.
MOMMA, IS IT GOOD? JEW? BUT HANS SAID...
HANNAH, REMEMBER, IF ANYONE EVER SAYS ANYTHING LIKE THAT, BE PROUD.
IF ONE IS ATTACKED AS A JEW, ONE MUST DEFEND ONESELF AS A JEW.
NOW, DO YOUR HOMEWORK.

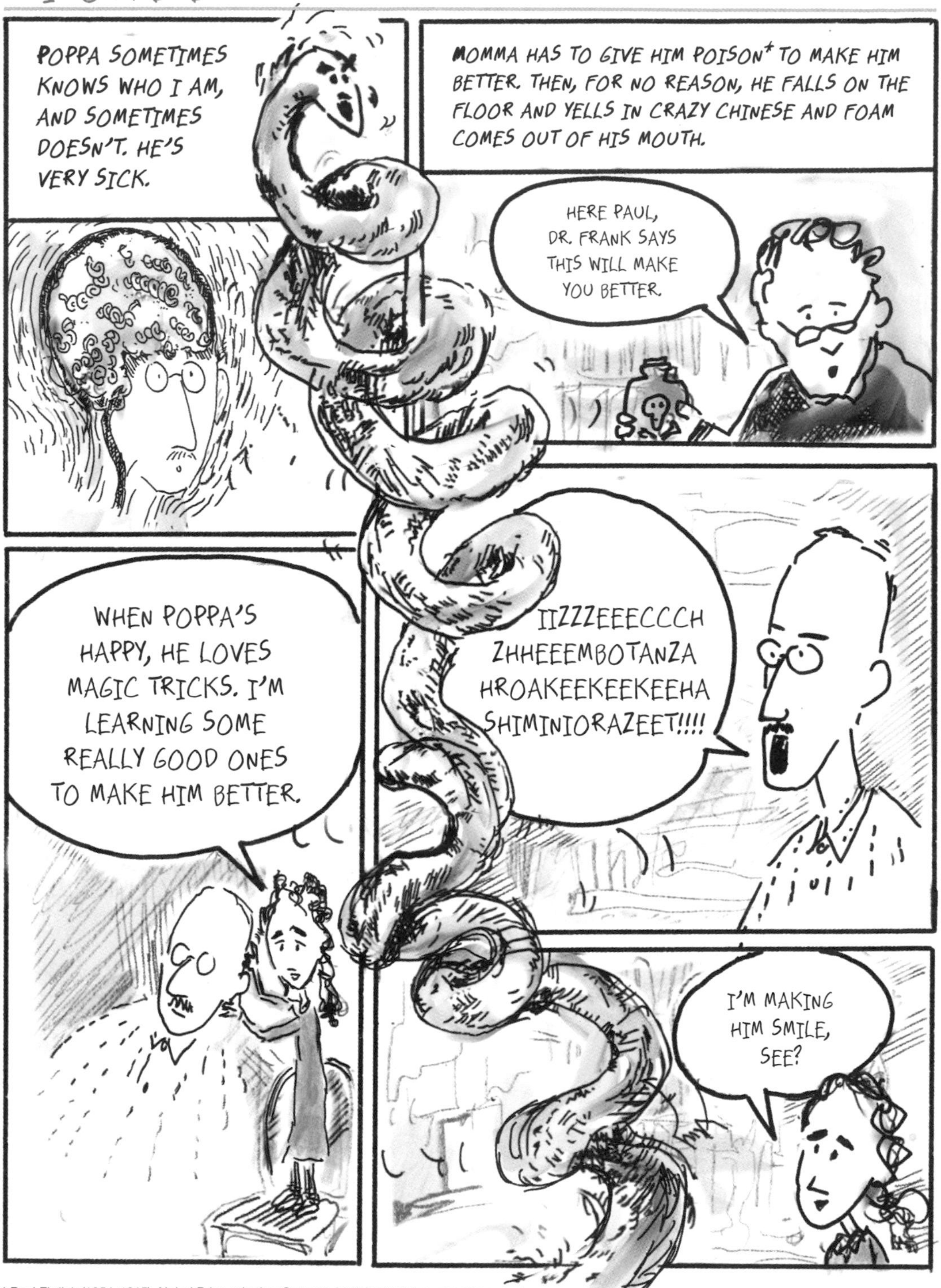
POPPA SOMETIMES KNOWS WHO I AM, AND SOMETIMES DOESN'T. HE'S VERY SICK.
MOMMA HAS TO GIVE HIM POISON* TO MAKE HIM BETTER. THEN, FOR NO REASON, HE FALLS ON THE FLOOR AND YELLS IN CRAZY CHINESE AND FOAM COMES OUT OF HIS MOUTH.
HERE PAUL, DR. FRANK SAYS THIS WILL MAKE YOU BETTER.
WHEN POPPA'S HAPPY, HE LOVES MAGIC TRICKS. I'M LEARNING SOME REALLY GOOD ONES TO MAKE HIM BETTER.
IIZZZEEECCCH ZHHEEEMBOTANZA HROAKEEKEEKEEHA SHIMINIORAZEET!!!!
I'M MAKING HIM SMILE, SEE?

* Paul Ehrlich (1854–1915). Nobel Prize–winning German Jewish physician who discovered the first effective medical treatment for syphilis, unfortunately a year or so too late for Paul Arendt. His story was made into a strange and wonderful 1940 biopic by Warner Bros., *Dr. Ehrlich's Magic Bullet*, starring Edward G. Robinson (born Emanuel Goldenberg).

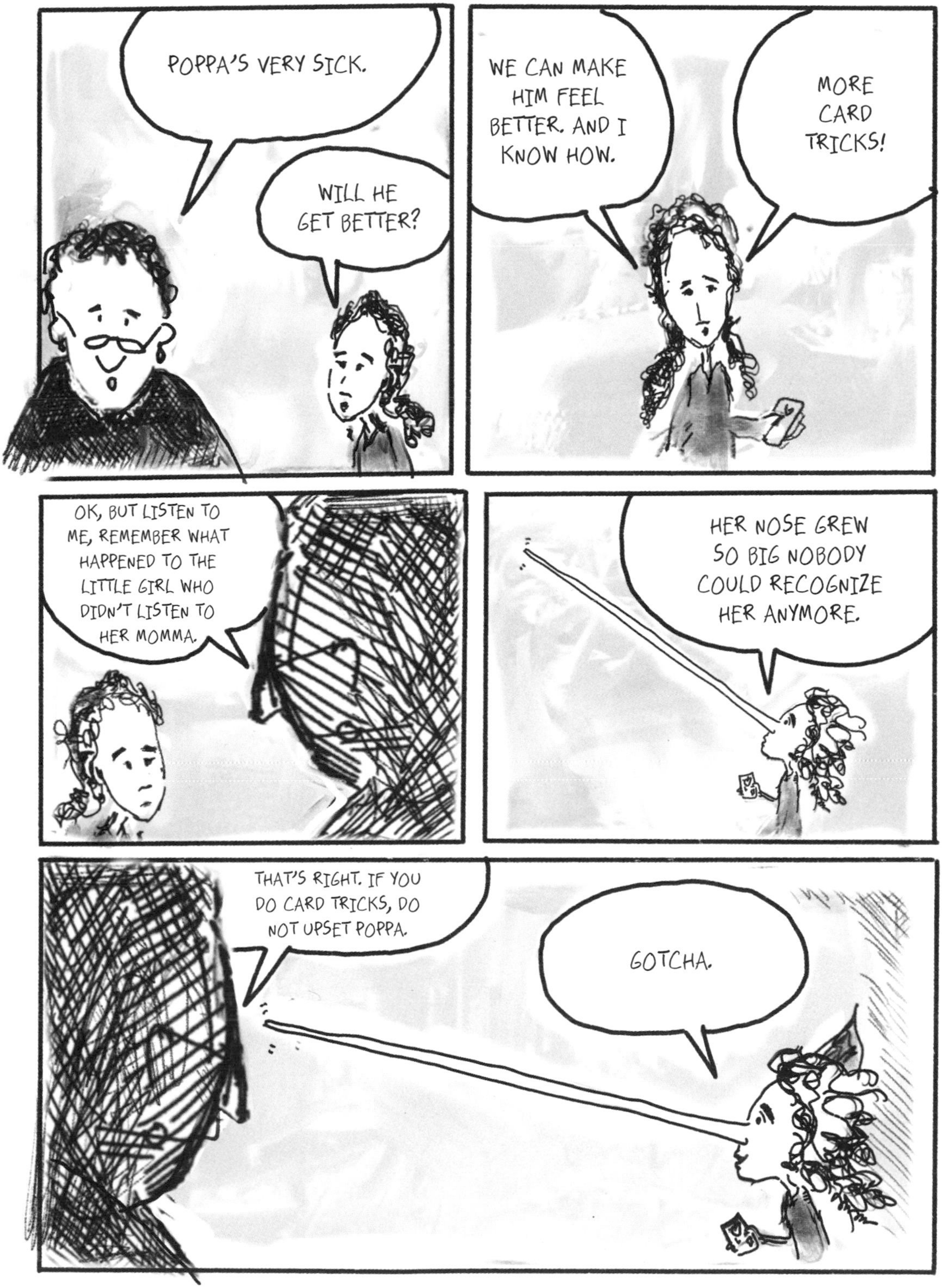
POPPA'S VERY SICK.
WILL HE GET BETTER?
WE CAN MAKE HIM FEEL BETTER. AND I KNOW HOW.
MORE CARD TRICKS!
OK, BUT LISTEN TO ME, REMEMBER WHAT HAPPENED TO THE LITTLE GIRL WHO DIDN'T LISTEN TO HER MOMMA.
HER NOSE GREW SO BIG NOBODY COULD RECOGNIZE HER ANYMORE.
THAT'S RIGHT. IF YOU DO CARD TRICKS, DO NOT UPSET POPPA.
GOTCHA.

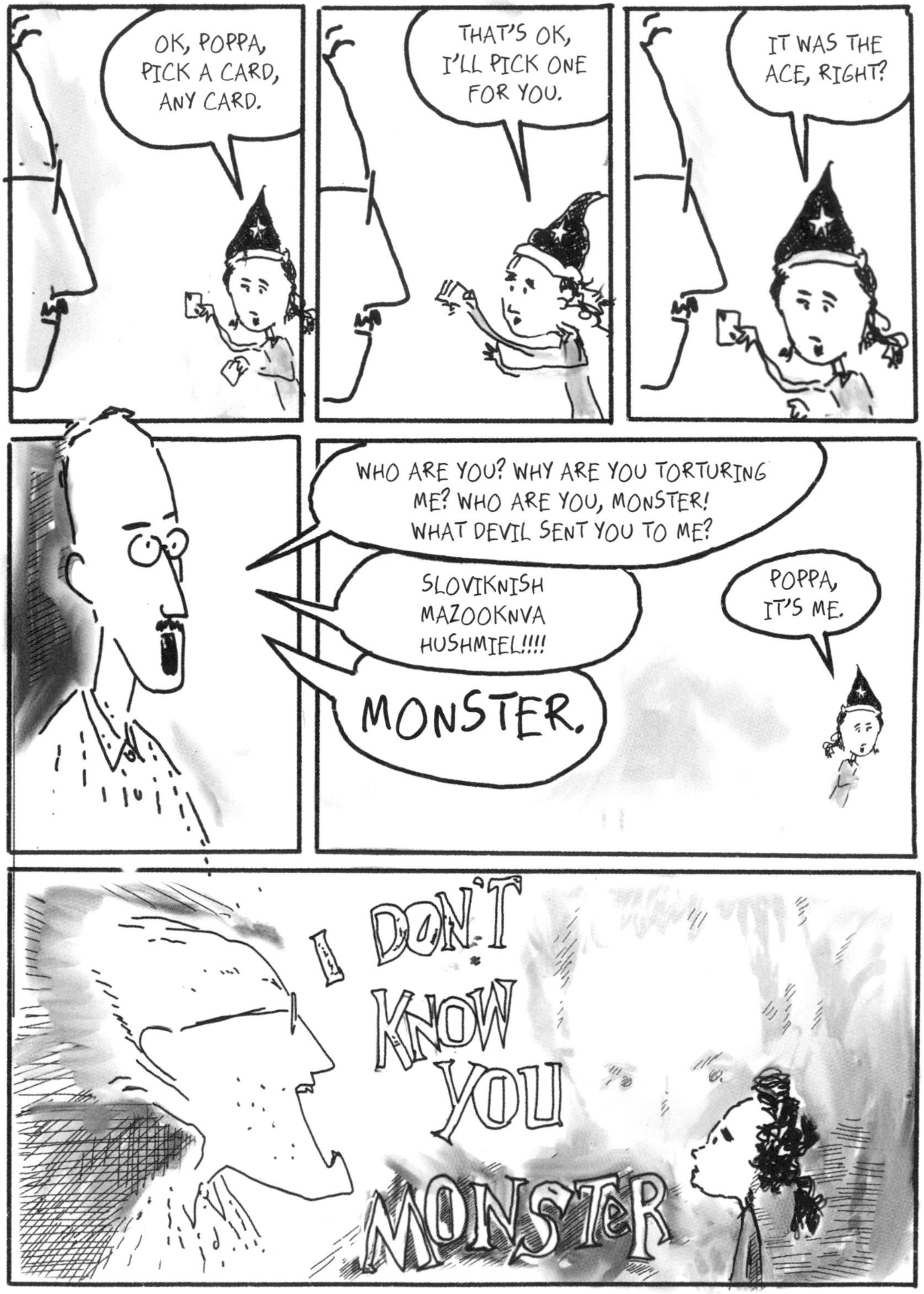
OK, POPPA, PICK A CARD, ANY CARD.
THAT'S OK, I'LL PICK ONE FOR YOU.
IT WAS THE ACE, RIGHT?
WHO ARE YOU? WHY ARE YOU TORTURING ME? WHO ARE YOU, MONSTER! WHAT DEVIL SENT YOU TO ME?
SLOVIKNISH MAZOOKNVA HUSHMIEL!!!!
MONSTER.
POPPA, IT'S ME.
I DON'T KNOW YOU MONSTER

THERE'S A STRANGE WORD I KEEP HEARING THE GROWN-UPS WHISPERING.

SO OF COURSE I GO TO THE LIBRARY AND LOOK IT UP IN THE GIGANTIC DICTIONARY YOU HAVE TO CLIMB ON THE CHAIR TO READ.

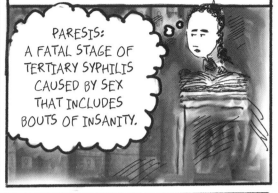

PARESIS: A FATAL STAGE OF TERTIARY SYPHILIS CAUSED BY SEX THAT INCLUDES BOUTS OF INSANITY.

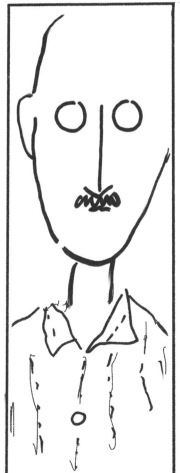

AND ONE DAY, POPPA IS NO MORE.

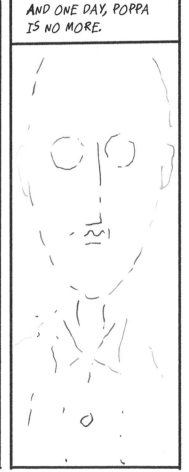

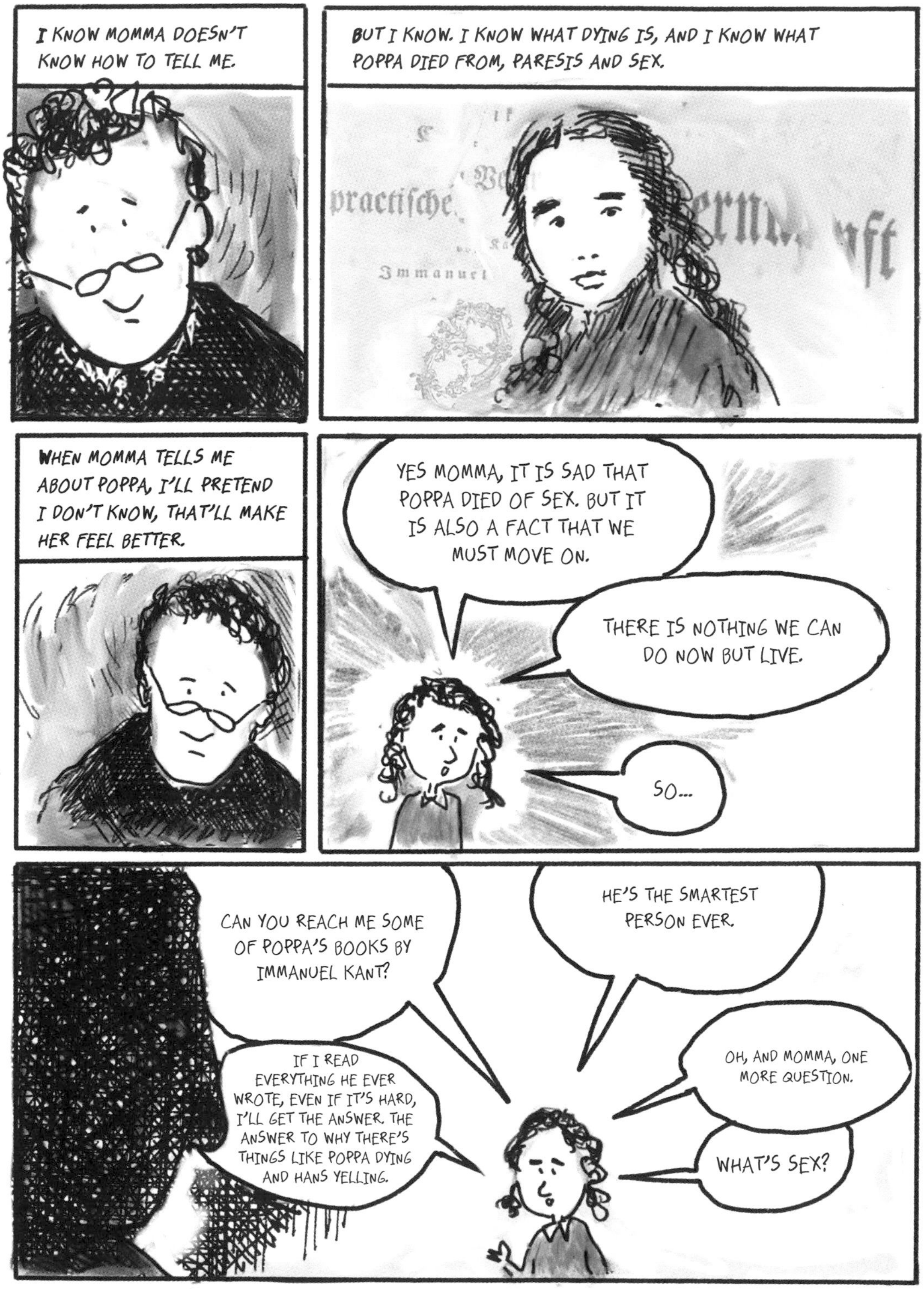
I KNOW MOMMA DOESN'T KNOW HOW TO TELL ME.
BUT I KNOW. I KNOW WHAT DYING IS, AND I KNOW WHAT POPPA DIED FROM, PARESIS AND SEX.
WHEN MOMMA TELLS ME ABOUT POPPA, I'LL PRETEND I DON'T KNOW, THAT'LL MAKE HER FEEL BETTER.
YES MOMMA, IT IS SAD THAT POPPA DIED OF SEX. BUT IT IS ALSO A FACT THAT WE MUST MOVE ON.
THERE IS NOTHING WE CAN DO NOW BUT LIVE.
SO...
CAN YOU REACH ME SOME OF POPPA'S BOOKS BY IMMANUEL KANT?
HE'S THE SMARTEST PERSON EVER.
IF I READ EVERYTHING HE EVER WROTE, EVEN IF IT'S HARD, I'LL GET THE ANSWER. THE ANSWER TO WHY THERE'S THINGS LIKE POPPA DYING AND HANS YELLING.
OH, AND MOMMA, ONE MORE QUESTION.
WHAT'S SEX?

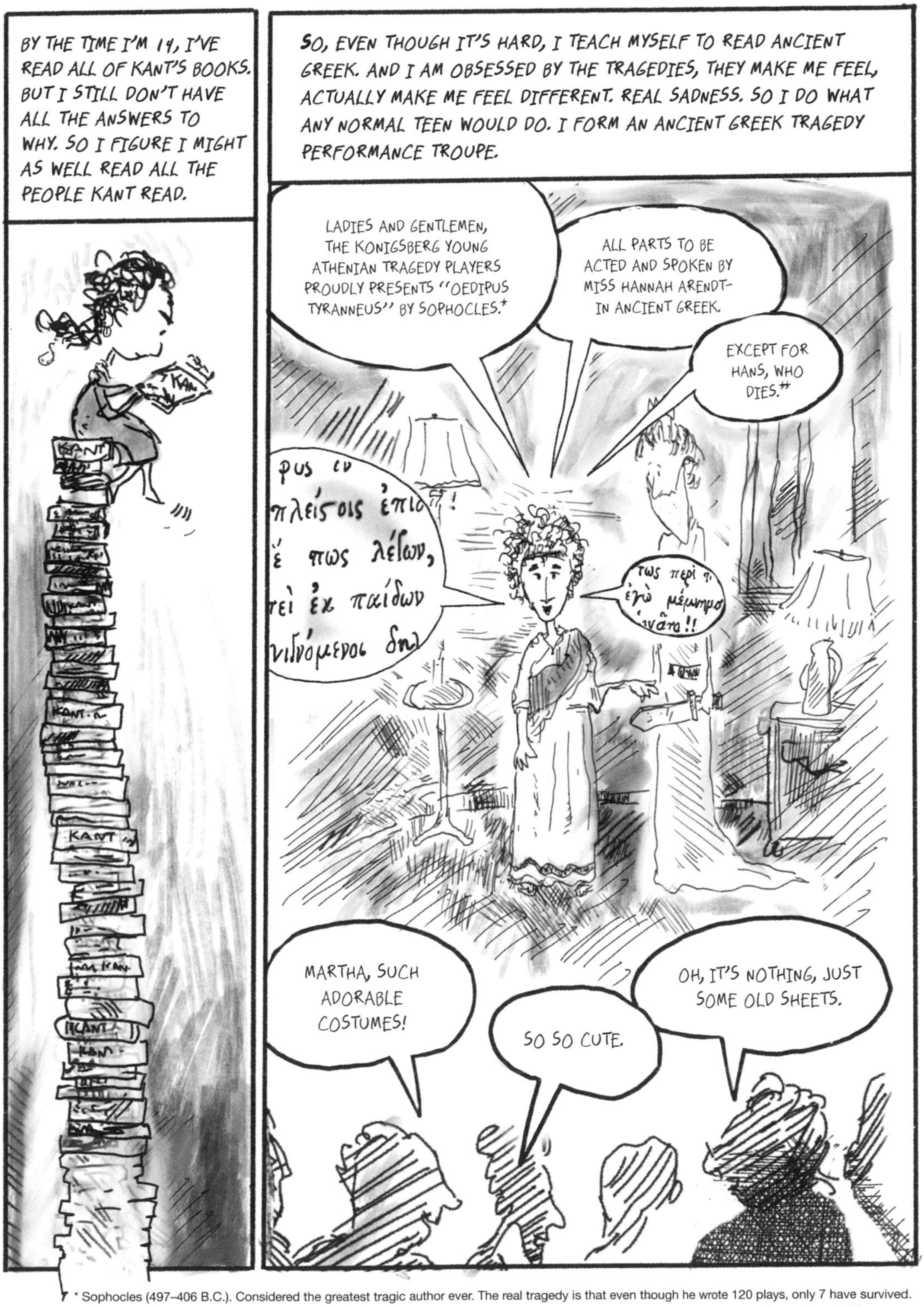
BY THE TIME I'M 14, I'VE READ ALL OF KANT'S BOOKS. BUT I STILL DON'T HAVE ALL THE ANSWERS TO WHY. SO I FIGURE I MIGHT AS WELL READ ALL THE PEOPLE KANT READ.
KANT
SO, EVEN THOUGH IT'S HARD, I TEACH MYSELF TO READ ANCIENT GREEK. AND I AM OBSESSED BY THE TRAGEDIES, THEY MAKE ME FEEL, ACTUALLY MAKE ME FEEL DIFFERENT. REAL SADNESS. SO I DO WHAT ANY NORMAL TEEN WOULD DO. I FORM AN ANCIENT GREEK TRAGEDY PERFORMANCE TROUPE.
LADIES AND GENTLEMEN, THE KONIGSBERG YOUNG ATHENIAN TRAGEDY PLAYERS PROUDLY PRESENTS "OEDIPUS TYRANNEUS" BY SOPHOCLES.*
ALL PARTS TO BE ACTED AND SPOKEN BY MISS HANNAH ARENDT- IN ANCIENT GREEK.
EXCEPT FOR HANS, WHO DIES.**
MARTHA, SUCH ADORABLE COSTUMES!
SO SO CUTE.
OH, IT'S NOTHING, JUST SOME OLD SHEETS.

* Sophocles (497–406 B.C.). Considered the greatest tragic author ever. The real tragedy is that even though he wrote 120 plays, only 7 have survived.

** The only other person who'll come into the club is Hans (we're friends again). I got him to join by telling him there's lots of swords and killing and all he has to do is die. But I really think he joins up because he likes me.

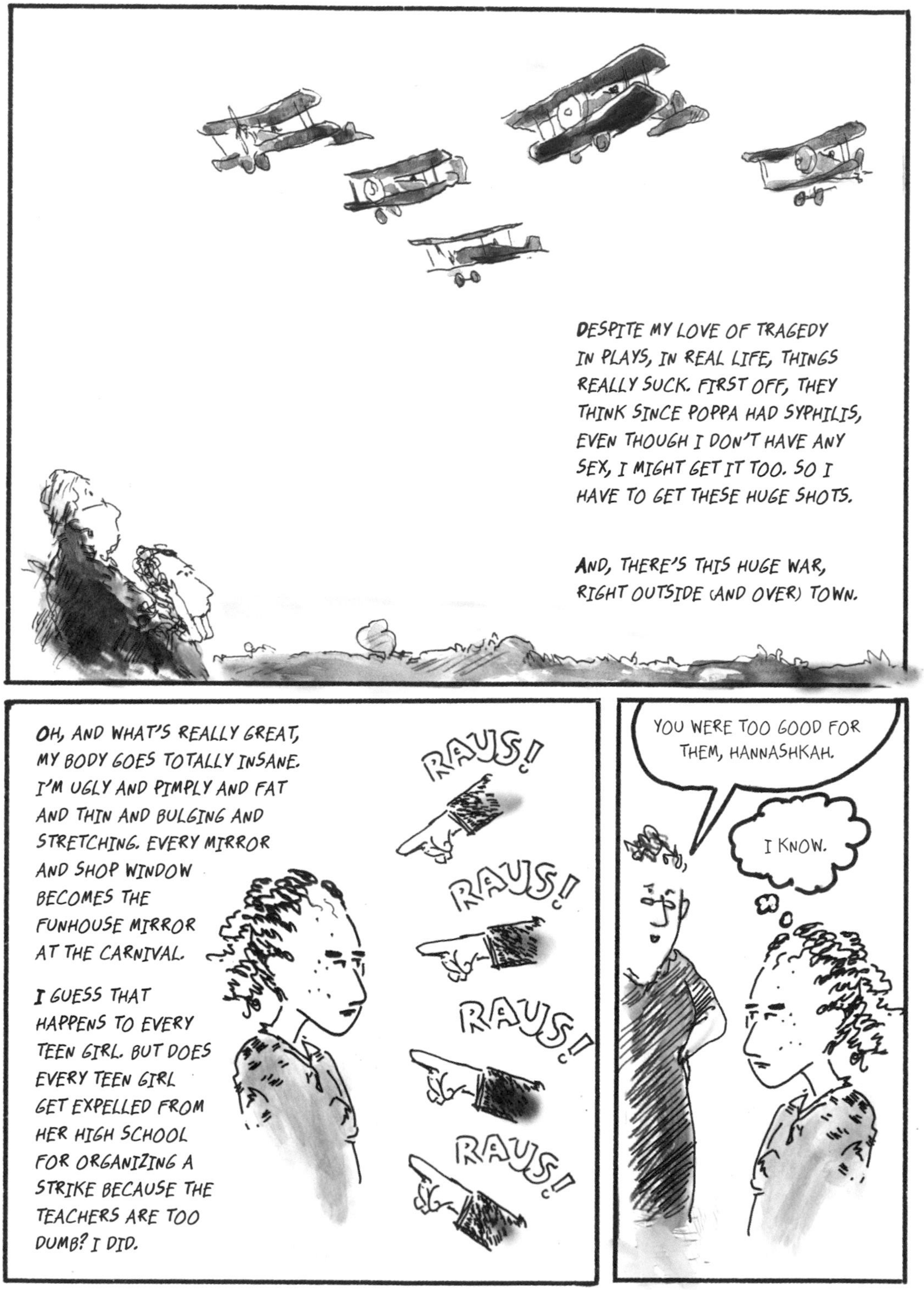
DESPITE MY LOVE OF TRAGEDY IN PLAYS, IN REAL LIFE, THINGS REALLY SUCK. FIRST OFF, THEY THINK SINCE POPPA HAD SYPHILIS, EVEN THOUGH I DON'T HAVE ANY SEX, I MIGHT GET IT TOO. SO I HAVE TO GET THESE HUGE SHOTS.
AND, THERE'S THIS HUGE WAR, RIGHT OUTSIDE (AND OVER) TOWN.
OH, AND WHAT'S REALLY GREAT, MY BODY GOES TOTALLY INSANE. I'M UGLY AND PIMPLY AND FAT AND THIN AND BULGING AND STRETCHING. EVERY MIRROR AND SHOP WINDOW BECOMES THE FUNHOUSE MIRROR AT THE CARNIVAL.
I GUESS THAT HAPPENS TO EVERY TEEN GIRL. BUT DOES EVERY TEEN GIRL GET EXPELLED FROM HER HIGH SCHOOL FOR ORGANIZING A STRIKE BECAUSE THE TEACHERS ARE TOO DUMB? I DID.
RAUS!
RAUS!
RAUS!
RAUS!
YOU WERE TOO GOOD FOR THEM, HANNASHKAH.
I KNOW.

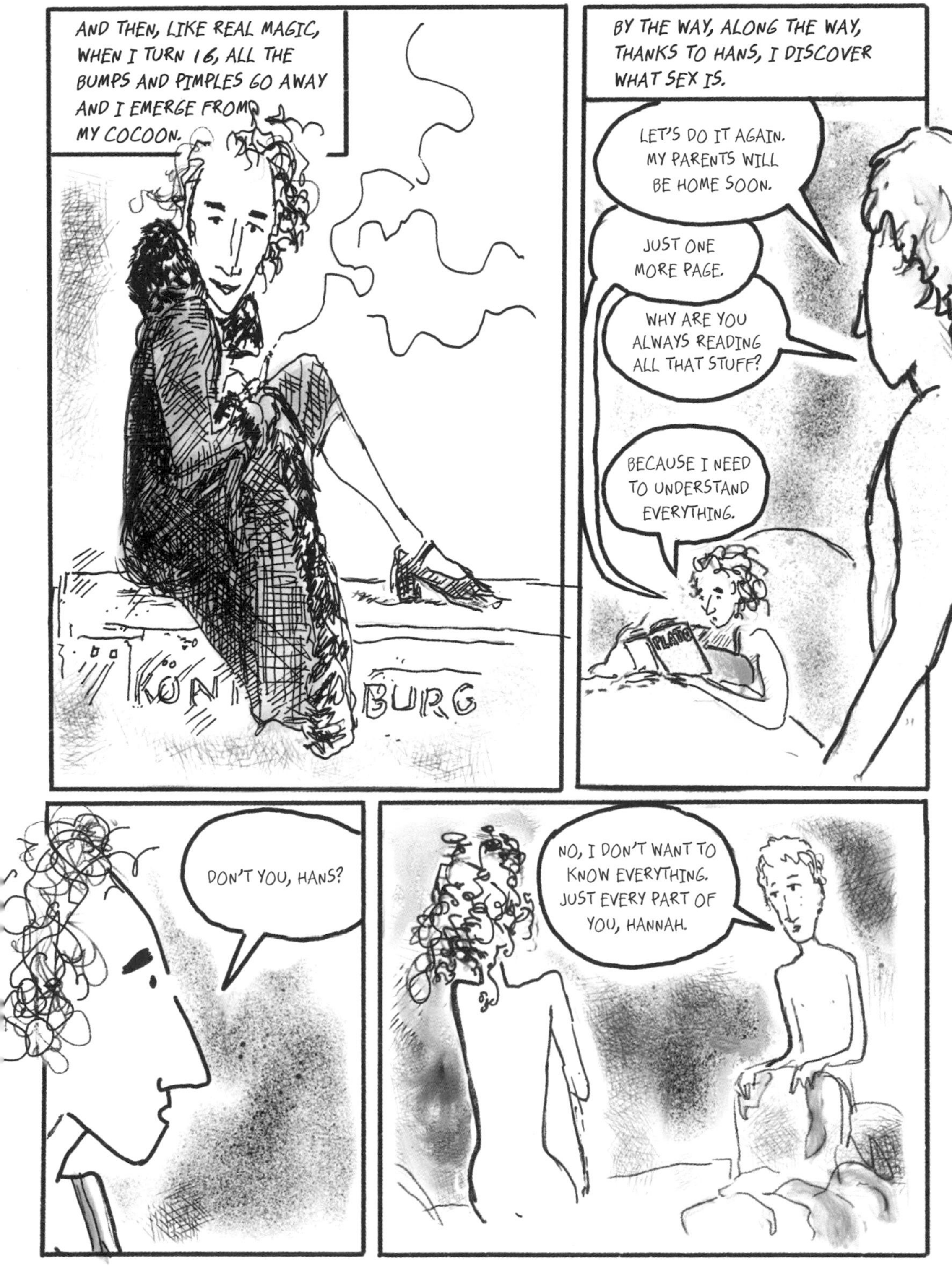
AND THEN, LIKE REAL MAGIC, WHEN I TURN 16, ALL THE BUMPS AND PIMPLES GO AWAY AND I EMERGE FROM MY COCOON.
KON
BURG
BY THE WAY, ALONG THE WAY, THANKS TO HANS, I DISCOVER WHAT SEX IS.
LET'S DO IT AGAIN. MY PARENTS WILL BE HOME SOON.
JUST ONE MORE PAGE.
WHY ARE YOU ALWAYS READING ALL THAT STUFF?
BECAUSE I NEED TO UNDERSTAND EVERYTHING.
PLATO
DON'T YOU, HANS?
NO, I DON'T WANT TO KNOW EVERYTHING. JUST EVERY PART OF YOU, HANNAH.

PEOPLE DON'T REALLY GET IT. THEY THINK I'M SUPPOSED TO BE KIND OF DUMB. (EXCEPT FOR MY MOM, THAT IS.) BUT, I SUPPOSE, TO BE TOTALLY HONEST, I REALLY AM DUMB. EXCEPT HERE'S SOMETHING YOU PROBABLY DON'T KNOW: IT TAKES ME A LOT OF HARD WORK, MORE THAN ANYONE EVER, I'M QUITE SURE, TO GET SMART. STUFF MOST NORMAL PEOPLE WOULD "GET" IN LIKE FIVE MINUTES, TAKES ME FIVE HOURS. I HAVE TO THINK AND THINK. BUT I PUT IN THE TIME AND THE WORK BECAUSE I NEED TO KNOW. TO UNDERSTAND. BUT NOBODY NOTICES HOW HARD I WORK. NO. THEY JUST SEE HOW SMART I'M SUPPOSED TO BE SO THEY GET ALL ENVIOUS. BUT GUESS WHAT ELSE? EVERY TIME THEY OPEN THEIR MOUTHS, THEY ARE REALLY STUPID. MANY ARE COMPLETE IDIOTS, SORRY. EVEN THOSE TEACHERS WHO THREW ME OUT OF SCHOOL. ESPECIALLY THEM.

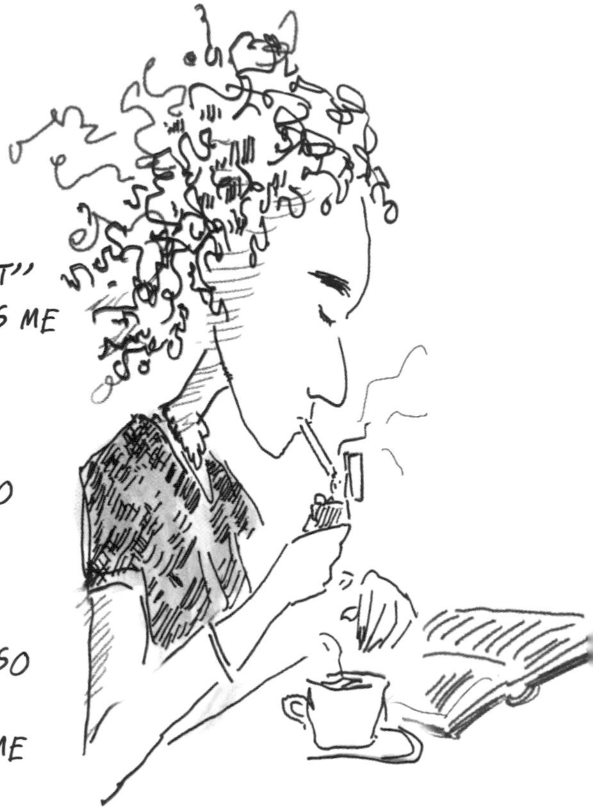

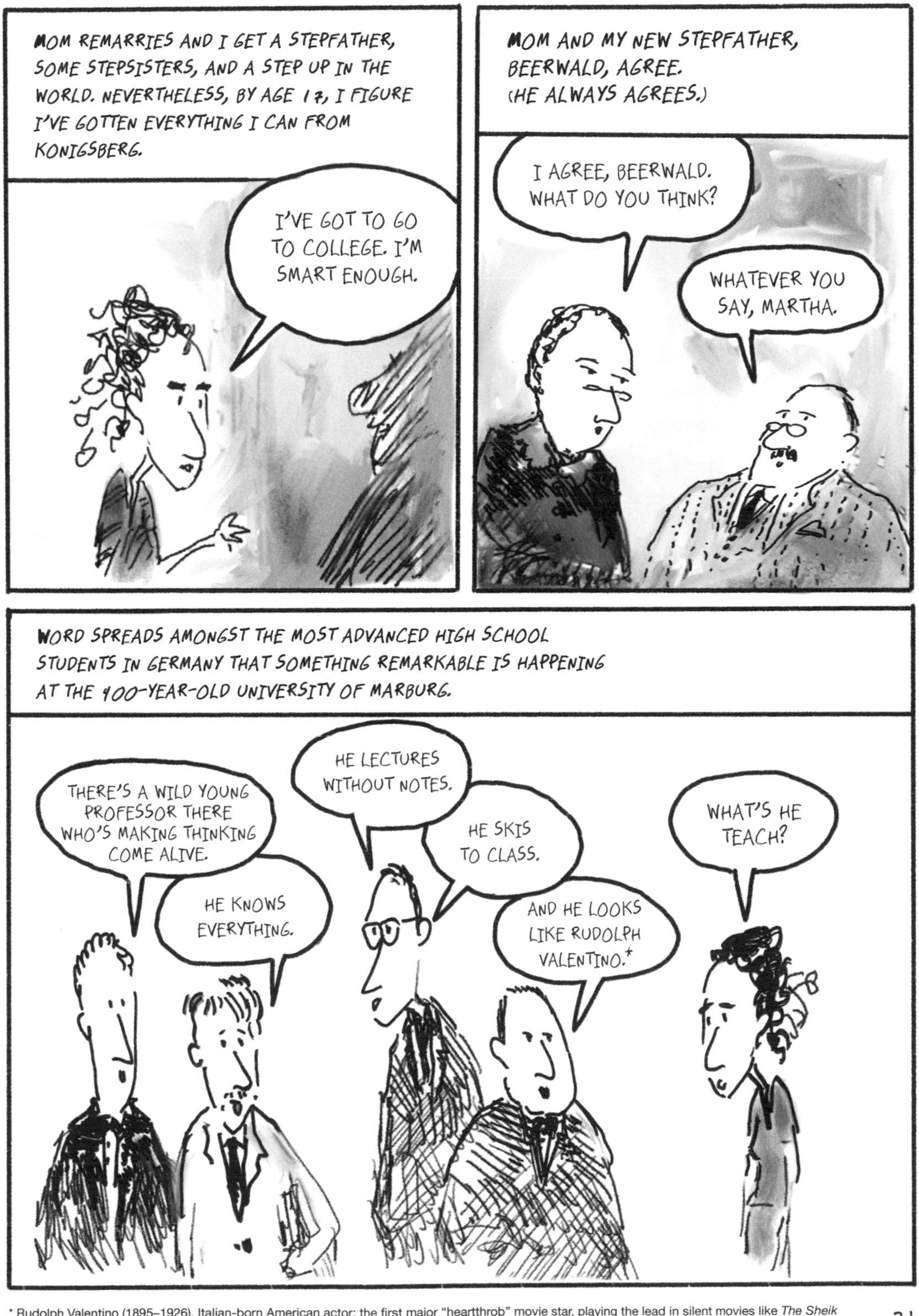
MOM REMARRIES AND I GET A STEPFATHER, SOME STEPSISTERS, AND A STEP UP IN THE WORLD. NEVERTHELESS, BY AGE 17, I FIGURE I'VE GOTTEN EVERYTHING I CAN FROM KONIGSBERG.
I'VE GOT TO GO TO COLLEGE. I'M SMART ENOUGH.
MOM AND MY NEW STEPFATHER, BEERWALD, AGREE. (HE ALWAYS AGREES.)
I AGREE, BEERWALD. WHAT DO YOU THINK?
WHATEVER YOU SAY, MARTHA.
WORD SPREADS AMONGST THE MOST ADVANCED HIGH SCHOOL STUDENTS IN GERMANY THAT SOMETHING REMARKABLE IS HAPPENING AT THE 400-YEAR-OLD UNIVERSITY OF MARBURG.
THERE'S A WILD YOUNG PROFESSOR THERE WHO'S MAKING THINKING COME ALIVE.
HE KNOWS EVERYTHING.
HE LECTURES WITHOUT NOTES.
HE SKIS TO CLASS.
AND HE LOOKS LIKE RUDOLPH VALENTINO.*
WHAT'S HE TEACH?

* Rudolph Valentino (1895–1926). Italian-born American actor; the first major "heartthrob" movie star, playing the lead in silent movies like *The Sheik* and *Blood and Sand*. When he died at age thirty-one, his was the largest celebrity funeral ever up to that time.

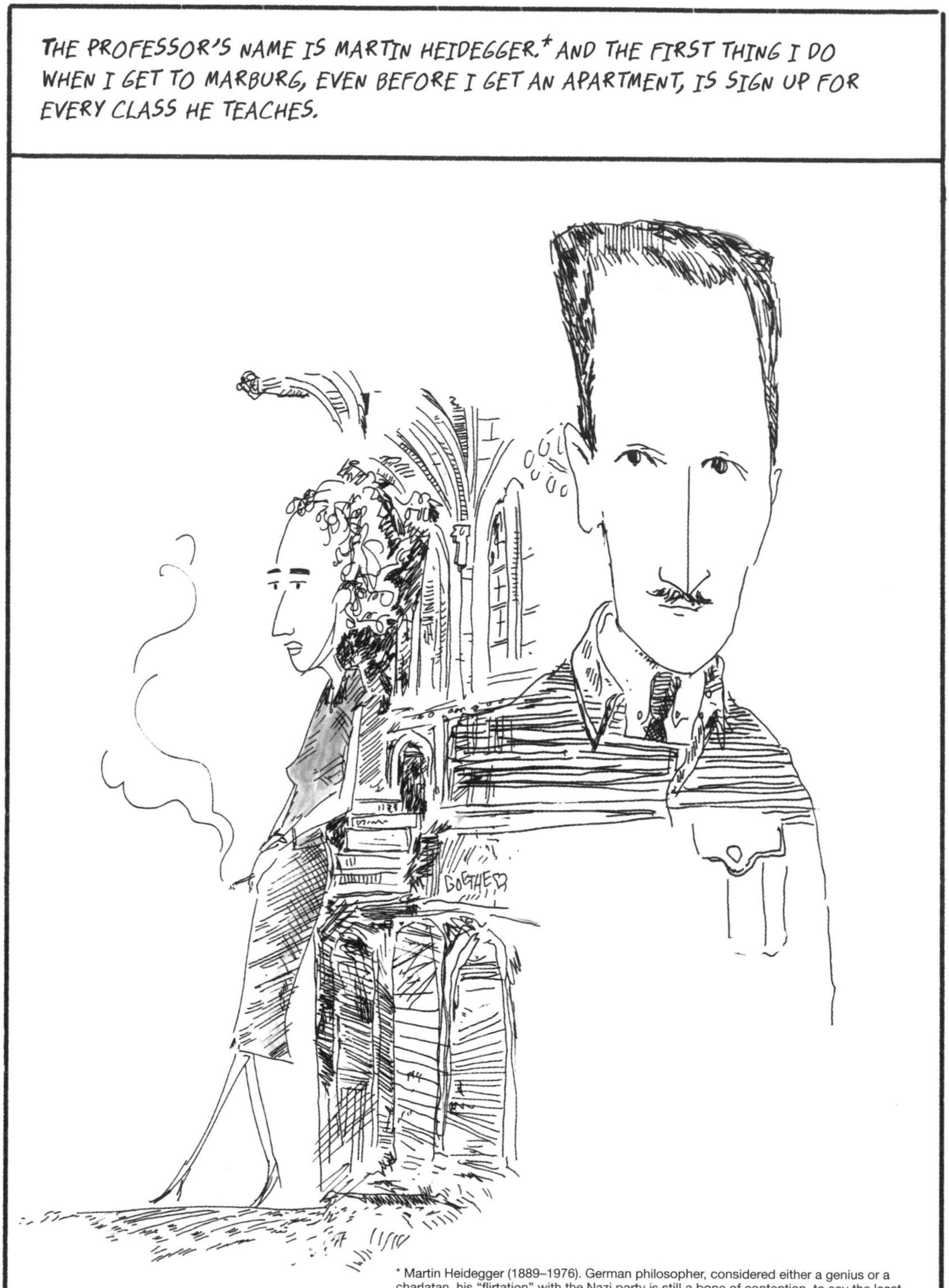
THE PROFESSOR'S NAME IS MARTIN HEIDEGGER.* AND THE FIRST THING I DO WHEN I GET TO MARBURG, EVEN BEFORE I GET AN APARTMENT, IS SIGN UP FOR EVERY CLASS HE TEACHES.
GOETHE

* Martin Heidegger (1889–1976). German philosopher, considered either a genius or a charlatan, his "flirtation" with the Nazi party is still a bone of contention, to say the least.

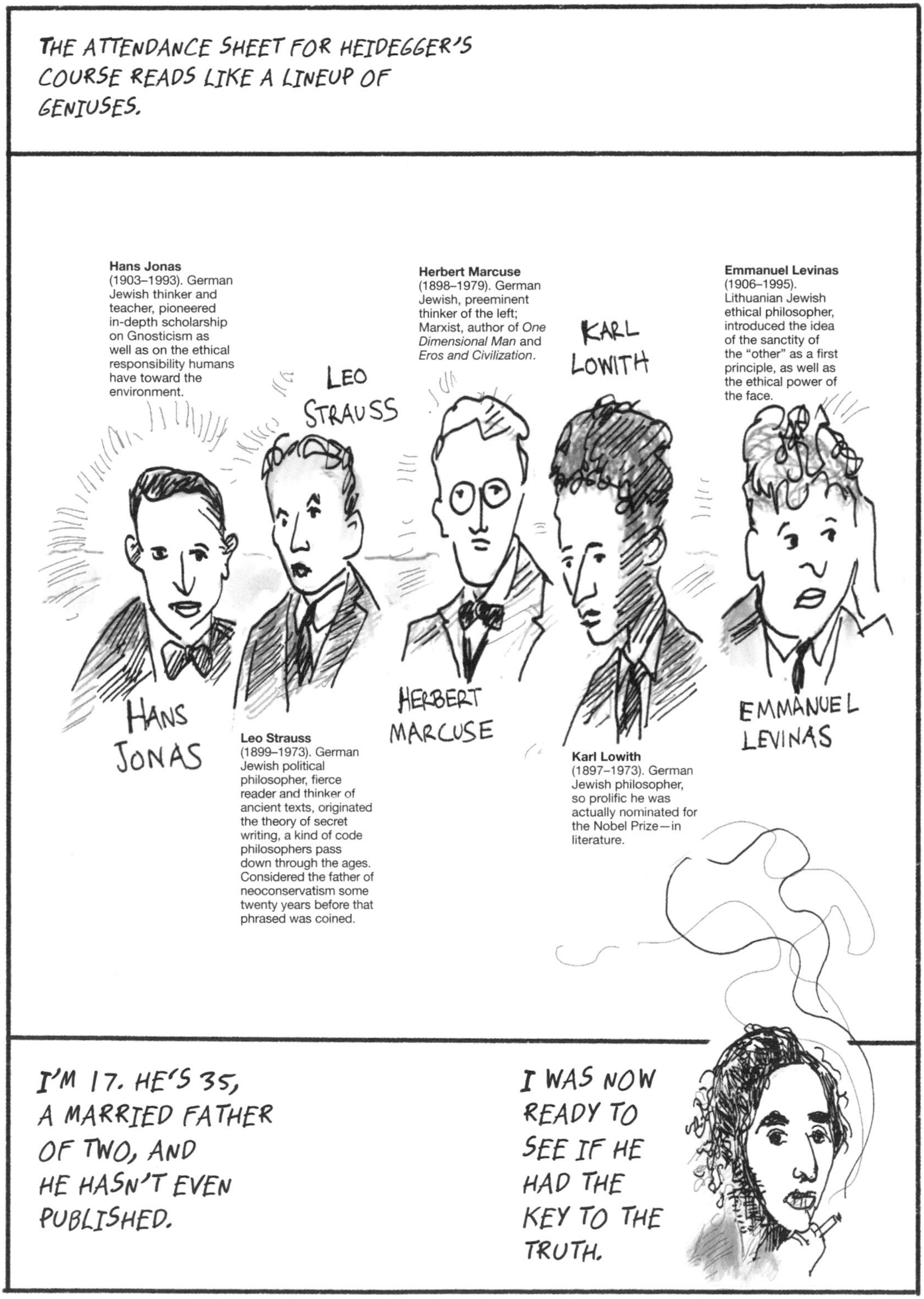
THE ATTENDANCE SHEET FOR HEIDEGGER'S COURSE READS LIKE A LINEUP OF GENIUSES.
Hans Jonas (1903–1993). German Jewish thinker and teacher, pioneered in-depth scholarship on Gnosticism as well as on the ethical responsibility humans have toward the environment.
HANS JONAS
LEO STRAUSS
Leo Strauss (1899–1973). German Jewish political philosopher, fierce reader and thinker of ancient texts, originated the theory of secret writing, a kind of code philosophers pass down through the ages. Considered the father of neoconservatism some twenty years before that phrased was coined.
Herbert Marcuse (1898–1979). German Jewish, preeminent thinker of the left; Marxist, author of *One Dimensional Man* and *Eros and Civilization*.
HERBERT MARCUSE
KARL LOWITH
Karl Lowith (1897–1973). German Jewish philosopher, so prolific he was actually nominated for the Nobel Prize—in literature.
Emmanuel Levinas (1906–1995). Lithuanian Jewish ethical philosopher, introduced the idea of the sanctity of the "other" as a first principle, as well as the ethical power of the face.
EMMANUEL LEVINAS
I'M 17. HE'S 35, A MARRIED FATHER OF TWO, AND HE HASN'T EVEN PUBLISHED.
I WAS NOW READY TO SEE IF HE HAD THE KEY TO THE TRUTH.

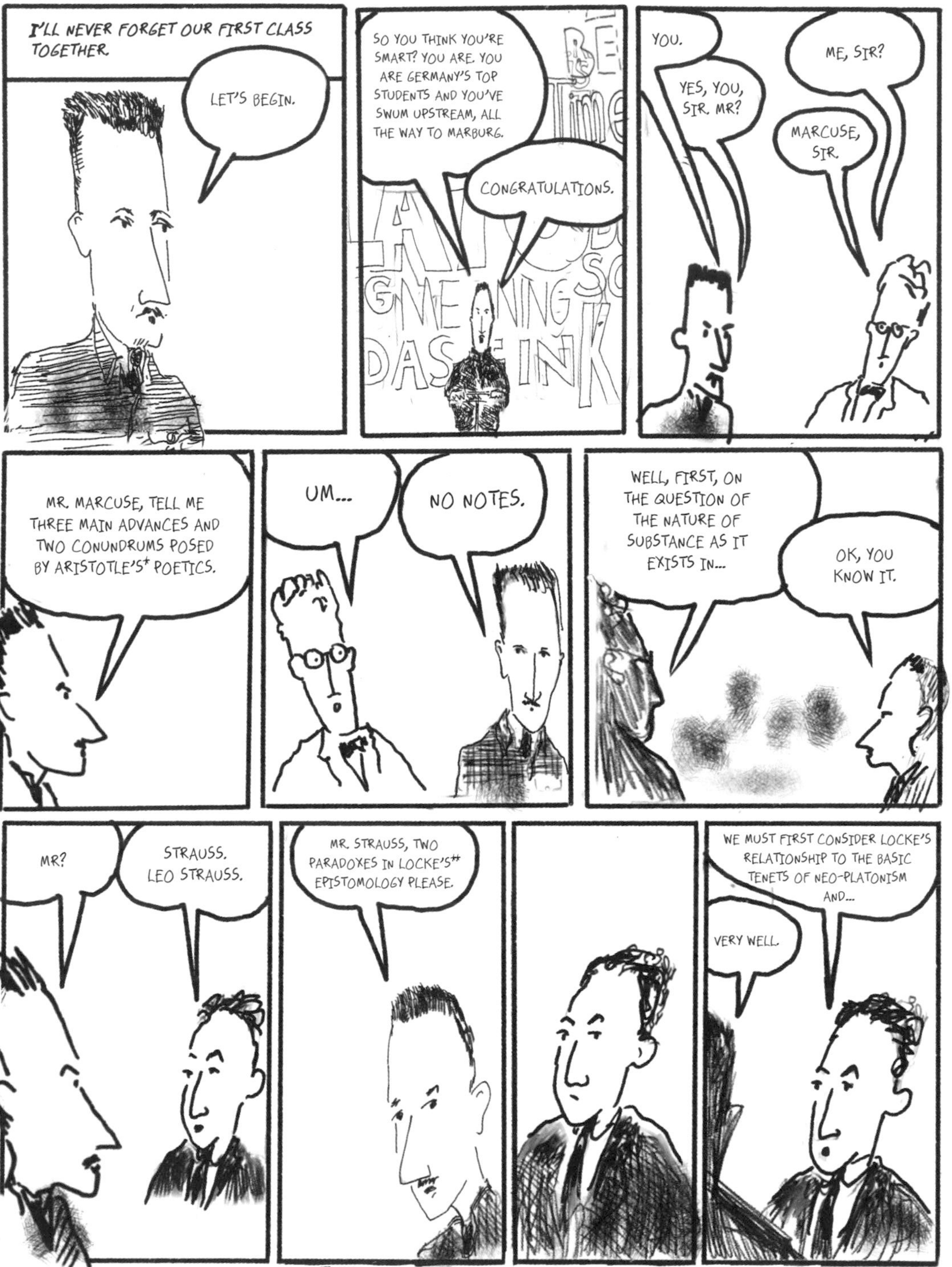

I'LL NEVER FORGET OUR FIRST CLASS TOGETHER.
LET'S BEGIN.
SO YOU THINK YOU'RE SMART? YOU ARE. YOU ARE GERMANY'S TOP STUDENTS AND YOU'VE SWUM UPSTREAM, ALL THE WAY TO MARBURG.
CONGRATULATIONS.
YOU.
ME, SIR?
YES, YOU, SIR. MR?
MARCUSE, SIR.
MR. MARCUSE, TELL ME THREE MAIN ADVANCES AND TWO CONUNDRUMS POSED BY ARISTOTLE'S* POETICS.
UM...
NO NOTES.
WELL, FIRST, ON THE QUESTION OF THE NATURE OF SUBSTANCE AS IT EXISTS IN...
OK, YOU KNOW IT.
MR?
STRAUSS. LEO STRAUSS.
MR. STRAUSS, TWO PARADOXES IN LOCKE'S** EPISTOMOLOGY PLEASE.
WE MUST FIRST CONSIDER LOCKE'S RELATIONSHIP TO THE BASIC TENETS OF NEO-PLATONISM AND...
VERY WELL.

* Aristotle (384–322 B.C.). Ancient Greek philosopher and scientist, student of Plato, who then split and started his own thing, along the way defining the fundamental way of thinking rationally about the world in subjects as diverse as how plants live to how to tell a joke.

** John Locke (1632–1704). English philosopher, super-rational, super-enlightenment, super skeptical—if you couldn't see it, prove it, he didn't buy it. His thinking inspired the men (and it seems, alas, they were all men) who framed the United States Constitution.

*** David Hume (1711–1776). Another super-skeptical Brit, of the Scottish variety, so unimpressed with habitual thinking that if you said to him, "The sun will rise tomorrow," he'd say, "How do you know? It's not tomorrow yet."

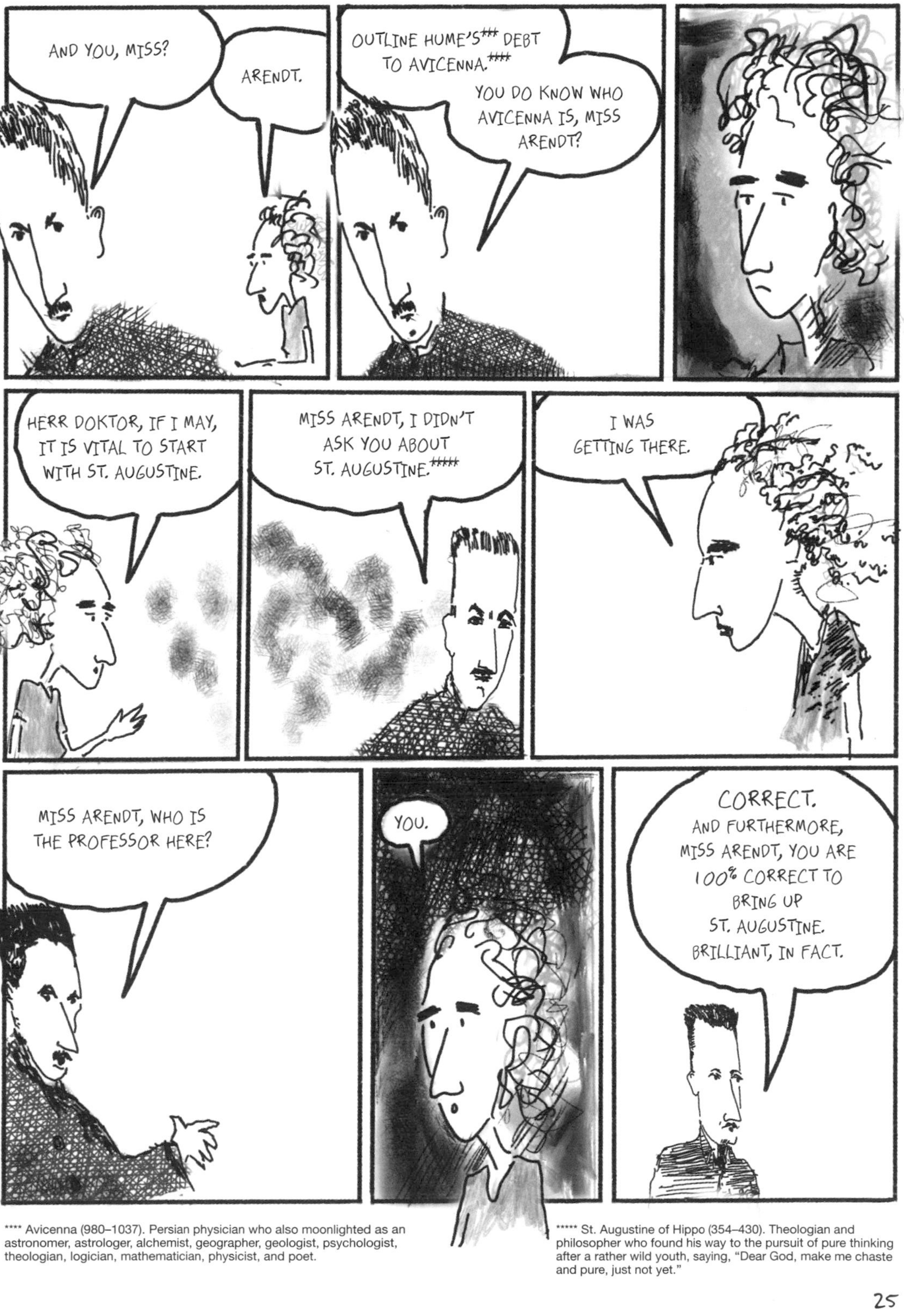
AND YOU, MISS?
ARENDT.
OUTLINE HUME'S*** DEBT TO AVICENNA.****
YOU DO KNOW WHO AVICENNA IS, MISS ARENDT?
HERR DOKTOR, IF I MAY, IT IS VITAL TO START WITH ST. AUGUSTINE.
MISS ARENDT, I DIDN'T ASK YOU ABOUT ST. AUGUSTINE.*****
I WAS GETTING THERE.
MISS ARENDT, WHO IS THE PROFESSOR HERE?
YOU.
CORRECT.
AND FURTHERMORE, MISS ARENDT, YOU ARE 100% CORRECT TO BRING UP ST. AUGUSTINE. BRILLIANT, IN FACT.

**** Avicenna (980–1037). Persian physician who also moonlighted as an astronomer, astrologer, alchemist, geographer, geologist, psychologist, theologian, logician, mathematician, physicist, and poet.

***** St. Augustine of Hippo (354–430). Theologian and philosopher who found his way to the pursuit of pure thinking after a rather wild youth, saying, "Dear God, make me chaste and pure, just not yet."

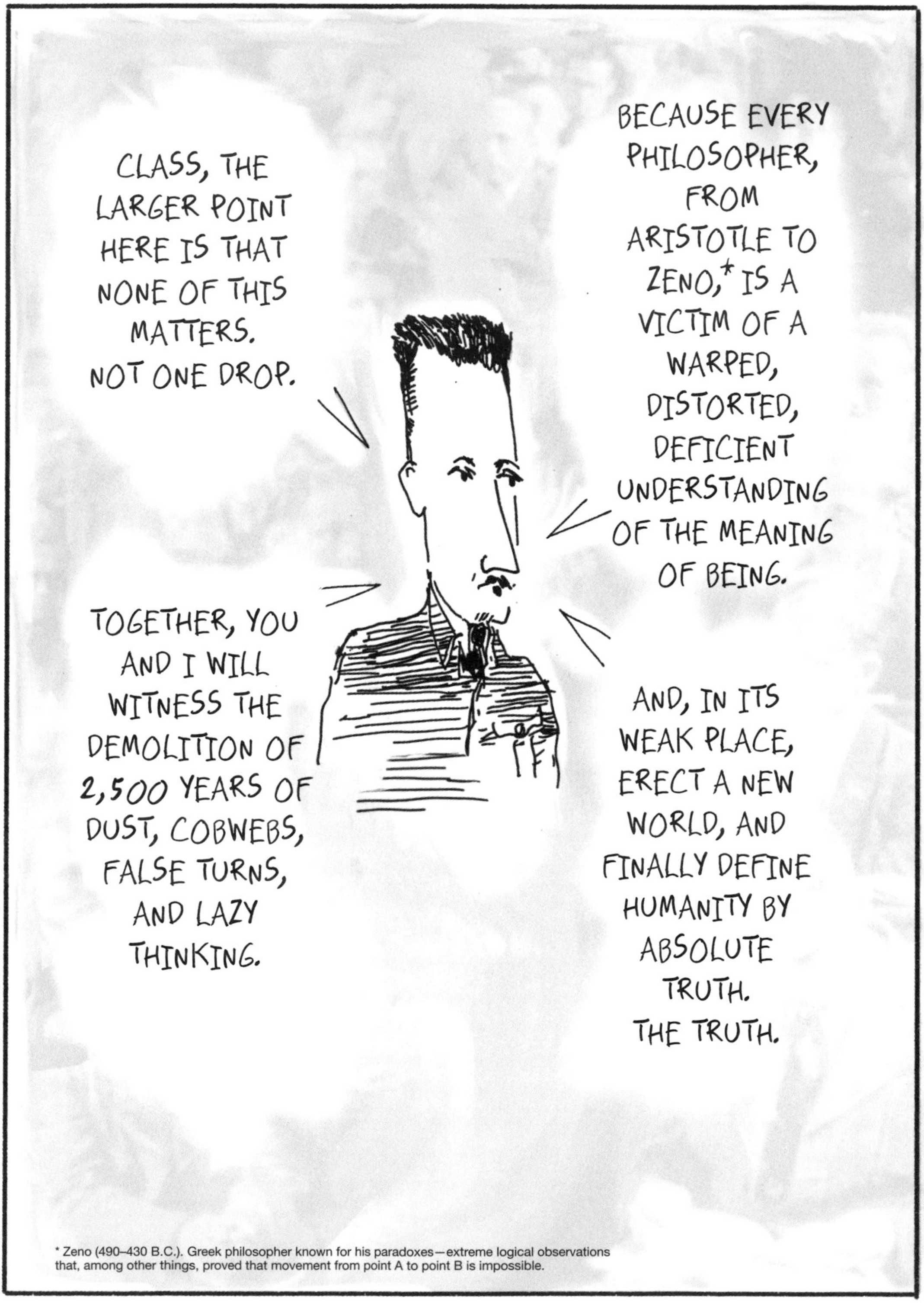
CLASS, THE LARGER POINT HERE IS THAT NONE OF THIS MATTERS. NOT ONE DROP.
BECAUSE EVERY PHILOSOPHER, FROM ARISTOTLE TO ZENO,* IS A VICTIM OF A WARPED, DISTORTED, DEFICIENT UNDERSTANDING OF THE MEANING OF BEING.
TOGETHER, YOU AND I WILL WITNESS THE DEMOLITION OF 2,500 YEARS OF DUST, COBWEBS, FALSE TURNS, AND LAZY THINKING.
AND, IN ITS WEAK PLACE, ERECT A NEW WORLD, AND FINALLY DEFINE HUMANITY BY ABSOLUTE TRUTH. THE TRUTH.

* Zeno (490–430 B.C.). Greek philosopher known for his paradoxes—extreme logical observations that, among other things, proved that movement from point A to point B is impossible.

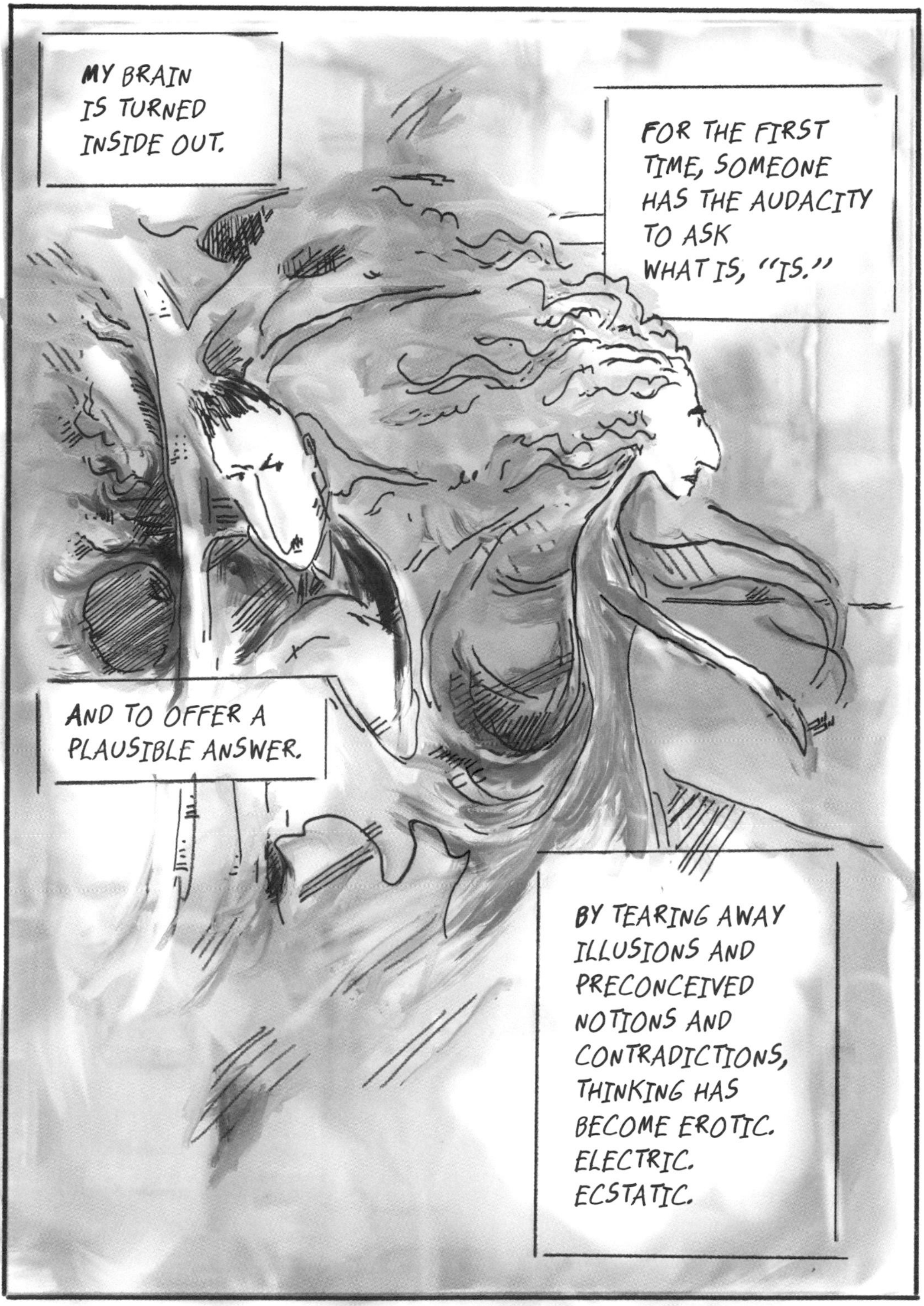
MY BRAIN IS TURNED INSIDE OUT.
FOR THE FIRST TIME, SOMEONE HAS THE AUDACITY TO ASK WHAT IS, "IS."
AND TO OFFER A PLAUSIBLE ANSWER.
BY TEARING AWAY ILLUSIONS AND PRECONCEIVED NOTIONS AND CONTRADICTIONS, THINKING HAS BECOME EROTIC. ELECTRIC. ECSTATIC.

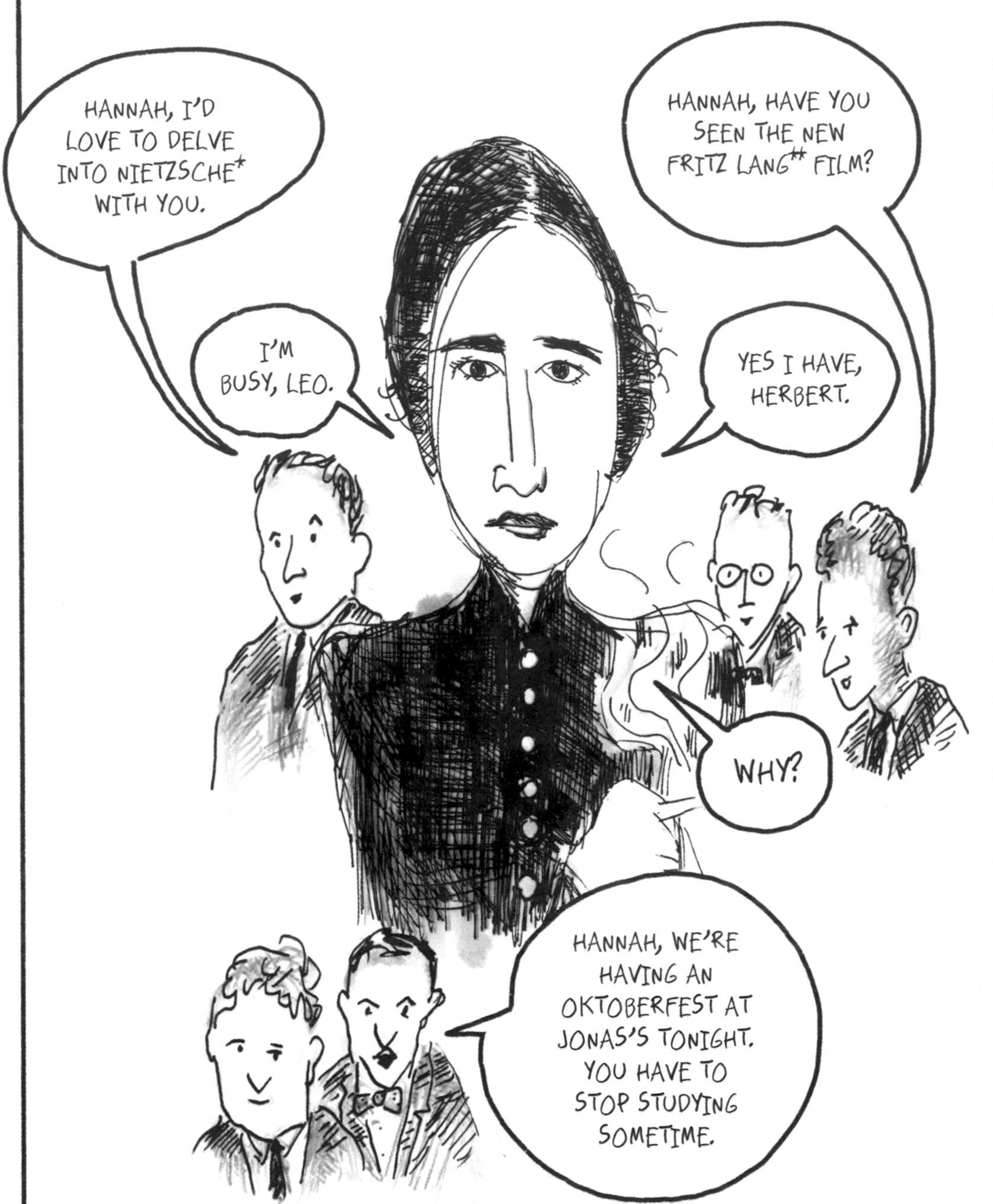
HANNAH, I'D LOVE TO DELVE INTO NIETZSCHE* WITH YOU.
I'M BUSY, LEO.
HANNAH, HAVE YOU SEEN THE NEW FRITZ LANG** FILM?
YES I HAVE, HERBERT.
WHY?
HANNAH, WE'RE HAVING AN OKTOBERFEST AT JONAS'S TONIGHT. YOU HAVE TO STOP STUDYING SOMETIME.

* Friedrich Nietzsche (1844–1900). German philosopher, famous for nihilism, aphorisms, and a very large moustache. He said, "God is dead," to which God supposedly replied in 1900, "Nietzsche is dead." His idea of the *ubermensch*, or Superman, led to some pretty dire consequences, although Siegel and Schuster's (two Jewish kids from Cleveland) Superman comic books weren't one of them. In fact, the "Man of Steel" has been traced to the Jewish mystical man of clay, the Golem.

** Fritz Lang (1890–1976). Monocle-sporting Austrian American half-Jewish filmmaker, who contrasted his dark cinema with that of the German-trained but British director Alfred Hitchcock. If Hitchcock was the "master of suspense," at least according to the British Film Institute, Lang can be called the "master of darkness." He invented the sci-fi movie, the film noir, and the super-spy movie. Kept a pet monkey.

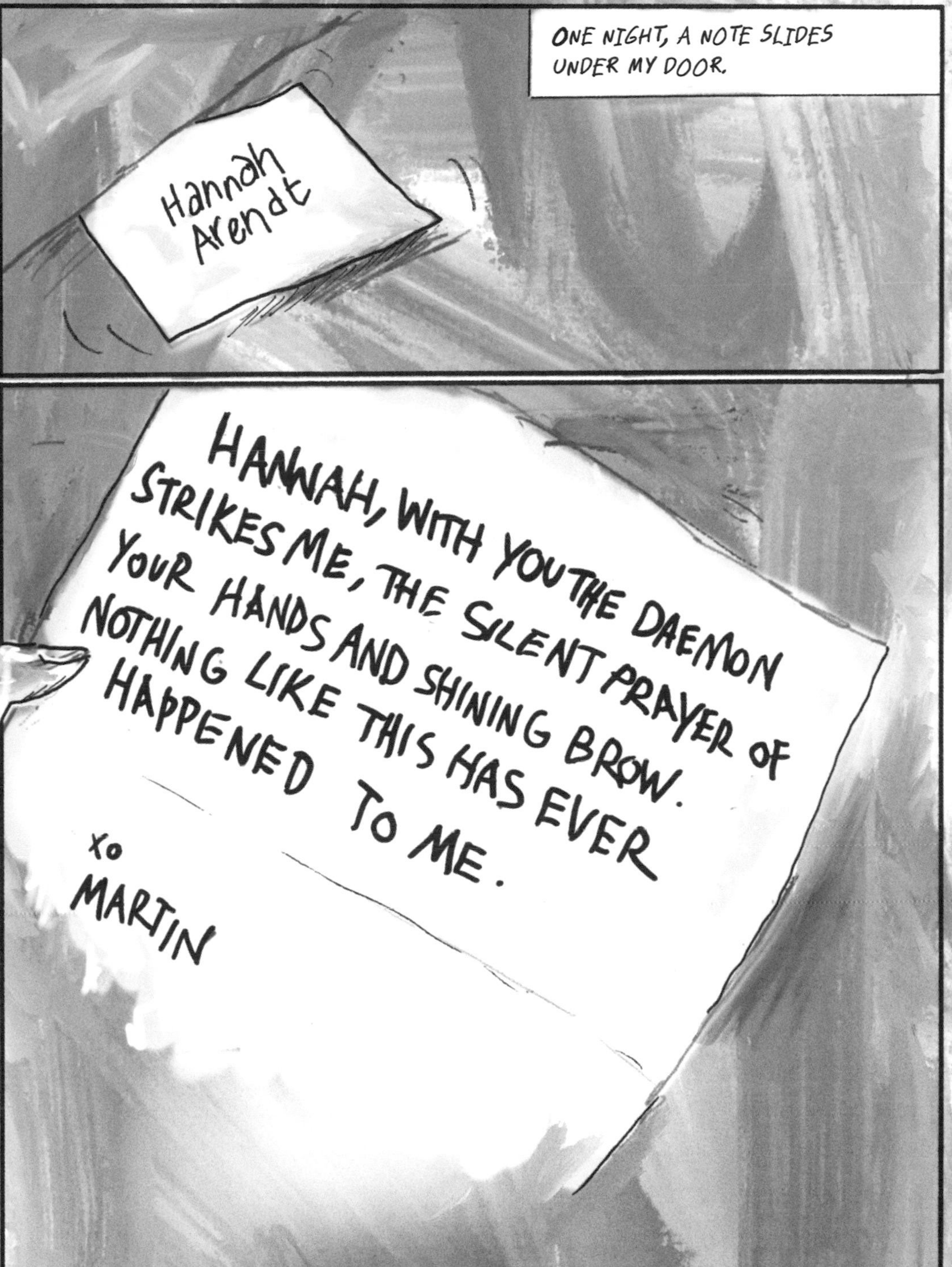
ONE NIGHT, A NOTE SLIDES UNDER MY DOOR.
Hannah Arendt
HANNAH, WITH YOU THE DAEMON STRIKES ME, THE SILENT PRAYER OF YOUR HANDS AND SHINING BROW. NOTHING LIKE THIS HAS EVER HAPPENED TO ME.
xo
MARTIN

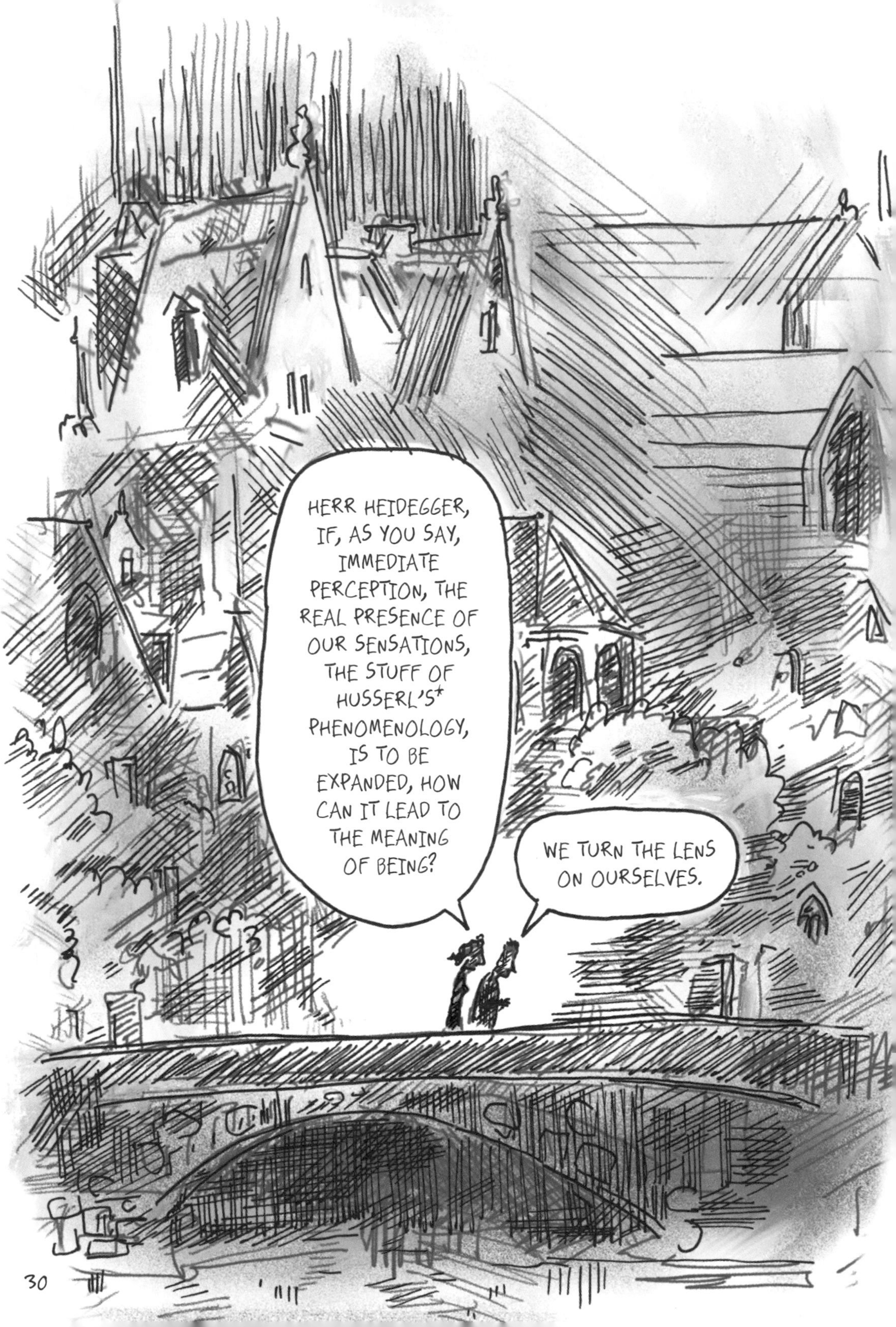
HERR HEIDEGGER, IF, AS YOU SAY, IMMEDIATE PERCEPTION, THE REAL PRESENCE OF OUR SENSATIONS, THE STUFF OF HUSSERL'S* PHENOMENOLOGY, IS TO BE EXPANDED, HOW CAN IT LEAD TO THE MEANING OF BEING?
WE TURN THE LENS ON OURSELVES.

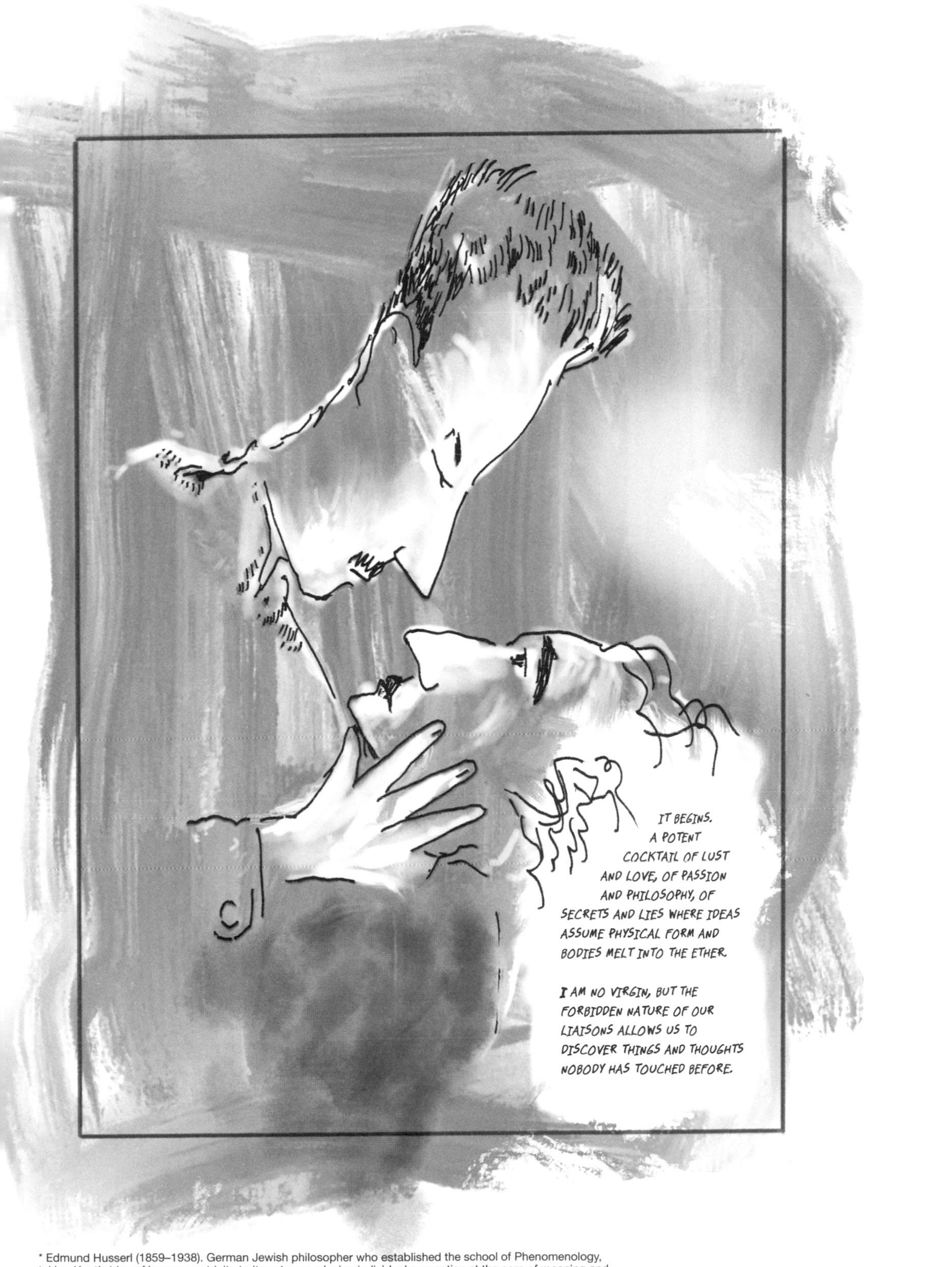
IT BEGINS.
A POTENT COCKTAIL OF LUST AND LOVE, OF PASSION AND PHILOSOPHY, OF SECRETS AND LIES WHERE IDEAS ASSUME PHYSICAL FORM AND BODIES MELT INTO THE ETHER.
I AM NO VIRGIN, BUT THE FORBIDDEN NATURE OF OUR LIAISONS ALLOWS US TO DISCOVER THINGS AND THOUGHTS NOBODY HAS TOUCHED BEFORE.

* Edmund Husserl (1859–1938). German Jewish philosopher who established the school of Phenomenology, taking Kant's idea of human centricity to its extreme, placing individual perception at the core of meaning and being. Heidegger's teacher, mentor, partner, boss, and then, according to some, victim.

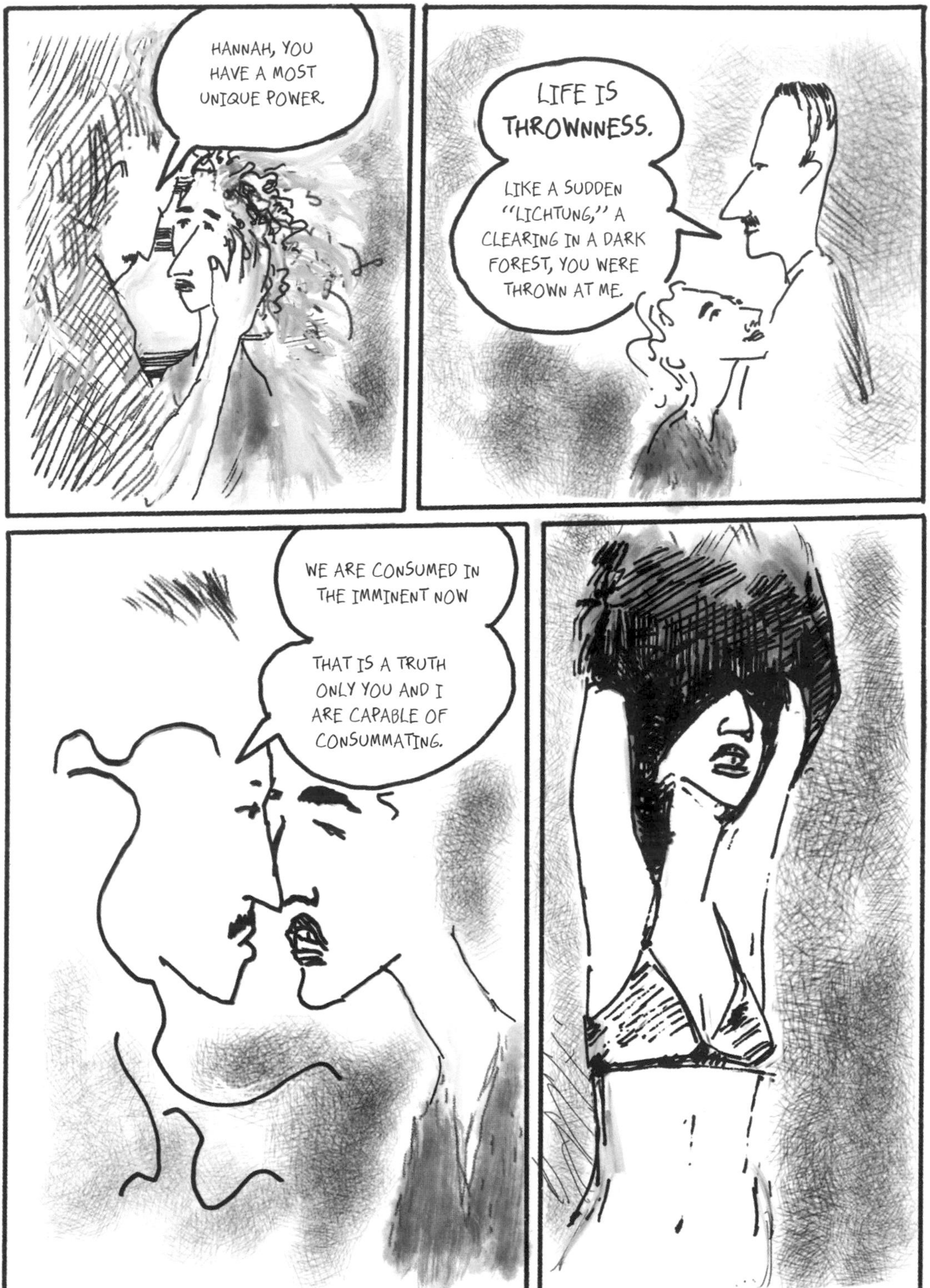
HANNAH, YOU HAVE A MOST UNIQUE POWER.
LIFE IS THROWNNESS.
LIKE A SUDDEN "LICHTUNG," A CLEARING IN A DARK FOREST, YOU WERE THROWN AT ME.
WE ARE CONSUMED IN THE IMMINENT NOW
THAT IS A TRUTH ONLY YOU AND I ARE CAPABLE OF CONSUMMATING.

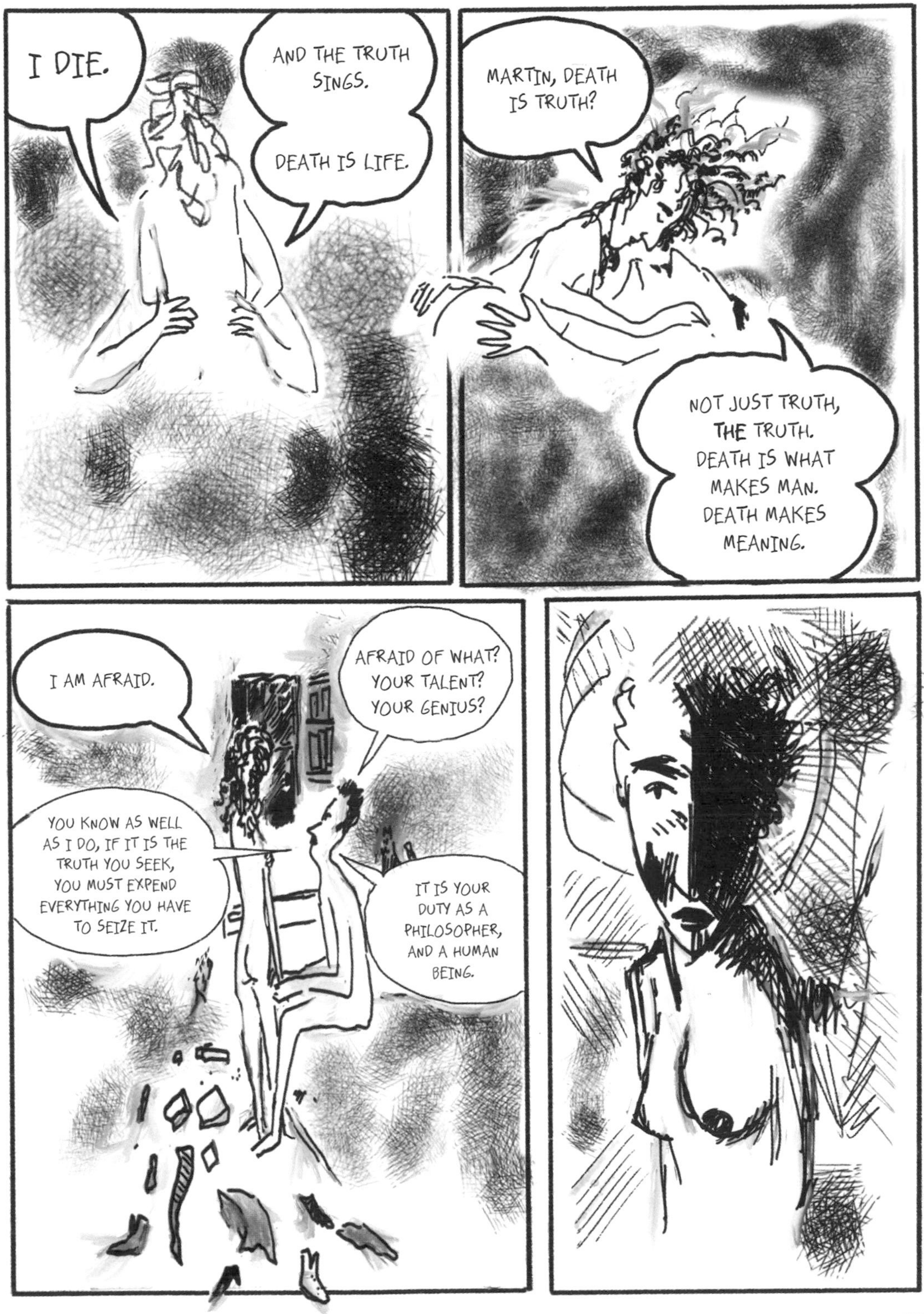
I DIE.
AND THE TRUTH SINGS.
DEATH IS LIFE.
MARTIN, DEATH IS TRUTH?
NOT JUST TRUTH, THE TRUTH. DEATH IS WHAT MAKES MAN. DEATH MAKES MEANING.
I AM AFRAID.
AFRAID OF WHAT? YOUR TALENT? YOUR GENIUS?
YOU KNOW AS WELL AS I DO, IF IT IS THE TRUTH YOU SEEK, YOU MUST EXPEND EVERYTHING YOU HAVE TO SEIZE IT.
IT IS YOUR DUTY AS A PHILOSOPHER, AND A HUMAN BEING.

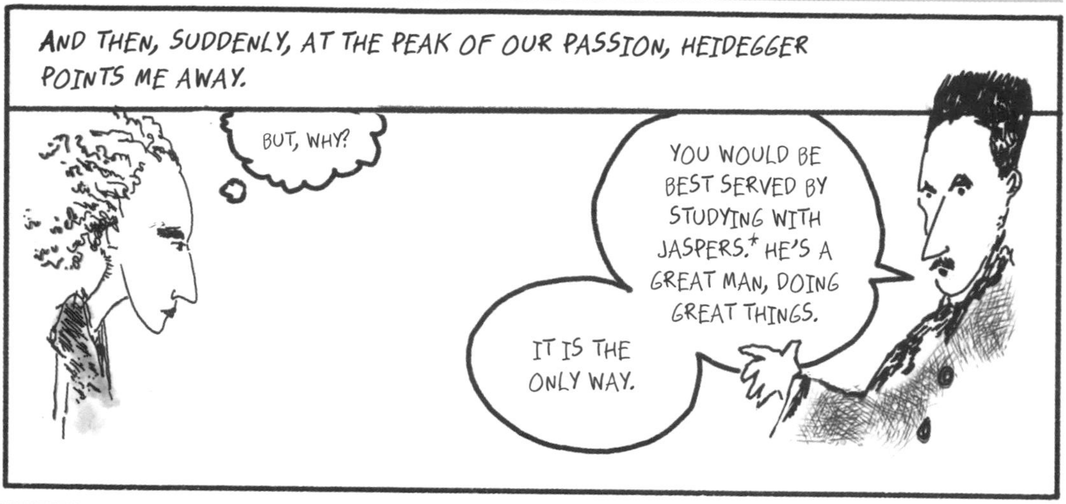
AND THEN, SUDDENLY, AT THE PEAK OF OUR PASSION, HEIDEGGER POINTS ME AWAY.
BUT, WHY?
YOU WOULD BE BEST SERVED BY STUDYING WITH JASPERS.* HE'S A GREAT MAN, DOING GREAT THINGS.
IT IS THE ONLY WAY.

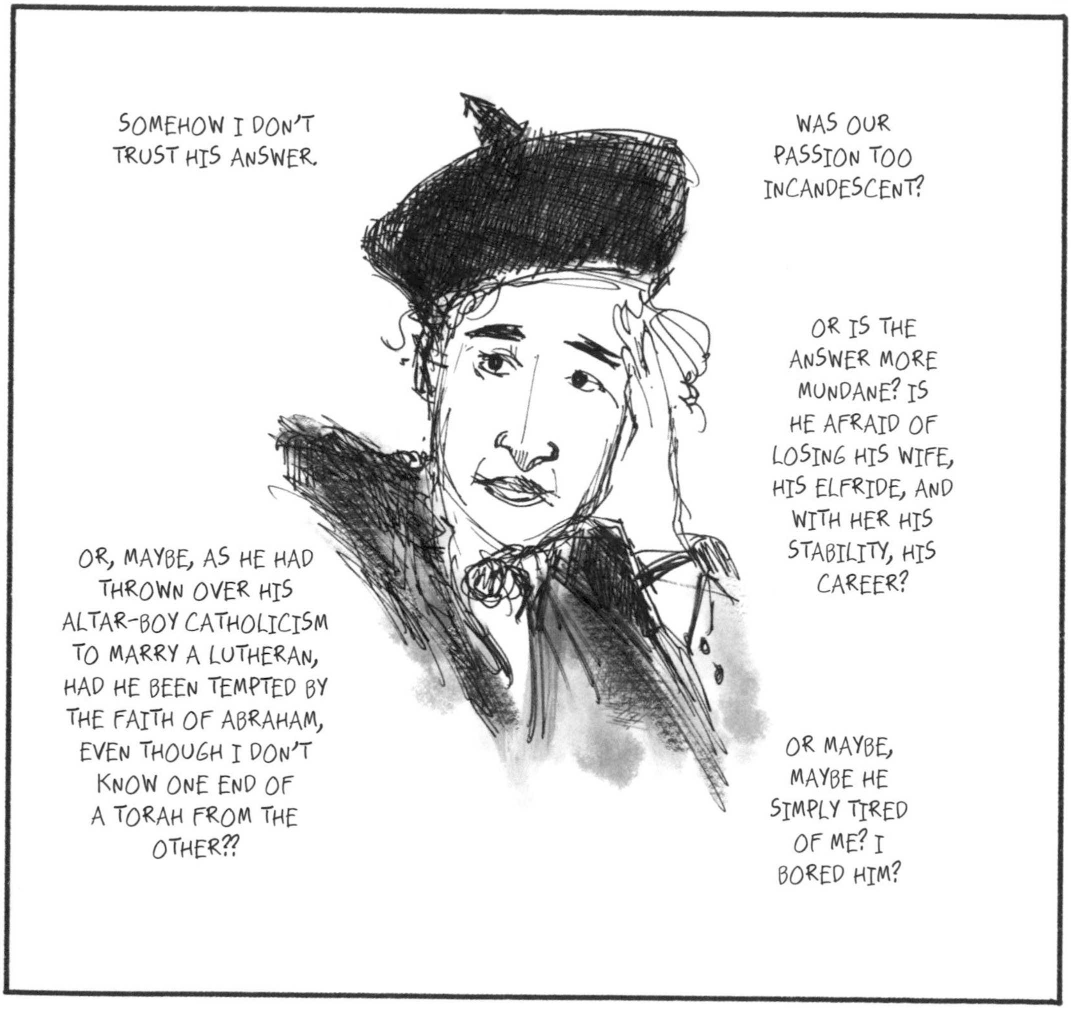
SOMEHOW I DON'T TRUST HIS ANSWER.
WAS OUR PASSION TOO INCANDESCENT?
OR IS THE ANSWER MORE MUNDANE? IS HE AFRAID OF LOSING HIS WIFE, HIS ELFRIDE, AND WITH HER HIS STABILITY, HIS CAREER?
OR, MAYBE, AS HE HAD THROWN OVER HIS ALTAR-BOY CATHOLICISM TO MARRY A LUTHERAN, HAD HE BEEN TEMPTED BY THE FAITH OF ABRAHAM, EVEN THOUGH I DON'T KNOW ONE END OF A TORAH FROM THE OTHER??
OR MAYBE, MAYBE HE SIMPLY TIRED OF ME? I BORED HIM?

* Karl Jaspers (1883–1969). German philosopher, humanist existentialist, and lifelong friend, teacher, and mentor of Hannah Arendt. Married to a Jew himself, his is the "yang" to Heidegger's "yin."

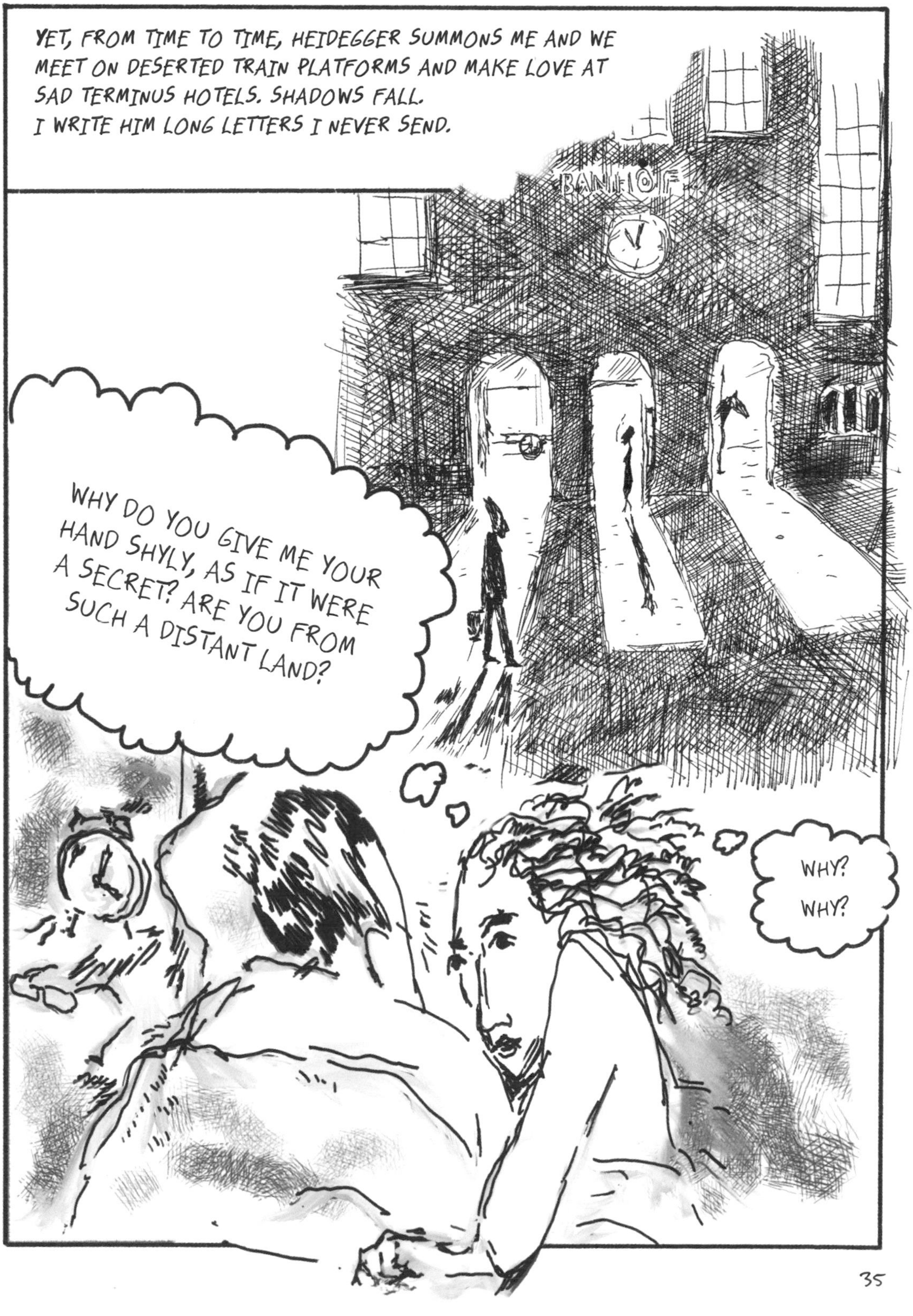
YET, FROM TIME TO TIME, HEIDEGGER SUMMONS ME AND WE MEET ON DESERTED TRAIN PLATFORMS AND MAKE LOVE AT SAD TERMINUS HOTELS. SHADOWS FALL. I WRITE HIM LONG LETTERS I NEVER SEND.
WHY DO YOU GIVE ME YOUR HAND SHYLY, AS IF IT WERE A SECRET? ARE YOU FROM SUCH A DISTANT LAND?
WHY? WHY?

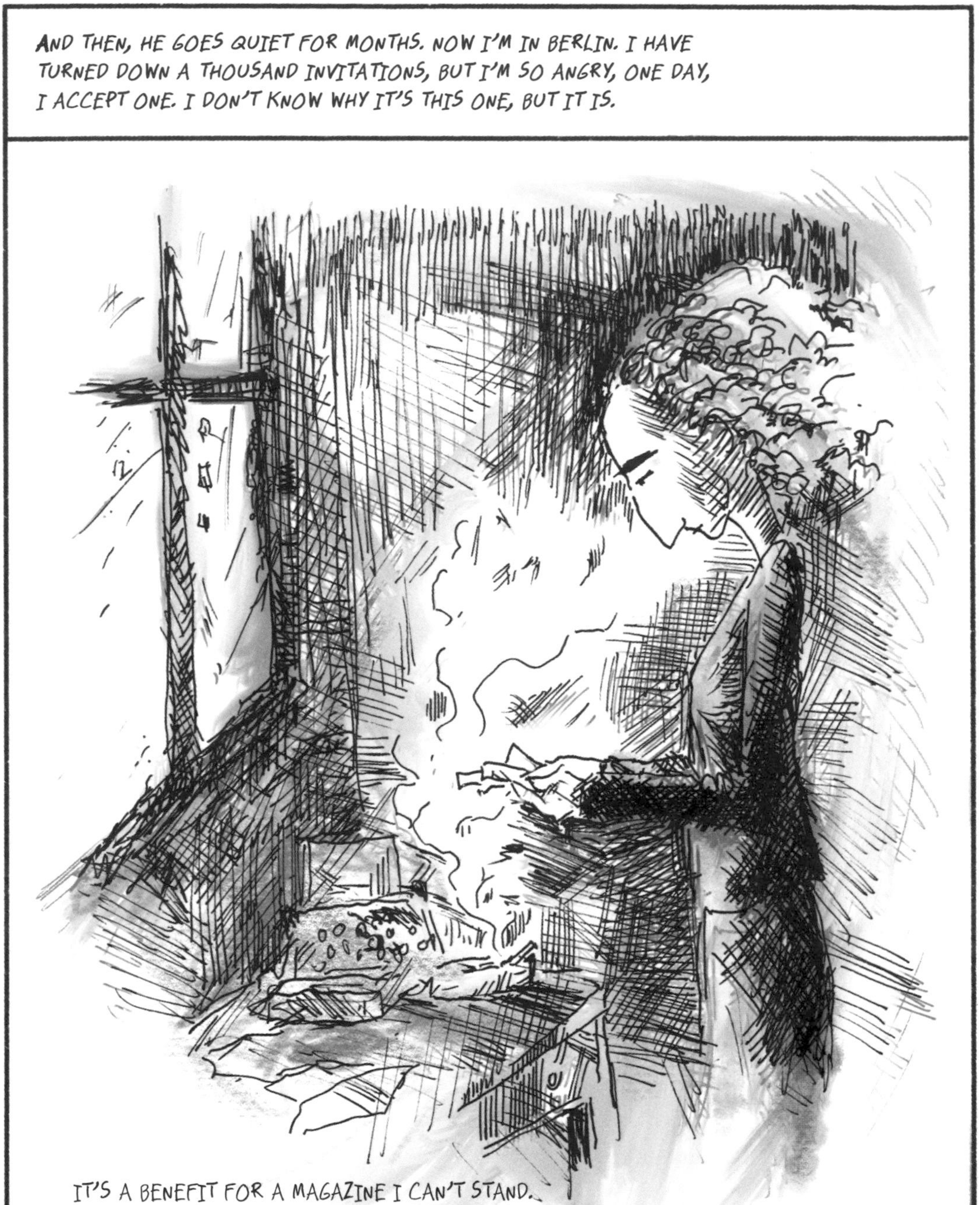
AND THEN, HE GOES QUIET FOR MONTHS. NOW I'M IN BERLIN. I HAVE TURNED DOWN A THOUSAND INVITATIONS, BUT I'M SO ANGRY, ONE DAY, I ACCEPT ONE. I DON'T KNOW WHY IT'S THIS ONE, BUT IT IS.
IT'S A BENEFIT FOR A MAGAZINE I CAN'T STAND. I'M NOT CRAZY ABOUT COMMUNISTS, I DON'T LIKE COSTUME PARTIES, I JUST WANT TO STAY HOME AND READ ARISTOTLE, BUT THAT BASTARD HEIDEGGER HASN'T WRITTEN IN MONTHS SO...

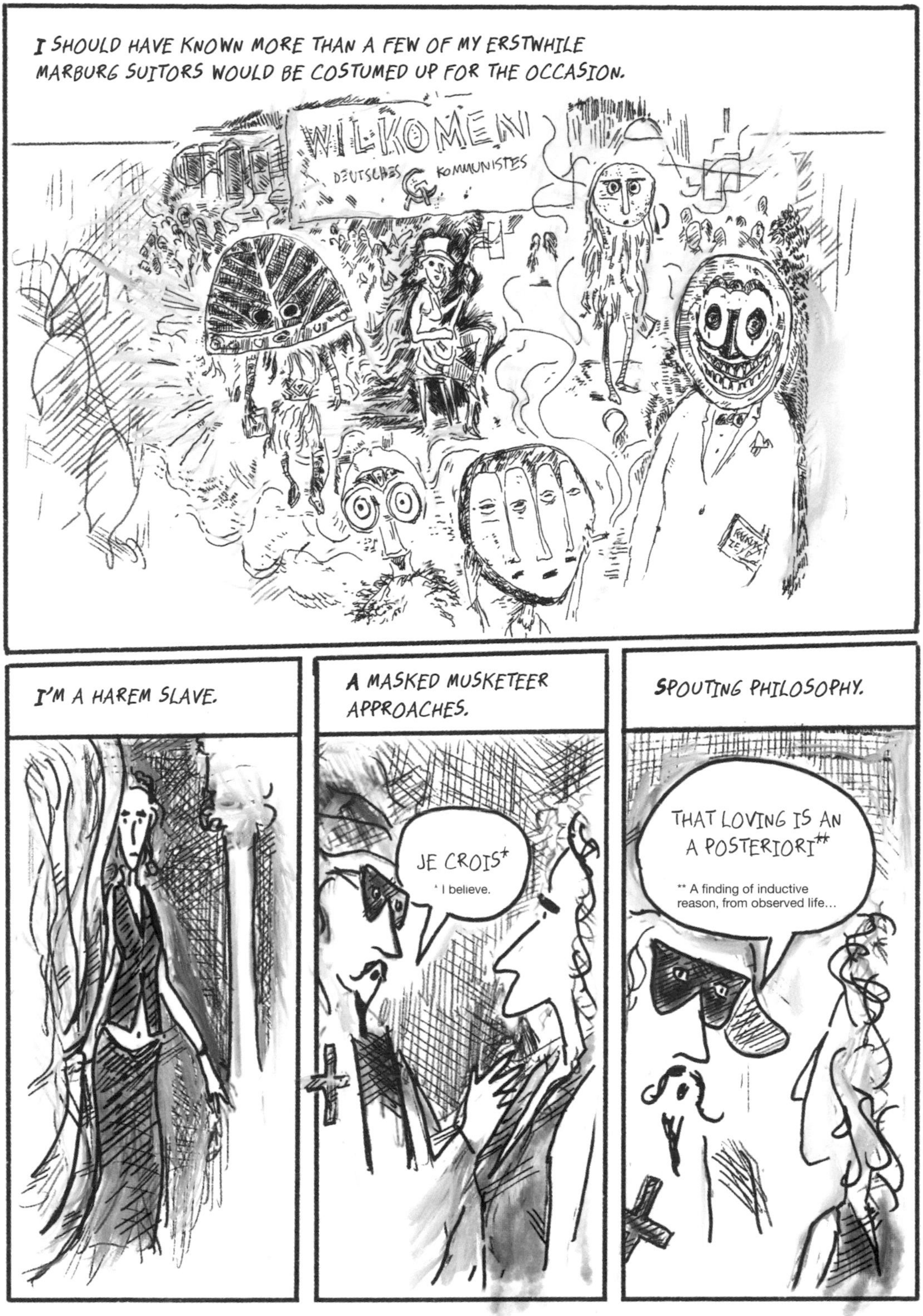
I SHOULD HAVE KNOWN MORE THAN A FEW OF MY ERSTWHILE MARBURG SUITORS WOULD BE COSTUMED UP FOR THE OCCASION.
WILKOMEN
DEUTSCHES KOMMUNISTES
I'M A HAREM SLAVE.
A MASKED MUSKETEER APPROACHES.
JE CROIS*
* I believe.
SPOUTING PHILOSOPHY.
THAT LOVING IS AN A POSTERIORI**
** A finding of inductive reason, from observed life…

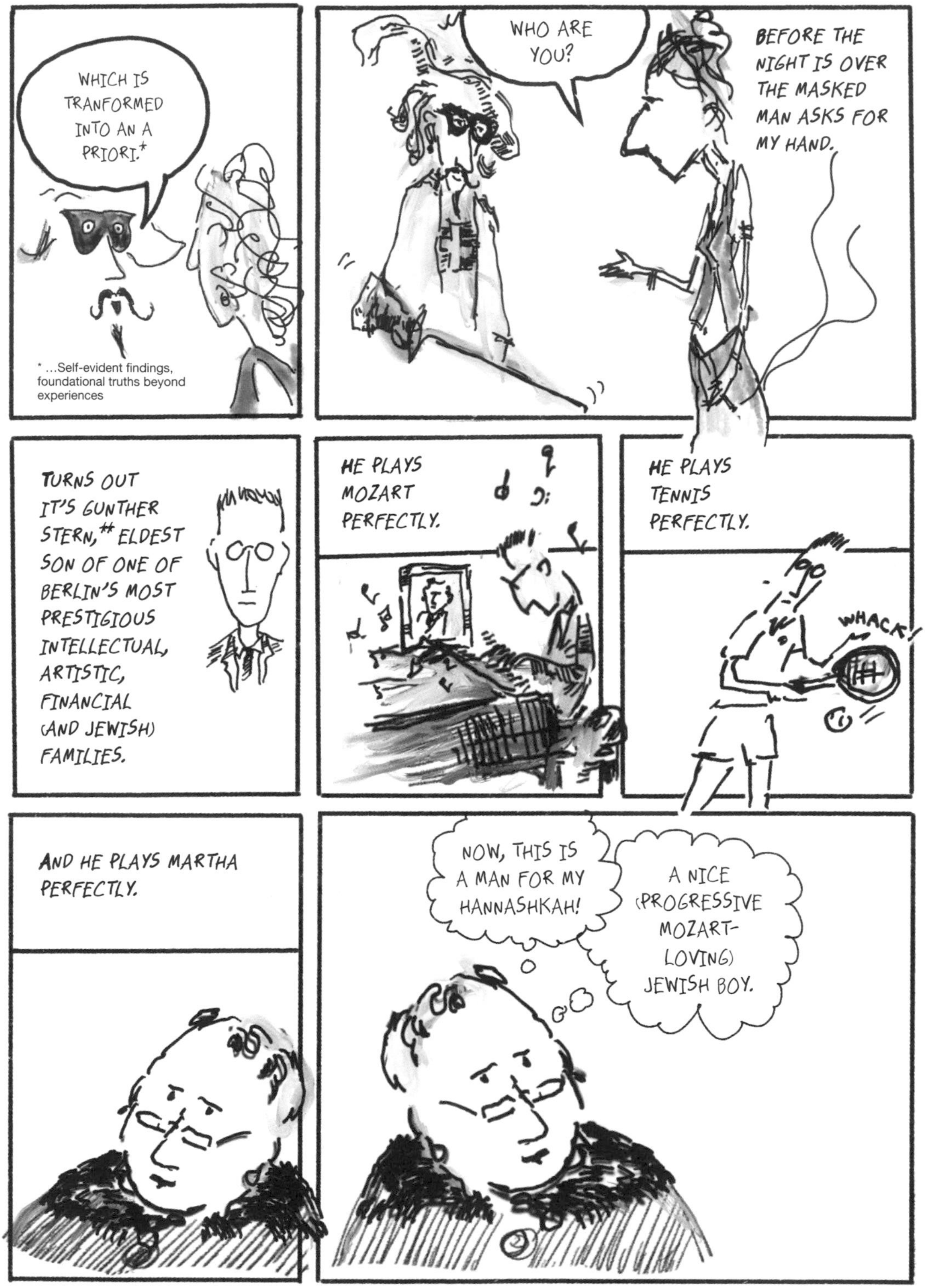
WHICH IS TRANFORMED INTO AN A PRIORI.*
* …Self-evident findings, foundational truths beyond experiences
WHO ARE YOU?
BEFORE THE NIGHT IS OVER THE MASKED MAN ASKS FOR MY HAND.
TURNS OUT IT'S GUNTHER STERN,** ELDEST SON OF ONE OF BERLIN'S MOST PRESTIGIOUS INTELLECTUAL, ARTISTIC, FINANCIAL (AND JEWISH) FAMILIES.
HE PLAYS MOZART PERFECTLY.
HE PLAYS TENNIS PERFECTLY.
WHACK!
AND HE PLAYS MARTHA PERFECTLY.
NOW, THIS IS A MAN FOR MY HANNASHKAH!
A NICE (PROGRESSIVE MOZART-LOVING) JEWISH BOY.

** Gunther Anders (1902–1992). German Jewish journalist, philosopher, critic, and stern anti-nuclear activist. (Born Gunther Stern.) Awarded the Sigmund Freud Prize.

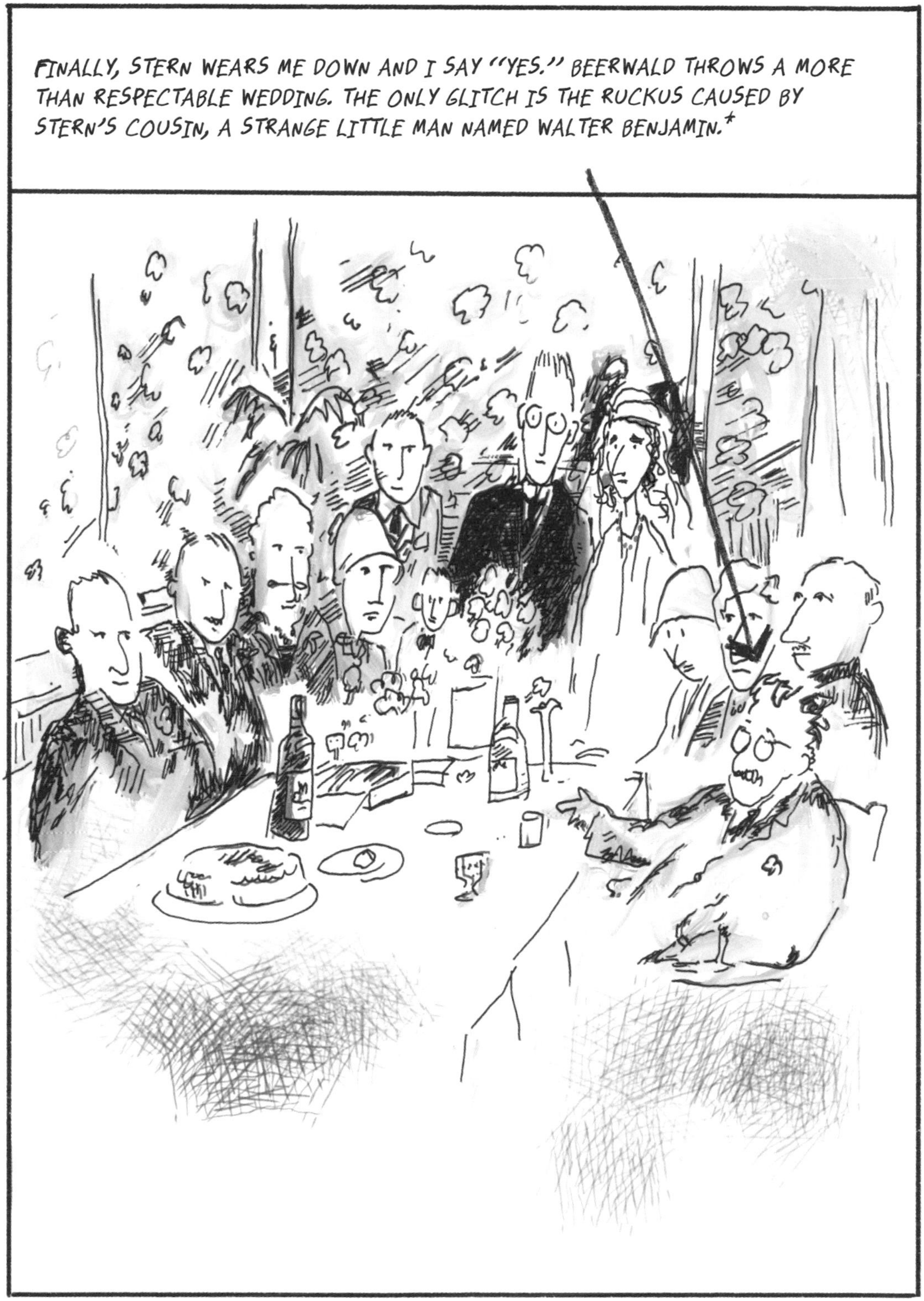
FINALLY, STERN WEARS ME DOWN AND I SAY "YES." BEERWALD THROWS A MORE THAN RESPECTABLE WEDDING. THE ONLY GLITCH IS THE RUCKUS CAUSED BY STERN'S COUSIN, A STRANGE LITTLE MAN NAMED WALTER BENJAMIN.*

* Walter Benjamin (1892–1940). German Jewish philosopher, critic, and flaneur. One of those thinkers who simply cannot fit into a box and yet whose influence continues to resonate in everything from urban planning to fine art to mysticism.

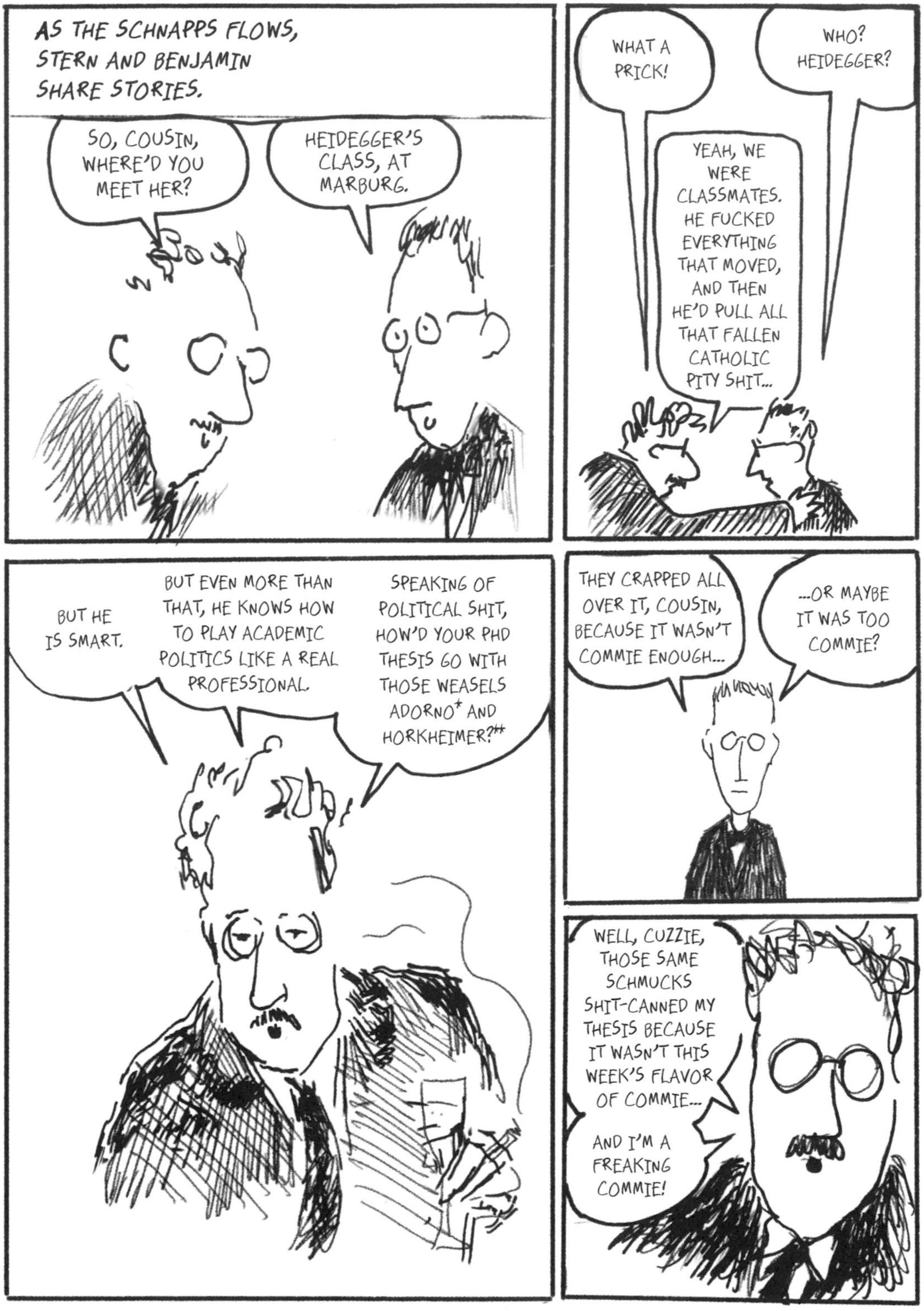
AS THE SCHNAPPS FLOWS, STERN AND BENJAMIN SHARE STORIES.
SO, COUSIN, WHERE'D YOU MEET HER?
HEIDEGGER'S CLASS, AT MARBURG.
WHAT A PRICK!
WHO? HEIDEGGER?
YEAH, WE WERE CLASSMATES. HE FUCKED EVERYTHING THAT MOVED, AND THEN HE'D PULL ALL THAT FALLEN CATHOLIC PITY SHIT...
BUT HE IS SMART.
BUT EVEN MORE THAN THAT, HE KNOWS HOW TO PLAY ACADEMIC POLITICS LIKE A REAL PROFESSIONAL.
SPEAKING OF POLITICAL SHIT, HOW'D YOUR PHD THESIS GO WITH THOSE WEASELS ADORNO* AND HORKHEIMER?**
THEY CRAPPED ALL OVER IT, COUSIN, BECAUSE IT WASN'T COMMIE ENOUGH...
...OR MAYBE IT WAS TOO COMMIE?
WELL, CUZZIE, THOSE SAME SCHMUCKS SHIT-CANNED MY THESIS BECAUSE IT WASN'T THIS WEEK'S FLAVOR OF COMMIE...
AND I'M A FREAKING COMMIE!

* Theodor Adorno (1903–1969). German Jewish thinker, key figure in the Frankfurt School of social theory, a neo-Marxian interpretation of everything. (Born as Theodore Weissengrad.) Some of his colleagues smelled a rat since he assumed a flagrantly Italian name and Italianate mannerisms to mask his Semitic roots.

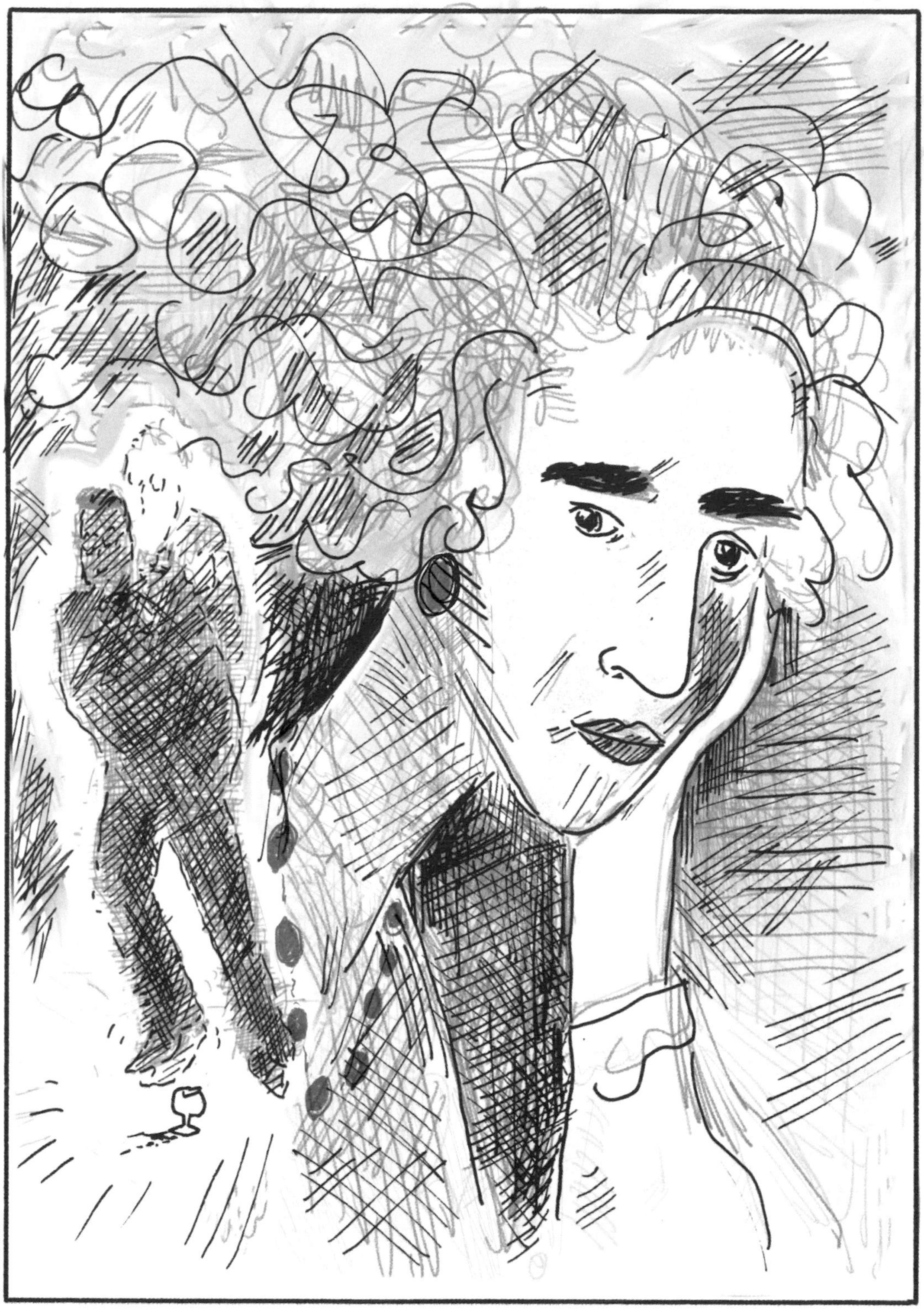

** Max Horkheimer (1895–1973). German Jewish philosopher and social critic, foundational member of the Frankfurt School.

Hannah's First Escape

Berlin

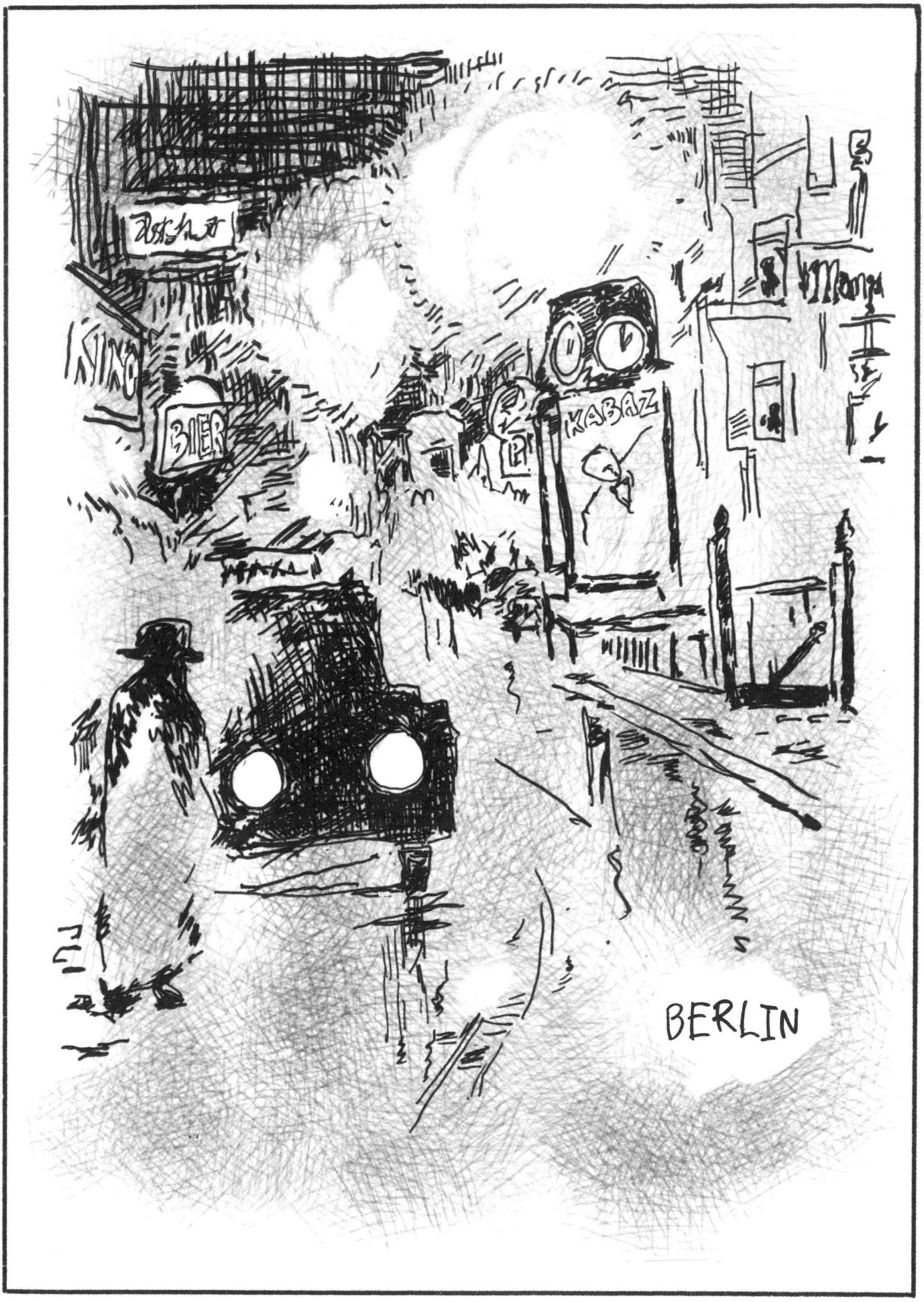
KINO
BIER
BERLIN

THE ROMANISCHES 1933

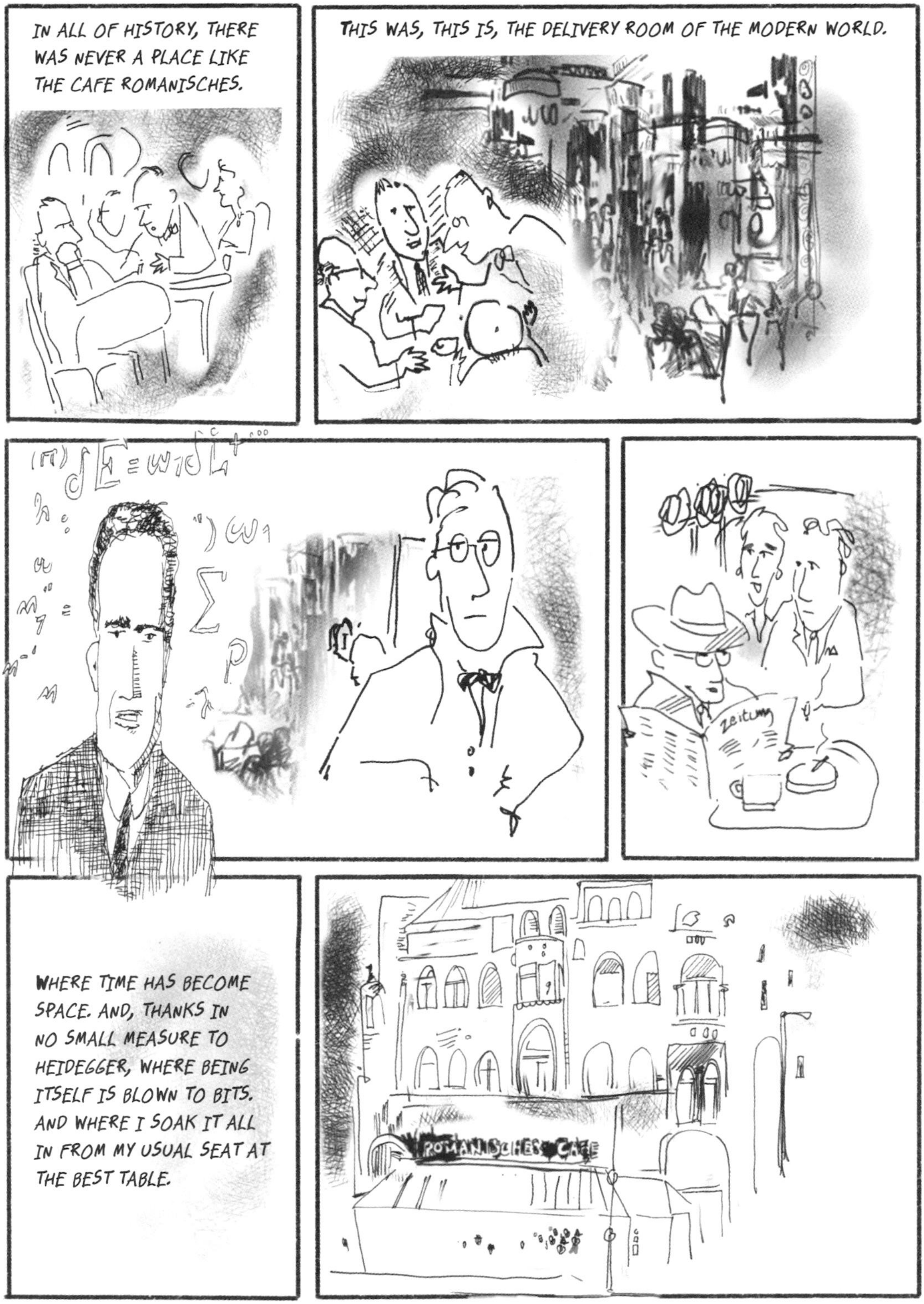
IN ALL OF HISTORY, THERE WAS NEVER A PLACE LIKE THE CAFE ROMANISCHES.
THIS WAS, THIS IS, THE DELIVERY ROOM OF THE MODERN WORLD.
Zeitung
WHERE TIME HAS BECOME SPACE. AND, THANKS IN NO SMALL MEASURE TO HEIDEGGER, WHERE BEING ITSELF IS BLOWN TO BITS. AND WHERE I SOAK IT ALL IN FROM MY USUAL SEAT AT THE BEST TABLE.
ROMANISCHES CAFE

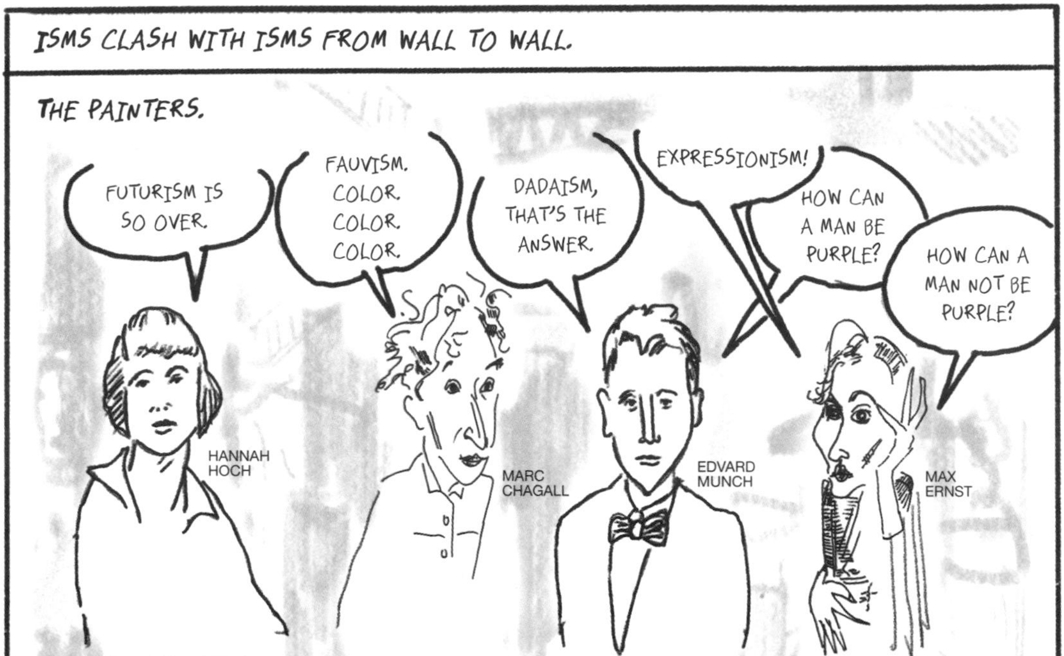
ISMS CLASH WITH ISMS FROM WALL TO WALL.
THE PAINTERS.
FUTURISM IS SO OVER.
FAUVISM. COLOR. COLOR. COLOR.
DADAISM, THAT'S THE ANSWER.
EXPRESSIONISM!
HOW CAN A MAN BE PURPLE?
HOW CAN A MAN NOT BE PURPLE?
HANNAH HOCH
MARC CHAGALL
EDVARD MUNCH
MAX ERNST

(1) Hannah Hoch (1889–1978): German Jewish artist, credited with refining the art of photomontage and with it the entire notion of the "mash-up," a very postmodern idea that drives much of the world of art and music today. (2) Mark Chagall (1887–1985). Russian Jewish artist born Moishe Shagalov, his embrace of the naïve masked an intense sophistication regarding color, myth, and story. His fans ranged from ardent Jungians to Mayor Richard J. Daley of the Great City of Chicago. (3) Edvard Munch (1863–1944). Neo-mystical Norwegian painter who plumbed his personal despair to create one of the icons of modern art (and times), *The Scream*. (4) Max Ernst (1891–1976). German artist, refugee from Hitler, and a foundational figure in a-rational (as if there is any other kind) art movements like dada and surrealism. (5) Artur Schnabel (1882–1951). Austrian Jewish pianist, the *New York Times* dubbed him "the man who invented Beethoven." Nazi music critics decried his playing as "too Jewish." He managed to escape but his mother and father perished in the camps during the war. (6) Arnold Schoenberg (1874–1951). Austrian Jewish composer and painter, credited with inventing modern atonal music. The Nazis labeled his art "degenerate." He fled to Hollywood (of all places), fearing the number 8 above all things.

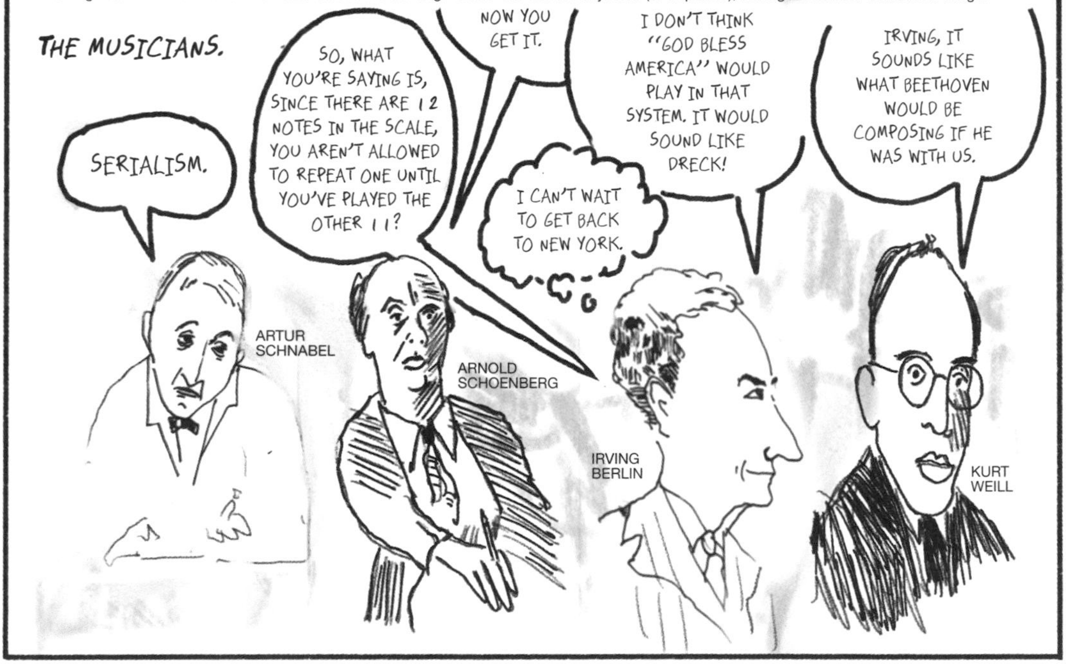
THE MUSICIANS.
SERIALISM.
SO, WHAT YOU'RE SAYING IS, SINCE THERE ARE 12 NOTES IN THE SCALE, YOU AREN'T ALLOWED TO REPEAT ONE UNTIL YOU'VE PLAYED THE OTHER 11?
NOW YOU GET IT.
I CAN'T WAIT TO GET BACK TO NEW YORK.
I DON'T THINK "GOD BLESS AMERICA" WOULD PLAY IN THAT SYSTEM. IT WOULD SOUND LIKE DRECK!
IRVING, IT SOUNDS LIKE WHAT BEETHOVEN WOULD BE COMPOSING IF HE WAS WITH US.
ARTUR SCHNABEL
ARNOLD SCHOENBERG
IRVING BERLIN
KURT WEILL

(7) Irving Berlin (1888–1989). Russian Jewish composer and lyricist, his "White Christmas" is the biggest-selling, most-recorded song ever. He eloped to Europe with his second wife, and headed straight to Berlin in the late 1920s to get away from it all. A difficult man and a source of great envy, his fellow composer Harry Warren quipped during World War II that the Allied Forces were "bombing the wrong Berlin." (8) Kurt Weill (1900–1950). German Jewish composer, known for his subversive political collaboration with Bertolt Brecht, his dystopian Weimar ditty "Mack the Knife" was a peculiar hit in Eisenhower's 1950s America for both Bobby Darin and Ella Fitzgerald.

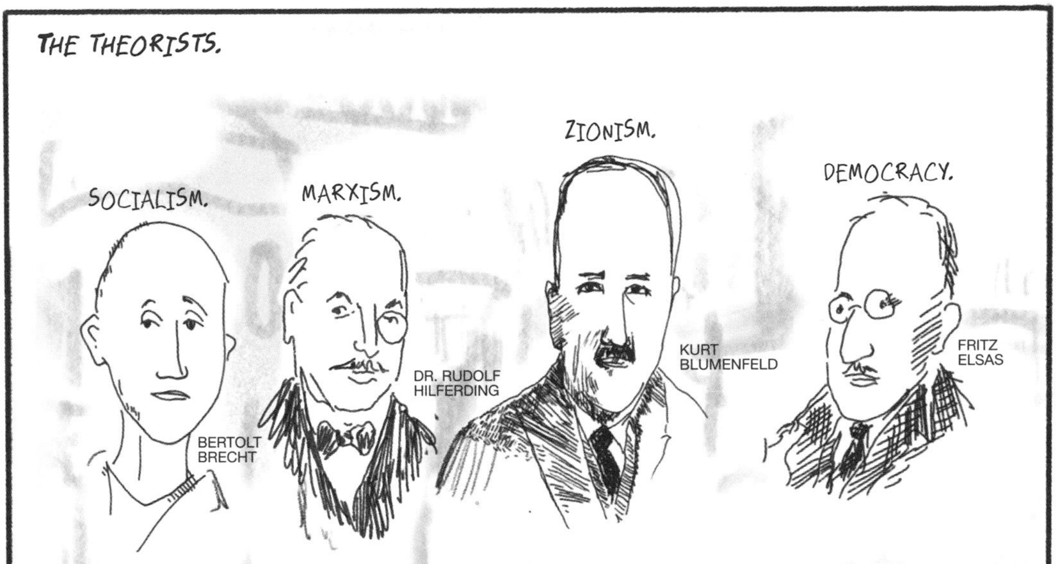
THE THEORISTS.
SOCIALISM.
MARXISM.
ZIONISM.
DEMOCRACY.
BERTOLT BRECHT
DR. RUDOLF HILFERDING
KURT BLUMENFELD
FRITZ ELSAS

(1) Bertolt Brecht (1898–1956). German poet and playwright, infused modern popular theater with strong political, anti-fascist messages. Pioneered "distancing" techniques (*Verfremdungseffekt*) to make it impossible for audiences to simply be swept away in the illusion of spectacle, but to truly *feel*. (2) Dr. Rudolf Hilferding (1877–1941). Austrian Jewish Marxist, economist, and physician. (3) Kurt Blumenfeld (1884–1963). German Jewish politician, key figure in the development of modern political Zionism as an organized response to persecution, and, like Hannah Arendt, from Konigsberg. (4) Fritz Elsas (1890–1945). Jewish German mayor of Berlin from 1931 until 1933. Executed at Sachhausen concentration camp by the Nazis. (5) Sir Alfred Hitchcock (1899–1980). English film director and producer, he learned his craft working at the legendary UFA film studios in Berlin in the 1920s. (6) Fritz Lang (1890–1976). (See page 28.)

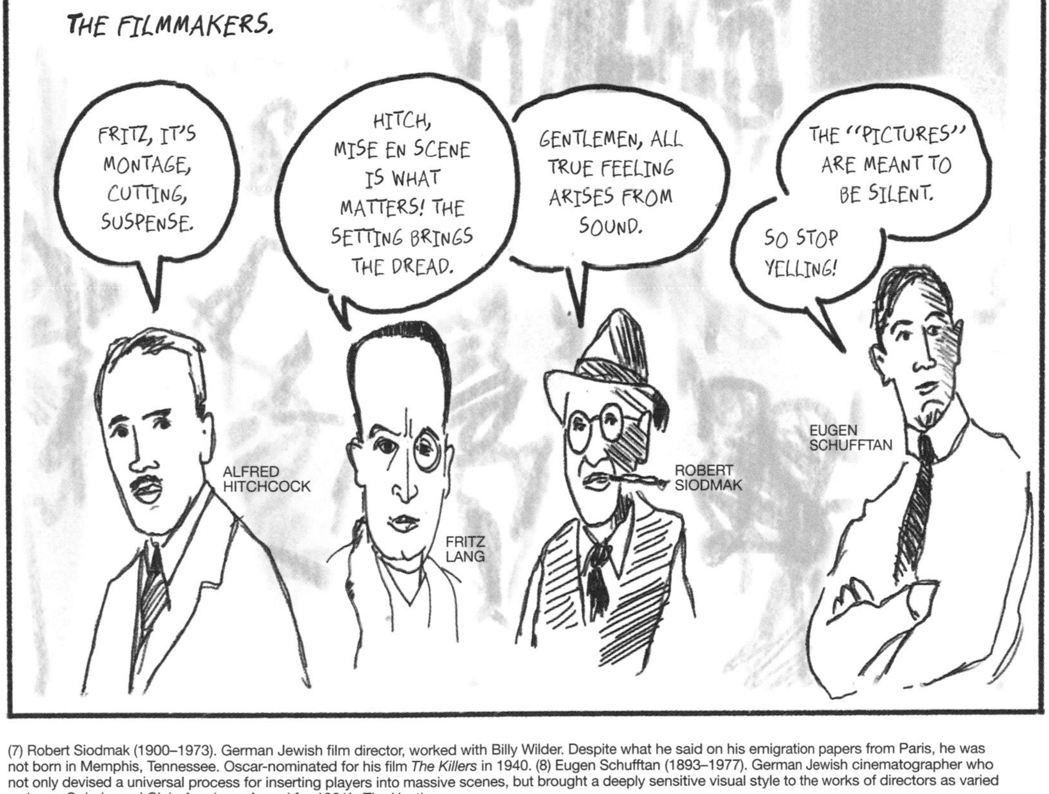
THE FILMMAKERS.
FRITZ, IT'S MONTAGE, CUTTING, SUSPENSE.
HITCH, MISE EN SCENE IS WHAT MATTERS! THE SETTING BRINGS THE DREAD.
GENTLEMEN, ALL TRUE FEELING ARISES FROM SOUND.
THE "PICTURES" ARE MEANT TO BE SILENT.
SO STOP YELLING!
ALFRED HITCHCOCK
FRITZ LANG
ROBERT SIODMAK
EUGEN SCHUFFTAN

(7) Robert Siodmak (1900–1973). German Jewish film director, worked with Billy Wilder. Despite what he said on his emigration papers from Paris, he was not born in Memphis, Tennessee. Oscar-nominated for his film *The Killers* in 1940. (8) Eugen Schufftan (1893–1977). German Jewish cinematographer who not only devised a universal process for inserting players into massive scenes, but brought a deeply sensitive visual style to the works of directors as varied as Lang, Ophuls, and Clair. Academy Award for 1961's *The Hustler*.

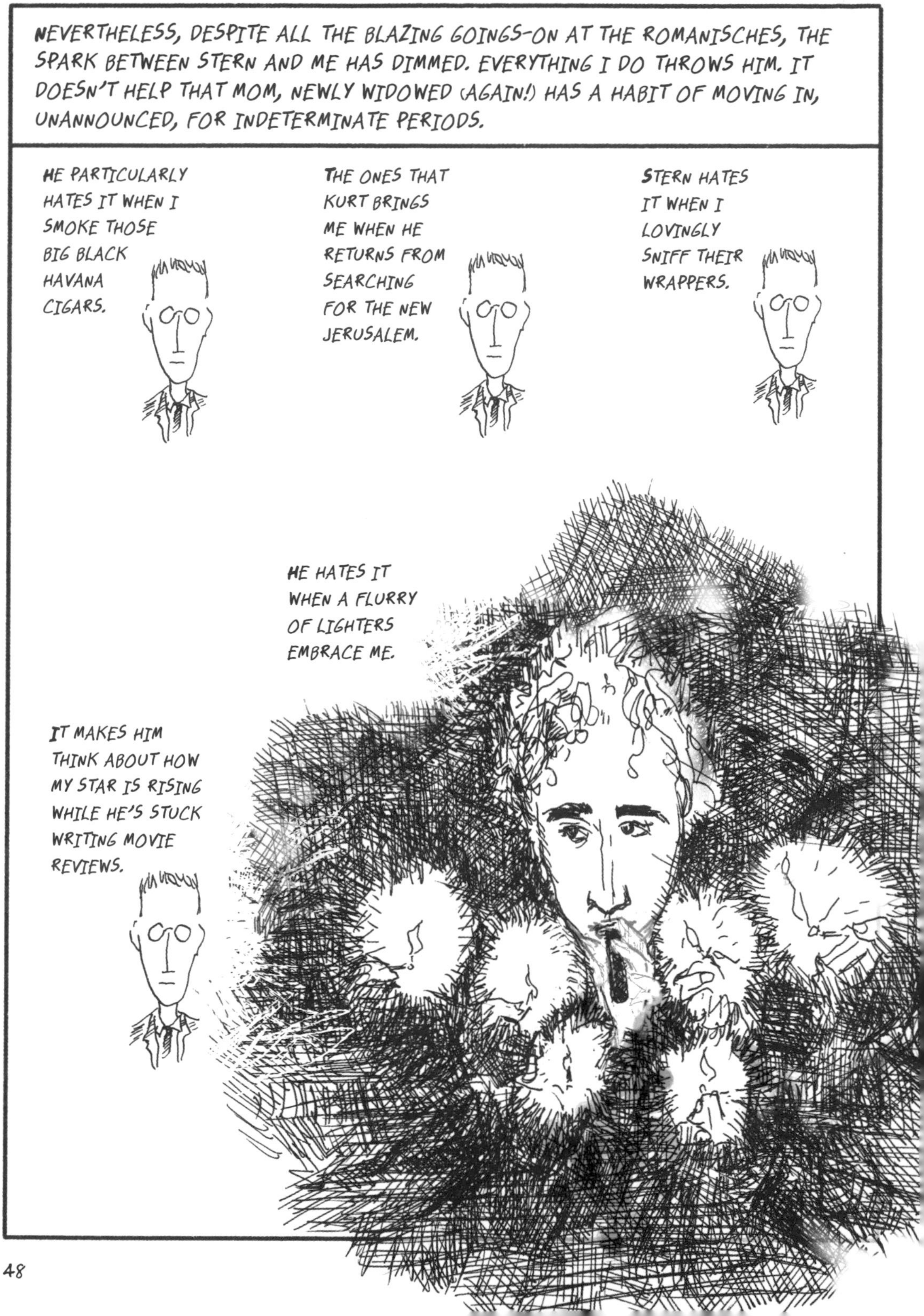
NEVERTHELESS, DESPITE ALL THE BLAZING GOINGS-ON AT THE ROMANISCHES, THE SPARK BETWEEN STERN AND ME HAS DIMMED. EVERYTHING I DO THROWS HIM. IT DOESN'T HELP THAT MOM, NEWLY WIDOWED (AGAIN!) HAS A HABIT OF MOVING IN, UNANNOUNCED, FOR INDETERMINATE PERIODS.
HE PARTICULARLY HATES IT WHEN I SMOKE THOSE BIG BLACK HAVANA CIGARS.
THE ONES THAT KURT BRINGS ME WHEN HE RETURNS FROM SEARCHING FOR THE NEW JERUSALEM.
STERN HATES IT WHEN I LOVINGLY SNIFF THEIR WRAPPERS.
HE HATES IT WHEN A FLURRY OF LIGHTERS EMBRACE ME.
IT MAKES HIM THINK ABOUT HOW MY STAR IS RISING WHILE HE'S STUCK WRITING MOVIE REVIEWS.

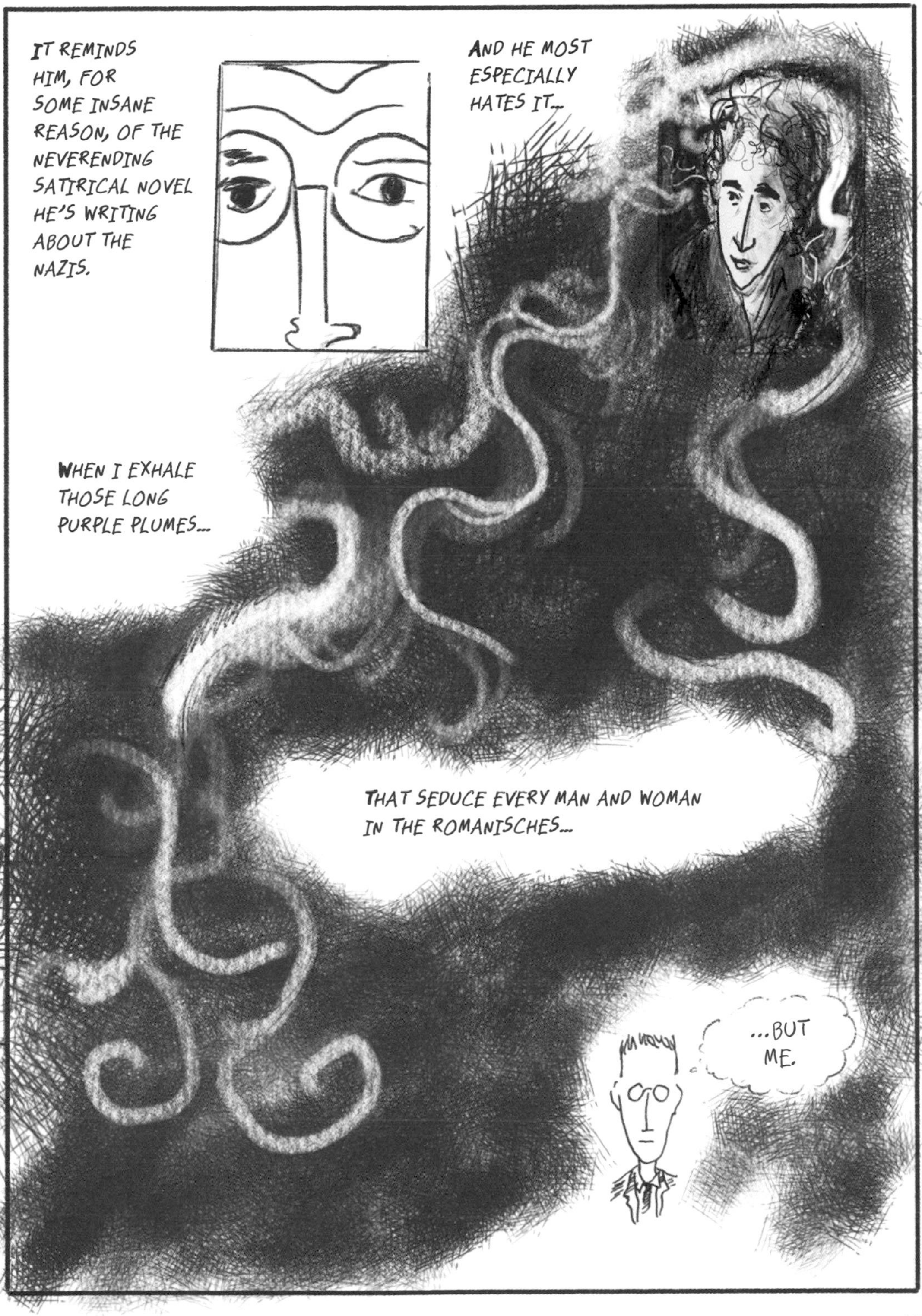
IT REMINDS HIM, FOR SOME INSANE REASON, OF THE NEVERENDING SATIRICAL NOVEL HE'S WRITING ABOUT THE NAZIS.
AND HE MOST ESPECIALLY HATES IT...
WHEN I EXHALE THOSE LONG PURPLE PLUMES...
THAT SEDUCE EVERY MAN AND WOMAN IN THE ROMANISCHES...
...BUT ME.

KANGAROO COURT IS IN SESSION: FEB. 27, 1933

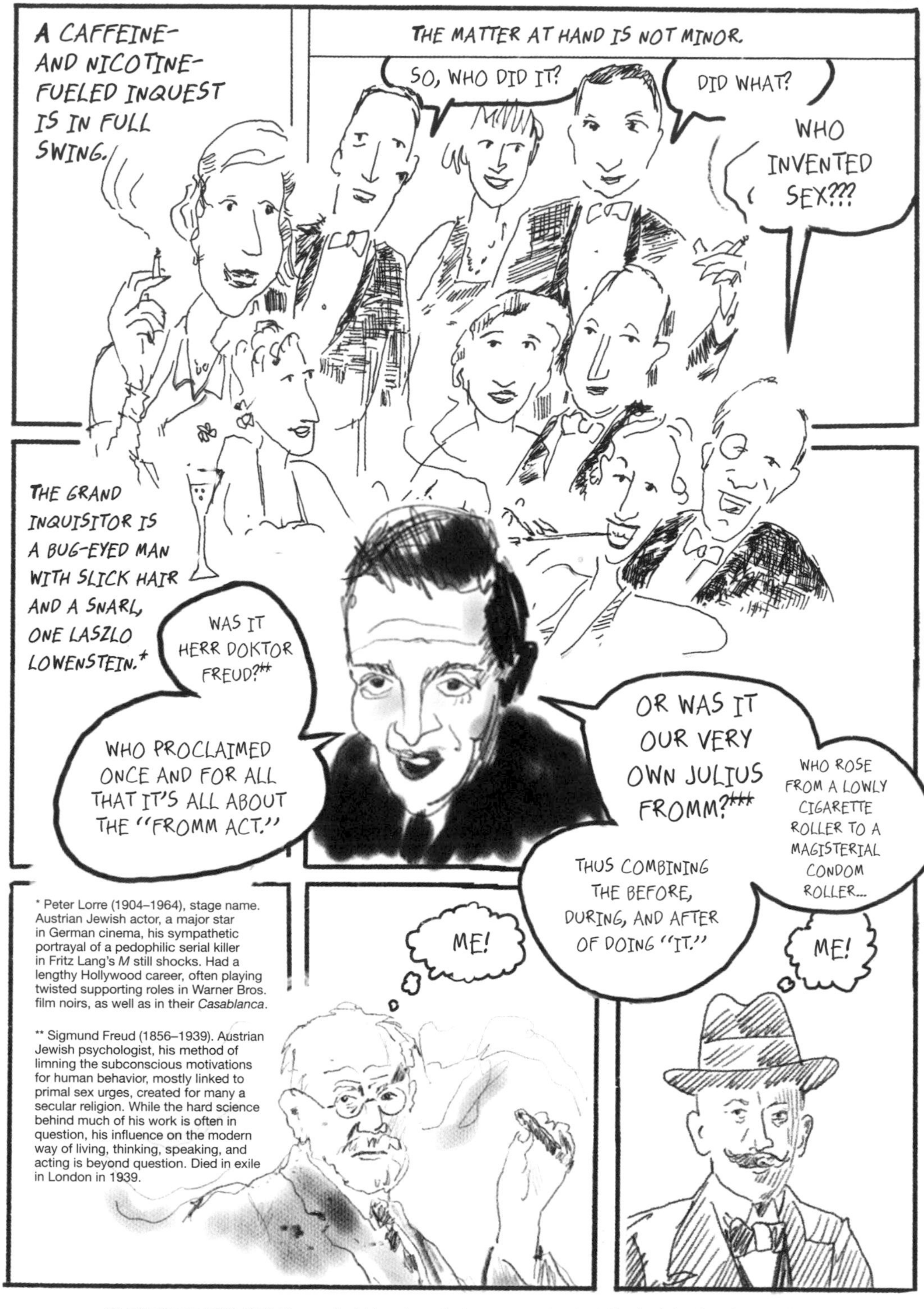
A CAFFEINE- AND NICOTINE-FUELED INQUEST IS IN FULL SWING.
THE MATTER AT HAND IS NOT MINOR.
SO, WHO DID IT?
DID WHAT?
WHO INVENTED SEX???
THE GRAND INQUISITOR IS A BUG-EYED MAN WITH SLICK HAIR AND A SNARL, ONE LASZLO LOWENSTEIN.*
WAS IT HERR DOKTOR FREUD?**
WHO PROCLAIMED ONCE AND FOR ALL THAT IT'S ALL ABOUT THE "FROMM ACT."
OR WAS IT OUR VERY OWN JULIUS FROMM?***
WHO ROSE FROM A LOWLY CIGARETTE ROLLER TO A MAGISTERIAL CONDOM ROLLER...
THUS COMBINING THE BEFORE, DURING, AND AFTER OF DOING "IT."
ME!
ME!

* Peter Lorre (1904–1964), stage name. Austrian Jewish actor, a major star in German cinema, his sympathetic portrayal of a pedophilic serial killer in Fritz Lang's *M* still shocks. Had a lengthy Hollywood career, often playing twisted supporting roles in Warner Bros. film noirs, as well as in their *Casablanca*.

** Sigmund Freud (1856–1939). Austrian Jewish psychologist, his method of limning the subconscious motivations for human behavior, mostly linked to primal sex urges, created for many a secular religion. While the hard science behind much of his work is often in question, his influence on the modern way of living, thinking, speaking, and acting is beyond question. Died in exile in London in 1939.

*** Julius Fromm (1883–1945). German Jewish inventor and entrepreneur, parlayed a night-school chemistry degree and a hardscrabble career as a lowly cigarette roller into his invention of the modern latex condom. His "Fromm's Act" condoms were so pervasive, in fact, that the phrase "doing the Fromm Act" became generic for having sex, just as "hand me a Kleenex" has become generic for "hand me a tissue." The Nazis stole his business empire from him, gave it to Hermann Goering's godmother, and forced him to flee to London, where he died in penury.

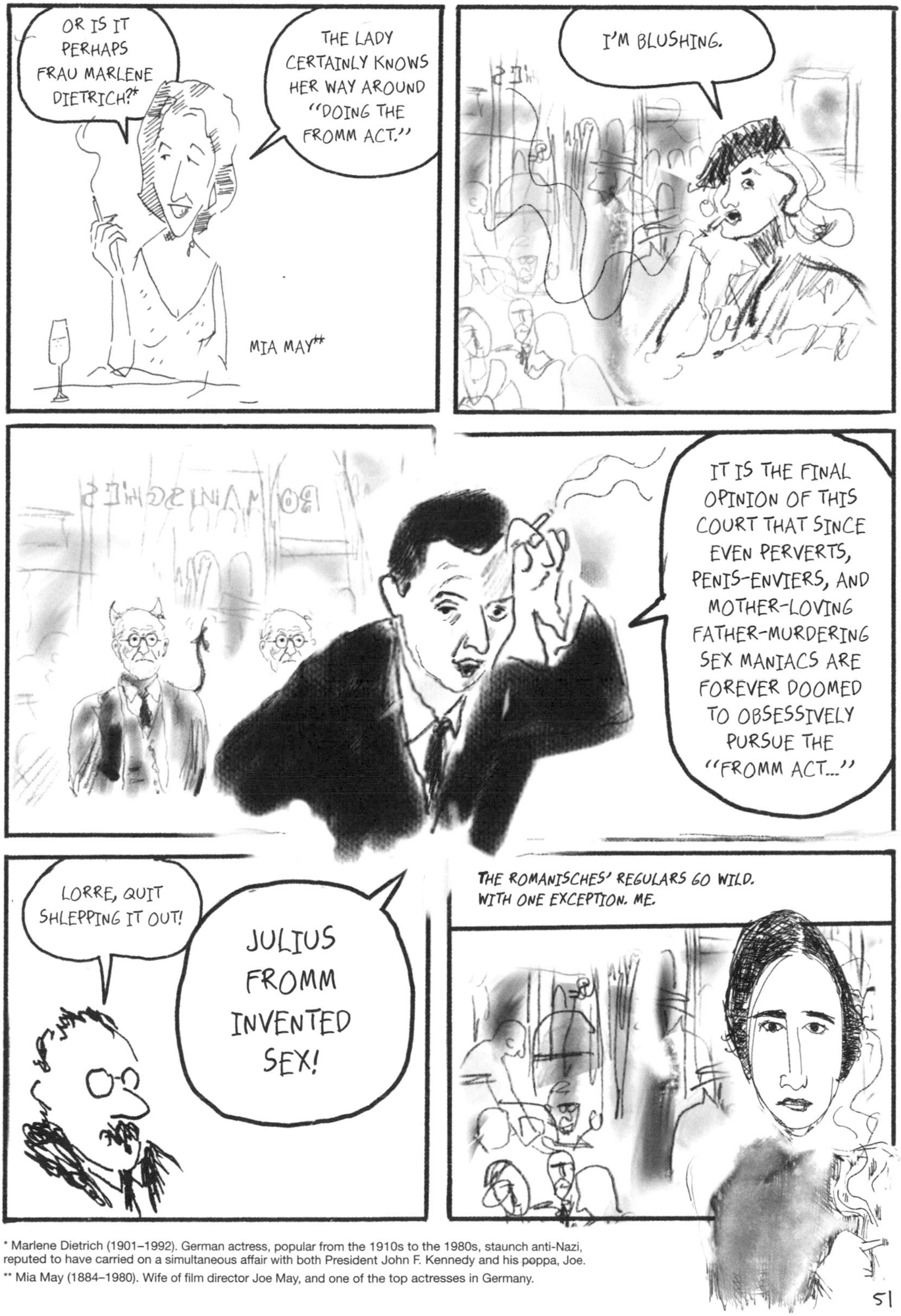
OR IS IT PERHAPS FRAU MARLENE DIETRICH?*
THE LADY CERTAINLY KNOWS HER WAY AROUND "DOING THE FROMM ACT."
MIA MAY**
I'M BLUSHING.
IT IS THE FINAL OPINION OF THIS COURT THAT SINCE EVEN PERVERTS, PENIS-ENVIERS, AND MOTHER-LOVING FATHER-MURDERING SEX MANIACS ARE FOREVER DOOMED TO OBSESSIVELY PURSUE THE "FROMM ACT..."
LORRE, QUIT SHLEPPING IT OUT!
JULIUS FROMM INVENTED SEX!
THE ROMANISCHES' REGULARS GO WILD. WITH ONE EXCEPTION. ME.

* Marlene Dietrich (1901–1992). German actress, popular from the 1910s to the 1980s, staunch anti-Nazi, reputed to have carried on a simultaneous affair with both President John F. Kennedy and his poppa, Joe.

** Mia May (1884–1980). Wife of film director Joe May, and one of the top actresses in Germany.

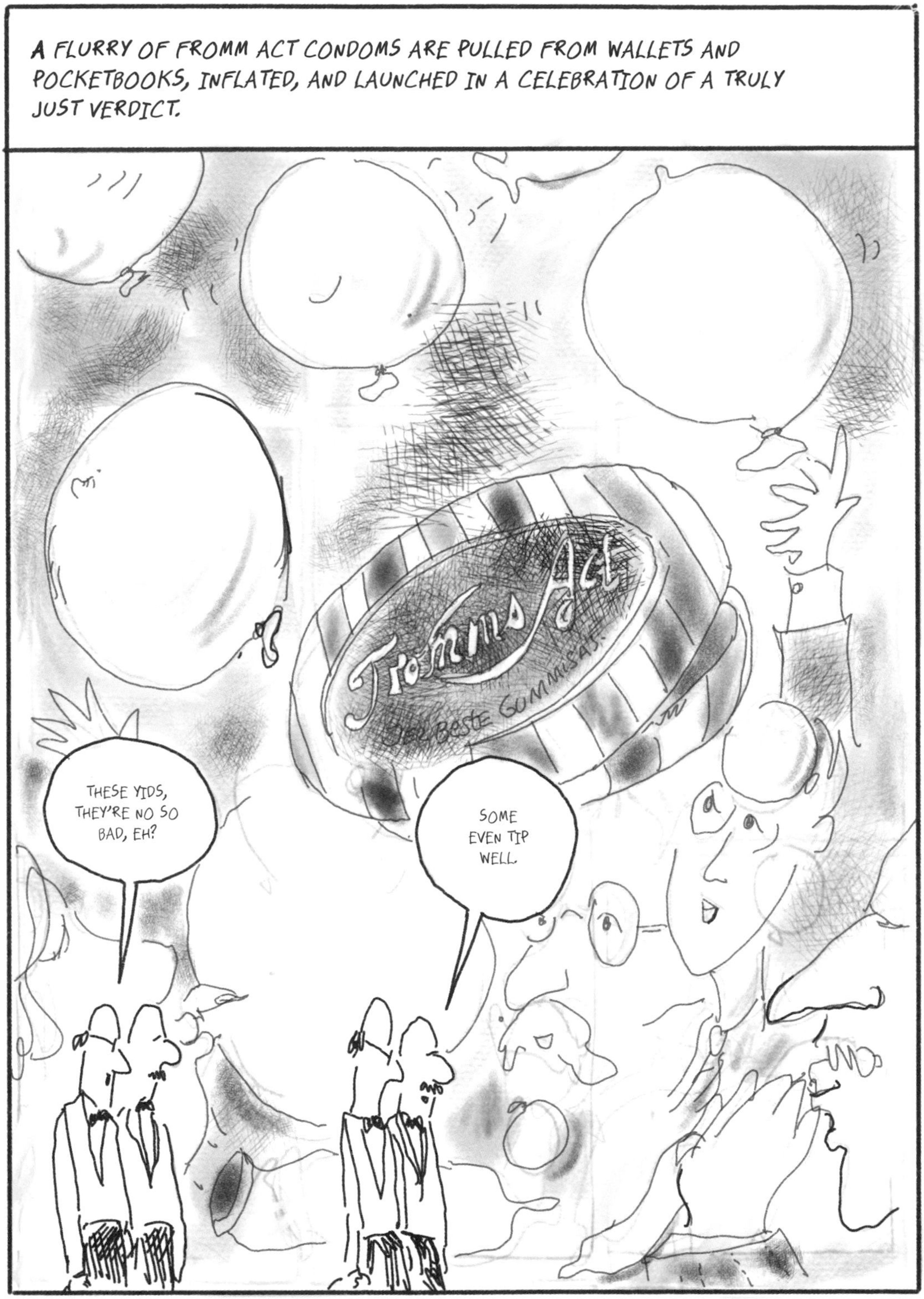
A FLURRY OF FROMM ACT CONDOMS ARE PULLED FROM WALLETS AND POCKETBOOKS, INFLATED, AND LAUNCHED IN A CELEBRATION OF A TRULY JUST VERDICT.
THESE YIDS, THEY'RE NO SO BAD, EH?
SOME EVEN TIP WELL.

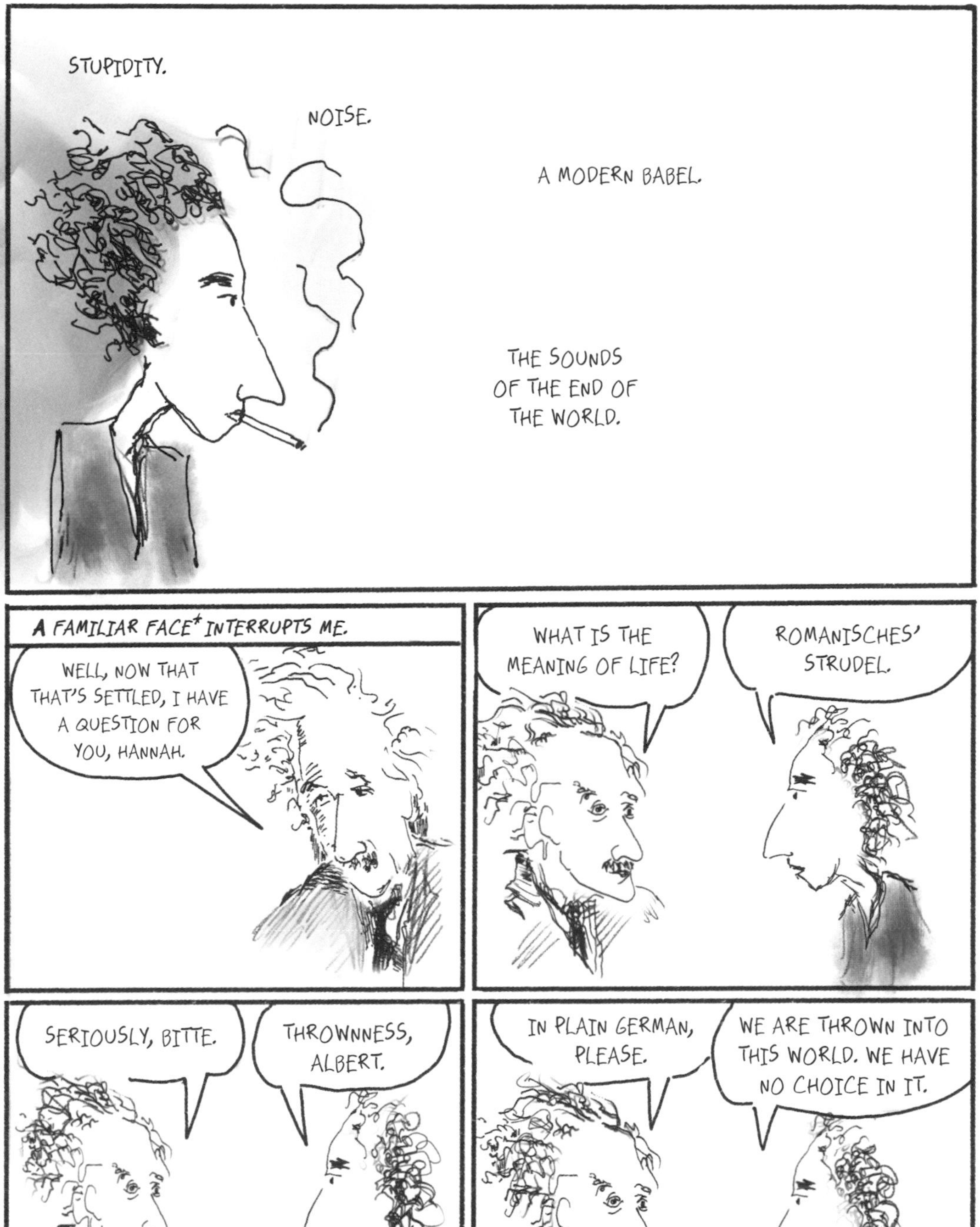
STUPIDITY.
NOISE.
A MODERN BABEL.
THE SOUNDS OF THE END OF THE WORLD.
A FAMILIAR FACE* INTERRUPTS ME.
WELL, NOW THAT THAT'S SETTLED, I HAVE A QUESTION FOR YOU, HANNAH.
WHAT IS THE MEANING OF LIFE?
ROMANISCHES' STRUDEL.
SERIOUSLY, BITTE.
THROWNNESS, ALBERT.
IN PLAIN GERMAN, PLEASE.
WE ARE THROWN INTO THIS WORLD. WE HAVE NO CHOICE IN IT.

* Albert Einstein (1879–1955). German Jewish physicist who changed the universe.

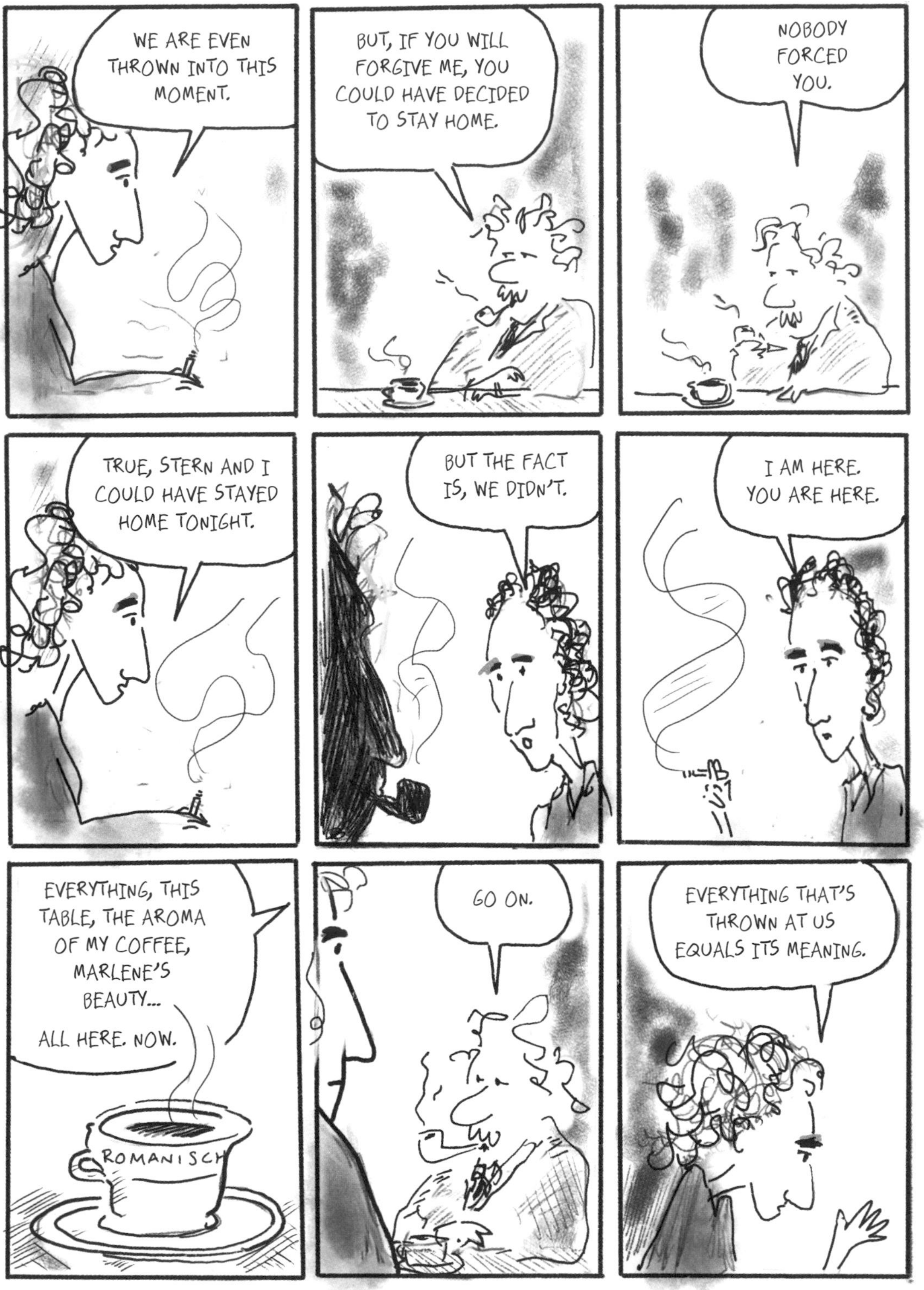
WE ARE EVEN THROWN INTO THIS MOMENT.
BUT, IF YOU WILL FORGIVE ME, YOU COULD HAVE DECIDED TO STAY HOME.
NOBODY FORCED YOU.
TRUE, STERN AND I COULD HAVE STAYED HOME TONIGHT.
BUT THE FACT IS, WE DIDN'T.
I AM HERE. YOU ARE HERE.
EVERYTHING, THIS TABLE, THE AROMA OF MY COFFEE, MARLENE'S BEAUTY...
ALL HERE. NOW.
ROMANISCH
GO ON.
EVERYTHING THAT'S THROWN AT US EQUALS ITS MEANING.

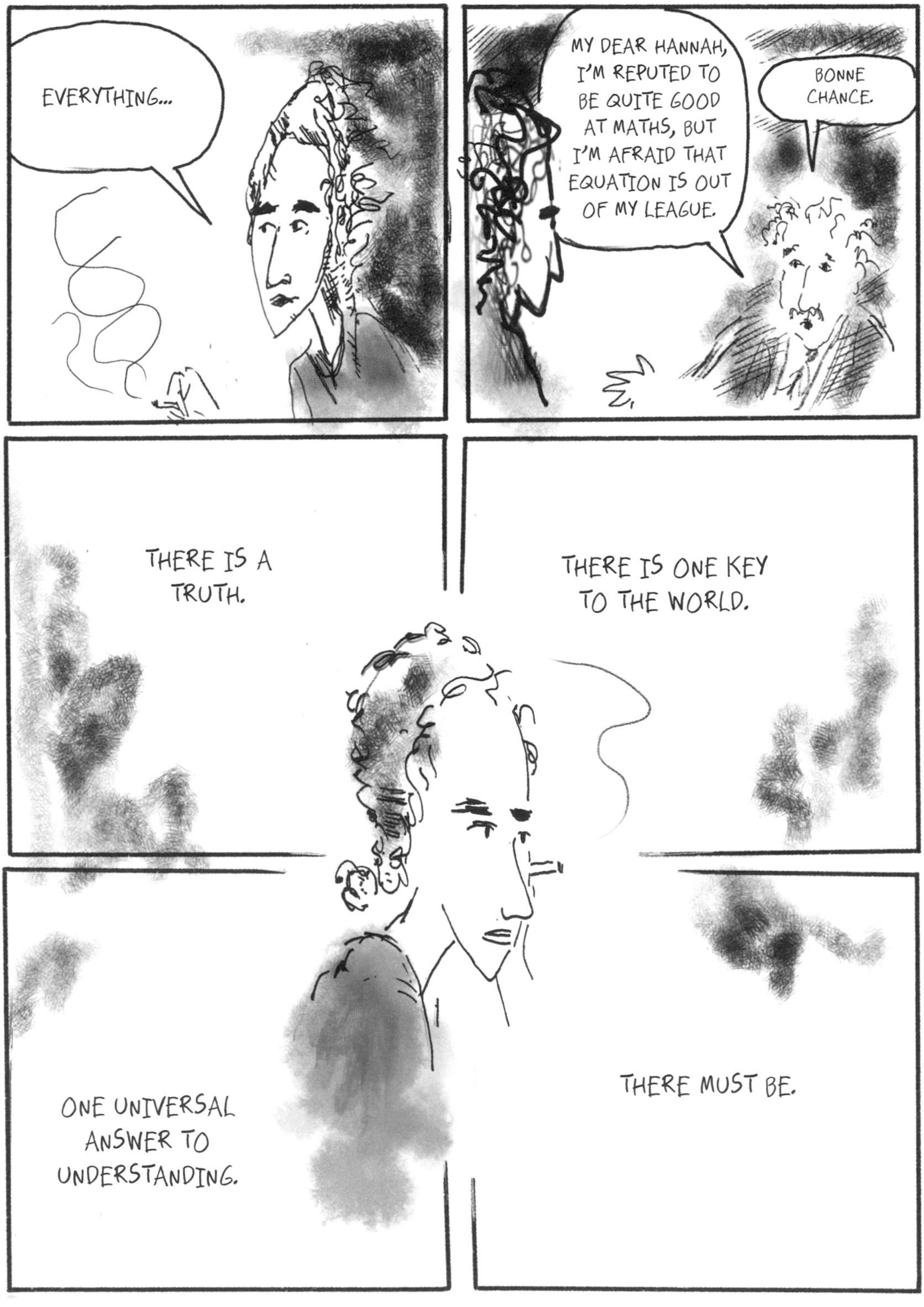
EVERYTHING...
MY DEAR HANNAH, I'M REPUTED TO BE QUITE GOOD AT MATHS, BUT I'M AFRAID THAT EQUATION IS OUT OF MY LEAGUE.
BONNE CHANCE.
THERE IS A TRUTH.
THERE IS ONE KEY TO THE WORLD.
ONE UNIVERSAL ANSWER TO UNDERSTANDING.
THERE MUST BE.

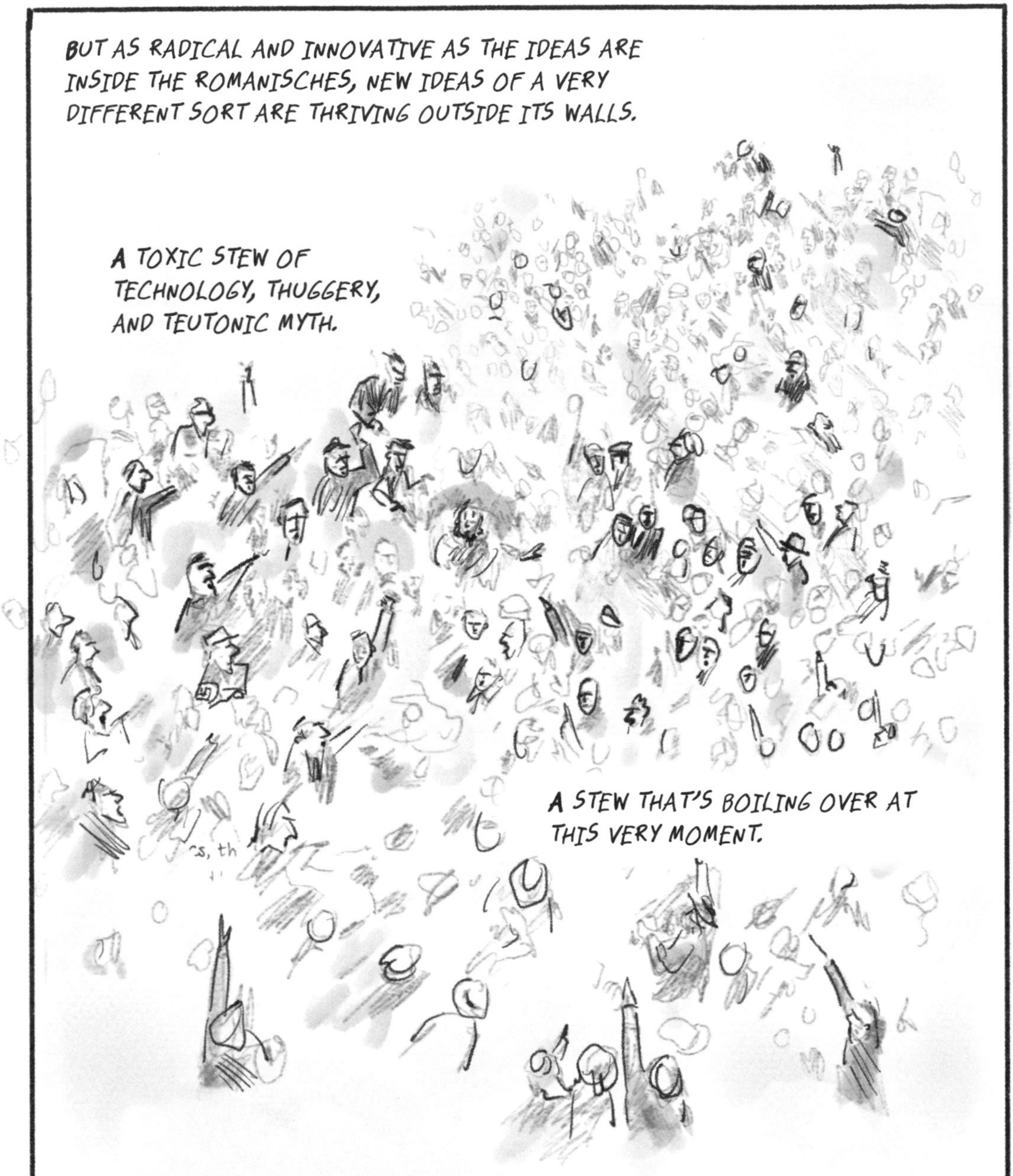
BUT AS RADICAL AND INNOVATIVE AS THE IDEAS ARE INSIDE THE ROMANISCHES, NEW IDEAS OF A VERY DIFFERENT SORT ARE THRIVING OUTSIDE ITS WALLS.
A TOXIC STEW OF TECHNOLOGY, THUGGERY, AND TEUTONIC MYTH.
A STEW THAT'S BOILING OVER AT THIS VERY MOMENT.

(1) W. H. Auden (1907–1973). English poet, inspiration for the Beats (such as Allen Ginsberg) and whose love poems and social poems still resonate. His "September 1, 1939" became a kind of healing psalm in New York City after the attacks of September 11, 2001. (2) Christopher Isherwood (1904–1986). English novelist, his Berlin stories were the basis of the play, the Broadway musical, and the film *Cabaret*. (3) Niels Bohr (1885–1962). Danish physicist who both challenged and furthered Einstein's work with his contributions to quantum theory. Won the 1922 Nobel Prize. (4) Artur Schnabel (1882–1951). (See page 46.) (5) Rudolf Breitscheid (1874–1944). Jewish German politician and journalist, a vocal proponent of democracy, despite fleeing to France, he was singled out by Hitler, the Gestapo tracked him down, and he was murdered.

CAROLA NEHER,* SINGER, ACTOR, MUSE TO POETS AND PLAYWRIGHTS, BURSTS IN WITH BREAKING NEWS.

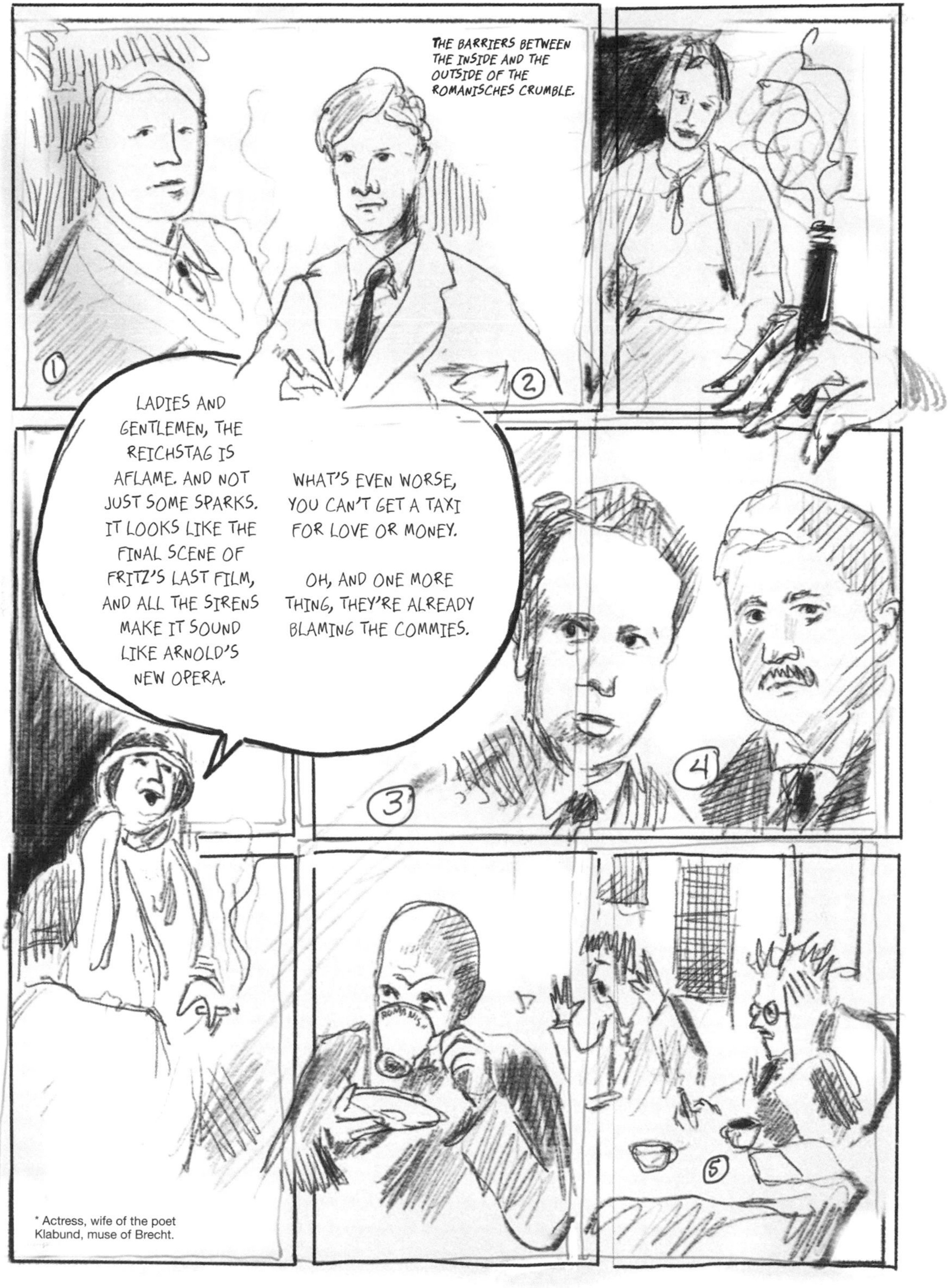
THE BARRIERS BETWEEN THE INSIDE AND THE OUTSIDE OF THE ROMANISCHES CRUMBLE.
LADIES AND GENTLEMEN, THE REICHSTAG IS AFLAME. AND NOT JUST SOME SPARKS. IT LOOKS LIKE THE FINAL SCENE OF FRITZ'S LAST FILM, AND ALL THE SIRENS MAKE IT SOUND LIKE ARNOLD'S NEW OPERA.
WHAT'S EVEN WORSE, YOU CAN'T GET A TAXI FOR LOVE OR MONEY.
OH, AND ONE MORE THING, THEY'RE ALREADY BLAMING THE COMMIES.

* Actress, wife of the poet Klabund, muse of Brecht.

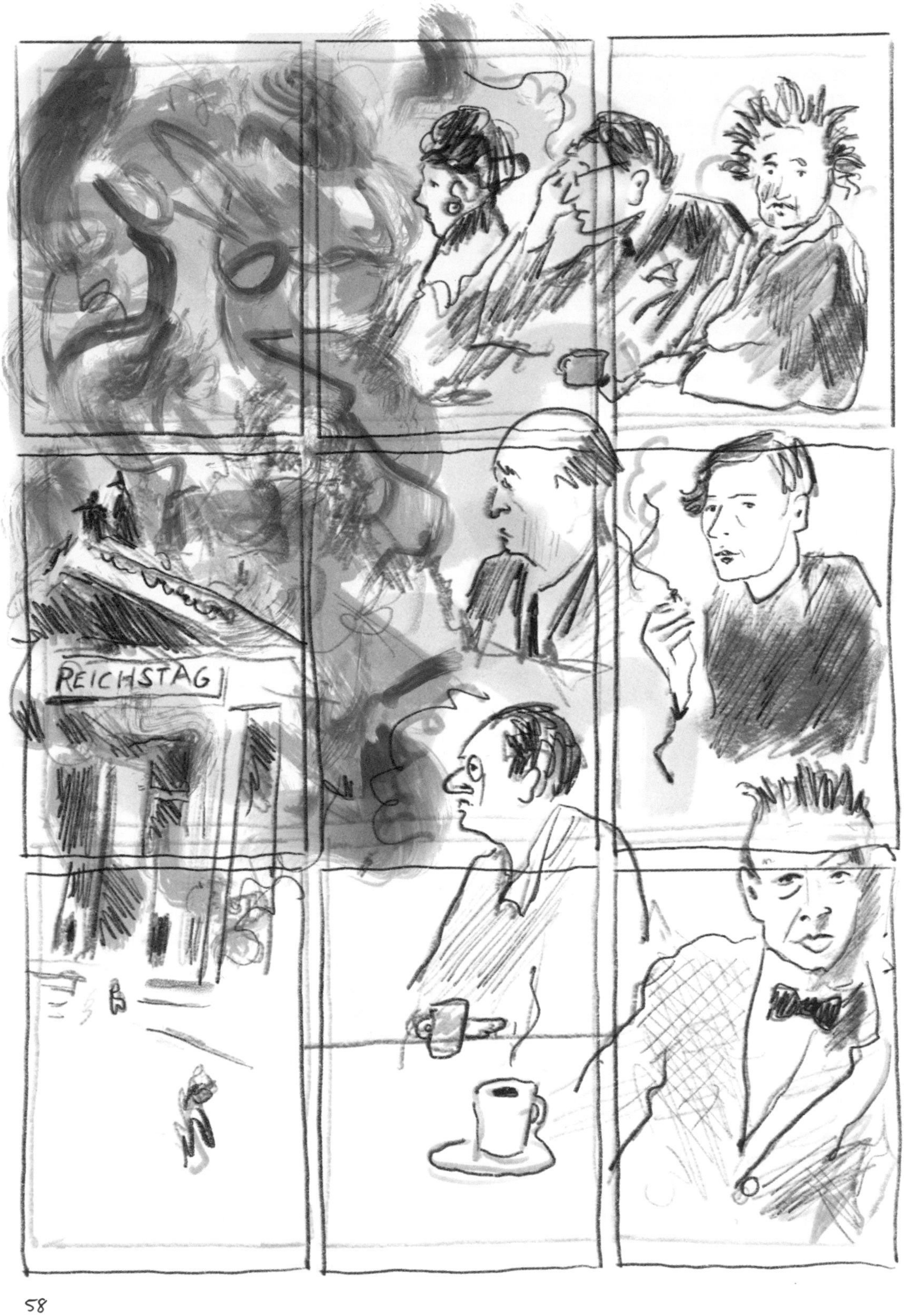
REICHSTAG

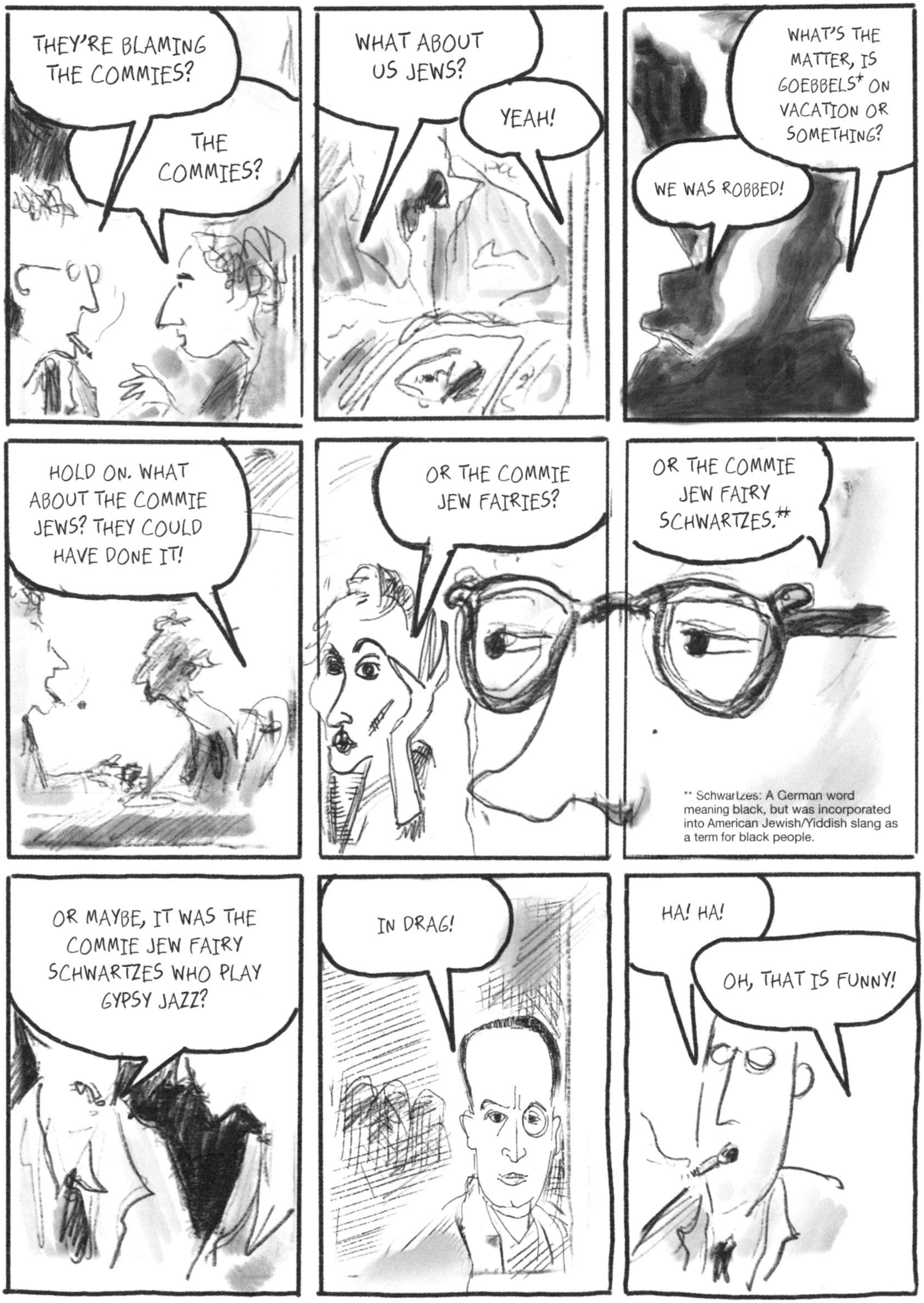
THEY'RE BLAMING THE COMMIES?
THE COMMIES?
WHAT ABOUT US JEWS?
YEAH!
WHAT'S THE MATTER, IS GOEBBELS* ON VACATION OR SOMETHING?
WE WAS ROBBED!
HOLD ON. WHAT ABOUT THE COMMIE JEWS? THEY COULD HAVE DONE IT!
OR THE COMMIE JEW FAIRIES?
OR THE COMMIE JEW FAIRY SCHWARTZES.**
** Schwartzes: A German word meaning black, but was incorporated into American Jewish/Yiddish slang as a term for black people.
OR MAYBE, IT WAS THE COMMIE JEW FAIRY SCHWARTZES WHO PLAY GYPSY JAZZ?
IN DRAG!
HA! HA!
OH, THAT IS FUNNY!

* Joseph Goebbels (1897–1945). German politician and Nazi head of propaganda. His sensitivity to modern mass media channels like radio, movies, and spectacle made him Hitler's de facto ad agency. His main pitch: "Kill the Jews, all of them."

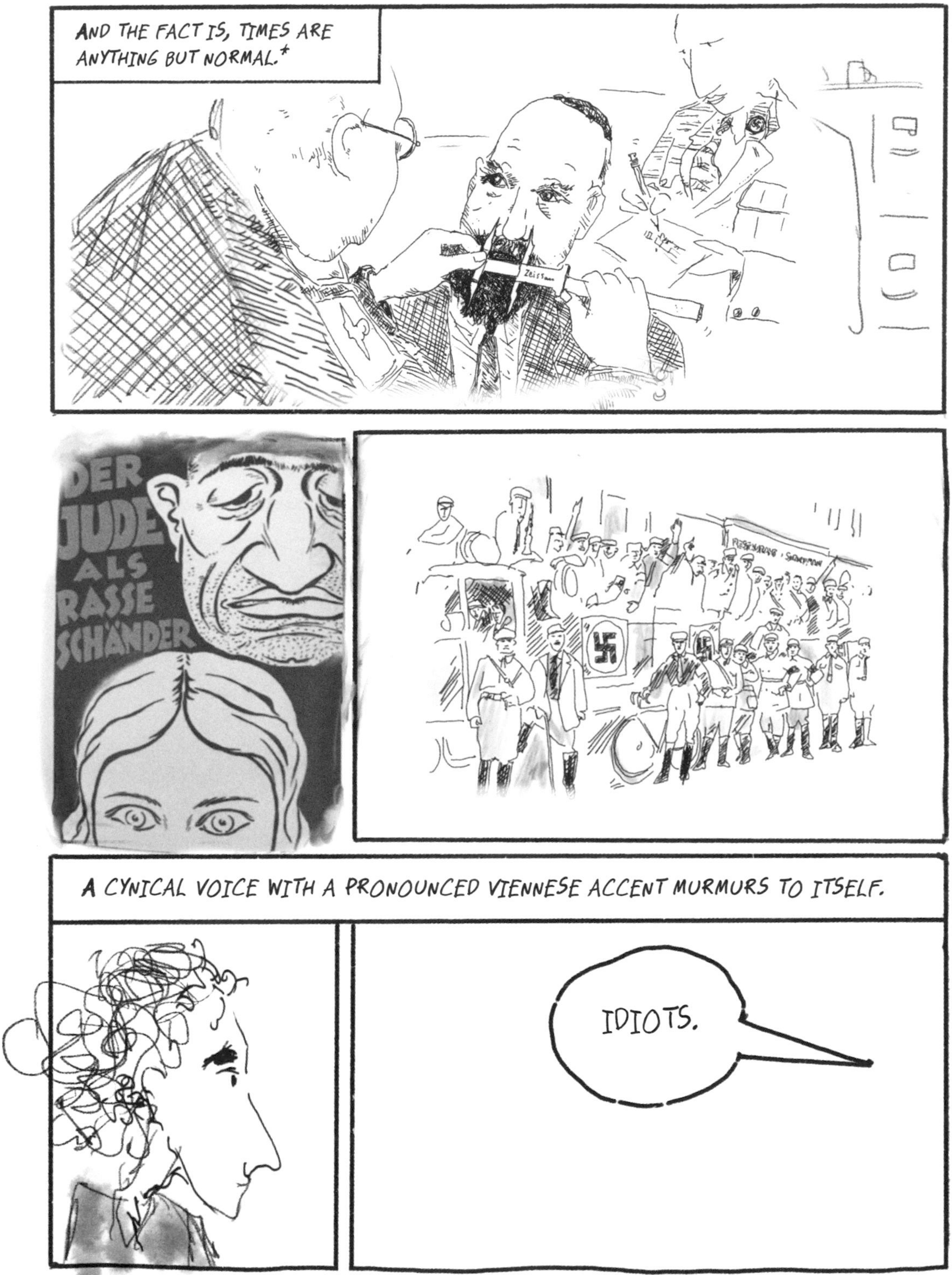
AND THE FACT IS, TIMES ARE ANYTHING BUT NORMAL.*
DER JUDE ALS RASSE SCHÄNDER
A CYNICAL VOICE WITH A PRONOUNCED VIENNESE ACCENT MURMURS TO ITSELF.
IDIOTS.

* Nazi scientists actually went as far as measuring and cataloguing the size of Jews' noses.

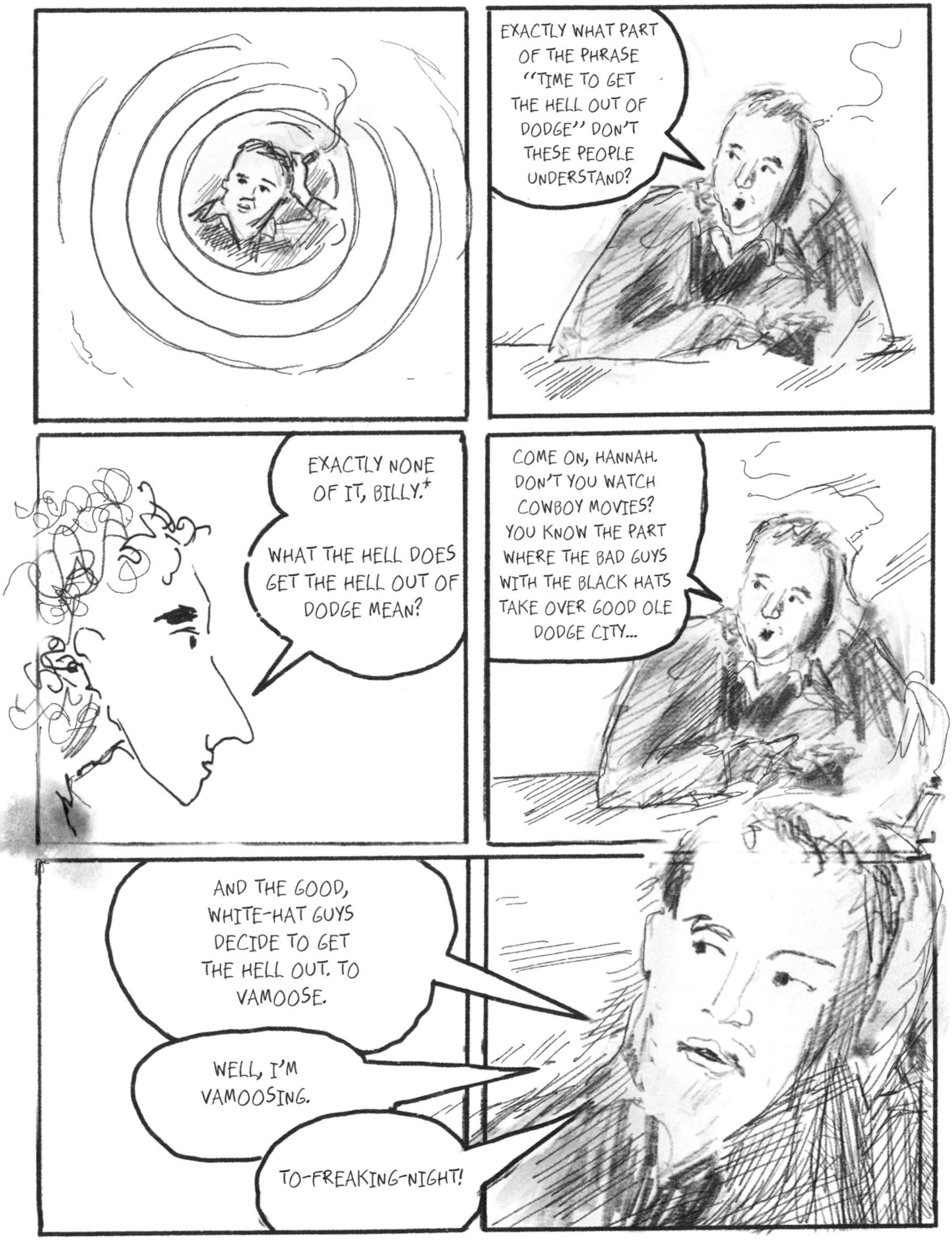
EXACTLY WHAT PART OF THE PHRASE "TIME TO GET THE HELL OUT OF DODGE" DON'T THESE PEOPLE UNDERSTAND?
EXACTLY NONE OF IT, BILLY.*
WHAT THE HELL DOES GET THE HELL OUT OF DODGE MEAN?
COME ON, HANNAH. DON'T YOU WATCH COWBOY MOVIES? YOU KNOW THE PART WHERE THE BAD GUYS WITH THE BLACK HATS TAKE OVER GOOD OLE DODGE CITY...
AND THE GOOD, WHITE-HAT GUYS DECIDE TO GET THE HELL OUT. TO VAMOOSE.
WELL, I'M VAMOOSING.
TO-FREAKING-NIGHT!

* Samuel "Billy" Wilder (1906–2002). Austrian Jewish filmmaker, responsible for bringing a subversive Weimar sensibility to Hollywood blockbusters, like *Some Like It Hot*, widely acclaimed as the greatest comedy of all time, but which extended to film noir in *Double Indemnity*. His satire *The Apartment* made him the first person to win the Academy Award as writer, producer, and director for the same movie.

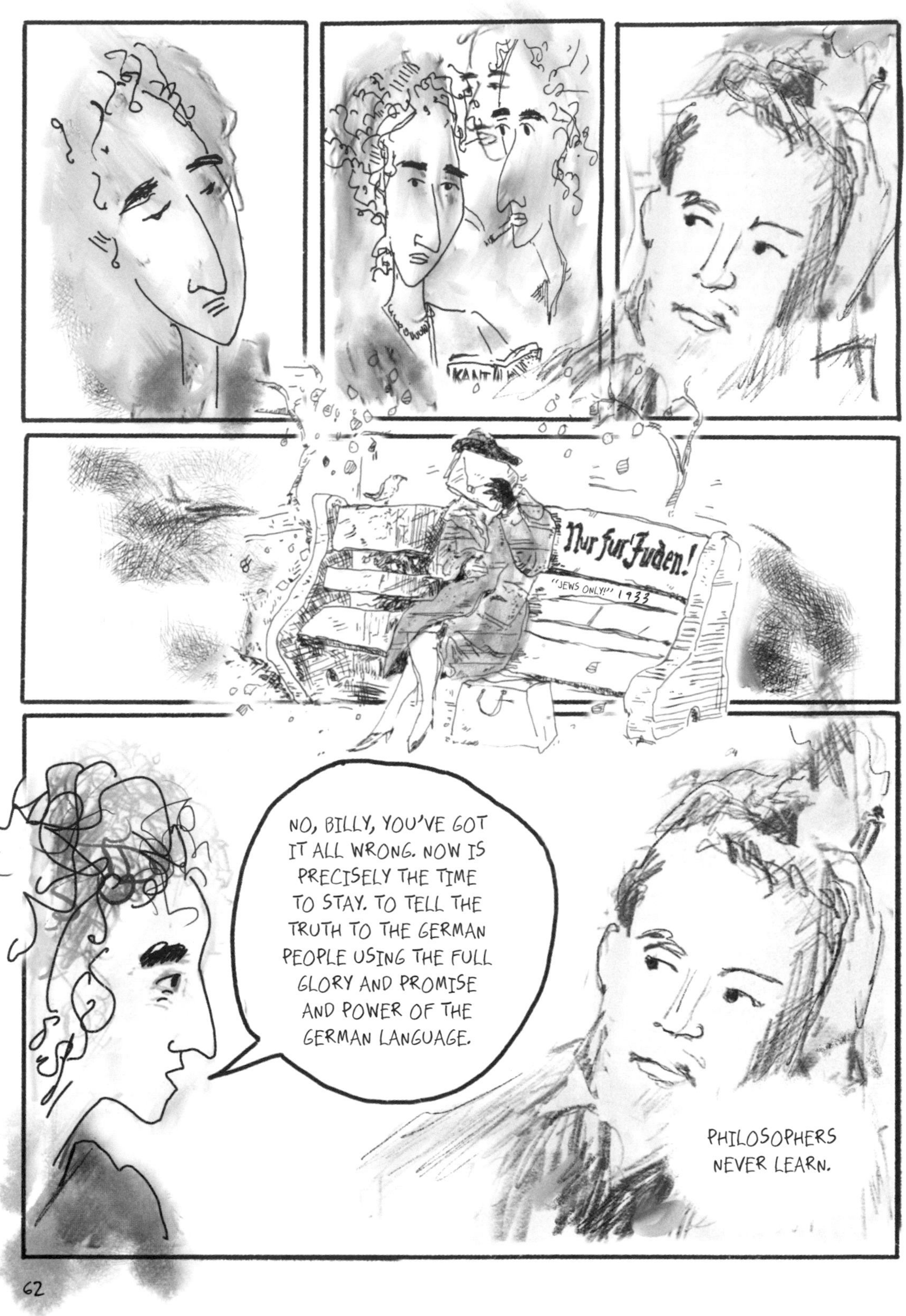
KANT
Nur fur Juden!
"JEWS ONLY!" 1933
NO, BILLY, YOU'VE GOT IT ALL WRONG. NOW IS PRECISELY THE TIME TO STAY. TO TELL THE TRUTH TO THE GERMAN PEOPLE USING THE FULL GLORY AND PROMISE AND POWER OF THE GERMAN LANGUAGE.
PHILOSOPHERS NEVER LEARN.

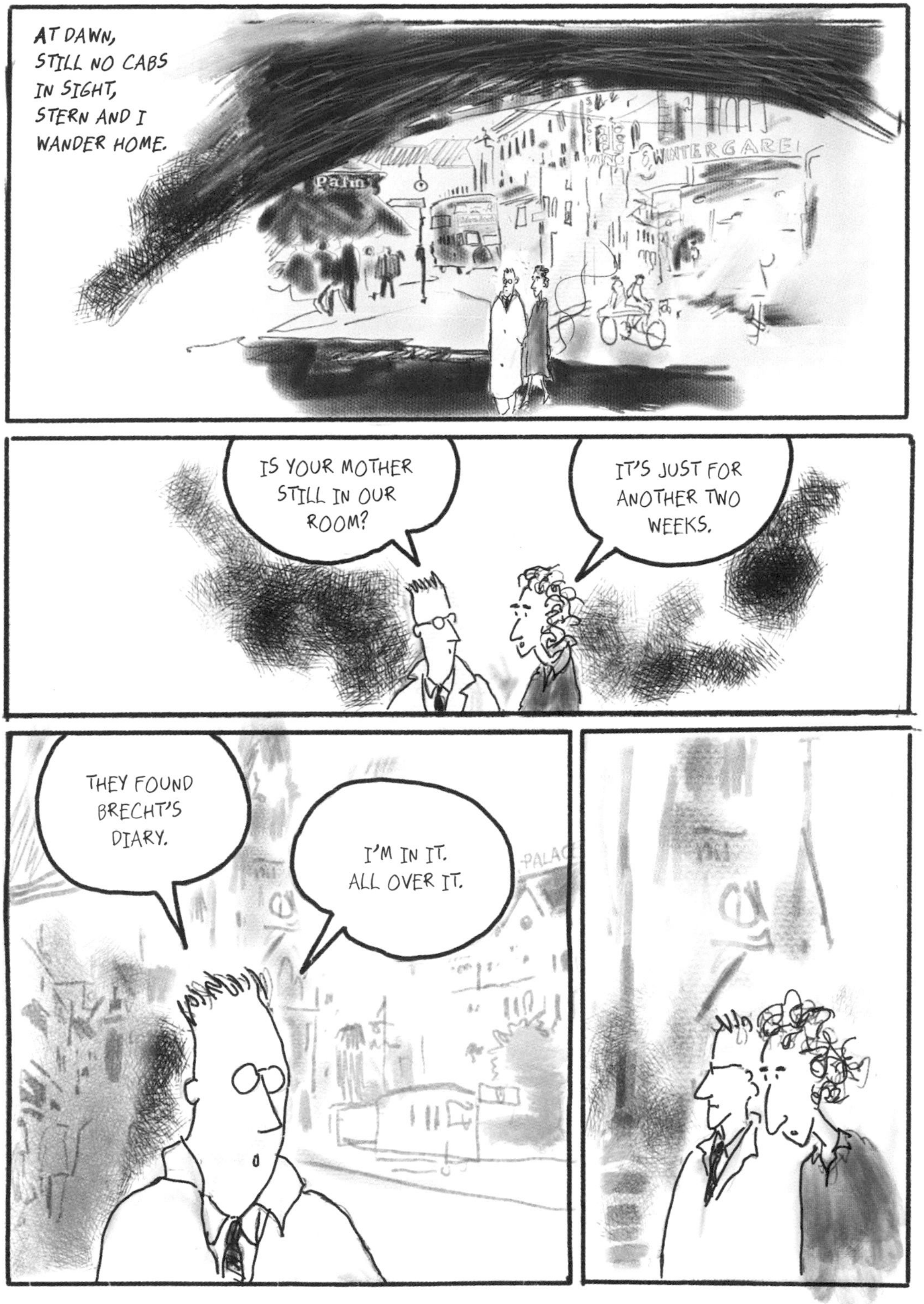
AT DAWN, STILL NO CABS IN SIGHT, STERN AND I WANDER HOME.
WINTERGARE
IS YOUR MOTHER STILL IN OUR ROOM?
IT'S JUST FOR ANOTHER TWO WEEKS.
THEY FOUND BRECHT'S DIARY.
I'M IN IT. ALL OVER IT.
PALAC

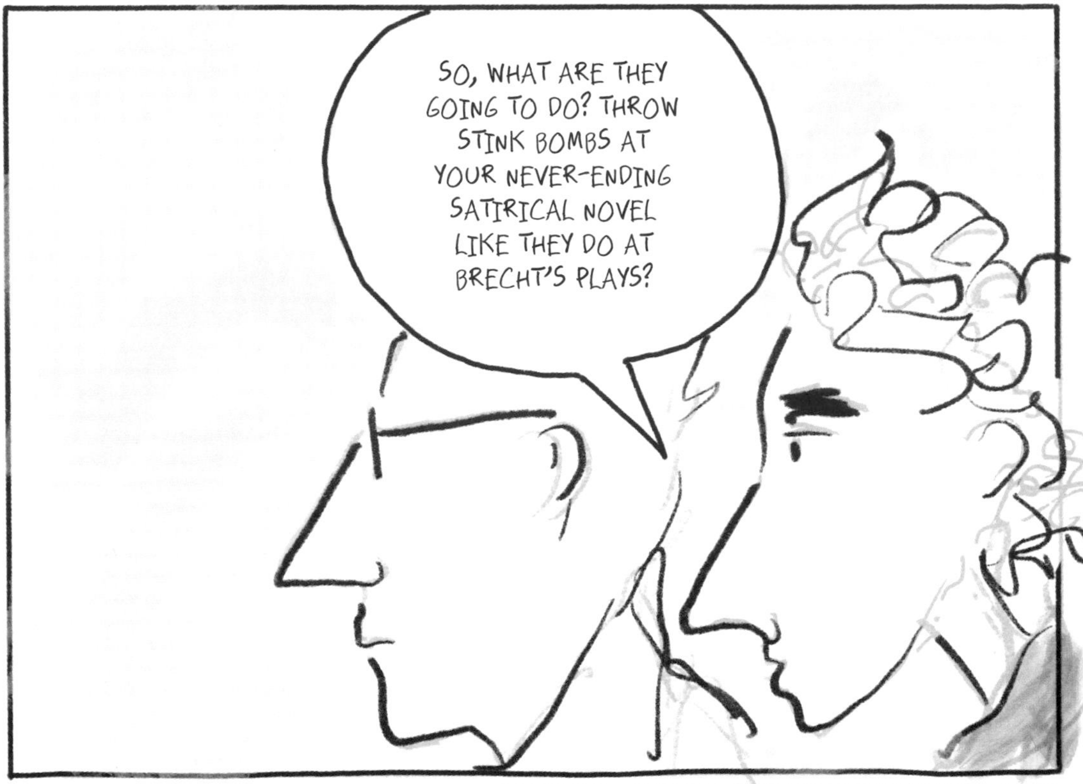
SO, WHAT ARE THEY GOING TO DO? THROW STINK BOMBS AT YOUR NEVER-ENDING SATIRICAL NOVEL LIKE THEY DO AT BRECHT'S PLAYS?

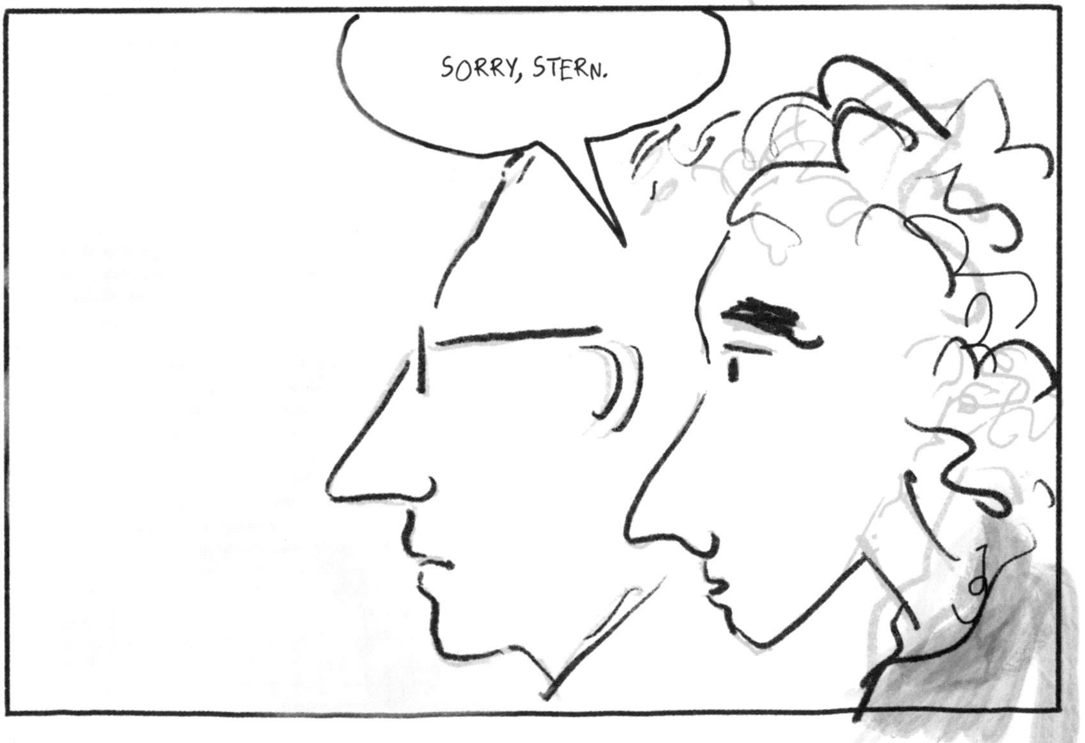
SORRY, STERN.

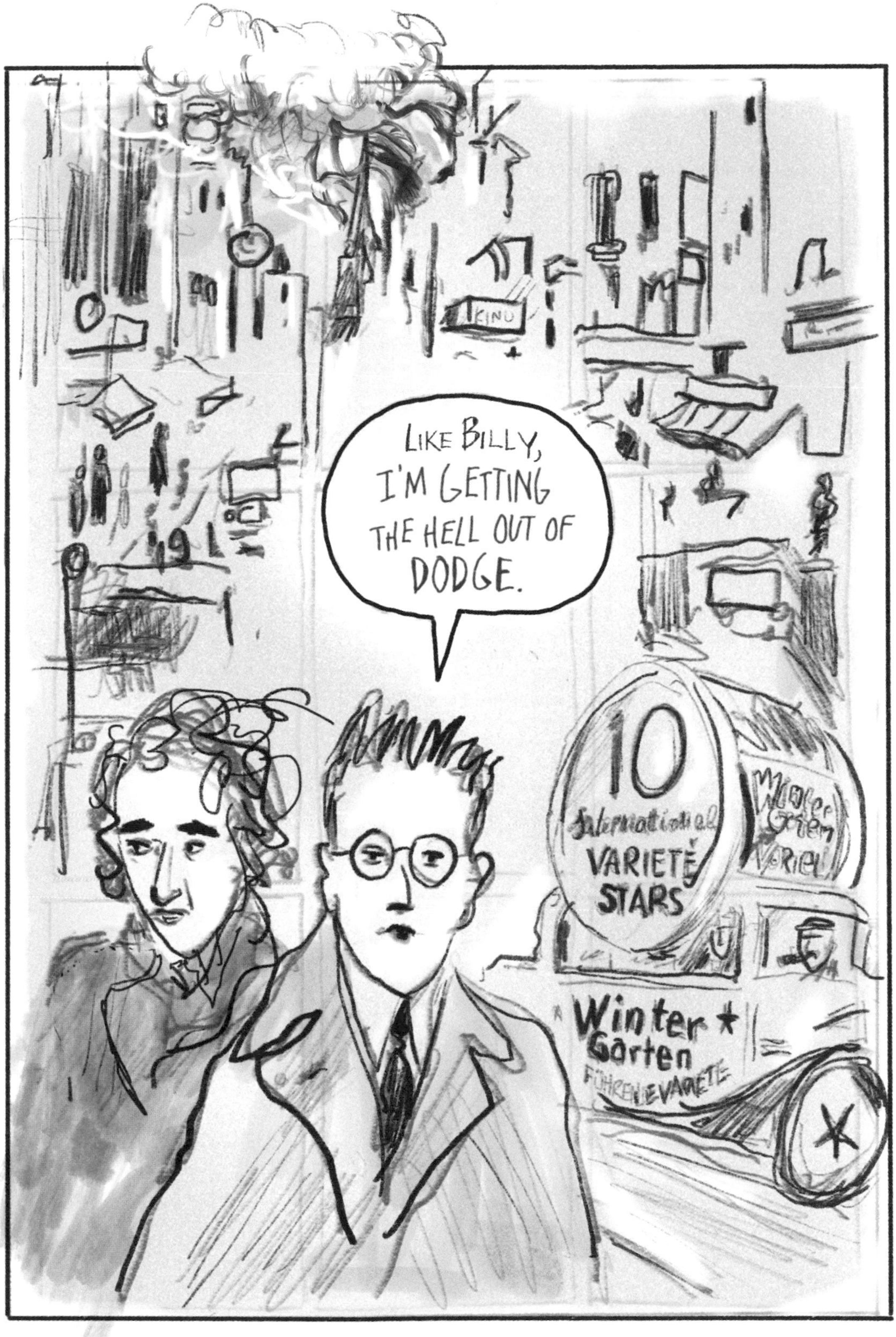
LIKE BILLY, I'M GETTING THE HELL OUT OF DODGE.
KINO
10
VARIETÉ
STARS
Winter ★
Garten

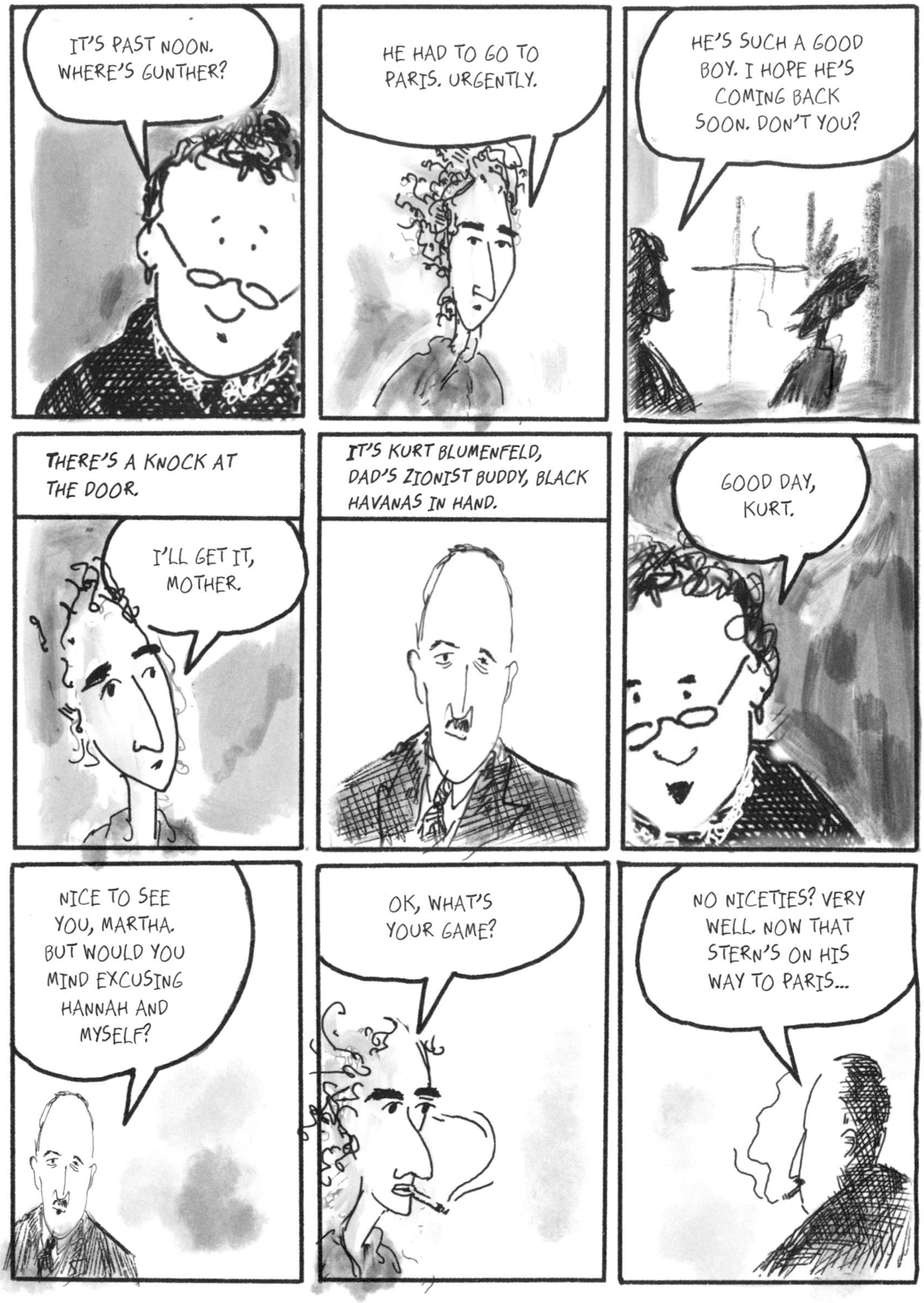
IT'S PAST NOON. WHERE'S GUNTHER?
HE HAD TO GO TO PARIS. URGENTLY.
HE'S SUCH A GOOD BOY. I HOPE HE'S COMING BACK SOON. DON'T YOU?
THERE'S A KNOCK AT THE DOOR.
I'LL GET IT, MOTHER.
IT'S KURT BLUMENFELD, DAD'S ZIONIST BUDDY, BLACK HAVANAS IN HAND.
GOOD DAY, KURT.
NICE TO SEE YOU, MARTHA. BUT WOULD YOU MIND EXCUSING HANNAH AND MYSELF?
OK, WHAT'S YOUR GAME?
NO NICETIES? VERY WELL. NOW THAT STERN'S ON HIS WAY TO PARIS...

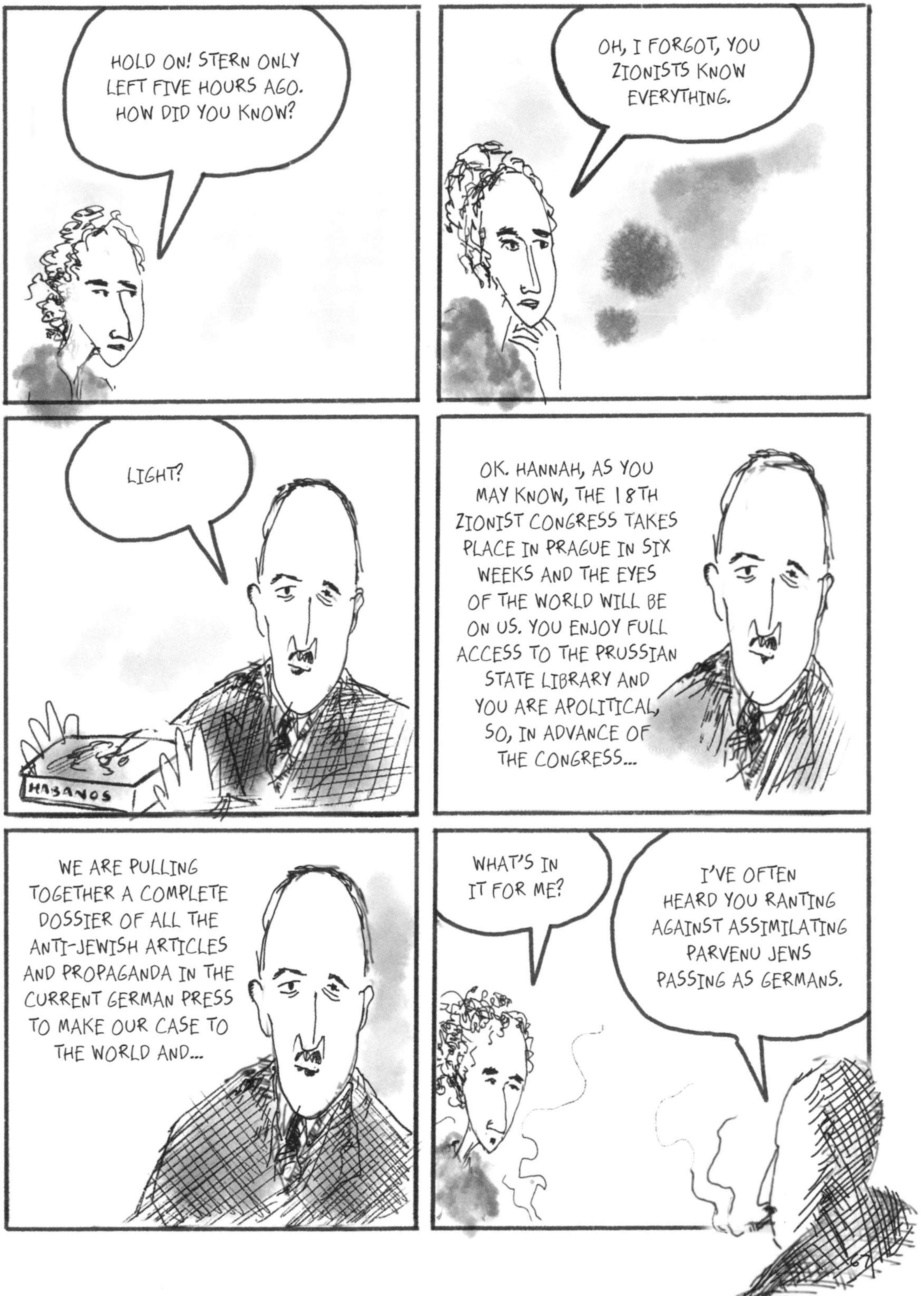
HOLD ON! STERN ONLY LEFT FIVE HOURS AGO. HOW DID YOU KNOW?
OH, I FORGOT, YOU ZIONISTS KNOW EVERYTHING.
LIGHT?
HABANOS
OK. HANNAH, AS YOU MAY KNOW, THE 18TH ZIONIST CONGRESS TAKES PLACE IN PRAGUE IN SIX WEEKS AND THE EYES OF THE WORLD WILL BE ON US. YOU ENJOY FULL ACCESS TO THE PRUSSIAN STATE LIBRARY AND YOU ARE APOLITICAL, SO, IN ADVANCE OF THE CONGRESS...
WE ARE PULLING TOGETHER A COMPLETE DOSSIER OF ALL THE ANTI-JEWISH ARTICLES AND PROPAGANDA IN THE CURRENT GERMAN PRESS TO MAKE OUR CASE TO THE WORLD AND...
WHAT'S IN IT FOR ME?
I'VE OFTEN HEARD YOU RANTING AGAINST ASSIMILATING PARVENU JEWS PASSING AS GERMANS.

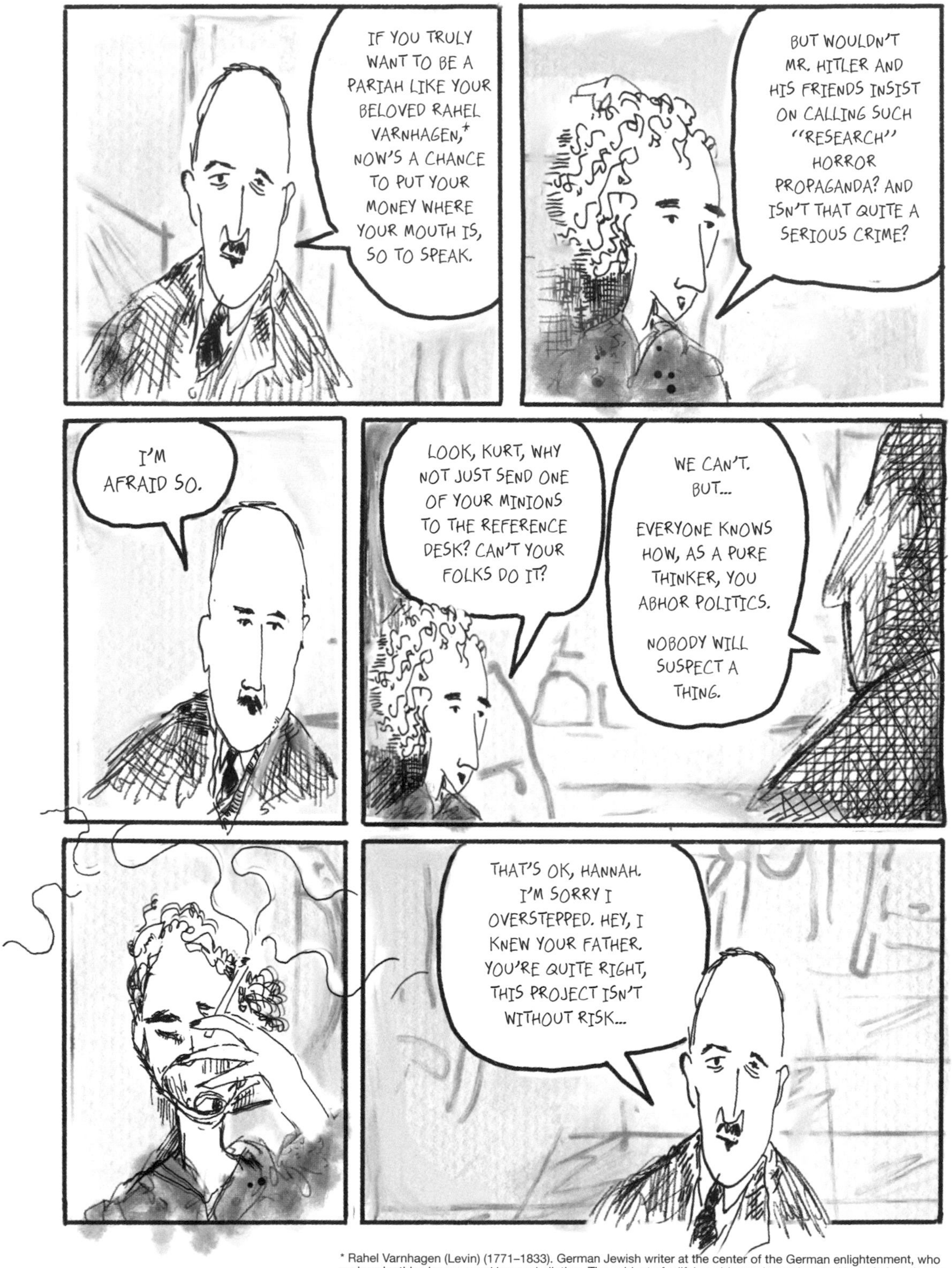
IF YOU TRULY WANT TO BE A PARIAH LIKE YOUR BELOVED RAHEL VARNHAGEN,* NOW'S A CHANCE TO PUT YOUR MONEY WHERE YOUR MOUTH IS, SO TO SPEAK.
BUT WOULDN'T MR. HITLER AND HIS FRIENDS INSIST ON CALLING SUCH "RESEARCH" HORROR PROPAGANDA? AND ISN'T THAT QUITE A SERIOUS CRIME?
I'M AFRAID SO.
LOOK, KURT, WHY NOT JUST SEND ONE OF YOUR MINIONS TO THE REFERENCE DESK? CAN'T YOUR FOLKS DO IT?
WE CAN'T. BUT...
EVERYONE KNOWS HOW, AS A PURE THINKER, YOU ABHOR POLITICS.
NOBODY WILL SUSPECT A THING.
THAT'S OK, HANNAH. I'M SORRY I OVERSTEPPED. HEY, I KNEW YOUR FATHER. YOU'RE QUITE RIGHT, THIS PROJECT ISN'T WITHOUT RISK...

* Rahel Varnhagen (Levin) (1771–1833). German Jewish writer at the center of the German enlightenment, who on her deathbed renounced her assimilation. The subject of a lifelong biography project by Hannah Arendt, she was often described by Arendt as "my closest friend, even though she's been dead for some hundred years."

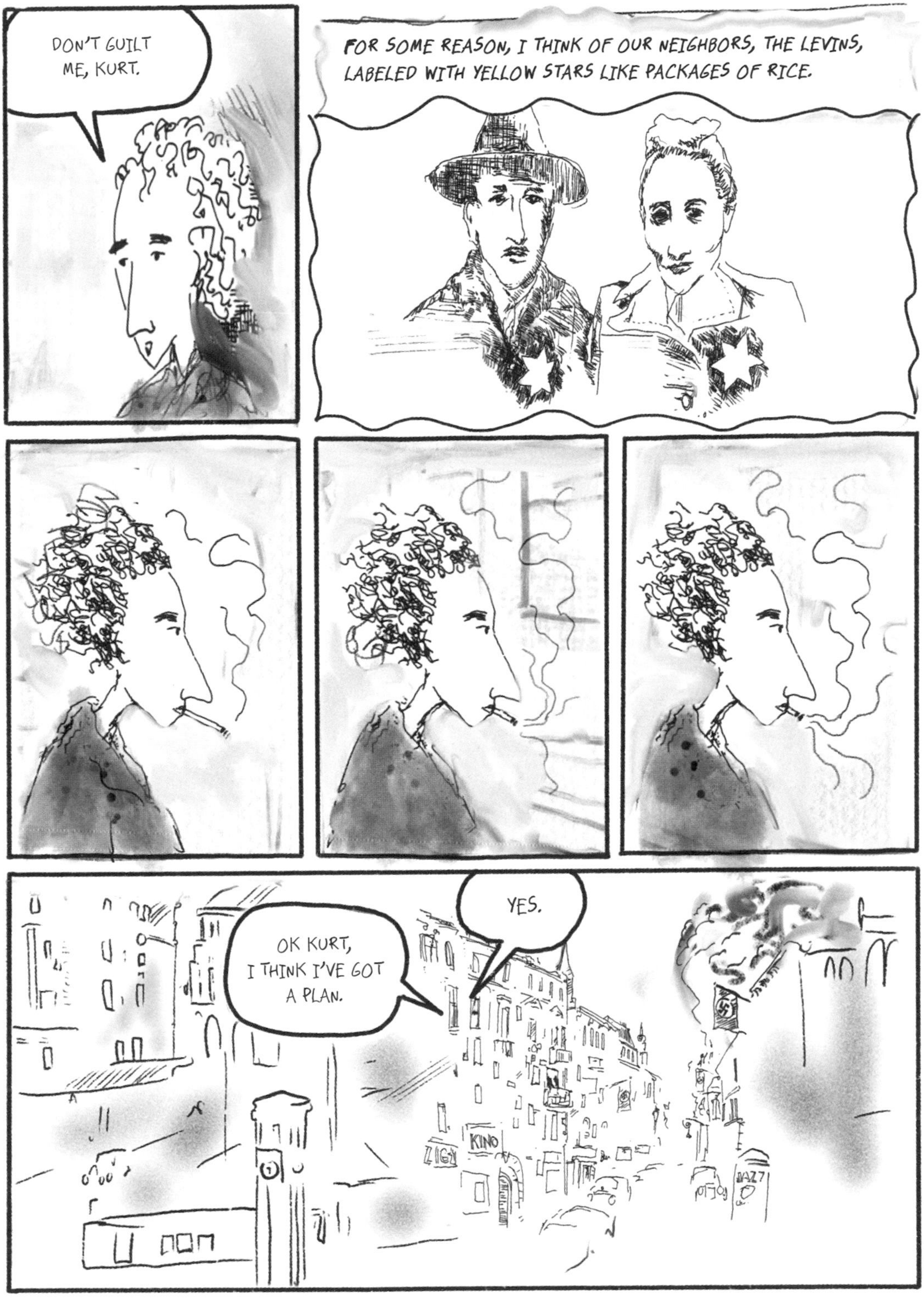
DON'T GUILT ME, KURT.
FOR SOME REASON, I THINK OF OUR NEIGHBORS, THE LEVINS, LABELED WITH YELLOW STARS LIKE PACKAGES OF RICE.
OK KURT, I THINK I'VE GOT A PLAN.
YES.
KINO
JAZZ

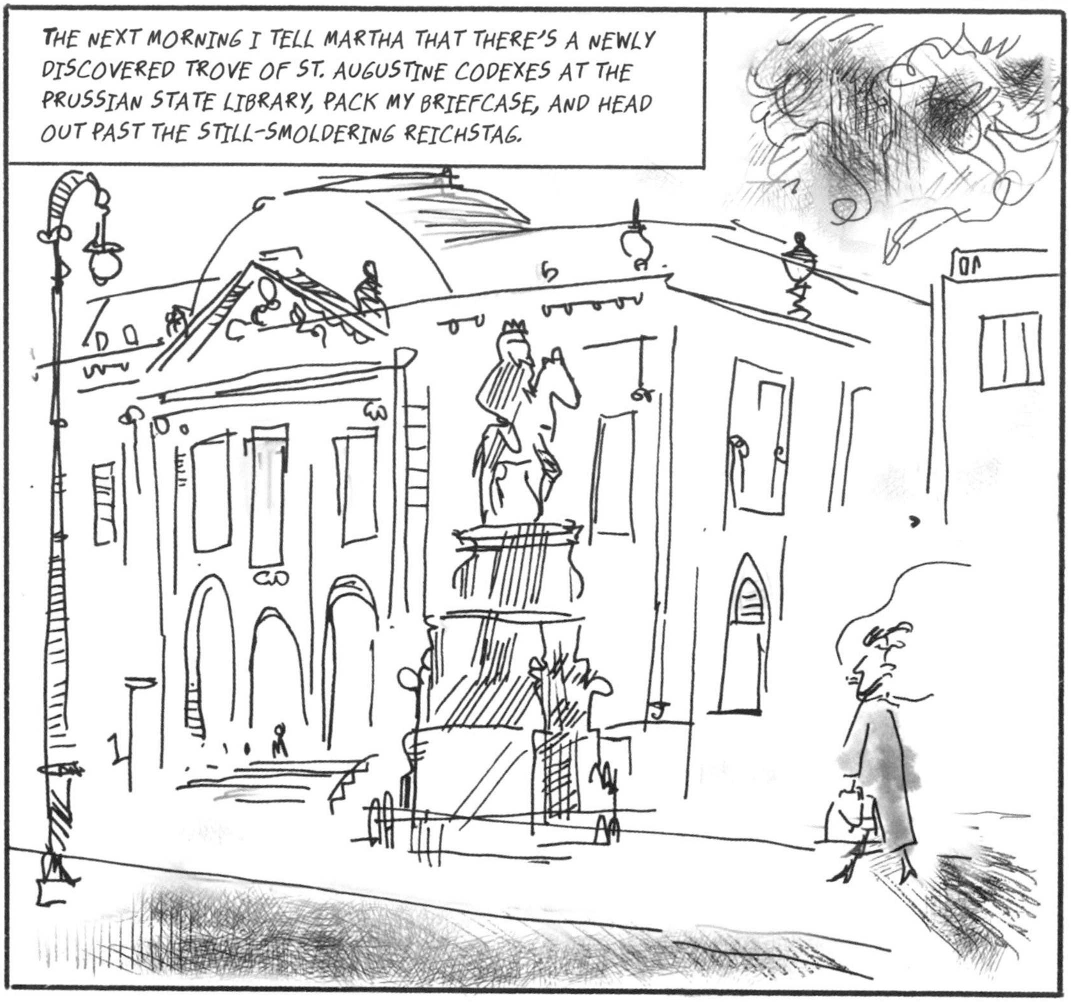
THE NEXT MORNING I TELL MARTHA THAT THERE'S A NEWLY DISCOVERED TROVE OF ST. AUGUSTINE CODEXES AT THE PRUSSIAN STATE LIBRARY, PACK MY BRIEFCASE, AND HEAD OUT PAST THE STILL-SMOLDERING REICHSTAG.

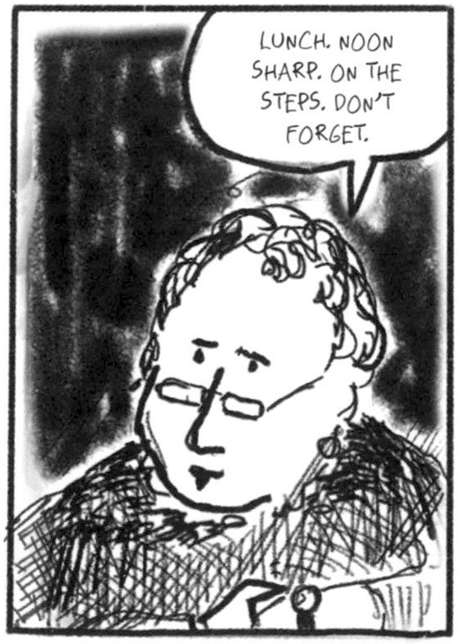
LUNCH. NOON SHARP. ON THE STEPS. DON'T FORGET.

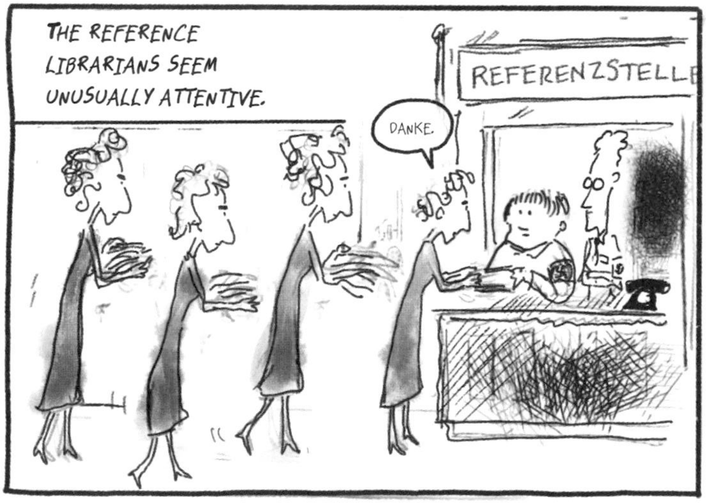
THE REFERENCE LIBRARIANS SEEM UNUSUALLY ATTENTIVE.
REFERENZSTELLE
DANKE.

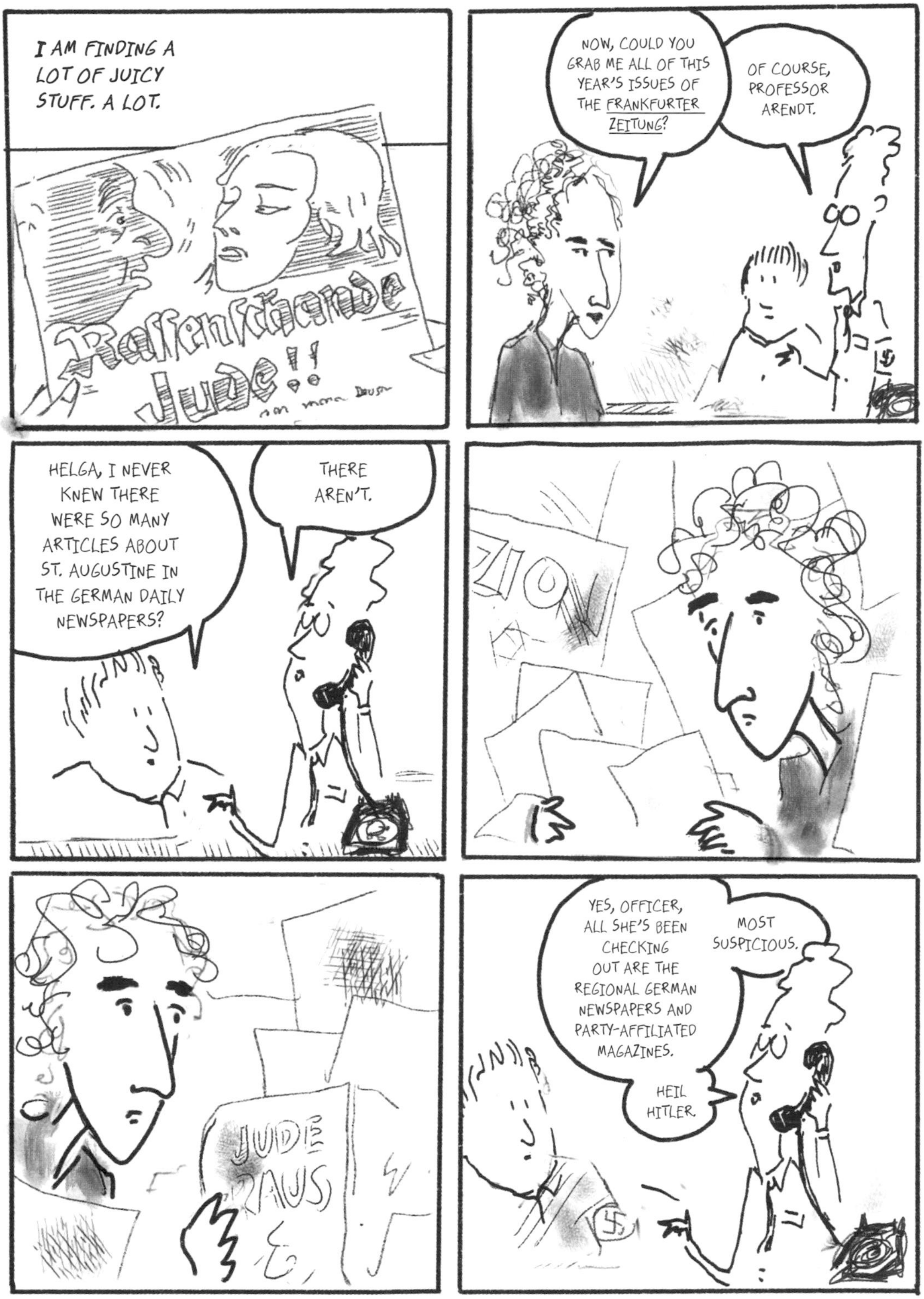
I AM FINDING A LOT OF JUICY STUFF. A LOT.
Rassenschande Jude!!
NOW, COULD YOU GRAB ME ALL OF THIS YEAR'S ISSUES OF THE FRANKFURTER ZEITUNG?
OF COURSE, PROFESSOR ARENDT.
HELGA, I NEVER KNEW THERE WERE SO MANY ARTICLES ABOUT ST. AUGUSTINE IN THE GERMAN DAILY NEWSPAPERS?
THERE AREN'T.
ZION
JUDE RAUS
YES, OFFICER, ALL SHE'S BEEN CHECKING OUT ARE THE REGIONAL GERMAN NEWSPAPERS AND PARTY-AFFILIATED MAGAZINES.
MOST SUSPICIOUS.
HEIL HITLER.

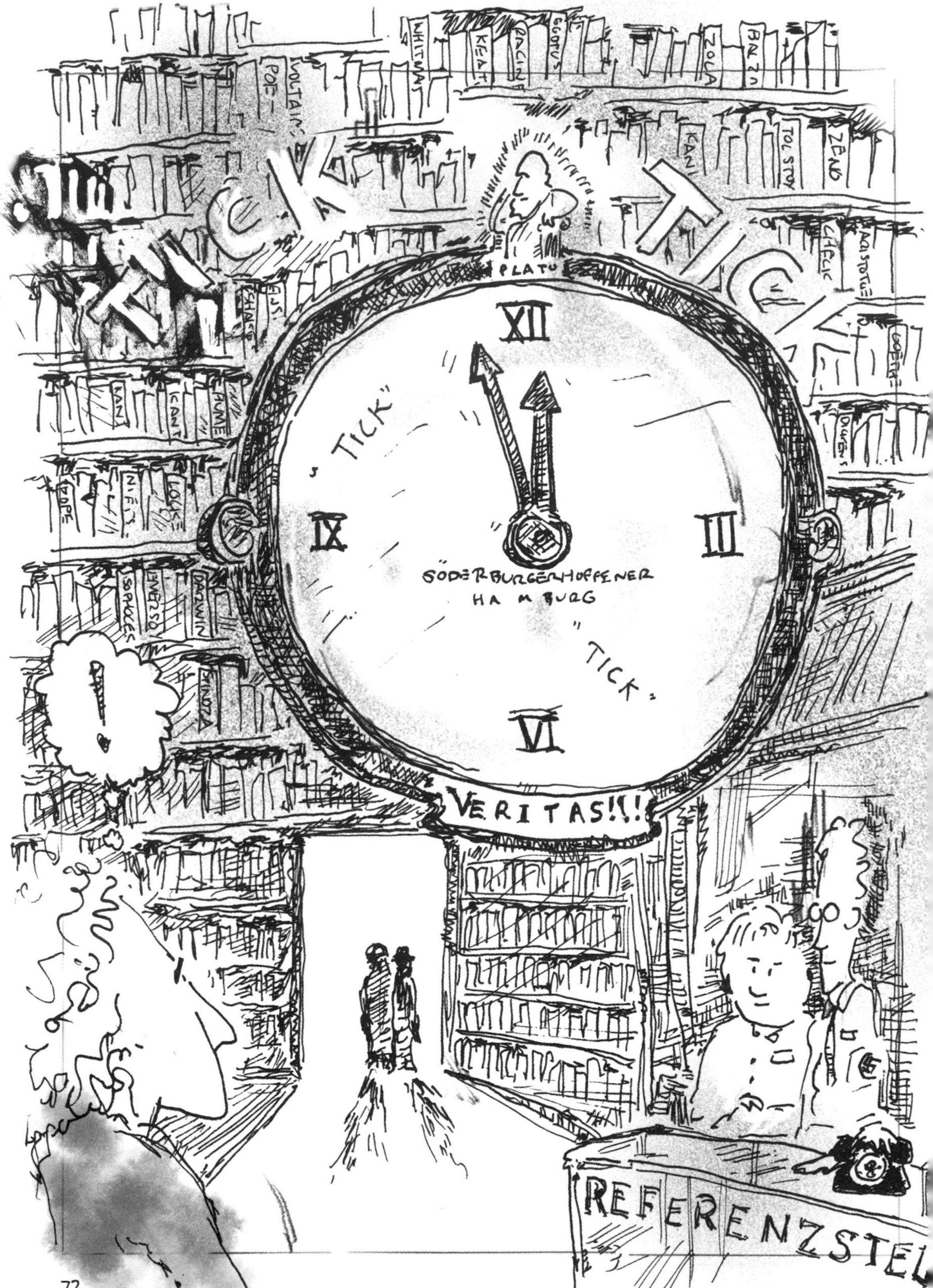
PLATO
XII
IX
III
VI
"TICK"
"TICK"
SÖDERBURGERHOFFENER
HA M BURG
VERITAS!!!
REFERENZSTEL
WHITMAN
ZOLA
TOLSTOY
HUME
KANT
LOCKE
DARWIN
SPINOZA

HOW'S ST. AUGUSTINE?

DEAD.

I'M STARVING.

ME TOO, MOM.

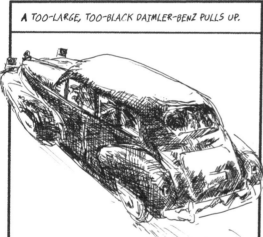

A TOO-LARGE, TOO-BLACK DAIMLER-BENZ PULLS UP.

A TOO-HANDSOME, TOO-YOUNG SA* OFFICER WAVES OUT THE WINDOW.

YES, OFFICER. YOU ARE AN OFFICER? YOU LOOK AWFULLY YOUNG TO BE AN OFFICER.

EXCUSE ME, MISS ARENDT.

AND YES, I AM AN OFFICER. NEWLY MINTED. MY UNCLE WERNER SAID MOVING TO THE POLITICAL SECTION WOULD BE A GOOD CAREER MOVE.

IT'S MY FIRST WEEK.

I STILL HAVE TO REFER TO THE INSTRUCTION MANUAL.

YOU'RE DOING A GREAT JOB. BUT HERR OFFICER, MY MOTHER AND I HAVE LUNCH RESERVATIONS AT KEMPINSKI.

* Hitler's hand-picked, brown-shirted "thugs," precursor to the Gestapo

73

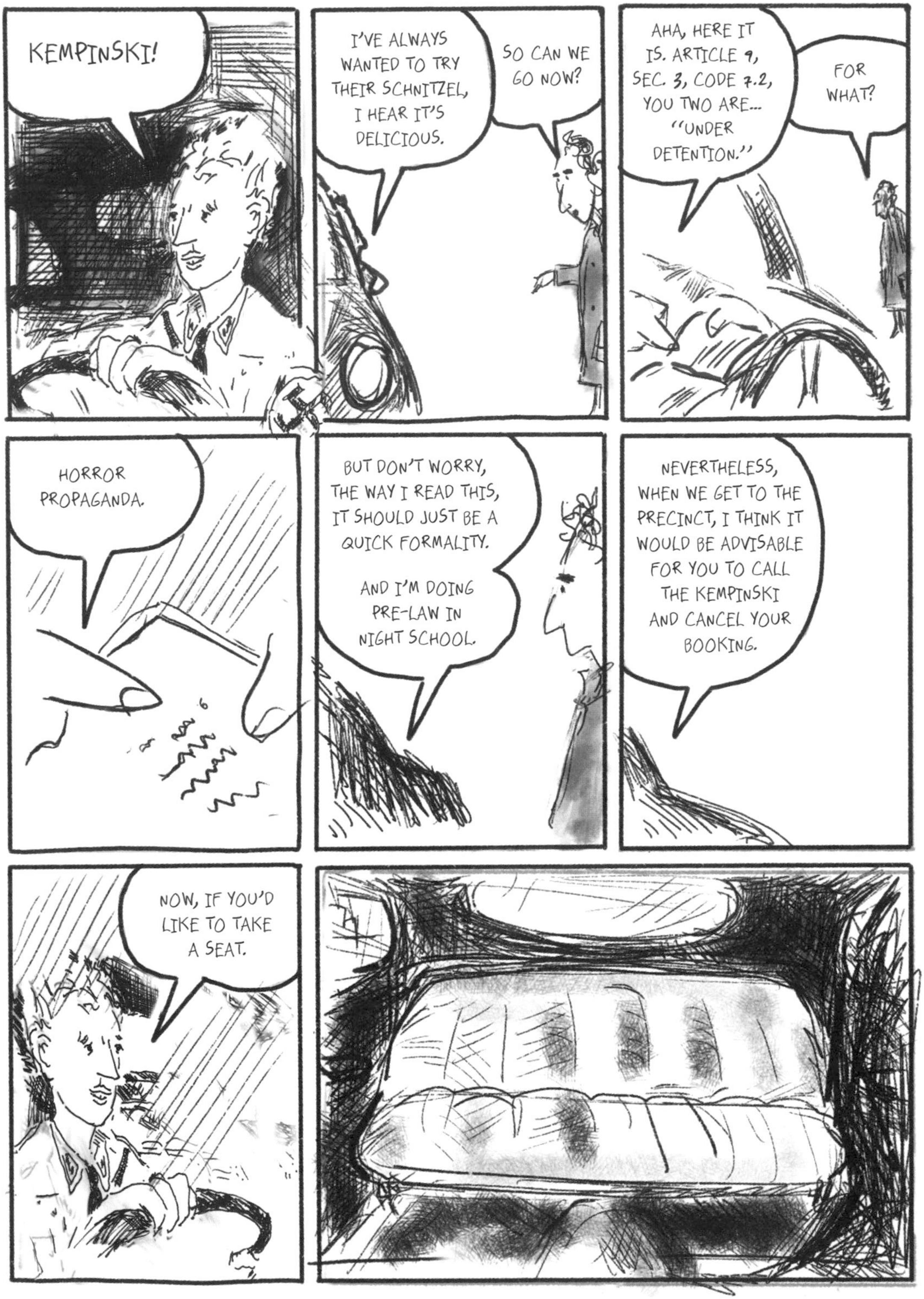
KEMPINSKI!
I'VE ALWAYS WANTED TO TRY THEIR SCHNITZEL, I HEAR IT'S DELICIOUS.
SO CAN WE GO NOW?
AHA, HERE IT IS. ARTICLE 9, SEC. 3, CODE 7.2, YOU TWO ARE... "UNDER DETENTION."
FOR WHAT?
HORROR PROPAGANDA.
BUT DON'T WORRY, THE WAY I READ THIS, IT SHOULD JUST BE A QUICK FORMALITY.
AND I'M DOING PRE-LAW IN NIGHT SCHOOL.
NEVERTHELESS, WHEN WE GET TO THE PRECINCT, I THINK IT WOULD BE ADVISABLE FOR YOU TO CALL THE KEMPINSKI AND CANCEL YOUR BOOKING.
NOW, IF YOU'D LIKE TO TAKE A SEAT.

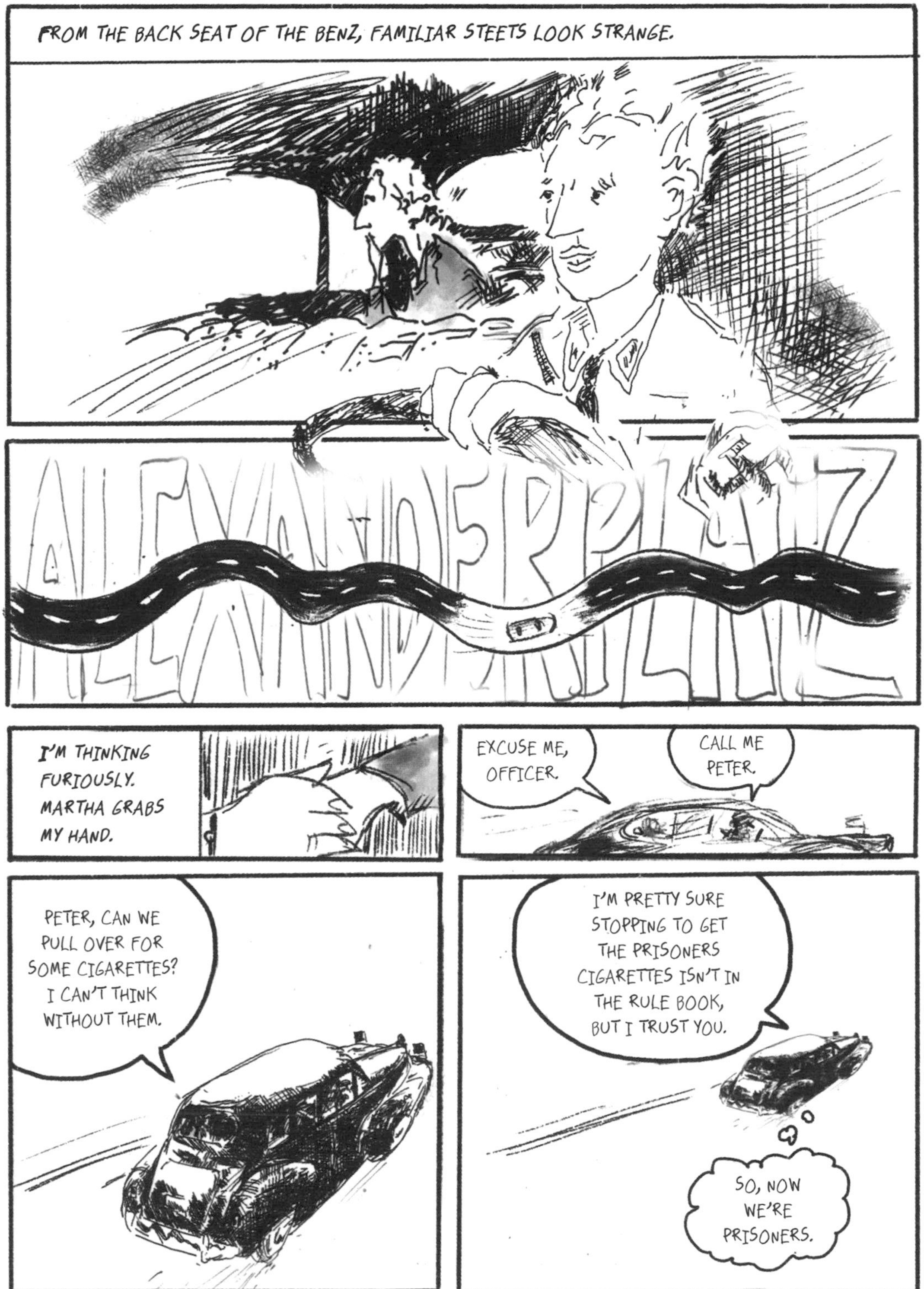
FROM THE BACK SEAT OF THE BENZ, FAMILIAR STEETS LOOK STRANGE.
ALEXANDERPLATZ
I'M THINKING FURIOUSLY. MARTHA GRABS MY HAND.
EXCUSE ME, OFFICER.
CALL ME PETER.
PETER, CAN WE PULL OVER FOR SOME CIGARETTES? I CAN'T THINK WITHOUT THEM.
I'M PRETTY SURE STOPPING TO GET THE PRISONERS CIGARETTES ISN'T IN THE RULE BOOK, BUT I TRUST YOU.
SO, NOW WE'RE PRISONERS.

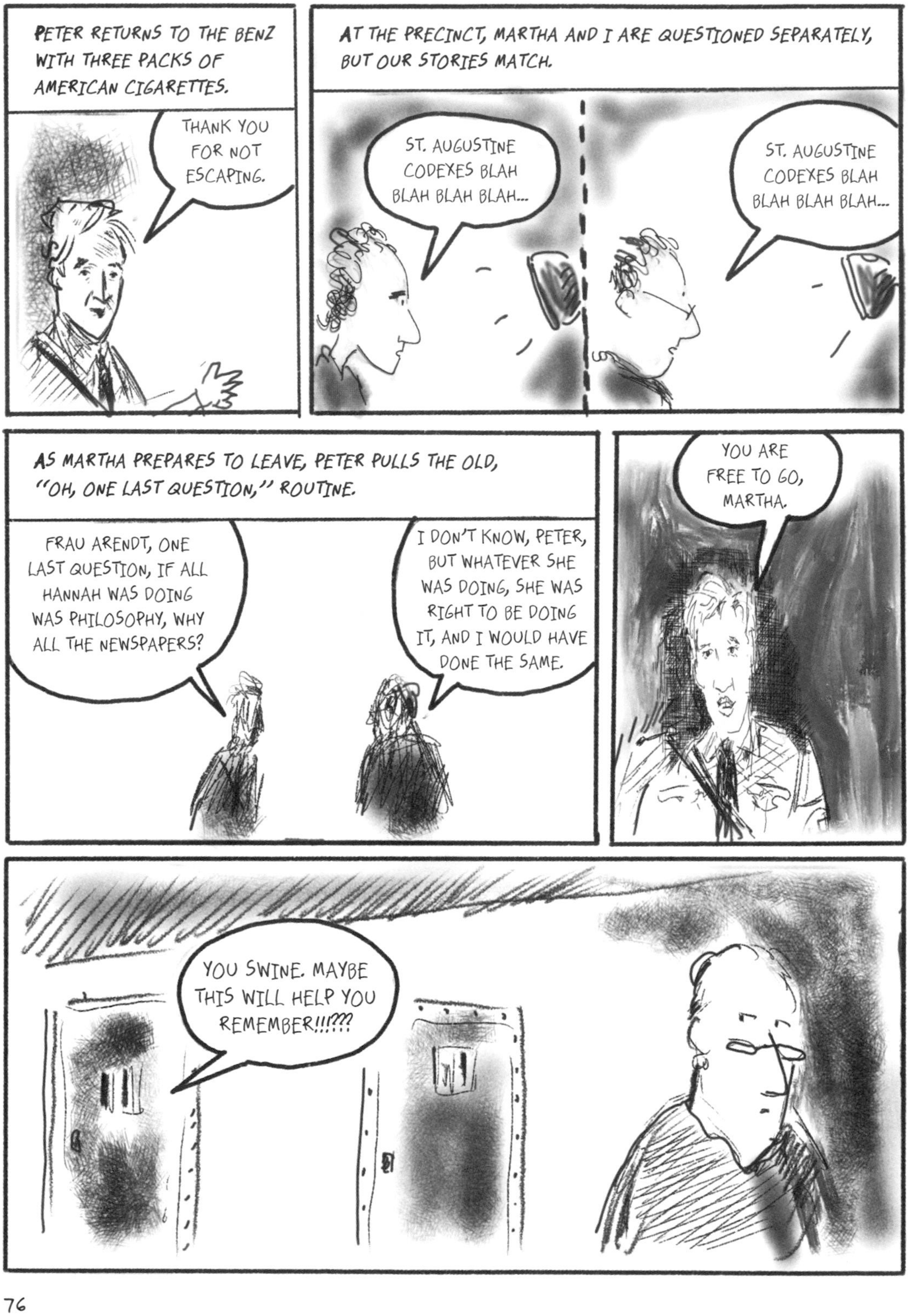
PETER RETURNS TO THE BENZ WITH THREE PACKS OF AMERICAN CIGARETTES.
THANK YOU FOR NOT ESCAPING.
AT THE PRECINCT, MARTHA AND I ARE QUESTIONED SEPARATELY, BUT OUR STORIES MATCH.
ST. AUGUSTINE CODEXES BLAH BLAH BLAH BLAH...
ST. AUGUSTINE CODEXES BLAH BLAH BLAH BLAH...
AS MARTHA PREPARES TO LEAVE, PETER PULLS THE OLD, "OH, ONE LAST QUESTION," ROUTINE.
FRAU ARENDT, ONE LAST QUESTION, IF ALL HANNAH WAS DOING WAS PHILOSOPHY, WHY ALL THE NEWSPAPERS?
I DON'T KNOW, PETER, BUT WHATEVER SHE WAS DOING, SHE WAS RIGHT TO BE DOING IT, AND I WOULD HAVE DONE THE SAME.
YOU ARE FREE TO GO, MARTHA.
YOU SWINE. MAYBE THIS WILL HELP YOU REMEMBER!!!???

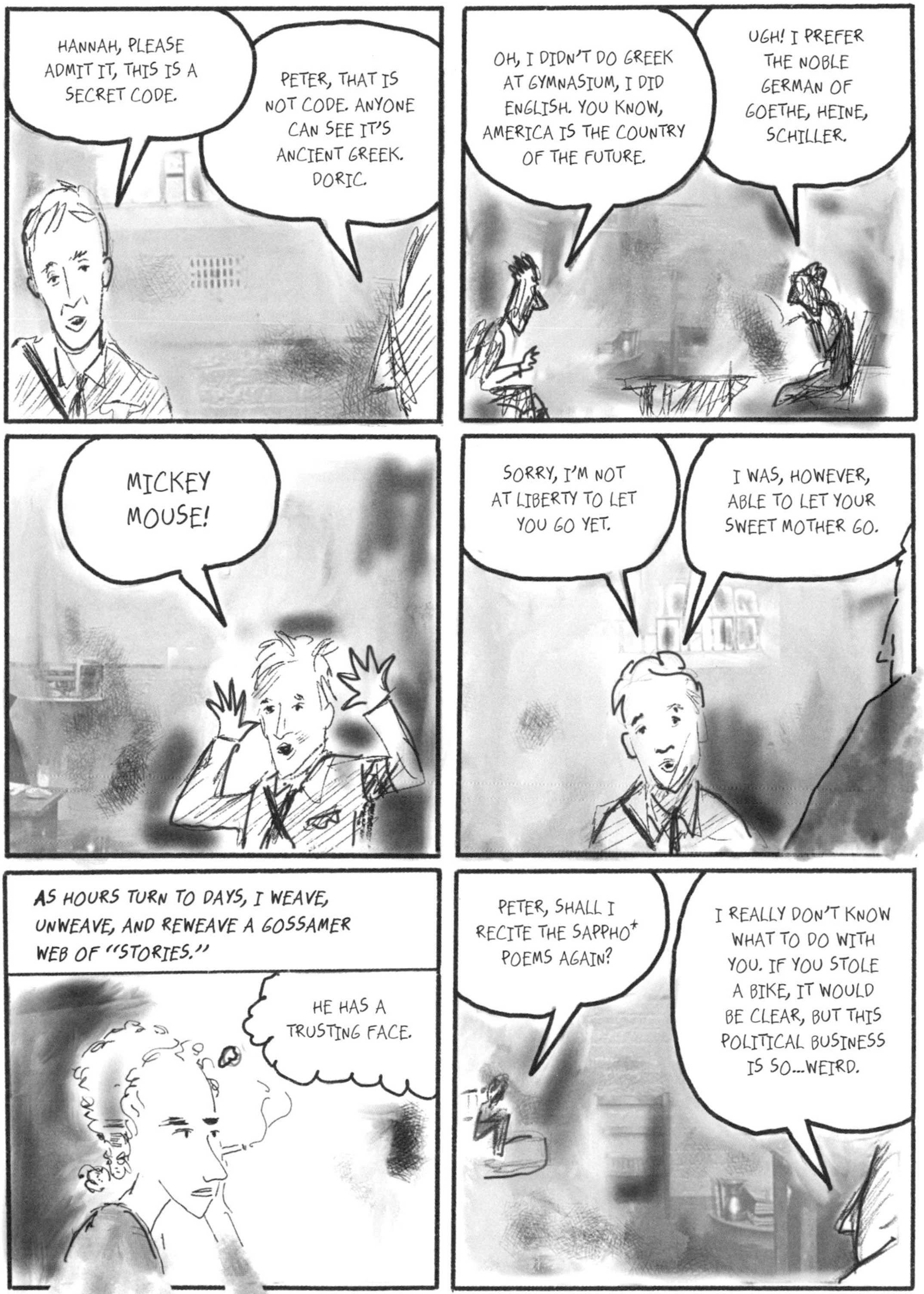
HANNAH, PLEASE ADMIT IT, THIS IS A SECRET CODE.
PETER, THAT IS NOT CODE. ANYONE CAN SEE IT'S ANCIENT GREEK. DORIC.
OH, I DIDN'T DO GREEK AT GYMNASIUM, I DID ENGLISH. YOU KNOW, AMERICA IS THE COUNTRY OF THE FUTURE.
UGH! I PREFER THE NOBLE GERMAN OF GOETHE, HEINE, SCHILLER.
MICKEY MOUSE!
SORRY, I'M NOT AT LIBERTY TO LET YOU GO YET.
I WAS, HOWEVER, ABLE TO LET YOUR SWEET MOTHER GO.
AS HOURS TURN TO DAYS, I WEAVE, UNWEAVE, AND REWEAVE A GOSSAMER WEB OF "STORIES."
HE HAS A TRUSTING FACE.
PETER, SHALL I RECITE THE SAPPHO* POEMS AGAIN?
I REALLY DON'T KNOW WHAT TO DO WITH YOU. IF YOU STOLE A BIKE, IT WOULD BE CLEAR, BUT THIS POLITICAL BUSINESS IS SO...WEIRD.

* Sappho (630–570 B.C.). Female Greek poet from the island of Lesbos, her lyric poetry celebrates sensuality, love, and ardor.

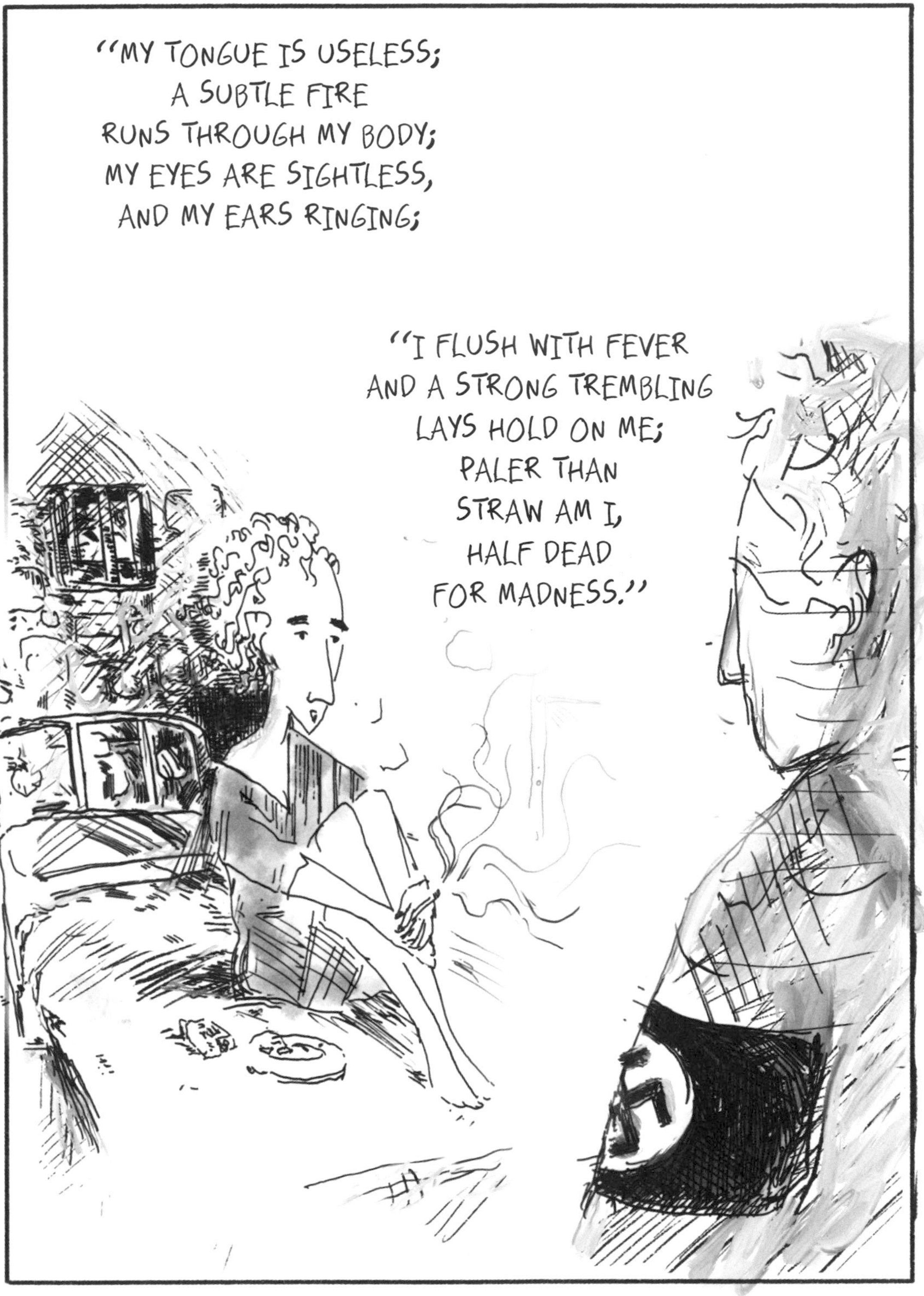
"MY TONGUE IS USELESS; A SUBTLE FIRE RUNS THROUGH MY BODY; MY EYES ARE SIGHTLESS, AND MY EARS RINGING;
"I FLUSH WITH FEVER AND A STRONG TREMBLING LAYS HOLD ON ME; PALER THAN STRAW AM I, HALF DEAD FOR MADNESS."

NO. (TWO DAYS LATER.)

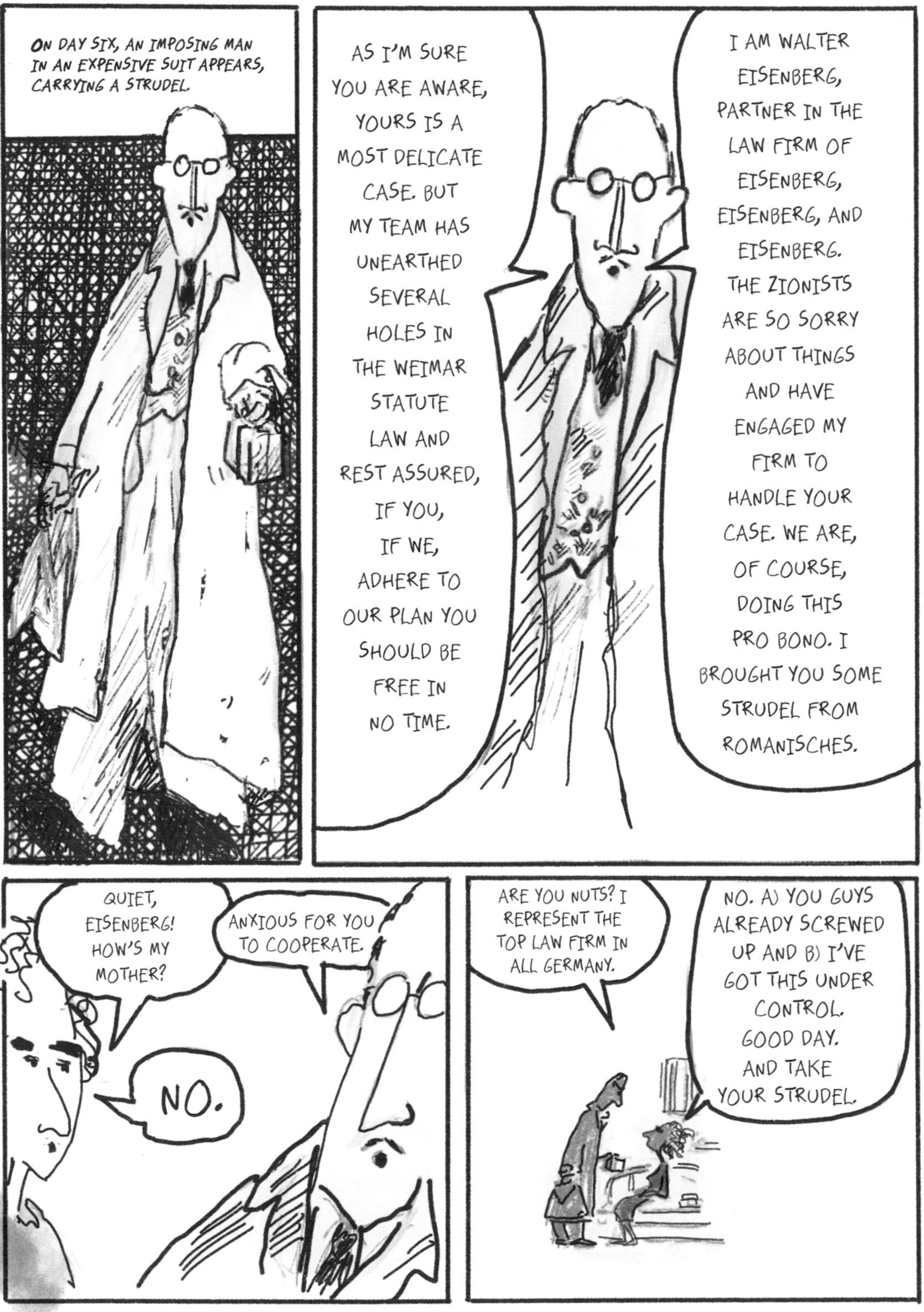
ON DAY SIX, AN IMPOSING MAN IN AN EXPENSIVE SUIT APPEARS, CARRYING A STRUDEL.
I AM WALTER EISENBERG, PARTNER IN THE LAW FIRM OF EISENBERG, EISENBERG, AND EISENBERG. THE ZIONISTS ARE SO SORRY ABOUT THINGS AND HAVE ENGAGED MY FIRM TO HANDLE YOUR CASE. WE ARE, OF COURSE, DOING THIS PRO BONO. I BROUGHT YOU SOME STRUDEL FROM ROMANISCHES.
AS I'M SURE YOU ARE AWARE, YOURS IS A MOST DELICATE CASE. BUT MY TEAM HAS UNEARTHED SEVERAL HOLES IN THE WEIMAR STATUTE LAW AND REST ASSURED, IF YOU, IF WE, ADHERE TO OUR PLAN YOU SHOULD BE FREE IN NO TIME.
QUIET, EISENBERG! HOW'S MY MOTHER?
ANXIOUS FOR YOU TO COOPERATE.
NO.
ARE YOU NUTS? I REPRESENT THE TOP LAW FIRM IN ALL GERMANY.
NO. A) YOU GUYS ALREADY SCREWED UP AND B) I'VE GOT THIS UNDER CONTROL. GOOD DAY. AND TAKE YOUR STRUDEL.

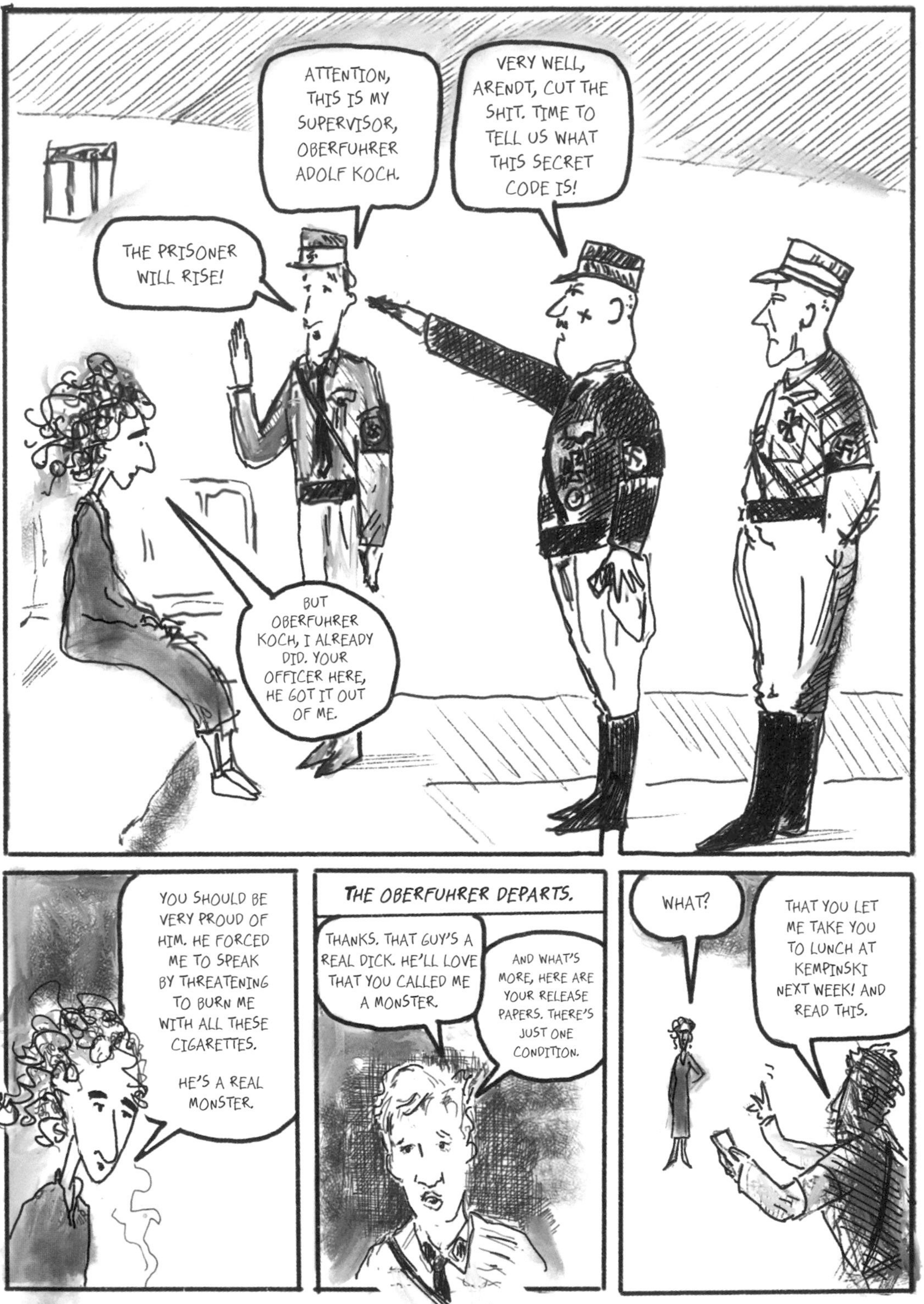
ATTENTION, THIS IS MY SUPERVISOR, OBERFUHRER ADOLF KOCH.
VERY WELL, ARENDT, CUT THE SHIT. TIME TO TELL US WHAT THIS SECRET CODE IS!
THE PRISONER WILL RISE!
BUT OBERFUHRER KOCH, I ALREADY DID. YOUR OFFICER HERE, HE GOT IT OUT OF ME.
YOU SHOULD BE VERY PROUD OF HIM. HE FORCED ME TO SPEAK BY THREATENING TO BURN ME WITH ALL THESE CIGARETTES.
HE'S A REAL MONSTER.
THE OBERFUHRER DEPARTS.
THANKS. THAT GUY'S A REAL DICK. HE'LL LOVE THAT YOU CALLED ME A MONSTER.
AND WHAT'S MORE, HERE ARE YOUR RELEASE PAPERS. THERE'S JUST ONE CONDITION.
WHAT?
THAT YOU LET ME TAKE YOU TO LUNCH AT KEMPINSKI NEXT WEEK! AND READ THIS.

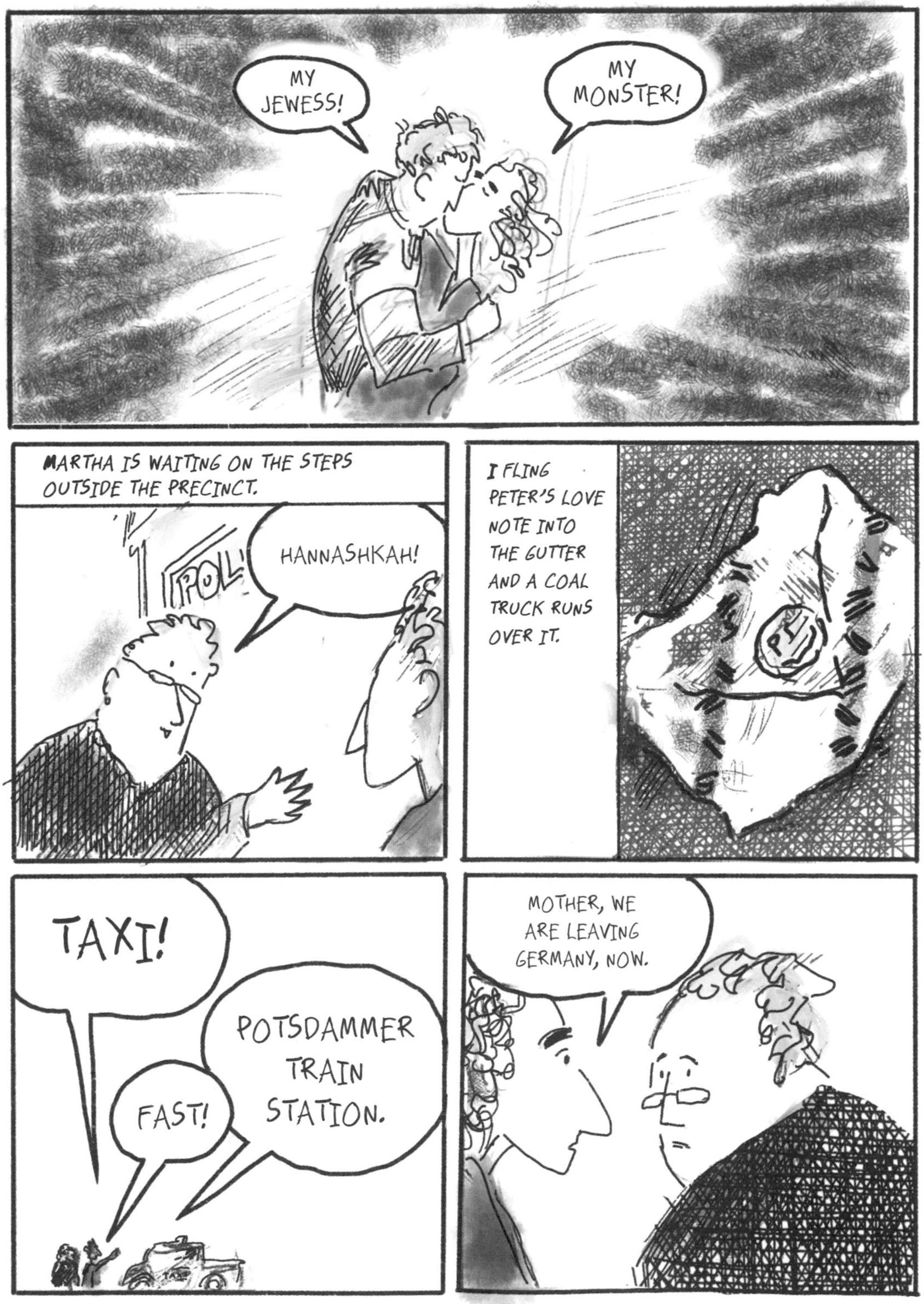
MY JEWESS!
MY MONSTER!
MARTHA IS WAITING ON THE STEPS OUTSIDE THE PRECINCT.
POL
HANNASHKAH!
I FLING PETER'S LOVE NOTE INTO THE GUTTER AND A COAL TRUCK RUNS OVER IT.
TAXI!
FAST!
POTSDAMMER TRAIN STATION.
MOTHER, WE ARE LEAVING GERMANY, NOW.

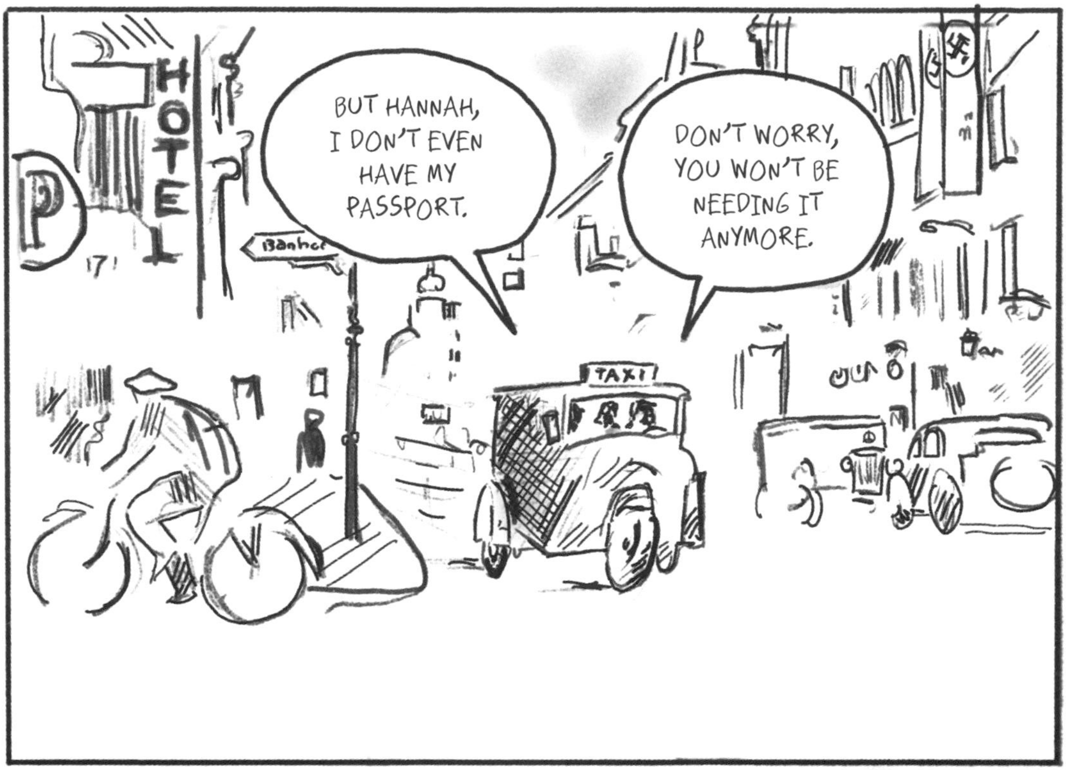
HOTEL
Bahnhof
BUT HANNAH, I DON'T EVEN HAVE MY PASSPORT.
DON'T WORRY, YOU WON'T BE NEEDING IT ANYMORE.
TAXI

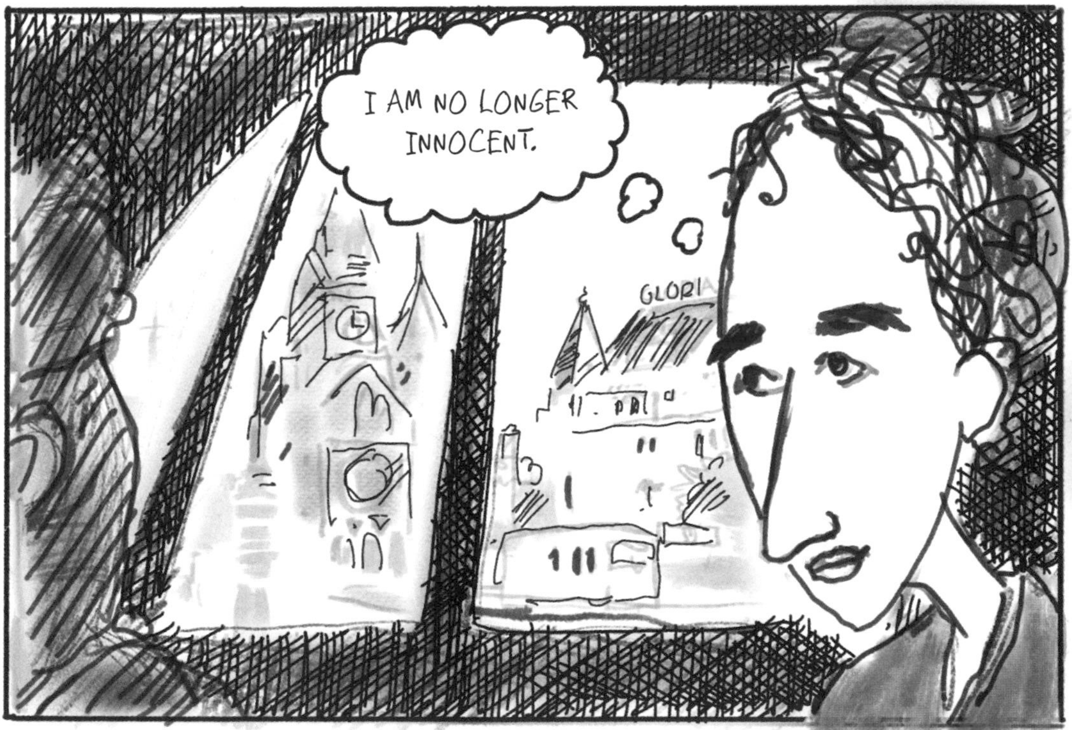
I AM NO LONGER INNOCENT.
GLORI

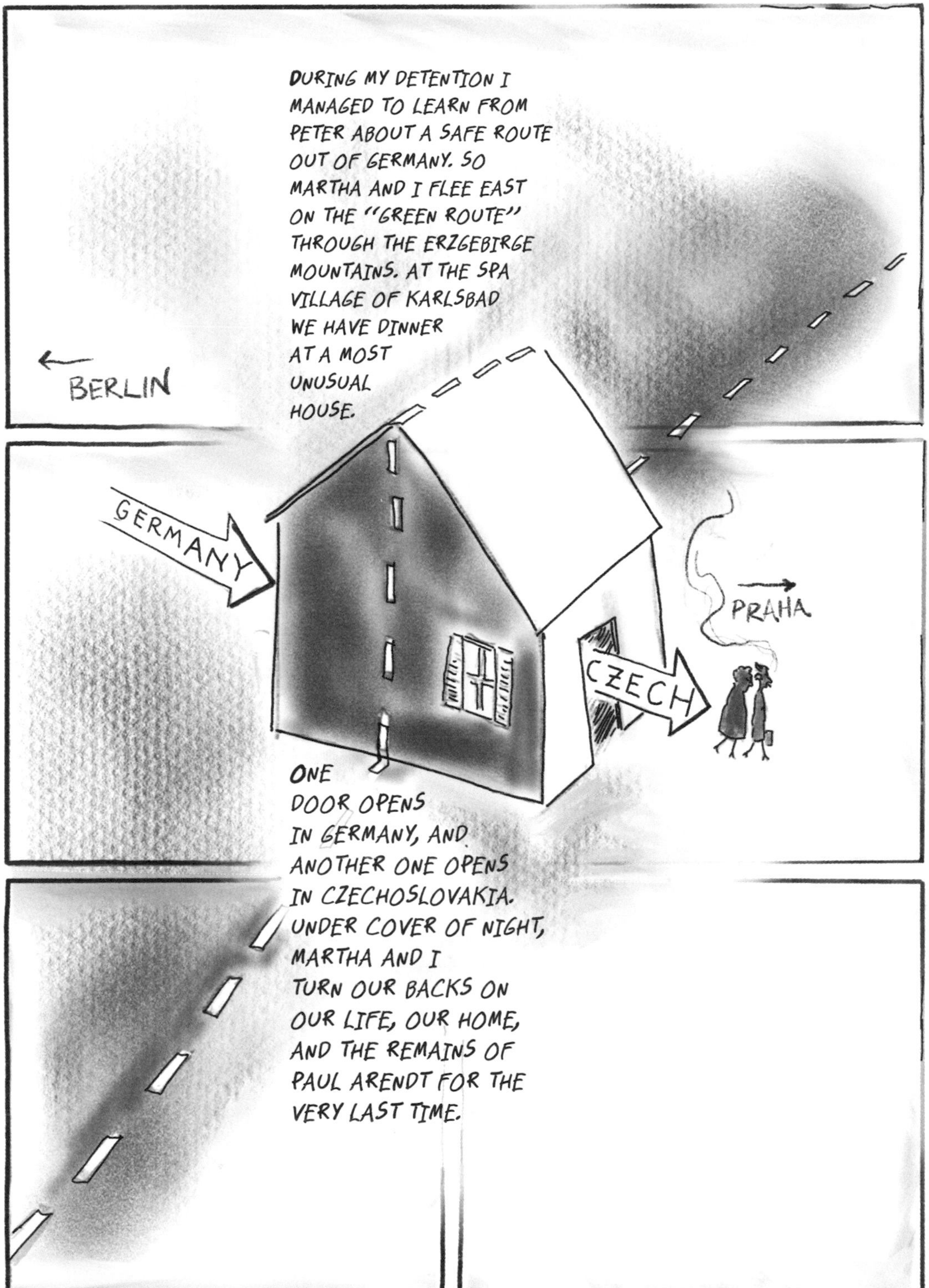
DURING MY DETENTION I MANAGED TO LEARN FROM PETER ABOUT A SAFE ROUTE OUT OF GERMANY. SO MARTHA AND I FLEE EAST ON THE "GREEN ROUTE" THROUGH THE ERZGEBIRGE MOUNTAINS. AT THE SPA VILLAGE OF KARLSBAD WE HAVE DINNER AT A MOST UNUSUAL HOUSE.
BERLIN
GERMANY
CZECH
PRAHA
ONE DOOR OPENS IN GERMANY, AND ANOTHER ONE OPENS IN CZECHOSLOVAKIA. UNDER COVER OF NIGHT, MARTHA AND I TURN OUR BACKS ON OUR LIFE, OUR HOME, AND THE REMAINS OF PAUL ARENDT FOR THE VERY LAST TIME.

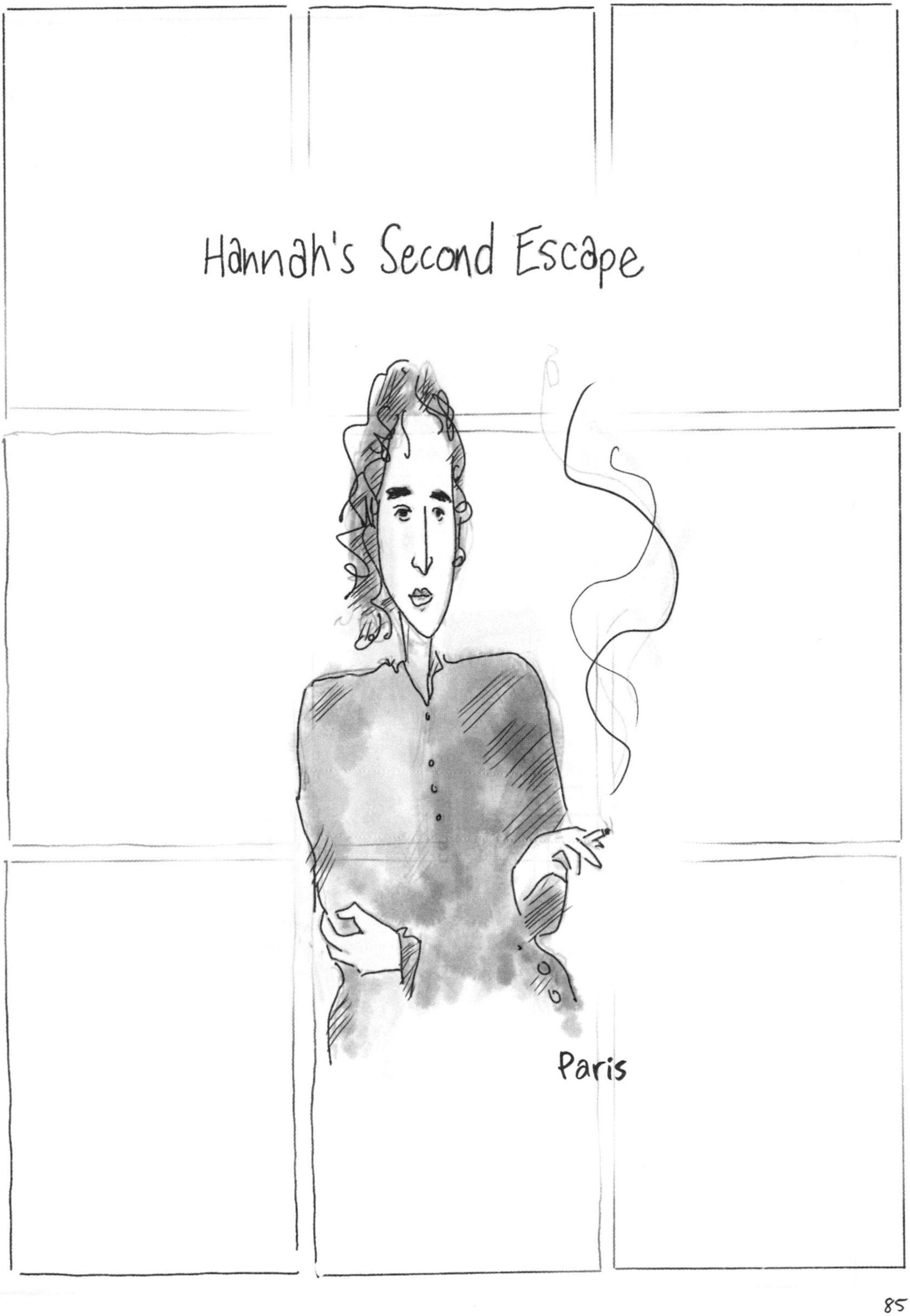
Hannah's Second Escape
Paris

TRIPLING DOWN ON THE TRUTH IN PARIS 1933

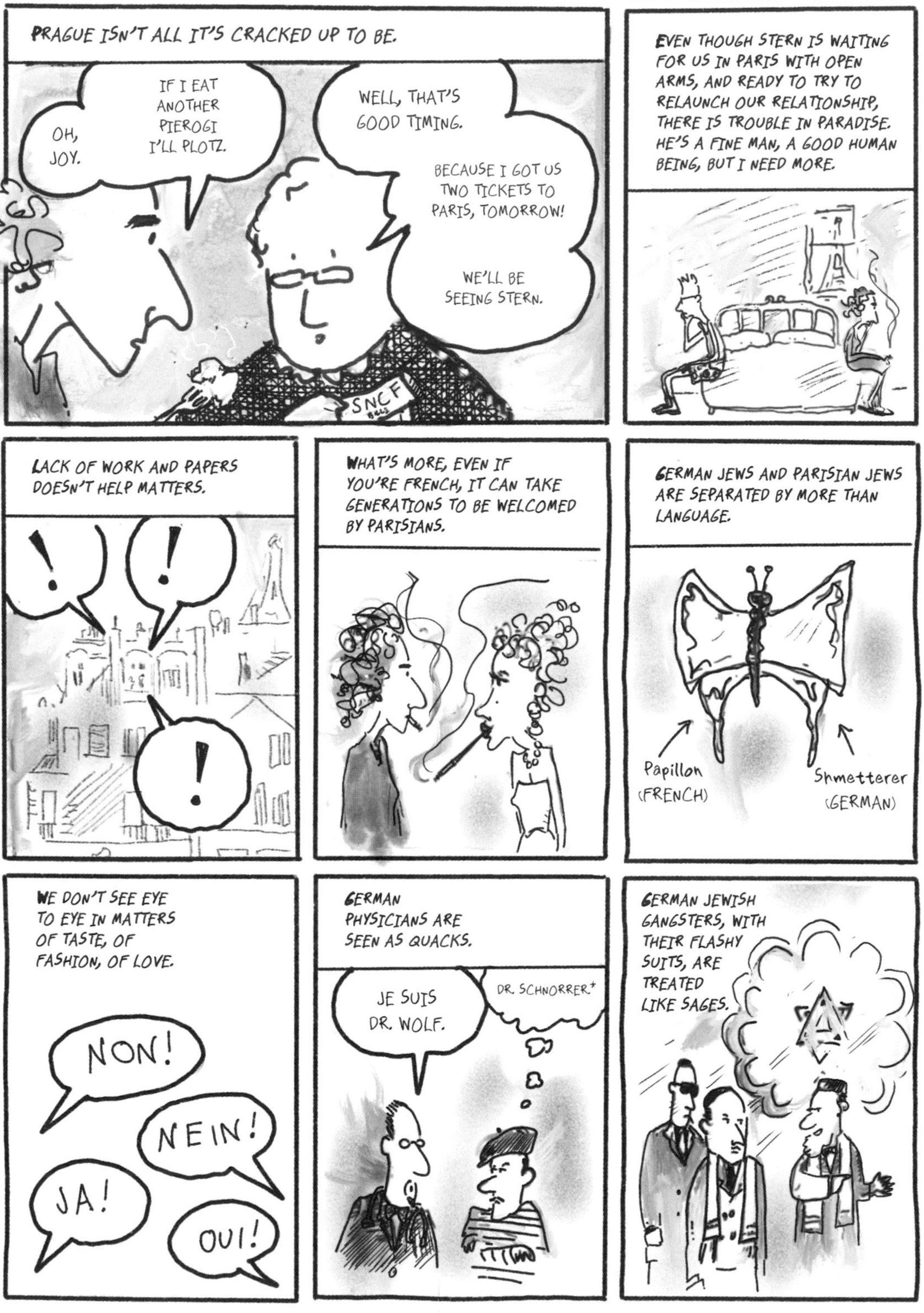
PRAGUE ISN'T ALL IT'S CRACKED UP TO BE.
OH, JOY.
IF I EAT ANOTHER PIEROGI I'LL PLOTZ.
WELL, THAT'S GOOD TIMING.
BECAUSE I GOT US TWO TICKETS TO PARIS, TOMORROW!
WE'LL BE SEEING STERN.
SNCF
EVEN THOUGH STERN IS WAITING FOR US IN PARIS WITH OPEN ARMS, AND READY TO TRY TO RELAUNCH OUR RELATIONSHIP, THERE IS TROUBLE IN PARADISE. HE'S A FINE MAN, A GOOD HUMAN BEING, BUT I NEED MORE.
LACK OF WORK AND PAPERS DOESN'T HELP MATTERS.
!
!
!
WHAT'S MORE, EVEN IF YOU'RE FRENCH, IT CAN TAKE GENERATIONS TO BE WELCOMED BY PARISIANS.
GERMAN JEWS AND PARISIAN JEWS ARE SEPARATED BY MORE THAN LANGUAGE.
Papillon (FRENCH)
Shmetterer (GERMAN)
WE DON'T SEE EYE TO EYE IN MATTERS OF TASTE, OF FASHION, OF LOVE.
NON!
NEIN!
JA!
OUI!
GERMAN PHYSICIANS ARE SEEN AS QUACKS.
JE SUIS DR. WOLF.
DR. SCHNORRER.*
GERMAN JEWISH GANGSTERS, WITH THEIR FLASHY SUITS, ARE TREATED LIKE SAGES.

* Cheap, borrowing, "Oh I forgot my wallet" type person

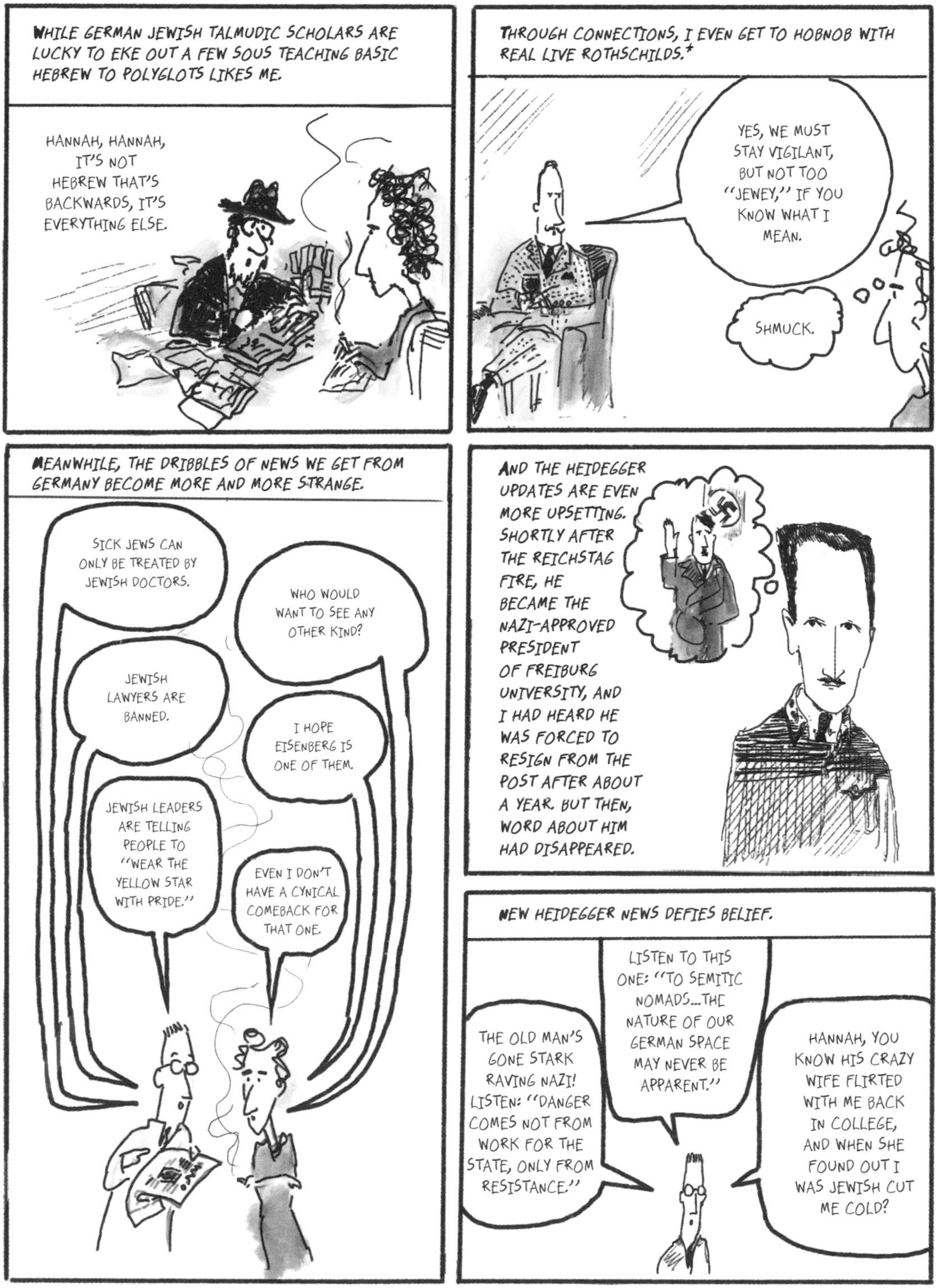
WHILE GERMAN JEWISH TALMUDIC SCHOLARS ARE LUCKY TO EKE OUT A FEW SOUS TEACHING BASIC HEBREW TO POLYGLOTS LIKES ME.
HANNAH, HANNAH, IT'S NOT HEBREW THAT'S BACKWARDS, IT'S EVERYTHING ELSE.
THROUGH CONNECTIONS, I EVEN GET TO HOBNOB WITH REAL LIVE ROTHSCHILDS.*
YES, WE MUST STAY VIGILANT, BUT NOT TOO "JEWEY," IF YOU KNOW WHAT I MEAN.
SHMUCK.
MEANWHILE, THE DRIBBLES OF NEWS WE GET FROM GERMANY BECOME MORE AND MORE STRANGE.
SICK JEWS CAN ONLY BE TREATED BY JEWISH DOCTORS.
WHO WOULD WANT TO SEE ANY OTHER KIND?
JEWISH LAWYERS ARE BANNED.
I HOPE EISENBERG IS ONE OF THEM.
JEWISH LEADERS ARE TELLING PEOPLE TO "WEAR THE YELLOW STAR WITH PRIDE."
EVEN I DON'T HAVE A CYNICAL COMEBACK FOR THAT ONE.
AND THE HEIDEGGER UPDATES ARE EVEN MORE UPSETTING. SHORTLY AFTER THE REICHSTAG FIRE, HE BECAME THE NAZI-APPROVED PRESIDENT OF FREIBURG UNIVERSITY, AND I HAD HEARD HE WAS FORCED TO RESIGN FROM THE POST AFTER ABOUT A YEAR. BUT THEN, WORD ABOUT HIM HAD DISAPPEARED.
NEW HEIDEGGER NEWS DEFIES BELIEF.
THE OLD MAN'S GONE STARK RAVING NAZI! LISTEN: "DANGER COMES NOT FROM WORK FOR THE STATE, ONLY FROM RESISTANCE."
LISTEN TO THIS ONE: "TO SEMITIC NOMADS...THE NATURE OF OUR GERMAN SPACE MAY NEVER BE APPARENT."
HANNAH, YOU KNOW HIS CRAZY WIFE FLIRTED WITH ME BACK IN COLLEGE, AND WHEN SHE FOUND OUT I WAS JEWISH CUT ME COLD?

* The Rothschild family. Jewish banking dynasty, founded by Mayer Rothschild in 1769, parlayed a Protestant "problem" with issuing credit into the first international finance business. Among other accomplishments, devised a system of lights connecting castles to get financial news transmitted around Europe faster than ever before.

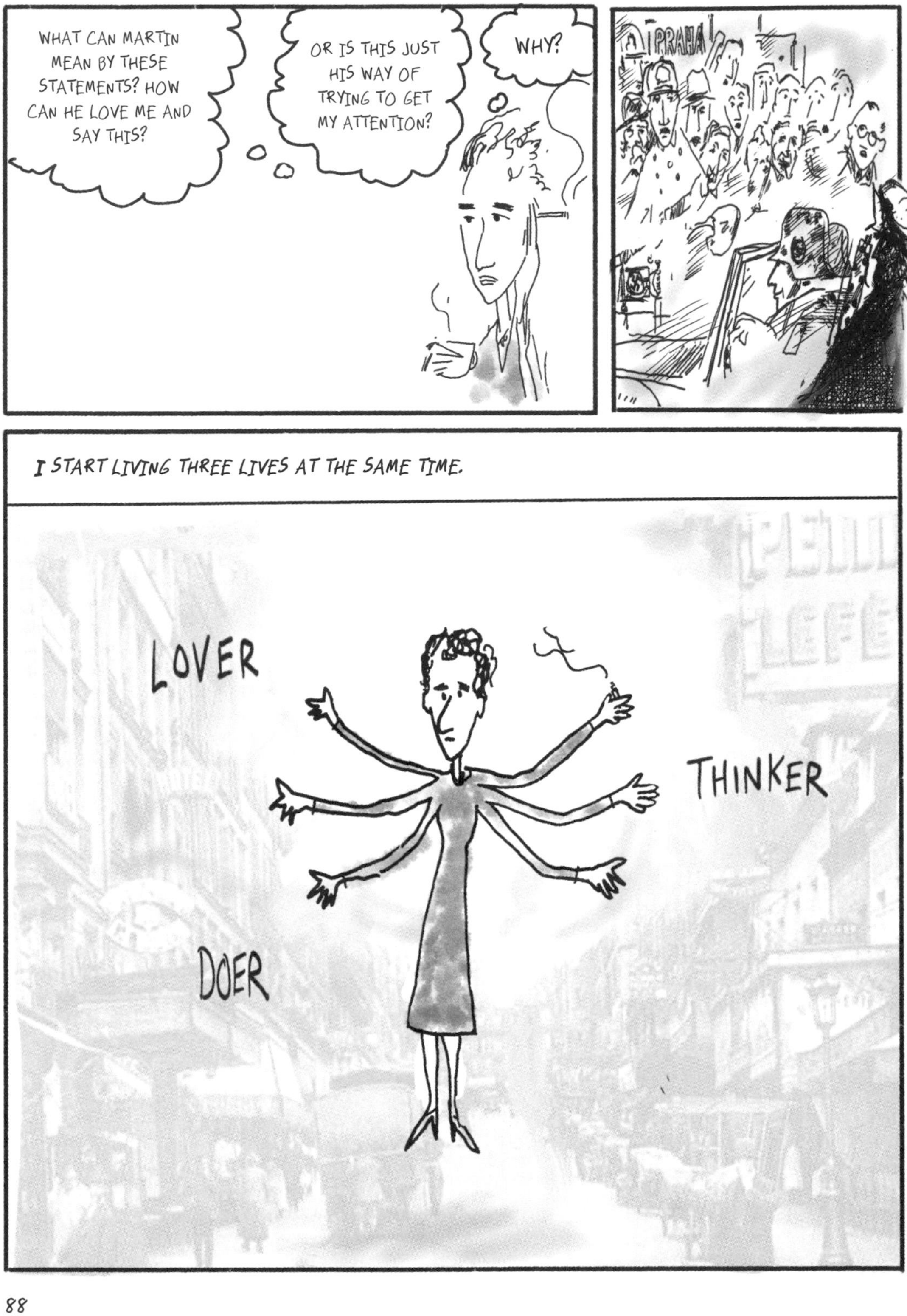
WHAT CAN MARTIN MEAN BY THESE STATEMENTS? HOW CAN HE LOVE ME AND SAY THIS?
OR IS THIS JUST HIS WAY OF TRYING TO GET MY ATTENTION?
WHY?
PRAHA
I START LIVING THREE LIVES AT THE SAME TIME.
LOVER
THINKER
DOER

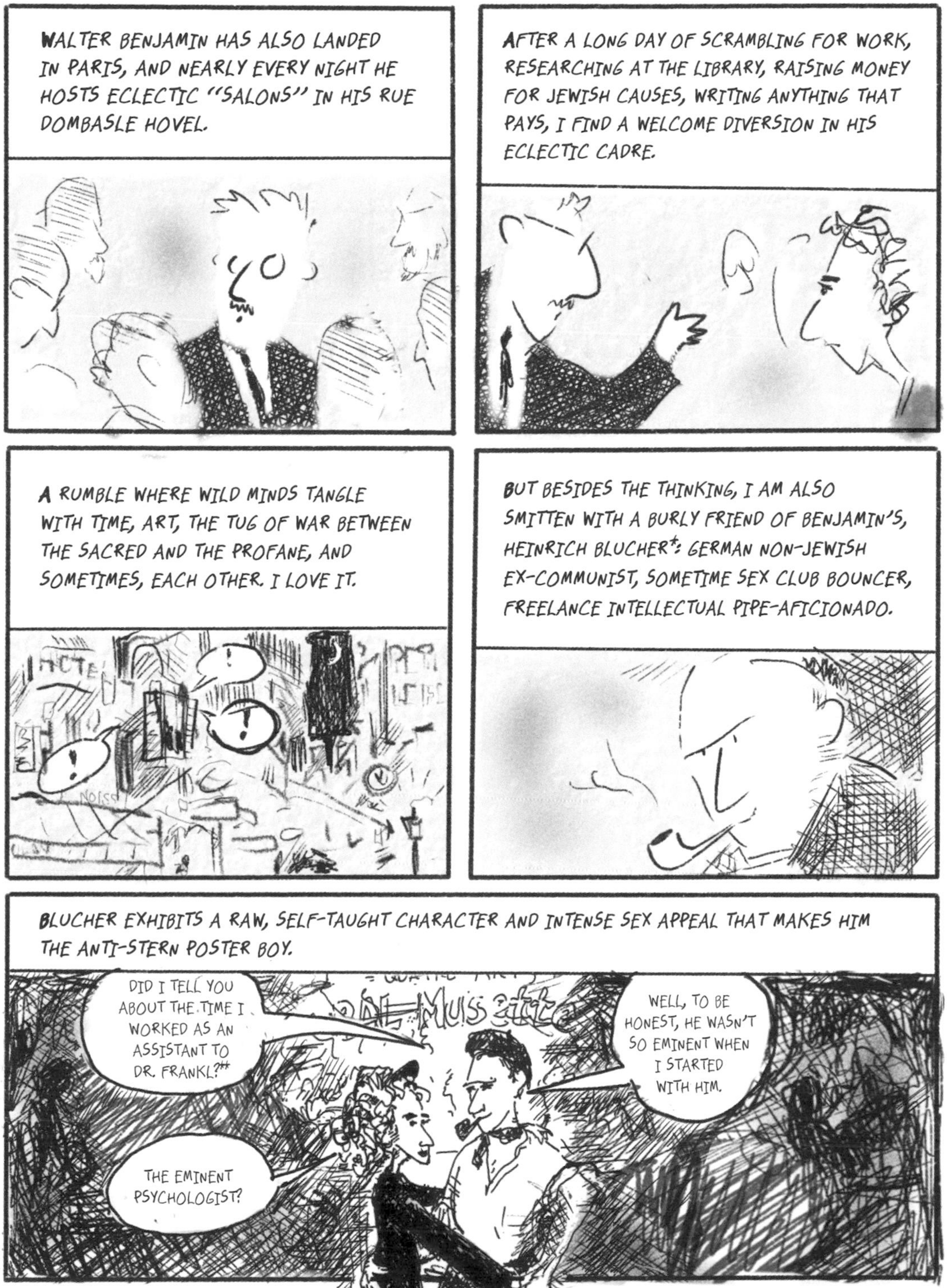
WALTER BENJAMIN HAS ALSO LANDED IN PARIS, AND NEARLY EVERY NIGHT HE HOSTS ECLECTIC "SALONS" IN HIS RUE DOMBASLE HOVEL.
AFTER A LONG DAY OF SCRAMBLING FOR WORK, RESEARCHING AT THE LIBRARY, RAISING MONEY FOR JEWISH CAUSES, WRITING ANYTHING THAT PAYS, I FIND A WELCOME DIVERSION IN HIS ECLECTIC CADRE.
A RUMBLE WHERE WILD MINDS TANGLE WITH TIME, ART, THE TUG OF WAR BETWEEN THE SACRED AND THE PROFANE, AND SOMETIMES, EACH OTHER. I LOVE IT.
!
!
!
BUT BESIDES THE THINKING, I AM ALSO SMITTEN WITH A BURLY FRIEND OF BENJAMIN'S, HEINRICH BLUCHER*: GERMAN NON-JEWISH EX-COMMUNIST, SOMETIME SEX CLUB BOUNCER, FREELANCE INTELLECTUAL PIPE-AFICIONADO.
BLUCHER EXHIBITS A RAW, SELF-TAUGHT CHARACTER AND INTENSE SEX APPEAL THAT MAKES HIM THE ANTI-STERN POSTER BOY.
DID I TELL YOU ABOUT THE TIME I WORKED AS AN ASSISTANT TO DR. FRANKL?**
THE EMINENT PSYCHOLOGIST?
WELL, TO BE HONEST, HE WASN'T SO EMINENT WHEN I STARTED WITH HIM.

* Heinrich Blucher (1899–1970). German poet, teacher, revolutionary, philosopher, and dancehall bouncer. Hannah Arendt's second husband.

** Dr. Viktor Frankl (1905–1997). Berlin Freudian psychologist, who, after his encounter with Blucher and their "shock" techniques, became less of a Freudian and more of a Blucherian.

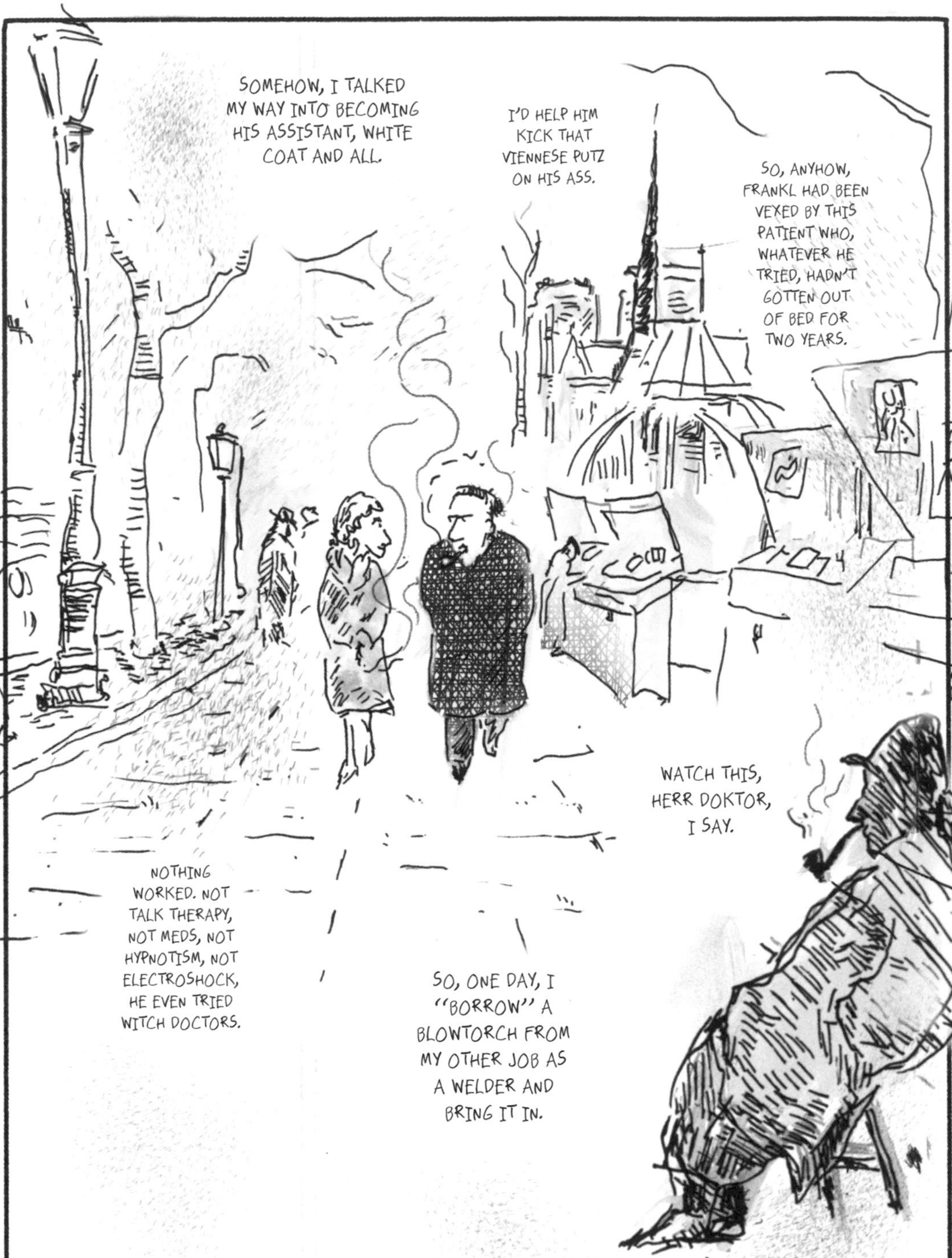
SOMEHOW, I TALKED MY WAY INTO BECOMING HIS ASSISTANT, WHITE COAT AND ALL.
I'D HELP HIM KICK THAT VIENNESE PUTZ ON HIS ASS.
SO, ANYHOW, FRANKL HAD BEEN VEXED BY THIS PATIENT WHO, WHATEVER HE TRIED, HADN'T GOTTEN OUT OF BED FOR TWO YEARS.
NOTHING WORKED. NOT TALK THERAPY, NOT MEDS, NOT HYPNOTISM, NOT ELECTROSHOCK, HE EVEN TRIED WITCH DOCTORS.
SO, ONE DAY, I "BORROW" A BLOWTORCH FROM MY OTHER JOB AS A WELDER AND BRING IT IN.
WATCH THIS, HERR DOKTOR, I SAY.

* Roscoe "Fatty" Arbuckle (1887–1933). American filmmaker, discovered Bob Hope and Buster Keaton, and mentored Charlie Chaplin. One of the top stars of the silent era, his career was destroyed by a rumor-mongering scandal-sheet press attack. After his banishment from Hollywood, he was set to relaunch his career in Berlin until his sudden death.

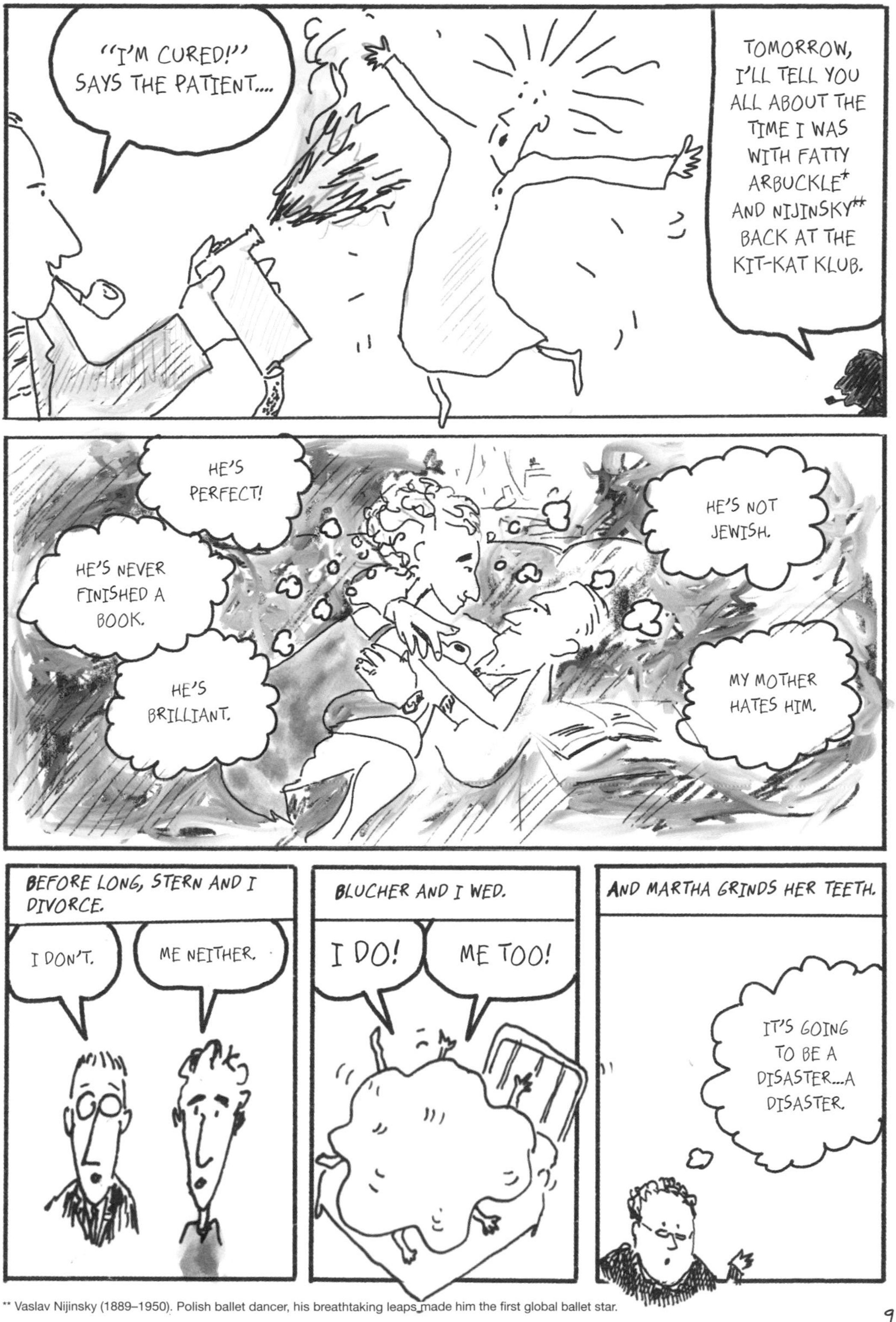
"I'M CURED!" SAYS THE PATIENT....
TOMORROW, I'LL TELL YOU ALL ABOUT THE TIME I WAS WITH FATTY ARBUCKLE* AND NIJINSKY** BACK AT THE KIT-KAT KLUB.
HE'S PERFECT!
HE'S NEVER FINISHED A BOOK.
HE'S BRILLIANT.
HE'S NOT JEWISH.
MY MOTHER HATES HIM.
BEFORE LONG, STERN AND I DIVORCE.
I DON'T.
ME NEITHER.
BLUCHER AND I WED.
I DO!
ME TOO!
AND MARTHA GRINDS HER TEETH.
IT'S GOING TO BE A DISASTER...A DISASTER.

** Vaslav Nijinsky (1889–1950). Polish ballet dancer, his breathtaking leaps made him the first global ballet star.

HANNAH'S PARIS TRIPTYCH PART TWO: THINKER 1937

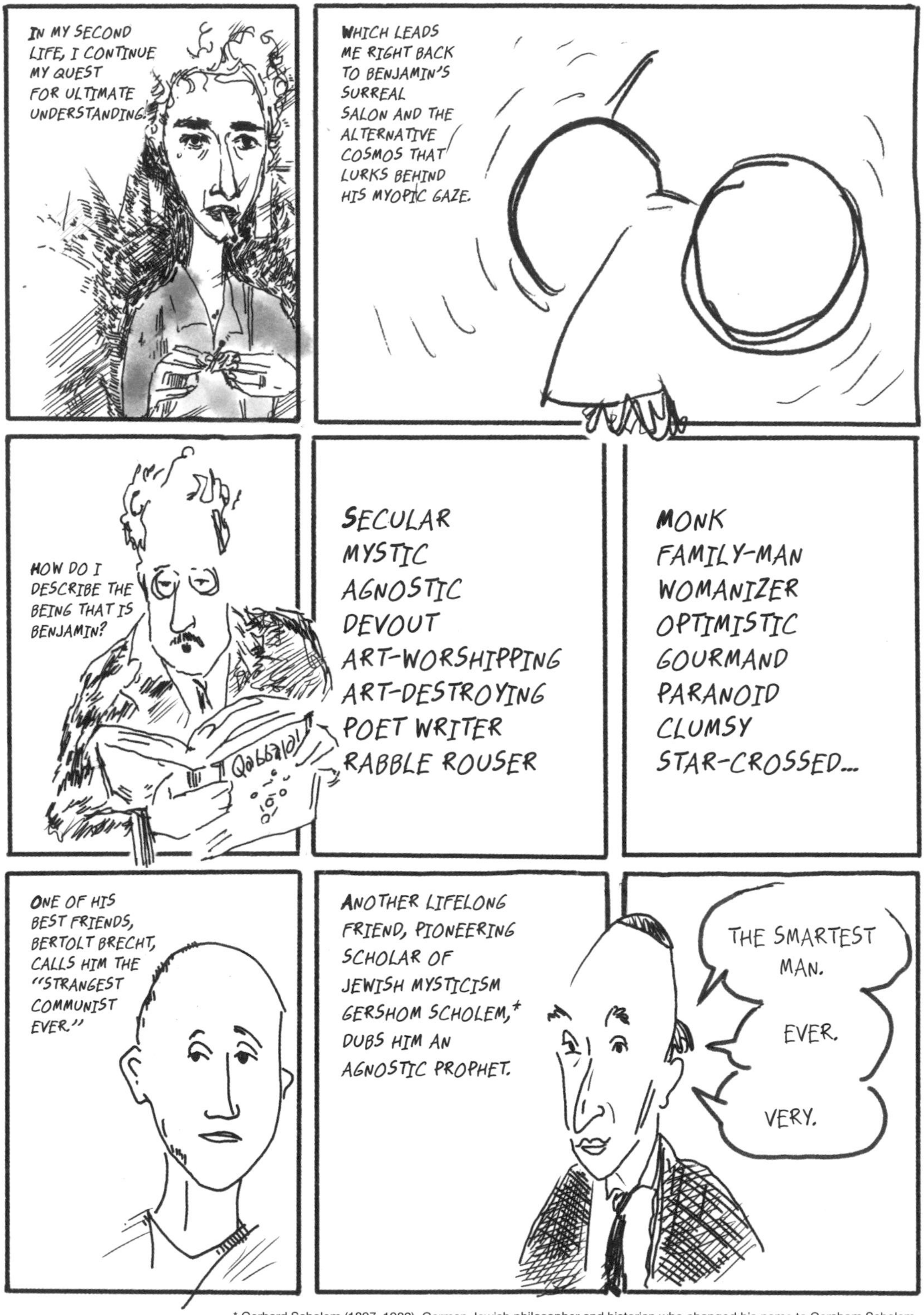
IN MY SECOND LIFE, I CONTINUE MY QUEST FOR ULTIMATE UNDERSTANDING.
WHICH LEADS ME RIGHT BACK TO BENJAMIN'S SURREAL SALON AND THE ALTERNATIVE COSMOS THAT LURKS BEHIND HIS MYOPIC GAZE.
HOW DO I DESCRIBE THE BEING THAT IS BENJAMIN?
SECULAR
MYSTIC
AGNOSTIC
DEVOUT
ART-WORSHIPPING
ART-DESTROYING
POET WRITER
RABBLE ROUSER
MONK
FAMILY-MAN
WOMANIZER
OPTIMISTIC
GOURMAND
PARANOID
CLUMSY
STAR-CROSSED...
ONE OF HIS BEST FRIENDS, BERTOLT BRECHT, CALLS HIM THE "STRANGEST COMMUNIST EVER."
ANOTHER LIFELONG FRIEND, PIONEERING SCHOLAR OF JEWISH MYSTICISM GERSHOM SCHOLEM,* DUBS HIM AN AGNOSTIC PROPHET.
THE SMARTEST MAN.
EVER.
VERY.

* Gerhard Scholem (1897–1982). German Jewish philosopher and historian who changed his name to Gershom Scholem. Founded the modern academic study of Jewish mysticism, Kabbalah, and lifelong best friend of Walter Benjamin.

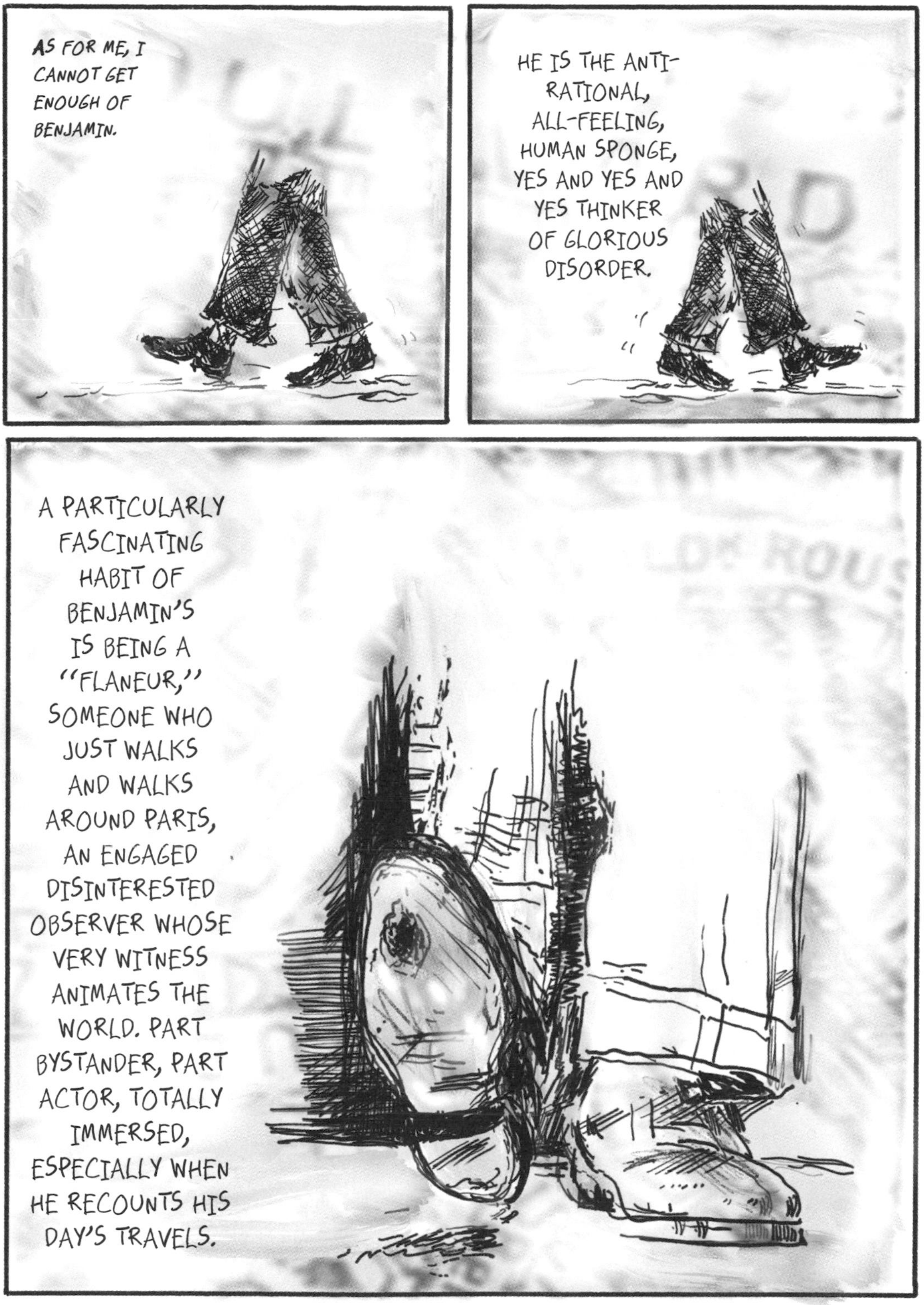
AS FOR ME, I CANNOT GET ENOUGH OF BENJAMIN.
HE IS THE ANTI-RATIONAL, ALL-FEELING, HUMAN SPONGE, YES AND YES AND YES THINKER OF GLORIOUS DISORDER.
A PARTICULARLY FASCINATING HABIT OF BENJAMIN'S IS BEING A "FLANEUR," SOMEONE WHO JUST WALKS AND WALKS AROUND PARIS, AN ENGAGED DISINTERESTED OBSERVER WHOSE VERY WITNESS ANIMATES THE WORLD. PART BYSTANDER, PART ACTOR, TOTALLY IMMERSED, ESPECIALLY WHEN HE RECOUNTS HIS DAY'S TRAVELS.

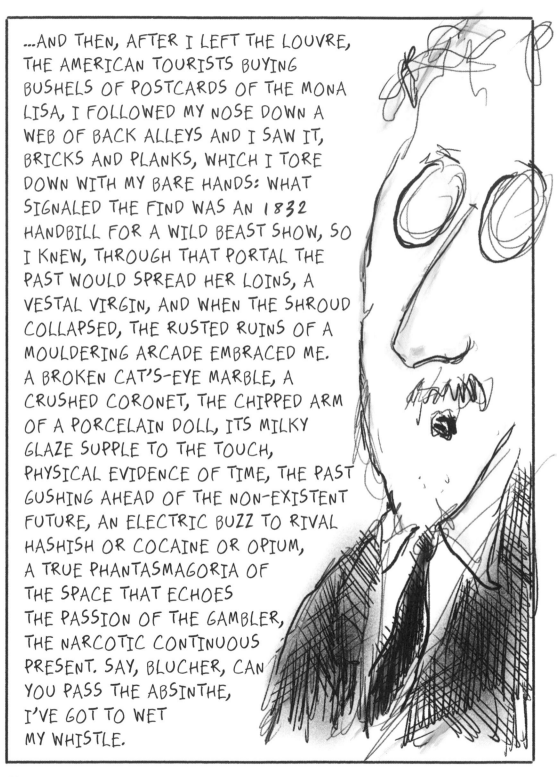

...AND THEN, AFTER I LEFT THE LOUVRE, THE AMERICAN TOURISTS BUYING BUSHELS OF POSTCARDS OF THE MONA LISA, I FOLLOWED MY NOSE DOWN A WEB OF BACK ALLEYS AND I SAW IT, BRICKS AND PLANKS, WHICH I TORE DOWN WITH MY BARE HANDS: WHAT SIGNALED THE FIND WAS AN 1832 HANDBILL FOR A WILD BEAST SHOW, SO I KNEW, THROUGH THAT PORTAL THE PAST WOULD SPREAD HER LOINS, A VESTAL VIRGIN, AND WHEN THE SHROUD COLLAPSED, THE RUSTED RUINS OF A MOULDERING ARCADE EMBRACED ME. A BROKEN CAT'S-EYE MARBLE, A CRUSHED CORONET, THE CHIPPED ARM OF A PORCELAIN DOLL, ITS MILKY GLAZE SUPPLE TO THE TOUCH, PHYSICAL EVIDENCE OF TIME, THE PAST GUSHING AHEAD OF THE NON-EXISTENT FUTURE, AN ELECTRIC BUZZ TO RIVAL HASHISH OR COCAINE OR OPIUM, A TRUE PHANTASMAGORIA OF THE SPACE THAT ECHOES THE PASSION OF THE GAMBLER, THE NARCOTIC CONTINUOUS PRESENT. SAY, BLUCHER, CAN YOU PASS THE ABSINTHE, I'VE GOT TO WET MY WHISTLE.

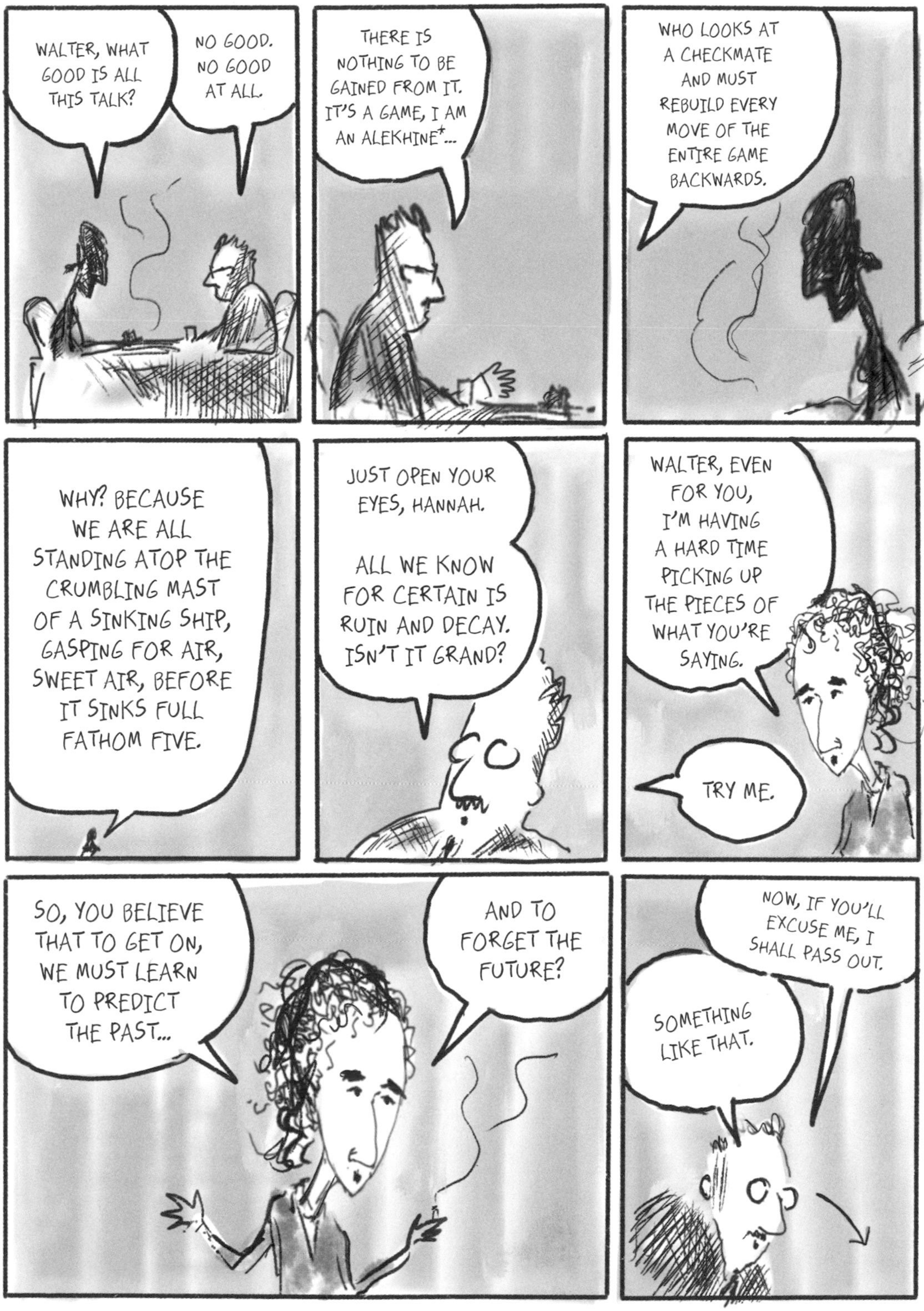
WALTER, WHAT GOOD IS ALL THIS TALK?
NO GOOD. NO GOOD AT ALL.
THERE IS NOTHING TO BE GAINED FROM IT. IT'S A GAME, I AM AN ALEKHINE*...
WHO LOOKS AT A CHECKMATE AND MUST REBUILD EVERY MOVE OF THE ENTIRE GAME BACKWARDS.
WHY? BECAUSE WE ARE ALL STANDING ATOP THE CRUMBLING MAST OF A SINKING SHIP, GASPING FOR AIR, SWEET AIR, BEFORE IT SINKS FULL FATHOM FIVE.
JUST OPEN YOUR EYES, HANNAH.
ALL WE KNOW FOR CERTAIN IS RUIN AND DECAY. ISN'T IT GRAND?
WALTER, EVEN FOR YOU, I'M HAVING A HARD TIME PICKING UP THE PIECES OF WHAT YOU'RE SAYING.
TRY ME.
SO, YOU BELIEVE THAT TO GET ON, WE MUST LEARN TO PREDICT THE PAST...
AND TO FORGET THE FUTURE?
SOMETHING LIKE THAT.
NOW, IF YOU'LL EXCUSE ME, I SHALL PASS OUT.

* Alexander Alekhine (1892–1946). Russian chess master and refugee, considered the bravest player in the history of the game.

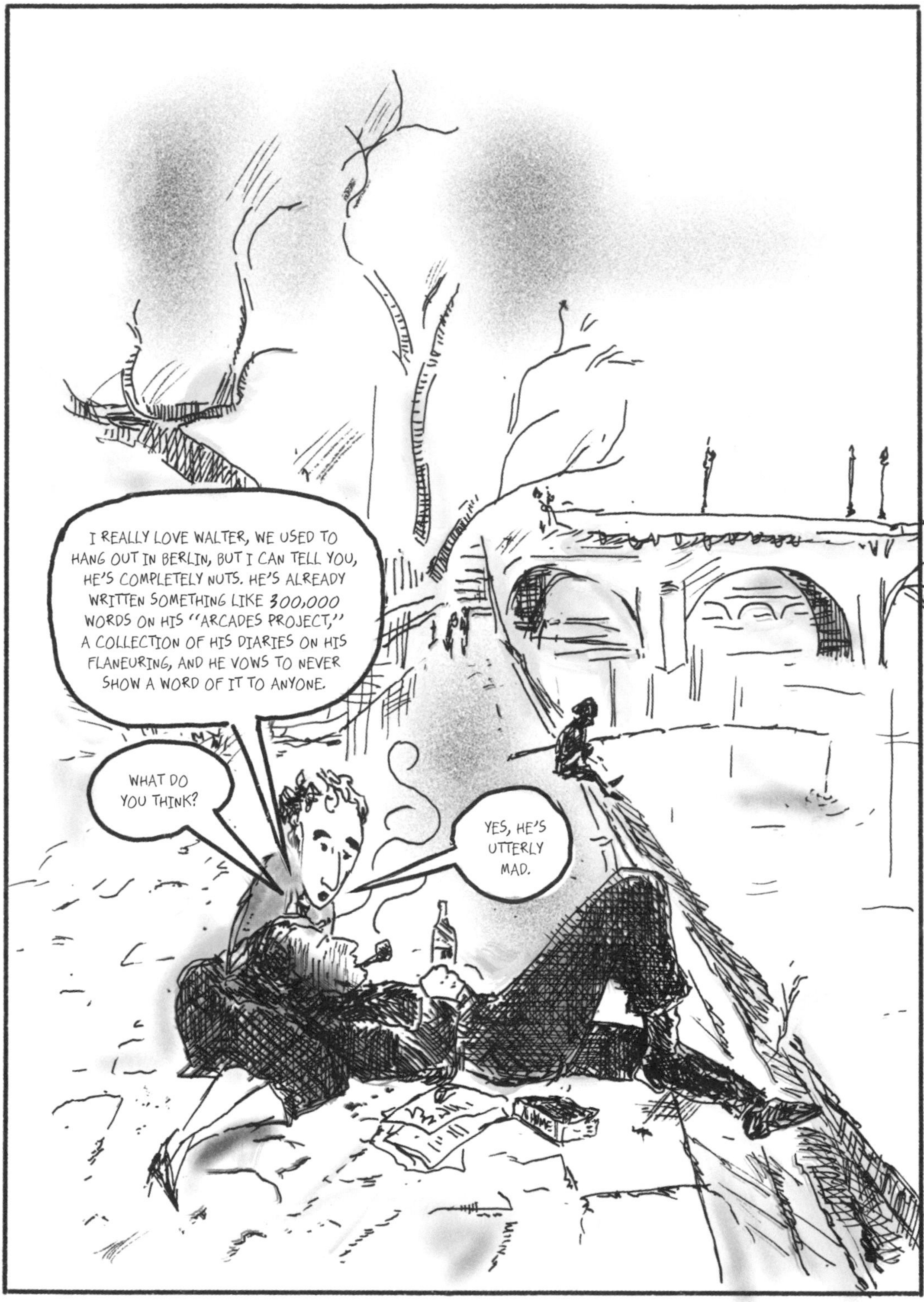
I REALLY LOVE WALTER, WE USED TO HANG OUT IN BERLIN, BUT I CAN TELL YOU, HE'S COMPLETELY NUTS. HE'S ALREADY WRITTEN SOMETHING LIKE 300,000 WORDS ON HIS "ARCADES PROJECT," A COLLECTION OF HIS DIARIES ON HIS FLANEURING, AND HE VOWS TO NEVER SHOW A WORD OF IT TO ANYONE.
WHAT DO YOU THINK?
YES, HE'S UTTERLY MAD.

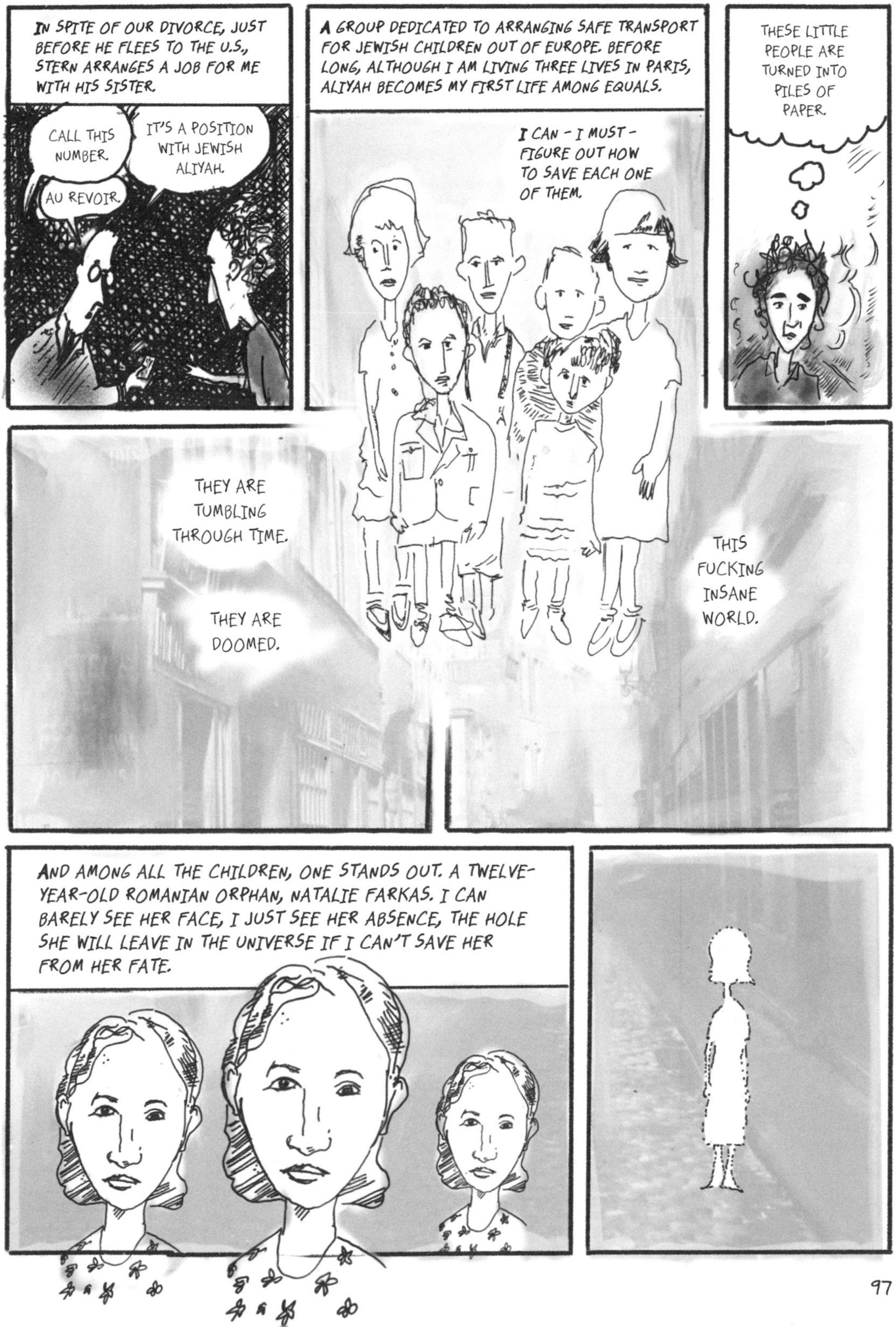
IN SPITE OF OUR DIVORCE, JUST BEFORE HE FLEES TO THE U.S., STERN ARRANGES A JOB FOR ME WITH HIS SISTER.
CALL THIS NUMBER.
IT'S A POSITION WITH JEWISH ALIYAH.
AU REVOIR.
A GROUP DEDICATED TO ARRANGING SAFE TRANSPORT FOR JEWISH CHILDREN OUT OF EUROPE. BEFORE LONG, ALTHOUGH I AM LIVING THREE LIVES IN PARIS, ALIYAH BECOMES MY FIRST LIFE AMONG EQUALS.
I CAN - I MUST - FIGURE OUT HOW TO SAVE EACH ONE OF THEM.
THESE LITTLE PEOPLE ARE TURNED INTO PILES OF PAPER.
THEY ARE TUMBLING THROUGH TIME.
THEY ARE DOOMED.
THIS FUCKING INSANE WORLD.
AND AMONG ALL THE CHILDREN, ONE STANDS OUT. A TWELVE-YEAR-OLD ROMANIAN ORPHAN, NATALIE FARKAS. I CAN BARELY SEE HER FACE, I JUST SEE HER ABSENCE, THE HOLE SHE WILL LEAVE IN THE UNIVERSE IF I CAN'T SAVE HER FROM HER FATE.

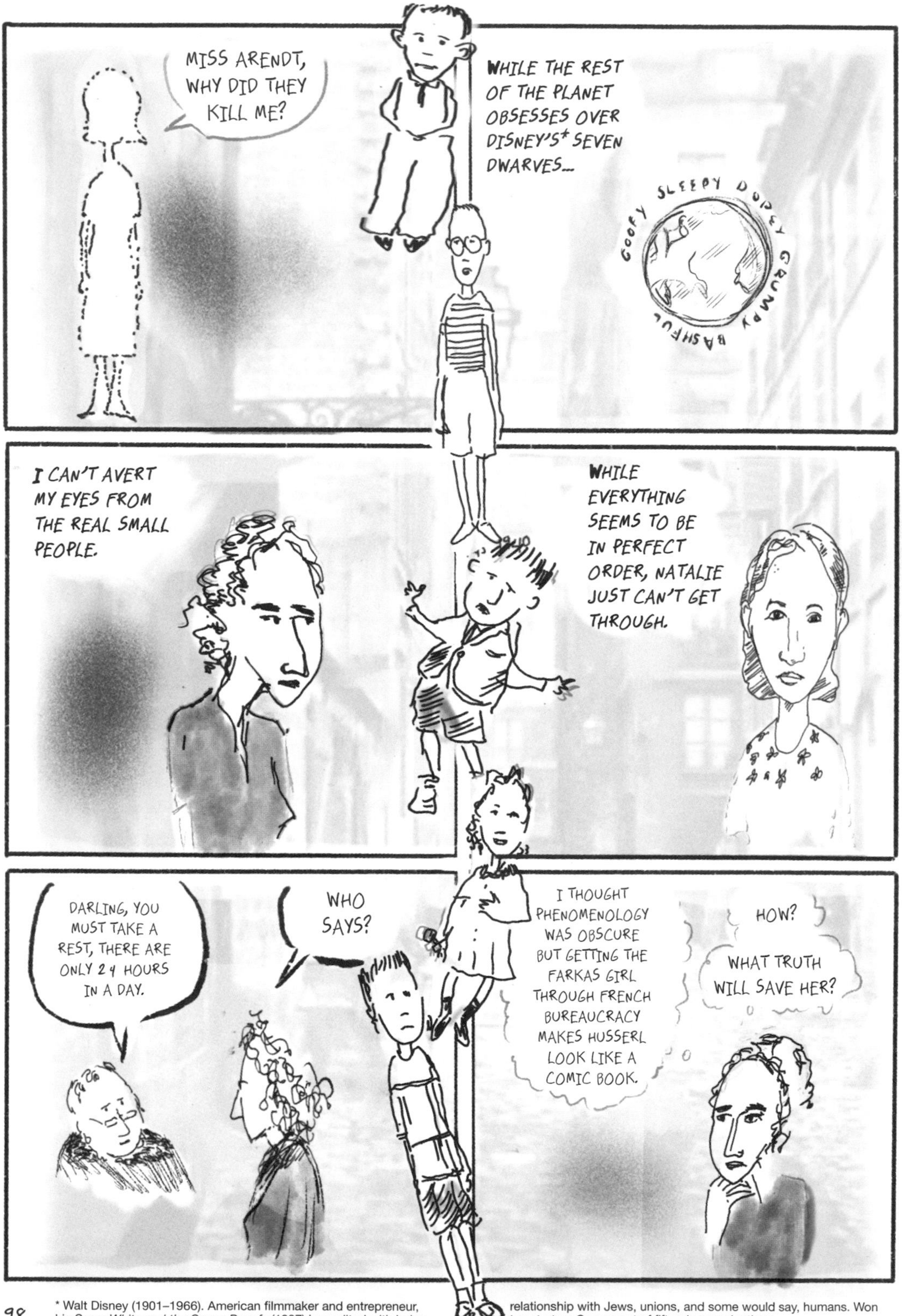
MISS ARENDT, WHY DID THEY KILL ME?
WHILE THE REST OF THE PLANET OBSESSES OVER DISNEY'S* SEVEN DWARVES...
GOOFY SLEEPY DOPEY GRUMPY BASHFUL
I CAN'T AVERT MY EYES FROM THE REAL SMALL PEOPLE.
WHILE EVERYTHING SEEMS TO BE IN PERFECT ORDER, NATALIE JUST CAN'T GET THROUGH.
DARLING, YOU MUST TAKE A REST, THERE ARE ONLY 24 HOURS IN A DAY.
WHO SAYS?
I THOUGHT PHENOMENOLOGY WAS OBSCURE BUT GETTING THE FARKAS GIRL THROUGH FRENCH BUREAUCRACY MAKES HUSSERL LOOK LIKE A COMIC BOOK.
HOW?
WHAT TRUTH WILL SAVE HER?

* Walt Disney (1901–1966). American filmmaker and entrepreneur, his *Snow White and the Seven Dwarfs* (1937) is credited with being the first full-length color animated motion picture. Had a troubled relationship with Jews, unions, and some would say, humans. Won twenty-two Oscars out of fifty-nine nominations.

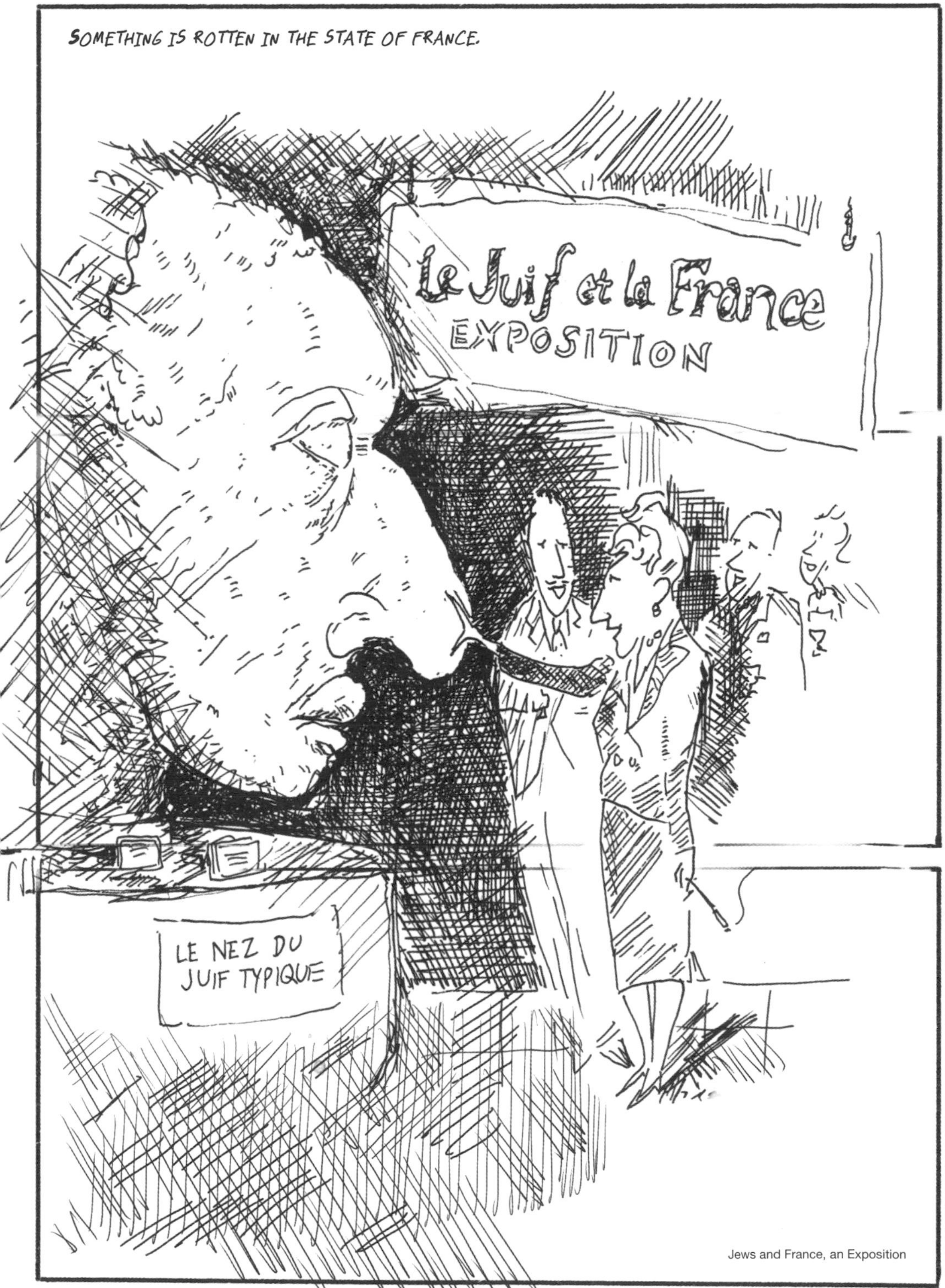
SOMETHING IS ROTTEN IN THE STATE OF FRANCE.
Le Juif et la France
EXPOSITION
LE NEZ DU JUIF TYPIQUE

Jews and France, an Exposition

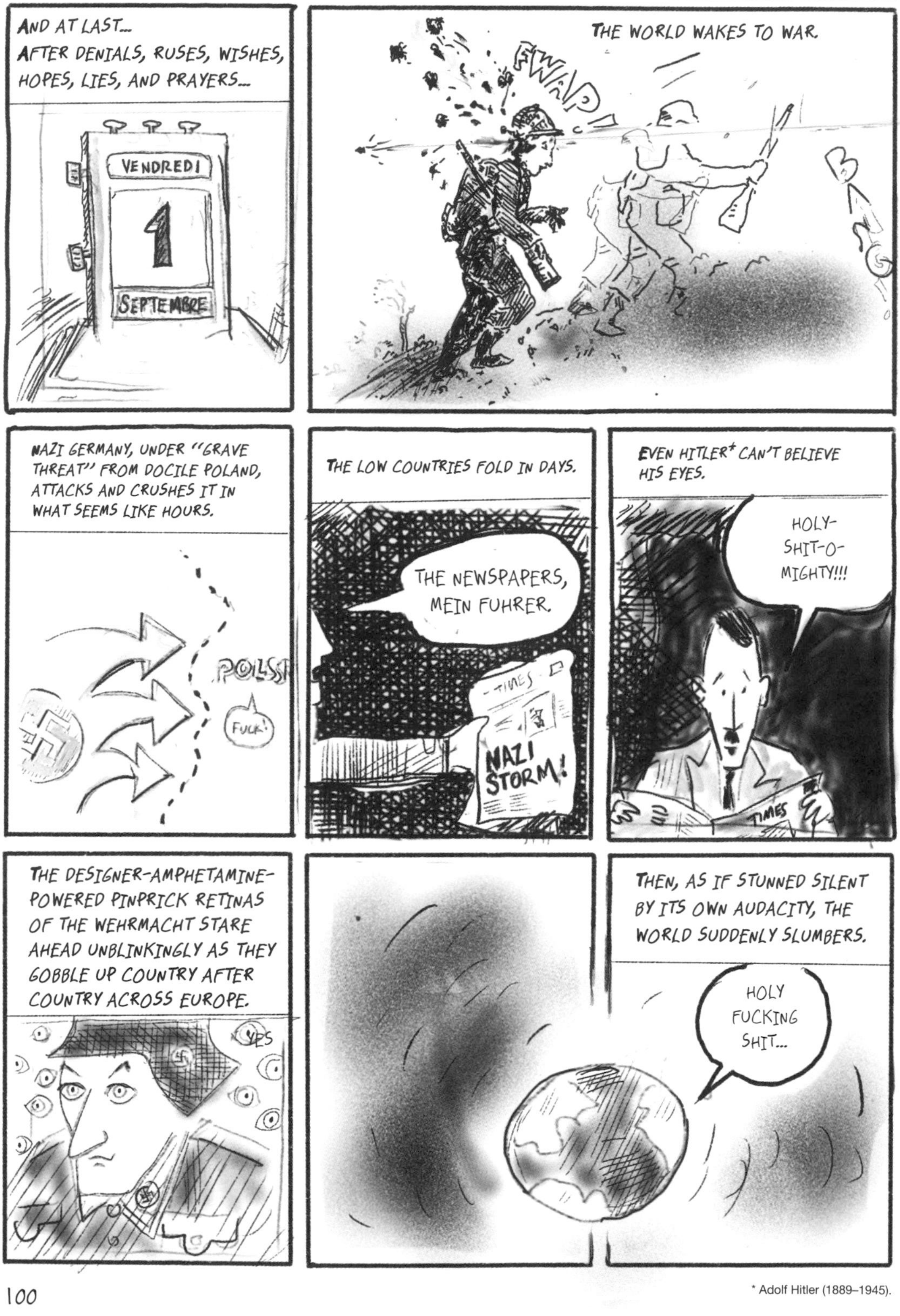
AND AT LAST...
AFTER DENIALS, RUSES, WISHES, HOPES, LIES, AND PRAYERS...
VENDREDI
1
SEPTEMBRE
THE WORLD WAKES TO WAR.
NAZI GERMANY, UNDER "GRAVE THREAT" FROM DOCILE POLAND, ATTACKS AND CRUSHES IT IN WHAT SEEMS LIKE HOURS.
FUCK!
THE LOW COUNTRIES FOLD IN DAYS.
THE NEWSPAPERS, MEIN FUHRER.
TIMES
NAZI STORM!
EVEN HITLER* CAN'T BELIEVE HIS EYES.
HOLY-SHIT-O-MIGHTY!!!
TIMES
THE DESIGNER-AMPHETAMINE-POWERED PINPRICK RETINAS OF THE WEHRMACHT STARE AHEAD UNBLINKINGLY AS THEY GOBBLE UP COUNTRY AFTER COUNTRY ACROSS EUROPE.
YES
THEN, AS IF STUNNED SILENT BY ITS OWN AUDACITY, THE WORLD SUDDENLY SLUMBERS.
HOLY FUCKING SHIT...

* Adolf Hitler (1889–1945).

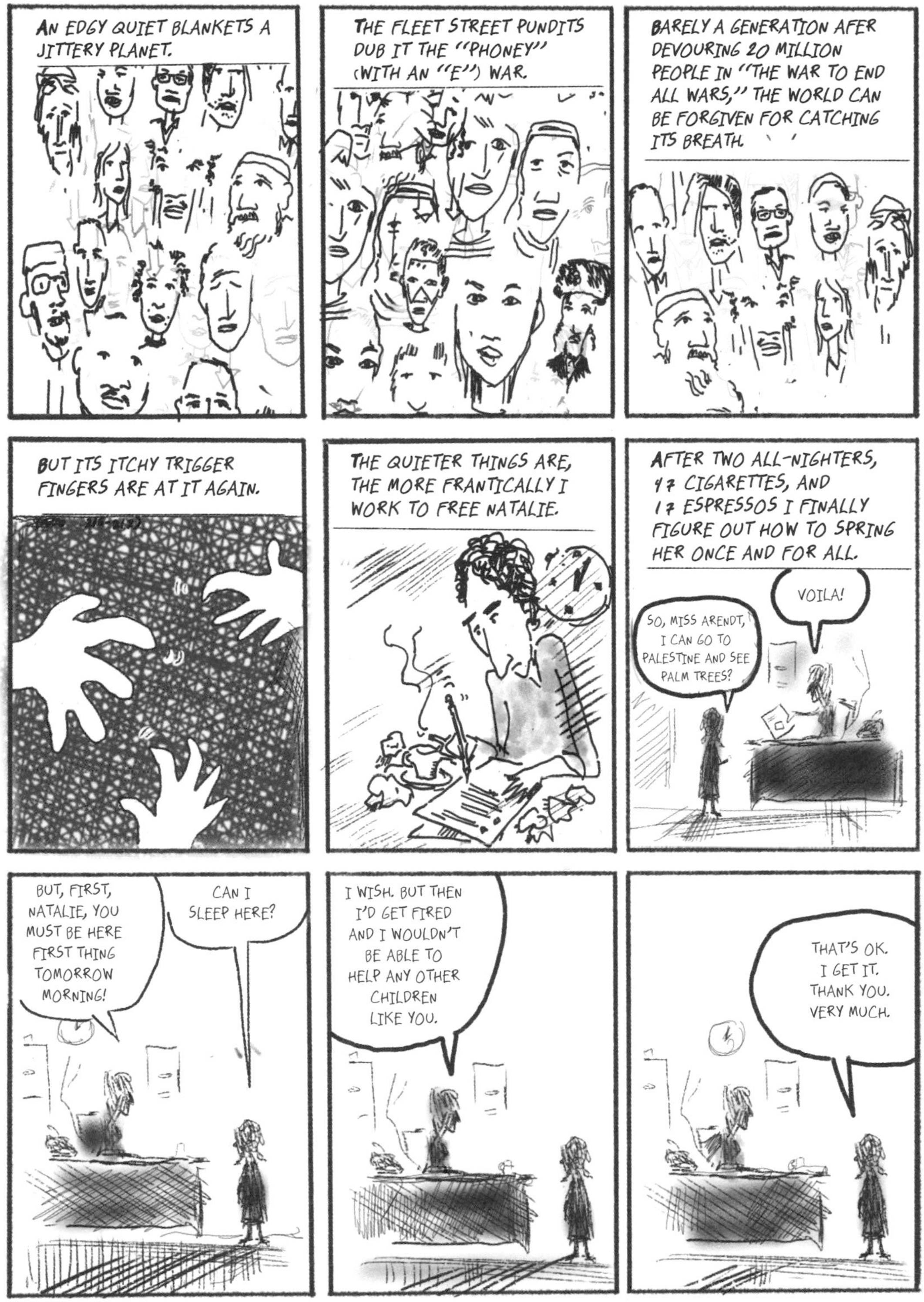
AN EDGY QUIET BLANKETS A JITTERY PLANET.
THE FLEET STREET PUNDITS DUB IT THE "PHONEY" (WITH AN "E") WAR.
BARELY A GENERATION AFER DEVOURING 20 MILLION PEOPLE IN "THE WAR TO END ALL WARS," THE WORLD CAN BE FORGIVEN FOR CATCHING ITS BREATH.
BUT ITS ITCHY TRIGGER FINGERS ARE AT IT AGAIN.
THE QUIETER THINGS ARE, THE MORE FRANTICALLY I WORK TO FREE NATALIE.
AFTER TWO ALL-NIGHTERS, 47 CIGARETTES, AND 17 ESPRESSOS I FINALLY FIGURE OUT HOW TO SPRING HER ONCE AND FOR ALL.
VOILA!
SO, MISS ARENDT, I CAN GO TO PALESTINE AND SEE PALM TREES?
BUT, FIRST, NATALIE, YOU MUST BE HERE FIRST THING TOMORROW MORNING!
CAN I SLEEP HERE?
I WISH. BUT THEN I'D GET FIRED AND I WOULDN'T BE ABLE TO HELP ANY OTHER CHILDREN LIKE YOU.
THAT'S OK. I GET IT. THANK YOU. VERY MUCH.

MAY 5, 1940

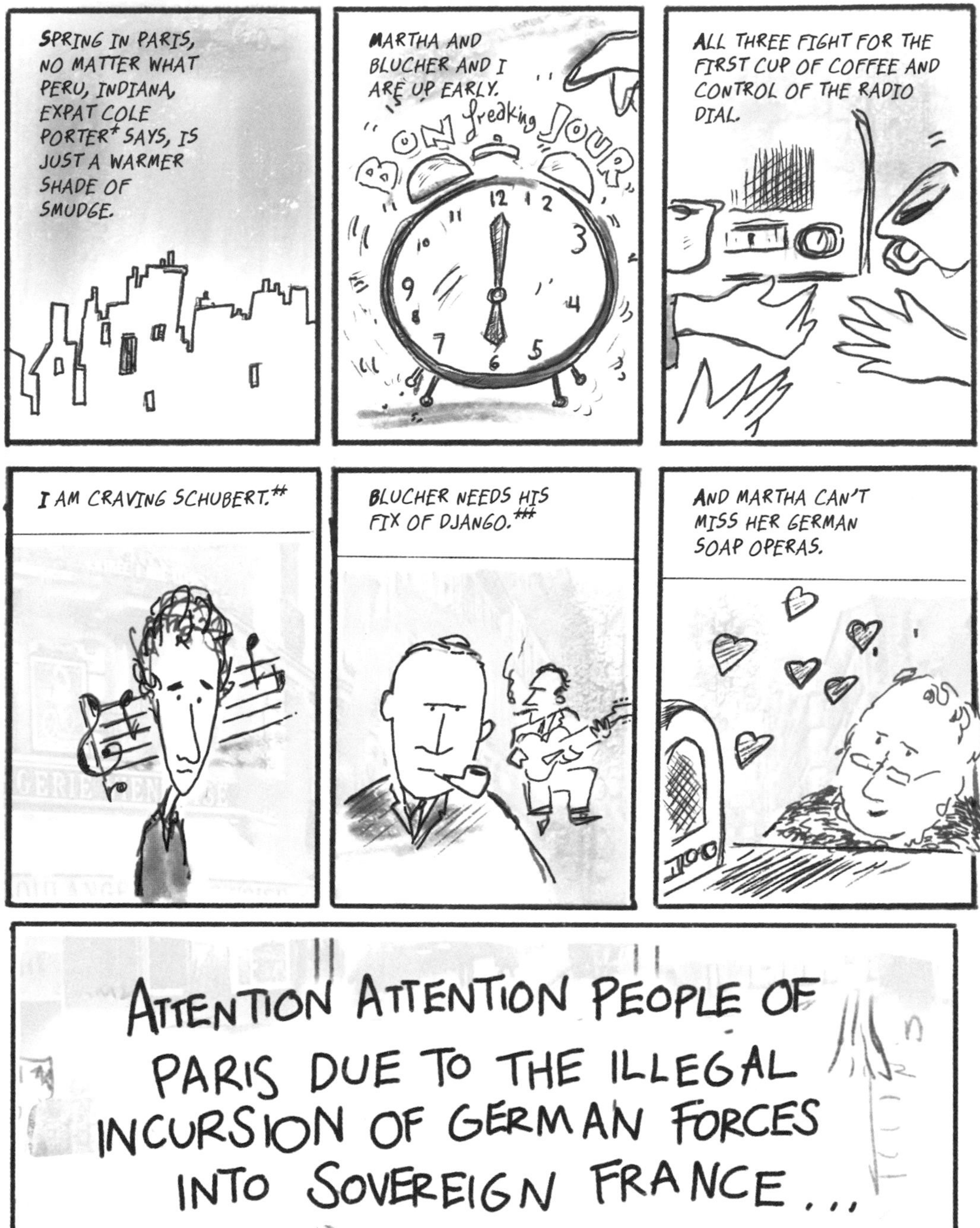
SPRING IN PARIS, NO MATTER WHAT PERU, INDIANA, EXPAT COLE PORTER* SAYS, IS JUST A WARMER SHADE OF SMUDGE.
MARTHA AND BLUCHER AND I ARE UP EARLY.
BON freaking JOUR
ALL THREE FIGHT FOR THE FIRST CUP OF COFFEE AND CONTROL OF THE RADIO DIAL.
I AM CRAVING SCHUBERT.**
BLUCHER NEEDS HIS FIX OF DJANGO.***
AND MARTHA CAN'T MISS HER GERMAN SOAP OPERAS.
ATTENTION ATTENTION PEOPLE OF PARIS DUE TO THE ILLEGAL INCURSION OF GERMAN FORCES INTO SOVEREIGN FRANCE...

* Cole Porter (1891–1964). American composer, a.k.a. the only non-Jew among the leading composers of the American popular songbook. A long-time expat in Paris. The Hollywood biopic made of his life starring Cary Grant managed to dodge his very gay, or at least very bi, personal life.

** Franz Schubert (1797–1828). Austrian composer. Before his death at age thirty-two, he created a body of work that still resonates for its melodic sensitivity and harmonic invention. Mostly ignored and misunderstood in his lifetime.

*** Jean "Django" Reinhardt (1910–1953). Romani jazz guitarist who did more with three fingers than most guitarists could do with twenty.

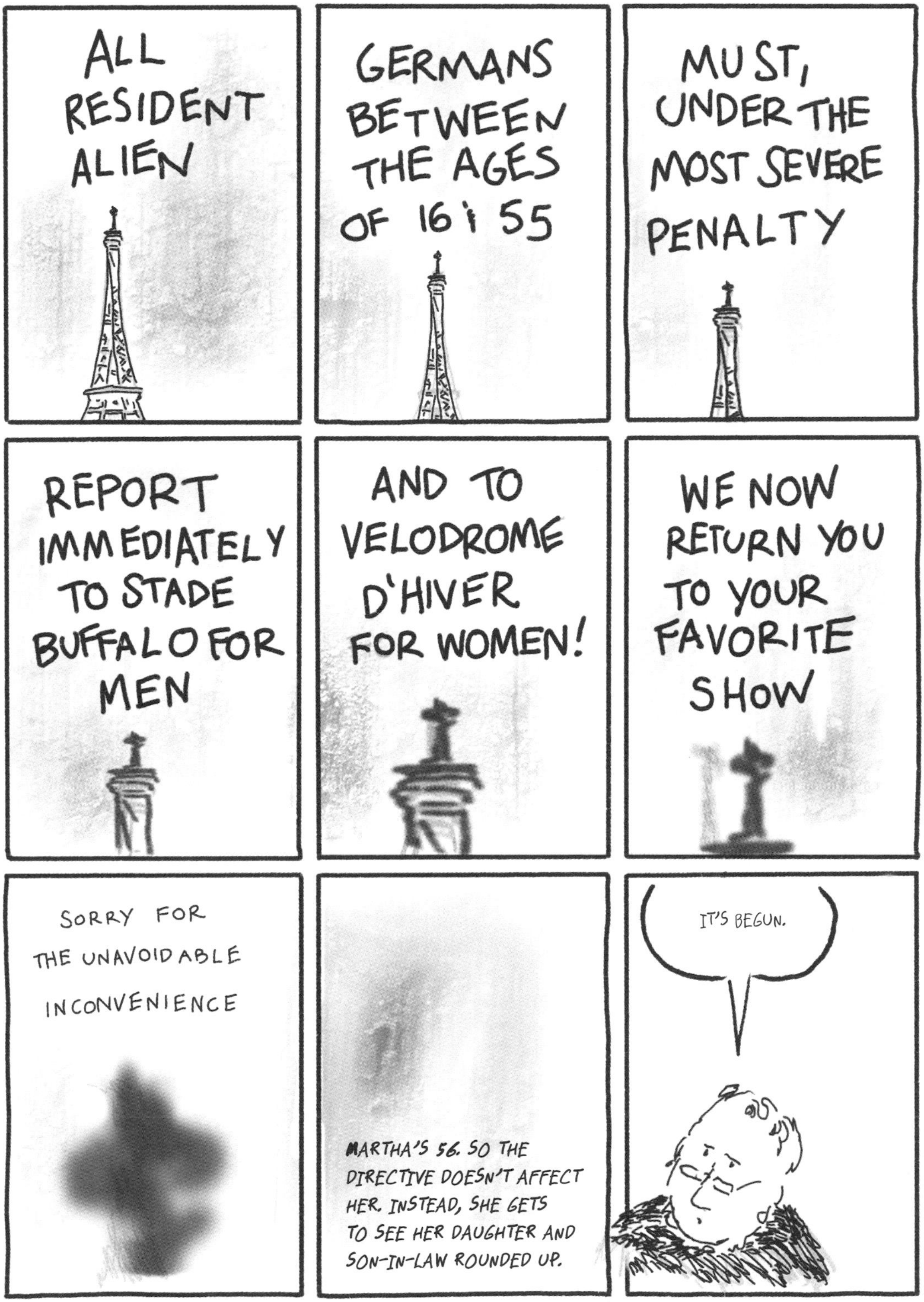
ALL RESIDENT ALIEN
GERMANS BETWEEN THE AGES OF 16 & 55
MUST, UNDER THE MOST SEVERE PENALTY
REPORT IMMEDIATELY TO STADE BUFFALO FOR MEN
AND TO VELODROME D'HIVER FOR WOMEN!
WE NOW RETURN YOU TO YOUR FAVORITE SHOW
SORRY FOR THE UNAVOIDABLE INCONVENIENCE
MARTHA'S 56. SO THE DIRECTIVE DOESN'T AFFECT HER. INSTEAD, SHE GETS TO SEE HER DAUGHTER AND SON-IN-LAW ROUNDED UP.
IT'S BEGUN.

THE VEL D'HIV A TRIUMPH OF FRENCH TECHNOLOGY!

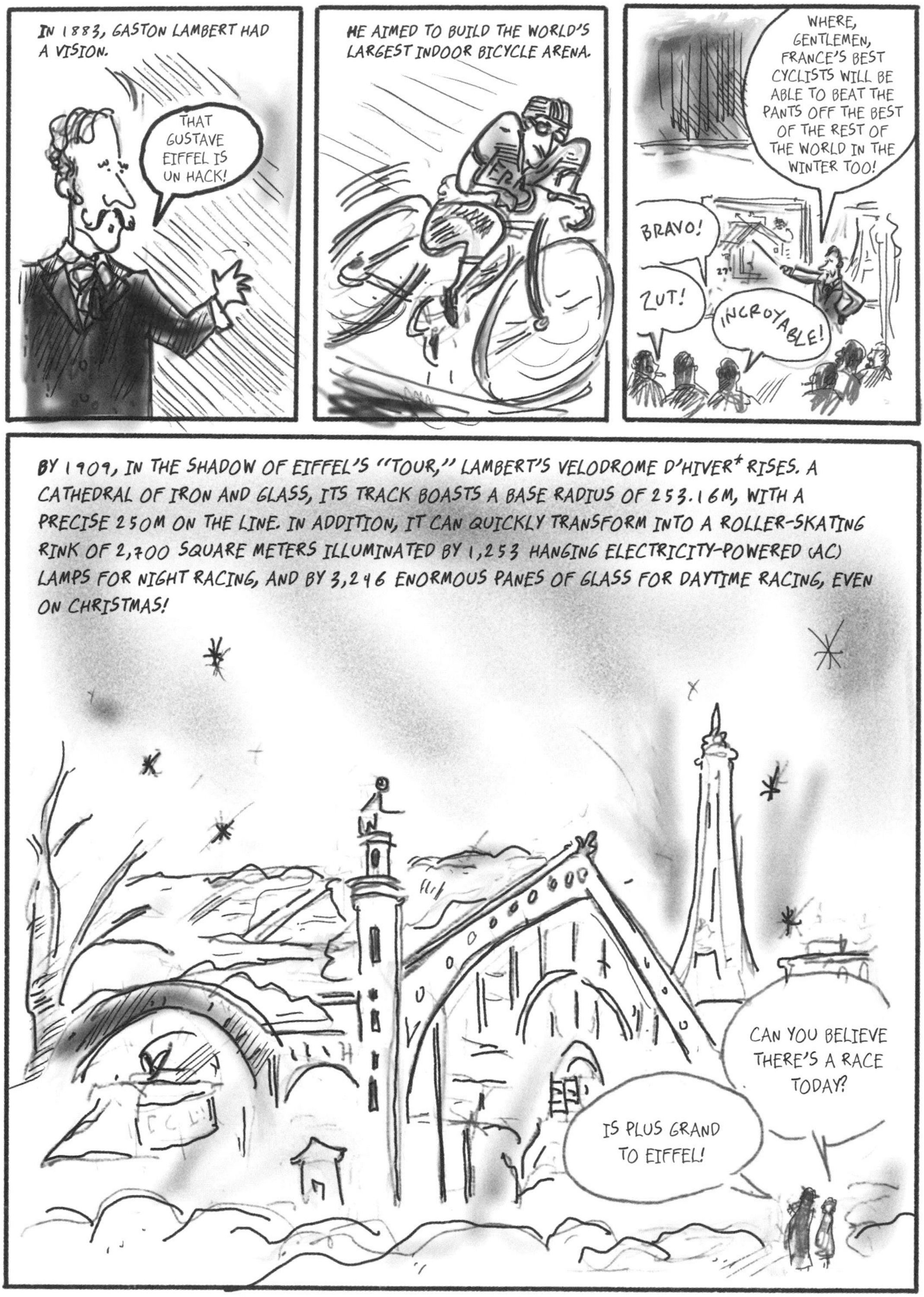
IN 1883, GASTON LAMBERT HAD A VISION.
THAT GUSTAVE EIFFEL IS UN HACK!
HE AIMED TO BUILD THE WORLD'S LARGEST INDOOR BICYCLE ARENA.
WHERE, GENTLEMEN, FRANCE'S BEST CYCLISTS WILL BE ABLE TO BEAT THE PANTS OFF THE BEST OF THE REST OF THE WORLD IN THE WINTER TOO!
BRAVO!
ZUT!
INCROYABLE!
BY 1909, IN THE SHADOW OF EIFFEL'S "TOUR," LAMBERT'S VELODROME D'HIVER* RISES. A CATHEDRAL OF IRON AND GLASS, ITS TRACK BOASTS A BASE RADIUS OF 253.16M, WITH A PRECISE 250M ON THE LINE. IN ADDITION, IT CAN QUICKLY TRANSFORM INTO A ROLLER-SKATING RINK OF 2,700 SQUARE METERS ILLUMINATED BY 1,253 HANGING ELECTRICITY-POWERED (AC) LAMPS FOR NIGHT RACING, AND BY 3,246 ENORMOUS PANES OF GLASS FOR DAYTIME RACING, EVEN ON CHRISTMAS!
CAN YOU BELIEVE THERE'S A RACE TODAY?
IS PLUS GRAND TO EIFFEL!

* Literally "Winter Bicycle Race Place," a.k.a. "Vel d'Hiv"

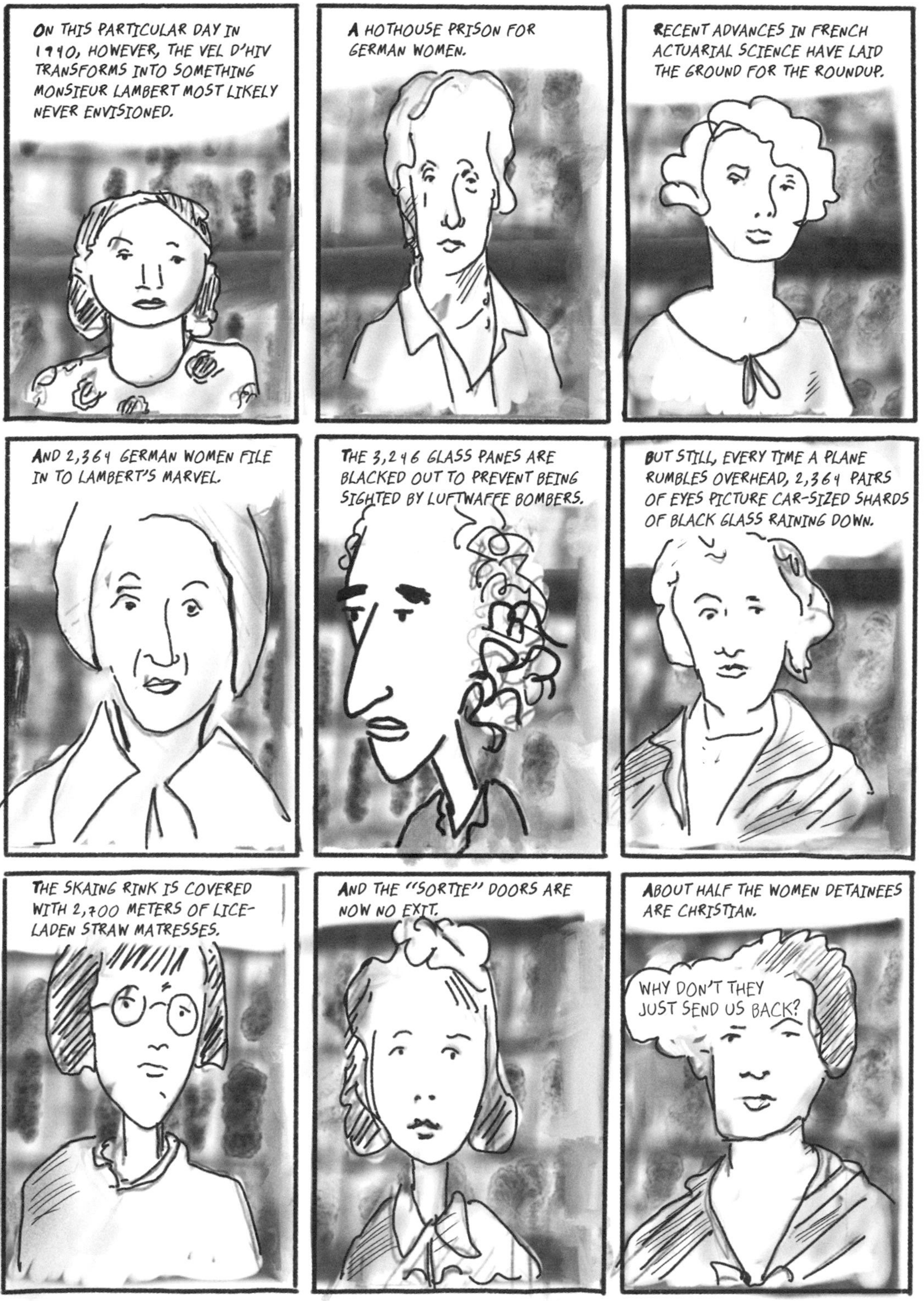
ON THIS PARTICULAR DAY IN 1940, HOWEVER, THE VEL D'HIV TRANSFORMS INTO SOMETHING MONSIEUR LAMBERT MOST LIKELY NEVER ENVISIONED.
A HOTHOUSE PRISON FOR GERMAN WOMEN.
RECENT ADVANCES IN FRENCH ACTUARIAL SCIENCE HAVE LAID THE GROUND FOR THE ROUNDUP.
AND 2,364 GERMAN WOMEN FILE IN TO LAMBERT'S MARVEL.
THE 3,246 GLASS PANES ARE BLACKED OUT TO PREVENT BEING SIGHTED BY LUFTWAFFE BOMBERS.
BUT STILL, EVERY TIME A PLANE RUMBLES OVERHEAD, 2,364 PAIRS OF EYES PICTURE CAR-SIZED SHARDS OF BLACK GLASS RAINING DOWN.
THE SKAING RINK IS COVERED WITH 2,700 METERS OF LICE-LADEN STRAW MATRESSES.
AND THE "SORTIE" DOORS ARE NOW NO EXIT.
ABOUT HALF THE WOMEN DETAINEES ARE CHRISTIAN.
WHY DON'T THEY JUST SEND US BACK?

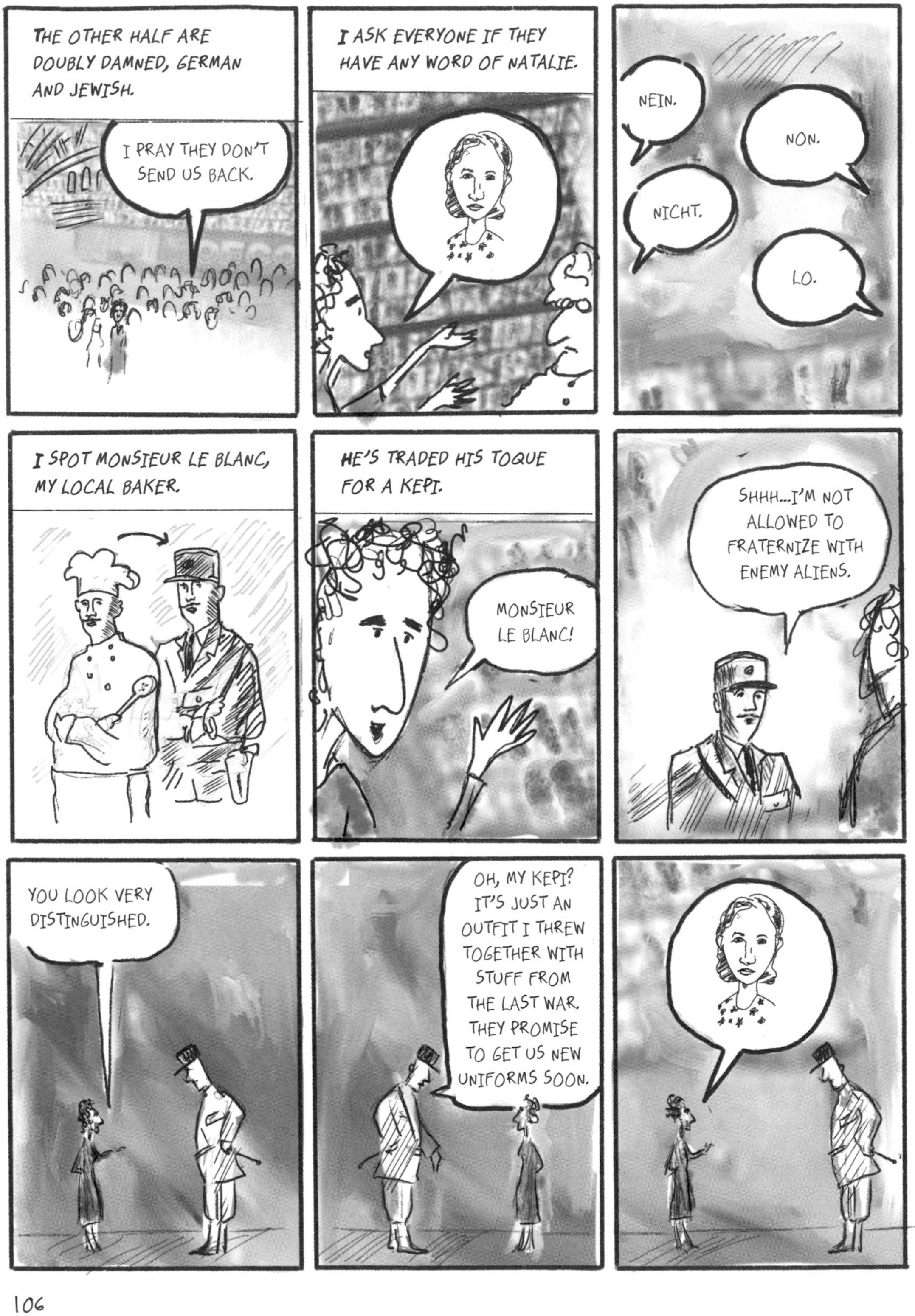
THE OTHER HALF ARE DOUBLY DAMNED, GERMAN AND JEWISH.
I PRAY THEY DON'T SEND US BACK.
I ASK EVERYONE IF THEY HAVE ANY WORD OF NATALIE.
NEIN.
NON.
NICHT.
LO.
I SPOT MONSIEUR LE BLANC, MY LOCAL BAKER.
HE'S TRADED HIS TOQUE FOR A KEPI.
MONSIEUR LE BLANC!
SHHH...I'M NOT ALLOWED TO FRATERNIZE WITH ENEMY ALIENS.
YOU LOOK VERY DISTINGUISHED.
OH, MY KEPI? IT'S JUST AN OUTFIT I THREW TOGETHER WITH STUFF FROM THE LAST WAR. THEY PROMISE TO GET US NEW UNIFORMS SOON.

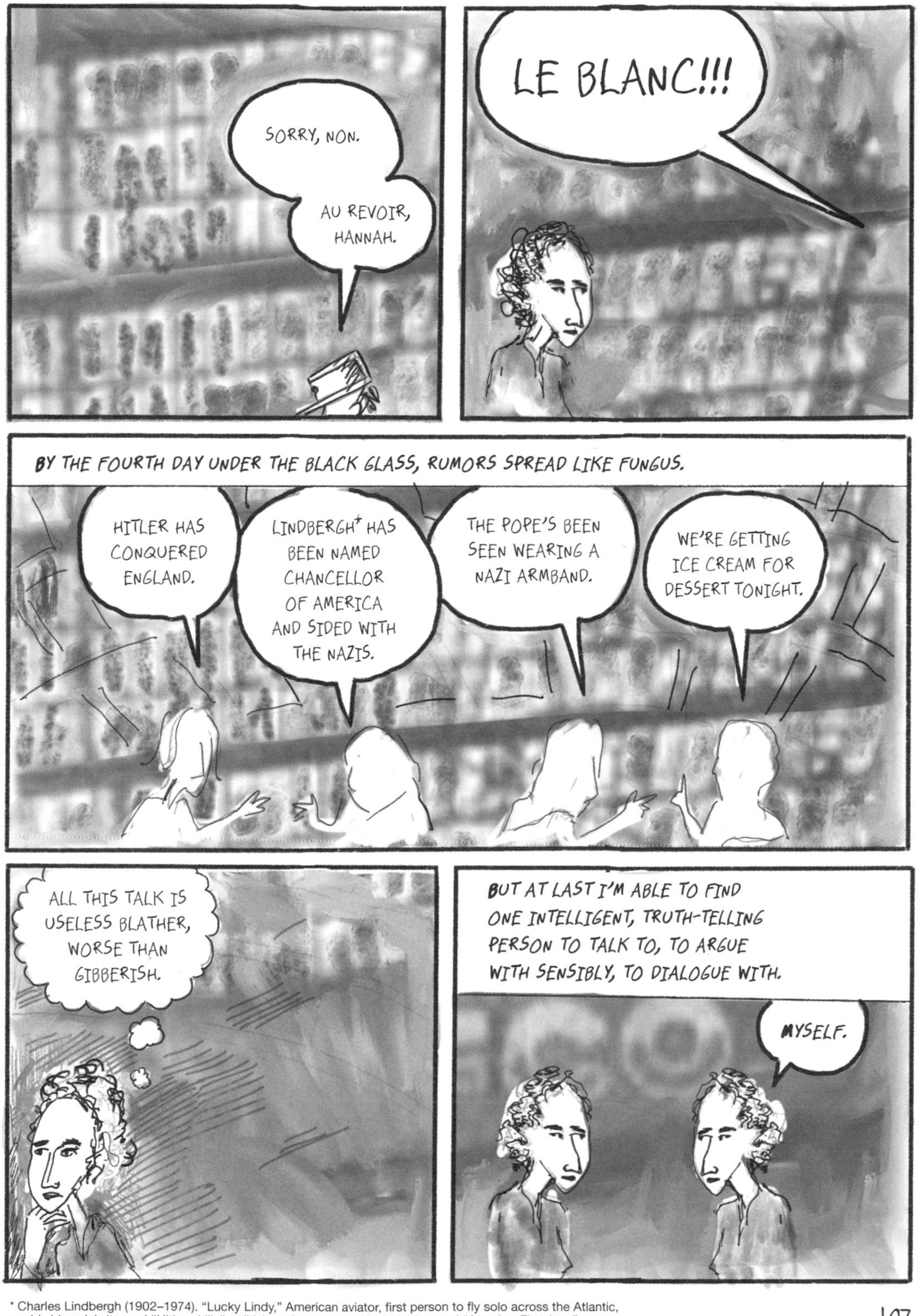
SORRY, NON.
AU REVOIR, HANNAH.
LE BLANC!!!
BY THE FOURTH DAY UNDER THE BLACK GLASS, RUMORS SPREAD LIKE FUNGUS.
HITLER HAS CONQUERED ENGLAND.
LINDBERGH* HAS BEEN NAMED CHANCELLOR OF AMERICA AND SIDED WITH THE NAZIS.
THE POPE'S BEEN SEEN WEARING A NAZI ARMBAND.
WE'RE GETTING ICE CREAM FOR DESSERT TONIGHT.
ALL THIS TALK IS USELESS BLATHER, WORSE THAN GIBBERISH.
BUT AT LAST I'M ABLE TO FIND ONE INTELLIGENT, TRUTH-TELLING PERSON TO TALK TO, TO ARGUE WITH SENSIBLY, TO DIALOGUE WITH.
MYSELF.

* Charles Lindbergh (1902–1974). "Lucky Lindy," American aviator, first person to fly solo across the Atlantic, worldwide celebrity, and "Hitler-philic" politician who espoused isolationism and "America-First-ism."

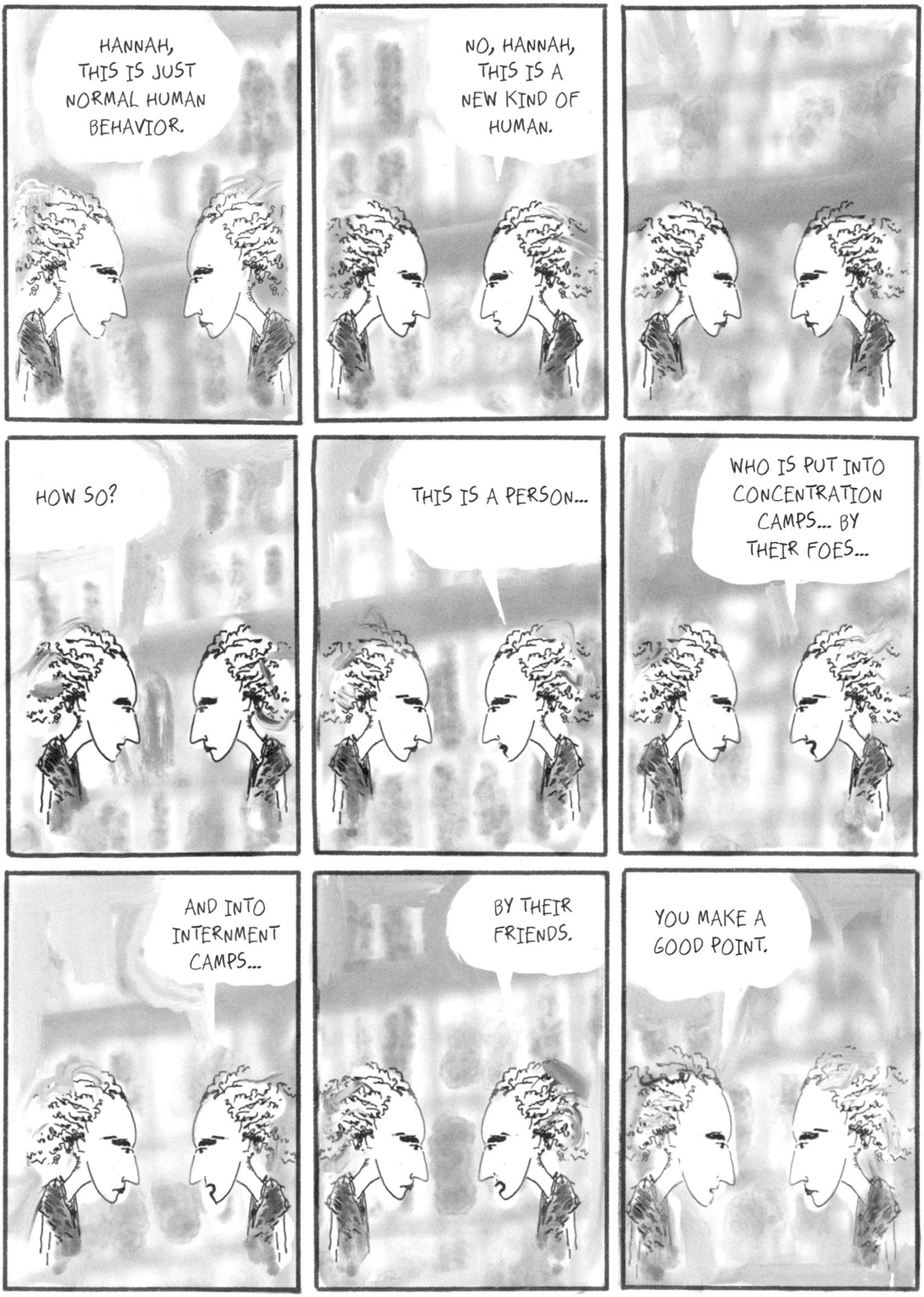
HANNAH, THIS IS JUST NORMAL HUMAN BEHAVIOR.
NO, HANNAH, THIS IS A NEW KIND OF HUMAN.
HOW SO?
THIS IS A PERSON...
WHO IS PUT INTO CONCENTRATION CAMPS... BY THEIR FOES...
AND INTO INTERNMENT CAMPS...
BY THEIR FRIENDS.
YOU MAKE A GOOD POINT.

TO GURS: MAY 23, 1940

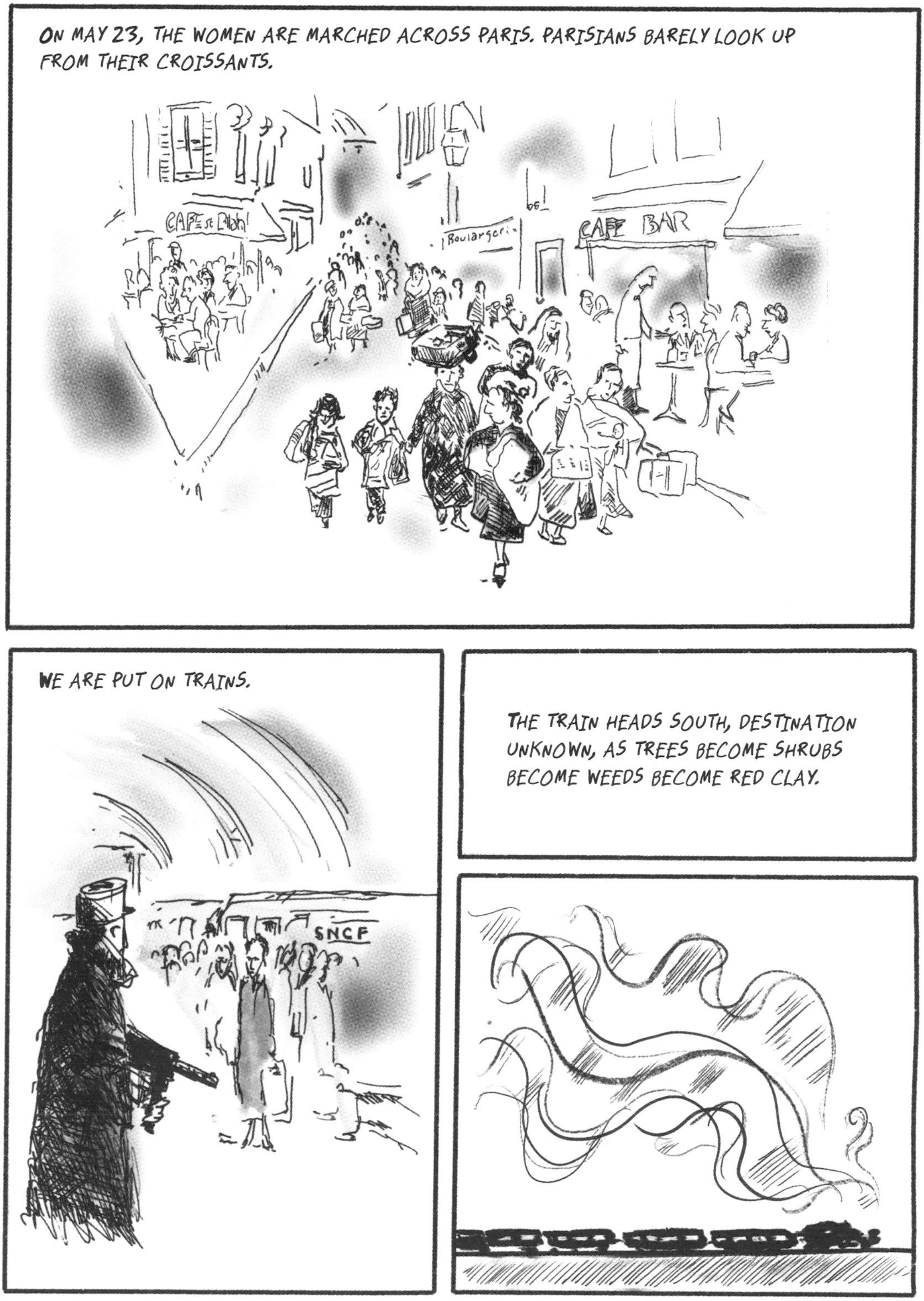
ON MAY 23, THE WOMEN ARE MARCHED ACROSS PARIS. PARISIANS BARELY LOOK UP FROM THEIR CROISSANTS.
CAFE BAR
WE ARE PUT ON TRAINS.
SNCF
THE TRAIN HEADS SOUTH, DESTINATION UNKNOWN, AS TREES BECOME SHRUBS BECOME WEEDS BECOME RED CLAY.

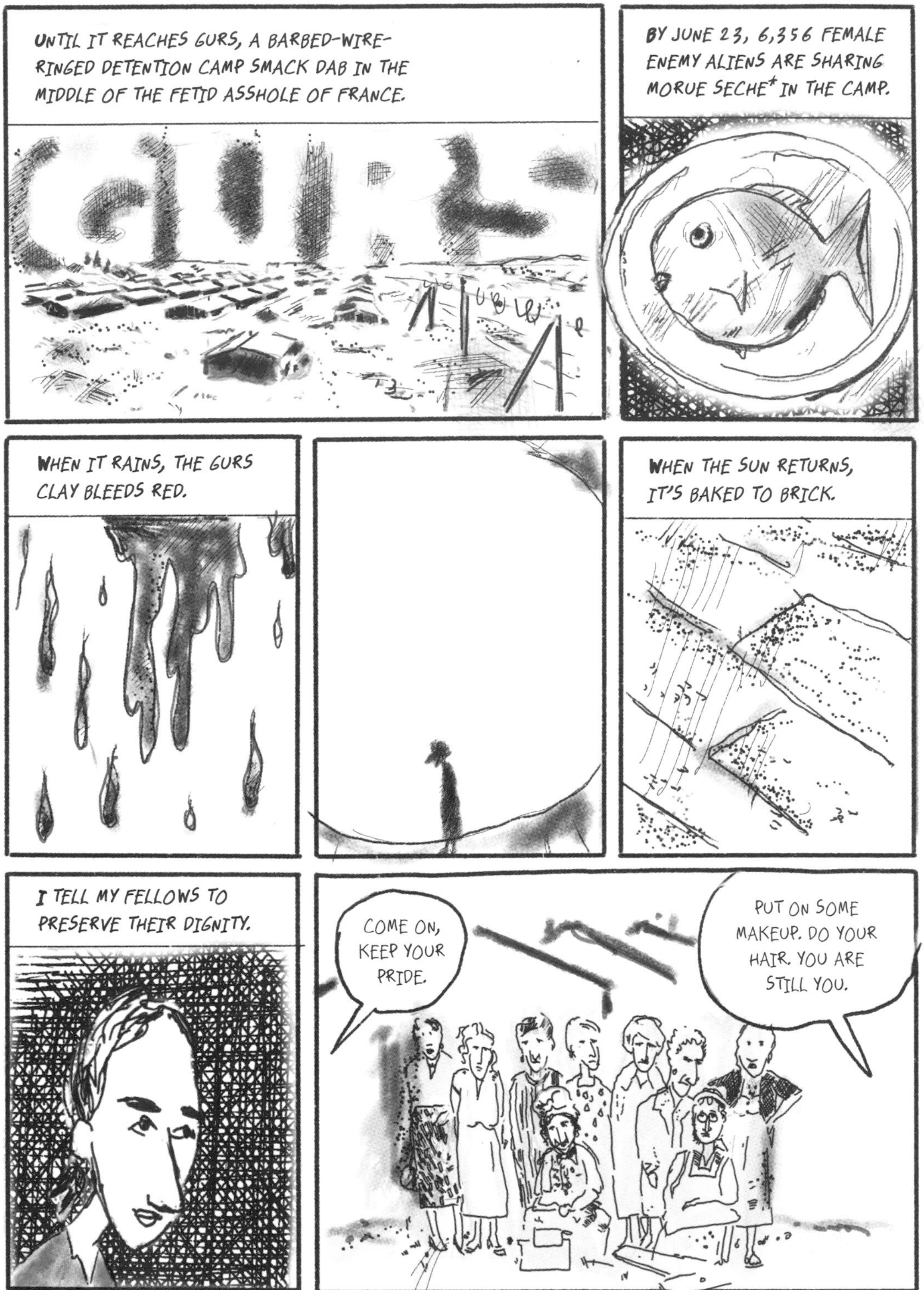
UNTIL IT REACHES GURS, A BARBED-WIRE-RINGED DETENTION CAMP SMACK DAB IN THE MIDDLE OF THE FETID ASSHOLE OF FRANCE.
GURS
BY JUNE 23, 6,356 FEMALE ENEMY ALIENS ARE SHARING MORUE SECHE* IN THE CAMP.
WHEN IT RAINS, THE GURS CLAY BLEEDS RED.
WHEN THE SUN RETURNS, IT'S BAKED TO BRICK.
I TELL MY FELLOWS TO PRESERVE THEIR DIGNITY.
COME ON, KEEP YOUR PRIDE.
PUT ON SOME MAKEUP. DO YOUR HAIR. YOU ARE STILL YOU.

* Morue seche: dried salted fish

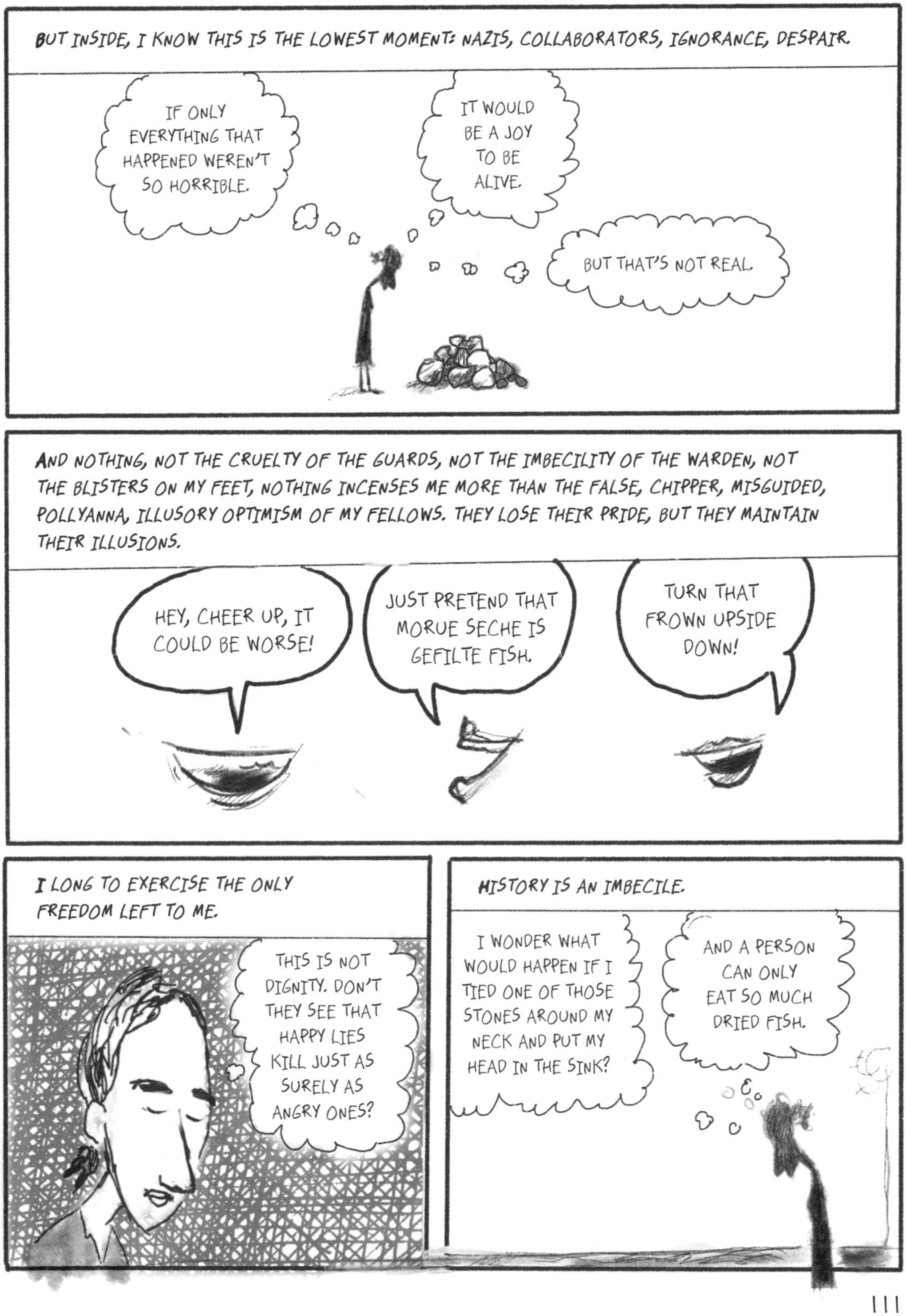
BUT INSIDE, I KNOW THIS IS THE LOWEST MOMENT: NAZIS, COLLABORATORS, IGNORANCE, DESPAIR.
IF ONLY EVERYTHING THAT HAPPENED WEREN'T SO HORRIBLE.
IT WOULD BE A JOY TO BE ALIVE.
BUT THAT'S NOT REAL.
AND NOTHING, NOT THE CRUELTY OF THE GUARDS, NOT THE IMBECILITY OF THE WARDEN, NOT THE BLISTERS ON MY FEET, NOTHING INCENSES ME MORE THAN THE FALSE, CHIPPER, MISGUIDED, POLLYANNA, ILLUSORY OPTIMISM OF MY FELLOWS. THEY LOSE THEIR PRIDE, BUT THEY MAINTAIN THEIR ILLUSIONS.
HEY, CHEER UP, IT COULD BE WORSE!
JUST PRETEND THAT MORUE SECHE IS GEFILTE FISH.
TURN THAT FROWN UPSIDE DOWN!
I LONG TO EXERCISE THE ONLY FREEDOM LEFT TO ME.
THIS IS NOT DIGNITY. DON'T THEY SEE THAT HAPPY LIES KILL JUST AS SURELY AS ANGRY ONES?
HISTORY IS AN IMBECILE.
I WONDER WHAT WOULD HAPPEN IF I TIED ONE OF THOSE STONES AROUND MY NECK AND PUT MY HEAD IN THE SINK?
AND A PERSON CAN ONLY EAT SO MUCH DRIED FISH.

THE SUBLIMITY OF SNAFU* JUNE 14, 1940

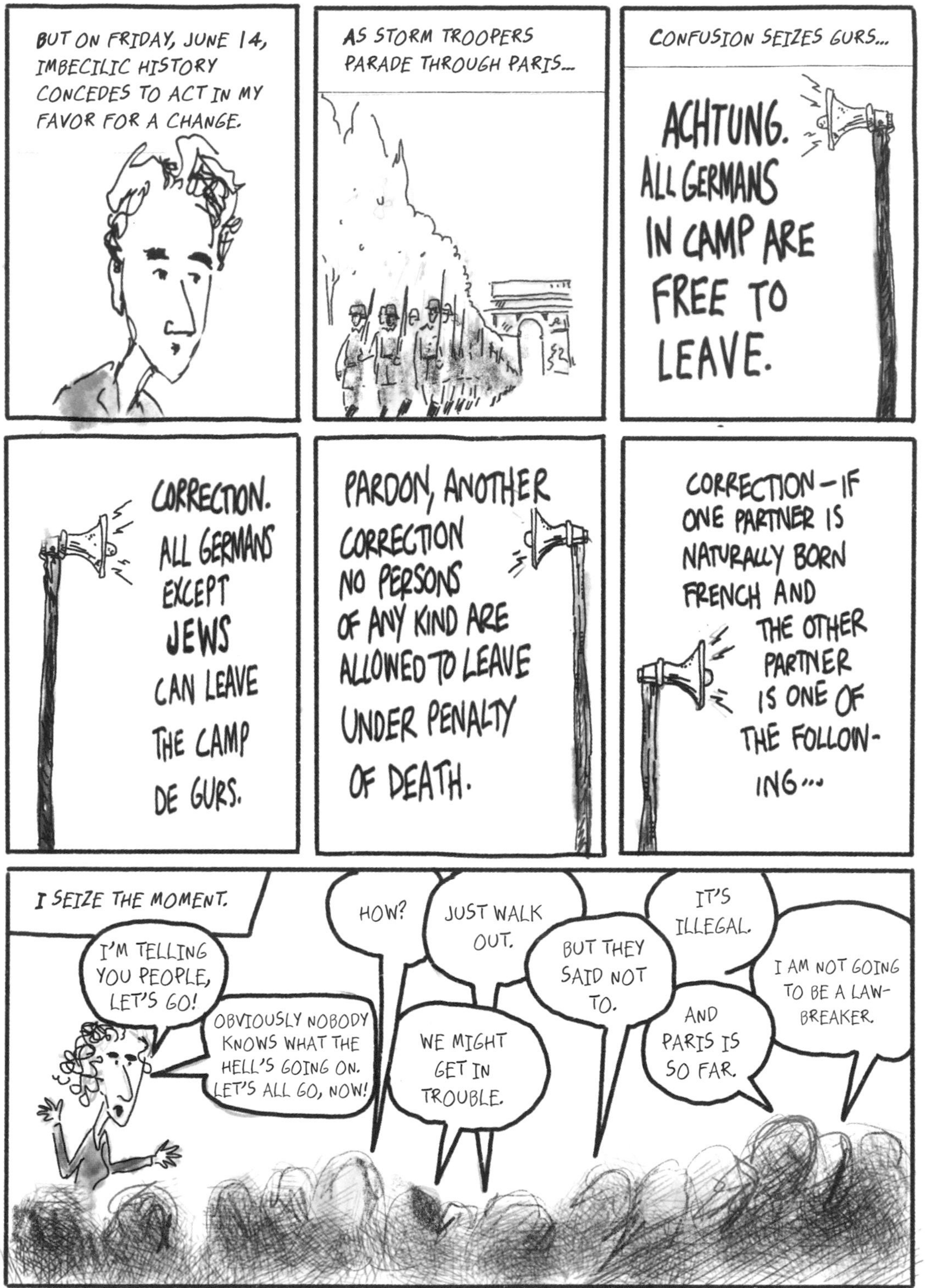

BUT ON FRIDAY, JUNE 14, IMBECILIC HISTORY CONCEDES TO ACT IN MY FAVOR FOR A CHANGE.
AS STORM TROOPERS PARADE THROUGH PARIS...
CONFUSION SEIZES GURS...
ACHTUNG. ALL GERMANS IN CAMP ARE FREE TO LEAVE.
CORRECTION. ALL GERMANS EXCEPT JEWS CAN LEAVE THE CAMP DE GURS.
PARDON, ANOTHER CORRECTION NO PERSONS OF ANY KIND ARE ALLOWED TO LEAVE UNDER PENALTY OF DEATH.
CORRECTION—IF ONE PARTNER IS NATURALLY BORN FRENCH AND THE OTHER PARTNER IS ONE OF THE FOLLOW-ING...
I SEIZE THE MOMENT.
I'M TELLING YOU PEOPLE, LET'S GO!
OBVIOUSLY NOBODY KNOWS WHAT THE HELL'S GOING ON. LET'S ALL GO, NOW!
HOW?
JUST WALK OUT.
WE MIGHT GET IN TROUBLE.
BUT THEY SAID NOT TO.
IT'S ILLEGAL.
AND PARIS IS SO FAR.
I AM NOT GOING TO BE A LAW-BREAKER.

* Situation Normal, All Fucked Up! U.S. Navy phrase from WWII

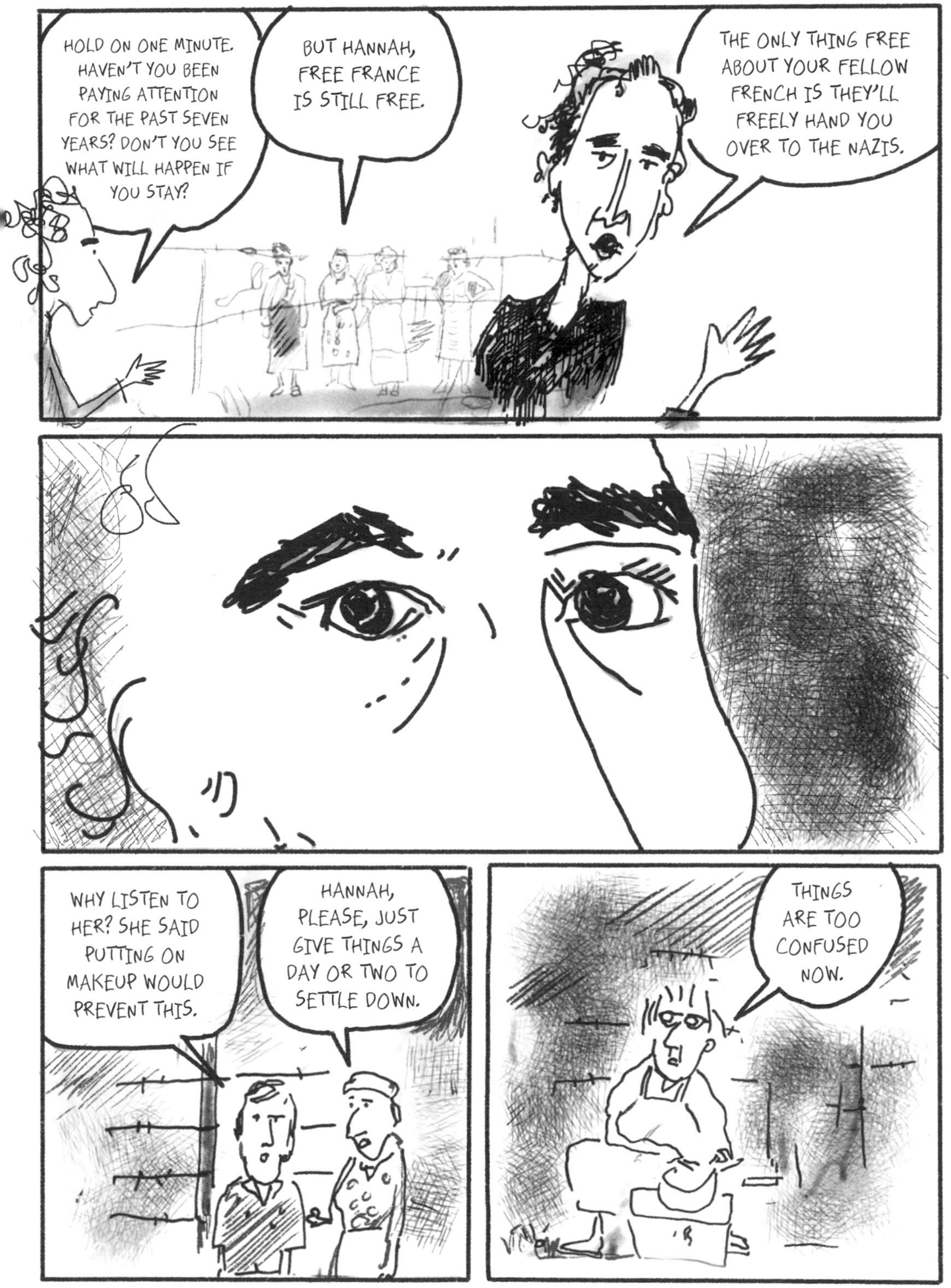
HOLD ON ONE MINUTE. HAVEN'T YOU BEEN PAYING ATTENTION FOR THE PAST SEVEN YEARS? DON'T YOU SEE WHAT WILL HAPPEN IF YOU STAY?
BUT HANNAH, FREE FRANCE IS STILL FREE.
THE ONLY THING FREE ABOUT YOUR FELLOW FRENCH IS THEY'LL FREELY HAND YOU OVER TO THE NAZIS.
WHY LISTEN TO HER? SHE SAID PUTTING ON MAKEUP WOULD PREVENT THIS.
HANNAH, PLEASE, JUST GIVE THINGS A DAY OR TWO TO SETTLE DOWN.
THINGS ARE TOO CONFUSED NOW.

THE CONFUSION IS OUR FRIEND.

BUT OUR FRIEND IS FADING FAST.

GO ON, HANNAH.

WE'LL CATCH UP WITH YOU IN A DAY OR TWO, ONCE THINGS SETTLE DOWN.

SO I SIMPLY WALK OUT!

6,800 WOMEN SIT TIGHT.

AND LIKE I SAID, FRENCH ENTROPY IS FAST REPLACED WITH NEEDLE-SHARP GERMAN EFFICIENCY.

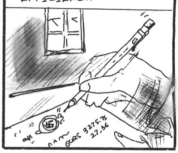

IN GURS, 6,800 WOMEN WATCH AS NEW, STRONG, KRUPP STEEL GERMAN FENCES RISE.

IN GURS, 6,800 WOMEN GREET ANOTHER 6,800 JEWISH WOMEN INGENIOUSLY TRANSPORTED ACROSS THE BORDER FROM BADEN AND SAARPFALZ, AND DELIVERED RIGHT ON TIME BY A FAST-RISING YOUNG SS OFFICER.

AN OFFICER BY THE NAME OF ADOLF EICHMANN.*

FOR THE HIGHEST ORDER OF THE EFFICIENT TRANSPORT OF VITAL ENEMY CONTAMINANTS, OFFICER EICHMANN IS AWARDED THIS VERY IMPORTANT MEDAL!

MY DUTY.

* Adolf Eichmann (1906–1962). German SS officer in charge of making the trains run on time to the concentration camps, and making sure they were full of Jews.

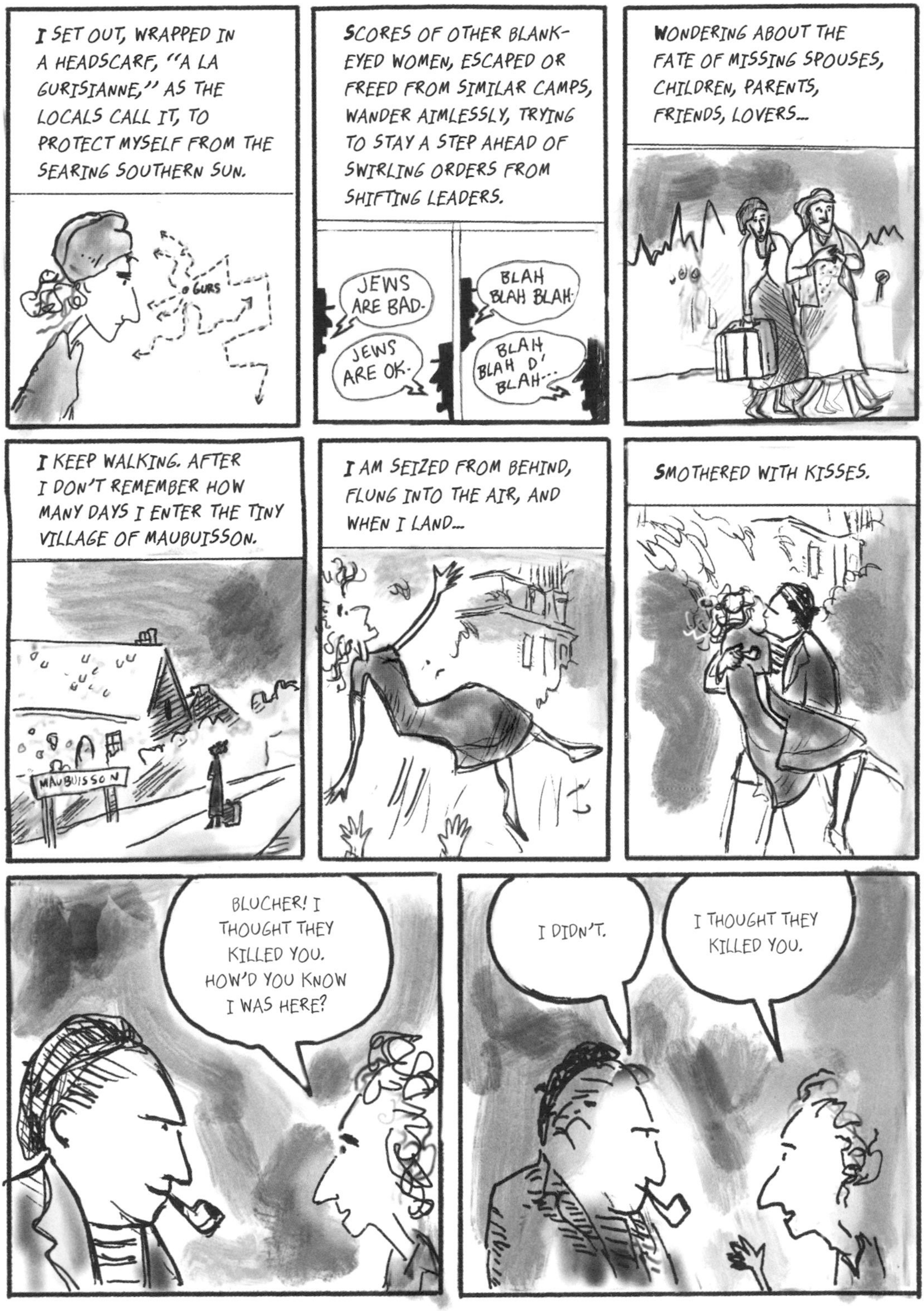
I SET OUT, WRAPPED IN A HEADSCARF, "A LA GURISIANNE," AS THE LOCALS CALL IT, TO PROTECT MYSELF FROM THE SEARING SOUTHERN SUN.
GURS
SCORES OF OTHER BLANK-EYED WOMEN, ESCAPED OR FREED FROM SIMILAR CAMPS, WANDER AIMLESSLY, TRYING TO STAY A STEP AHEAD OF SWIRLING ORDERS FROM SHIFTING LEADERS.
JEWS ARE BAD.
JEWS ARE OK.
BLAH BLAH BLAH.
BLAH BLAH D' BLAH...
WONDERING ABOUT THE FATE OF MISSING SPOUSES, CHILDREN, PARENTS, FRIENDS, LOVERS...
I KEEP WALKING. AFTER I DON'T REMEMBER HOW MANY DAYS I ENTER THE TINY VILLAGE OF MAUBUISSON.
MAUBUISSON
I AM SEIZED FROM BEHIND, FLUNG INTO THE AIR, AND WHEN I LAND...
SMOTHERED WITH KISSES.
BLUCHER! I THOUGHT THEY KILLED YOU. HOW'D YOU KNOW I WAS HERE?
I DIDN'T.
I THOUGHT THEY KILLED YOU.

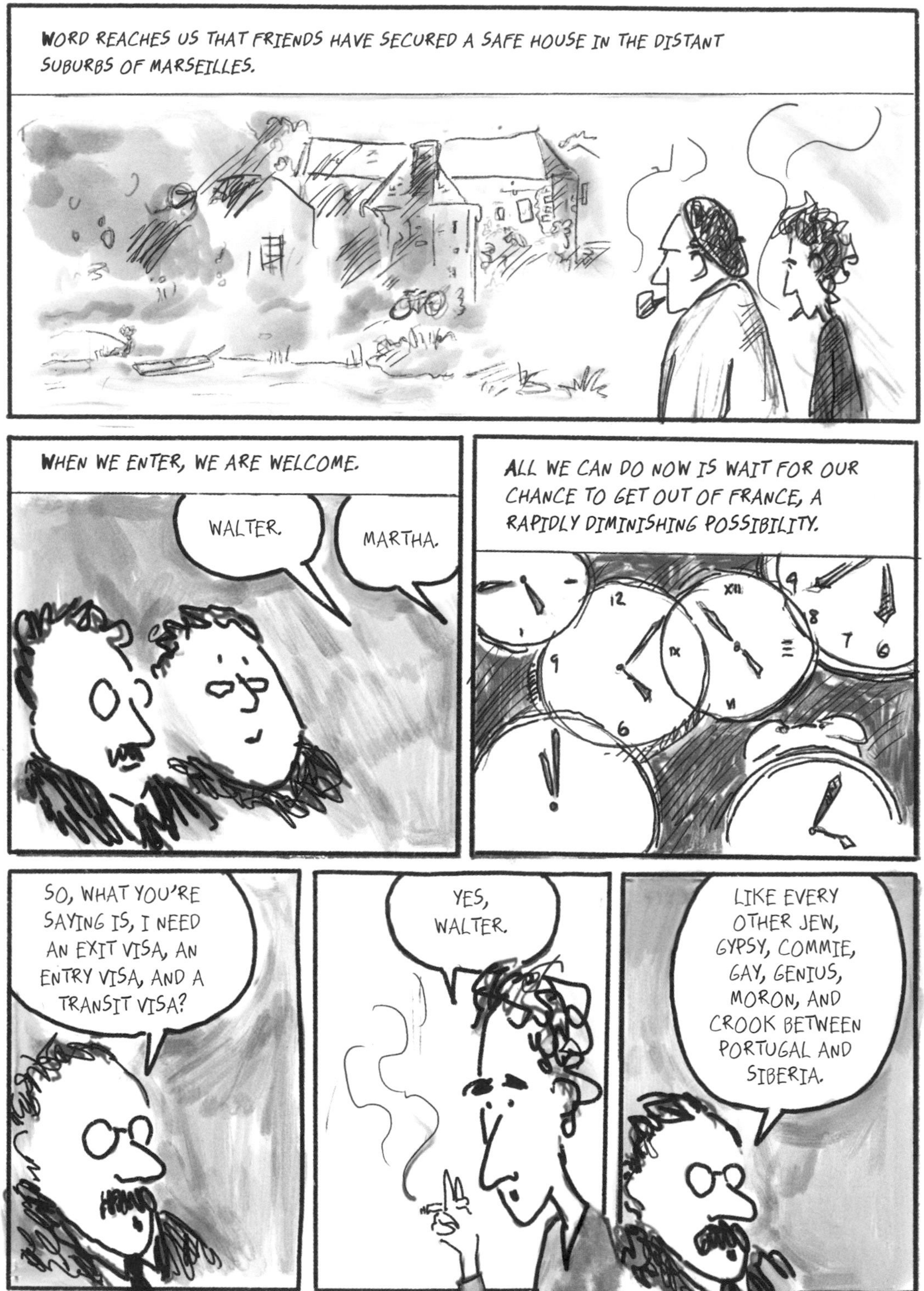
WORD REACHES US THAT FRIENDS HAVE SECURED A SAFE HOUSE IN THE DISTANT SUBURBS OF MARSEILLES.
WHEN WE ENTER, WE ARE WELCOME.
WALTER.
MARTHA.
ALL WE CAN DO NOW IS WAIT FOR OUR CHANCE TO GET OUT OF FRANCE, A RAPIDLY DIMINISHING POSSIBILITY.
SO, WHAT YOU'RE SAYING IS, I NEED AN EXIT VISA, AN ENTRY VISA, AND A TRANSIT VISA?
YES, WALTER.
LIKE EVERY OTHER JEW, GYPSY, COMMIE, GAY, GENIUS, MORON, AND CROOK BETWEEN PORTUGAL AND SIBERIA.

DOOMED ATHENS ON THE MEDITERRANEAN

MARSEILLES, HANGING ON THE SOUTHERN LIP OF EUROPE, HOSTS THE VISA OFFICE AND A MENAGERIE OF WHARVES, CAFES, BARS, AND BORDELLOS CLOTTED WITH THE BEST AND WORST THAT EUROPE HAS TO OFFER. IT'S AN ARDUOUS 40 KM FROM OUR SAFE HOUSE, AND ITS ELUSIVE VISA OFFICE OPENS AND CLOSES ON A WHIM.

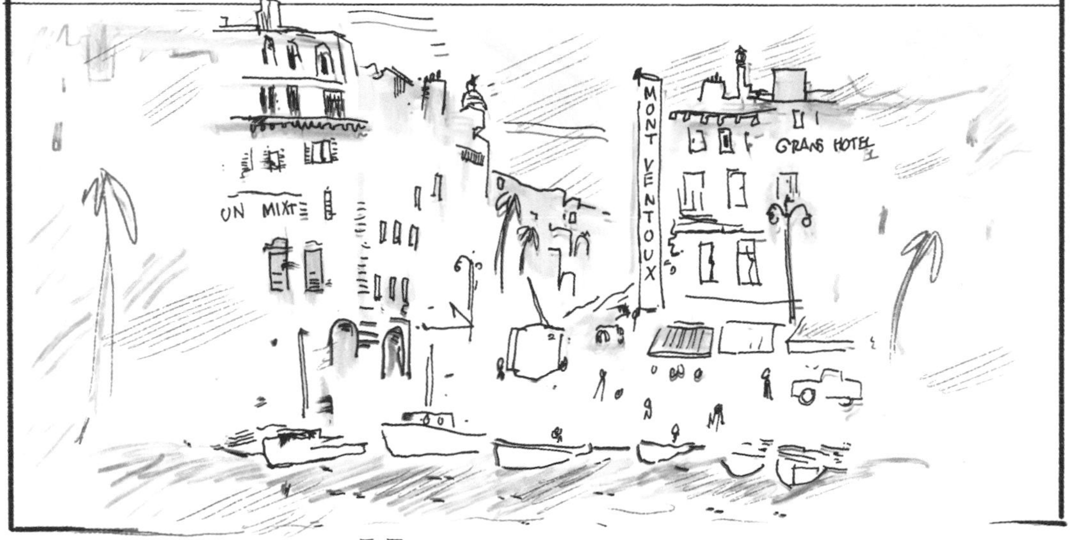
MONT VENTOUX
GRANS HOTEL
ON MIXTE

ON THOSE ODD MOMENTS WHEN THE OFFICE IS OPEN, A MOST ECLECTIC MOB QUEUES UP FOR THEIR CHANCE AT FREEDOM.

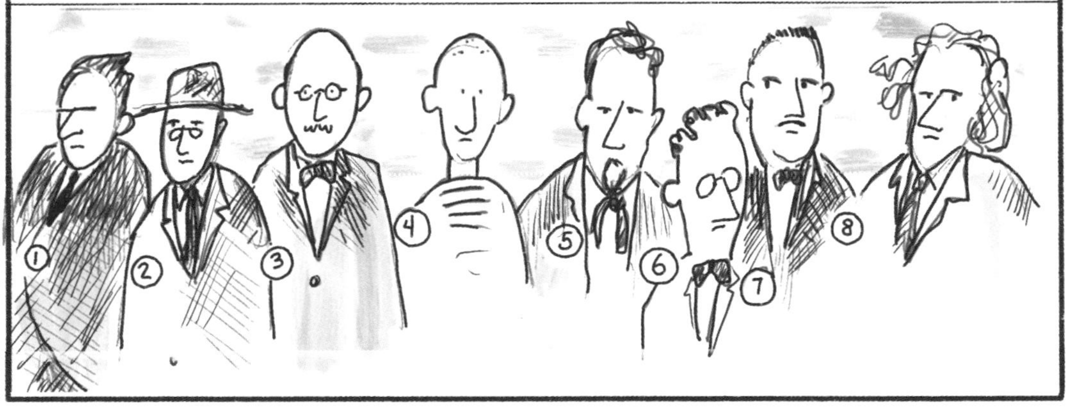
1
2
3
4
5
6
7
8

(1) Arthur Koestler CBE (1905–1983). Hungarian Jewish writer, who, after a stint as a communist, wrote his 1940 novel *Darkness at Noon*, as an early attack on what Hannah Arendt would later define as "Totalitarianism." (2) Claude Levi-Strauss (1908–2009). French Jewish anthropologist, credited for systematizing "structural" theory, which says humans are deeply wired for behavior through primal languages that extend far beyond spoken or written words. Escaped the Nazis through Marseilles via Martinique to New York. (3) Franz Werfel (1890–1945). Austrian Jewish writer, early chronicler of the Armenian genocide of 1915, his novel *The Song of Bernadette* was made into a Hollywood blockbuster about a religious mystic. Friend and mentor of Franz Kafka. (4) Andre Breton (1896–1966). French writer, founding father of surrealism, which he dubbed pure psychic automatism, whatever that means! (5) Heinrich Mann (1871–1950). German writer who fled for his life in 1933. His 1915 essay about Emile Zola's defense of a Jewish officer from institutional anti-Semitism was a loosely veiled attack on German aggression in World War One—during World War One! (6) Varian Fry (1907–1967). American journalist who ran a rescue network in France that helped nearly four thousand Jews and other oppressed people escape. (7) Andre Masson (1896–1987). French artist and hashish buddy of Walter Benjamin. (8) Lion Feuchtwanger (1884–1958). German Jewish writer, who, while strenuous in his criticism of the Nazis, was sometimes criticized for turning a blind eye to the brutal rule of Russia's Joseph Stalin.

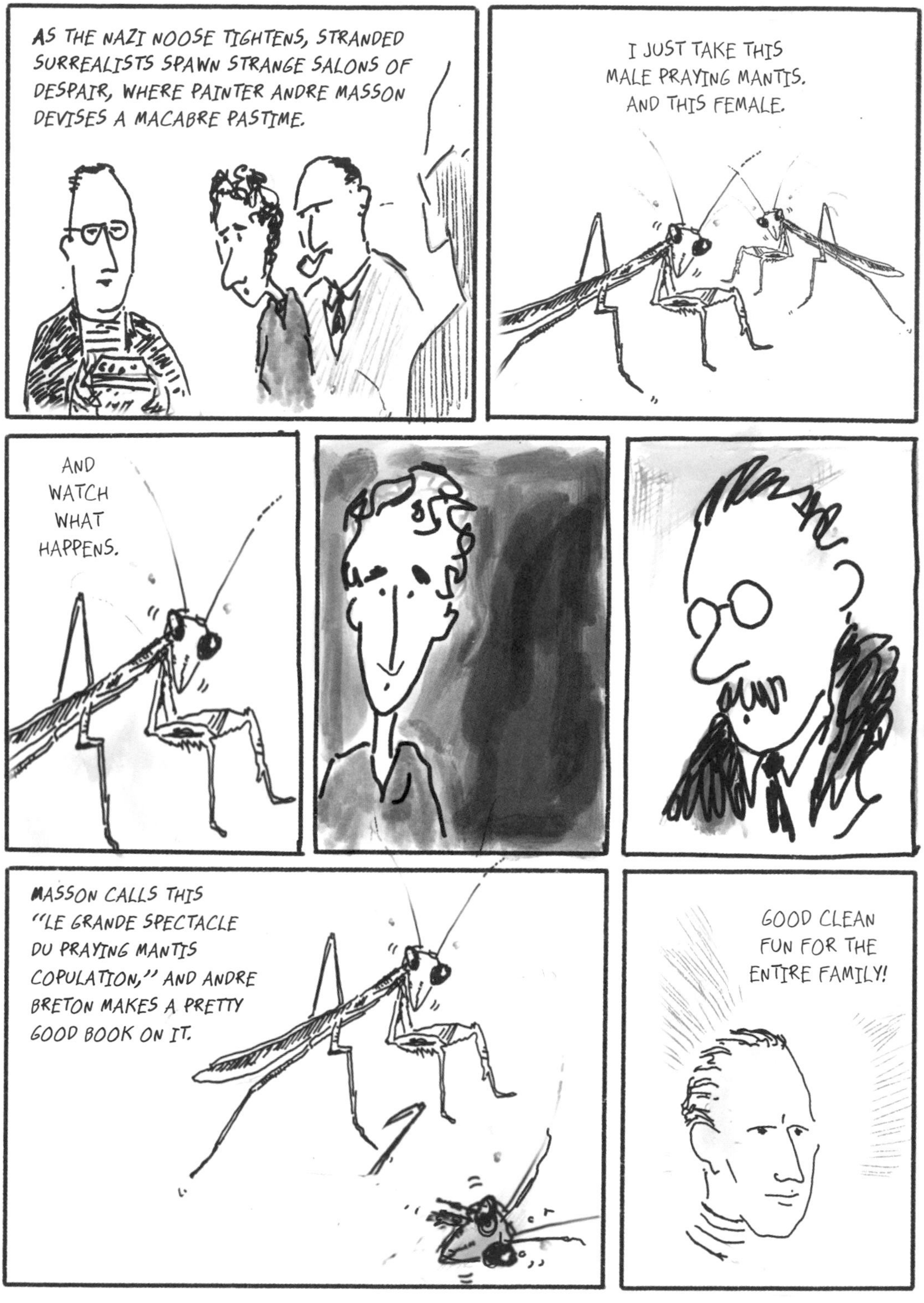
AS THE NAZI NOOSE TIGHTENS, STRANDED SURREALISTS SPAWN STRANGE SALONS OF DESPAIR, WHERE PAINTER ANDRE MASSON DEVISES A MACABRE PASTIME.
I JUST TAKE THIS MALE PRAYING MANTIS. AND THIS FEMALE.
AND WATCH WHAT HAPPENS.
MASSON CALLS THIS "LE GRANDE SPECTACLE DU PRAYING MANTIS COPULATION," AND ANDRE BRETON MAKES A PRETTY GOOD BOOK ON IT.
GOOD CLEAN FUN FOR THE ENTIRE FAMILY!

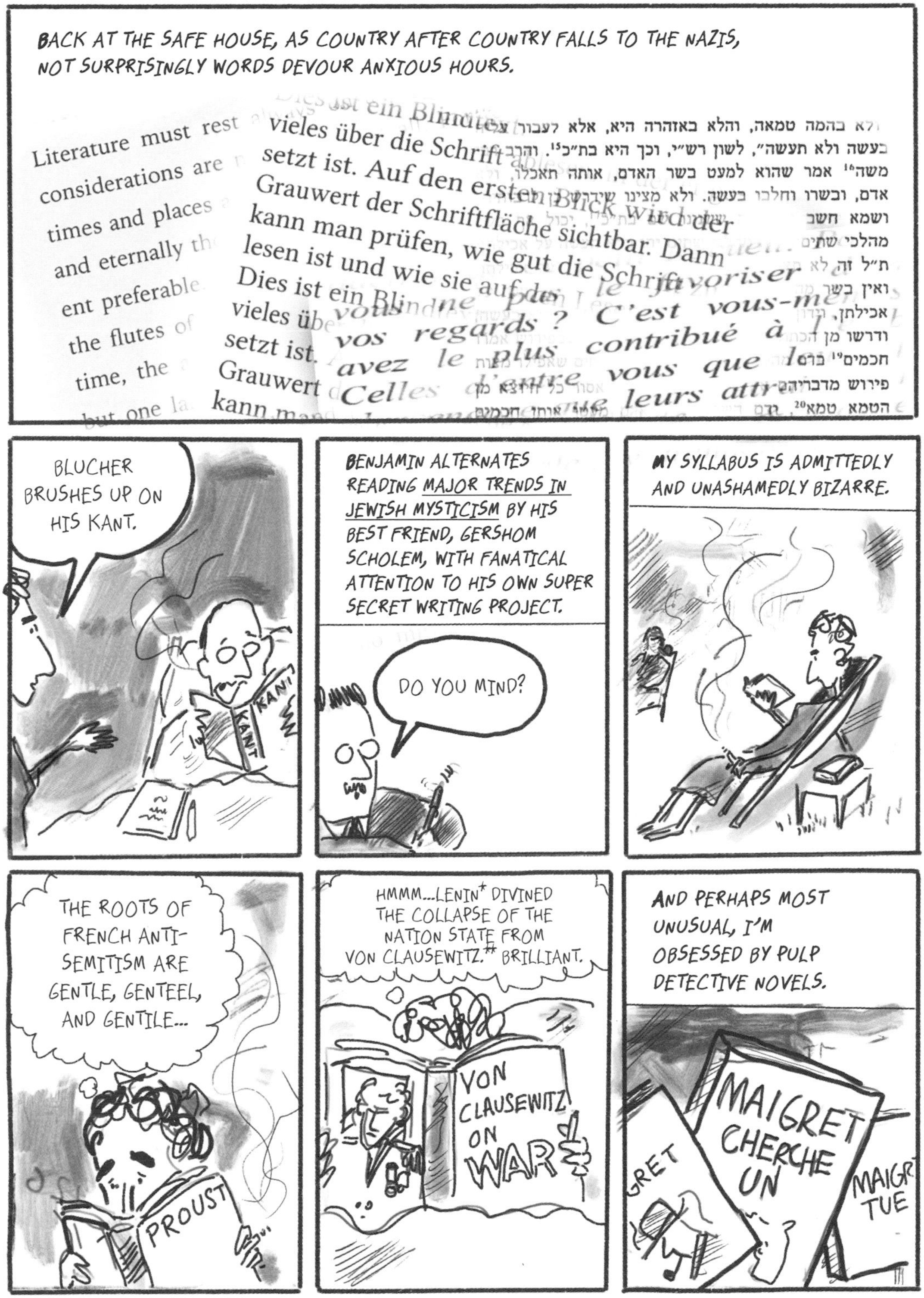
BACK AT THE SAFE HOUSE, AS COUNTRY AFTER COUNTRY FALLS TO THE NAZIS, NOT SURPRISINGLY WORDS DEVOUR ANXIOUS HOURS.
BLUCHER BRUSHES UP ON HIS KANT.
KANT
BENJAMIN ALTERNATES READING MAJOR TRENDS IN JEWISH MYSTICISM BY HIS BEST FRIEND, GERSHOM SCHOLEM, WITH FANATICAL ATTENTION TO HIS OWN SUPER SECRET WRITING PROJECT.
DO YOU MIND?
MY SYLLABUS IS ADMITTEDLY AND UNASHAMEDLY BIZARRE.
THE ROOTS OF FRENCH ANTI-SEMITISM ARE GENTLE, GENTEEL, AND GENTILE...
PROUST
HMMM...LENIN* DIVINED THE COLLAPSE OF THE NATION STATE FROM VON CLAUSEWITZ.** BRILLIANT.
VON CLAUSEWITZ ON WAR
AND PERHAPS MOST UNUSUAL, I'M OBSESSED BY PULP DETECTIVE NOVELS.
MAIGRET CHERCHE UN
GRET
MAIGR TUE

* Vladimir Lenin (1870–1924). Russian communist revolutionary, turned from a childhood of middle-class respectability to a life of fierce, even violent commitment to changing the world, starting with getting rid of the Czar and all his ministers.

** Carl Von Clausewitz (1780–1831). Prussian general and military theorist who stressed the psychological nature of war. His *On War* is still studied, as is his insight that "war is the advancement of policy by other means."

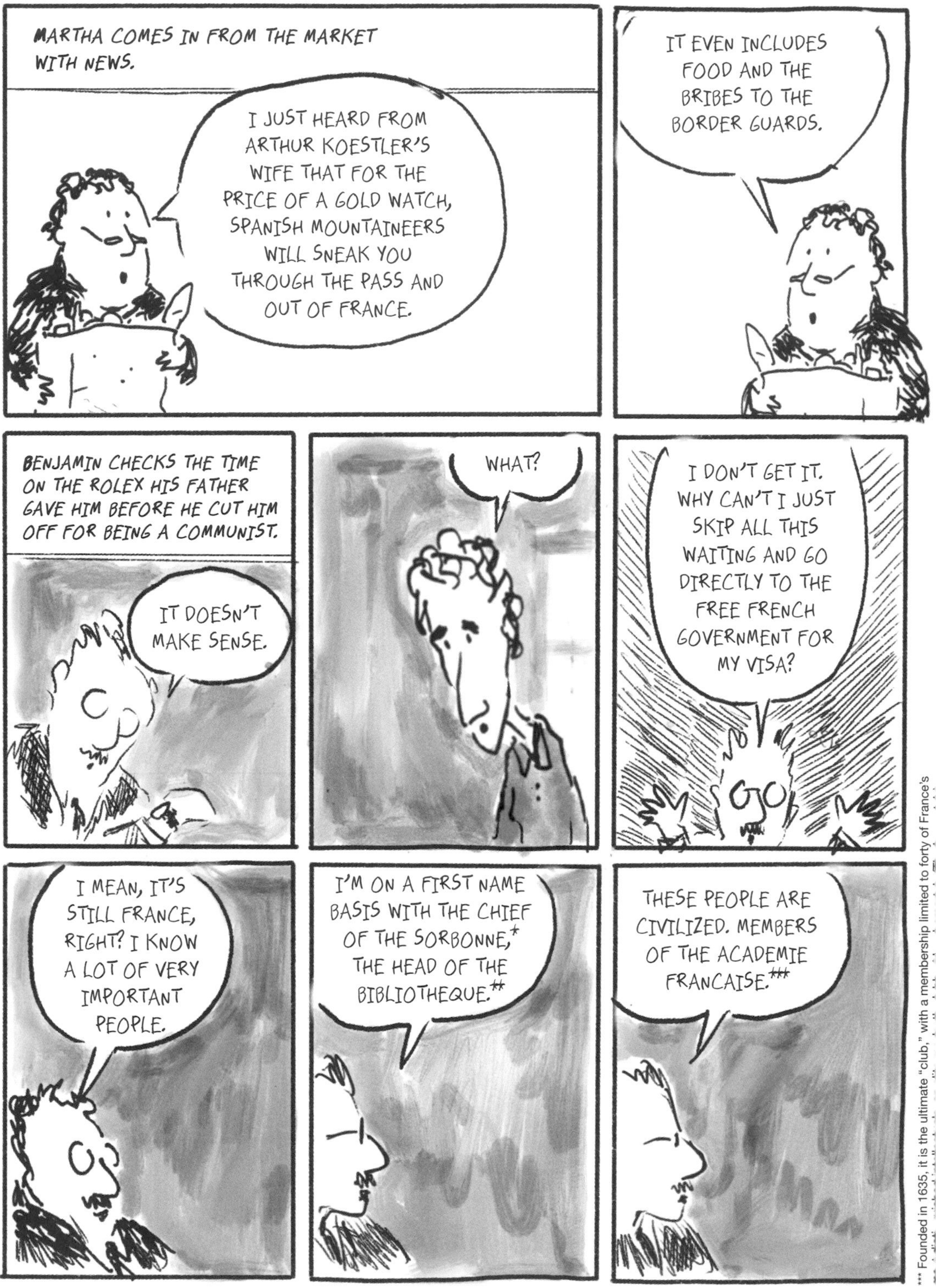
MARTHA COMES IN FROM THE MARKET WITH NEWS.
I JUST HEARD FROM ARTHUR KOESTLER'S WIFE THAT FOR THE PRICE OF A GOLD WATCH, SPANISH MOUNTAINEERS WILL SNEAK YOU THROUGH THE PASS AND OUT OF FRANCE.
IT EVEN INCLUDES FOOD AND THE BRIBES TO THE BORDER GUARDS.
BENJAMIN CHECKS THE TIME ON THE ROLEX HIS FATHER GAVE HIM BEFORE HE CUT HIM OFF FOR BEING A COMMUNIST.
IT DOESN'T MAKE SENSE.
WHAT?
I DON'T GET IT. WHY CAN'T I JUST SKIP ALL THIS WAITING AND GO DIRECTLY TO THE FREE FRENCH GOVERNMENT FOR MY VISA?
I MEAN, IT'S STILL FRANCE, RIGHT? I KNOW A LOT OF VERY IMPORTANT PEOPLE.
I'M ON A FIRST NAME BASIS WITH THE CHIEF OF THE SORBONNE,* THE HEAD OF THE BIBLIOTHEQUE.**
THESE PEOPLE ARE CIVILIZED. MEMBERS OF THE ACADEMIE FRANCAISE.***

*** Founded in 1635, it is the ultimate "club," with a membership limited to forty of France's

* The most prestigious university in France—Oxford, Harvard, Cambridge, Princeton, Stanford, and MIT all rolled into one.

** The state library of France, established in 1461, with the largest collection of medieval and modern manuscripts in the world.

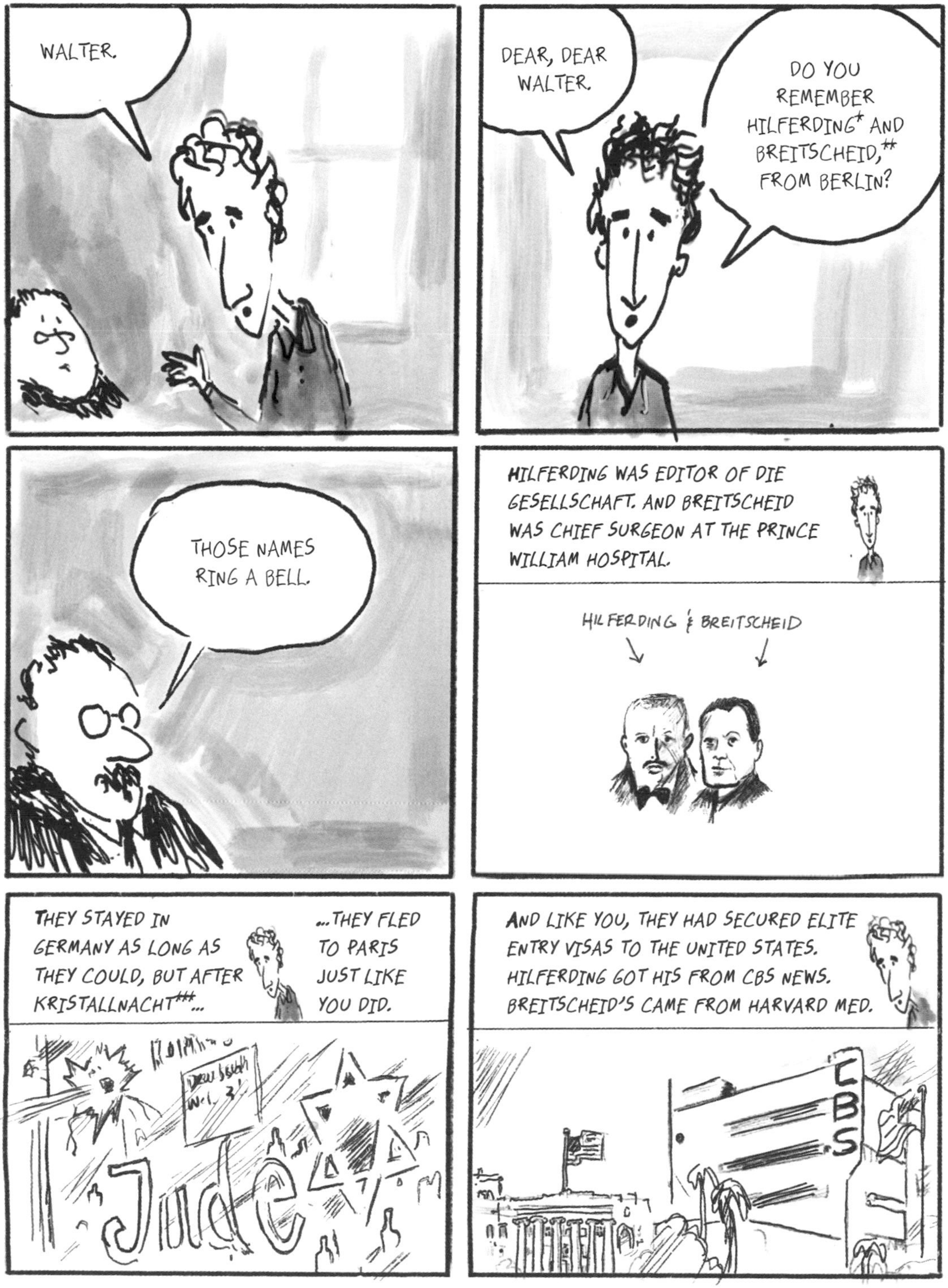
WALTER.
DEAR, DEAR WALTER.
DO YOU REMEMBER HILFERDING* AND BREITSCHEID,** FROM BERLIN?
THOSE NAMES RING A BELL.
HILFERDING WAS EDITOR OF DIE GESELLSCHAFT. AND BREITSCHEID WAS CHIEF SURGEON AT THE PRINCE WILLIAM HOSPITAL.
HILFERDING & BREITSCHEID
THEY STAYED IN GERMANY AS LONG AS THEY COULD, BUT AFTER KRISTALLNACHT***...
...THEY FLED TO PARIS JUST LIKE YOU DID.
Jude
AND LIKE YOU, THEY HAD SECURED ELITE ENTRY VISAS TO THE UNITED STATES. HILFERDING GOT HIS FROM CBS NEWS. BREITSCHEID'S CAME FROM HARVARD MED.
CBS

* Dr. Rudolf Hilferding (1877–1941). (See page 47.)

** Rudolf Breitscheid (1874–1944). (See page 56.)

*** November 9, 1938, literally "the night of broken glass," when mobs of Nazis (and ordinary Germans and Austrians) destroyed Jewish homes, businesses, and people.

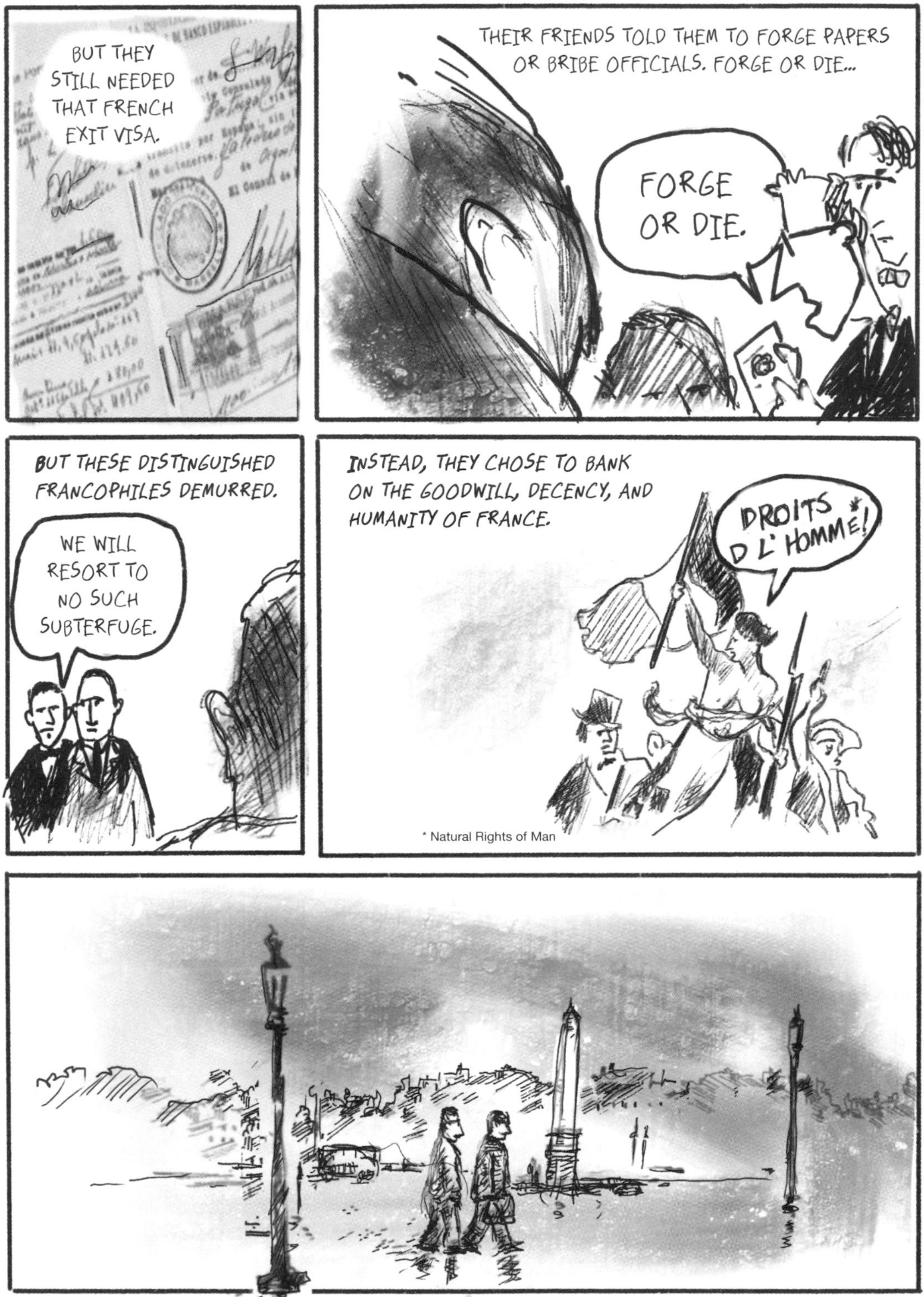
BUT THEY STILL NEEDED THAT FRENCH EXIT VISA.
THEIR FRIENDS TOLD THEM TO FORGE PAPERS OR BRIBE OFFICIALS. FORGE OR DIE...
FORGE OR DIE.
BUT THESE DISTINGUISHED FRANCOPHILES DEMURRED.
WE WILL RESORT TO NO SUCH SUBTERFUGE.
INSTEAD, THEY CHOSE TO BANK ON THE GOODWILL, DECENCY, AND HUMANITY OF FRANCE.
DROITS D L'HOMME!*
* Natural Rights of Man

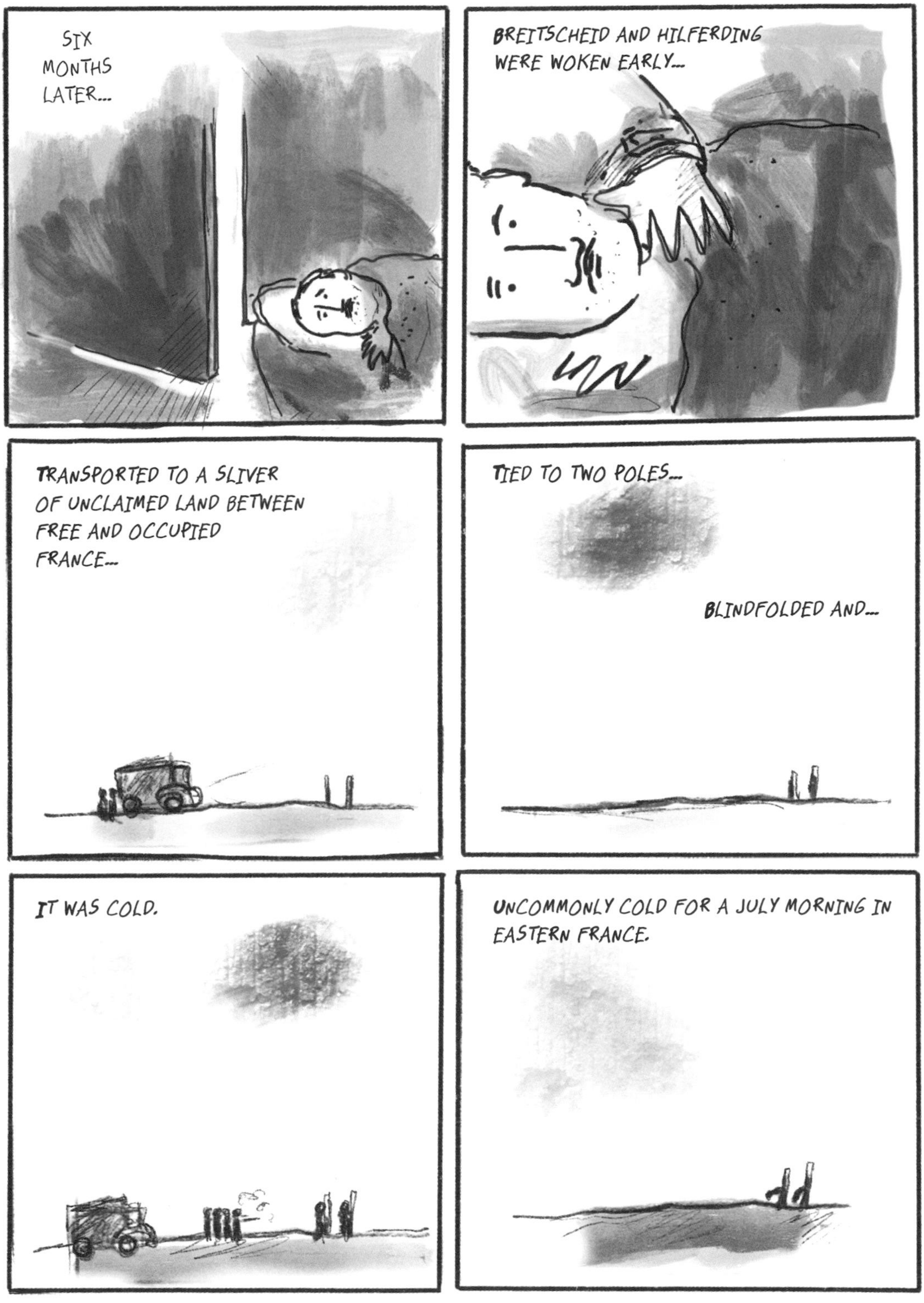
SIX MONTHS LATER...
BREITSCHEID AND HILFERDING WERE WOKEN EARLY...
TRANSPORTED TO A SLIVER OF UNCLAIMED LAND BETWEEN FREE AND OCCUPIED FRANCE...
TIED TO TWO POLES...
BLINDFOLDED AND...
IT WAS COLD.
UNCOMMONLY COLD FOR A JULY MORNING IN EASTERN FRANCE.

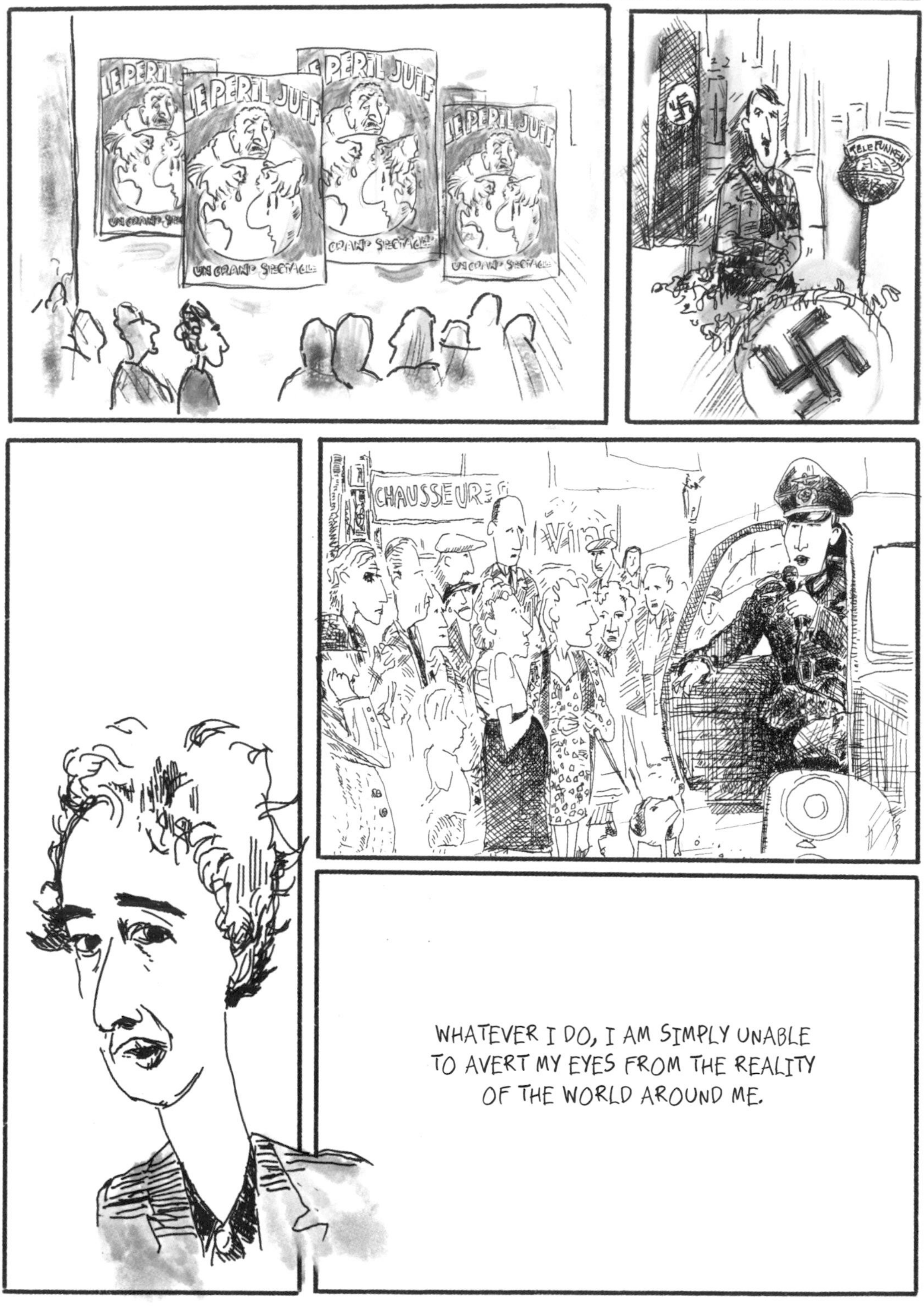
LE PERIL JUIF
UN GRAND SPECTACLE
TELEFUNKEN
CHAUSSEUR
WHATEVER I DO, I AM SIMPLY UNABLE TO AVERT MY EYES FROM THE REALITY OF THE WORLD AROUND ME.

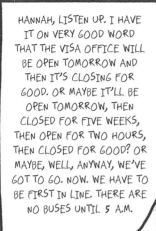

HANNAH, LISTEN UP. I HAVE IT ON VERY GOOD WORD THAT THE VISA OFFICE WILL BE OPEN TOMORROW AND THEN IT'S CLOSING FOR GOOD. OR MAYBE IT'LL BE OPEN TOMORROW, THEN CLOSED FOR FIVE WEEKS, THEN OPEN FOR TWO HOURS, THEN CLOSED FOR GOOD? OR MAYBE, WELL, ANYWAY, WE'VE GOT TO GO. NOW. WE HAVE TO BE FIRST IN LINE. THERE ARE NO BUSES UNTIL 5 A.M.

KAFKA* WOULD BE FLUMMOXED BY MY REALITY.

AS WE GET READY, BENJAMIN CREEPS OVER AND HANDS ME A TIGHTLY WRAPPED MANUSCRIPT.

I WANT YOU TO TAKE THIS.

WHAT IS IT?

THE BEST THING I'VE EVER DONE. I WANT YOU TO TAKE IT.

AND, THIS IS CRUCIAL, UNDER ANY CIRCUSTANCES YOU, AND ONLY YOU, ARE NOT TO READ IT UNTIL **JUST THE RIGHT TIME**.

WHY? EVEN FOR YOU, WALTER, YOU'RE NOT MAKING SENSE.

I'VE FINALLY DONE IT. I MARRIED THE JEWISH MYSTICISM OF THE LURIANIC** KABBALAH WITH THE PHENOMENOLOGY OF HEIDEGGER AND HUSSERL, AND THROWN IN MORE THAN A DASH OF PAUL KLEE.

FOR HANNAH ARENDT'S EYES ONLY!
Walter Benjamin

* Franz Kafka (1883–1924). German-speaking Jewish Czech writer, credited with creating modern literature with parables that fluently mix fantasy, reality, myth, fact, circumstance, and fate. Asked, and answered, the question, "I wonder what it would be like to wake up one morning as a gigantic cockroach?"

** Isaac Luria (1534–1572). Born in Jerusalem to German parents, Jewish rabbi and mystic, major figure in Kabbalah, his writings in what is referred to as the Lurianic Kabbalah skirt the line between the sublime and the subversive.

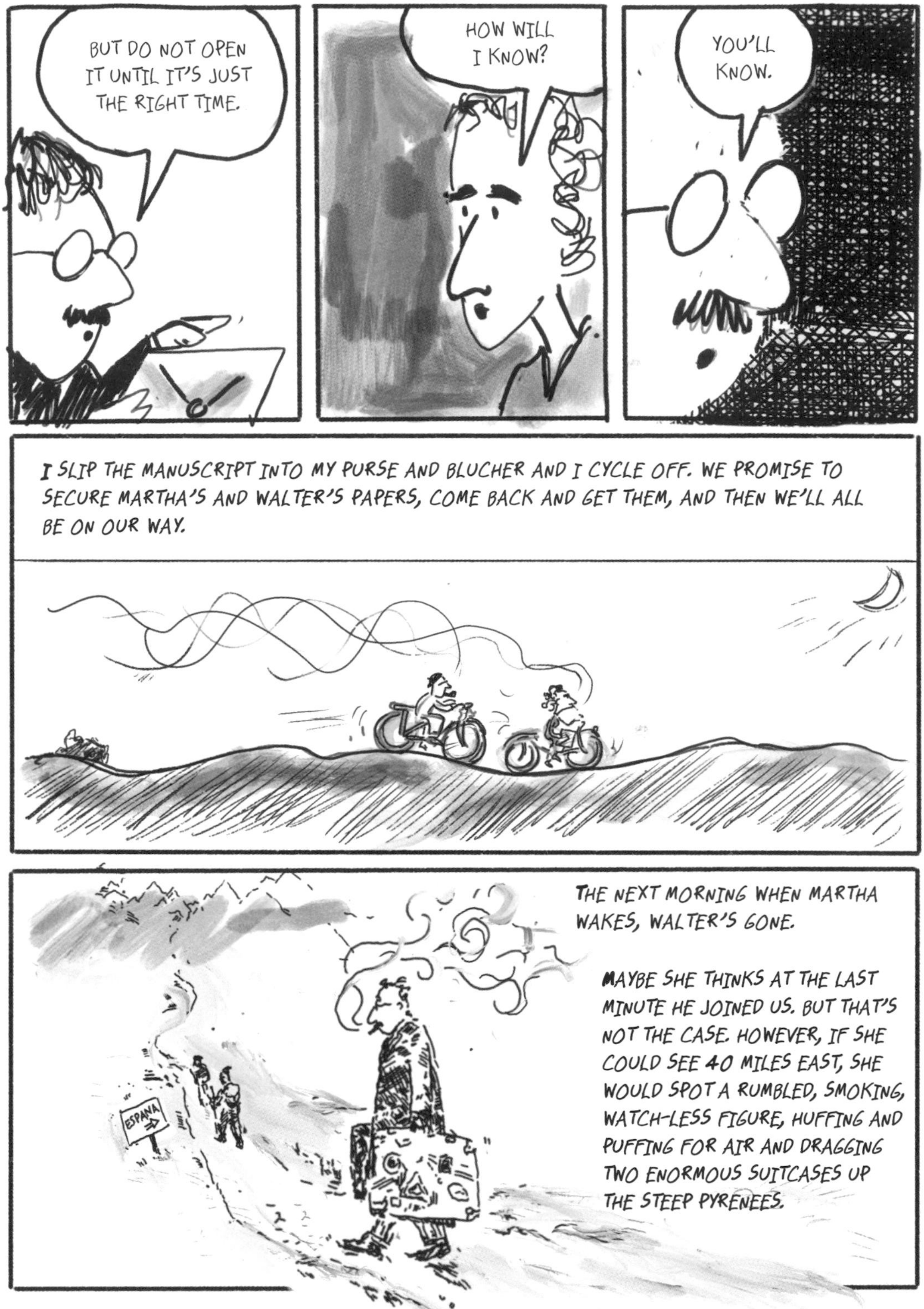
BUT DO NOT OPEN IT UNTIL IT'S JUST THE RIGHT TIME.
HOW WILL I KNOW?
YOU'LL KNOW.
I SLIP THE MANUSCRIPT INTO MY PURSE AND BLUCHER AND I CYCLE OFF. WE PROMISE TO SECURE MARTHA'S AND WALTER'S PAPERS, COME BACK AND GET THEM, AND THEN WE'LL ALL BE ON OUR WAY.
THE NEXT MORNING WHEN MARTHA WAKES, WALTER'S GONE.
MAYBE SHE THINKS AT THE LAST MINUTE HE JOINED US. BUT THAT'S NOT THE CASE. HOWEVER, IF SHE COULD SEE 40 MILES EAST, SHE WOULD SPOT A RUMBLED, SMOKING, WATCH-LESS FIGURE, HUFFING AND PUFFING FOR AIR AND DRAGGING TWO ENORMOUS SUITCASES UP THE STEEP PYRENEES.
ESPANA

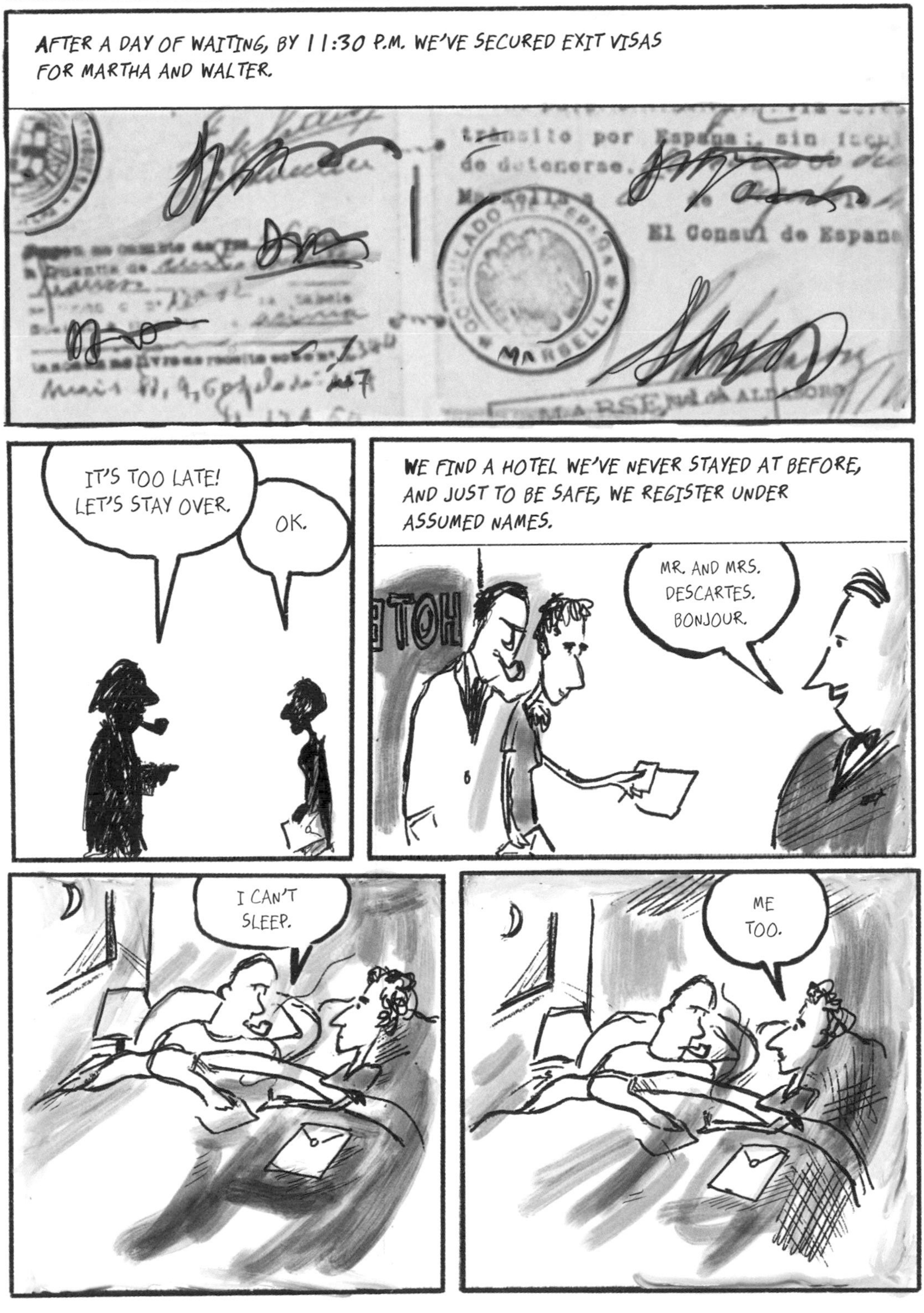
AFTER A DAY OF WAITING, BY 11:30 P.M. WE'VE SECURED EXIT VISAS FOR MARTHA AND WALTER.
IT'S TOO LATE! LET'S STAY OVER.
OK.
WE FIND A HOTEL WE'VE NEVER STAYED AT BEFORE, AND JUST TO BE SAFE, WE REGISTER UNDER ASSUMED NAMES.
HOTEL
MR. AND MRS. DESCARTES. BONJOUR.
I CAN'T SLEEP.
ME TOO.

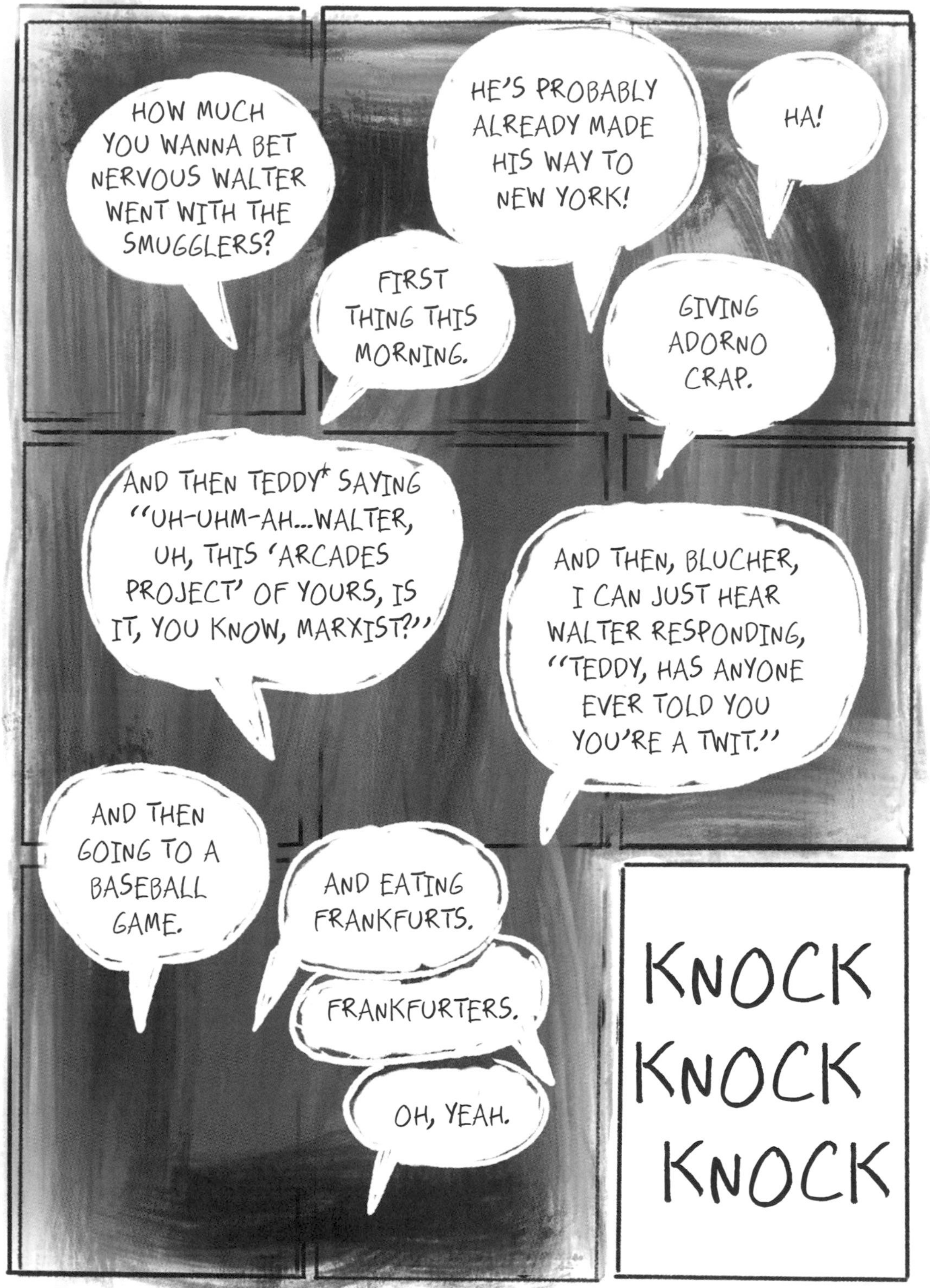
HOW MUCH YOU WANNA BET NERVOUS WALTER WENT WITH THE SMUGGLERS?
HE'S PROBABLY ALREADY MADE HIS WAY TO NEW YORK!
HA!
FIRST THING THIS MORNING.
GIVING ADORNO CRAP.
AND THEN TEDDY* SAYING "UH-UHM-AH...WALTER, UH, THIS 'ARCADES PROJECT' OF YOURS, IS IT, YOU KNOW, MARXIST?"
AND THEN, BLUCHER, I CAN JUST HEAR WALTER RESPONDING, "TEDDY, HAS ANYONE EVER TOLD YOU YOU'RE A TWIT."
AND THEN GOING TO A BASEBALL GAME.
AND EATING FRANKFURTS.
FRANKFURTERS.
OH, YEAH.
KNOCK KNOCK KNOCK

* Theodore Adorno

4:00 A.M.

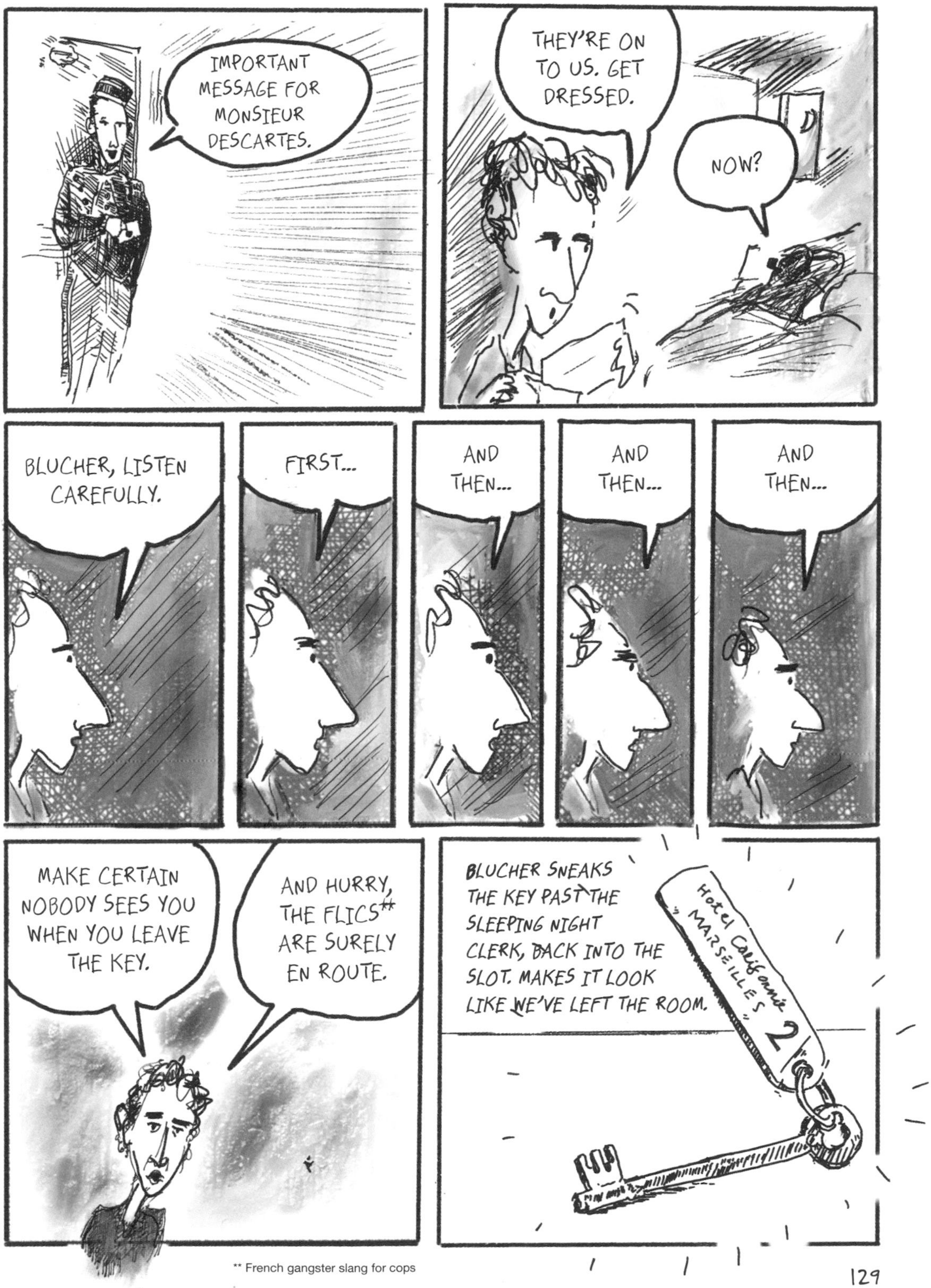
IMPORTANT MESSAGE FOR MONSIEUR DESCARTES.
THEY'RE ON TO US. GET DRESSED.
NOW?
BLUCHER, LISTEN CAREFULLY.
FIRST...
AND THEN...
AND THEN...
AND THEN...
MAKE CERTAIN NOBODY SEES YOU WHEN YOU LEAVE THE KEY.
AND HURRY, THE FLICS** ARE SURELY EN ROUTE.
BLUCHER SNEAKS THE KEY PAST THE SLEEPING NIGHT CLERK, BACK INTO THE SLOT. MAKES IT LOOK LIKE WE'VE LEFT THE ROOM.
Hotel California
"MARSEILLES"
2

** French gangster slang for cops

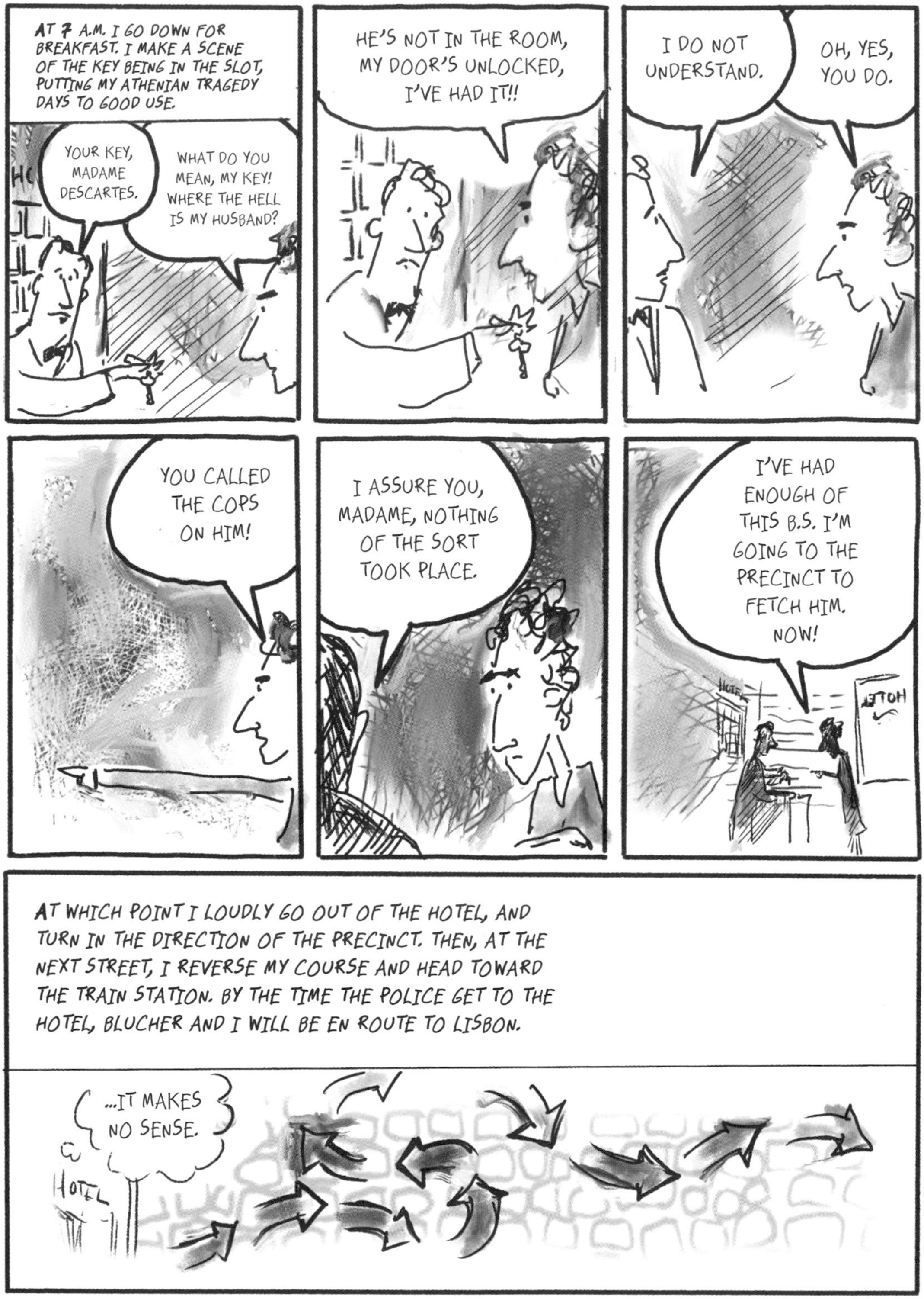
AT 7 A.M. I GO DOWN FOR BREAKFAST. I MAKE A SCENE OF THE KEY BEING IN THE SLOT, PUTTING MY ATHENIAN TRAGEDY DAYS TO GOOD USE.
YOUR KEY, MADAME DESCARTES.
WHAT DO YOU MEAN, MY KEY! WHERE THE HELL IS MY HUSBAND?
HE'S NOT IN THE ROOM, MY DOOR'S UNLOCKED, I'VE HAD IT!!
I DO NOT UNDERSTAND.
OH, YES, YOU DO.
YOU CALLED THE COPS ON HIM!
I ASSURE YOU, MADAME, NOTHING OF THE SORT TOOK PLACE.
I'VE HAD ENOUGH OF THIS B.S. I'M GOING TO THE PRECINCT TO FETCH HIM. NOW!
HOTEL
AT WHICH POINT I LOUDLY GO OUT OF THE HOTEL, AND TURN IN THE DIRECTION OF THE PRECINCT. THEN, AT THE NEXT STREET, I REVERSE MY COURSE AND HEAD TOWARD THE TRAIN STATION. BY THE TIME THE POLICE GET TO THE HOTEL, BLUCHER AND I WILL BE EN ROUTE TO LISBON.
...IT MAKES NO SENSE.
HOTEL

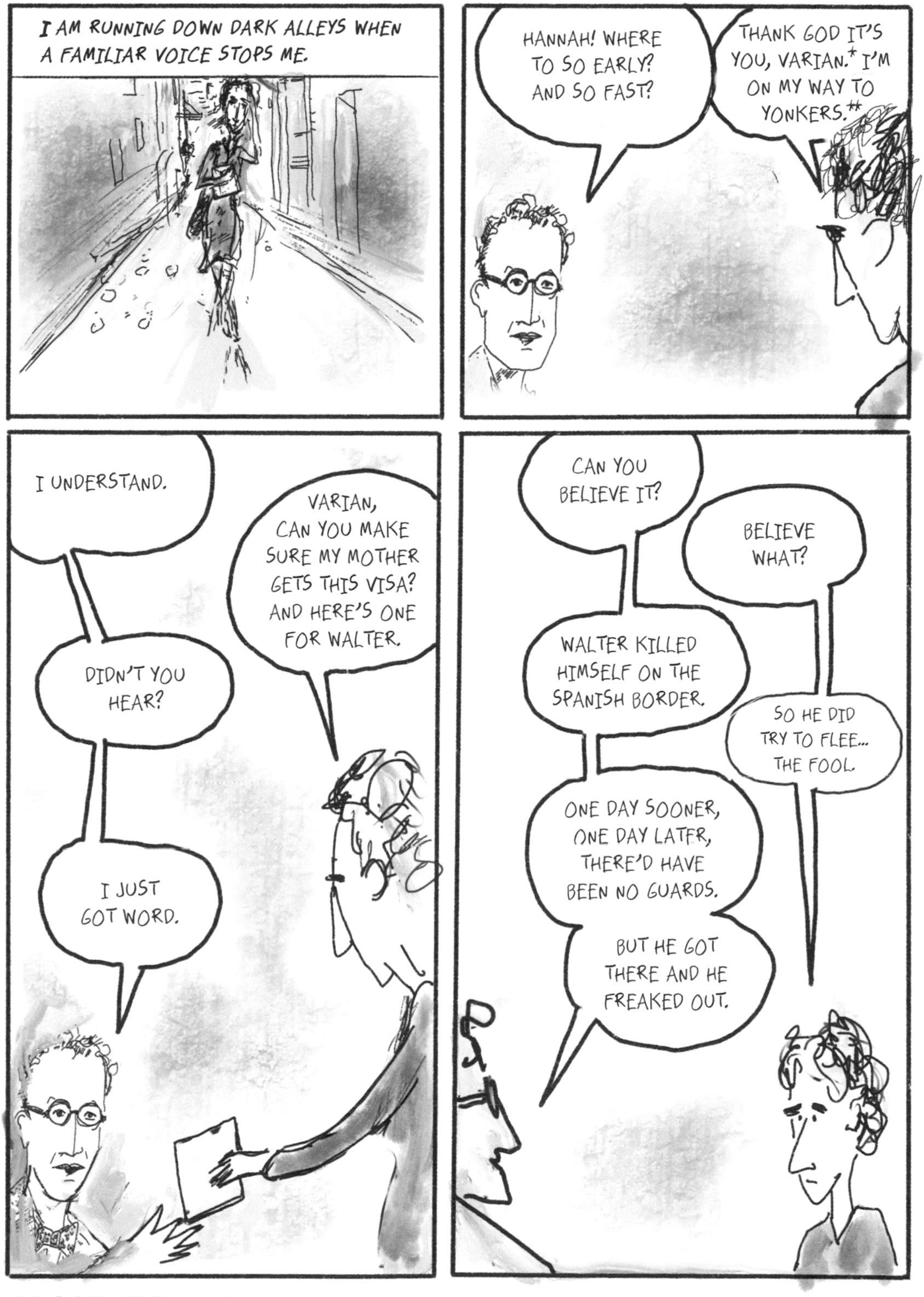
I AM RUNNING DOWN DARK ALLEYS WHEN A FAMILIAR VOICE STOPS ME.
HANNAH! WHERE TO SO EARLY? AND SO FAST?
THANK GOD IT'S YOU, VARIAN.* I'M ON MY WAY TO YONKERS.**
I UNDERSTAND.
VARIAN, CAN YOU MAKE SURE MY MOTHER GETS THIS VISA? AND HERE'S ONE FOR WALTER.
DIDN'T YOU HEAR?
I JUST GOT WORD.
CAN YOU BELIEVE IT?
BELIEVE WHAT?
WALTER KILLED HIMSELF ON THE SPANISH BORDER.
SO HE DID TRY TO FLEE... THE FOOL.
ONE DAY SOONER, ONE DAY LATER, THERE'D HAVE BEEN NO GUARDS.
BUT HE GOT THERE AND HE FREAKED OUT.

* Varian Fry (1907–1967). (See page 117.)

** Code for something you can't say

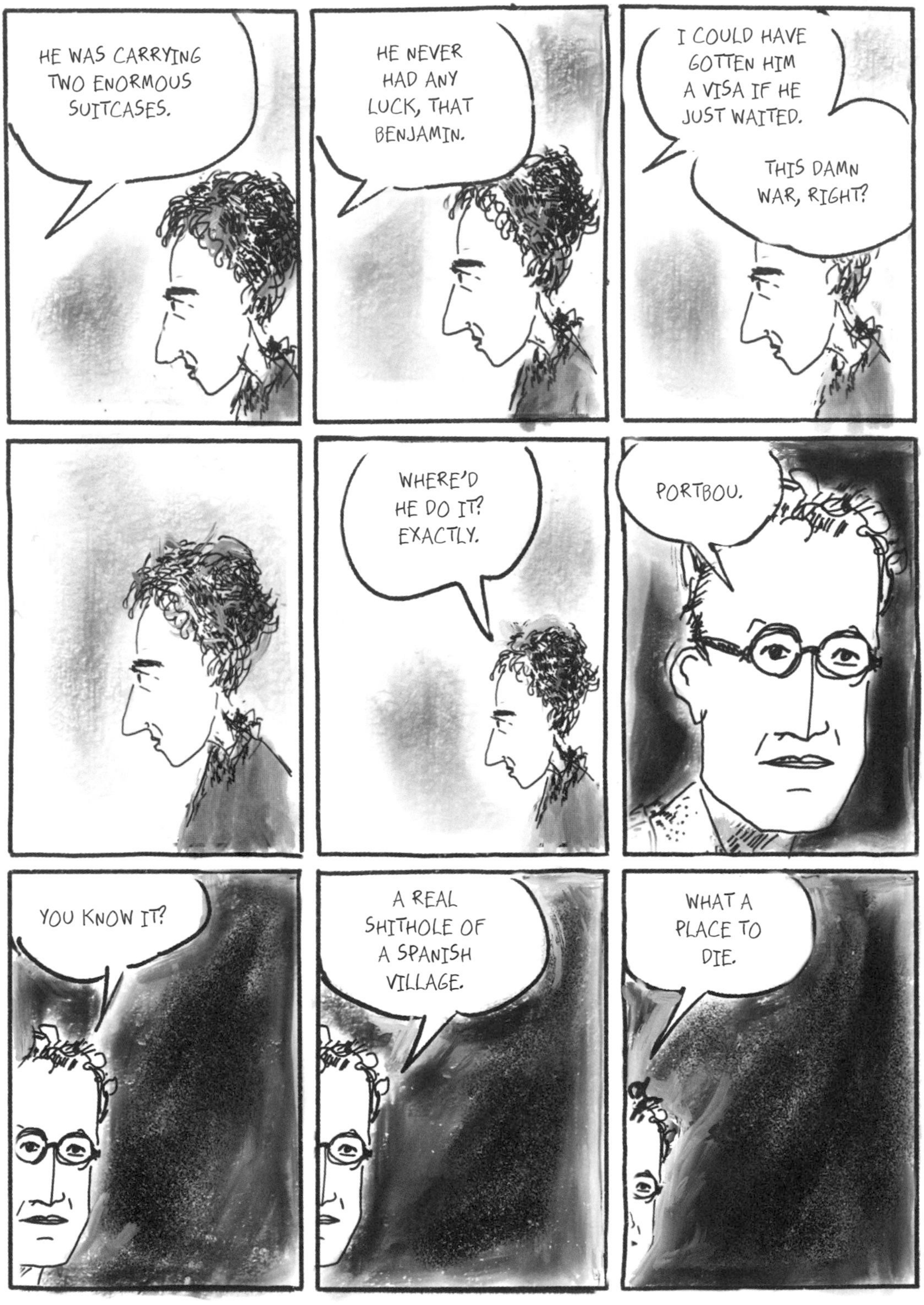
HE WAS CARRYING TWO ENORMOUS SUITCASES.
HE NEVER HAD ANY LUCK, THAT BENJAMIN.
I COULD HAVE GOTTEN HIM A VISA IF HE JUST WAITED.
THIS DAMN WAR, RIGHT?
WHERE'D HE DO IT? EXACTLY.
PORTBOU.
YOU KNOW IT?
A REAL SHITHOLE OF A SPANISH VILLAGE.
WHAT A PLACE TO DIE.

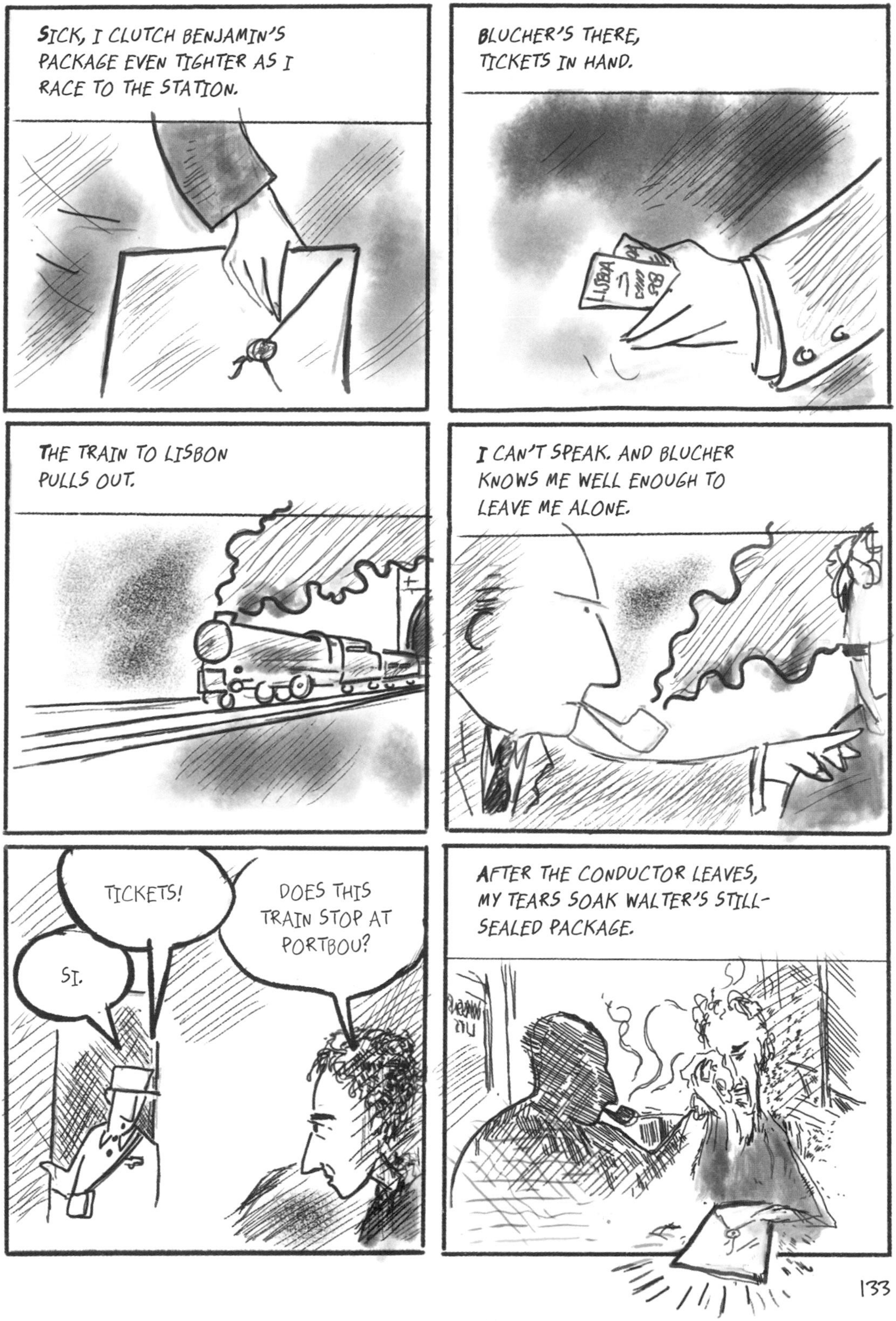
SICK, I CLUTCH BENJAMIN'S PACKAGE EVEN TIGHTER AS I RACE TO THE STATION.
BLUCHER'S THERE, TICKETS IN HAND.
LISBOA
THE TRAIN TO LISBON PULLS OUT.
I CAN'T SPEAK. AND BLUCHER KNOWS ME WELL ENOUGH TO LEAVE ME ALONE.
TICKETS!
SI.
DOES THIS TRAIN STOP AT PORTBOU?
AFTER THE CONDUCTOR LEAVES, MY TEARS SOAK WALTER'S STILL-SEALED PACKAGE.

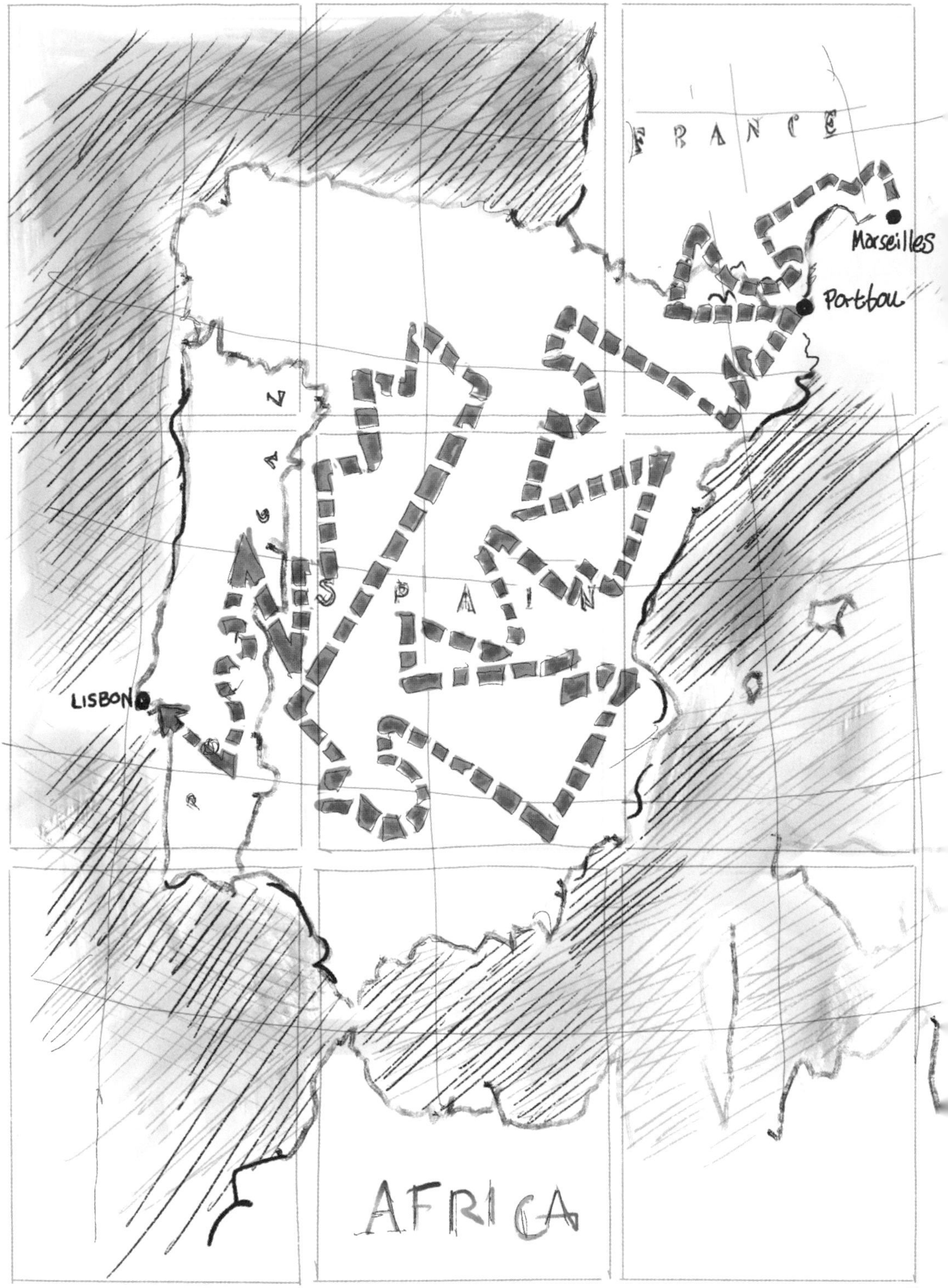
FRANCE
Marseilles
Portbou
SPAIN
LISBON
AFRICA

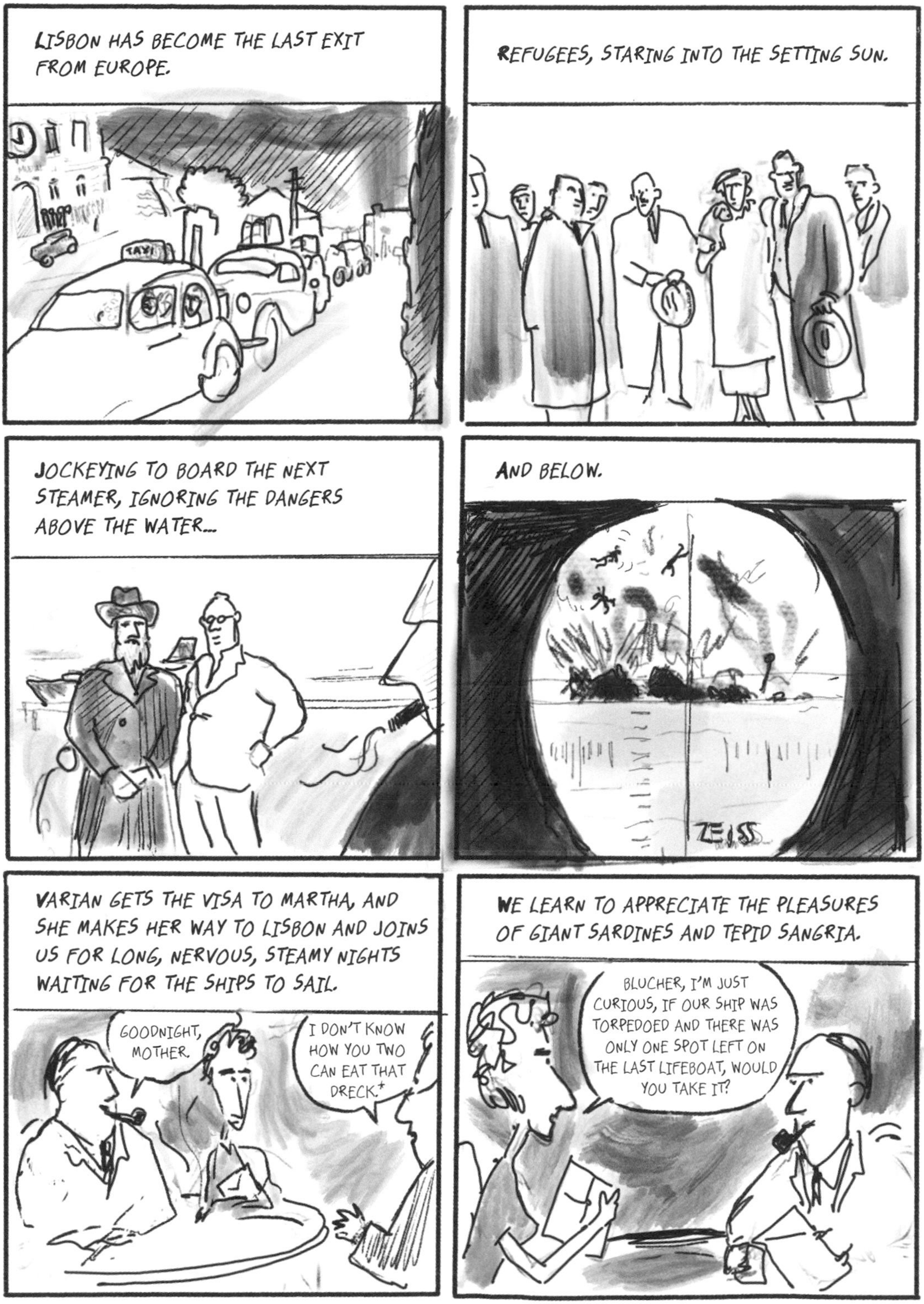
LISBON HAS BECOME THE LAST EXIT FROM EUROPE.
TAXI
REFUGEES, STARING INTO THE SETTING SUN.
JOCKEYING TO BOARD THE NEXT STEAMER, IGNORING THE DANGERS ABOVE THE WATER...
AND BELOW.
ZEISS
VARIAN GETS THE VISA TO MARTHA, AND SHE MAKES HER WAY TO LISBON AND JOINS US FOR LONG, NERVOUS, STEAMY NIGHTS WAITING FOR THE SHIPS TO SAIL.
GOODNIGHT, MOTHER.
I DON'T KNOW HOW YOU TWO CAN EAT THAT DRECK.*
WE LEARN TO APPRECIATE THE PLEASURES OF GIANT SARDINES AND TEPID SANGRIA.
BLUCHER, I'M JUST CURIOUS, IF OUR SHIP WAS TORPEDOED AND THERE WAS ONLY ONE SPOT LEFT ON THE LAST LIFEBOAT, WOULD YOU TAKE IT?

* Really awful stuff—Yiddish

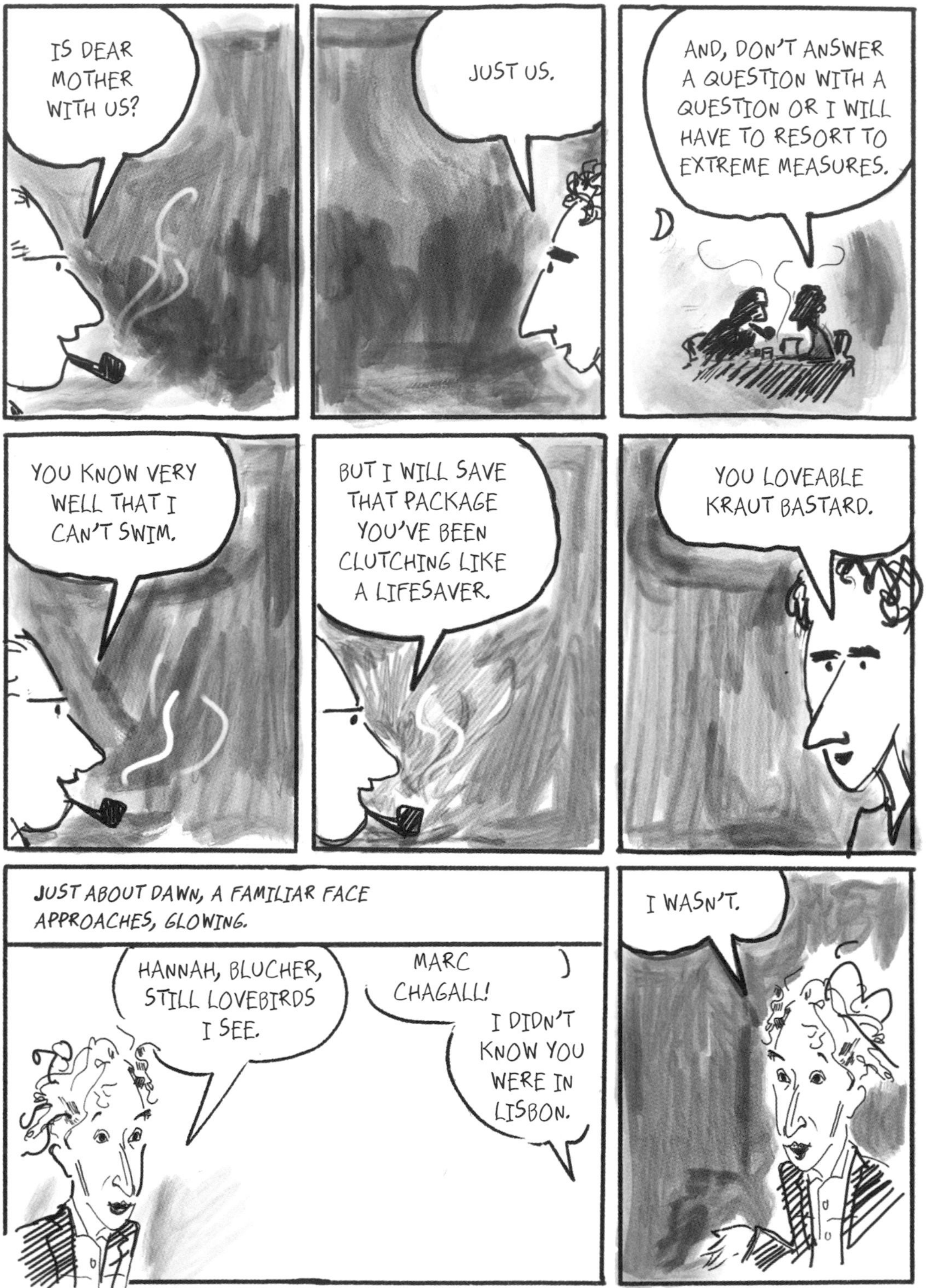
IS DEAR MOTHER WITH US?
JUST US.
AND, DON'T ANSWER A QUESTION WITH A QUESTION OR I WILL HAVE TO RESORT TO EXTREME MEASURES.
YOU KNOW VERY WELL THAT I CAN'T SWIM.
BUT I WILL SAVE THAT PACKAGE YOU'VE BEEN CLUTCHING LIKE A LIFESAVER.
YOU LOVEABLE KRAUT BASTARD.
JUST ABOUT DAWN, A FAMILIAR FACE APPROACHES, GLOWING.
HANNAH, BLUCHER, STILL LOVEBIRDS I SEE.
MARC CHAGALL!
I DIDN'T KNOW YOU WERE IN LISBON.
I WASN'T.

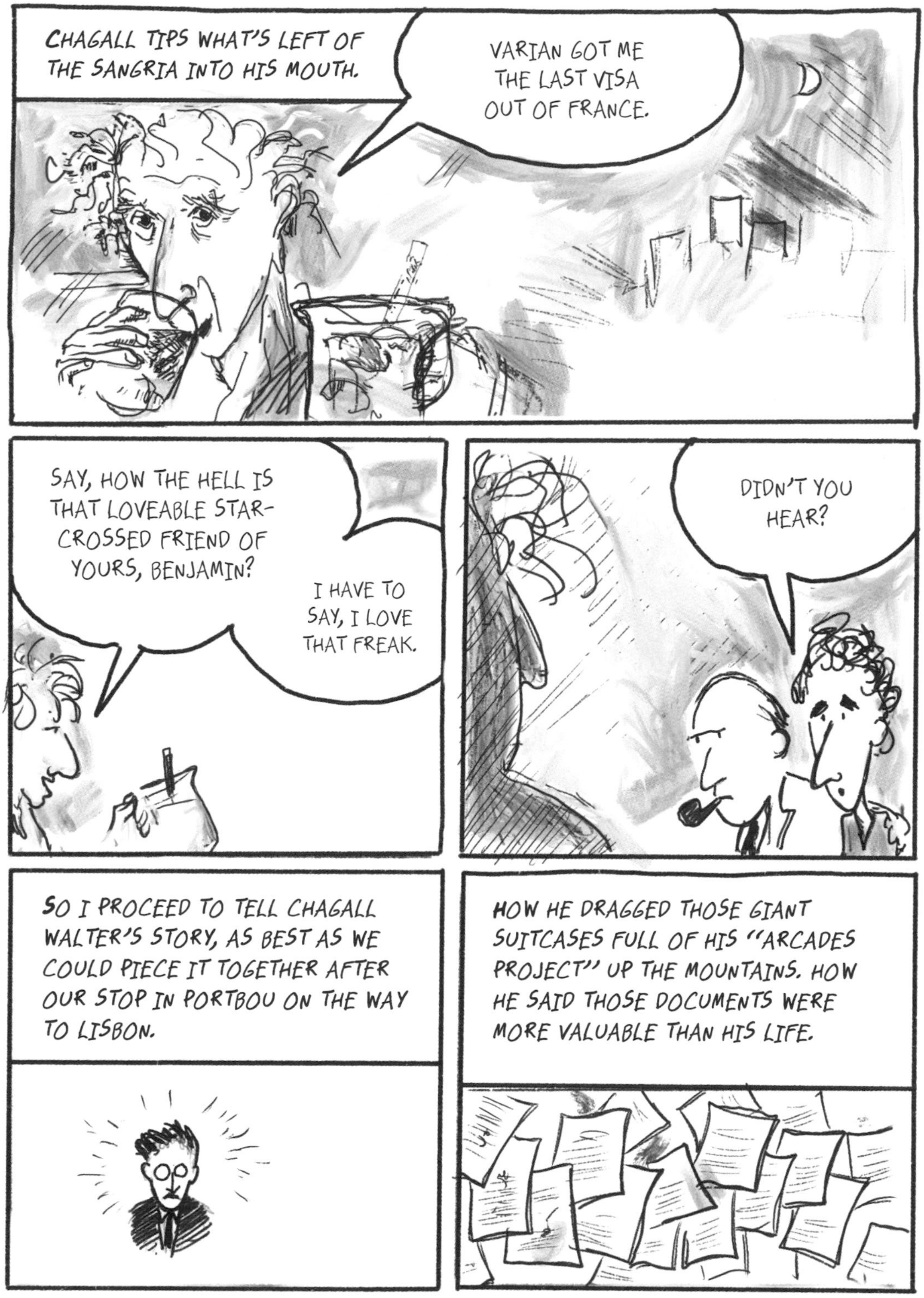
CHAGALL TIPS WHAT'S LEFT OF THE SANGRIA INTO HIS MOUTH.
VARIAN GOT ME THE LAST VISA OUT OF FRANCE.
SAY, HOW THE HELL IS THAT LOVEABLE STAR-CROSSED FRIEND OF YOURS, BENJAMIN?
I HAVE TO SAY, I LOVE THAT FREAK.
DIDN'T YOU HEAR?
SO I PROCEED TO TELL CHAGALL WALTER'S STORY, AS BEST AS WE COULD PIECE IT TOGETHER AFTER OUR STOP IN PORTBOU ON THE WAY TO LISBON.
HOW HE DRAGGED THOSE GIANT SUITCASES FULL OF HIS "ARCADES PROJECT" UP THE MOUNTAINS. HOW HE SAID THOSE DOCUMENTS WERE MORE VALUABLE THAN HIS LIFE.

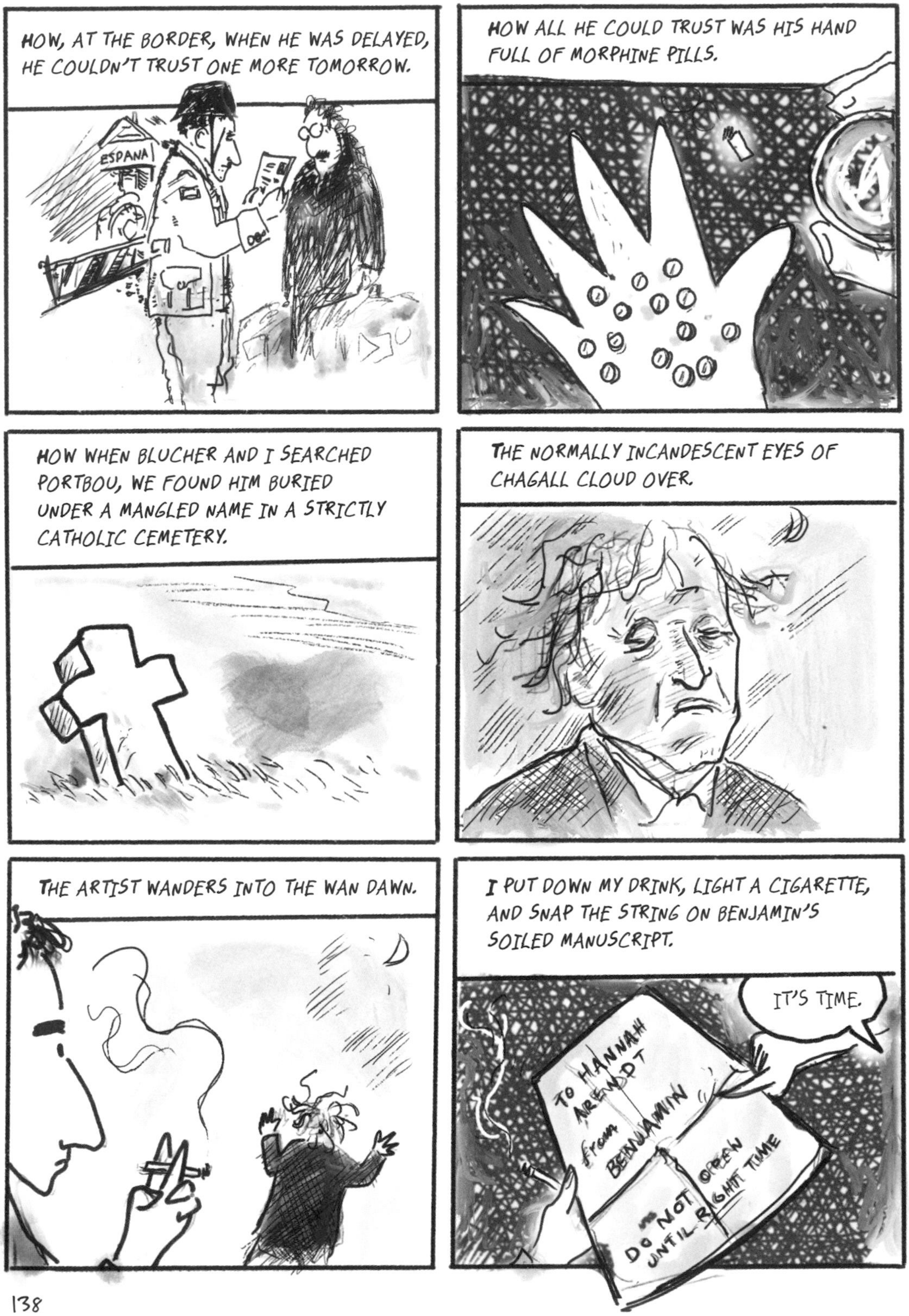
HOW, AT THE BORDER, WHEN HE WAS DELAYED, HE COULDN'T TRUST ONE MORE TOMORROW.
ESPANA
HOW ALL HE COULD TRUST WAS HIS HAND FULL OF MORPHINE PILLS.
HOW WHEN BLUCHER AND I SEARCHED PORTBOU, WE FOUND HIM BURIED UNDER A MANGLED NAME IN A STRICTLY CATHOLIC CEMETERY.
THE NORMALLY INCANDESCENT EYES OF CHAGALL CLOUD OVER.
THE ARTIST WANDERS INTO THE WAN DAWN.
I PUT DOWN MY DRINK, LIGHT A CIGARETTE, AND SNAP THE STRING ON BENJAMIN'S SOILED MANUSCRIPT.
IT'S TIME.
TO HANNAH ARENDT from BENJAMIN
DO NOT OPEN UNTIL RIGHT TIME

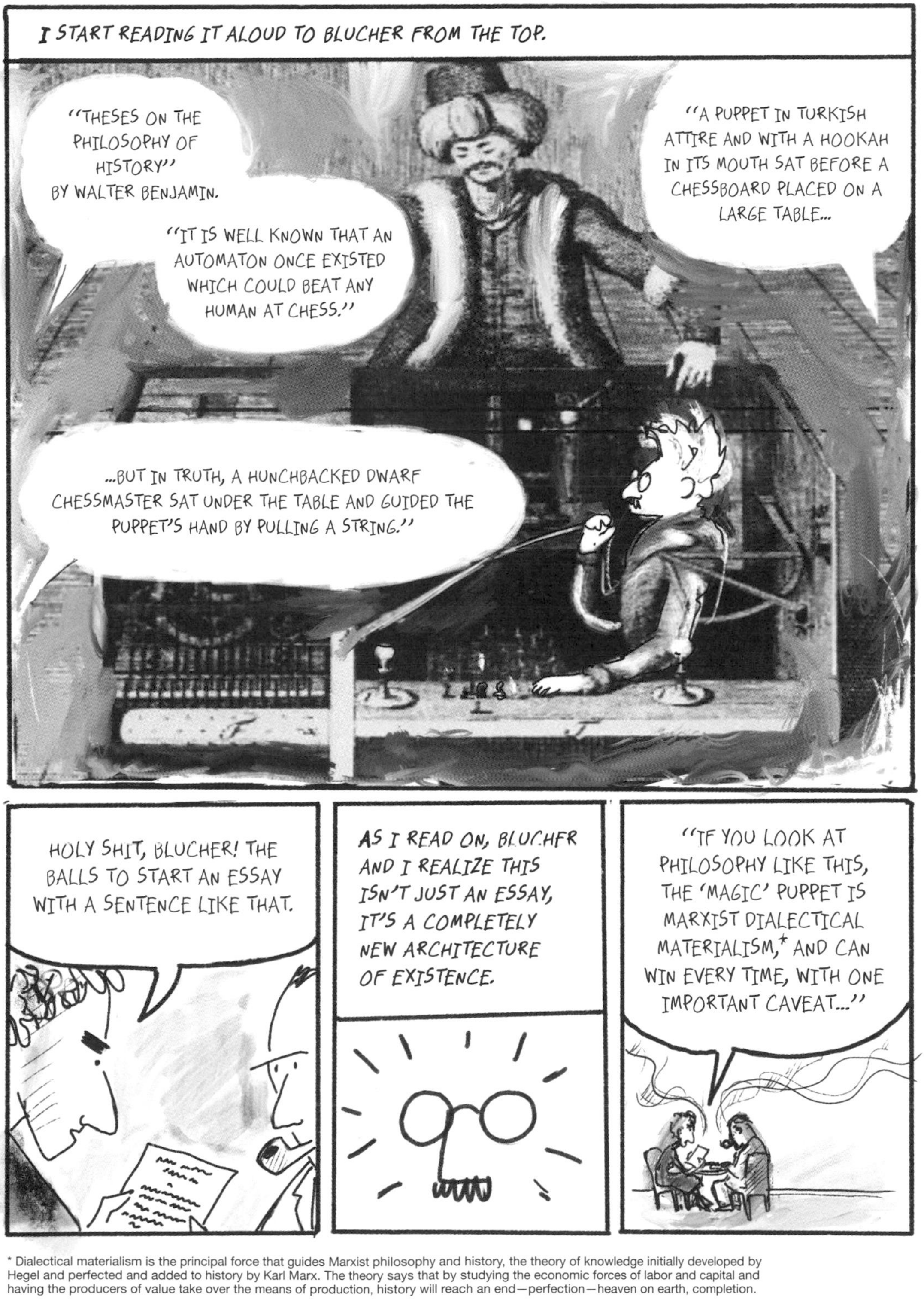
I START READING IT ALOUD TO BLUCHER FROM THE TOP.
"THESES ON THE PHILOSOPHY OF HISTORY" BY WALTER BENJAMIN.
"IT IS WELL KNOWN THAT AN AUTOMATON ONCE EXISTED WHICH COULD BEAT ANY HUMAN AT CHESS."
"A PUPPET IN TURKISH ATTIRE AND WITH A HOOKAH IN ITS MOUTH SAT BEFORE A CHESSBOARD PLACED ON A LARGE TABLE...
...BUT IN TRUTH, A HUNCHBACKED DWARF CHESSMASTER SAT UNDER THE TABLE AND GUIDED THE PUPPET'S HAND BY PULLING A STRING."
HOLY SHIT, BLUCHER! THE BALLS TO START AN ESSAY WITH A SENTENCE LIKE THAT.
AS I READ ON, BLUCHER AND I REALIZE THIS ISN'T JUST AN ESSAY, IT'S A COMPLETELY NEW ARCHITECTURE OF EXISTENCE.
"IF YOU LOOK AT PHILOSOPHY LIKE THIS, THE 'MAGIC' PUPPET IS MARXIST DIALECTICAL MATERIALISM,* AND CAN WIN EVERY TIME, WITH ONE IMPORTANT CAVEAT..."

* Dialectical materialism is the principal force that guides Marxist philosophy and history, the theory of knowledge initially developed by Hegel and perfected and added to history by Karl Marx. The theory says that by studying the economic forces of labor and capital and having the producers of value take over the means of production, history will reach an end—perfection—heaven on earth, completion.

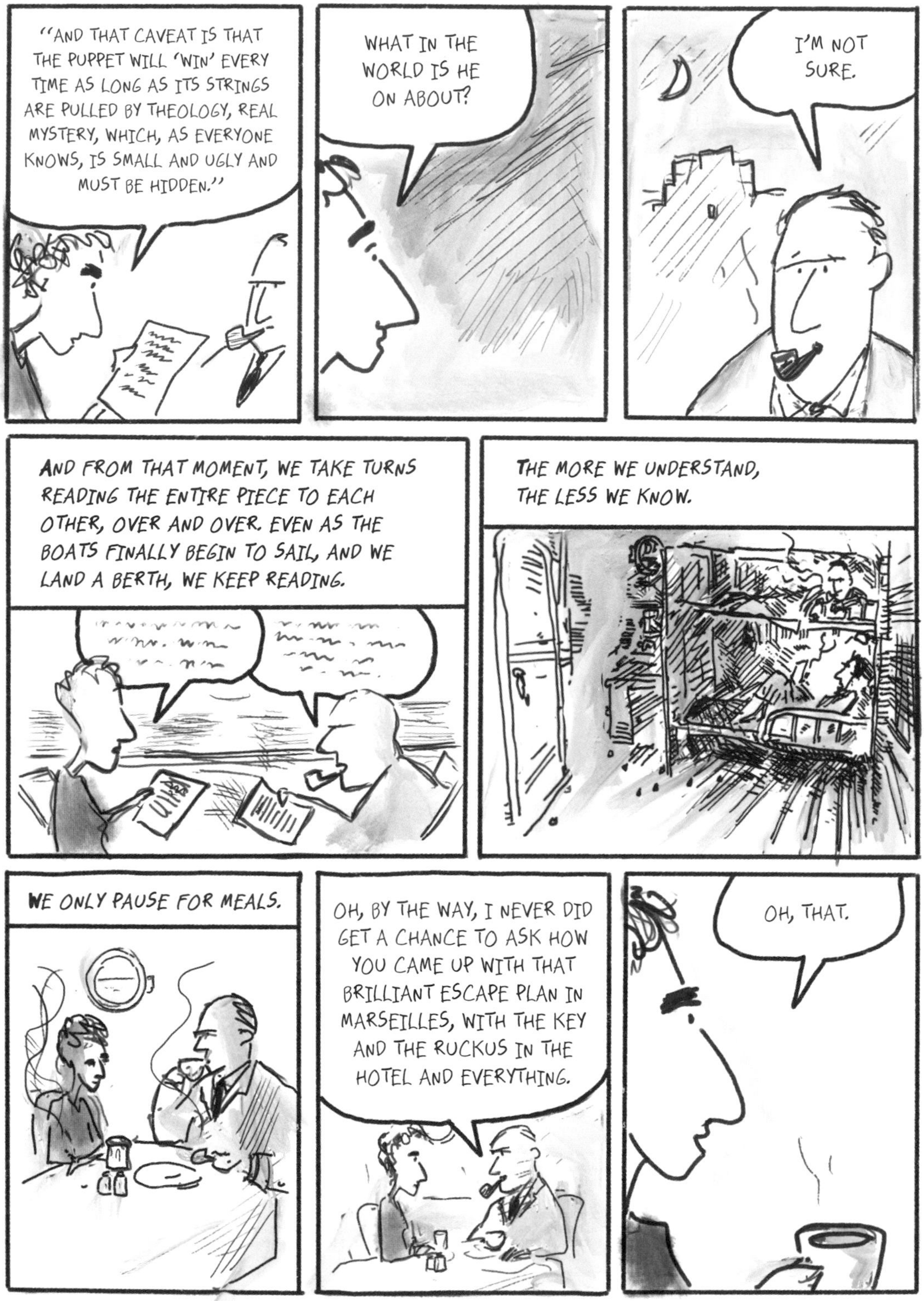
"AND THAT CAVEAT IS THAT THE PUPPET WILL 'WIN' EVERY TIME AS LONG AS ITS STRINGS ARE PULLED BY THEOLOGY, REAL MYSTERY, WHICH, AS EVERYONE KNOWS, IS SMALL AND UGLY AND MUST BE HIDDEN."
WHAT IN THE WORLD IS HE ON ABOUT?
I'M NOT SURE.
AND FROM THAT MOMENT, WE TAKE TURNS READING THE ENTIRE PIECE TO EACH OTHER, OVER AND OVER. EVEN AS THE BOATS FINALLY BEGIN TO SAIL, AND WE LAND A BERTH, WE KEEP READING.
THE MORE WE UNDERSTAND, THE LESS WE KNOW.
WE ONLY PAUSE FOR MEALS.
OH, BY THE WAY, I NEVER DID GET A CHANCE TO ASK HOW YOU CAME UP WITH THAT BRILLIANT ESCAPE PLAN IN MARSEILLES, WITH THE KEY AND THE RUCKUS IN THE HOTEL AND EVERYTHING.
OH, THAT.

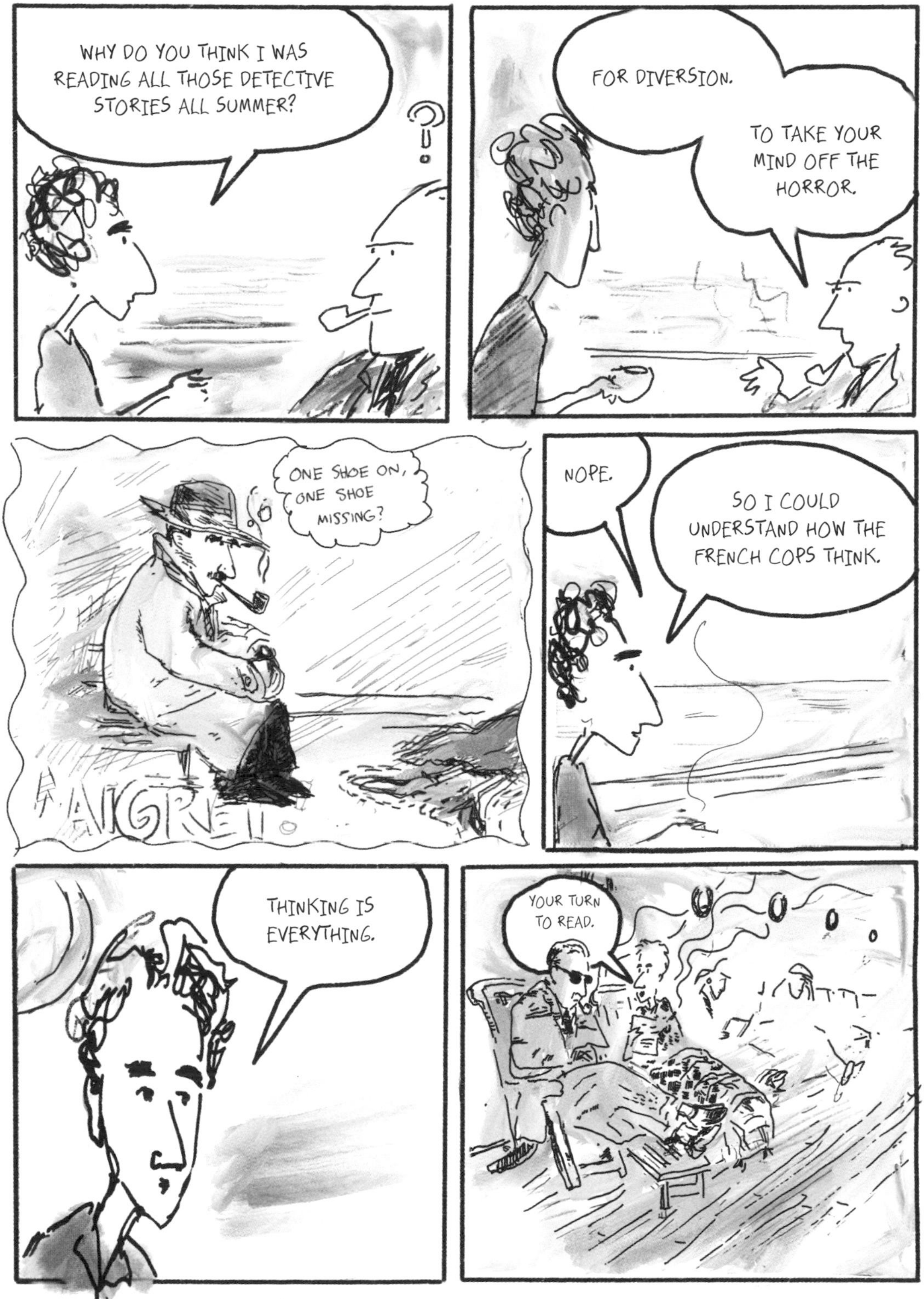
WHY DO YOU THINK I WAS READING ALL THOSE DETECTIVE STORIES ALL SUMMER?
FOR DIVERSION.
TO TAKE YOUR MIND OFF THE HORROR.
ONE SHOE ON, ONE SHOE MISSING?
NOPE.
SO I COULD UNDERSTAND HOW THE FRENCH COPS THINK.
THINKING IS EVERYTHING.
YOUR TURN TO READ.

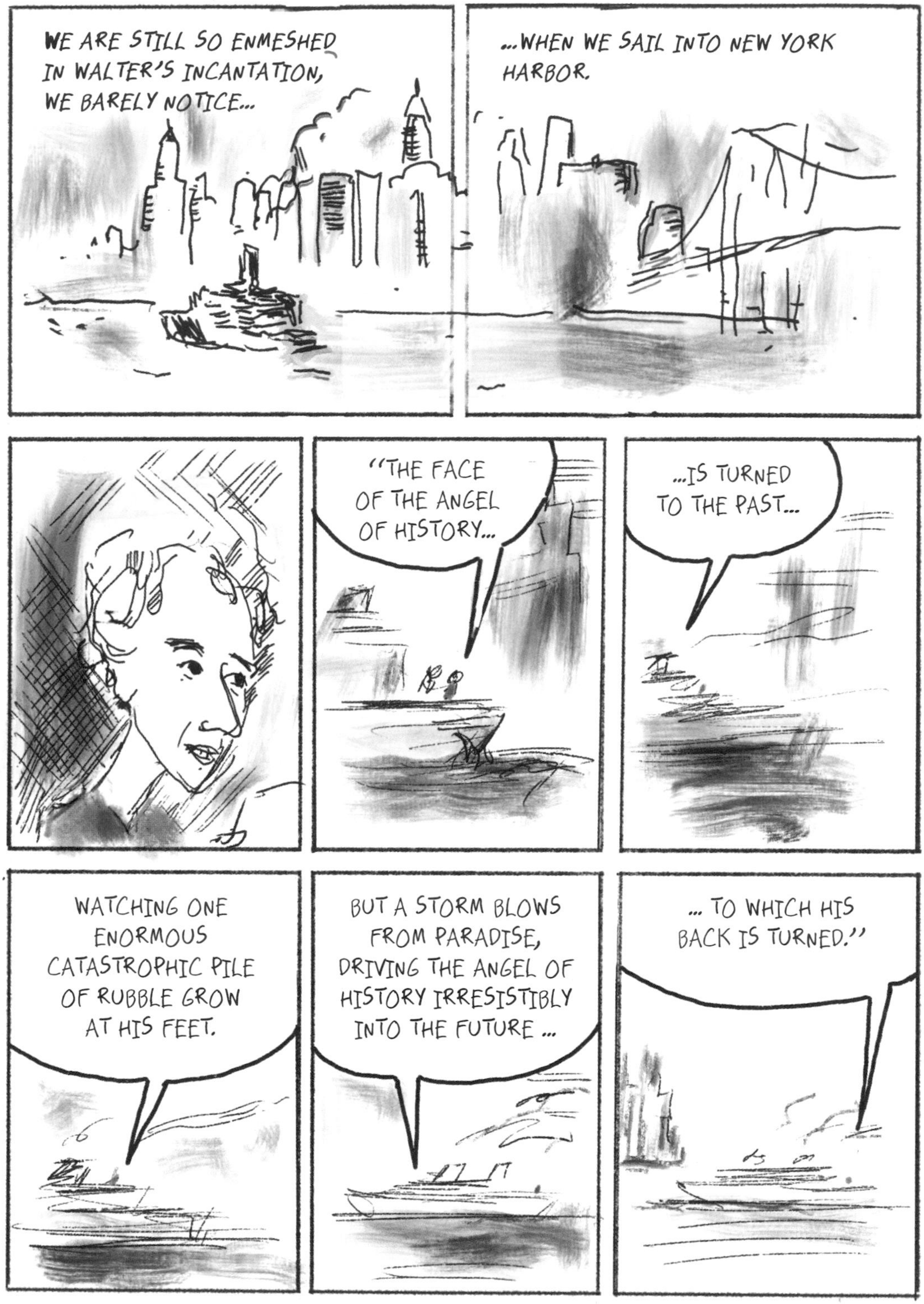
WE ARE STILL SO ENMESHED IN WALTER'S INCANTATION, WE BARELY NOTICE...
...WHEN WE SAIL INTO NEW YORK HARBOR.
"THE FACE OF THE ANGEL OF HISTORY...
...IS TURNED TO THE PAST...
WATCHING ONE ENORMOUS CATASTROPHIC PILE OF RUBBLE GROW AT HIS FEET.
BUT A STORM BLOWS FROM PARADISE, DRIVING THE ANGEL OF HISTORY IRRESISTIBLY INTO THE FUTURE ...
... TO WHICH HIS BACK IS TURNED."

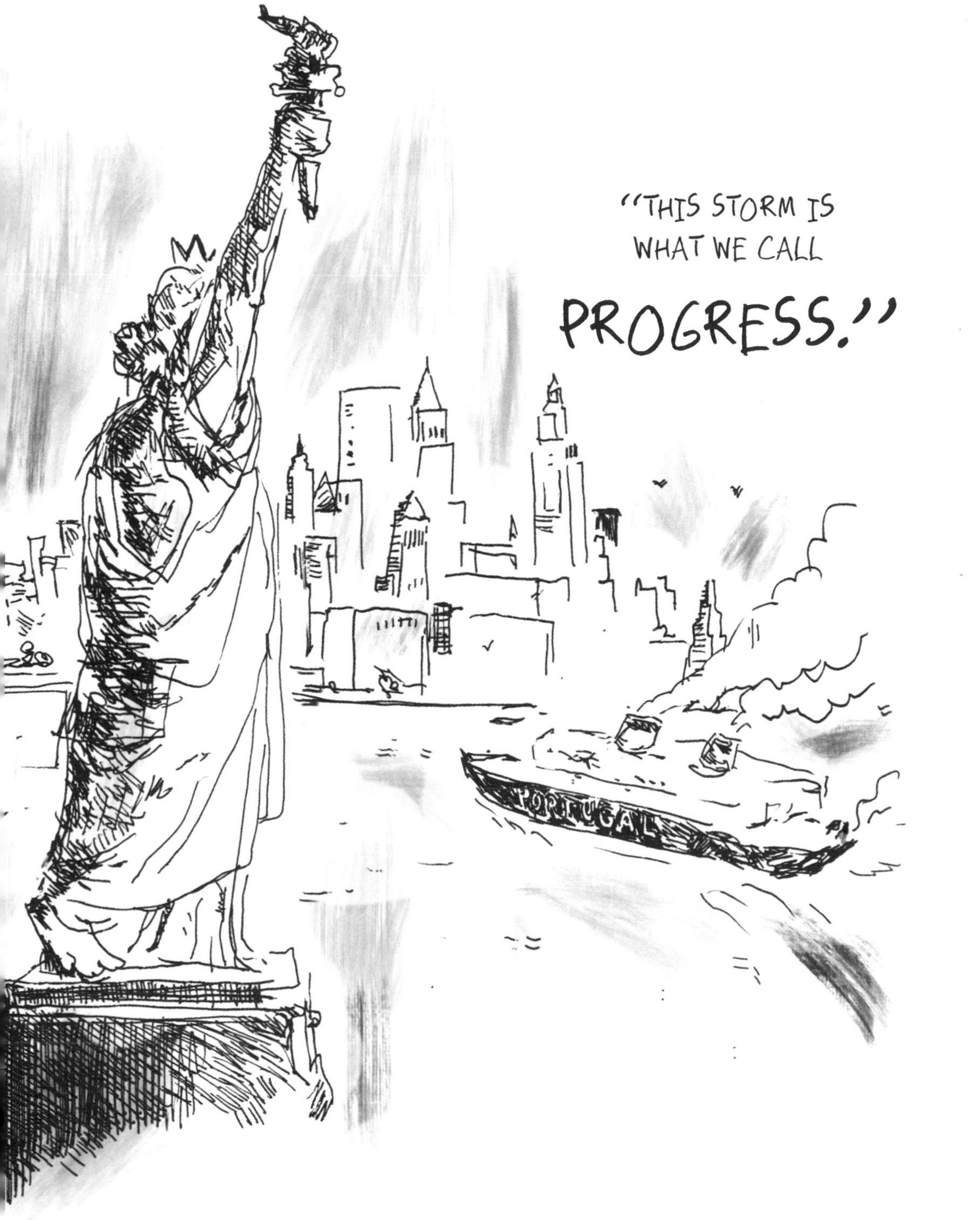
"THIS STORM IS WHAT WE CALL PROGRESS."
PORTUGAL

Hannah's Third Escape

New York

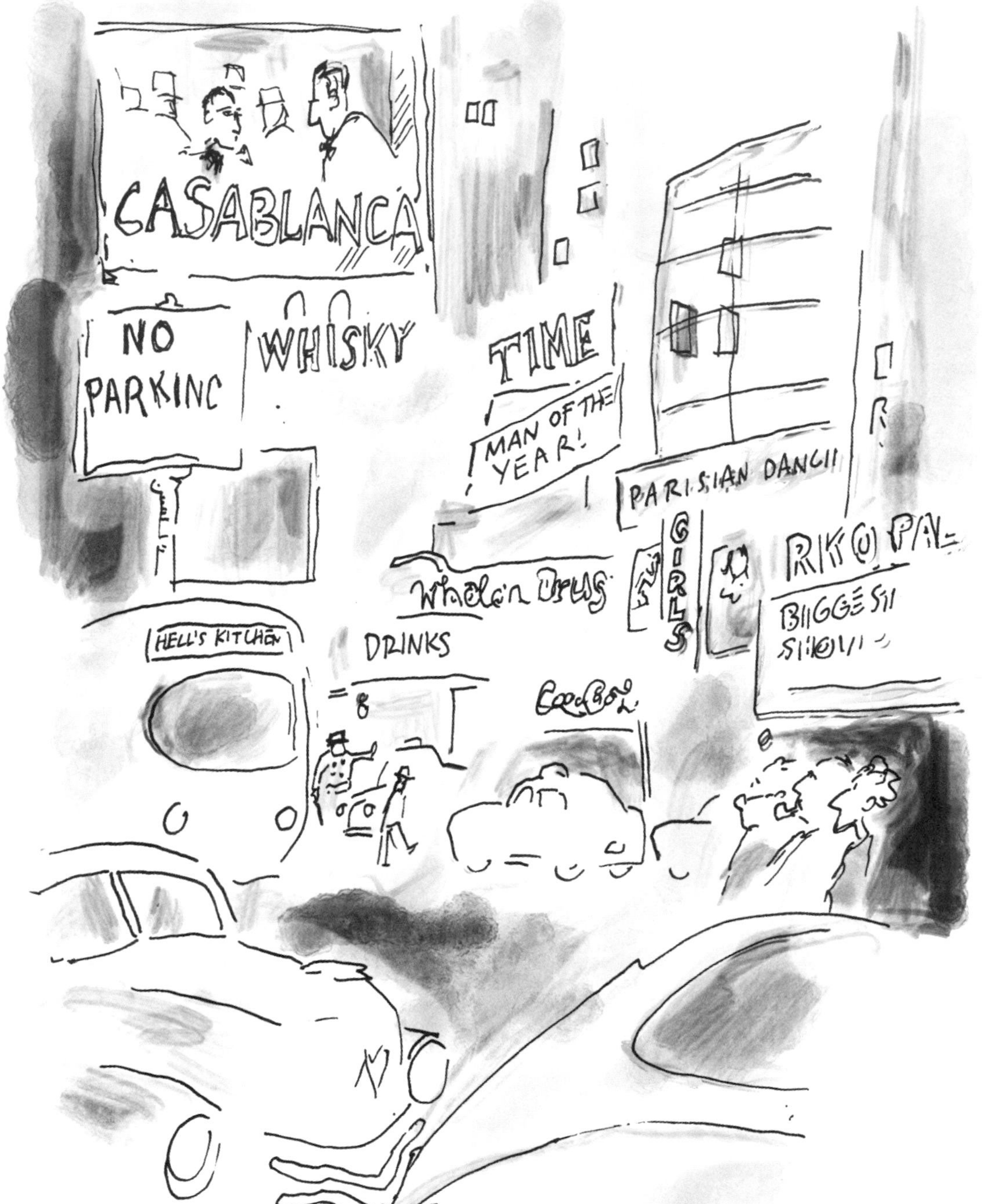
CASABLANCA
NO PARKINC
WHISKY
TIME
MAN OF THE YEAR!
PARISIAN DANC
GIRLS
RKO PAL
BIGGEST SHOW
Whelan Drugs
HELL'S KITCHEN
DRINKS

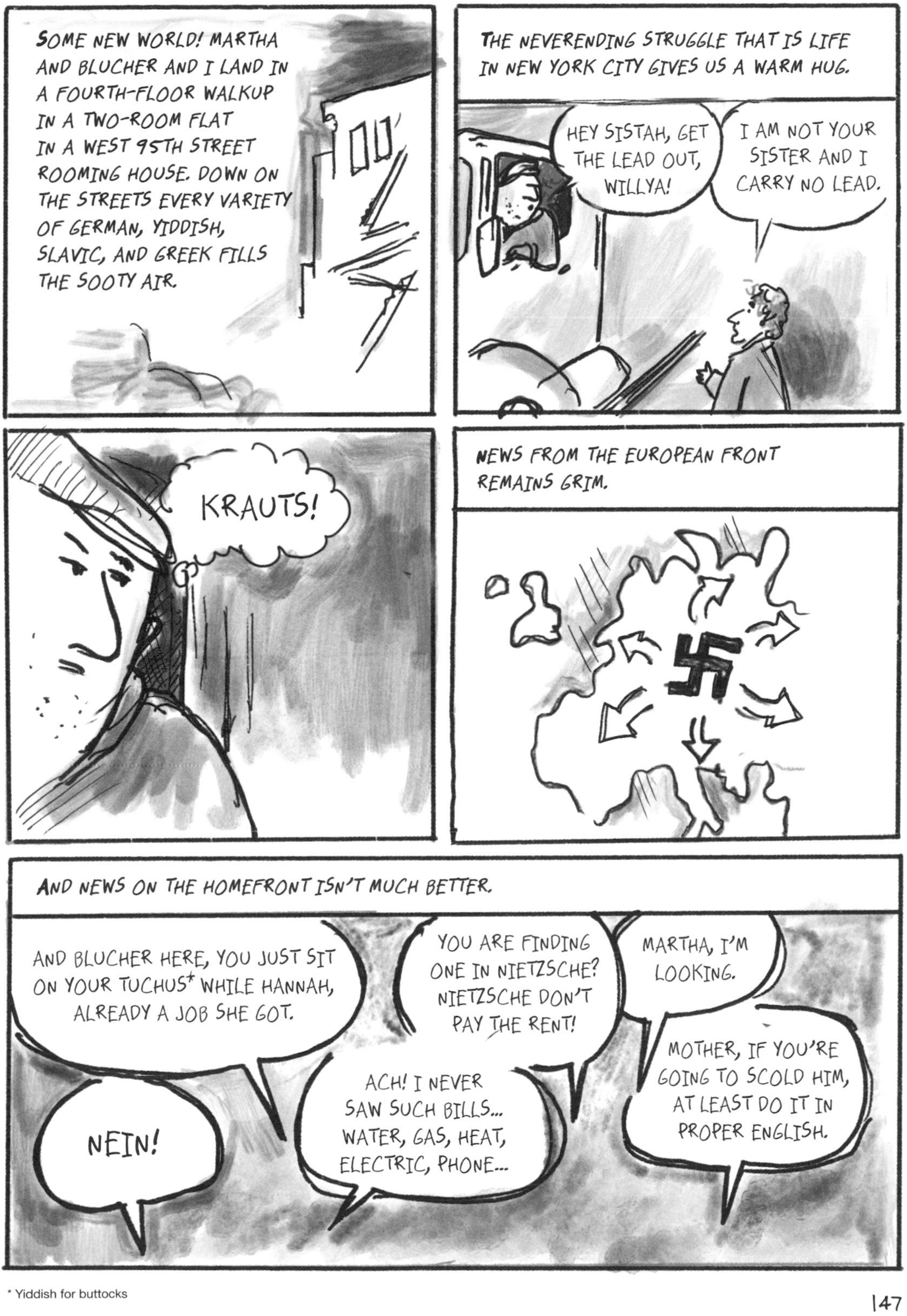
SOME NEW WORLD! MARTHA AND BLUCHER AND I LAND IN A FOURTH-FLOOR WALKUP IN A TWO-ROOM FLAT IN A WEST 95TH STREET ROOMING HOUSE. DOWN ON THE STREETS EVERY VARIETY OF GERMAN, YIDDISH, SLAVIC, AND GREEK FILLS THE SOOTY AIR.
THE NEVERENDING STRUGGLE THAT IS LIFE IN NEW YORK CITY GIVES US A WARM HUG.
HEY SISTAH, GET THE LEAD OUT, WILLYA!
I AM NOT YOUR SISTER AND I CARRY NO LEAD.
KRAUTS!
NEWS FROM THE EUROPEAN FRONT REMAINS GRIM.
AND NEWS ON THE HOMEFRONT ISN'T MUCH BETTER.
AND BLUCHER HERE, YOU JUST SIT ON YOUR TUCHUS* WHILE HANNAH, ALREADY A JOB SHE GOT.
NEIN!
YOU ARE FINDING ONE IN NIETZSCHE? NIETZSCHE DON'T PAY THE RENT!
ACH! I NEVER SAW SUCH BILLS... WATER, GAS, HEAT, ELECTRIC, PHONE...
MARTHA, I'M LOOKING.
MOTHER, IF YOU'RE GOING TO SCOLD HIM, AT LEAST DO IT IN PROPER ENGLISH.

* Yiddish for buttocks

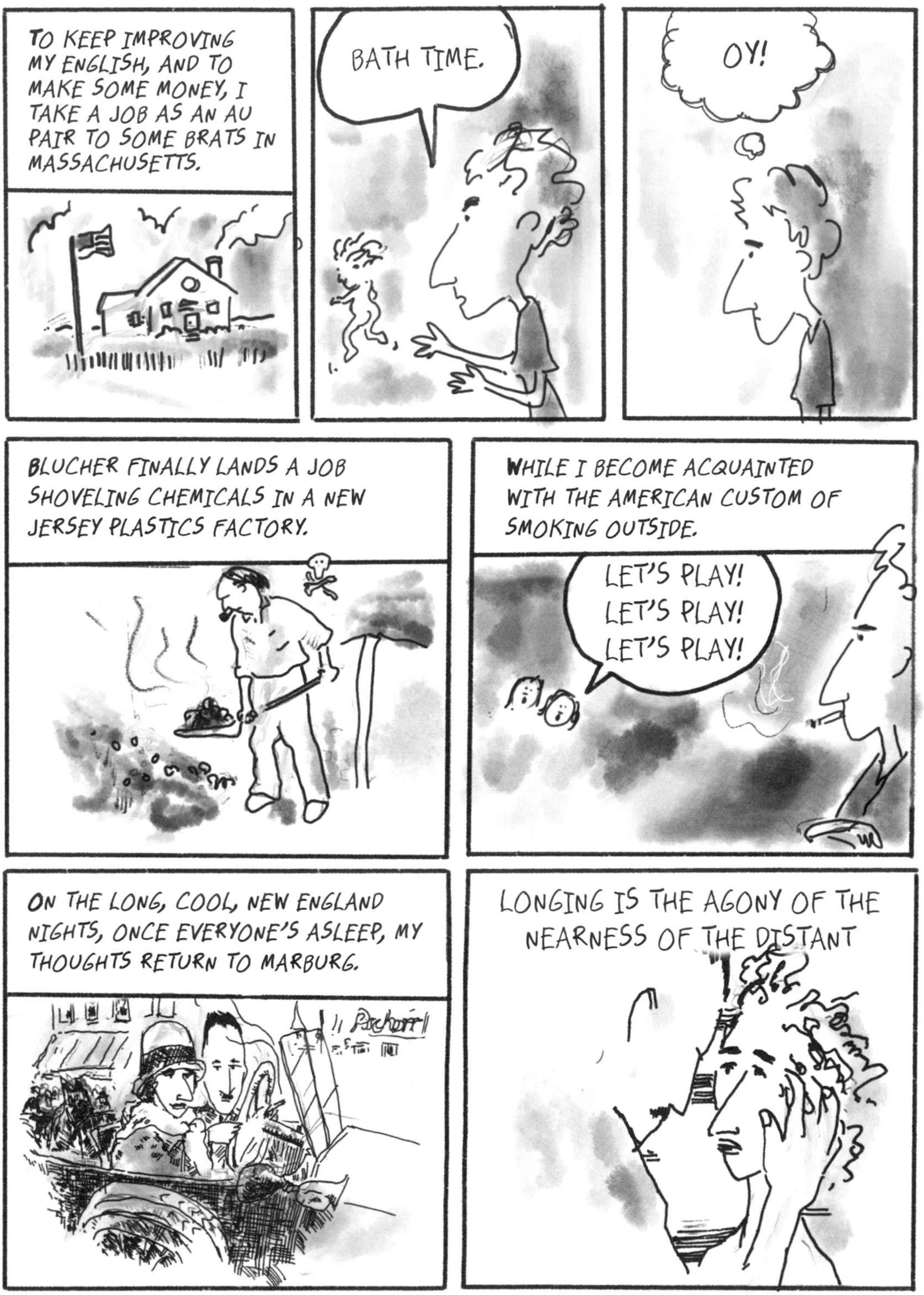
TO KEEP IMPROVING MY ENGLISH, AND TO MAKE SOME MONEY, I TAKE A JOB AS AN AU PAIR TO SOME BRATS IN MASSACHUSETTS.
BATH TIME.
OY!
BLUCHER FINALLY LANDS A JOB SHOVELING CHEMICALS IN A NEW JERSEY PLASTICS FACTORY.
WHILE I BECOME ACQUAINTED WITH THE AMERICAN CUSTOM OF SMOKING OUTSIDE.
LET'S PLAY! LET'S PLAY! LET'S PLAY!
ON THE LONG, COOL, NEW ENGLAND NIGHTS, ONCE EVERYONE'S ASLEEP, MY THOUGHTS RETURN TO MARBURG.
LONGING IS THE AGONY OF THE NEARNESS OF THE DISTANT

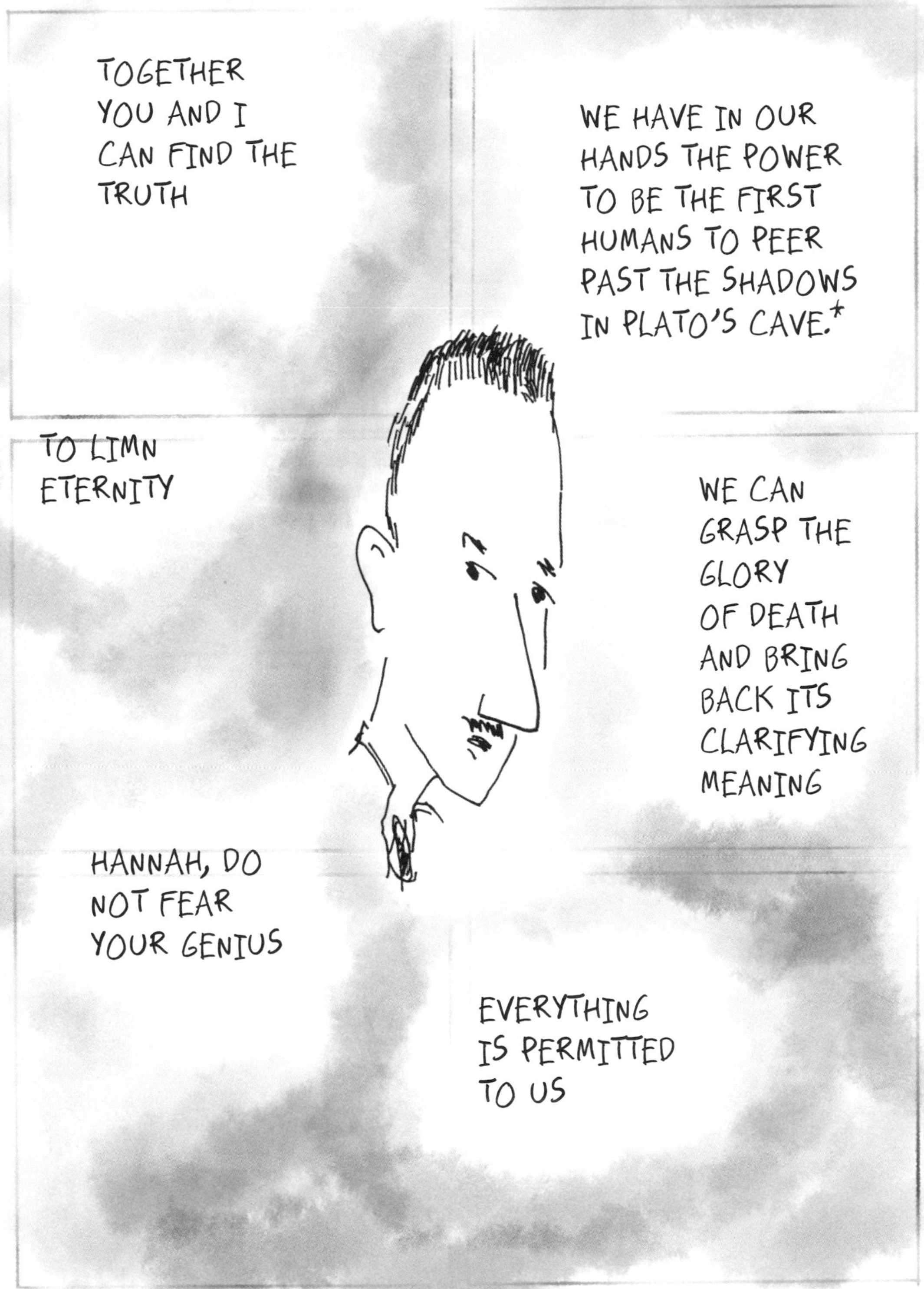
TOGETHER YOU AND I CAN FIND THE TRUTH
WE HAVE IN OUR HANDS THE POWER TO BE THE FIRST HUMANS TO PEER PAST THE SHADOWS IN PLATO'S CAVE.*
TO LIMN ETERNITY
WE CAN GRASP THE GLORY OF DEATH AND BRING BACK ITS CLARIFYING MEANING
HANNAH, DO NOT FEAR YOUR GENIUS
EVERYTHING IS PERMITTED TO US

* A story wherein Plato describes how all we can "see" of ultimate reality are the shadows cast by the true "forms" of existence. In other words, we, in this life, are basically many, many steps removed from the Truth with a capital *T*.

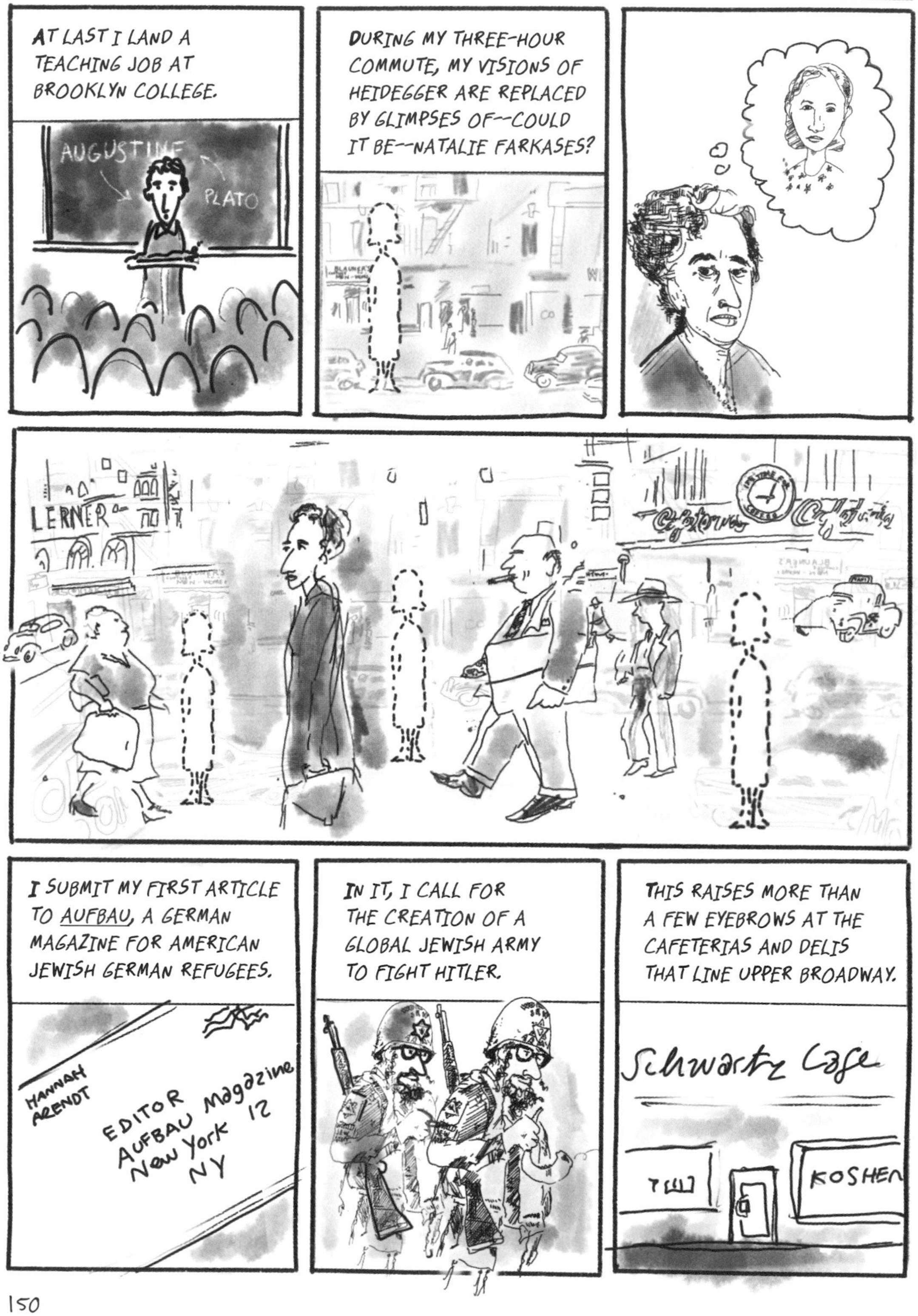
AT LAST I LAND A TEACHING JOB AT BROOKLYN COLLEGE.
AUGUSTINE
PLATO
DURING MY THREE-HOUR COMMUTE, MY VISIONS OF HEIDEGGER ARE REPLACED BY GLIMPSES OF--COULD IT BE--NATALIE FARKASES?
LERNER
I SUBMIT MY FIRST ARTICLE TO AUFBAU, A GERMAN MAGAZINE FOR AMERICAN JEWISH GERMAN REFUGEES.
HANNAH ARENDT
EDITOR
AUFBAU Magazine
New York 12
NY
IN IT, I CALL FOR THE CREATION OF A GLOBAL JEWISH ARMY TO FIGHT HITLER.
THIS RAISES MORE THAN A FEW EYEBROWS AT THE CAFETERIAS AND DELIS THAT LINE UPPER BROADWAY.
Schwartz Cafe

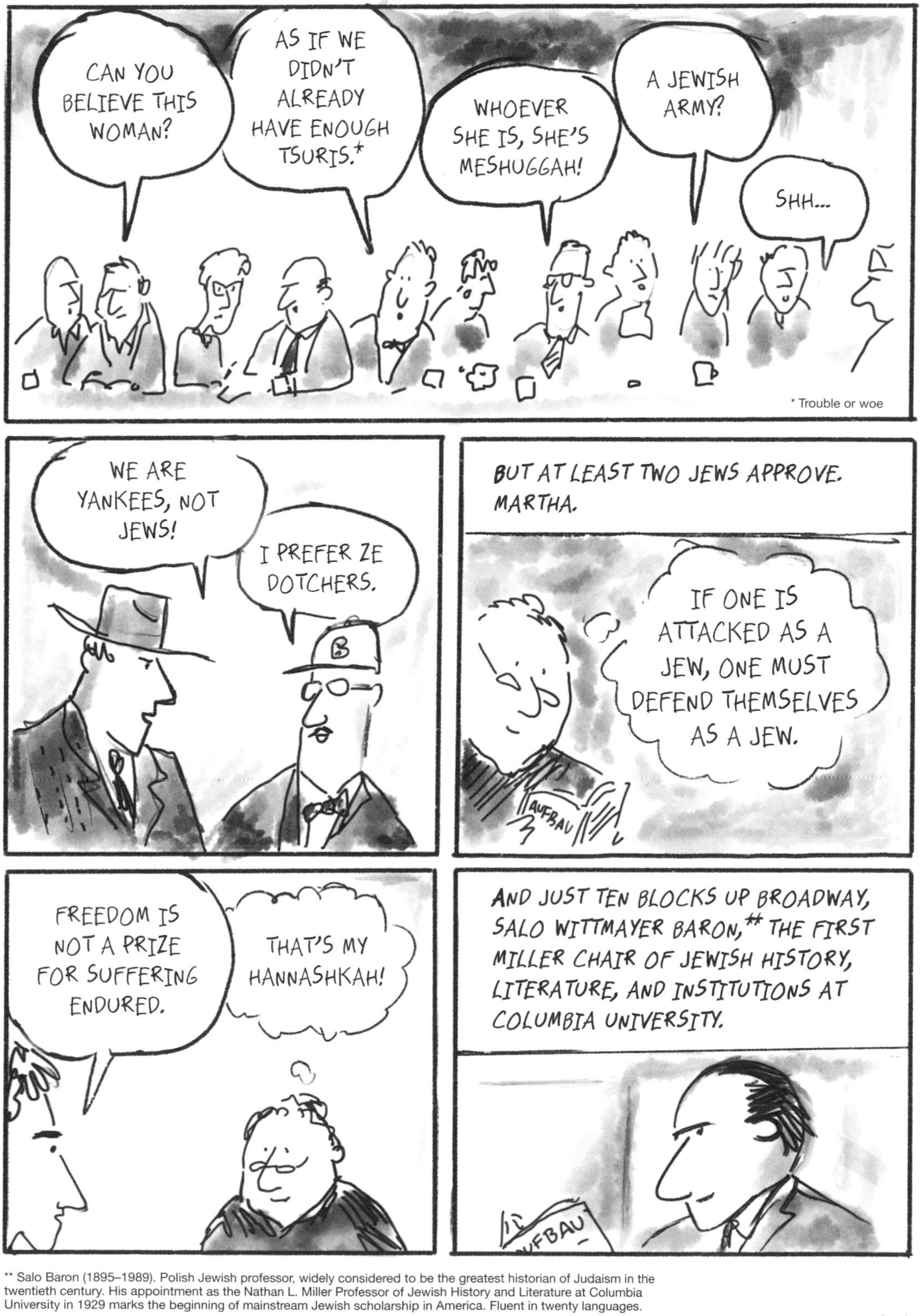
CAN YOU BELIEVE THIS WOMAN?
AS IF WE DIDN'T ALREADY HAVE ENOUGH TSURIS.*
WHOEVER SHE IS, SHE'S MESHUGGAH!
A JEWISH ARMY?
SHH...
WE ARE YANKEES, NOT JEWS!
I PREFER ZE DOTCHERS.
BUT AT LEAST TWO JEWS APPROVE. MARTHA.
IF ONE IS ATTACKED AS A JEW, ONE MUST DEFEND THEMSELVES AS A JEW.
AUFBAU
FREEDOM IS NOT A PRIZE FOR SUFFERING ENDURED.
THAT'S MY HANNASHKAH!
AND JUST TEN BLOCKS UP BROADWAY, SALO WITTMAYER BARON,** THE FIRST MILLER CHAIR OF JEWISH HISTORY, LITERATURE, AND INSTITUTIONS AT COLUMBIA UNIVERSITY.
AUFBAU

* Trouble or woe

** Salo Baron (1895–1989). Polish Jewish professor, widely considered to be the greatest historian of Judaism in the twentieth century. His appointment as the Nathan L. Miller Professor of Jewish History and Literature at Columbia University in 1929 marks the beginning of mainstream Jewish scholarship in America. Fluent in twenty languages.

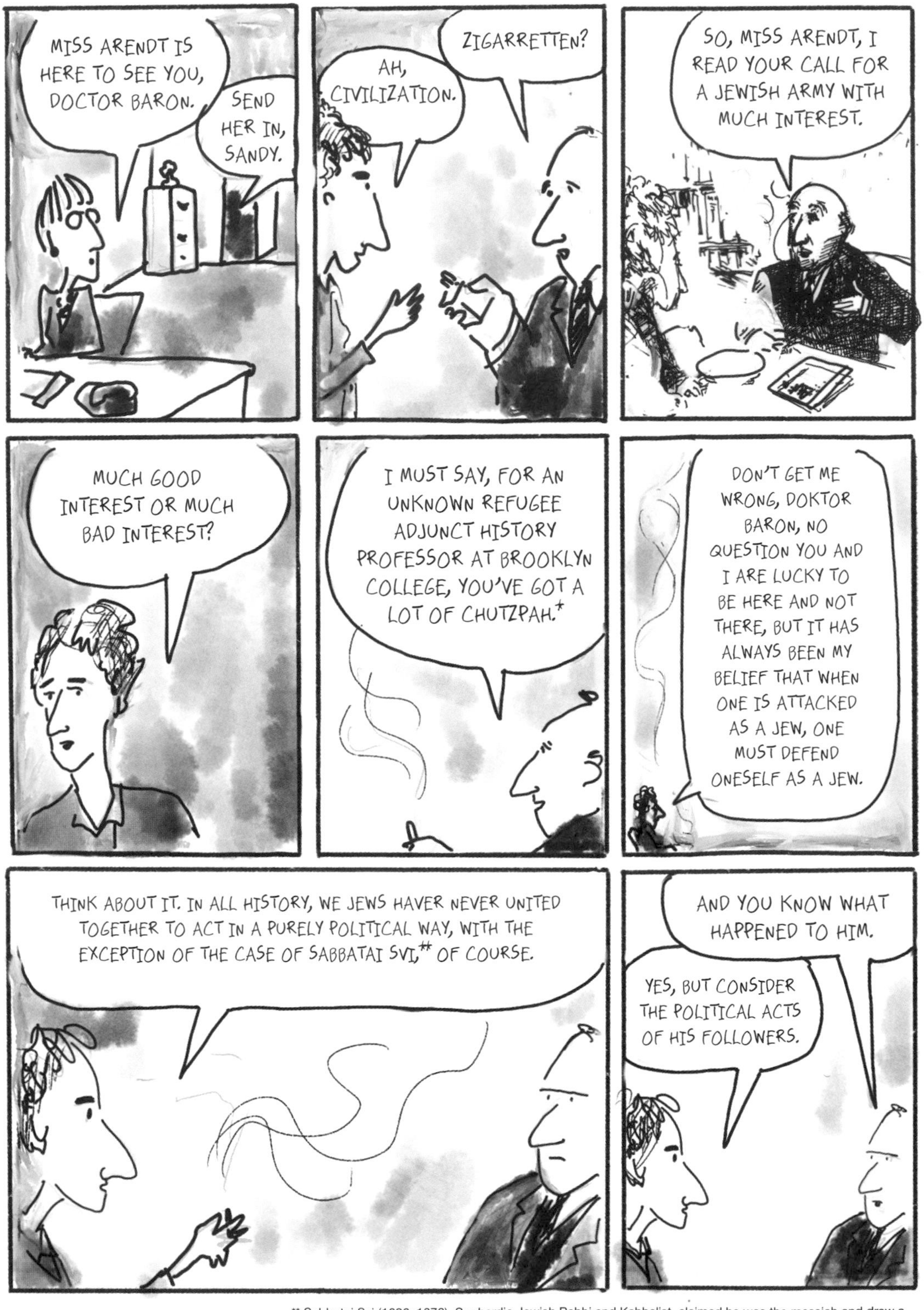
MISS ARENDT IS HERE TO SEE YOU, DOCTOR BARON.
SEND HER IN, SANDY.
ZIGARRETTEN?
AH, CIVILIZATION.
SO, MISS ARENDT, I READ YOUR CALL FOR A JEWISH ARMY WITH MUCH INTEREST.
MUCH GOOD INTEREST OR MUCH BAD INTEREST?
I MUST SAY, FOR AN UNKNOWN REFUGEE ADJUNCT HISTORY PROFESSOR AT BROOKLYN COLLEGE, YOU'VE GOT A LOT OF CHUTZPAH.*
DON'T GET ME WRONG, DOKTOR BARON, NO QUESTION YOU AND I ARE LUCKY TO BE HERE AND NOT THERE, BUT IT HAS ALWAYS BEEN MY BELIEF THAT WHEN ONE IS ATTACKED AS A JEW, ONE MUST DEFEND ONESELF AS A JEW.
THINK ABOUT IT. IN ALL HISTORY, WE JEWS HAVER NEVER UNITED TOGETHER TO ACT IN A PURELY POLITICAL WAY, WITH THE EXCEPTION OF THE CASE OF SABBATAI SVI,** OF COURSE.
AND YOU KNOW WHAT HAPPENED TO HIM.
YES, BUT CONSIDER THE POLITICAL ACTS OF HIS FOLLOWERS.

* Yiddish for audacious confidence, best described by the story about the guy who

** Sabbatai Svi (1626–1676). Sephardic Jewish Rabbi and Kabbalist, claimed he was the messiah and drew a massive, transnational following, until threat of execution by a doubting caliph spurred his conversion to Islam.

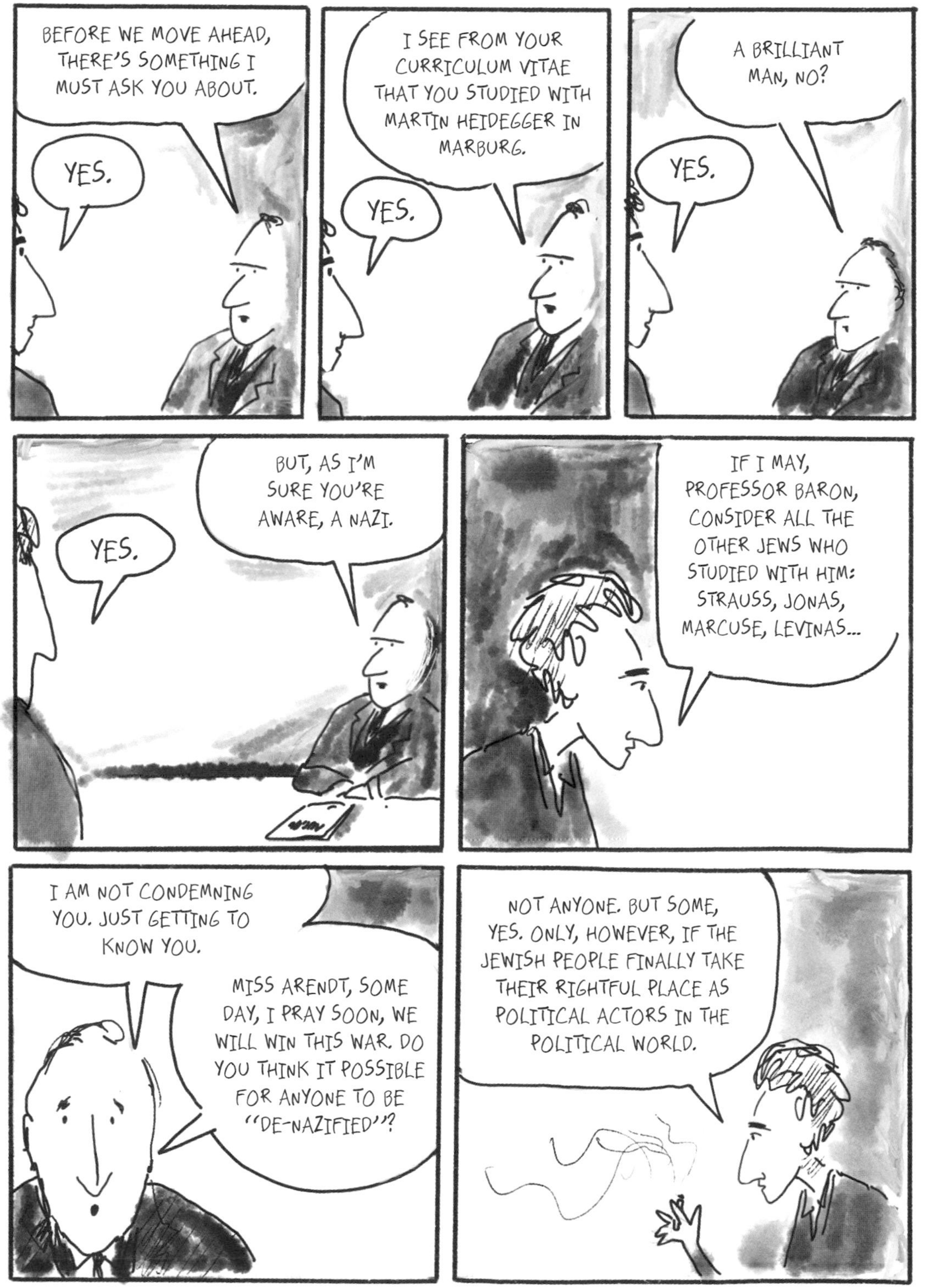

BEFORE WE MOVE AHEAD, THERE'S SOMETHING I MUST ASK YOU ABOUT.
YES.
I SEE FROM YOUR CURRICULUM VITAE THAT YOU STUDIED WITH MARTIN HEIDEGGER IN MARBURG.
YES.
A BRILLIANT MAN, NO?
YES.
BUT, AS I'M SURE YOU'RE AWARE, A NAZI.
YES.
IF I MAY, PROFESSOR BARON, CONSIDER ALL THE OTHER JEWS WHO STUDIED WITH HIM: STRAUSS, JONAS, MARCUSE, LEVINAS...
I AM NOT CONDEMNING YOU. JUST GETTING TO KNOW YOU.
MISS ARENDT, SOME DAY, I PRAY SOON, WE WILL WIN THIS WAR. DO YOU THINK IT POSSIBLE FOR ANYONE TO BE "DE-NAZIFIED"?
NOT ANYONE. BUT SOME, YES. ONLY, HOWEVER, IF THE JEWISH PEOPLE FINALLY TAKE THEIR RIGHTFUL PLACE AS POLITICAL ACTORS IN THE POLITICAL WORLD.

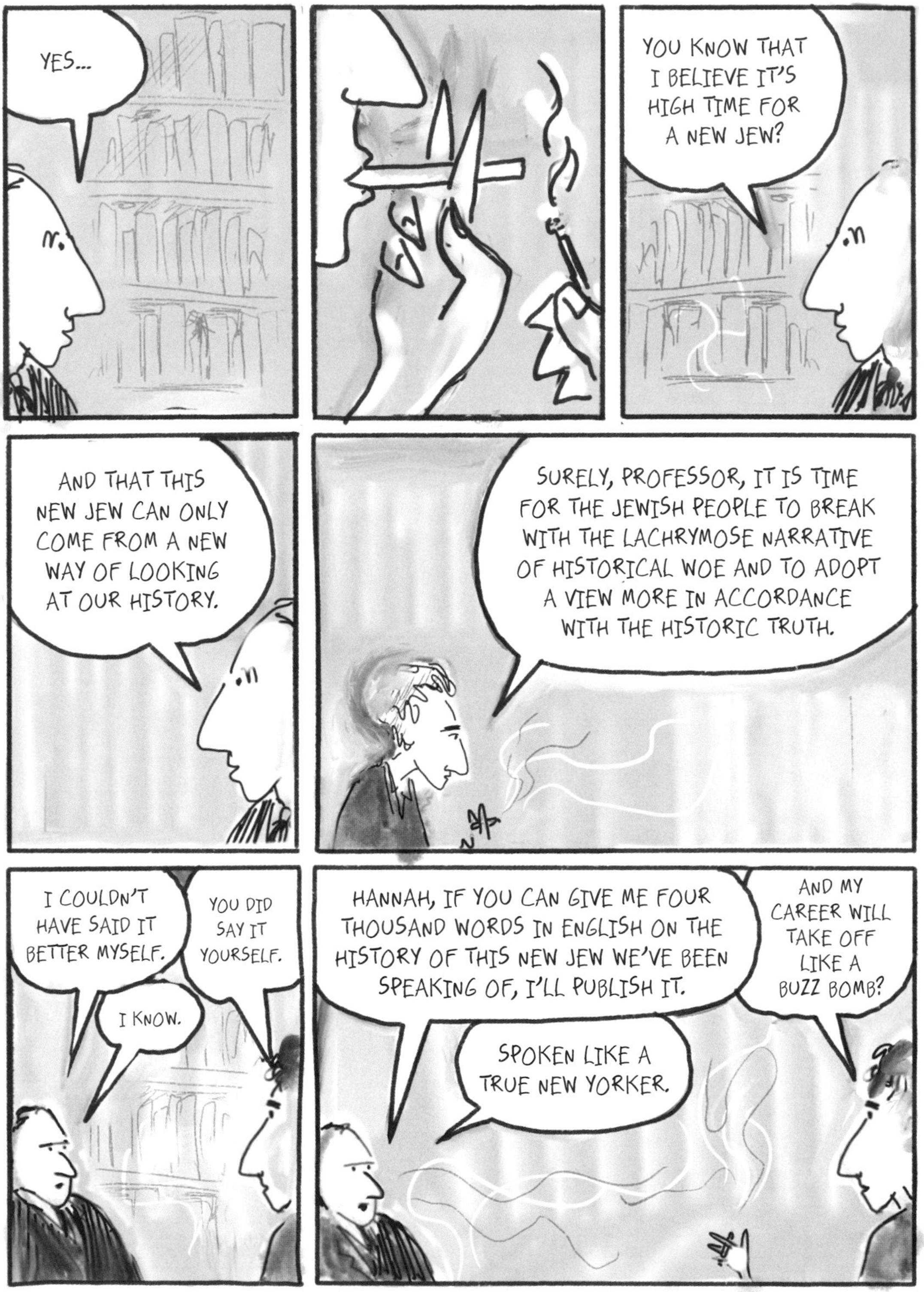
YES...
YOU KNOW THAT I BELIEVE IT'S HIGH TIME FOR A NEW JEW?
AND THAT THIS NEW JEW CAN ONLY COME FROM A NEW WAY OF LOOKING AT OUR HISTORY.
SURELY, PROFESSOR, IT IS TIME FOR THE JEWISH PEOPLE TO BREAK WITH THE LACHRYMOSE NARRATIVE OF HISTORICAL WOE AND TO ADOPT A VIEW MORE IN ACCORDANCE WITH THE HISTORIC TRUTH.
I COULDN'T HAVE SAID IT BETTER MYSELF.
YOU DID SAY IT YOURSELF.
I KNOW.
HANNAH, IF YOU CAN GIVE ME FOUR THOUSAND WORDS IN ENGLISH ON THE HISTORY OF THIS NEW JEW WE'VE BEEN SPEAKING OF, I'LL PUBLISH IT.
AND MY CAREER WILL TAKE OFF LIKE A BUZZ BOMB?
SPOKEN LIKE A TRUE NEW YORKER.

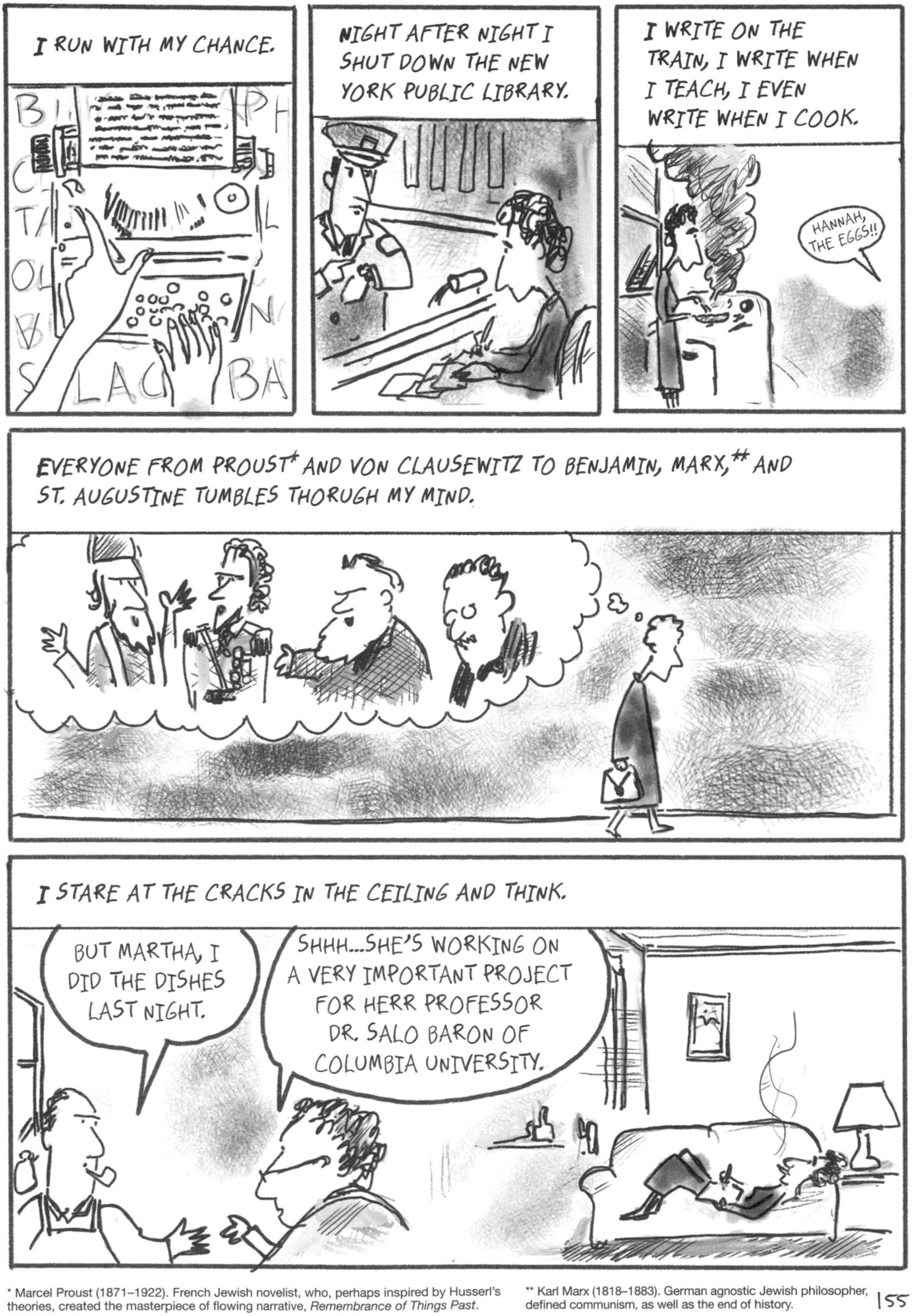
I RUN WITH MY CHANCE.
NIGHT AFTER NIGHT I SHUT DOWN THE NEW YORK PUBLIC LIBRARY.
I WRITE ON THE TRAIN, I WRITE WHEN I TEACH, I EVEN WRITE WHEN I COOK.
HANNAH, THE EGGS!!
EVERYONE FROM PROUST* AND VON CLAUSEWITZ TO BENJAMIN, MARX,** AND ST. AUGUSTINE TUMBLES THORUGH MY MIND.
I STARE AT THE CRACKS IN THE CEILING AND THINK.
BUT MARTHA, I DID THE DISHES LAST NIGHT.
SHHH...SHE'S WORKING ON A VERY IMPORTANT PROJECT FOR HERR PROFESSOR DR. SALO BARON OF COLUMBIA UNIVERSITY.

* Marcel Proust (1871–1922). French Jewish novelist, who, perhaps inspired by Husserl's theories, created the masterpiece of flowing narrative, *Remembrance of Things Past*.

** Karl Marx (1818–1883). German agnostic Jewish philosopher, defined communism, as well as the end of history.

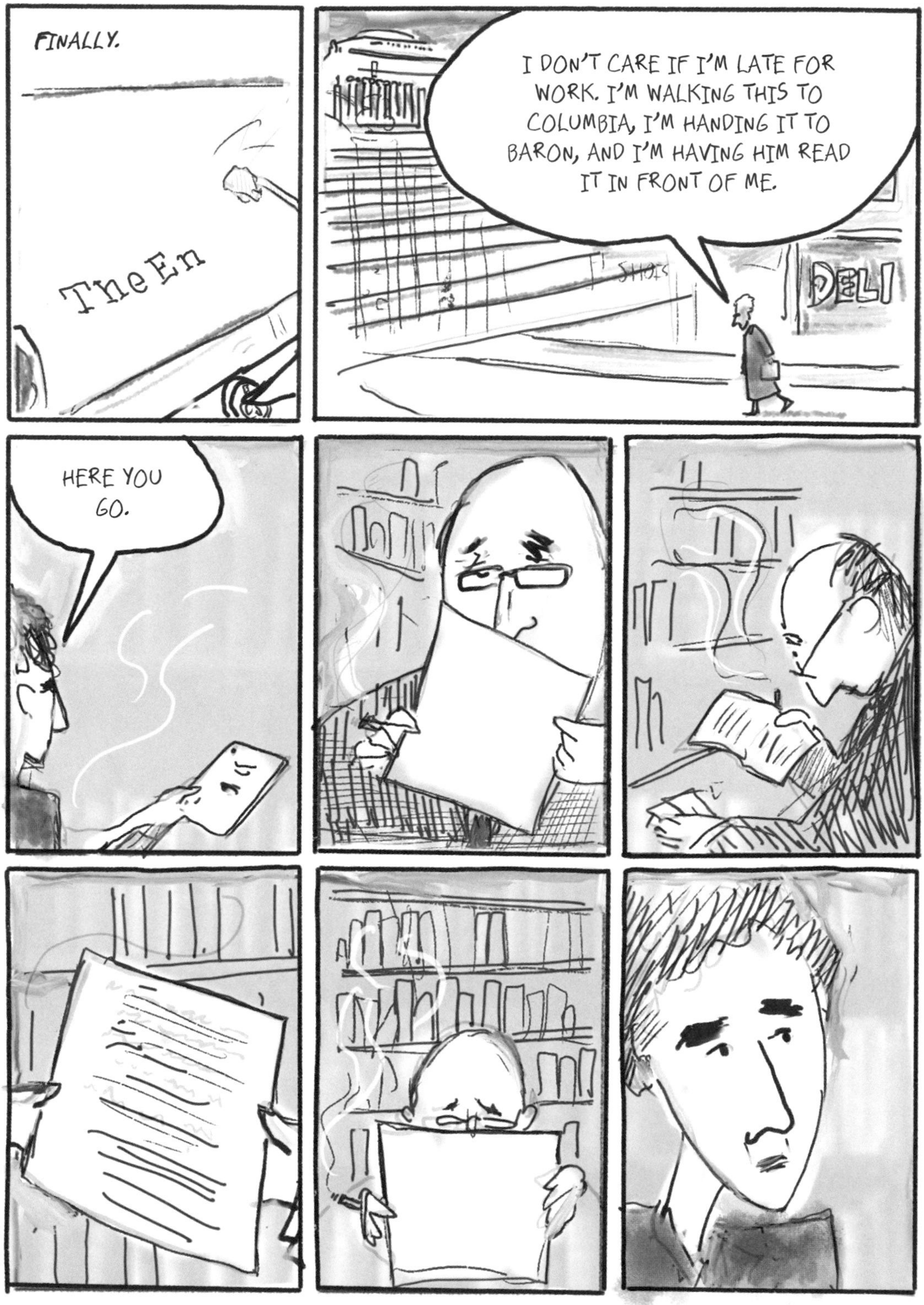
FINALLY.
The En
I DON'T CARE IF I'M LATE FOR WORK. I'M WALKING THIS TO COLUMBIA, I'M HANDING IT TO BARON, AND I'M HAVING HIM READ IT IN FRONT OF ME.
DELI
HERE YOU GO.

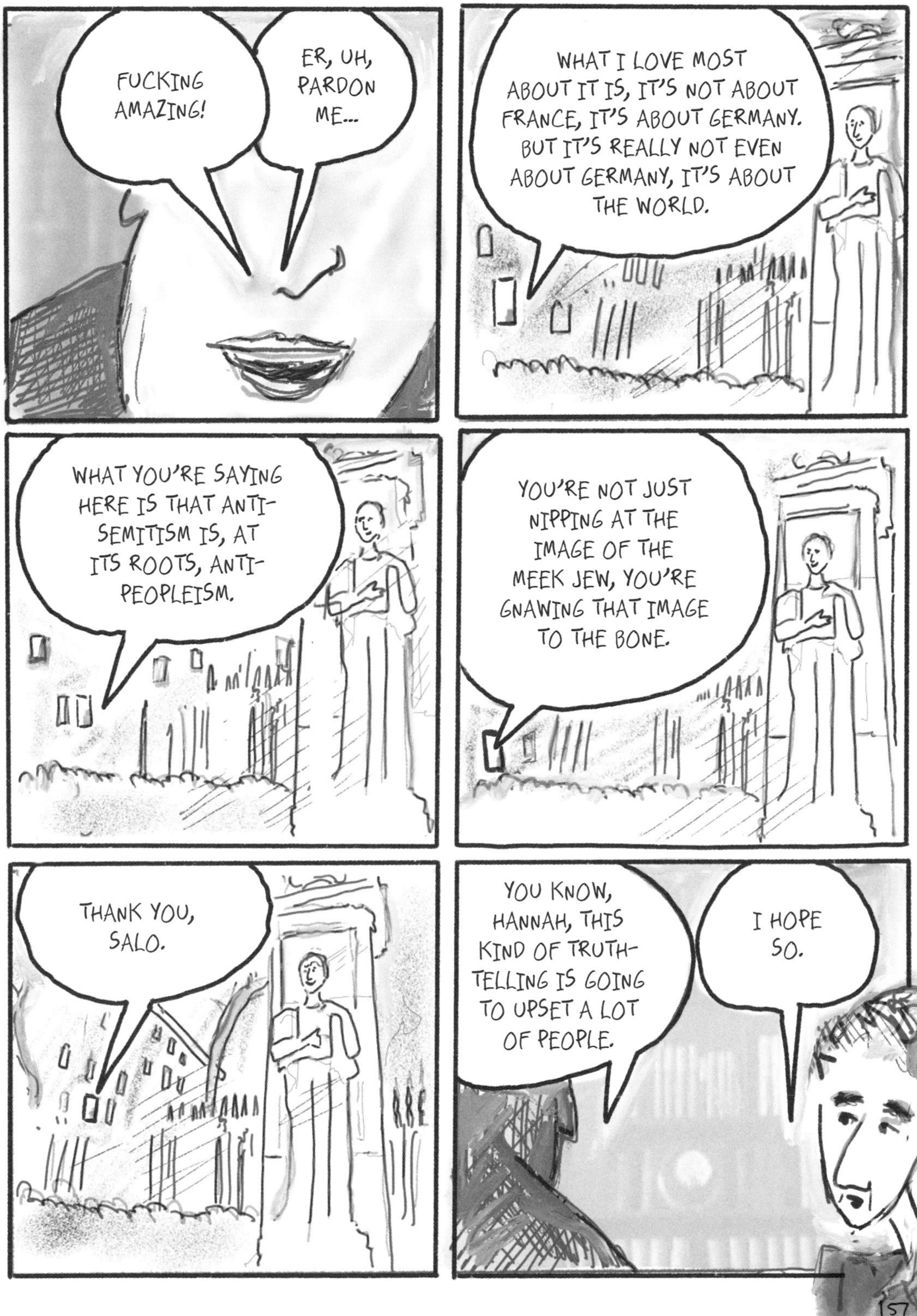
FUCKING AMAZING!
ER, UH, PARDON ME...
WHAT I LOVE MOST ABOUT IT IS, IT'S NOT ABOUT FRANCE, IT'S ABOUT GERMANY. BUT IT'S REALLY NOT EVEN ABOUT GERMANY, IT'S ABOUT THE WORLD.
WHAT YOU'RE SAYING HERE IS THAT ANTI-SEMITISM IS, AT ITS ROOTS, ANTI-PEOPLEISM.
YOU'RE NOT JUST NIPPING AT THE IMAGE OF THE MEEK JEW, YOU'RE GNAWING THAT IMAGE TO THE BONE.
THANK YOU, SALO.
YOU KNOW, HANNAH, THIS KIND OF TRUTH-TELLING IS GOING TO UPSET A LOT OF PEOPLE.
I HOPE SO.

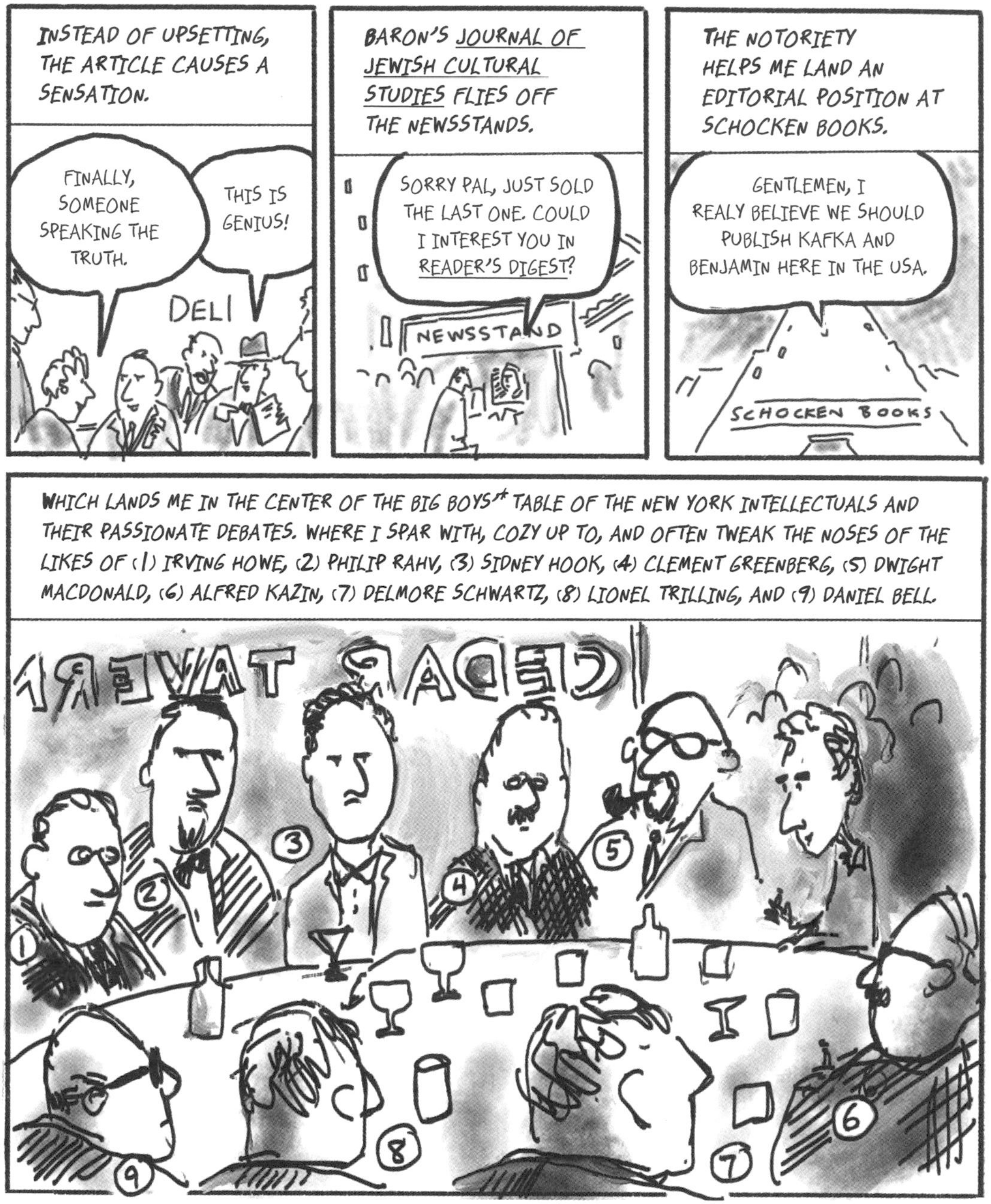
INSTEAD OF UPSETTING, THE ARTICLE CAUSES A SENSATION.
FINALLY, SOMEONE SPEAKING THE TRUTH.
THIS IS GENIUS!
DELI
BARON'S JOURNAL OF JEWISH CULTURAL STUDIES FLIES OFF THE NEWSSTANDS.
SORRY PAL, JUST SOLD THE LAST ONE. COULD I INTEREST YOU IN READER'S DIGEST?
NEWSSTAND
THE NOTORIETY HELPS ME LAND AN EDITORIAL POSITION AT SCHOCKEN BOOKS.
GENTLEMEN, I REALY BELIEVE WE SHOULD PUBLISH KAFKA AND BENJAMIN HERE IN THE USA.
SCHOCKEN BOOKS
WHICH LANDS ME IN THE CENTER OF THE BIG BOYS'* TABLE OF THE NEW YORK INTELLECTUALS AND THEIR PASSIONATE DEBATES. WHERE I SPAR WITH, COZY UP TO, AND OFTEN TWEAK THE NOSES OF THE LIKES OF (1) IRVING HOWE, (2) PHILIP RAHV, (3) SIDNEY HOOK, (4) CLEMENT GREENBERG, (5) DWIGHT MACDONALD, (6) ALFRED KAZIN, (7) DELMORE SCHWARTZ, (8) LIONEL TRILLING, AND (9) DANIEL BELL.
1
2
3
4
5
6
7
8
9

(1) Irving Howe (1920–1993). American Jewish writer and critic, born Irving Horenstein in the Bronx. (2) Philip Rahv (1908–1973). American Jewish writer and editor, born in Russia, co-founded the *Partisan Review*, one of the first editors to introduce Kafka to Americans. (3) Sidney Hook (1902–1989). American Jewish philosopher who, after embracing communism in his youth, became a vocal critic of totalitarianism as practiced by Stalin in Soviet Russia. (4) Clement Greenberg (1909–1994). American Jewish art critic who was a vocal supporter of Jackson Pollock and other abstract expressionists, thus shifting the epicenter of modern art from Paris to Manhattan. (5) Dwight Macdonald (1906–1982). American critic, college buddies with *Time* magazine founder Henry Luce, who quickly rose to reigning highbrow writer in America. He fell out with Luce when *Fortune* magazine severely edited an attack he penned on U.S. Steel.

(6) Alfred Kazin (1915–1998). American Jewish writer, rose from the ghettos of Brooklyn's Brownsville to the heights of literary influence as a chronicler of the universal immigrant experience. (7) Delmore Schwartz (1913–1966). American Jewish writer who mined his family traumas for revealing and searing stories. The youngest to ever win the Bollingen Prize for poetry. At Syracuse University, one of his prize students was American Jewish songwriter and rock star Lou Reed. (8) Lionel Trilling (1905–1975). American Jewish writer and critic of books, theater, music, you name it. A liberal, but opposed the Stalinist extreme-left, saying Liberalism had to "affirm the value of individual existence in all its variousness, complexity, and difficulty." (9) Daniel Bell (Bolotsky) (1919–2011). American Jewish sociologist, Harvard professor, and wrestler with the emergence of what he coined as "post-industrial society."

* And yes, they were mostly "boys."

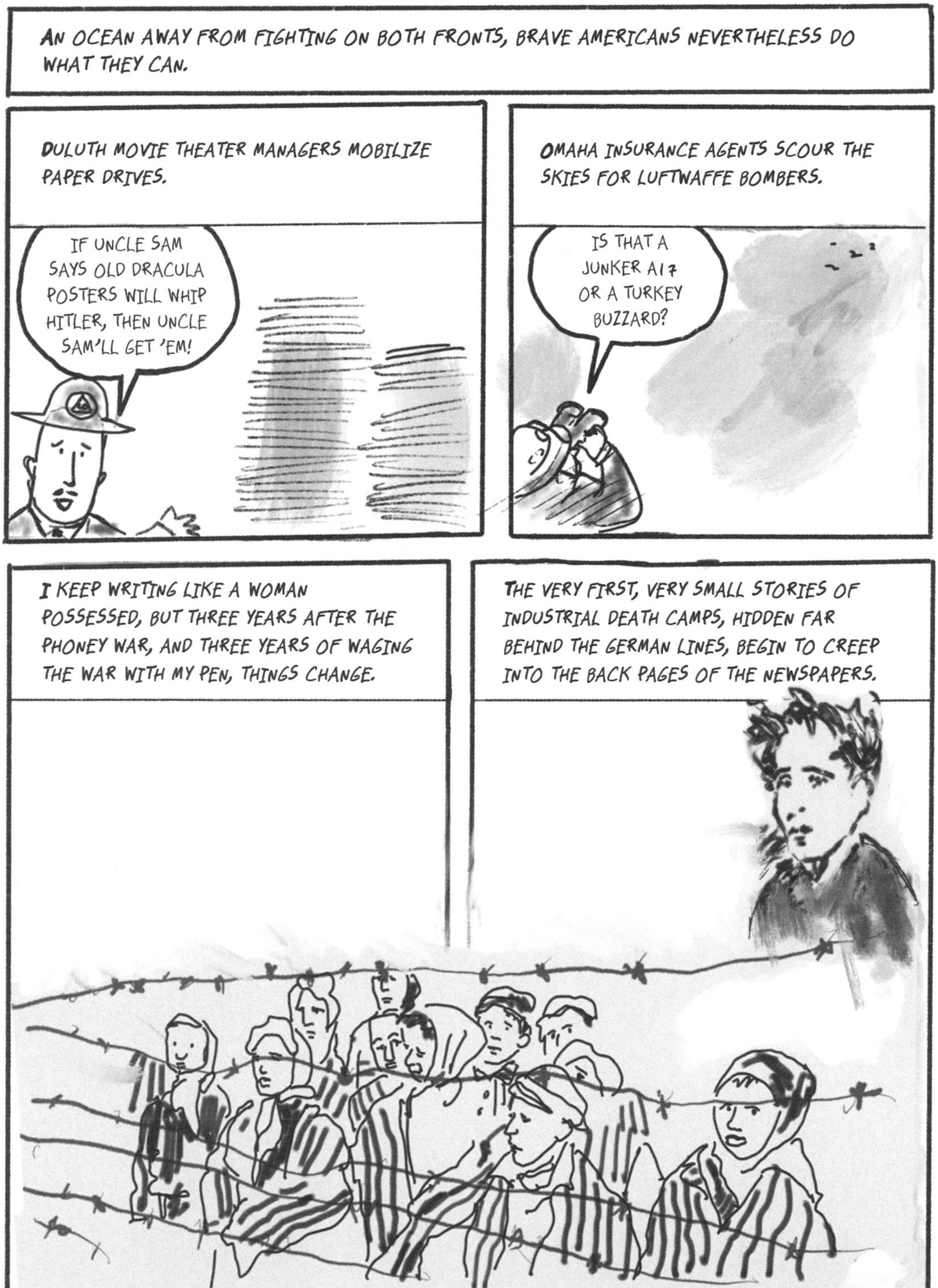
AN OCEAN AWAY FROM FIGHTING ON BOTH FRONTS, BRAVE AMERICANS NEVERTHELESS DO WHAT THEY CAN.
DULUTH MOVIE THEATER MANAGERS MOBILIZE PAPER DRIVES.
IF UNCLE SAM SAYS OLD DRACULA POSTERS WILL WHIP HITLER, THEN UNCLE SAM'LL GET 'EM!
OMAHA INSURANCE AGENTS SCOUR THE SKIES FOR LUFTWAFFE BOMBERS.
IS THAT A JUNKER A17 OR A TURKEY BUZZARD?
I KEEP WRITING LIKE A WOMAN POSSESSED, BUT THREE YEARS AFTER THE PHONEY WAR, AND THREE YEARS OF WAGING THE WAR WITH MY PEN, THINGS CHANGE.
THE VERY FIRST, VERY SMALL STORIES OF INDUSTRIAL DEATH CAMPS, HIDDEN FAR BEHIND THE GERMAN LINES, BEGIN TO CREEP INTO THE BACK PAGES OF THE NEWSPAPERS.

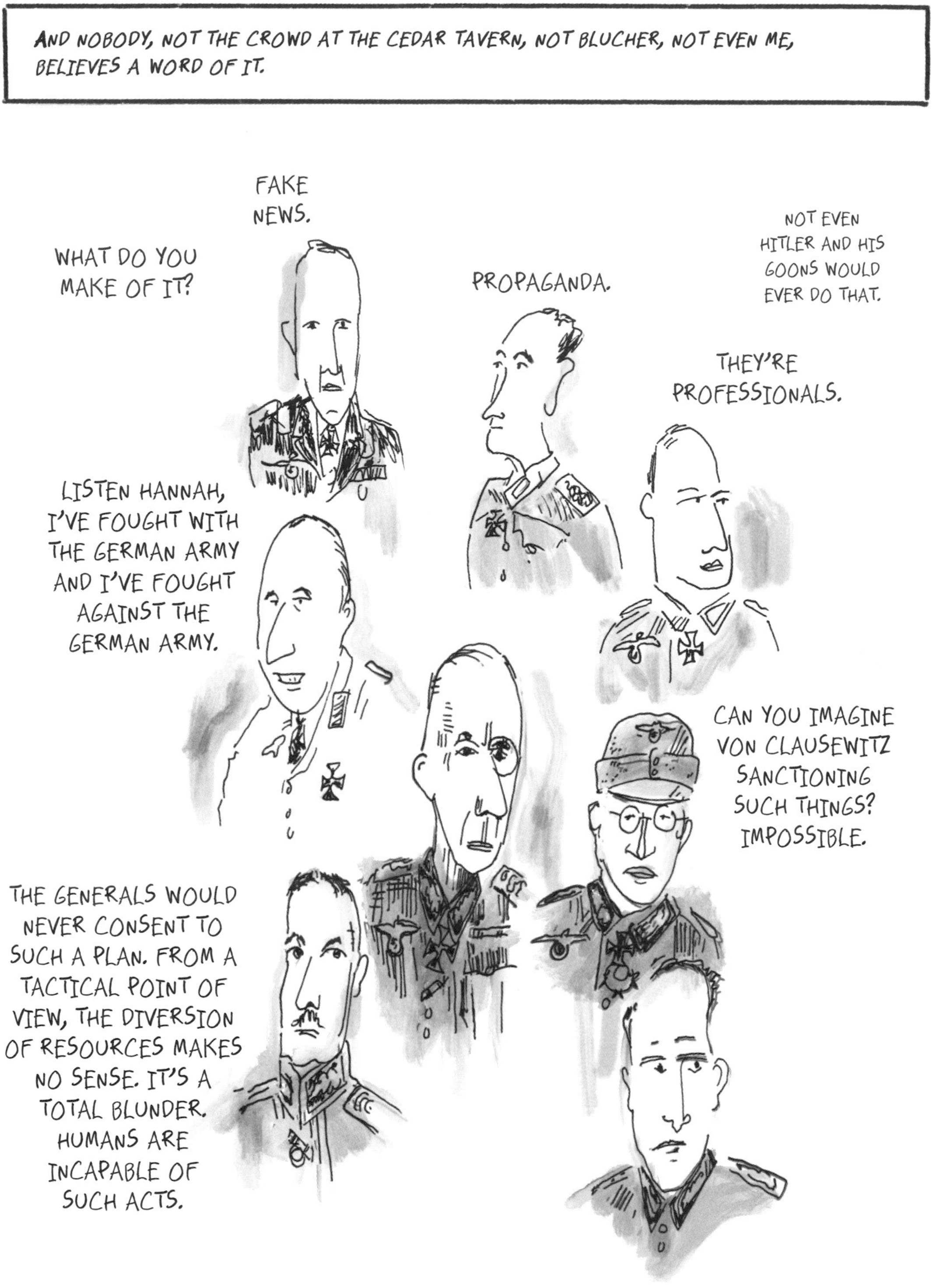
AND NOBODY, NOT THE CROWD AT THE CEDAR TAVERN, NOT BLUCHER, NOT EVEN ME, BELIEVES A WORD OF IT.
WHAT DO YOU MAKE OF IT?
FAKE NEWS.
PROPAGANDA.
NOT EVEN HITLER AND HIS GOONS WOULD EVER DO THAT.
THEY'RE PROFESSIONALS.
LISTEN HANNAH, I'VE FOUGHT WITH THE GERMAN ARMY AND I'VE FOUGHT AGAINST THE GERMAN ARMY.
CAN YOU IMAGINE VON CLAUSEWITZ SANCTIONING SUCH THINGS? IMPOSSIBLE.
THE GENERALS WOULD NEVER CONSENT TO SUCH A PLAN. FROM A TACTICAL POINT OF VIEW, THE DIVERSION OF RESOURCES MAKES NO SENSE. IT'S A TOTAL BLUNDER. HUMANS ARE INCAPABLE OF SUCH ACTS.

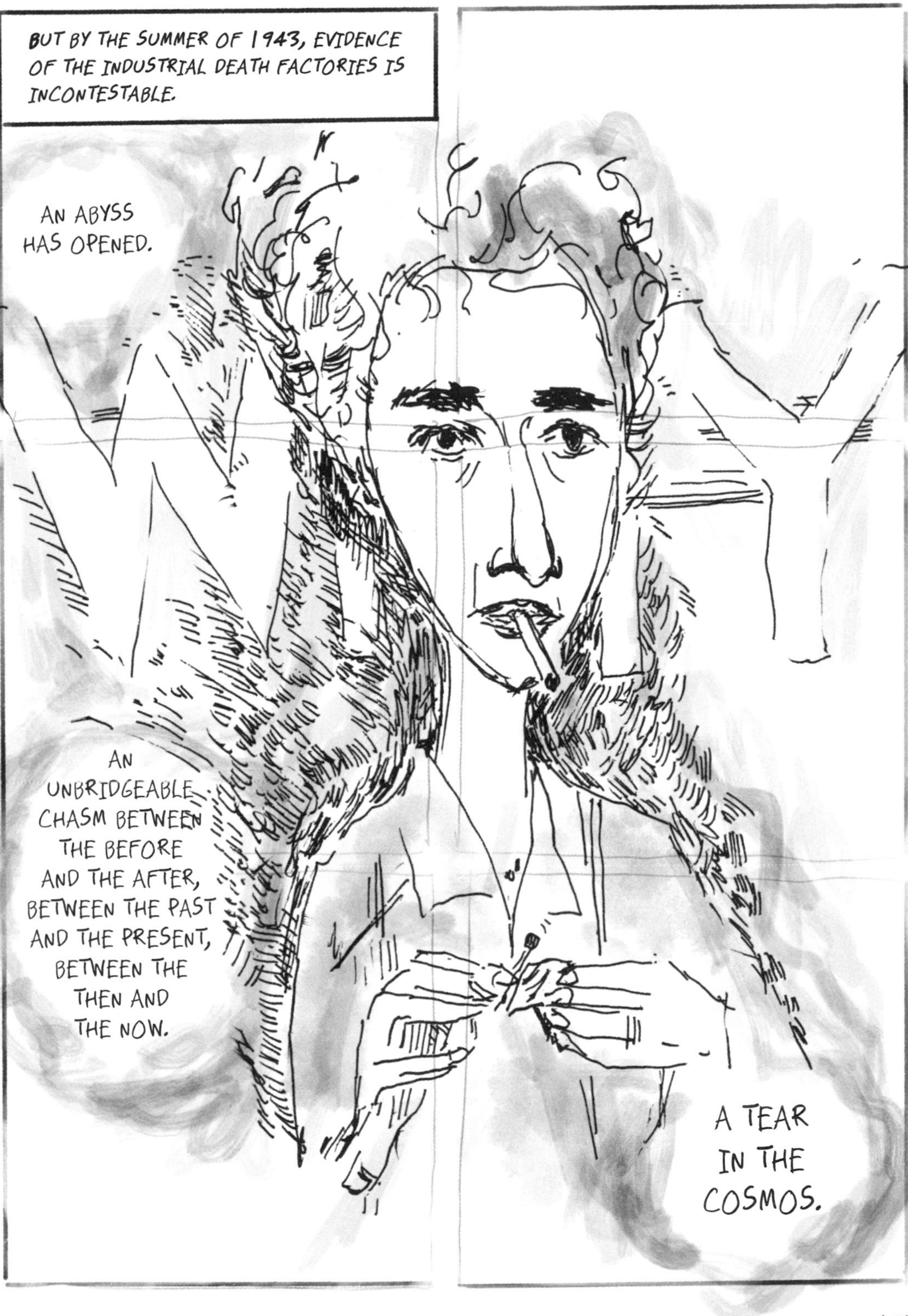
BUT BY THE SUMMER OF 1943, EVIDENCE OF THE INDUSTRIAL DEATH FACTORIES IS INCONTESTABLE.
AN ABYSS HAS OPENED.
AN UNBRIDGEABLE CHASM BETWEEN THE BEFORE AND THE AFTER, BETWEEN THE PAST AND THE PRESENT, BETWEEN THE THEN AND THE NOW.
A TEAR IN THE COSMOS.

AND WHILE I STRUGGLE TO COMPREHEND HOW MY BELOVED GERMAN LANGUAGE COULD BE TWISTED INTO GAS CHAMBERS, EINSTEIN'S INTELLECTUAL PROGENY STRETCH THE LANGUAGE OF GOETHE AND SCHILLER TO GIVE BIRTH TO A MACHINE THAT COULD SNUFF OUT THE ENTIRE PLANET. GERMANY FALLS, AND WITH IT HER ATOMIC PROJECT. NEVERTHELESS, NOT WANTING TO LEAVE GOOD SCIENCE ON THE TABLE, IN TWO HORRIFIC NANOSECONDS, THE ATOMIC BOMB TURNS TWO JAPANESE CITIES INTO FIRE, AND SNUFFS OUT THE WAR, WIDENING THE ABYSS EVEN FURTHER.

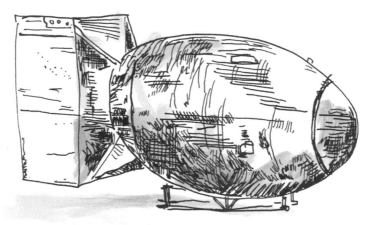

"Fat Man"
146,000 KILLED IN HIROSHIMA

"Little Boy"
80,000 KILLED IN NAGASAKI

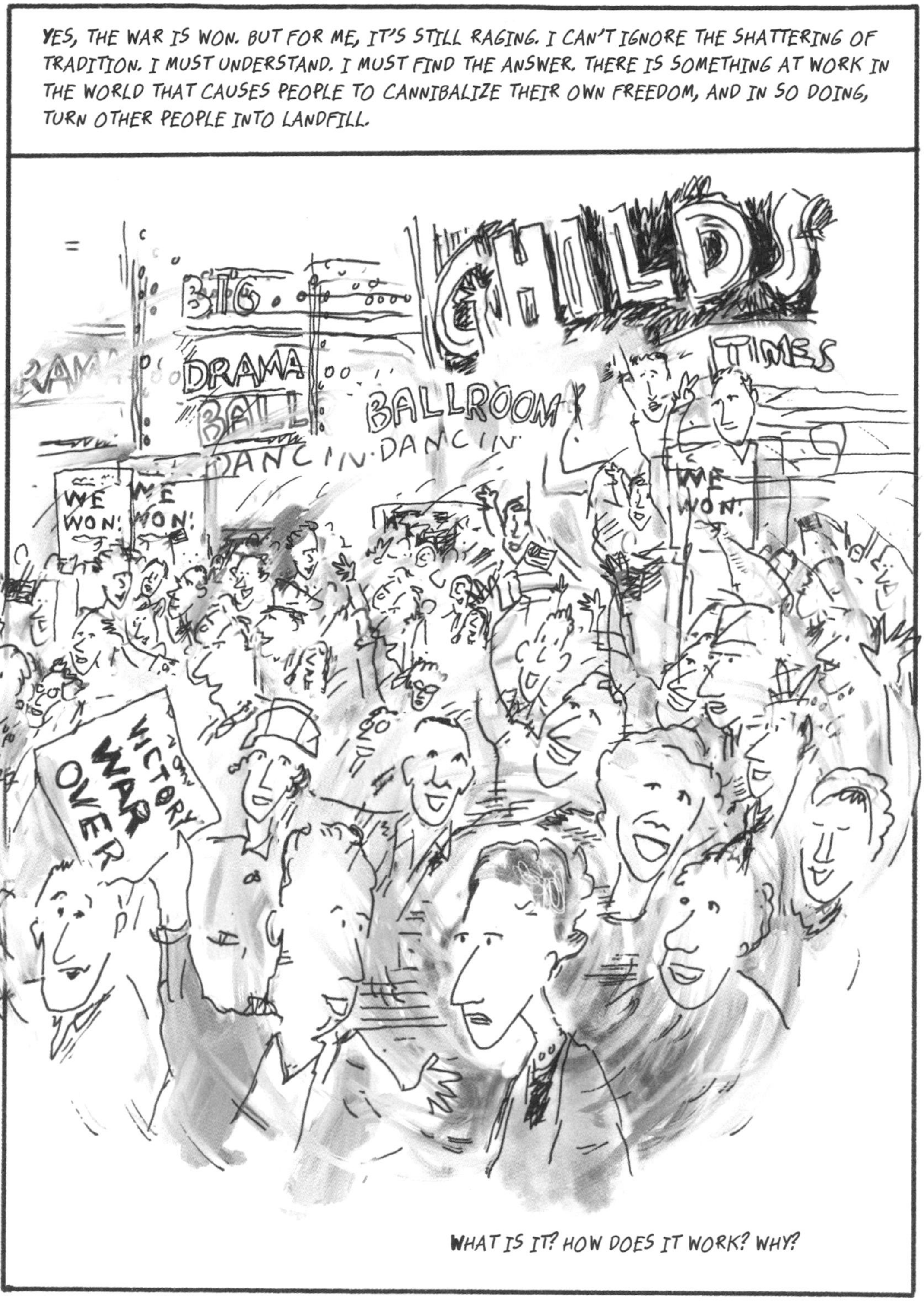
YES, THE WAR IS WON. BUT FOR ME, IT'S STILL RAGING. I CAN'T IGNORE THE SHATTERING OF TRADITION. I MUST UNDERSTAND. I MUST FIND THE ANSWER. THERE IS SOMETHING AT WORK IN THE WORLD THAT CAUSES PEOPLE TO CANNIBALIZE THEIR OWN FREEDOM, AND IN SO DOING, TURN OTHER PEOPLE INTO LANDFILL.
CHILDS
BIG
DRAMA
BALL
BALLROOM
DANCIN DANCIN
TIMES
WE WON!
WE WON!
WE WON!
VICTORY WAR OVER
WHAT IS IT? HOW DOES IT WORK? WHY?

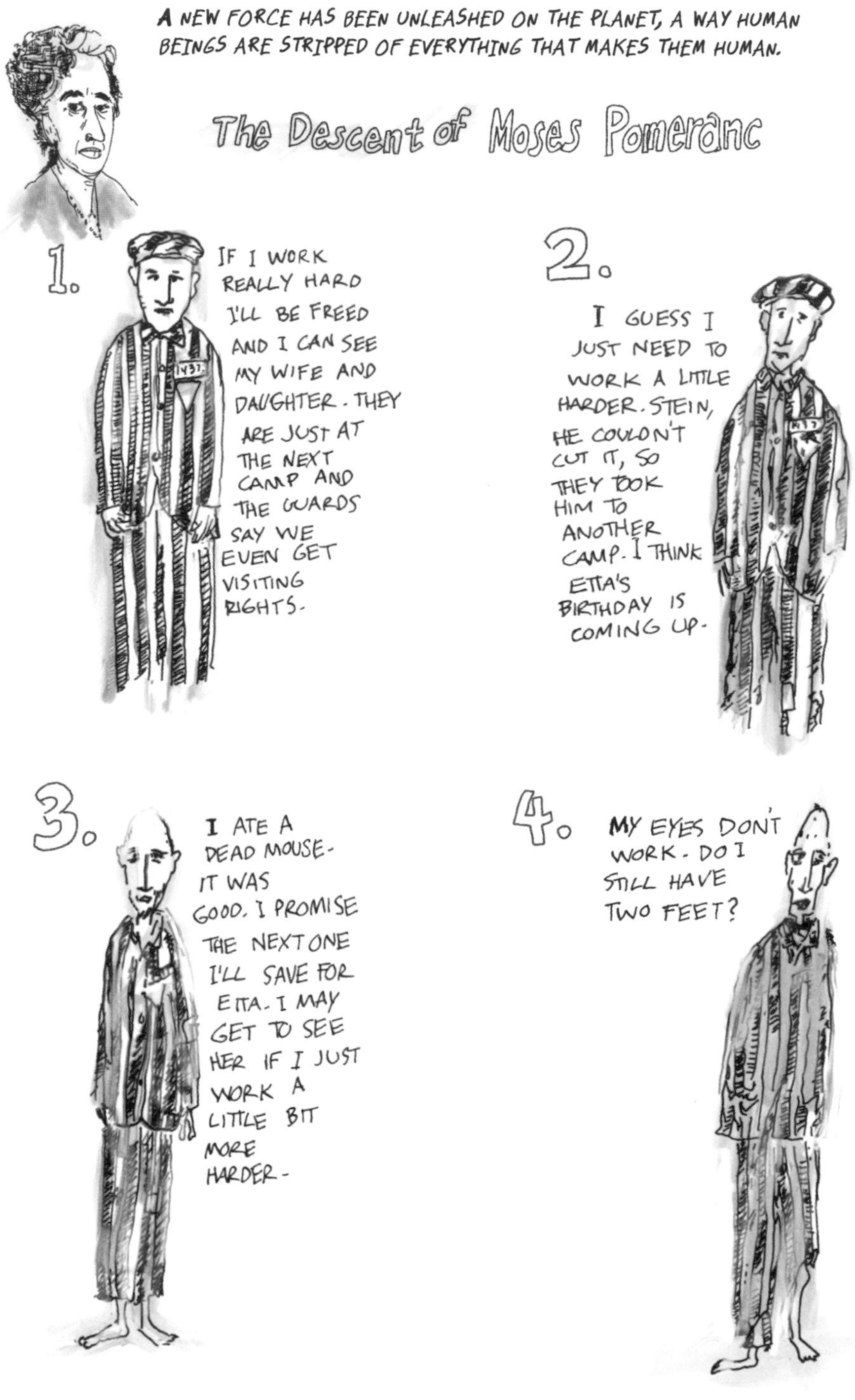
A NEW FORCE HAS BEEN UNLEASHED ON THE PLANET, A WAY HUMAN BEINGS ARE STRIPPED OF EVERYTHING THAT MAKES THEM HUMAN.
The Descent of Moses Pomeranc
1.
IF I WORK REALLY HARD I'LL BE FREED AND I CAN SEE MY WIFE AND DAUGHTER. THEY ARE JUST AT THE NEXT CAMP AND THE GUARDS SAY WE EVEN GET VISITING RIGHTS.
2.
I GUESS I JUST NEED TO WORK A LITTLE HARDER. STEIN, HE COULDN'T CUT IT, SO THEY TOOK HIM TO ANOTHER CAMP. I THINK ETTA'S BIRTHDAY IS COMING UP.
3.
I ATE A DEAD MOUSE. IT WAS GOOD. I PROMISE THE NEXT ONE I'LL SAVE FOR ETTA. I MAY GET TO SEE HER IF I JUST WORK A LITTLE BIT MORE HARDER.
4.
MY EYES DON'T WORK. DO I STILL HAVE TWO FEET?

* Joseph Stalin (1878–1953). Dictator of the Soviet Union from the mid-1920s until his death, who rewrote history both from the barrel of a gun and from a typewriter. He believed that he could bend the facts to conform to his vision of total domination and along the way had his scientists do the same thing, leading to mass starvation.

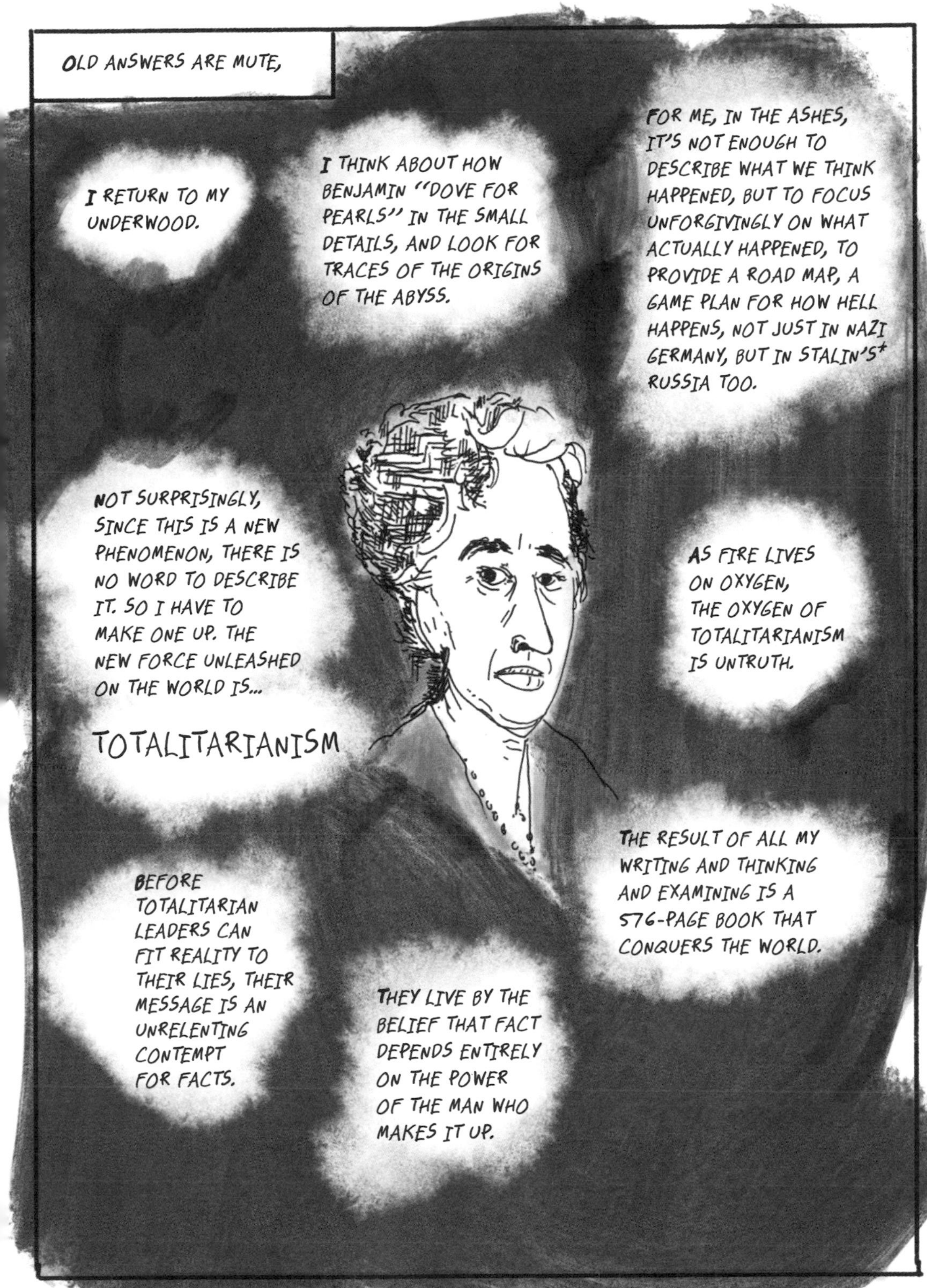
OLD ANSWERS ARE MUTE,
I RETURN TO MY UNDERWOOD.
I THINK ABOUT HOW BENJAMIN "DOVE FOR PEARLS" IN THE SMALL DETAILS, AND LOOK FOR TRACES OF THE ORIGINS OF THE ABYSS.
FOR ME, IN THE ASHES, IT'S NOT ENOUGH TO DESCRIBE WHAT WE THINK HAPPENED, BUT TO FOCUS UNFORGIVINGLY ON WHAT ACTUALLY HAPPENED, TO PROVIDE A ROAD MAP, A GAME PLAN FOR HOW HELL HAPPENS, NOT JUST IN NAZI GERMANY, BUT IN STALIN'S* RUSSIA TOO.
NOT SURPRISINGLY, SINCE THIS IS A NEW PHENOMENON, THERE IS NO WORD TO DESCRIBE IT. SO I HAVE TO MAKE ONE UP. THE NEW FORCE UNLEASHED ON THE WORLD IS...
TOTALITARIANISM
AS FIRE LIVES ON OXYGEN, THE OXYGEN OF TOTALITARIANISM IS UNTRUTH.
THE RESULT OF ALL MY WRITING AND THINKING AND EXAMINING IS A 576-PAGE BOOK THAT CONQUERS THE WORLD.
BEFORE TOTALITARIAN LEADERS CAN FIT REALITY TO THEIR LIES, THEIR MESSAGE IS AN UNRELENTING CONTEMPT FOR FACTS.
THEY LIVE BY THE BELIEF THAT FACT DEPENDS ENTIRELY ON THE POWER OF THE MAN WHO MAKES IT UP.

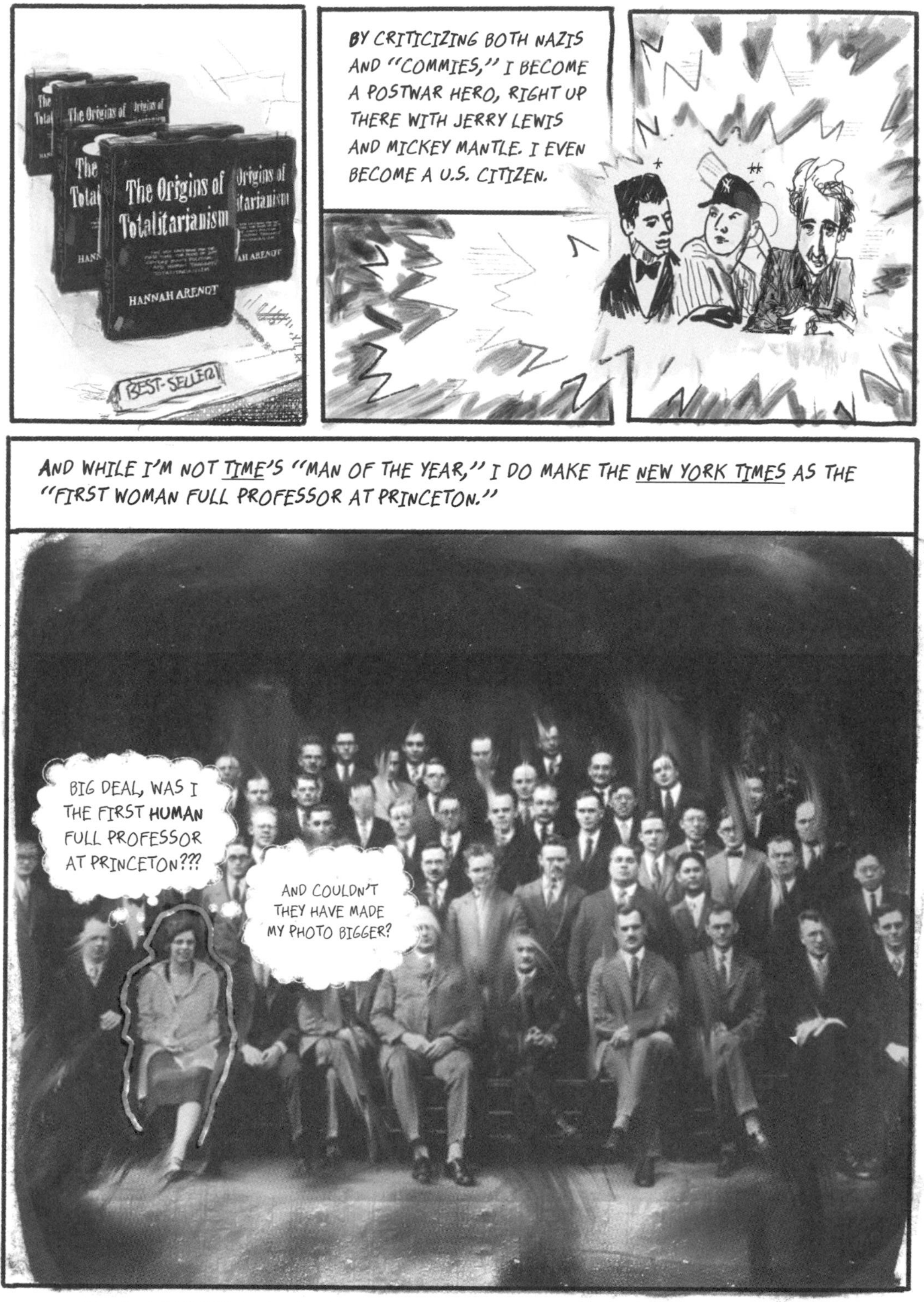
The Origins of Totalitarianism
HANNAH ARENDT
BEST-SELLER
BY CRITICIZING BOTH NAZIS AND "COMMIES," I BECOME A POSTWAR HERO, RIGHT UP THERE WITH JERRY LEWIS AND MICKEY MANTLE. I EVEN BECOME A U.S. CITIZEN.
*
**
AND WHILE I'M NOT TIME'S "MAN OF THE YEAR," I DO MAKE THE NEW YORK TIMES AS THE "FIRST WOMAN FULL PROFESSOR AT PRINCETON."
BIG DEAL, WAS I THE FIRST HUMAN FULL PROFESSOR AT PRINCETON???
AND COULDN'T THEY HAVE MADE MY PHOTO BIGGER?

* Jerry Lewis (1926–2017). American Jewish comedian and filmmaker. (Born Joseph Levitch.) He also invented the first video assist set-up which defined a large part of modern filmmaking technique.

** Mickey Mantle (1931–1995). American baseball player, regarded as the greatest switch-hitter ever.

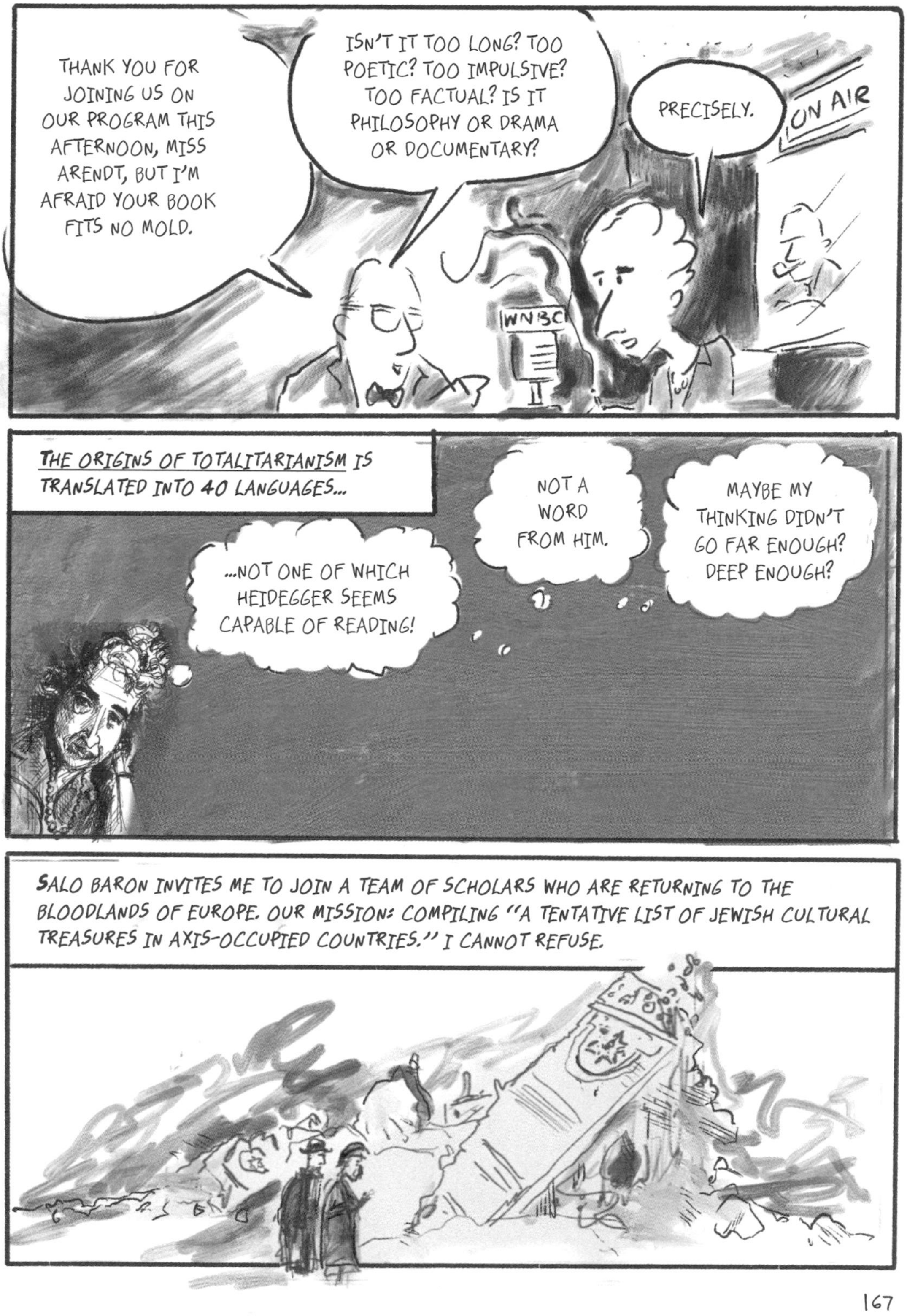
THANK YOU FOR JOINING US ON OUR PROGRAM THIS AFTERNOON, MISS ARENDT, BUT I'M AFRAID YOUR BOOK FITS NO MOLD.
ISN'T IT TOO LONG? TOO POETIC? TOO IMPULSIVE? TOO FACTUAL? IS IT PHILOSOPHY OR DRAMA OR DOCUMENTARY?
PRECISELY.
ON AIR
WNBC
THE ORIGINS OF TOTALITARIANISM IS TRANSLATED INTO 40 LANGUAGES...
...NOT ONE OF WHICH HEIDEGGER SEEMS CAPABLE OF READING!
NOT A WORD FROM HIM.
MAYBE MY THINKING DIDN'T GO FAR ENOUGH? DEEP ENOUGH?
SALO BARON INVITES ME TO JOIN A TEAM OF SCHOLARS WHO ARE RETURNING TO THE BLOODLANDS OF EUROPE. OUR MISSION: COMPILING "A TENTATIVE LIST OF JEWISH CULTURAL TREASURES IN AXIS-OCCUPIED COUNTRIES." I CANNOT REFUSE.

HEIDEGGER'S HUTTE

AT THE TAIL END OF THE EXPEDITION, I GIVE IN TO ANOTHER INVITATION.

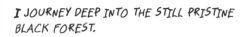

I JOURNEY DEEP INTO THE STILL PRISTINE BLACK FOREST.

WHERE HEIDEGGER WAITS FOR ME IN HIS "HUTTE," OUTSIDE THE REMOTE HAMLET OF TOTHENBERG.

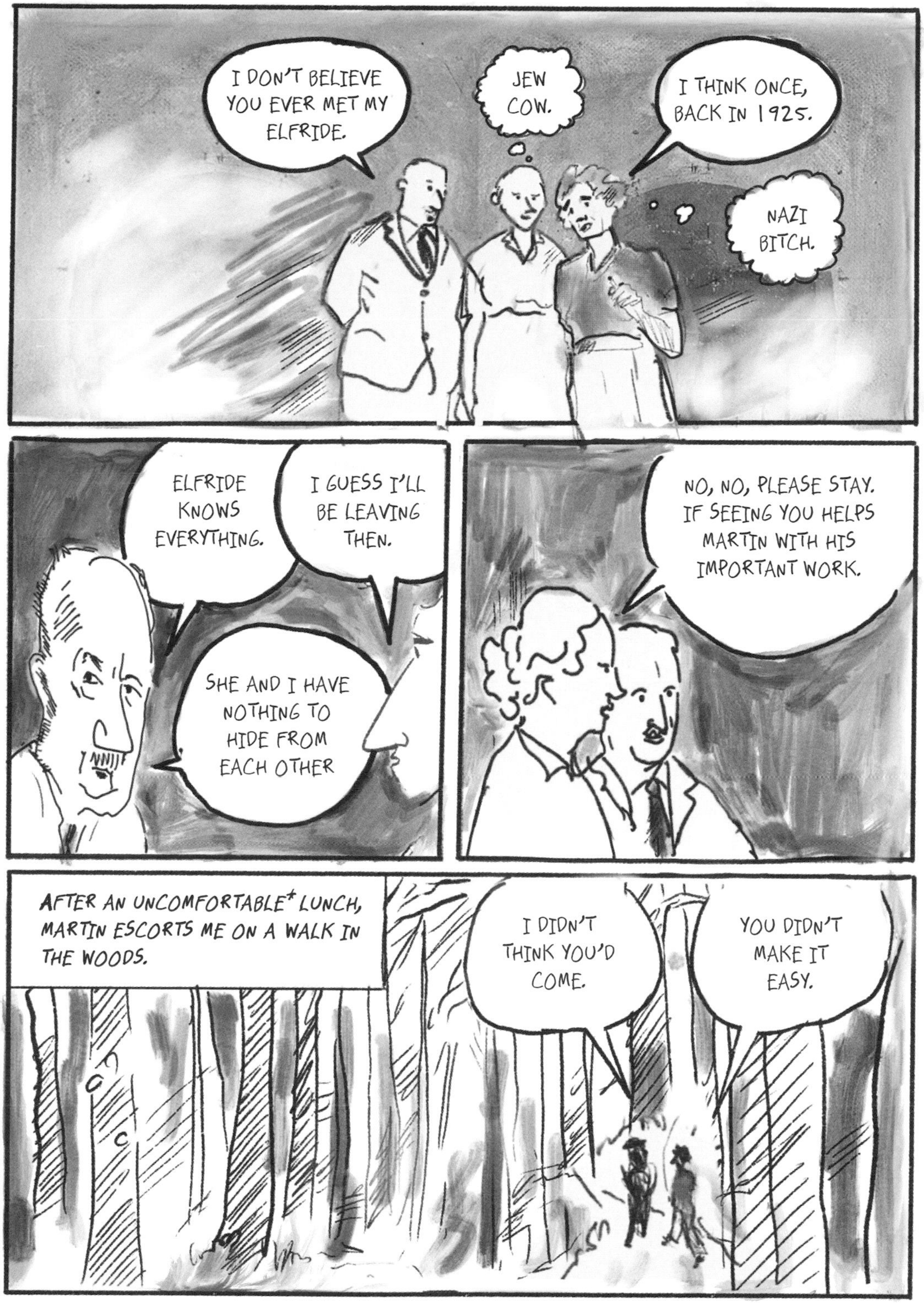
I DON'T BELIEVE YOU EVER MET MY ELFRIDE.
JEW COW.
I THINK ONCE, BACK IN 1925.
NAZI BITCH.
ELFRIDE KNOWS EVERYTHING.
I GUESS I'LL BE LEAVING THEN.
SHE AND I HAVE NOTHING TO HIDE FROM EACH OTHER
NO, NO, PLEASE STAY. IF SEEING YOU HELPS MARTIN WITH HIS IMPORTANT WORK.
AFTER AN UNCOMFORTABLE* LUNCH, MARTIN ESCORTS ME ON A WALK IN THE WOODS.
I DIDN'T THINK YOU'D COME.
YOU DIDN'T MAKE IT EASY.

* Massive understatement

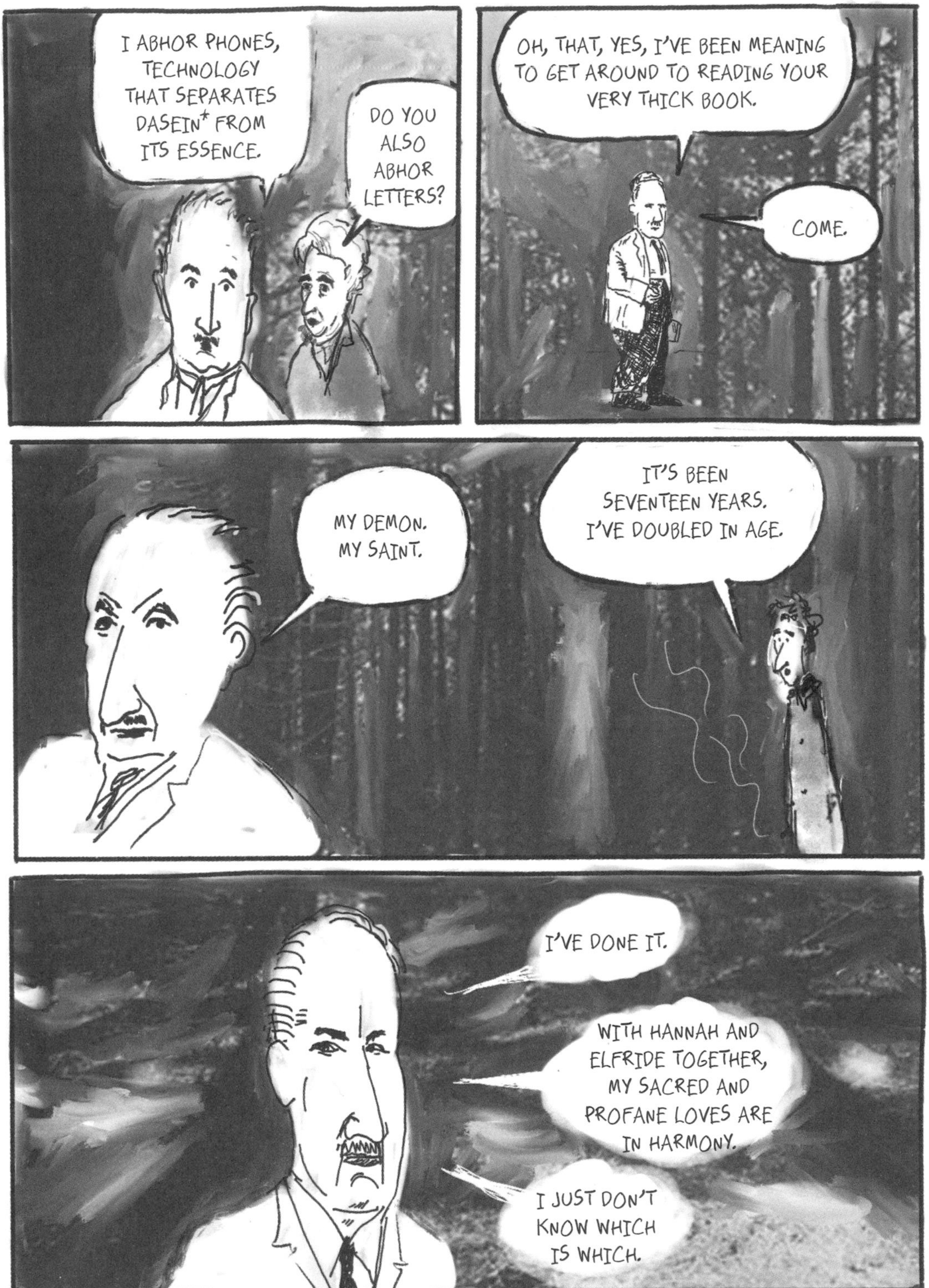
I ABHOR PHONES, TECHNOLOGY THAT SEPARATES DASEIN* FROM ITS ESSENCE.
DO YOU ALSO ABHOR LETTERS?
OH, THAT, YES, I'VE BEEN MEANING TO GET AROUND TO READING YOUR VERY THICK BOOK.
COME.
MY DEMON. MY SAINT.
IT'S BEEN SEVENTEEN YEARS. I'VE DOUBLED IN AGE.
I'VE DONE IT.
WITH HANNAH AND ELFRIDE TOGETHER, MY SACRED AND PROFANE LOVES ARE IN HARMONY.
I JUST DON'T KNOW WHICH IS WHICH.

* Dasein: that entity that says of itself, "I am that entity," the thrown "things-stuff-beings" that are walking around doing stuff, in other words, you.

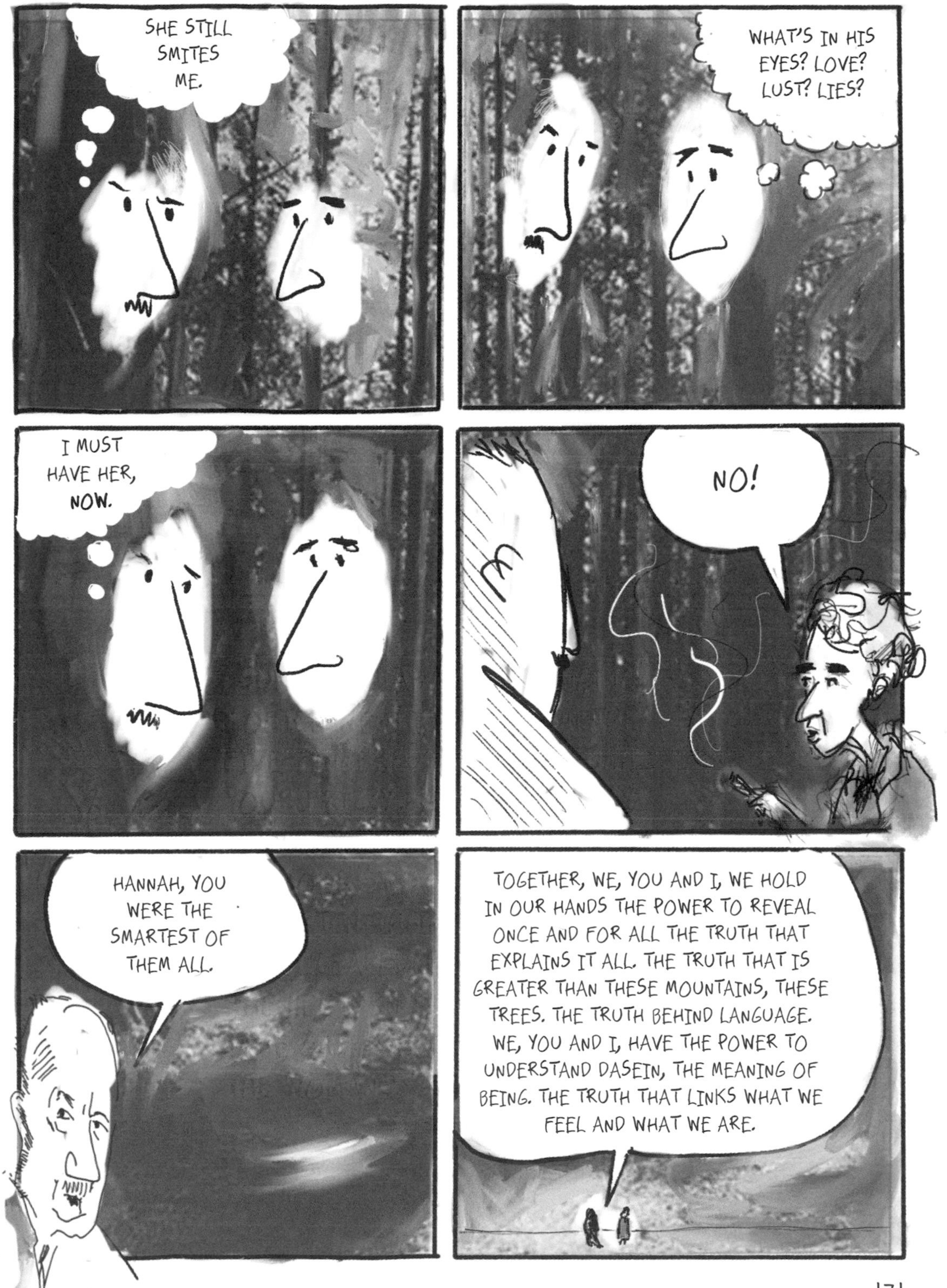
SHE STILL SMITES ME.
WHAT'S IN HIS EYES? LOVE? LUST? LIES?
I MUST HAVE HER, NOW.
NO!
HANNAH, YOU WERE THE SMARTEST OF THEM ALL.
TOGETHER, WE, YOU AND I, WE HOLD IN OUR HANDS THE POWER TO REVEAL ONCE AND FOR ALL THE TRUTH THAT EXPLAINS IT ALL. THE TRUTH THAT IS GREATER THAN THESE MOUNTAINS, THESE TREES. THE TRUTH BEHIND LANGUAGE. WE, YOU AND I, HAVE THE POWER TO UNDERSTAND DASEIN, THE MEANING OF BEING. THE TRUTH THAT LINKS WHAT WE FEEL AND WHAT WE ARE.

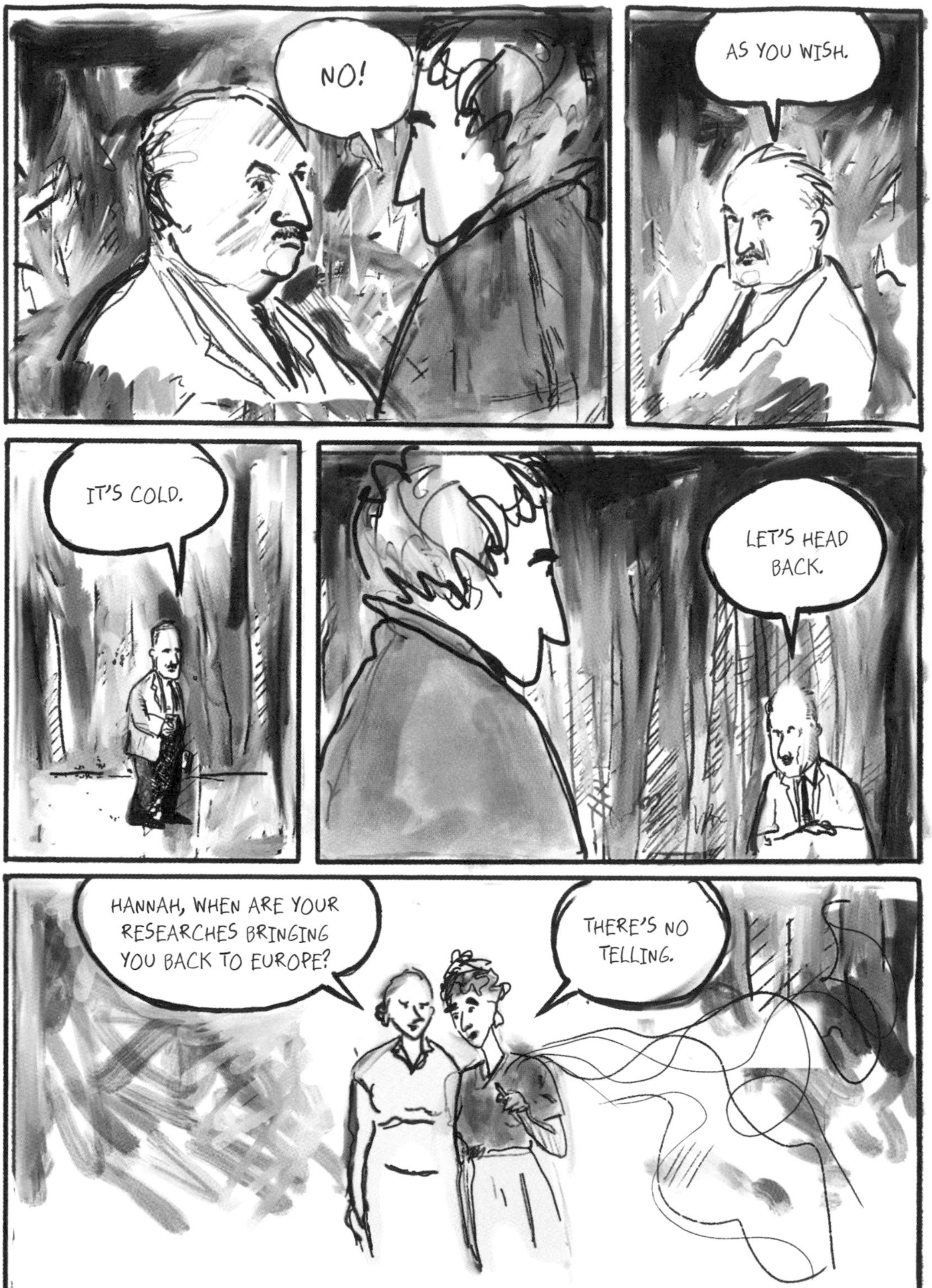
NO!
AS YOU WISH.
IT'S COLD.
LET'S HEAD BACK.
HANNAH, WHEN ARE YOUR RESEARCHES BRINGING YOU BACK TO EUROPE?
THERE'S NO TELLING.

NOT A WORD OF APOLOGY FROM HER! A TRUE GERMAN WOMAN WOULD HAVE KNOWN HOW TO BEHAVE.

AUF WIEDERSEHEN, HANNAH.

ELFRIDE, I MUST GO TO WORK NOW. I AM NOT TO BE DISTURBED.

IF THE JEW MAKES HIM HAPPY AND PRODUCTIVE, IT IS MY DUTY TO ALLOW IT.

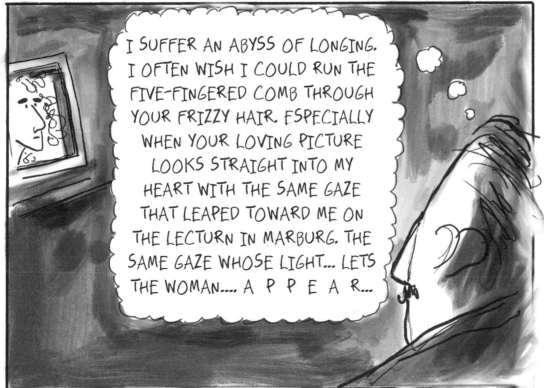

I SUFFER AN ABYSS OF LONGING. I OFTEN WISH I COULD RUN THE FIVE-FINGERED COMB THROUGH YOUR FRIZZY HAIR. ESPECIALLY WHEN YOUR LOVING PICTURE LOOKS STRAIGHT INTO MY HEART WITH THE SAME GAZE THAT LEAPED TOWARD ME ON THE LECTURN IN MARBURG. THE SAME GAZE WHOSE LIGHT... LETS THE WOMAN.... A P P E A R...

THE END OF MARTHA AND THE INFINITE WHY 1951

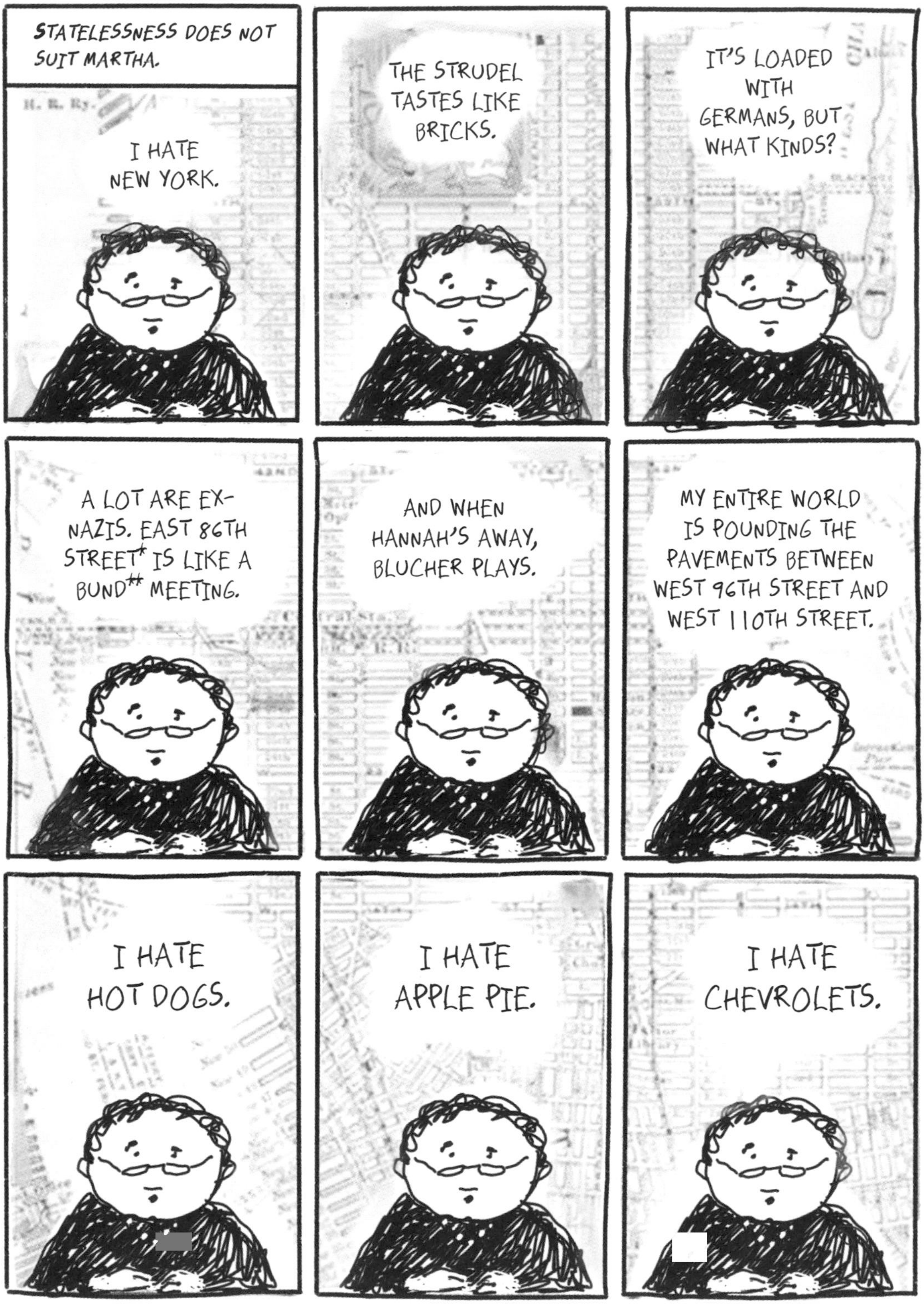
STATELESSNESS DOES NOT SUIT MARTHA.
I HATE NEW YORK.
THE STRUDEL TASTES LIKE BRICKS.
IT'S LOADED WITH GERMANS, BUT WHAT KINDS?
A LOT ARE EX-NAZIS. EAST 86TH STREET* IS LIKE A BUND** MEETING.
AND WHEN HANNAH'S AWAY, BLUCHER PLAYS.
MY ENTIRE WORLD IS POUNDING THE PAVEMENTS BETWEEN WEST 96TH STREET AND WEST 110TH STREET.
I HATE HOT DOGS.
I HATE APPLE PIE.
I HATE CHEVROLETS.

* "Sauerkraut Blvd" ** American Nazi Party

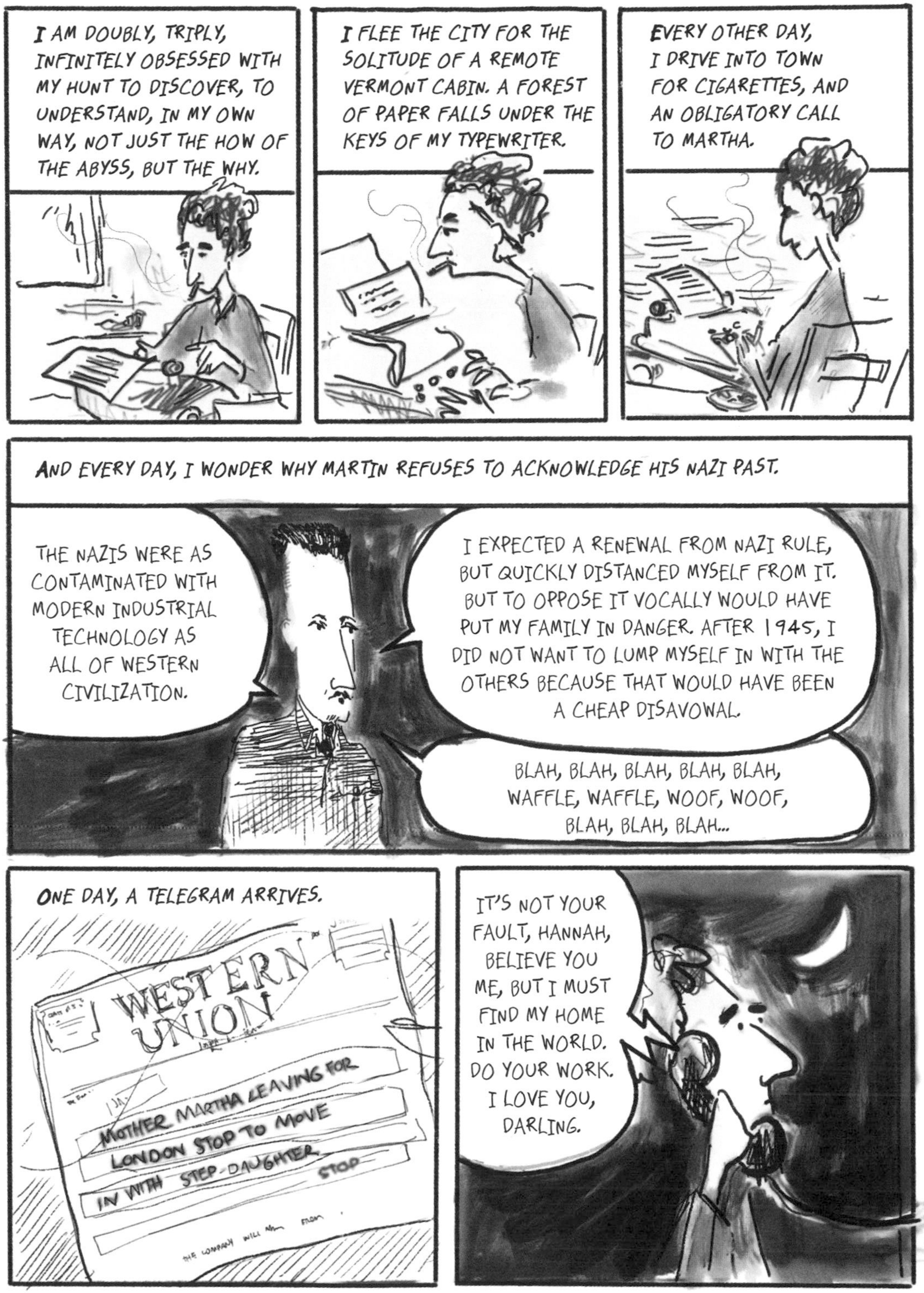
I AM DOUBLY, TRIPLY, INFINITELY OBSESSED WITH MY HUNT TO DISCOVER, TO UNDERSTAND, IN MY OWN WAY, NOT JUST THE HOW OF THE ABYSS, BUT THE WHY.
I FLEE THE CITY FOR THE SOLITUDE OF A REMOTE VERMONT CABIN. A FOREST OF PAPER FALLS UNDER THE KEYS OF MY TYPEWRITER.
EVERY OTHER DAY, I DRIVE INTO TOWN FOR CIGARETTES, AND AN OBLIGATORY CALL TO MARTHA.
AND EVERY DAY, I WONDER WHY MARTIN REFUSES TO ACKNOWLEDGE HIS NAZI PAST.
THE NAZIS WERE AS CONTAMINATED WITH MODERN INDUSTRIAL TECHNOLOGY AS ALL OF WESTERN CIVILIZATION.
I EXPECTED A RENEWAL FROM NAZI RULE, BUT QUICKLY DISTANCED MYSELF FROM IT. BUT TO OPPOSE IT VOCALLY WOULD HAVE PUT MY FAMILY IN DANGER. AFTER 1945, I DID NOT WANT TO LUMP MYSELF IN WITH THE OTHERS BECAUSE THAT WOULD HAVE BEEN A CHEAP DISAVOWAL.
BLAH, BLAH, BLAH, BLAH, BLAH, WAFFLE, WAFFLE, WOOF, WOOF, BLAH, BLAH, BLAH...
ONE DAY, A TELEGRAM ARRIVES.
WESTERN UNION
MOTHER MARTHA LEAVING FOR LONDON STOP TO MOVE IN WITH STEP-DAUGHTER STOP
IT'S NOT YOUR FAULT, HANNAH, BELIEVE YOU ME, BUT I MUST FIND MY HOME IN THE WORLD. DO YOUR WORK. I LOVE YOU, DARLING.

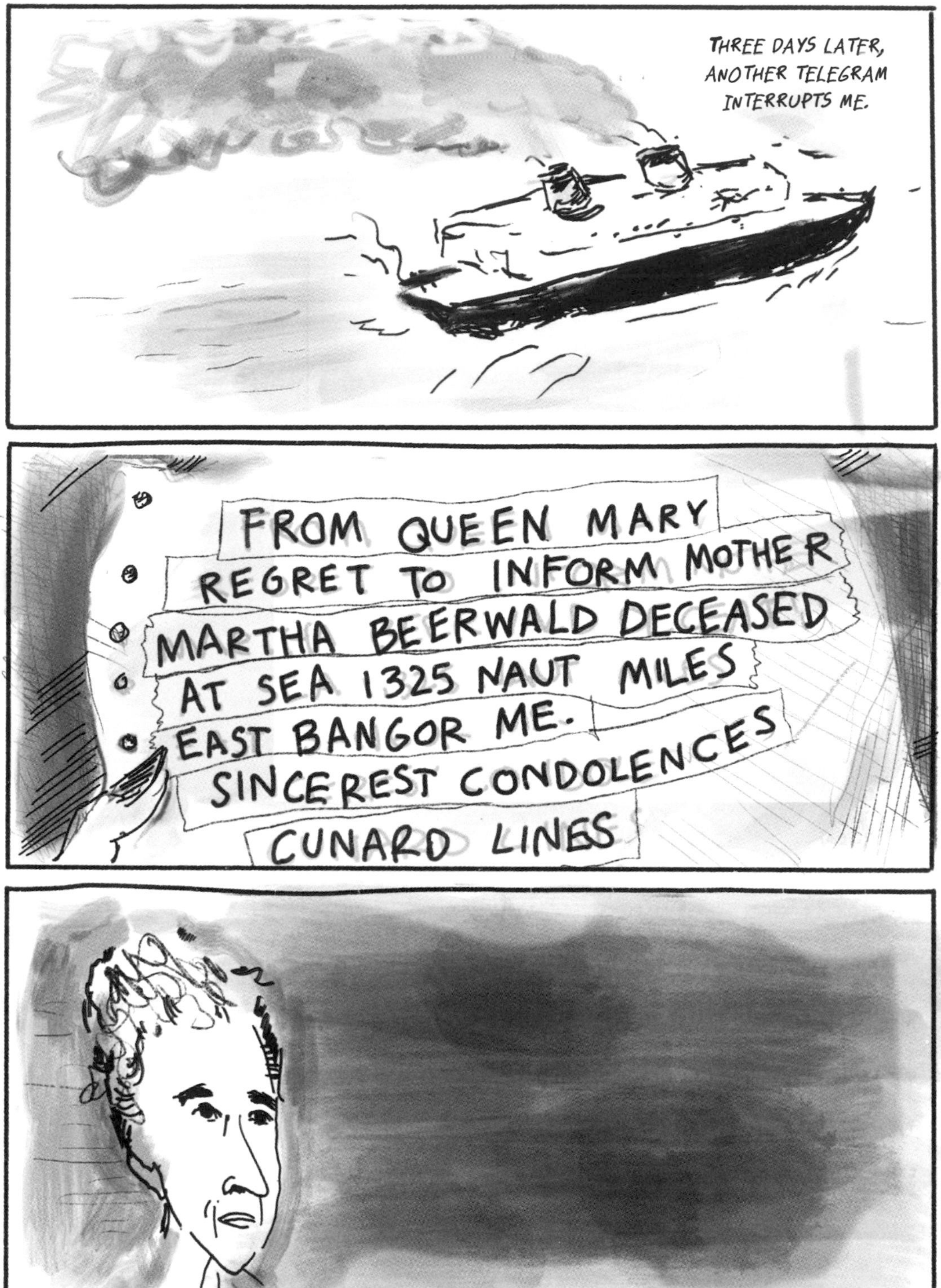
THREE DAYS LATER, ANOTHER TELEGRAM INTERRUPTS ME.
FROM QUEEN MARY
REGRET TO INFORM MOTHER
MARTHA BEERWALD DECEASED
AT SEA 1325 NAUT MILES
EAST BANGOR ME.
SINCEREST CONDOLENCES
CUNARD LINES

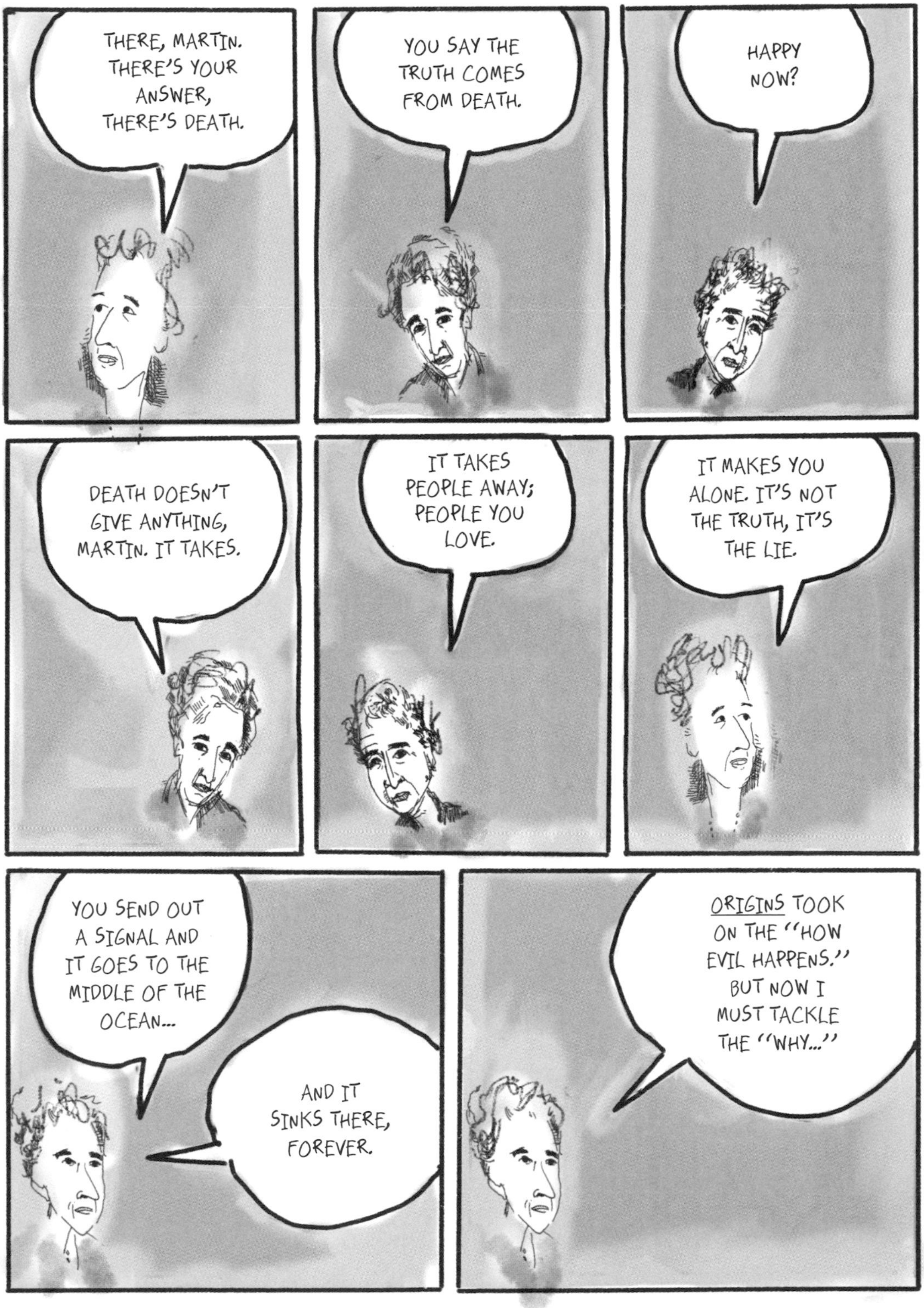
THERE, MARTIN. THERE'S YOUR ANSWER, THERE'S DEATH.
YOU SAY THE TRUTH COMES FROM DEATH.
HAPPY NOW?
DEATH DOESN'T GIVE ANYTHING, MARTIN. IT TAKES.
IT TAKES PEOPLE AWAY; PEOPLE YOU LOVE.
IT MAKES YOU ALONE. IT'S NOT THE TRUTH, IT'S THE LIE.
YOU SEND OUT A SIGNAL AND IT GOES TO THE MIDDLE OF THE OCEAN...
AND IT SINKS THERE, FOREVER.
ORIGINS TOOK ON THE "HOW EVIL HAPPENS." BUT NOW I MUST TACKLE THE "WHY..."

ORIGINS LETS US MOVE UPTOWN TO A MUCH NICER, FIVE-ROOM, TWO-BATH APARTMENT IN A DOORMAN BUILDING WITH AN ELEVATOR AND PARTIAL RIVER VIEWS.

IT IS FROM HERE THAT I DECIDE TO SET UP CAMP IN MY EFFORTS TO CRACK WHY THE ABYSS HAPPENS.

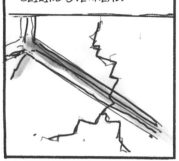

MY HEADQUARTERS IS A COUCH. MY METHOD IS STUDYING A CRACK IN THE PLASTER CEILING OVERHEAD.

AND DEBATING WITH THE ONLY ADVERSARY I TRULY TRUST.

HANNAH V. HANNAH.

THE ABYSS IS REAL.

YES, BUT WE ARE STILL IN THE WORLD.

BUT IN A NEW PLACE.

HOW DID WE GET HERE?

WHY?

YES, WHY?

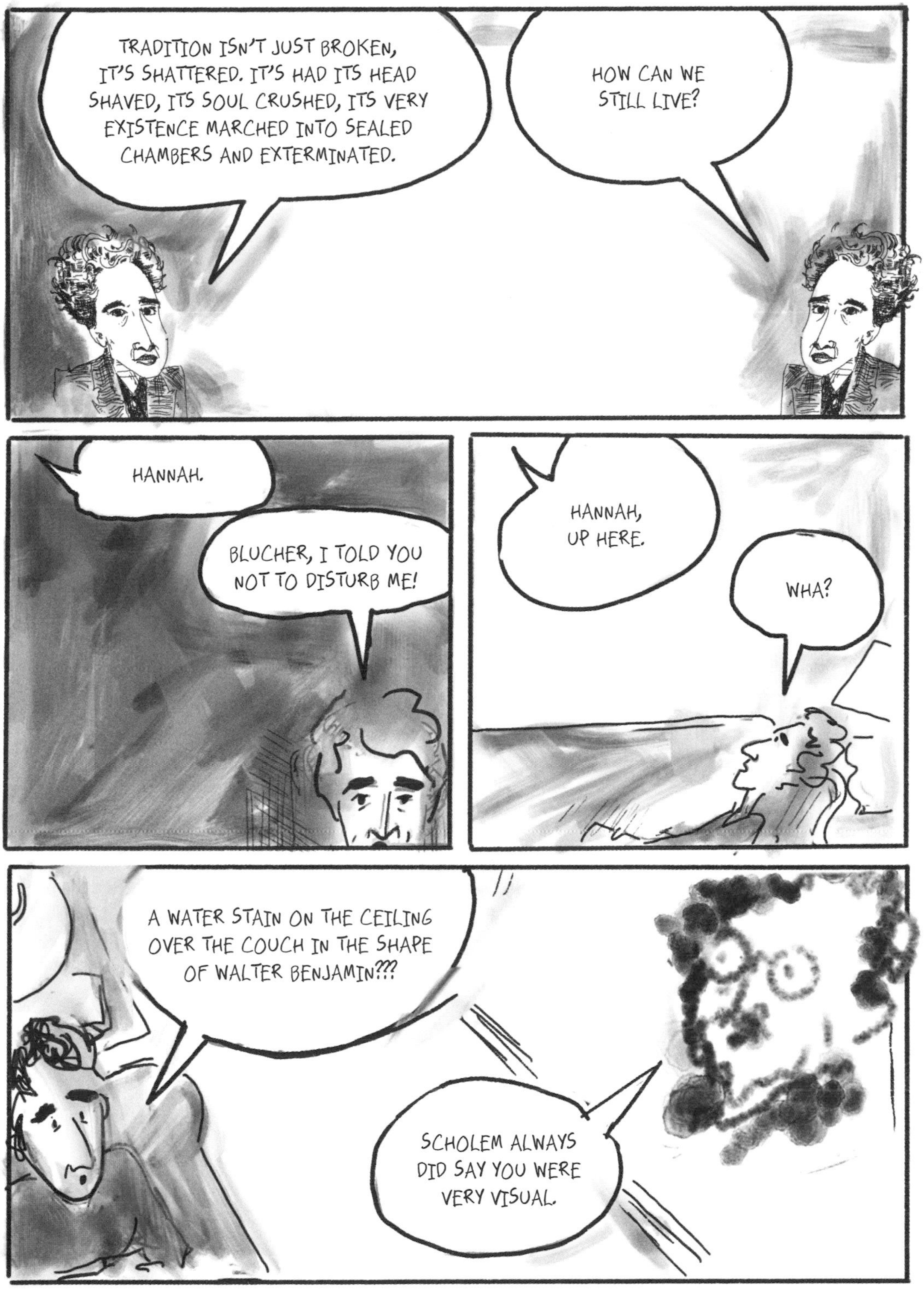
TRADITION ISN'T JUST BROKEN, IT'S SHATTERED. IT'S HAD ITS HEAD SHAVED, ITS SOUL CRUSHED, ITS VERY EXISTENCE MARCHED INTO SEALED CHAMBERS AND EXTERMINATED.
HOW CAN WE STILL LIVE?
HANNAH.
BLUCHER, I TOLD YOU NOT TO DISTURB ME!
HANNAH, UP HERE.
WHA?
A WATER STAIN ON THE CEILING OVER THE COUCH IN THE SHAPE OF WALTER BENJAMIN???
SCHOLEM ALWAYS DID SAY YOU WERE VERY VISUAL.

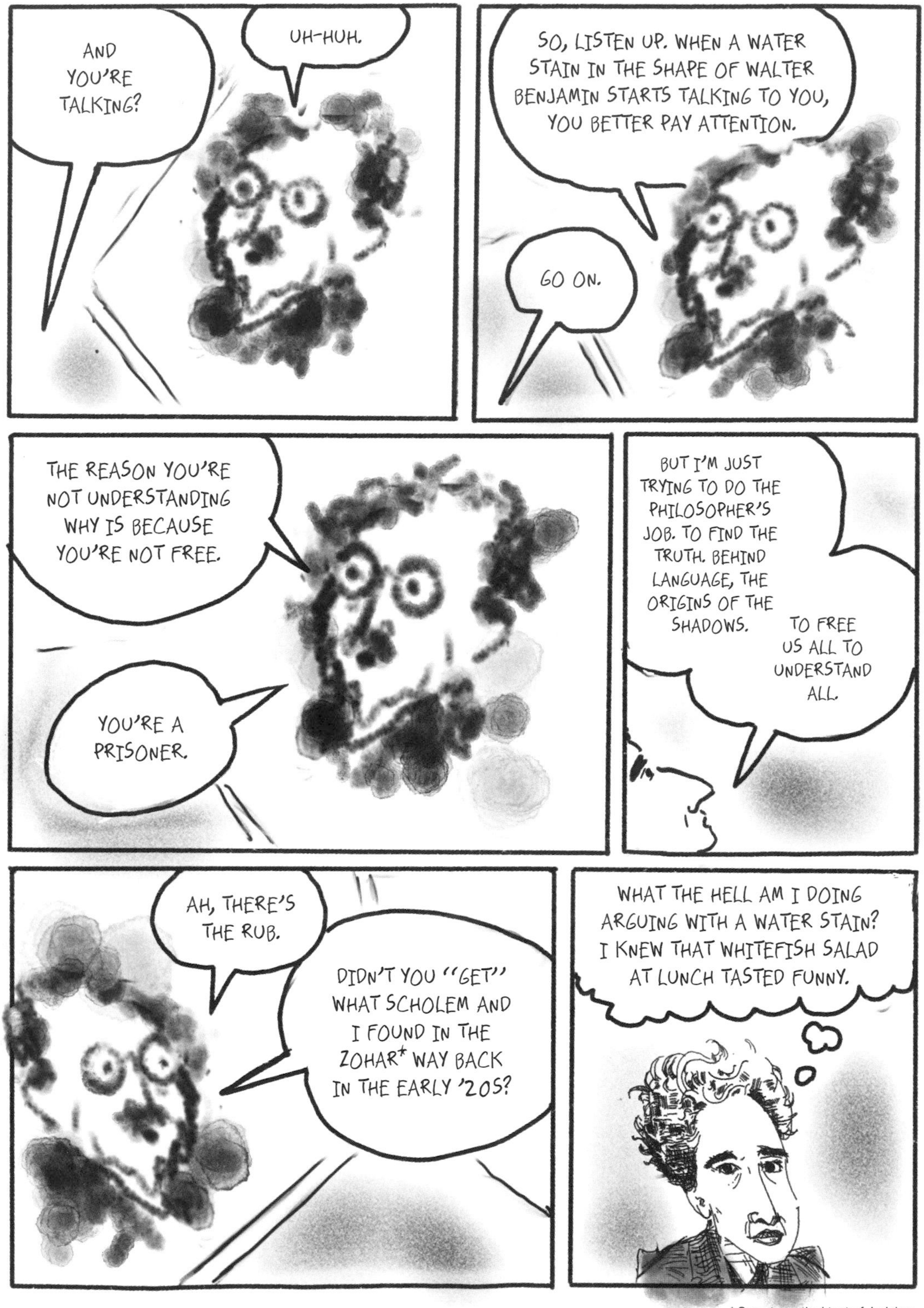
AND YOU'RE TALKING?
UH-HUH.
SO, LISTEN UP. WHEN A WATER STAIN IN THE SHAPE OF WALTER BENJAMIN STARTS TALKING TO YOU, YOU BETTER PAY ATTENTION.
GO ON.
THE REASON YOU'RE NOT UNDERSTANDING WHY IS BECAUSE YOU'RE NOT FREE.
YOU'RE A PRISONER.
BUT I'M JUST TRYING TO DO THE PHILOSOPHER'S JOB. TO FIND THE TRUTH. BEHIND LANGUAGE, THE ORIGINS OF THE SHADOWS.
TO FREE US ALL TO UNDERSTAND ALL.
AH, THERE'S THE RUB.
DIDN'T YOU "GET" WHAT SCHOLEM AND I FOUND IN THE ZOHAR* WAY BACK IN THE EARLY '20S?
WHAT THE HELL AM I DOING ARGUING WITH A WATER STAIN? I KNEW THAT WHITEFISH SALAD AT LUNCH TASTED FUNNY.

* Secret mystical text of Judaism

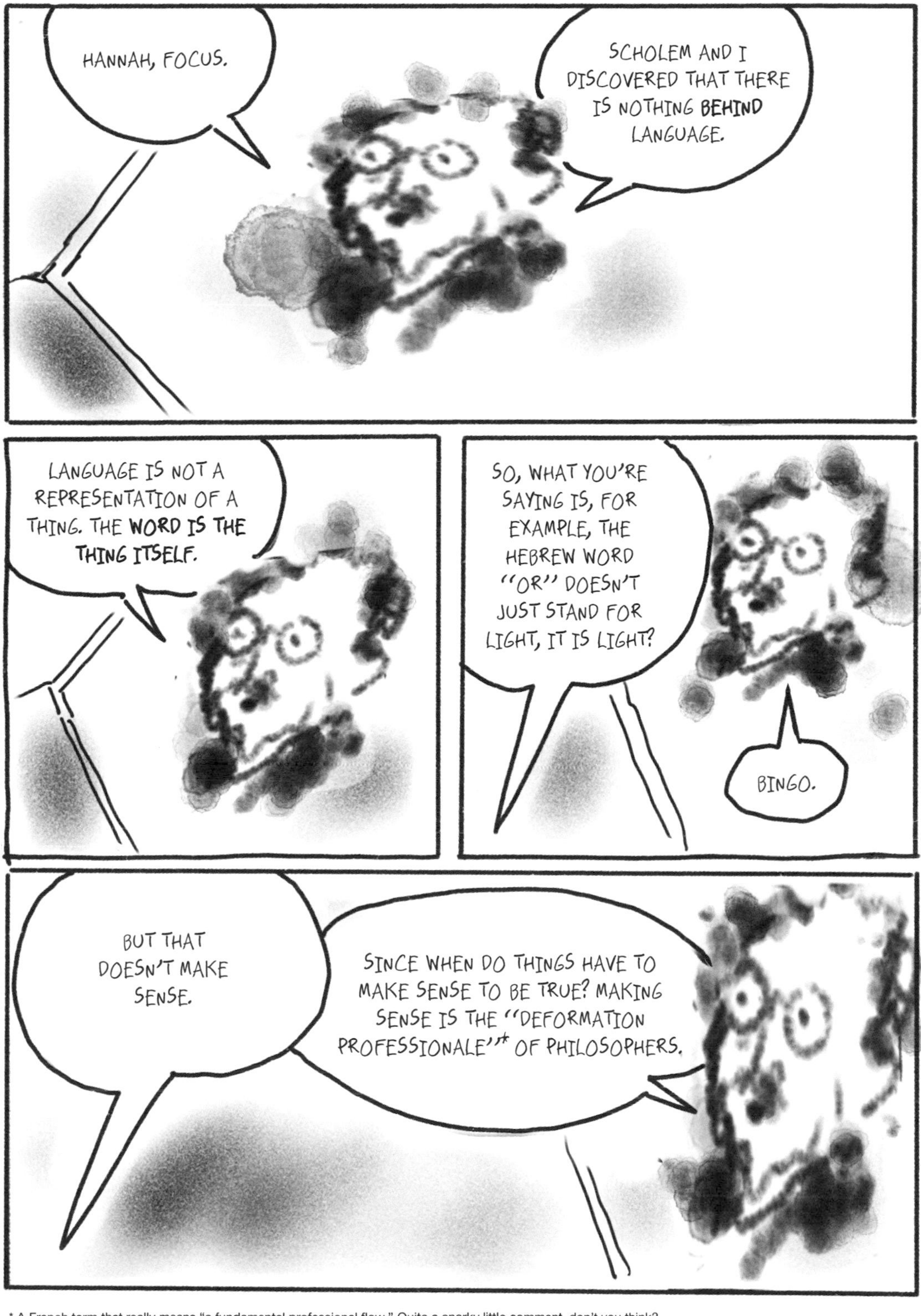
HANNAH, FOCUS.
SCHOLEM AND I DISCOVERED THAT THERE IS NOTHING BEHIND LANGUAGE.
LANGUAGE IS NOT A REPRESENTATION OF A THING. THE WORD IS THE THING ITSELF.
SO, WHAT YOU'RE SAYING IS, FOR EXAMPLE, THE HEBREW WORD "OR" DOESN'T JUST STAND FOR LIGHT, IT IS LIGHT?
BINGO.
BUT THAT DOESN'T MAKE SENSE.
SINCE WHEN DO THINGS HAVE TO MAKE SENSE TO BE TRUE? MAKING SENSE IS THE "DEFORMATION PROFESSIONALE"* OF PHILOSOPHERS.

* A French term that really means "a fundamental professional flaw." Quite a snarky little comment, don't you think?

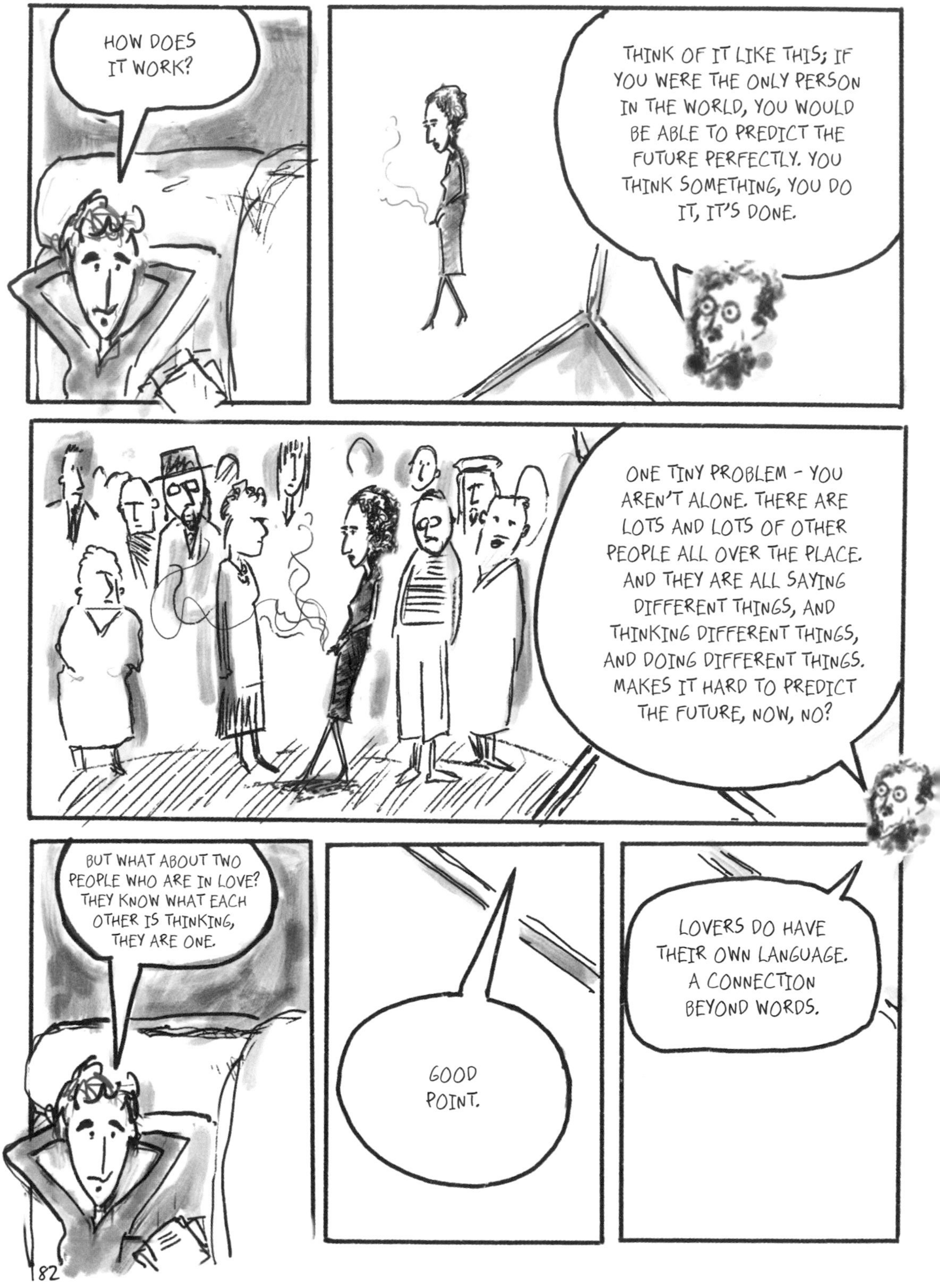
HOW DOES IT WORK?
THINK OF IT LIKE THIS; IF YOU WERE THE ONLY PERSON IN THE WORLD, YOU WOULD BE ABLE TO PREDICT THE FUTURE PERFECTLY. YOU THINK SOMETHING, YOU DO IT, IT'S DONE.
ONE TINY PROBLEM - YOU AREN'T ALONE. THERE ARE LOTS AND LOTS OF OTHER PEOPLE ALL OVER THE PLACE. AND THEY ARE ALL SAYING DIFFERENT THINGS, AND THINKING DIFFERENT THINGS, AND DOING DIFFERENT THINGS. MAKES IT HARD TO PREDICT THE FUTURE, NOW, NO?
BUT WHAT ABOUT TWO PEOPLE WHO ARE IN LOVE? THEY KNOW WHAT EACH OTHER IS THINKING, THEY ARE ONE.
GOOD POINT.
LOVERS DO HAVE THEIR OWN LANGUAGE. A CONNECTION BEYOND WORDS.

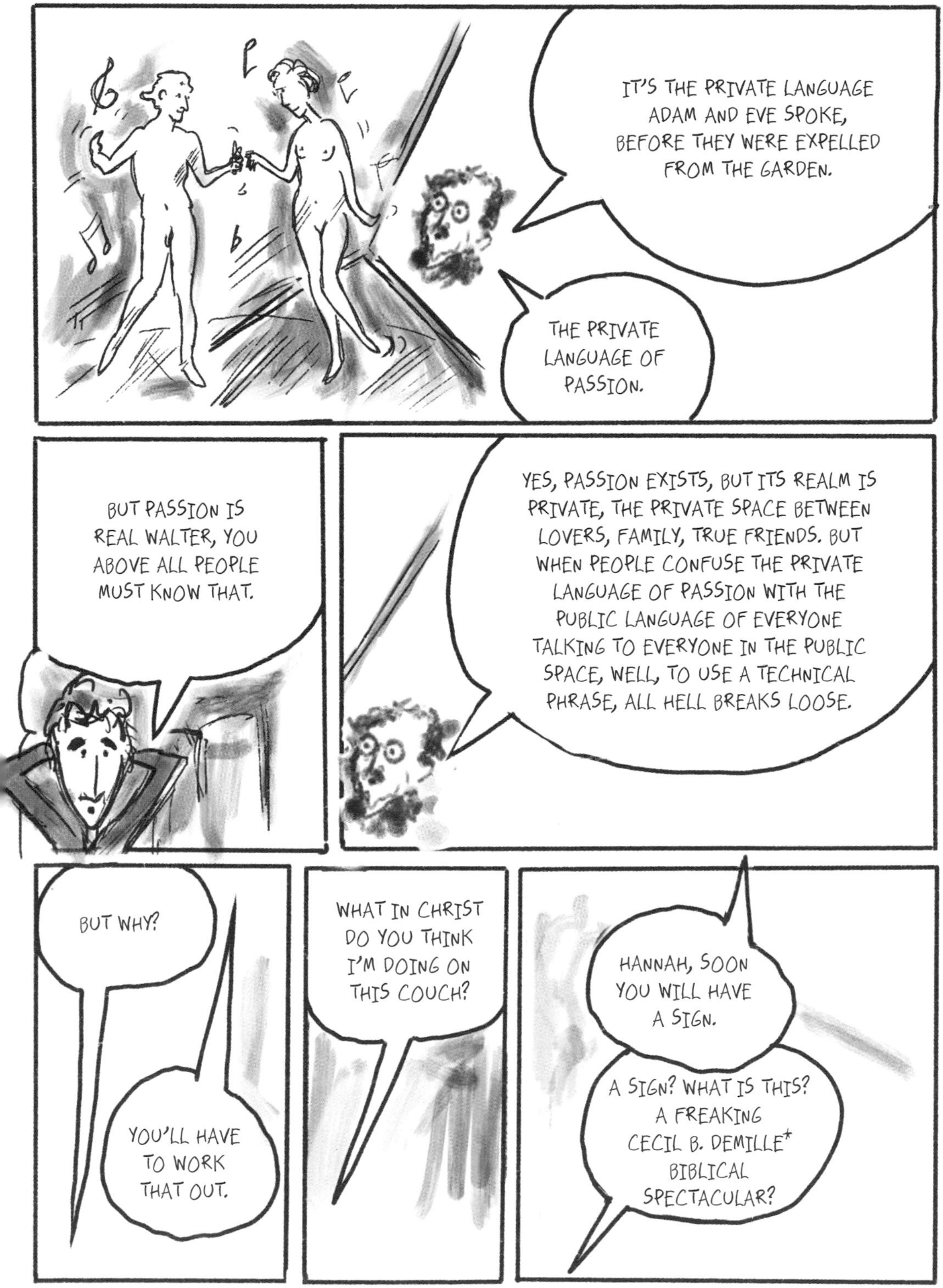
IT'S THE PRIVATE LANGUAGE ADAM AND EVE SPOKE, BEFORE THEY WERE EXPELLED FROM THE GARDEN.
THE PRIVATE LANGUAGE OF PASSION.
BUT PASSION IS REAL WALTER, YOU ABOVE ALL PEOPLE MUST KNOW THAT.
YES, PASSION EXISTS, BUT ITS REALM IS PRIVATE, THE PRIVATE SPACE BETWEEN LOVERS, FAMILY, TRUE FRIENDS. BUT WHEN PEOPLE CONFUSE THE PRIVATE LANGUAGE OF PASSION WITH THE PUBLIC LANGUAGE OF EVERYONE TALKING TO EVERYONE IN THE PUBLIC SPACE, WELL, TO USE A TECHNICAL PHRASE, ALL HELL BREAKS LOOSE.
BUT WHY?
YOU'LL HAVE TO WORK THAT OUT.
WHAT IN CHRIST DO YOU THINK I'M DOING ON THIS COUCH?
HANNAH, SOON YOU WILL HAVE A SIGN.
A SIGN? WHAT IS THIS? A FREAKING CECIL B. DEMILLE* BIBLICAL SPECTACULAR?

* Cecil B. DeMille (1881–1959). American film pioneer, created the "epic," and evinced some questionable moral and ethical choices in his films, most notoriously in his *The Birth of a Nation*.

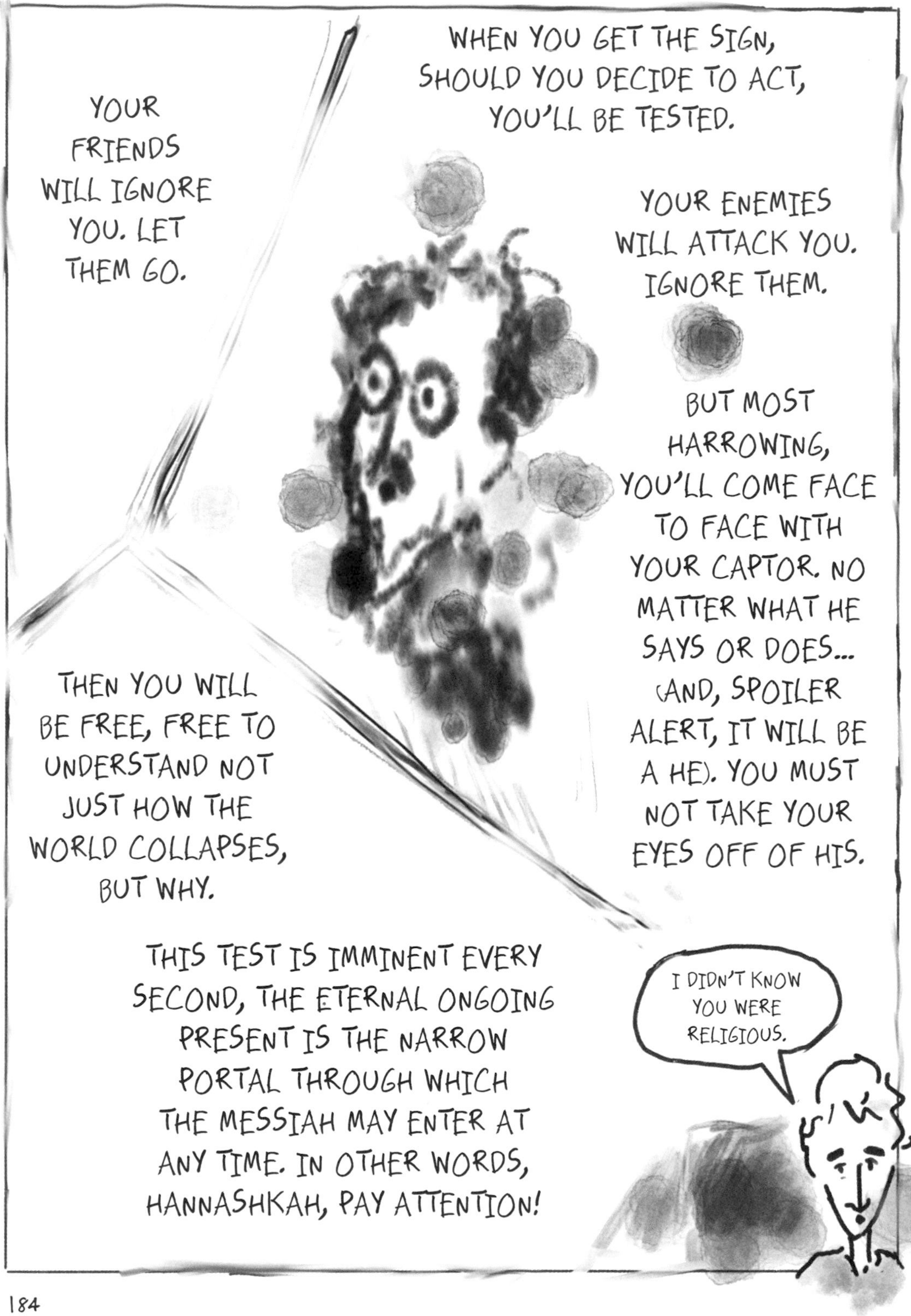
WHEN YOU GET THE SIGN, SHOULD YOU DECIDE TO ACT, YOU'LL BE TESTED.
YOUR FRIENDS WILL IGNORE YOU. LET THEM GO.
YOUR ENEMIES WILL ATTACK YOU. IGNORE THEM.
BUT MOST HARROWING, YOU'LL COME FACE TO FACE WITH YOUR CAPTOR. NO MATTER WHAT HE SAYS OR DOES... (AND, SPOILER ALERT, IT WILL BE A HE). YOU MUST NOT TAKE YOUR EYES OFF OF HIS.
THEN YOU WILL BE FREE, FREE TO UNDERSTAND NOT JUST HOW THE WORLD COLLAPSES, BUT WHY.
THIS TEST IS IMMINENT EVERY SECOND, THE ETERNAL ONGOING PRESENT IS THE NARROW PORTAL THROUGH WHICH THE MESSIAH MAY ENTER AT ANY TIME. IN OTHER WORDS, HANNASHKAH, PAY ATTENTION!
I DIDN'T KNOW YOU WERE RELIGIOUS.

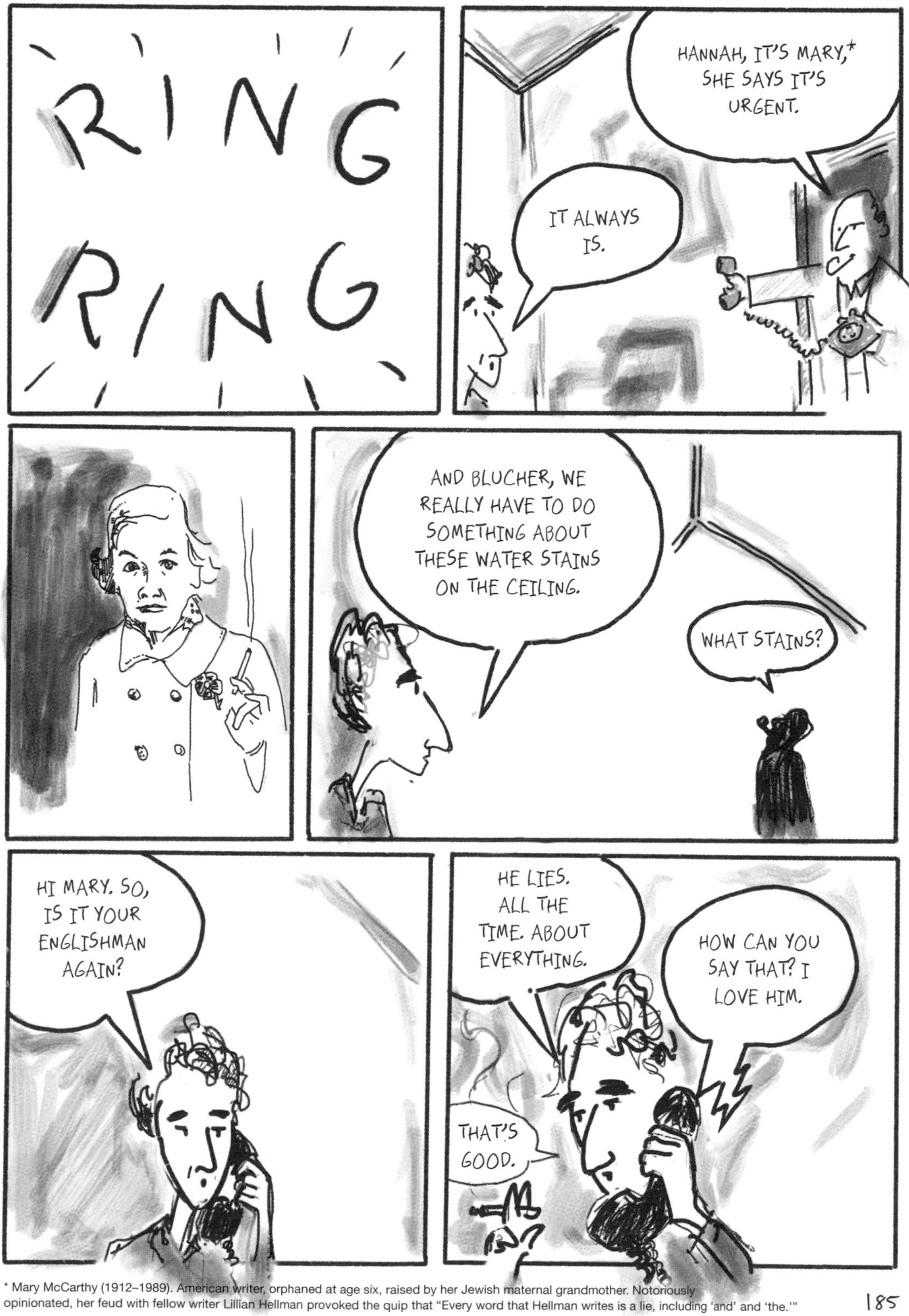
RING
RING
HANNAH, IT'S MARY,* SHE SAYS IT'S URGENT.
IT ALWAYS IS.
AND BLUCHER, WE REALLY HAVE TO DO SOMETHING ABOUT THESE WATER STAINS ON THE CEILING.
WHAT STAINS?
HI MARY. SO, IS IT YOUR ENGLISHMAN AGAIN?
HE LIES. ALL THE TIME. ABOUT EVERYTHING.
HOW CAN YOU SAY THAT? I LOVE HIM.
THAT'S GOOD.

* Mary McCarthy (1912–1989). American writer, orphaned at age six, raised by her Jewish maternal grandmother. Notoriously opinionated, her feud with fellow writer Lillian Hellman provoked the quip that "Every word that Hellman writes is a lie, including 'and' and 'the.'"

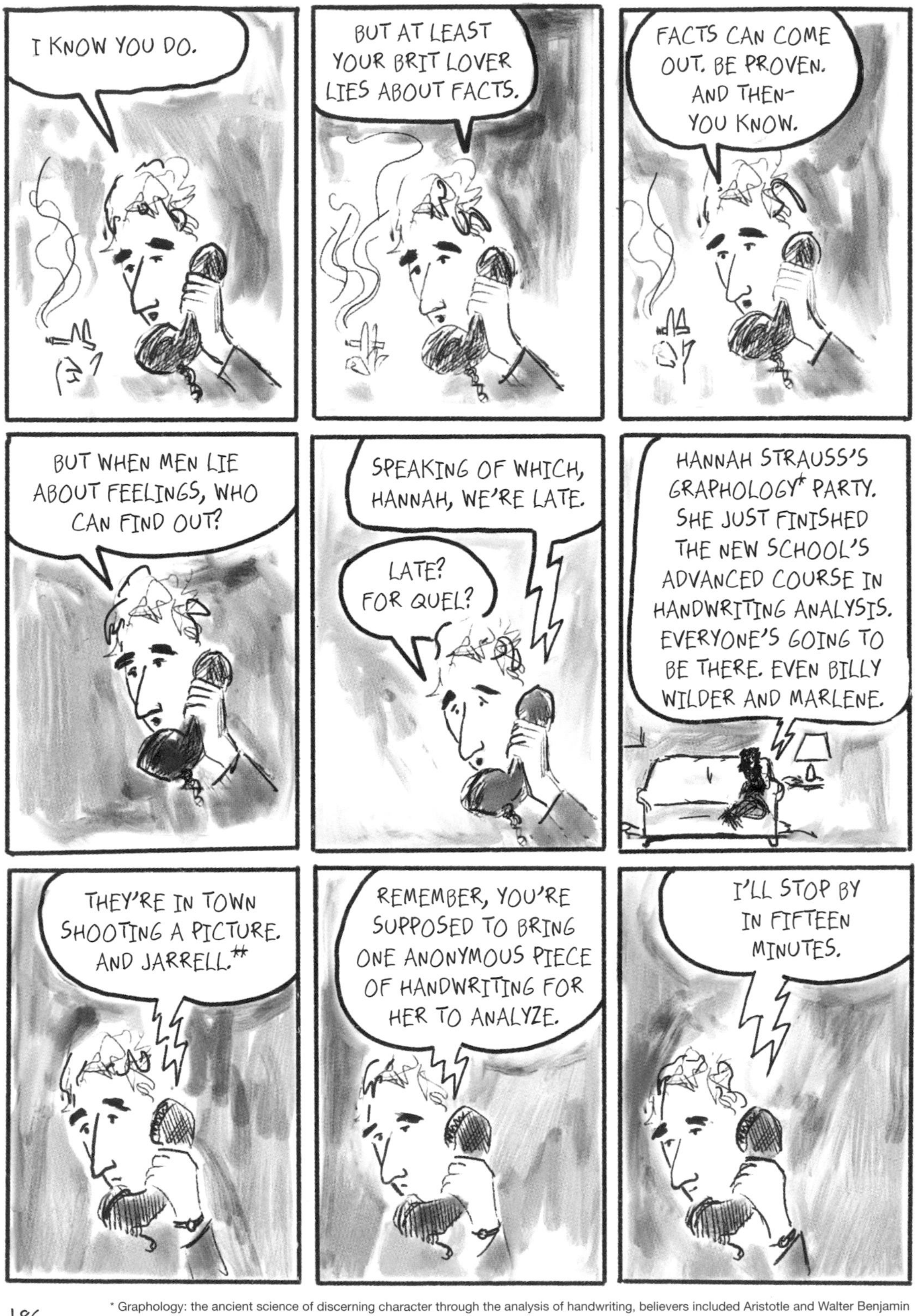
I KNOW YOU DO.
BUT AT LEAST YOUR BRIT LOVER LIES ABOUT FACTS.
FACTS CAN COME OUT. BE PROVEN. AND THEN- YOU KNOW.
BUT WHEN MEN LIE ABOUT FEELINGS, WHO CAN FIND OUT?
SPEAKING OF WHICH, HANNAH, WE'RE LATE.
LATE? FOR QUEL?
HANNAH STRAUSS'S GRAPHOLOGY* PARTY. SHE JUST FINISHED THE NEW SCHOOL'S ADVANCED COURSE IN HANDWRITING ANALYSIS. EVERYONE'S GOING TO BE THERE. EVEN BILLY WILDER AND MARLENE.
THEY'RE IN TOWN SHOOTING A PICTURE. AND JARRELL.**
REMEMBER, YOU'RE SUPPOSED TO BRING ONE ANONYMOUS PIECE OF HANDWRITING FOR HER TO ANALYZE.
I'LL STOP BY IN FIFTEEN MINUTES.

* Graphology: the ancient science of discerning character through the analysis of handwriting, believers included Aristotle and Walter Benjamin
** Randall Jarrell (1914–1965). American poet and critic, devoted friend of Hannah Arendt's, Poet Laureate of the U.S.

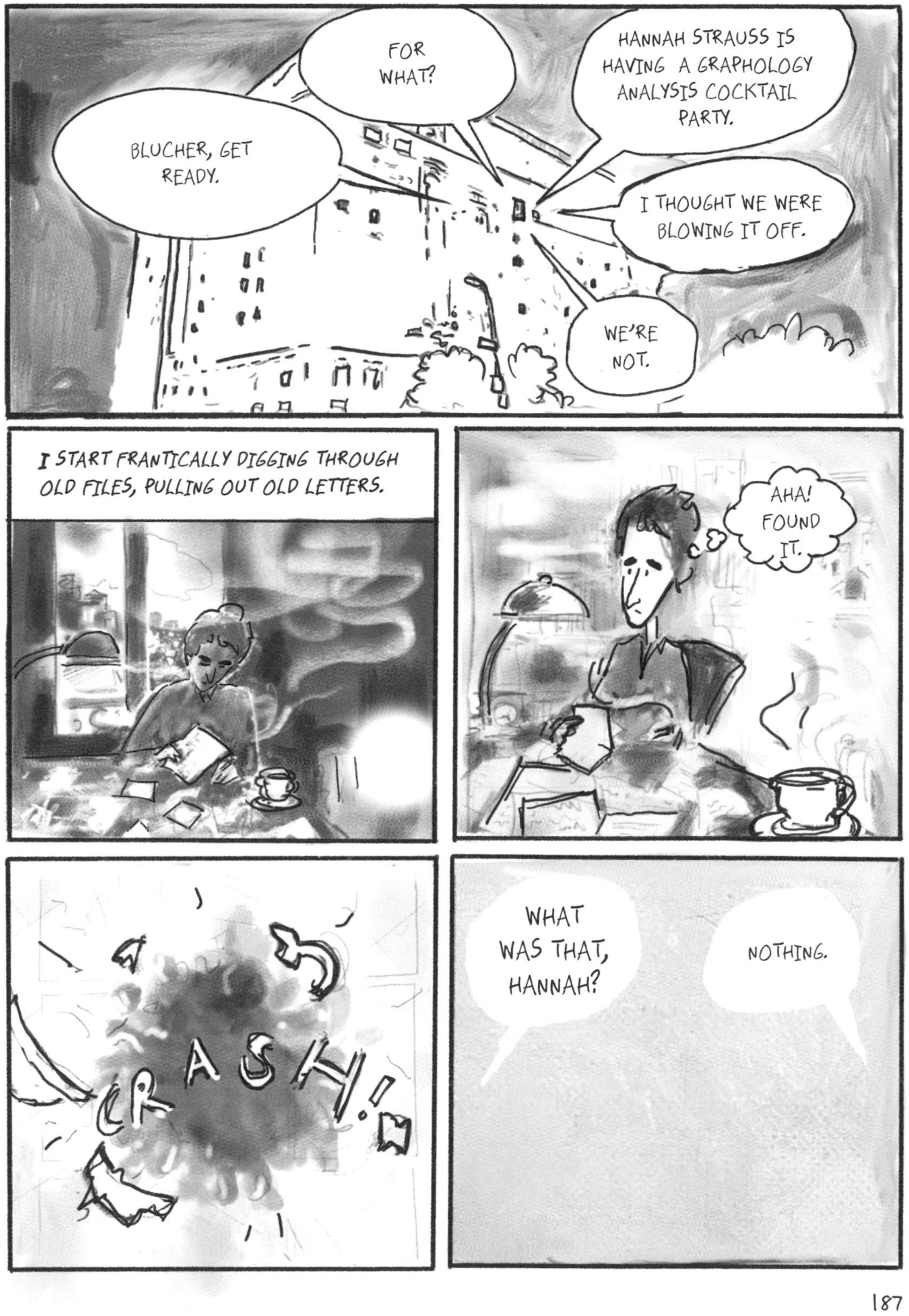
BLUCHER, GET READY.
FOR WHAT?
HANNAH STRAUSS IS HAVING A GRAPHOLOGY ANALYSIS COCKTAIL PARTY.
I THOUGHT WE WERE BLOWING IT OFF.
WE'RE NOT.
I START FRANTICALLY DIGGING THROUGH OLD FILES, PULLING OUT OLD LETTERS.
AHA! FOUND IT.
CRASH!
WHAT WAS THAT, HANNAH?
NOTHING.

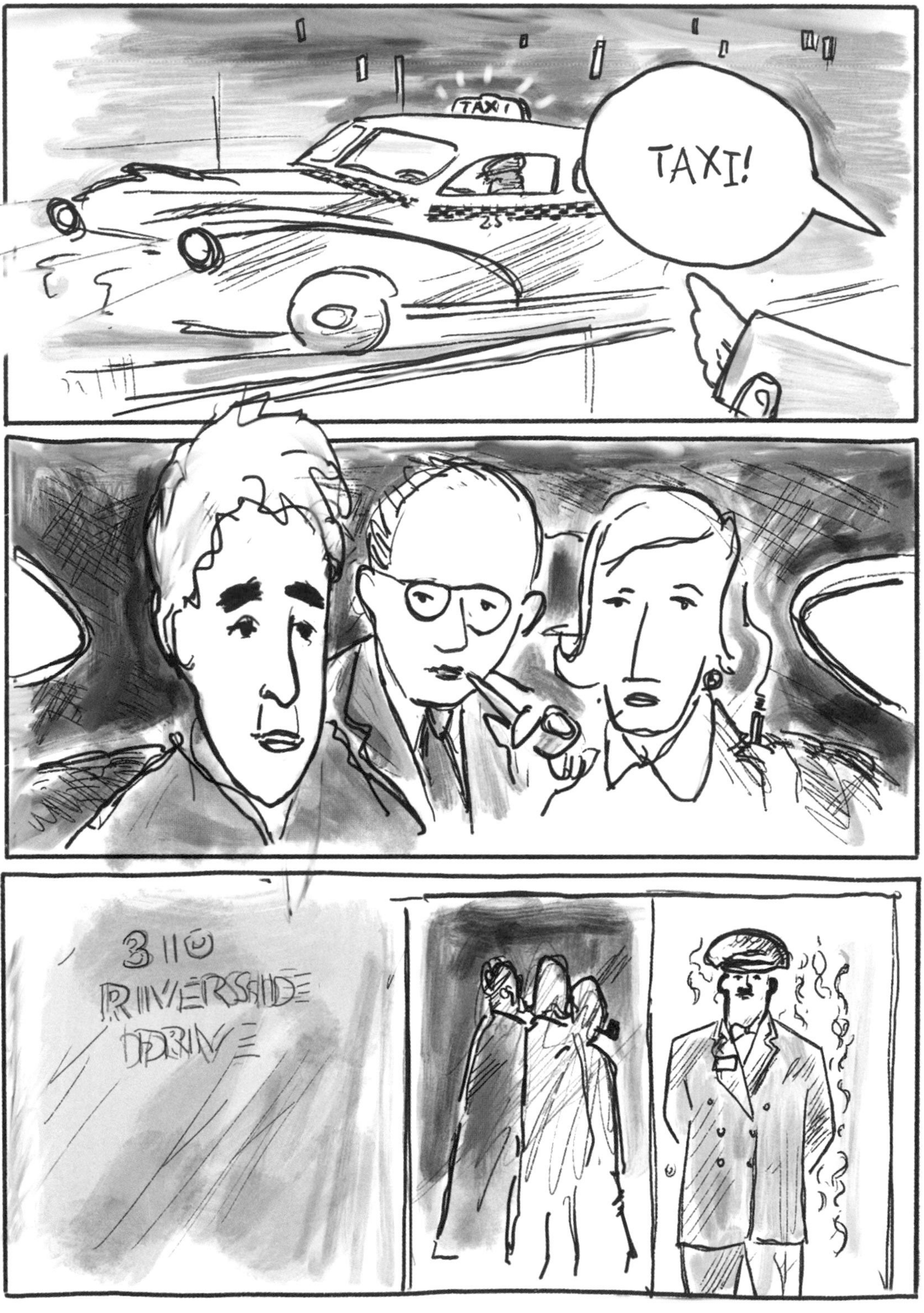
TAXI!
310
RIVERSIDE
DRIVE

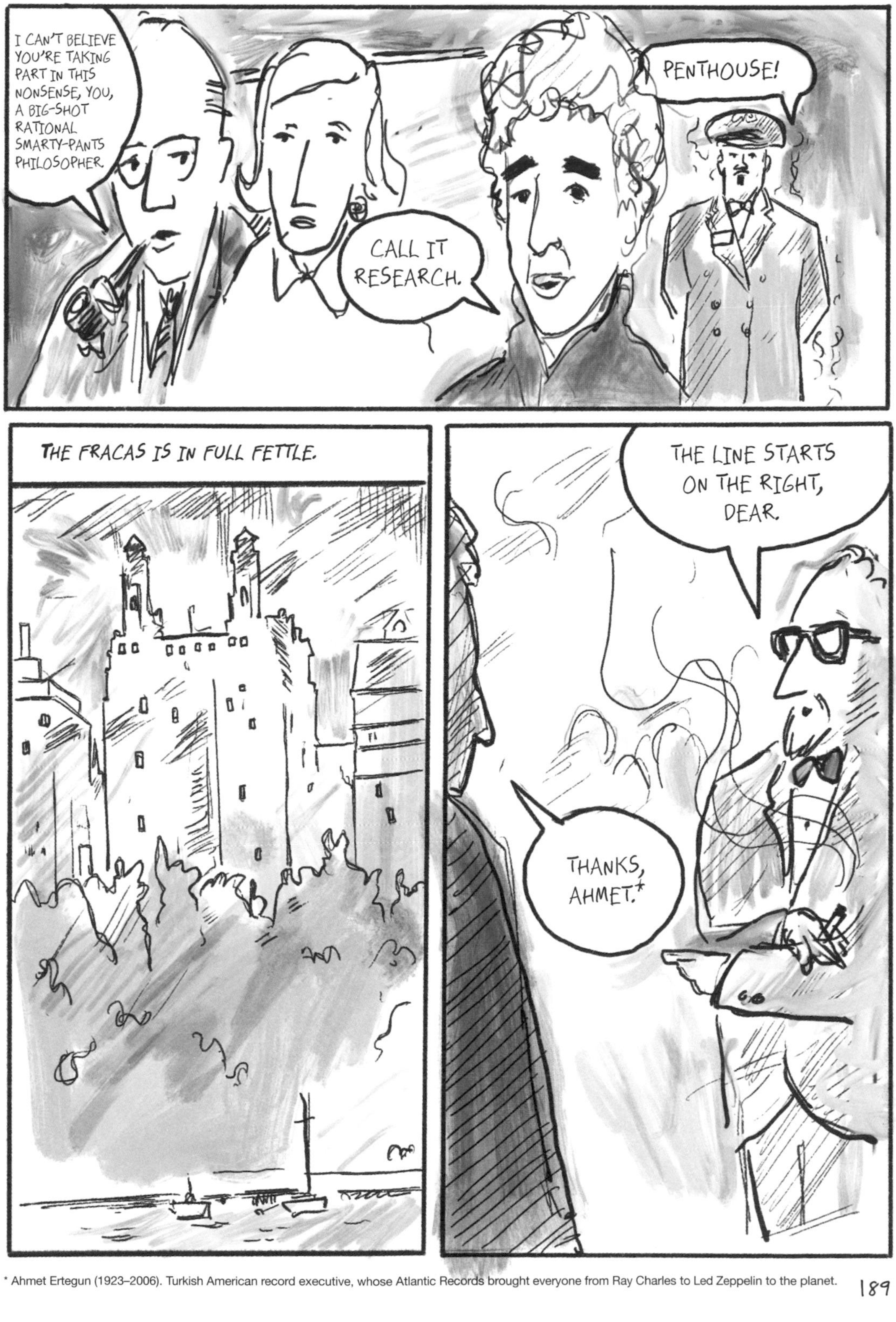
I CAN'T BELIEVE YOU'RE TAKING PART IN THIS NONSENSE, YOU, A BIG-SHOT RATIONAL SMARTY-PANTS PHILOSOPHER.
CALL IT RESEARCH.
PENTHOUSE!
THE FRACAS IS IN FULL FETTLE.
THE LINE STARTS ON THE RIGHT, DEAR.
THANKS, AHMET.*

* Ahmet Ertegun (1923–2006). Turkish American record executive, whose Atlantic Records brought everyone from Ray Charles to Led Zeppelin to the planet.

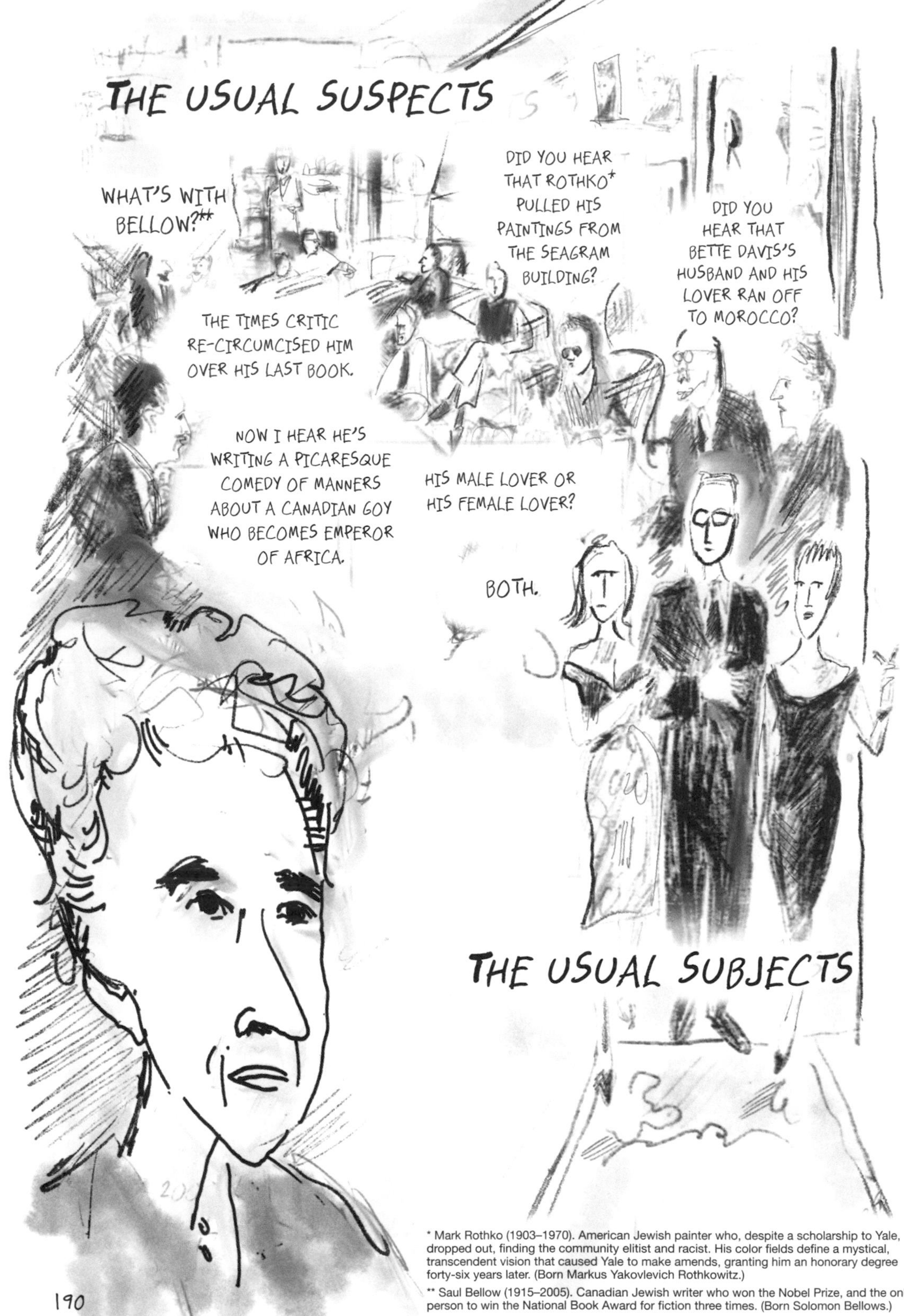
THE USUAL SUSPECTS
WHAT'S WITH BELLOW?**
THE TIMES CRITIC RE-CIRCUMCISED HIM OVER HIS LAST BOOK.
NOW I HEAR HE'S WRITING A PICARESQUE COMEDY OF MANNERS ABOUT A CANADIAN GOY WHO BECOMES EMPEROR OF AFRICA.
DID YOU HEAR THAT ROTHKO* PULLED HIS PAINTINGS FROM THE SEAGRAM BUILDING?
DID YOU HEAR THAT BETTE DAVIS'S HUSBAND AND HIS LOVER RAN OFF TO MOROCCO?
HIS MALE LOVER OR HIS FEMALE LOVER?
BOTH.
THE USUAL SUBJECTS

* Mark Rothko (1903–1970). American Jewish painter who, despite a scholarship to Yale, dropped out, finding the community elitist and racist. His color fields define a mystical, transcendent vision that caused Yale to make amends, granting him an honorary degree forty-six years later. (Born Markus Yakovlevich Rothkowitz.)

** Saul Bellow (1915–2005). Canadian Jewish writer who won the Nobel Prize, and the only person to win the National Book Award for fiction three times. (Born Solomon Bellows.)

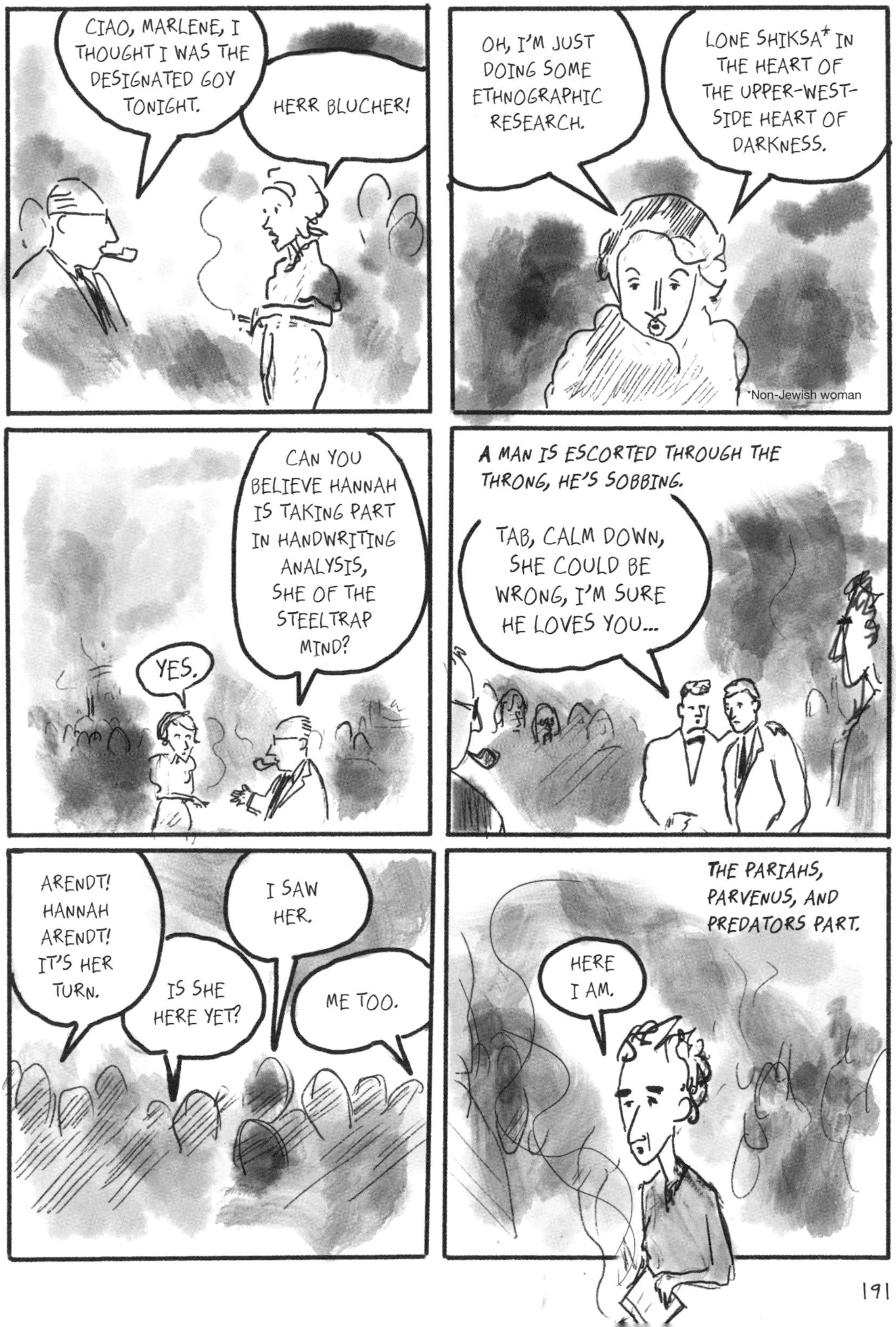
CIAO, MARLENE, I THOUGHT I WAS THE DESIGNATED GOY TONIGHT.
HERR BLUCHER!
OH, I'M JUST DOING SOME ETHNOGRAPHIC RESEARCH.
LONE SHIKSA* IN THE HEART OF THE UPPER-WEST-SIDE HEART OF DARKNESS.
*Non-Jewish woman
CAN YOU BELIEVE HANNAH IS TAKING PART IN HANDWRITING ANALYSIS, SHE OF THE STEELTRAP MIND?
YES.
A MAN IS ESCORTED THROUGH THE THRONG, HE'S SOBBING.
TAB, CALM DOWN, SHE COULD BE WRONG, I'M SURE HE LOVES YOU...
ARENDT! HANNAH ARENDT! IT'S HER TURN.
IS SHE HERE YET?
I SAW HER.
ME TOO.
THE PARIAHS, PARVENUS, AND PREDATORS PART.
HERE I AM.

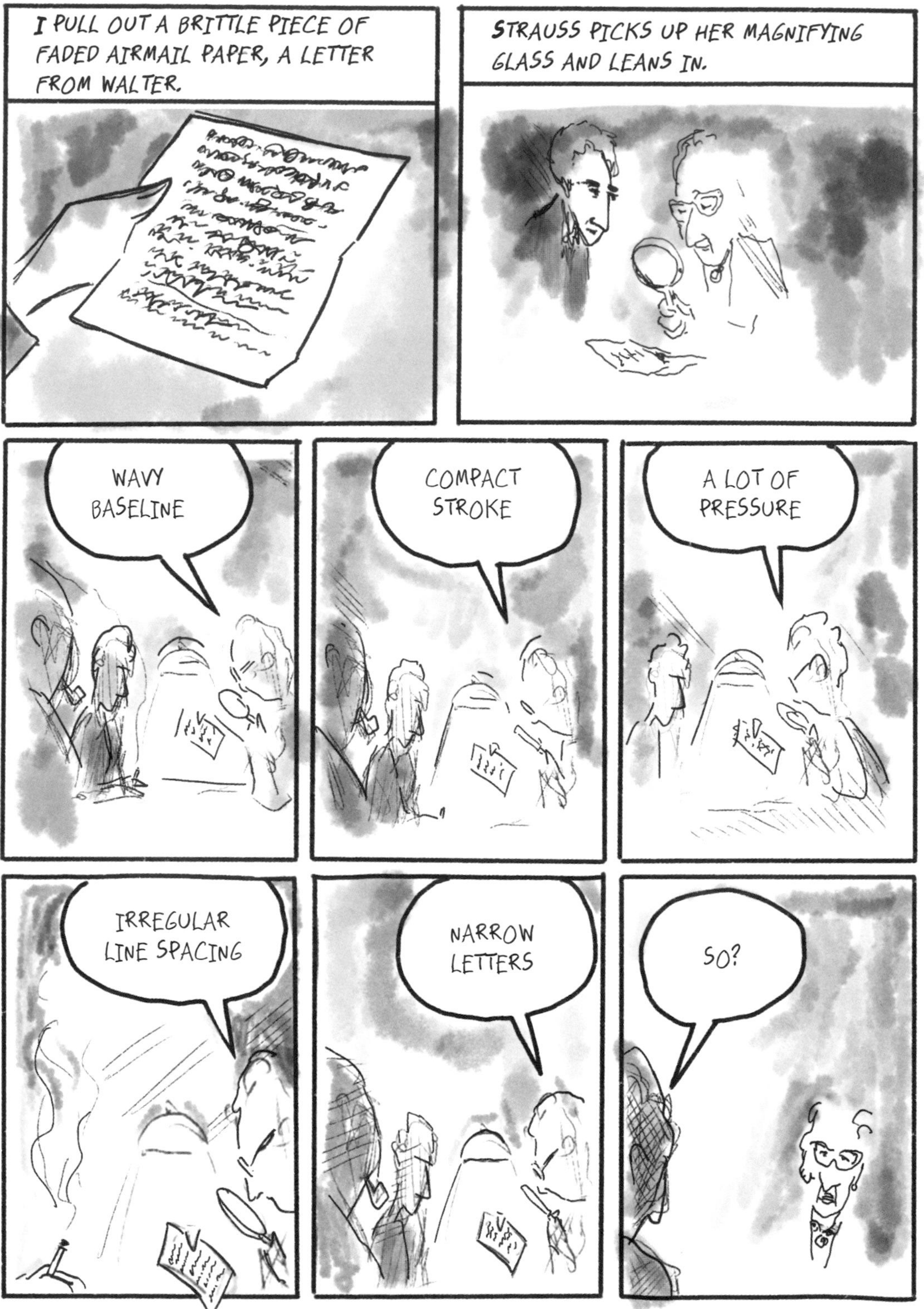
I PULL OUT A BRITTLE PIECE OF FADED AIRMAIL PAPER, A LETTER FROM WALTER.
STRAUSS PICKS UP HER MAGNIFYING GLASS AND LEANS IN.
WAVY BASELINE
COMPACT STROKE
A LOT OF PRESSURE
IRREGULAR LINE SPACING
NARROW LETTERS
SO?

IF THERE'S ONE THING THAT'S CLEAR, THIS MAN IS VERY SELF-DESTRUCTIVE.

YES, HE TOOK HIS LIFE NOT LONG AGO* ON THE SPANISH BORDER.

I AM SORRY.

* Even though it was 18 years!

I KNOW WE'RE ONLY SUPPOSED TO BRING ONE SAMPLE BUT...

THAT'S OK HANNAH, I'M SURE NOBODY WILL MIND IF I EXAMINE ANOTHER FOR YOU.

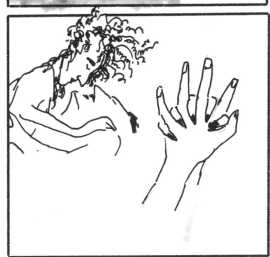

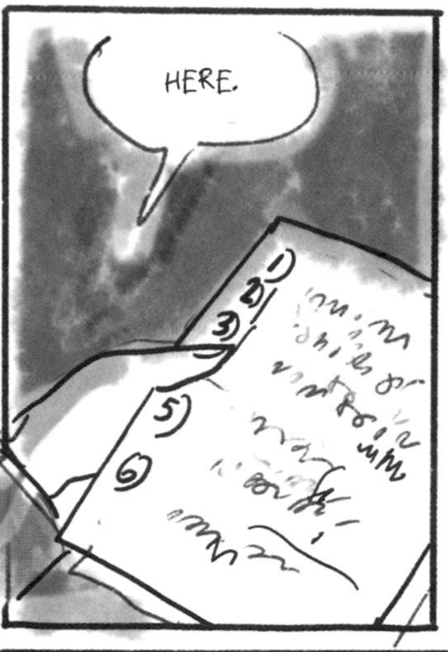
HERE.

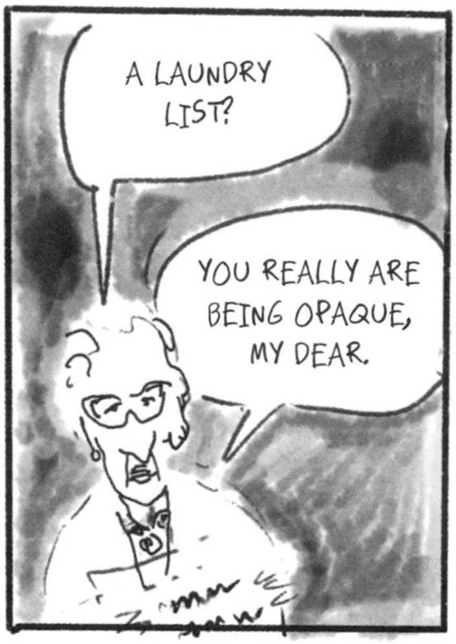
A LAUNDRY LIST?
YOU REALLY ARE BEING OPAQUE, MY DEAR.

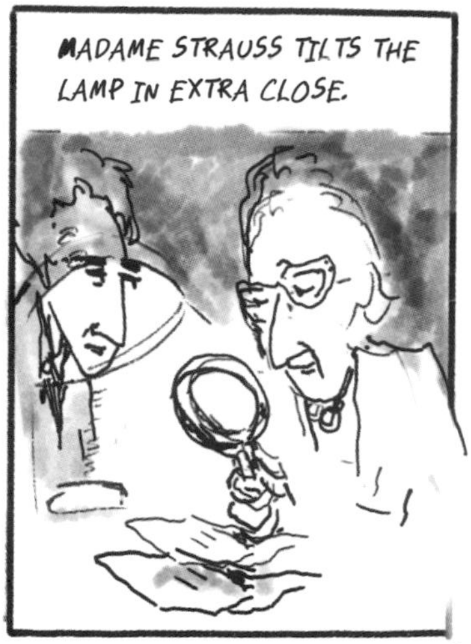
MADAME STRAUSS TILTS THE LAMP IN EXTRA CLOSE.

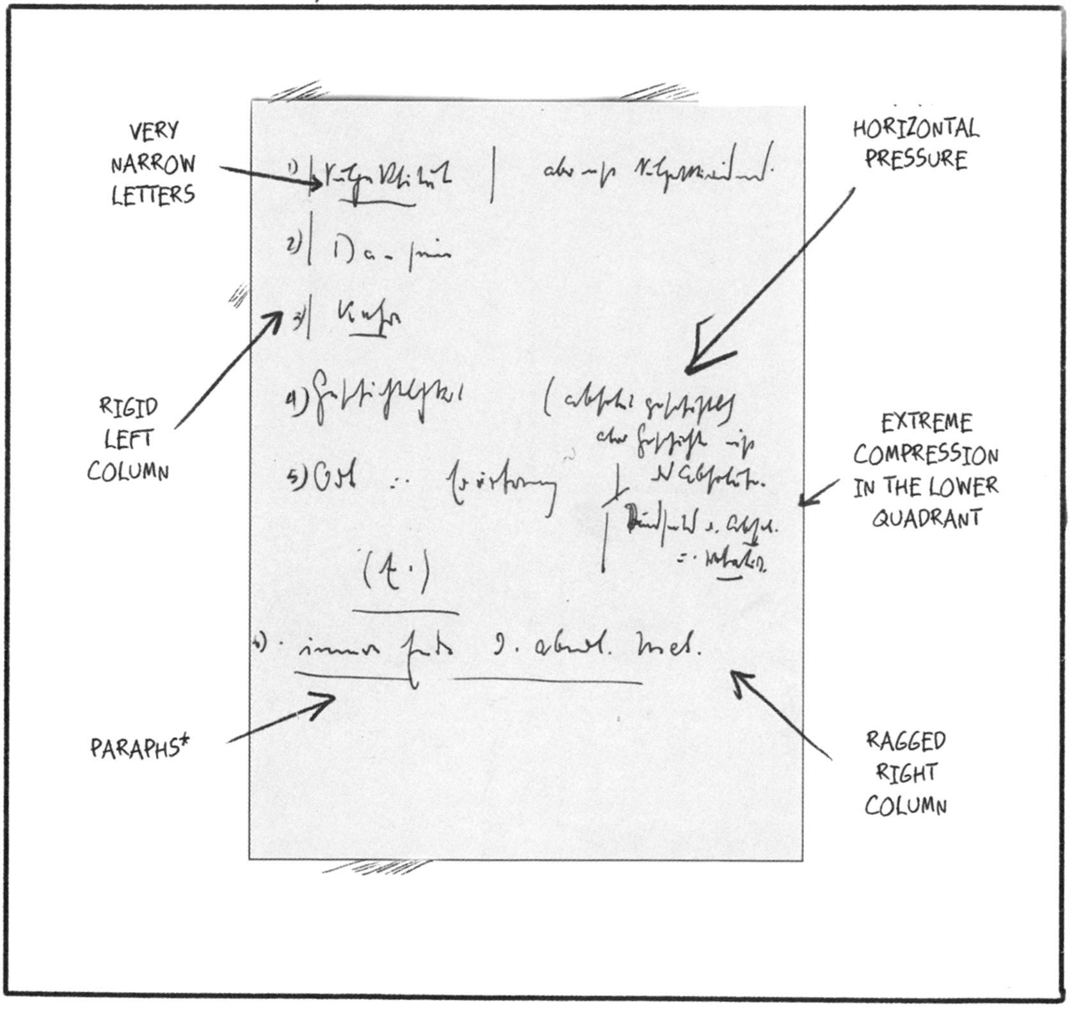
VERY NARROW LETTERS
HORIZONTAL PRESSURE
RIGID LEFT COLUMN
EXTREME COMPRESSION IN THE LOWER QUADRANT
PARAPHS*
RAGGED RIGHT COLUMN

* Underlinings

WHAT DOES IT MEAN?

THIS MAN IS FASCINATED WITH LANGUAGE, WITH WORDS. BUT NOT JUST THE WORDS. WITH THEIR ORIGINS, WHAT'S BEHIND THEM. AND JUST LIKE ERASMUS OF ROTTERDAM,* WHOSE SCRIPT IS IDENTICAL, THIS MAN VACILLATES IN HIS COMMITMENTS.

HOW DO YOU KNOW?

SEE HOW HE DOES HIS "W'S"?

A LOOPING ARC ON THE FIRST INCLINE, A SHARP ANGLE ON THE SECOND. IT INDICATES THAT HE ALLIES HIMSELF TO A CAUSE, THEN RETREATS INTO HIS OWN REALM.

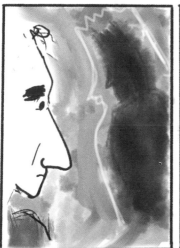

IS HE MARRIED?

YES, BUT THE MARRIAGE DOES NOT MATTER TO HIM.

* Erasmus of Rotterdam (1466–1536). Dutch thinker and priest, saw past the partisan squabbles of his times, a firm believer in free will, folly, and the "Via Media," the middle road, which basically succeeded in pissing off just about everyone on all sides of a debate.

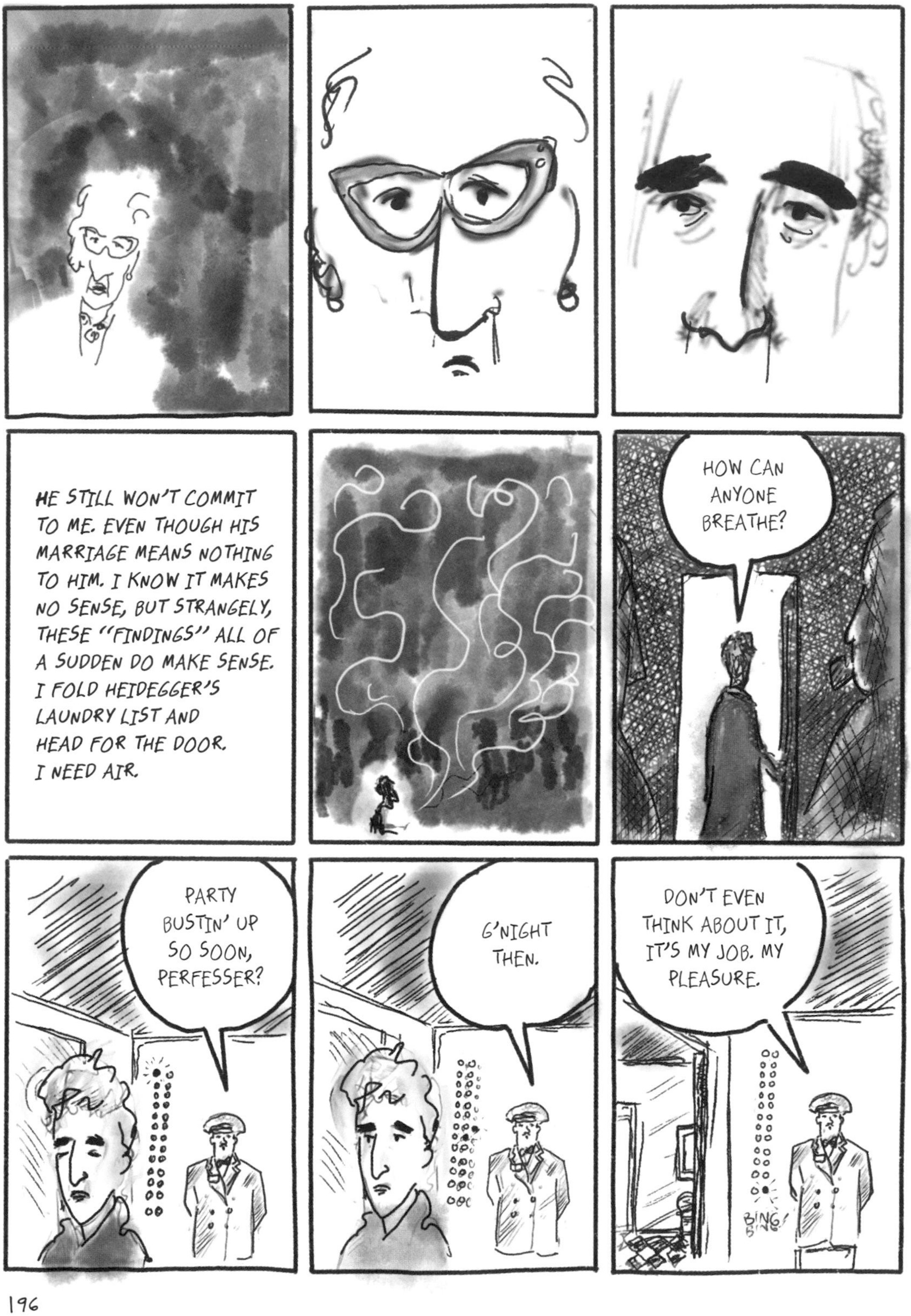
HE STILL WON'T COMMIT TO ME. EVEN THOUGH HIS MARRIAGE MEANS NOTHING TO HIM. I KNOW IT MAKES NO SENSE, BUT STRANGELY, THESE "FINDINGS" ALL OF A SUDDEN DO MAKE SENSE. I FOLD HEIDEGGER'S LAUNDRY LIST AND HEAD FOR THE DOOR. I NEED AIR.
HOW CAN ANYONE BREATHE?
PARTY BUSTIN' UP SO SOON, PERFESSER?
G'NIGHT THEN.
DON'T EVEN THINK ABOUT IT, IT'S MY JOB. MY PLEASURE.
BING!

KADDISH* ON RIVERSIDE

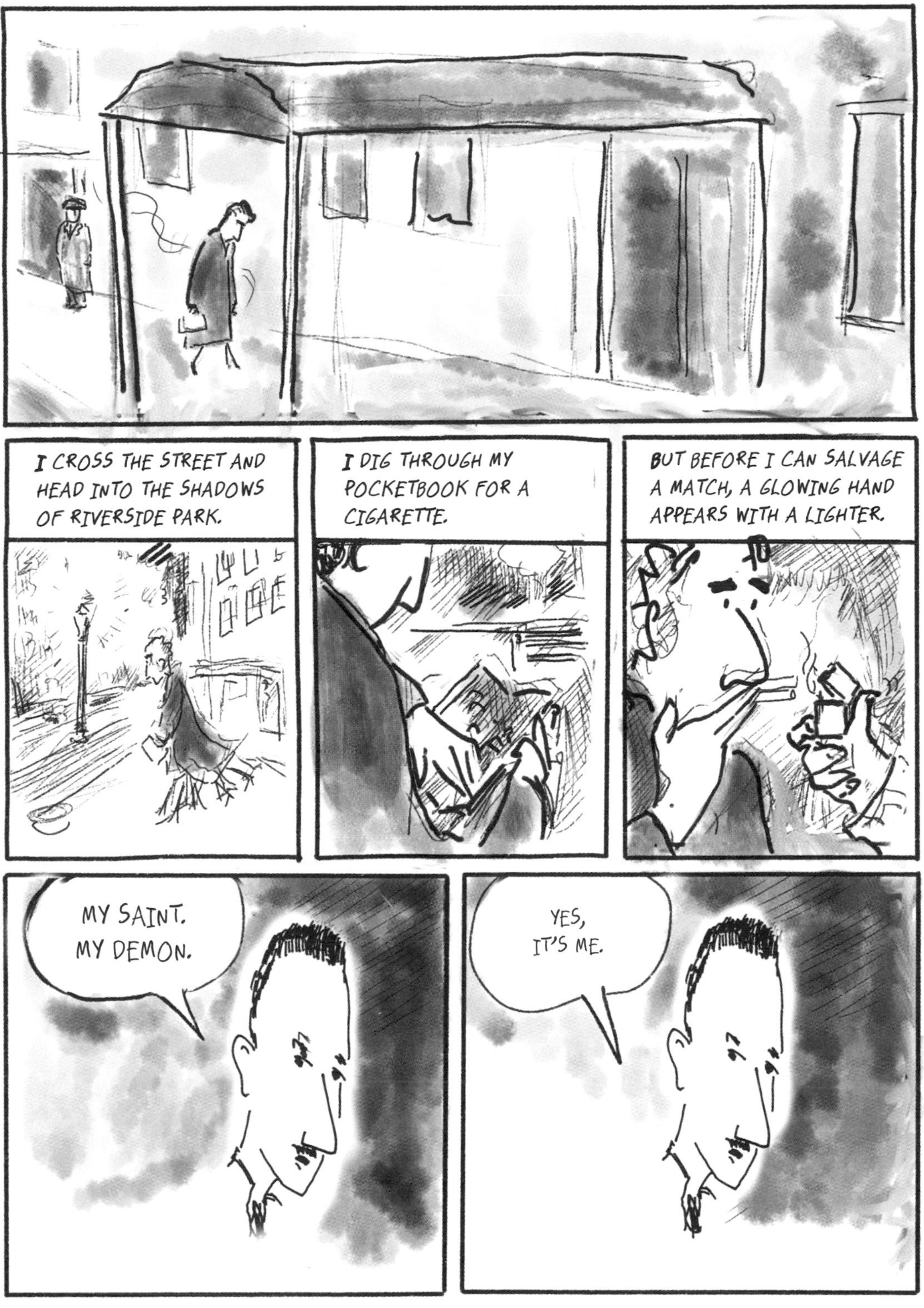

I CROSS THE STREET AND HEAD INTO THE SHADOWS OF RIVERSIDE PARK.
I DIG THROUGH MY POCKETBOOK FOR A CIGARETTE.
BUT BEFORE I CAN SALVAGE A MATCH, A GLOWING HAND APPEARS WITH A LIGHTER.
MY SAINT. MY DEMON.
YES, IT'S ME.

* Hebrew prayer for the dead.

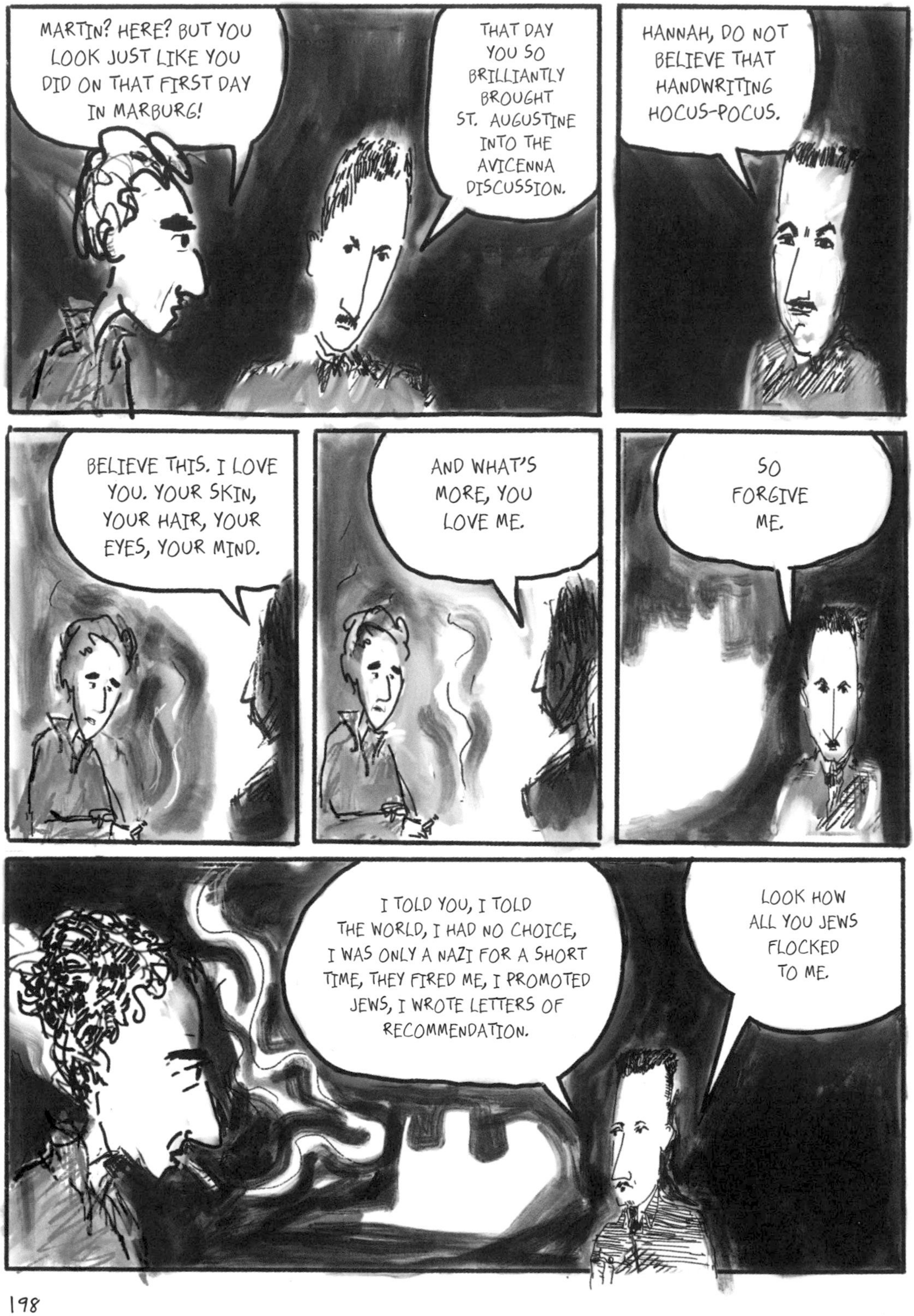
MARTIN? HERE? BUT YOU LOOK JUST LIKE YOU DID ON THAT FIRST DAY IN MARBURG!
THAT DAY YOU SO BRILLIANTLY BROUGHT ST. AUGUSTINE INTO THE AVICENNA DISCUSSION.
HANNAH, DO NOT BELIEVE THAT HANDWRITING HOCUS-POCUS.
BELIEVE THIS. I LOVE YOU. YOUR SKIN, YOUR HAIR, YOUR EYES, YOUR MIND.
AND WHAT'S MORE, YOU LOVE ME.
SO FORGIVE ME.
I TOLD YOU, I TOLD THE WORLD, I HAD NO CHOICE, I WAS ONLY A NAZI FOR A SHORT TIME, THEY FIRED ME, I PROMOTED JEWS, I WROTE LETTERS OF RECOMMENDATION.
LOOK HOW ALL YOU JEWS FLOCKED TO ME.

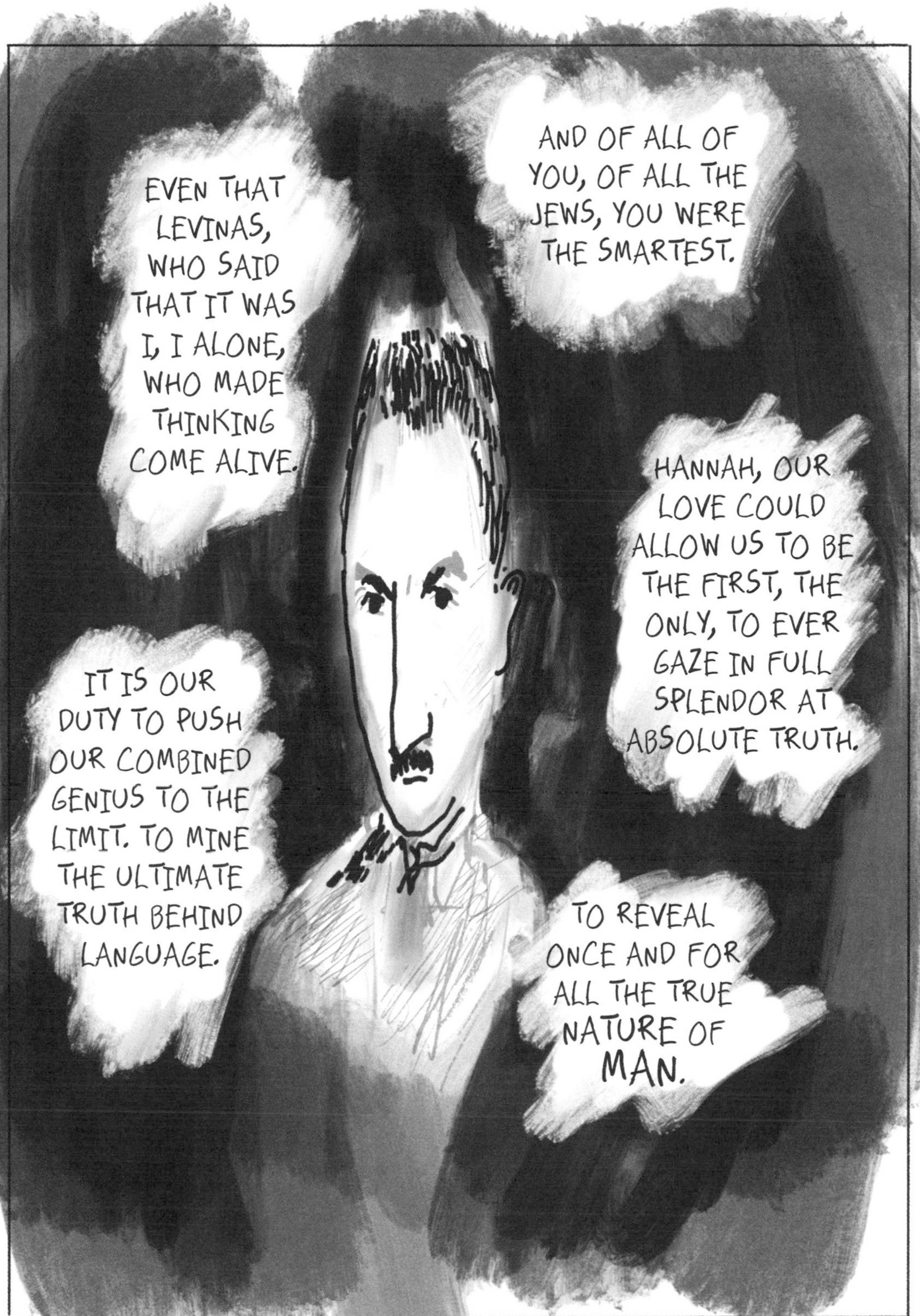
EVEN THAT LEVINAS, WHO SAID THAT IT WAS I, I ALONE, WHO MADE THINKING COME ALIVE.
AND OF ALL OF YOU, OF ALL THE JEWS, YOU WERE THE SMARTEST.
HANNAH, OUR LOVE COULD ALLOW US TO BE THE FIRST, THE ONLY, TO EVER GAZE IN FULL SPLENDOR AT ABSOLUTE TRUTH.
IT IS OUR DUTY TO PUSH OUR COMBINED GENIUS TO THE LIMIT. TO MINE THE ULTIMATE TRUTH BEHIND LANGUAGE.
TO REVEAL ONCE AND FOR ALL THE TRUE NATURE OF MAN.

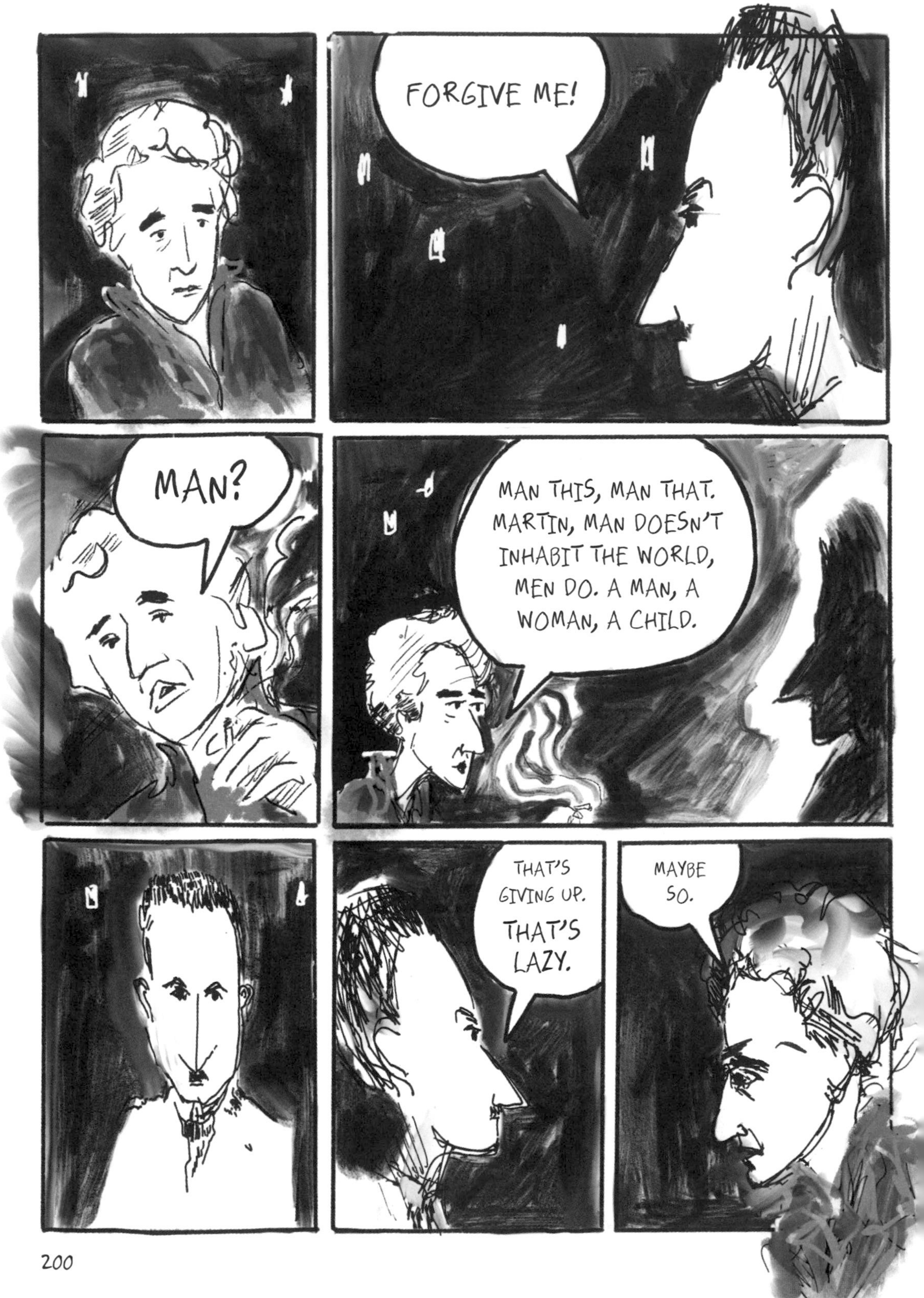
FORGIVE ME!
MAN?
MAN THIS, MAN THAT. MARTIN, MAN DOESN'T INHABIT THE WORLD, MEN DO. A MAN, A WOMAN, A CHILD.
THAT'S GIVING UP. THAT'S LAZY.
MAYBE SO.

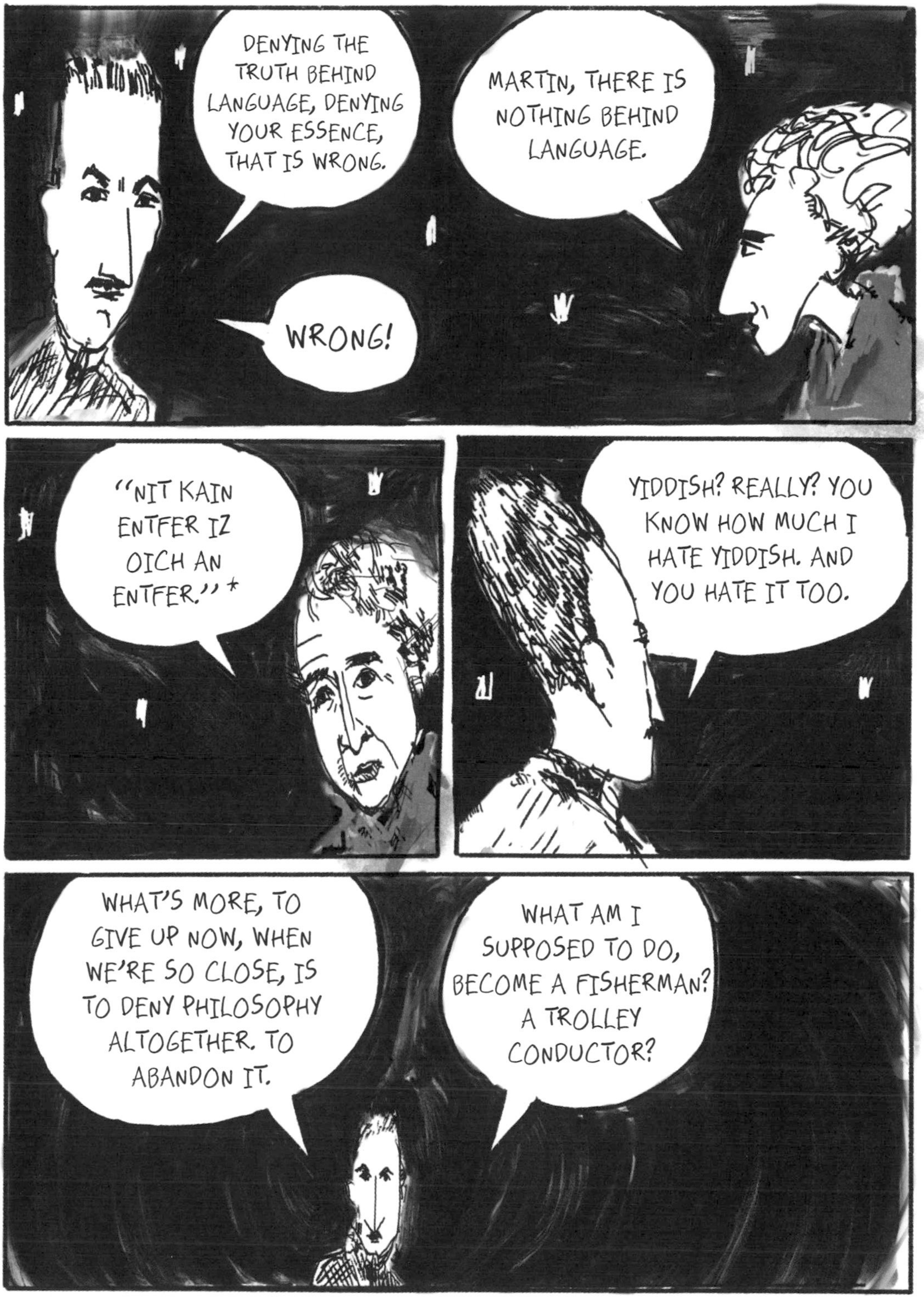

DENYING THE TRUTH BEHIND LANGUAGE, DENYING YOUR ESSENCE, THAT IS WRONG.
MARTIN, THERE IS NOTHING BEHIND LANGUAGE.
WRONG!
"NIT KAIN ENTFER IZ OICH AN ENTFER." *
YIDDISH? REALLY? YOU KNOW HOW MUCH I HATE YIDDISH. AND YOU HATE IT TOO.
WHAT'S MORE, TO GIVE UP NOW, WHEN WE'RE SO CLOSE, IS TO DENY PHILOSOPHY ALTOGETHER. TO ABANDON IT.
WHAT AM I SUPPOSED TO DO, BECOME A FISHERMAN? A TROLLEY CONDUCTOR?

* "No answer is also an answer," Yiddish proverb

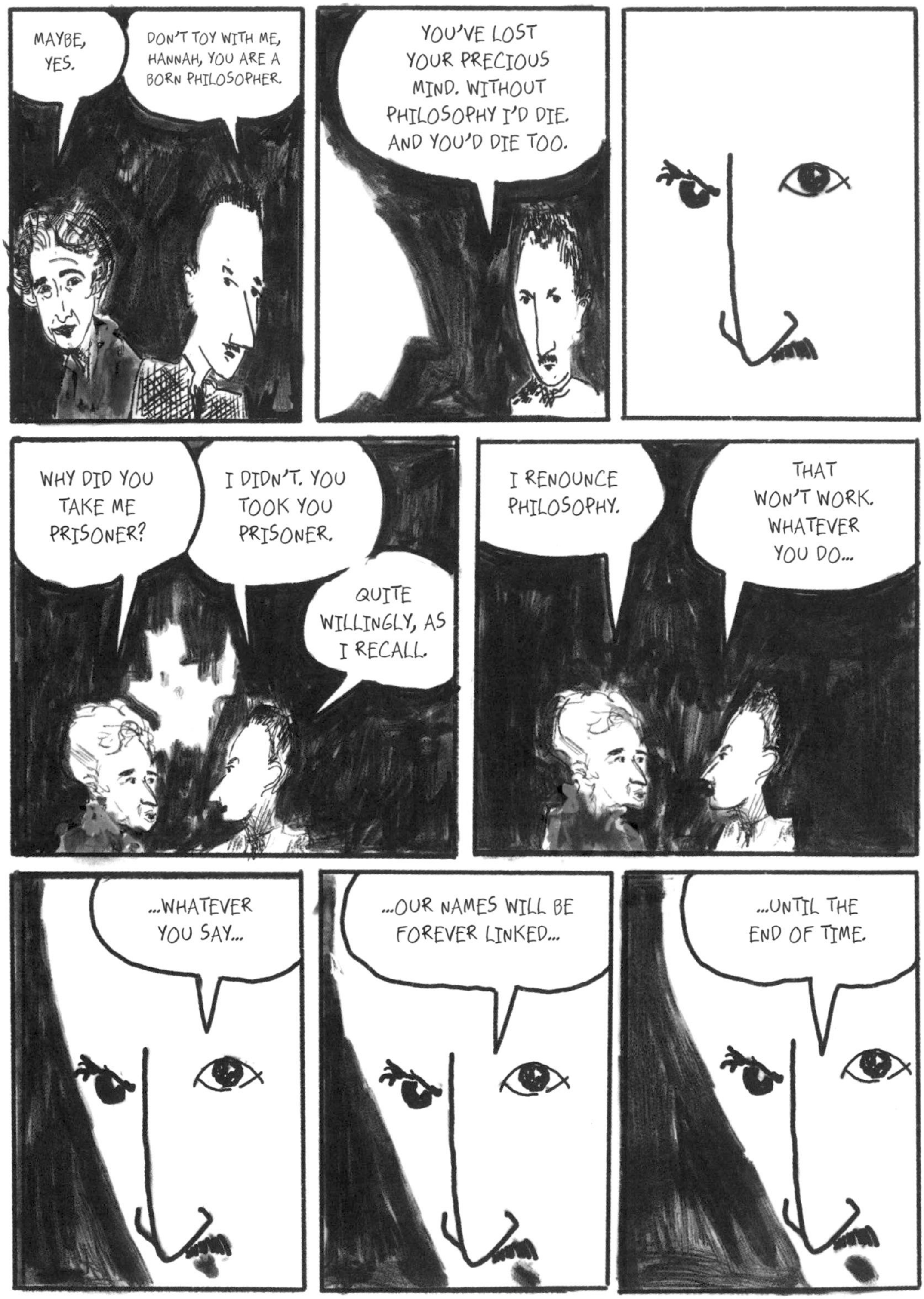
MAYBE, YES.
DON'T TOY WITH ME, HANNAH, YOU ARE A BORN PHILOSOPHER.
YOU'VE LOST YOUR PRECIOUS MIND. WITHOUT PHILOSOPHY I'D DIE. AND YOU'D DIE TOO.
WHY DID YOU TAKE ME PRISONER?
I DIDN'T. YOU TOOK YOU PRISONER.
QUITE WILLINGLY, AS I RECALL.
I RENOUNCE PHILOSOPHY.
THAT WON'T WORK. WHATEVER YOU DO...
...WHATEVER YOU SAY...
...OUR NAMES WILL BE FOREVER LINKED...
...UNTIL THE END OF TIME.

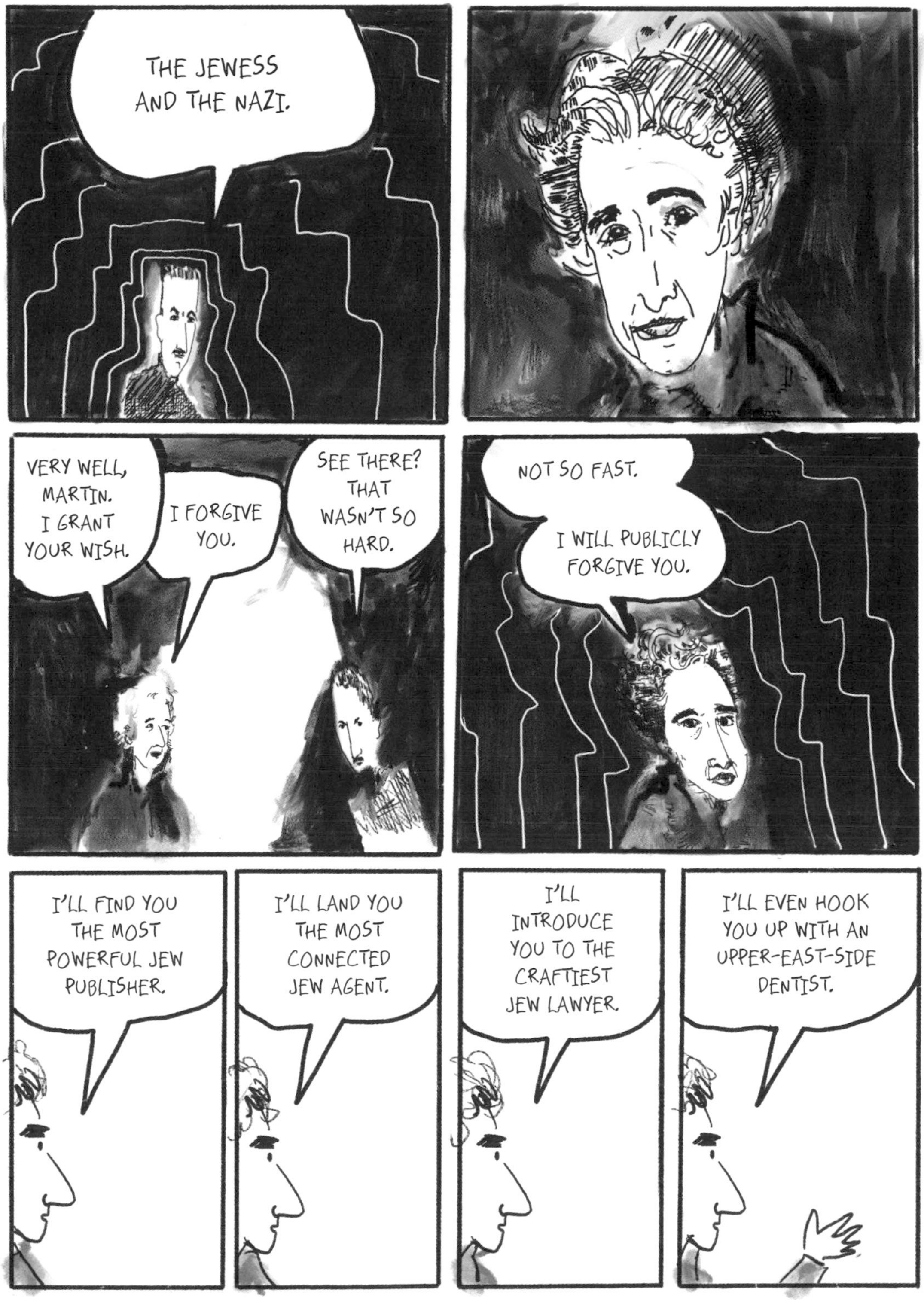
THE JEWESS AND THE NAZI.
VERY WELL, MARTIN. I GRANT YOUR WISH.
I FORGIVE YOU.
SEE THERE? THAT WASN'T SO HARD.
NOT SO FAST.
I WILL PUBLICLY FORGIVE YOU.
I'LL FIND YOU THE MOST POWERFUL JEW PUBLISHER.
I'LL LAND YOU THE MOST CONNECTED JEW AGENT.
I'LL INTRODUCE YOU TO THE CRAFTIEST JEW LAWYER.
I'LL EVEN HOOK YOU UP WITH AN UPPER-EAST-SIDE DENTIST.

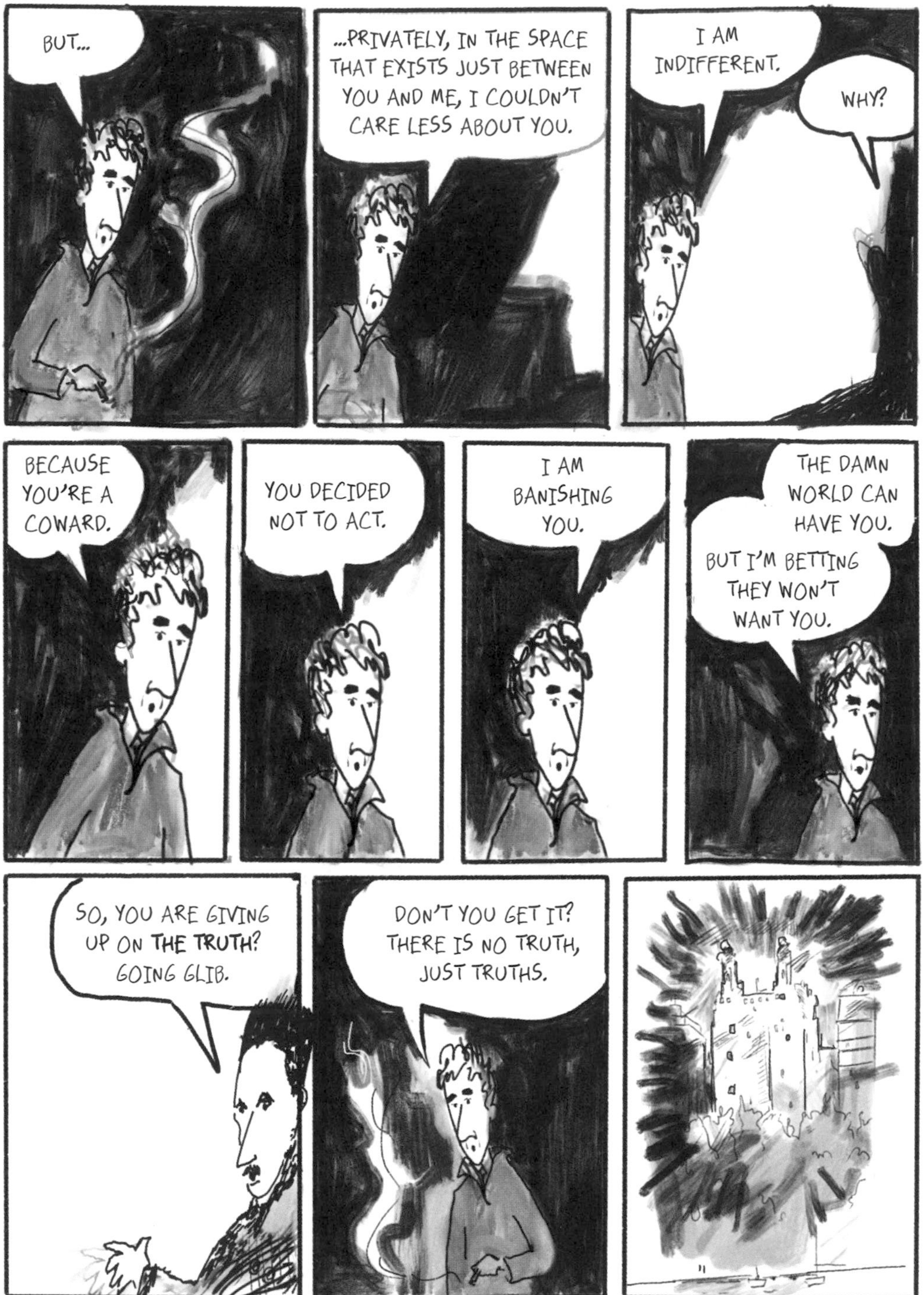
BUT...
...PRIVATELY, IN THE SPACE THAT EXISTS JUST BETWEEN YOU AND ME, I COULDN'T CARE LESS ABOUT YOU.
I AM INDIFFERENT.
WHY?
BECAUSE YOU'RE A COWARD.
YOU DECIDED NOT TO ACT.
I AM BANISHING YOU.
THE DAMN WORLD CAN HAVE YOU.
BUT I'M BETTING THEY WON'T WANT YOU.
SO, YOU ARE GIVING UP ON THE TRUTH? GOING GLIB.
DON'T YOU GET IT? THERE IS NO TRUTH, JUST TRUTHS.

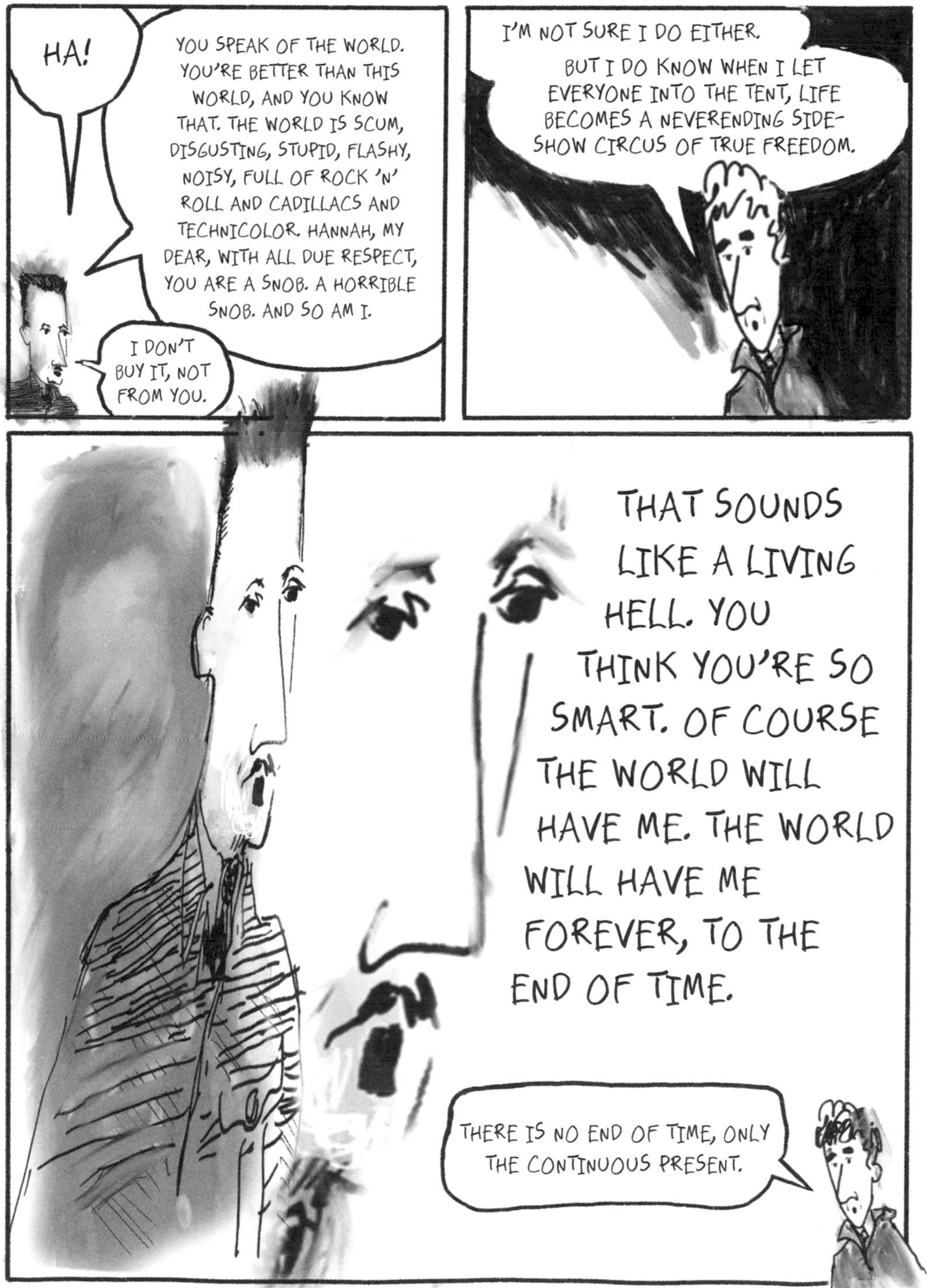
HA!
YOU SPEAK OF THE WORLD. YOU'RE BETTER THAN THIS WORLD, AND YOU KNOW THAT. THE WORLD IS SCUM, DISGUSTING, STUPID, FLASHY, NOISY, FULL OF ROCK 'N' ROLL AND CADILLACS AND TECHNICOLOR. HANNAH, MY DEAR, WITH ALL DUE RESPECT, YOU ARE A SNOB. A HORRIBLE SNOB. AND SO AM I.
I DON'T BUY IT, NOT FROM YOU.
I'M NOT SURE I DO EITHER.
BUT I DO KNOW WHEN I LET EVERYONE INTO THE TENT, LIFE BECOMES A NEVERENDING SIDE-SHOW CIRCUS OF TRUE FREEDOM.
THAT SOUNDS LIKE A LIVING HELL. YOU THINK YOU'RE SO SMART. OF COURSE THE WORLD WILL HAVE ME. THE WORLD WILL HAVE ME FOREVER, TO THE END OF TIME.
THERE IS NO END OF TIME, ONLY THE CONTINUOUS PRESENT.

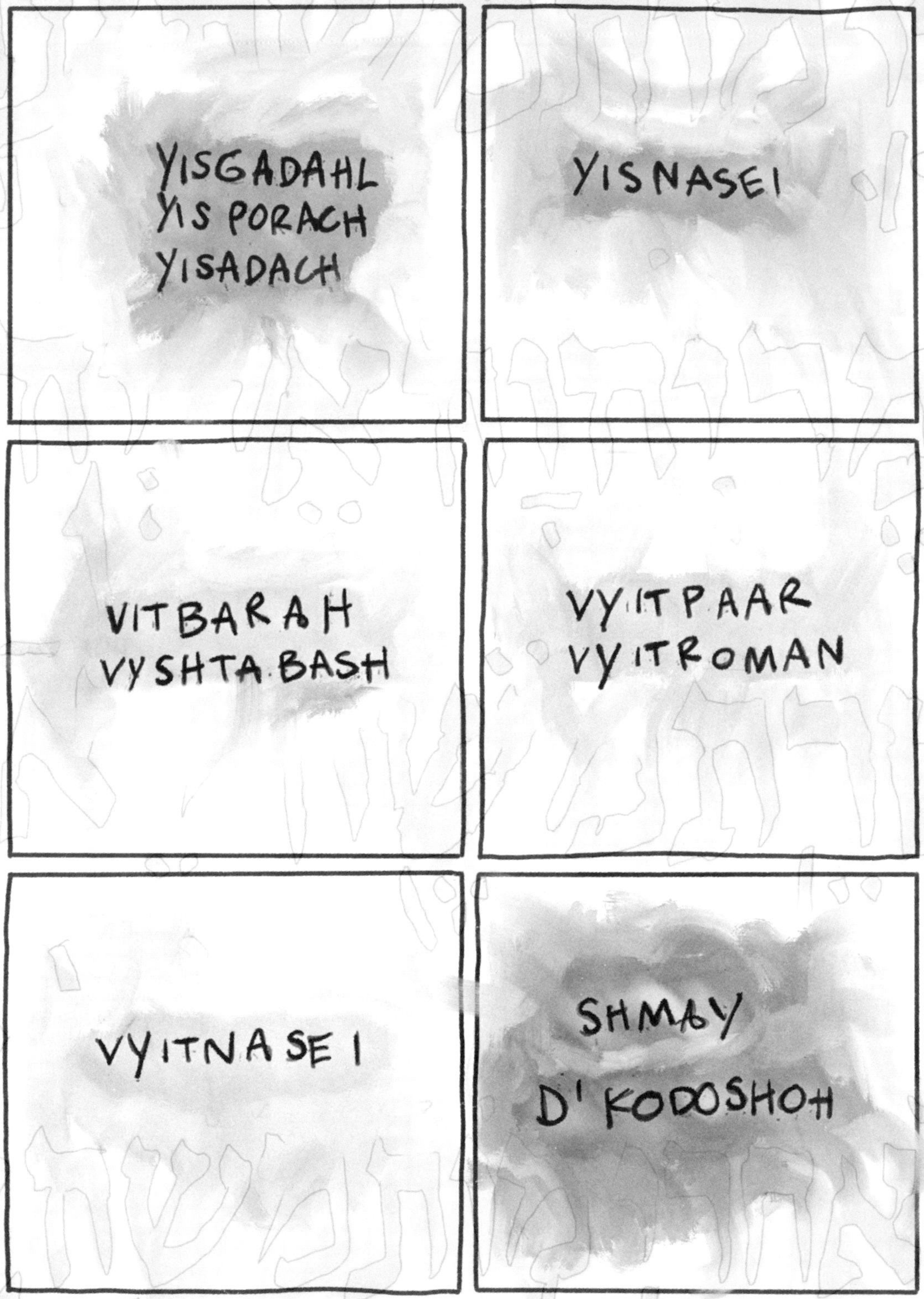
YISGADAHL
YIS PORACH
YISADACH
YISNASEI
VITBARAH
VYSHTA BASH
VYITPAAR
VYITROMAN
VYITNASEI
SHMAY
D' KODOSHOH

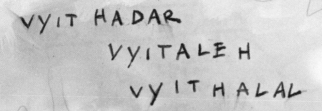

VYIT HADAR

VYITALEH

VYITHALAL

SH ME I

D KO DE SHA I

A M E N

Glorified and sanctified be God's great name throughout the world which He has created according to His will.
May He establish His kingdom in your lifetime and during your days, and within the life of the entire House of Israel, speedily and soon; and say, Amen.

May His great name be blessed forever and to all eternity.
Blessed and praised, glorified and exalted, extolled and honored, adored and lauded be the name of the Holy One, blessed be He, beyond all the blessings and hymns, praises and consolations that are ever spoken in the world; and LET US say, Amen.

Thinking without a Banister

Jerusalem
and beyond

SPACE-AGE THINKER

IN LATE *1958*, I PUBLISH MY MOST AMBITIOUS WORK.

IT PROCLAIMS DEFIANCE OF THE PHILOSOPHY INDUSTRY RIGHT FROM ITS TITLE.

THE HUMAN CONDITION
by Hannah Arendt

INSTEAD OF PROMISING TO DISCUSS HUMAN NATURE, OR NATURAL RIGHTS, I CHOOSE TO TALK ABOUT OUR IMMEDIATE HUMAN PLIGHT ON THE ONLY LIFE-SUPPORTING PLANET WE KNOW OF IN THE UNIVERSE. EARTH.

AT LAST, THE "WHY"!

EXPLAINED.

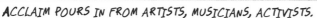

ACCLAIM POURS IN FROM ARTISTS, MUSICIANS, ACTIVISTS.

W.H. AUDEN

HANNAH, DARLING, IT SEEMS LIKE YOU WROTE THIS ESPECIALLY FOR ME.

THANK YOU. IT ANSWERS. PERIOD.

AND KNOW THIS, IF THE DIVINE BLUCHER EVER DIES, AND I KNOW HE WON'T SINCE HE'S A GOD AMONG MEN, BUT IF HE DOES, MAY I MARRY YOU, EVEN THOUGH, I AM, HOW SHALL I PUT IT, NOT INCLINED TOWARD WOMEN.

THE WORLD STILL DOESN'T UNDERSTAND THE ABYSS, OR WHY HORROR HAPPENS. IT HAPPENS WHEN PRIVATE EMOTIONS ENTER THE REALM OF THE PUBLIC SPACE. I VOW TO TRY TO SHARE MY UNDERSTANDING.

POLITICAL QUESTIONS ARE FAR TOO SERIOUS TO BE LEFT TO POLITICIANS.

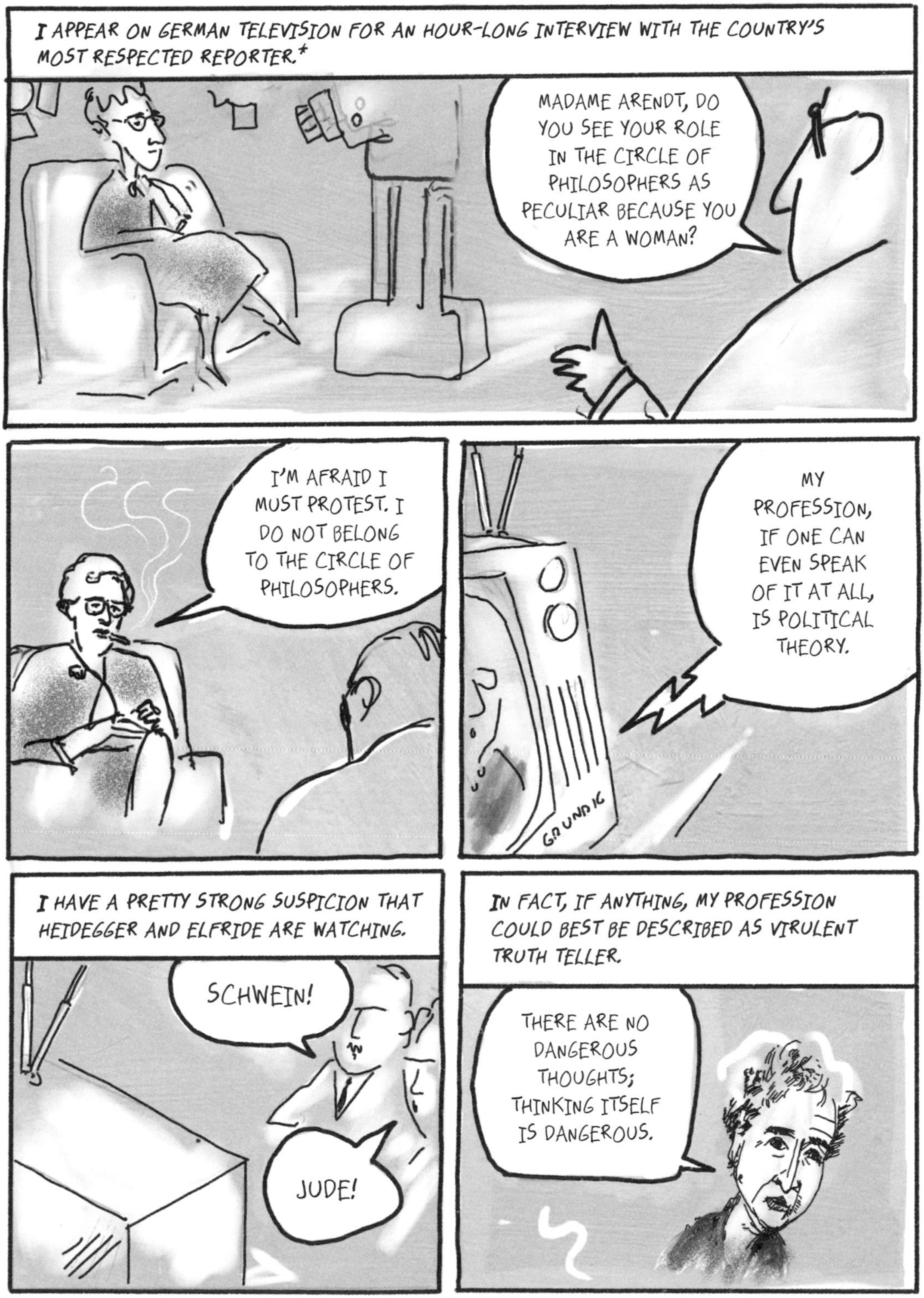
I APPEAR ON GERMAN TELEVISION FOR AN HOUR-LONG INTERVIEW WITH THE COUNTRY'S MOST RESPECTED REPORTER.*
MADAME ARENDT, DO YOU SEE YOUR ROLE IN THE CIRCLE OF PHILOSOPHERS AS PECULIAR BECAUSE YOU ARE A WOMAN?
I'M AFRAID I MUST PROTEST. I DO NOT BELONG TO THE CIRCLE OF PHILOSOPHERS.
MY PROFESSION, IF ONE CAN EVEN SPEAK OF IT AT ALL, IS POLITICAL THEORY.
GRUNDIG
I HAVE A PRETTY STRONG SUSPICION THAT HEIDEGGER AND ELFRIDE ARE WATCHING.
SCHWEIN!
JUDE!
IN FACT, IF ANYTHING, MY PROFESSION COULD BEST BE DESCRIBED AS VIRULENT TRUTH TELLER.
THERE ARE NO DANGEROUS THOUGHTS; THINKING ITSELF IS DANGEROUS.

* Gunter Gaus (1929–2004). Postwar German journalist and politician, key architect of the new, progressive reparation-minded, politically aware nation that rose from the ashes of Hitler's regime.

IN THOUGHT AND IN DEED, TO SURVIVE IN THE WORLD, I ERECT A FIRM WALL BETWEEN THE PUBLIC SPACE AND THE PRIVATE.

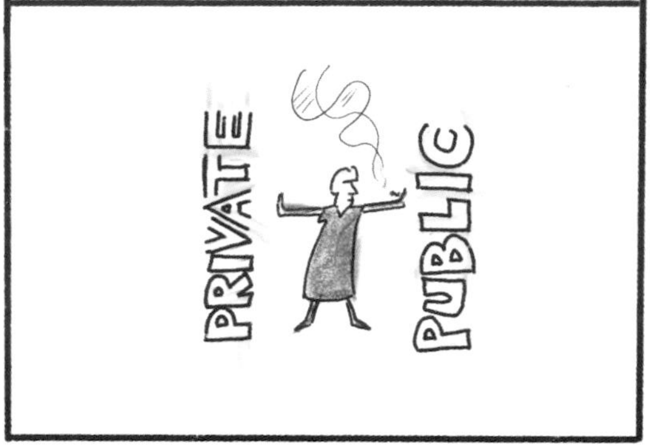
PRIVATE
PUBLIC

MY RATIONALE FOR THIS BARRIER IS PLAIN TO SEE.

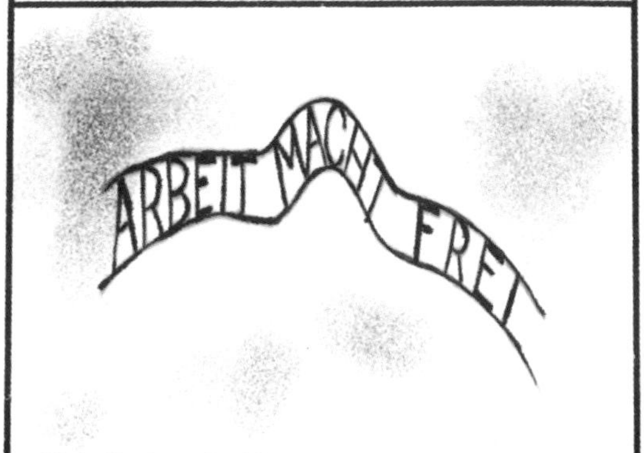
ARBEIT MACHT FREI

"Work will make you free." Sign over the entrance to Auschwitz.

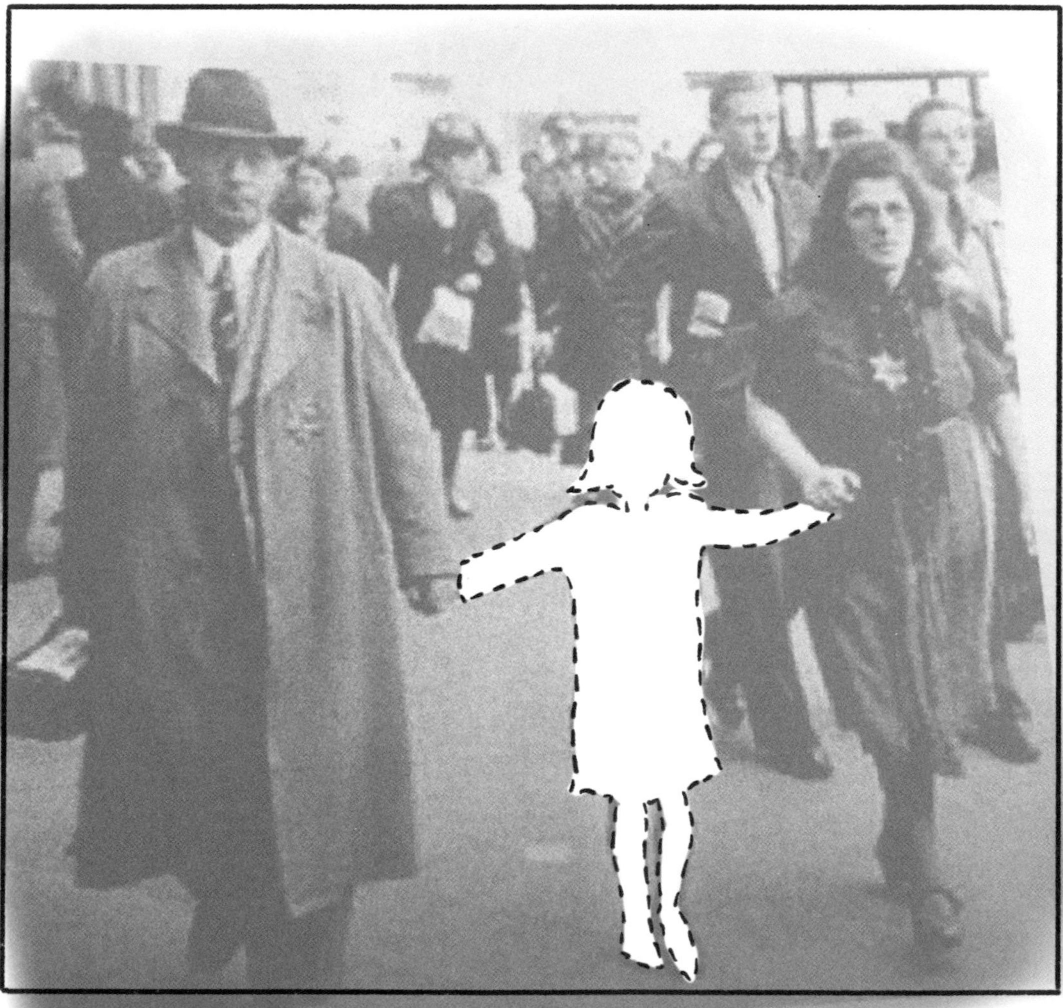

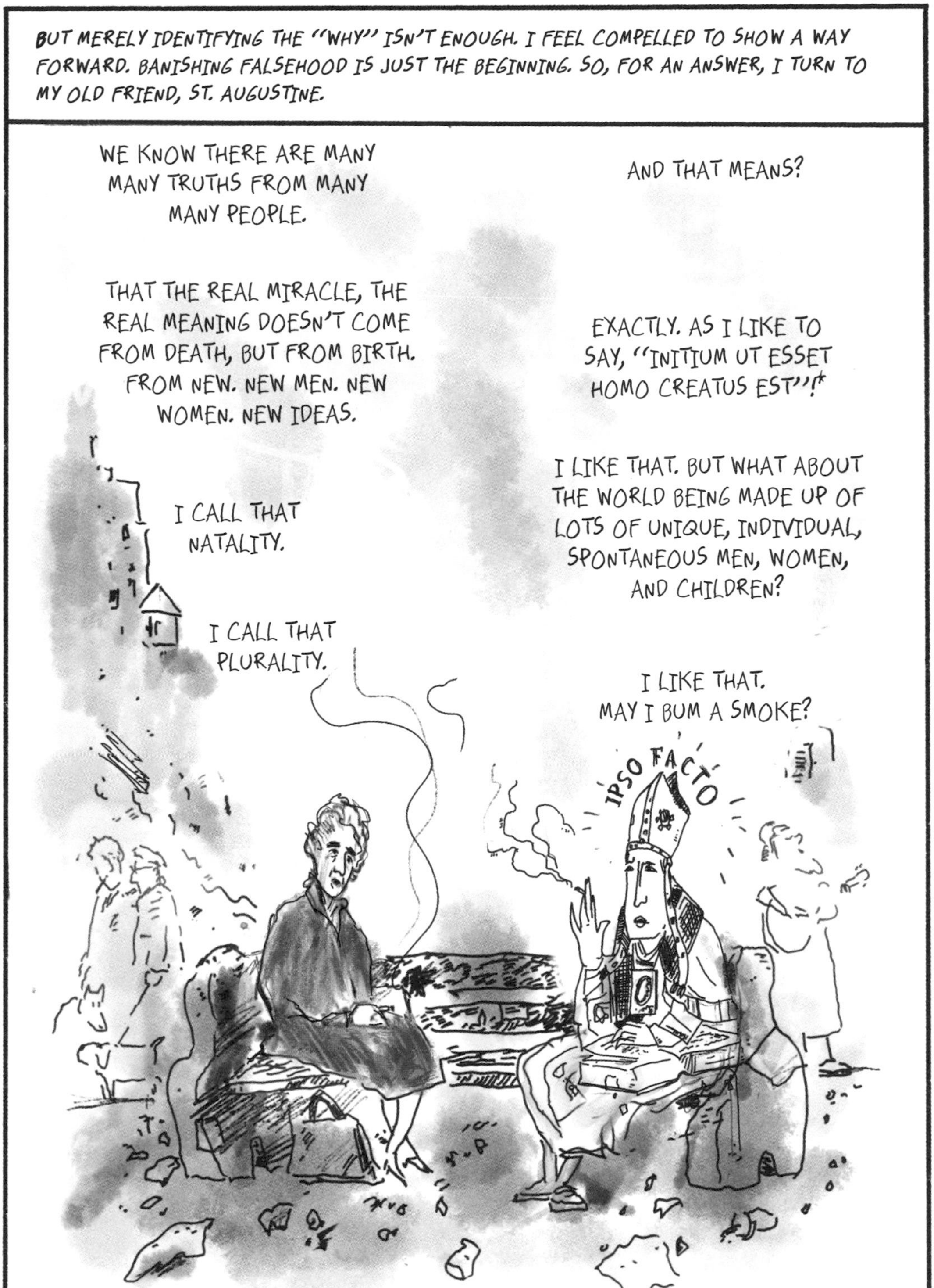
BUT MERELY IDENTIFYING THE "WHY" ISN'T ENOUGH. I FEEL COMPELLED TO SHOW A WAY FORWARD. BANISHING FALSEHOOD IS JUST THE BEGINNING. SO, FOR AN ANSWER, I TURN TO MY OLD FRIEND, ST. AUGUSTINE.
WE KNOW THERE ARE MANY MANY TRUTHS FROM MANY MANY PEOPLE.
AND THAT MEANS?
THAT THE REAL MIRACLE, THE REAL MEANING DOESN'T COME FROM DEATH, BUT FROM BIRTH. FROM NEW. NEW MEN. NEW WOMEN. NEW IDEAS.
EXACTLY. AS I LIKE TO SAY, "INITIUM UT ESSET HOMO CREATUS EST"!*
I CALL THAT NATALITY.
I LIKE THAT. BUT WHAT ABOUT THE WORLD BEING MADE UP OF LOTS OF UNIQUE, INDIVIDUAL, SPONTANEOUS MEN, WOMEN, AND CHILDREN?
I CALL THAT PLURALITY.
I LIKE THAT. MAY I BUM A SMOKE?
IPSO FACTO

* "That a beginning be made, Man was created."

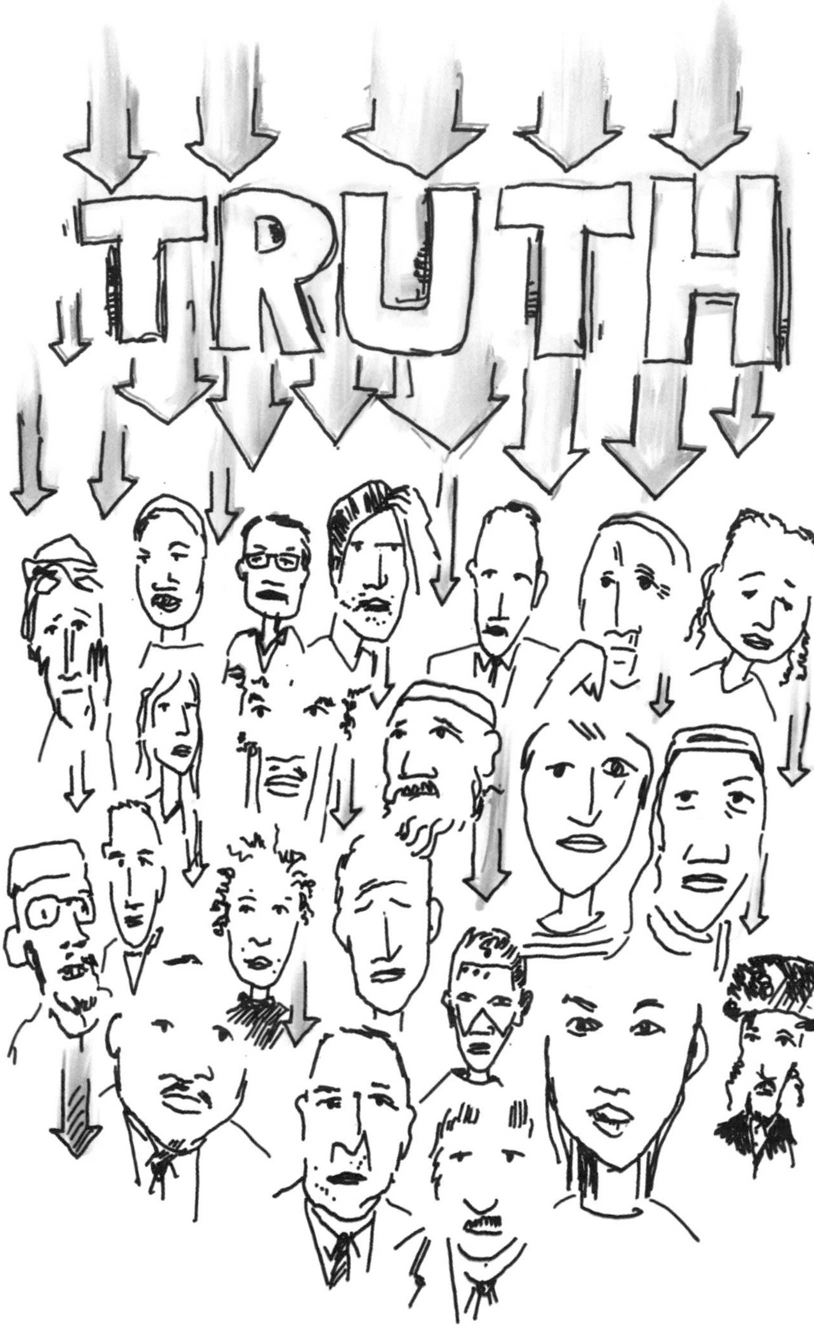
TRUTH

AND IT IS PRECISELY THIS FORCE, THE FACTS OF NATALITY AND PLURALITY, THAT TOTALITARIANISM IS DESIGNED TO SMOTHER. SO THEY CLAIM TO KNOW THE TRUTH. BUT INSTEAD OF ONE MONOLITHIC ALL-KNOWING TRUTH...

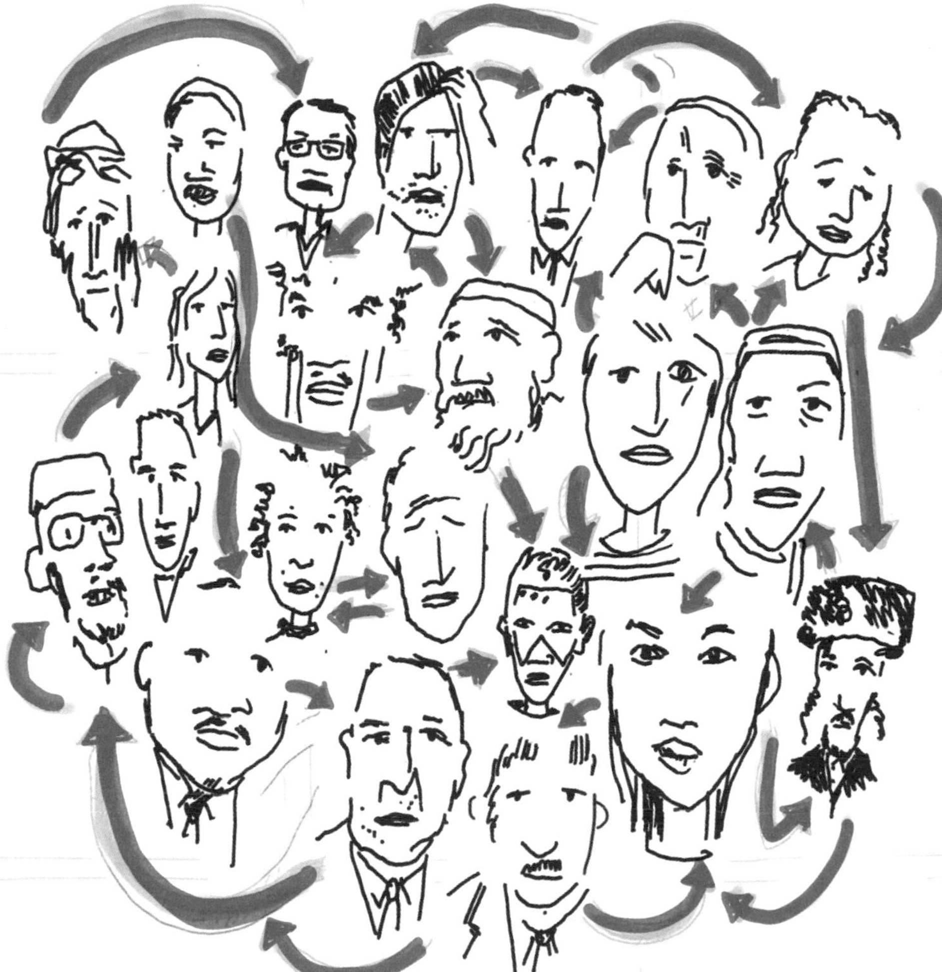

THIS IS MORE WHAT FREEDOM LOOKS LIKE. A MILLION BILLION TRUTHS, ACTED OUT IN PUBLIC, WITH EVERY PASSING SECOND.
MESSY? YOU BET.
BUT CONSIDER THE ALTERNATIVE.

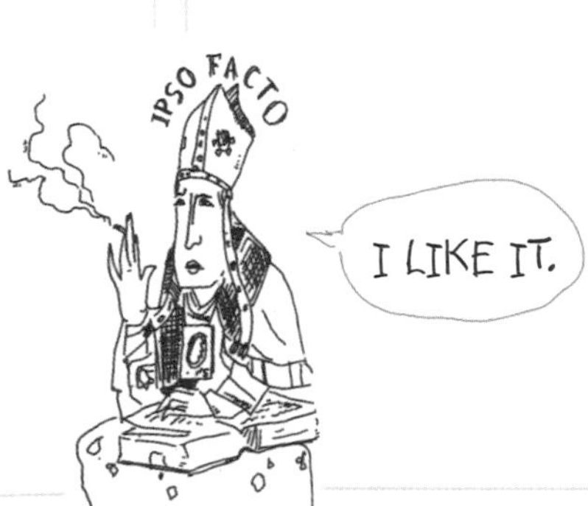
IPSO FACTO
I LIKE IT.

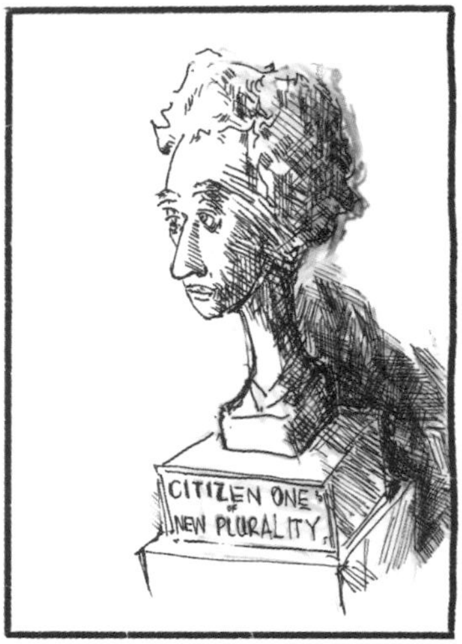
CITIZEN ONE of NEW PLURALITY

WITH THIS UNDERSTANDING IN HAND, I HAVE NO CHOICE. SO I JUST JUMP INTO THE FRAY AND ANOINT MYSELF CITIZEN ONE OF THE BRAVE NEW WORLD OF PLURALITY.

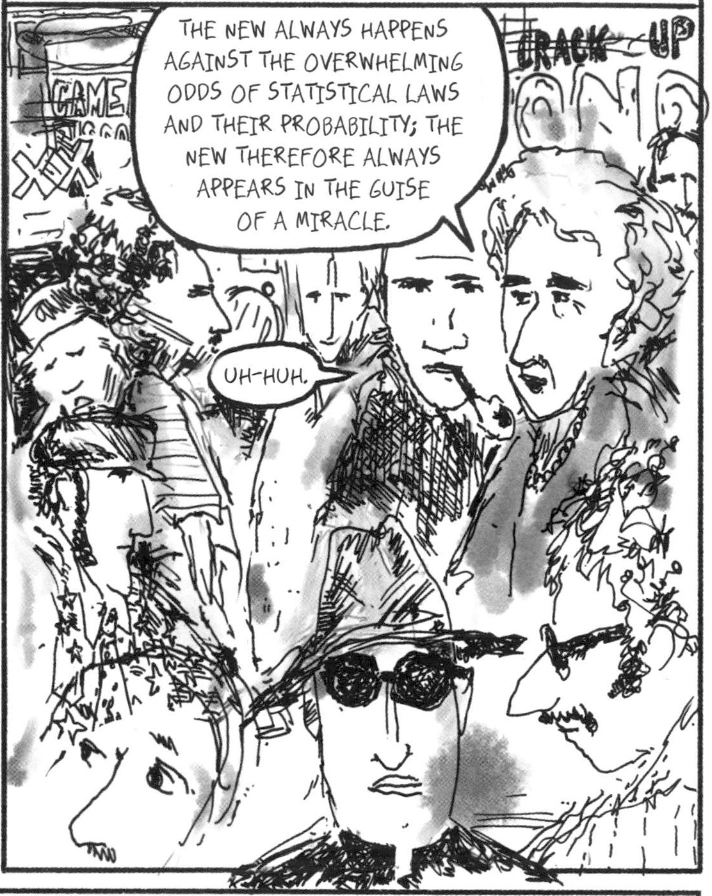
THE NEW ALWAYS HAPPENS AGAINST THE OVERWHELMING ODDS OF STATISTICAL LAWS AND THEIR PROBABILITY; THE NEW THEREFORE ALWAYS APPEARS IN THE GUISE OF A MIRACLE.
UH-HUH.

INSTEAD OF THINKING, WHICH PRESUMES COMING UP WITH THE ANSWER, I PRACTICE WHAT I CALL "THINKING THROUGH," WHICH RAISES MORE QUESTIONS.

YOU COULD SAY THAT IT MOST RESEMBLES THE PRACTICE OF ANOTHER "THINKER-THROUGHER" WHO PLIES HIS CRAFT 148 BLOCKS DOWNTOWN FROM MY APARTMENT. WHERE JOHN COLTRANE* TAKES THE WORLD ON A WILD RIDE OF THINKING AND MAKING AT THE SAME TIME.

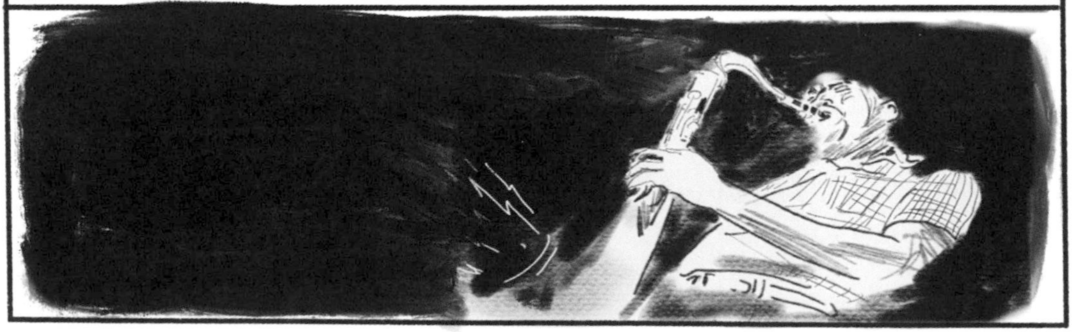

* John Coltrane (1926–1967). American jazz saxophonist who opened jazz up to long improvisations along modal lines, inspiring free, spiritual, and Eastern influences into Western music.

COULD HE BE CITIZEN TWO?

...AND SO... AND SO... AND SO... AND SO... AND THEN... WHAT? SO... HOW ABOUT? SO... AND THEN... BUT THEN... AND THEN... BUT? SO... HMM? ...WHAT IF? WHAT? HOW ABOUT? SO... BUT? HMM? AND THEN... HMM? ANOTHER? AND SO... BUT... IP

I TAKE MY NON-DOCTRINE OF "THINKING-THROUGH" ON THE ROAD.

SO, MADAME ARENDT, WHAT YOU'RE SAYING IS THE BEST WE CAN DO IS JUST MAKE IT UP AS WE GO?

American Philosop Society

EVERY SINGLE DAMN ONE OF US, YES. I'M AFRAID THAT'S ALL I'VE GOT. THERE IS NO RECIPE. BUT, ON THE UPSIDE, IF WE ARE CERTAIN TO INCLUDE EVERYONE EQUALLY, THIS BIG, ONGOING, FRANKLY FUCKED-UP MESS WON'T COUGH UP A HITLER OR A STALIN AGAIN.

AND WITH EVERY PUBLIC STATEMENT I MAKE DISAVOWING PHILOSOPHY...

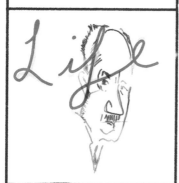

AND EVERY DENIAL OF SUPREME, DEATH-FOCUSED MEANING...

I TWIST THE KNIFE DEEPER INTO THE SIDE OF HEIDEGGER. AND PRIVATELY, I KIND OF ENJOY IT.*

* It's not revenge, per se, but privately I must confess, it feels good. No wonder the only big clumsy German word the Americans have adopted, besides *gesundheit*, is the delicious *schadenfreude*, taking pleasure in the misfortune of one's adversaries.

TANGO WITH THE DEVIL: BUENOS AIRES 1961

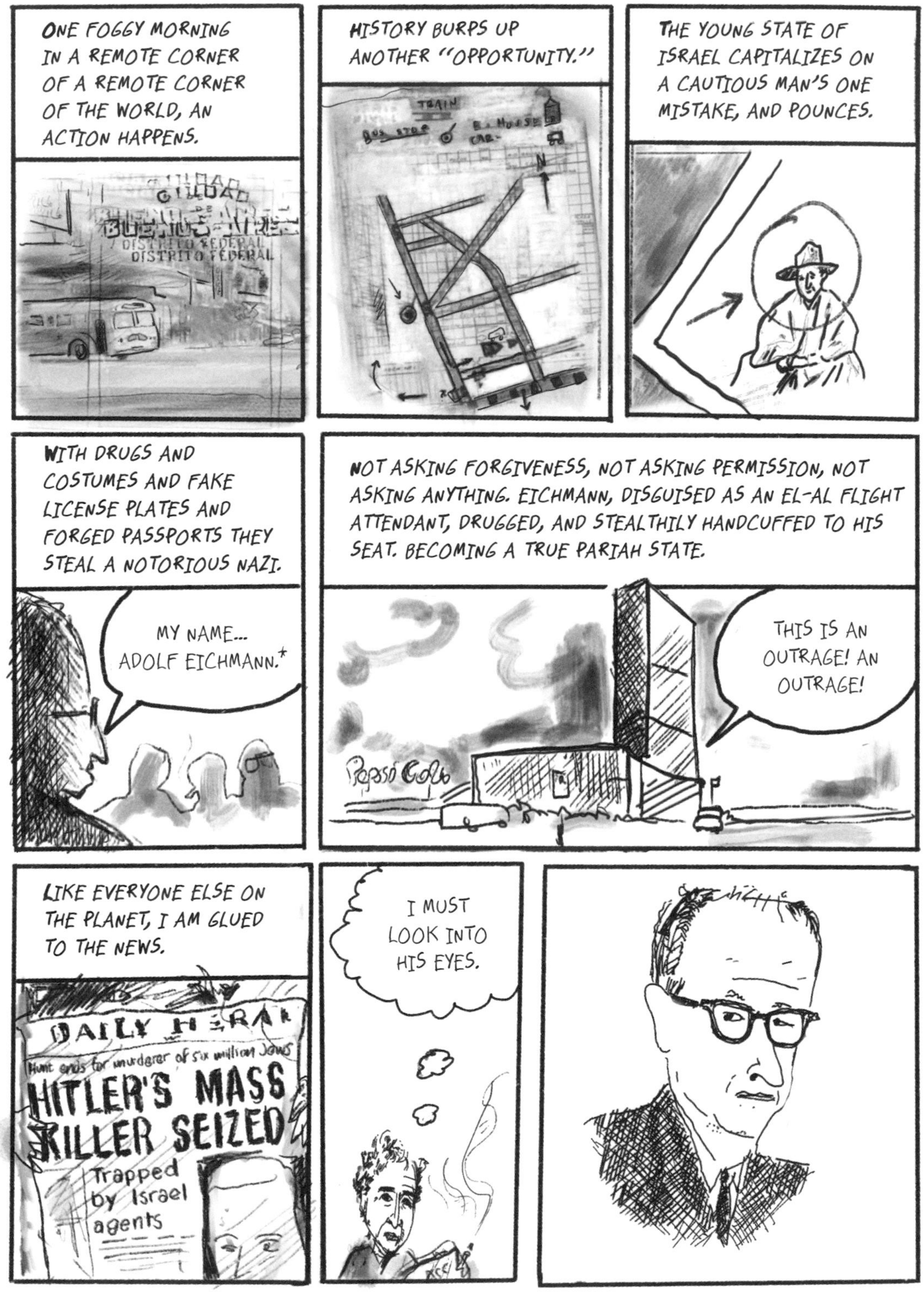
ONE FOGGY MORNING IN A REMOTE CORNER OF A REMOTE CORNER OF THE WORLD, AN ACTION HAPPENS.
CIUDAD
BUENOS AIRES
DISTRITO FEDERAL
HISTORY BURPS UP ANOTHER "OPPORTUNITY."
TRAIN
BUS STOP
E. HOUSE
CAR
N
THE YOUNG STATE OF ISRAEL CAPITALIZES ON A CAUTIOUS MAN'S ONE MISTAKE, AND POUNCES.
WITH DRUGS AND COSTUMES AND FAKE LICENSE PLATES AND FORGED PASSPORTS THEY STEAL A NOTORIOUS NAZI.
MY NAME... ADOLF EICHMANN.*
NOT ASKING FORGIVENESS, NOT ASKING PERMISSION, NOT ASKING ANYTHING. EICHMANN, DISGUISED AS AN EL-AL FLIGHT ATTENDANT, DRUGGED, AND STEALTHILY HANDCUFFED TO HIS SEAT. BECOMING A TRUE PARIAH STATE.
THIS IS AN OUTRAGE! AN OUTRAGE!
Pepsi Cola
LIKE EVERYONE ELSE ON THE PLANET, I AM GLUED TO THE NEWS.
DAILY HERAL
Hunt ends for murderer of six million Jews
HITLER'S MASS KILLER SEIZED
Trapped by Israel agents
I MUST LOOK INTO HIS EYES.

* Adolf Eichmann (1906–1962). (See page 114.)

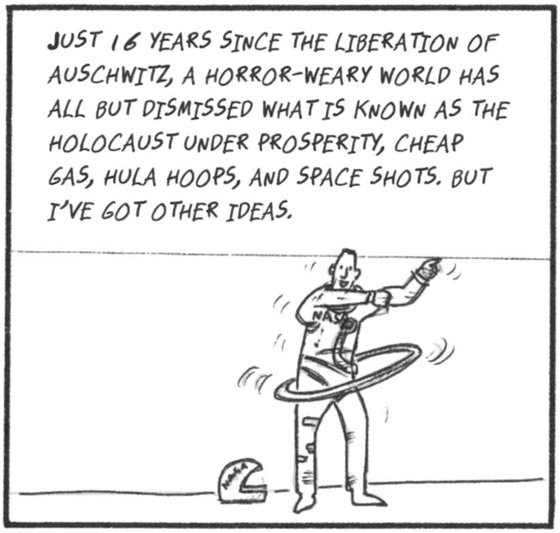
JUST 16 YEARS SINCE THE LIBERATION OF AUSCHWITZ, A HORROR-WEARY WORLD HAS ALL BUT DISMISSED WHAT IS KNOWN AS THE HOLOCAUST UNDER PROSPERITY, CHEAP GAS, HULA HOOPS, AND SPACE SHOTS. BUT I'VE GOT OTHER IDEAS.

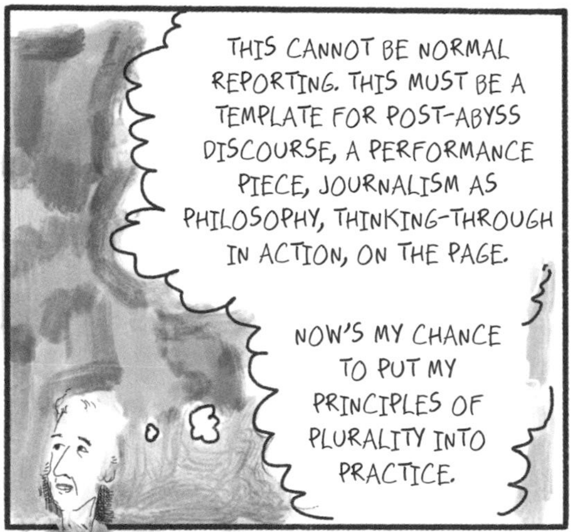
THIS CANNOT BE NORMAL REPORTING. THIS MUST BE A TEMPLATE FOR POST-ABYSS DISCOURSE, A PERFORMANCE PIECE, JOURNALISM AS PHILOSOPHY, THINKING-THROUGH IN ACTION, ON THE PAGE.
NOW'S MY CHANCE TO PUT MY PRINCIPLES OF PLURALITY INTO PRACTICE.

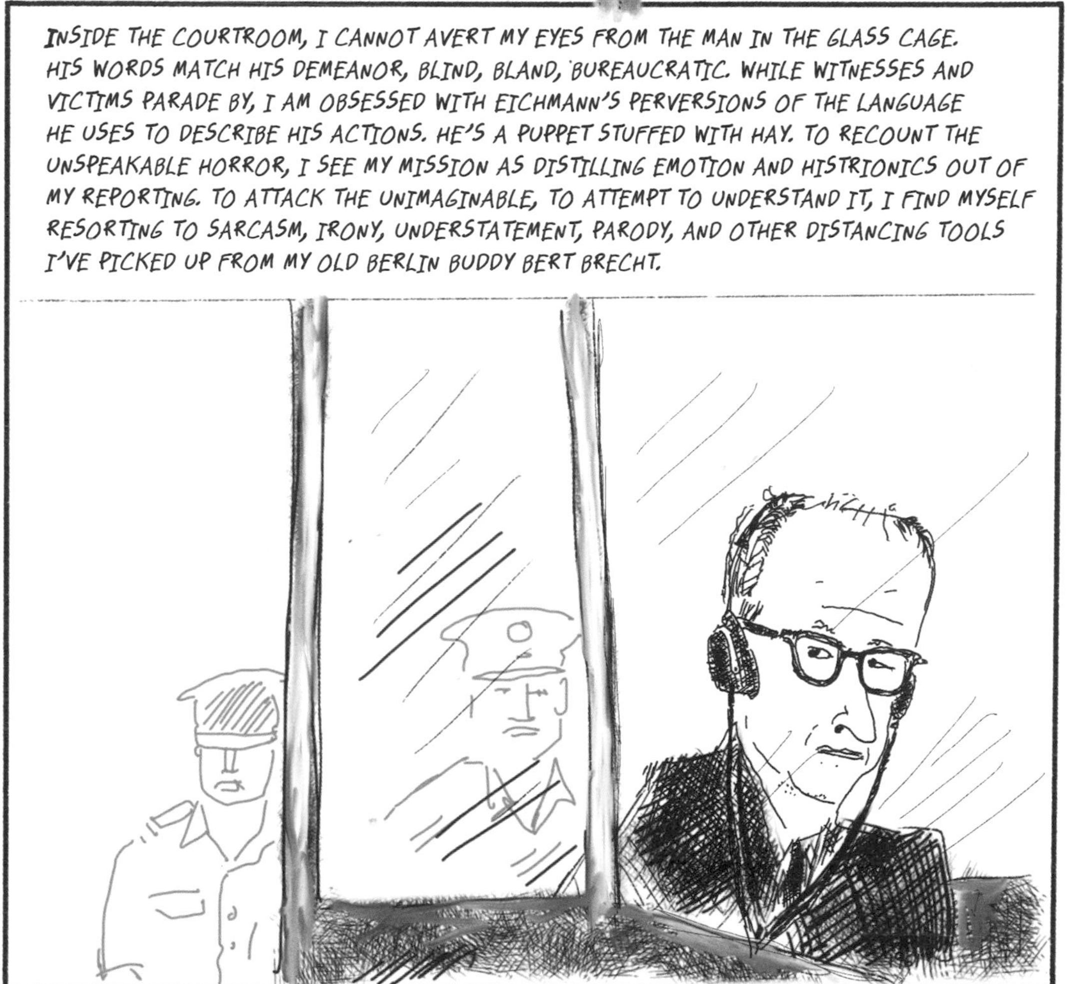
INSIDE THE COURTROOM, I CANNOT AVERT MY EYES FROM THE MAN IN THE GLASS CAGE. HIS WORDS MATCH HIS DEMEANOR, BLIND, BLAND, BUREAUCRATIC. WHILE WITNESSES AND VICTIMS PARADE BY, I AM OBSESSED WITH EICHMANN'S PERVERSIONS OF THE LANGUAGE HE USES TO DESCRIBE HIS ACTIONS. HE'S A PUPPET STUFFED WITH HAY. TO RECOUNT THE UNSPEAKABLE HORROR, I SEE MY MISSION AS DISTILLING EMOTION AND HISTRIONICS OUT OF MY REPORTING. TO ATTACK THE UNIMAGINABLE, TO ATTEMPT TO UNDERSTAND IT, I FIND MYSELF RESORTING TO SARCASM, IRONY, UNDERSTATEMENT, PARODY, AND OTHER DISTANCING TOOLS I'VE PICKED UP FROM MY OLD BERLIN BUDDY BERT BRECHT.

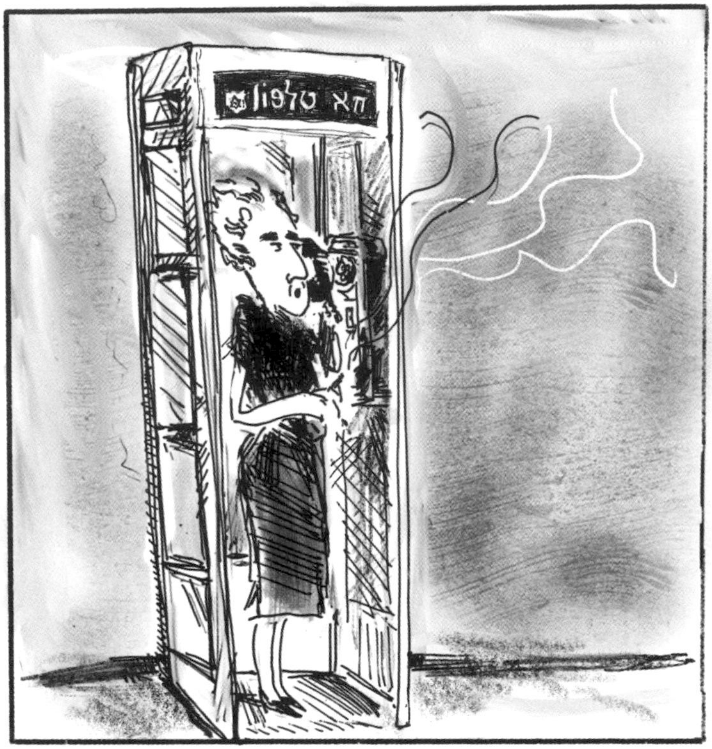

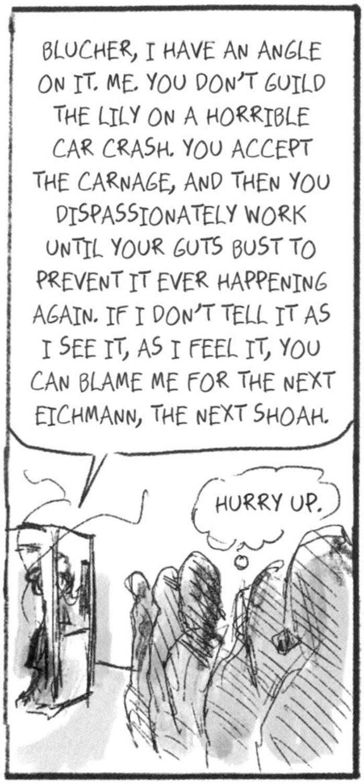

BLUCHER, I HAVE AN ANGLE ON IT. ME. YOU DON'T GUILD THE LILY ON A HORRIBLE CAR CRASH. YOU ACCEPT THE CARNAGE, AND THEN YOU DISPASSIONATELY WORK UNTIL YOUR GUTS BUST TO PREVENT IT EVER HAPPENING AGAIN. IF I DON'T TELL IT AS I SEE IT, AS I FEEL IT, YOU CAN BLAME ME FOR THE NEXT EICHMANN, THE NEXT SHOAH.
HURRY UP.

AS HARD AS I TRY, I CANNOT SEE A MONSTER IN THE GLASS BOOTH. I SEE A BORE, A CAREERIST FORMER VACUUM CLEANER SALESMAN SPOUTING EMPTY SALES PITCHES. HE'S ORDINARY, WHICH MAKES HIS CRIMES EVEN MORE HORRIBLE THAN A FRANKENSTEIN FANTASY.

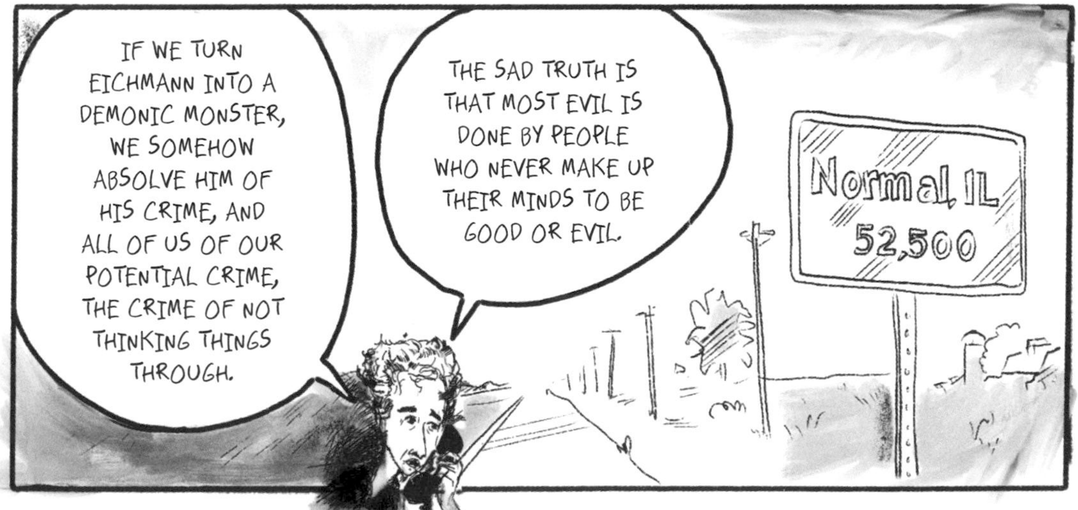

IF WE TURN EICHMANN INTO A DEMONIC MONSTER, WE SOMEHOW ABSOLVE HIM OF HIS CRIME, AND ALL OF US OF OUR POTENTIAL CRIME, THE CRIME OF NOT THINKING THINGS THROUGH.
THE SAD TRUTH IS THAT MOST EVIL IS DONE BY PEOPLE WHO NEVER MAKE UP THEIR MINDS TO BE GOOD OR EVIL.
Normal IL
52,500

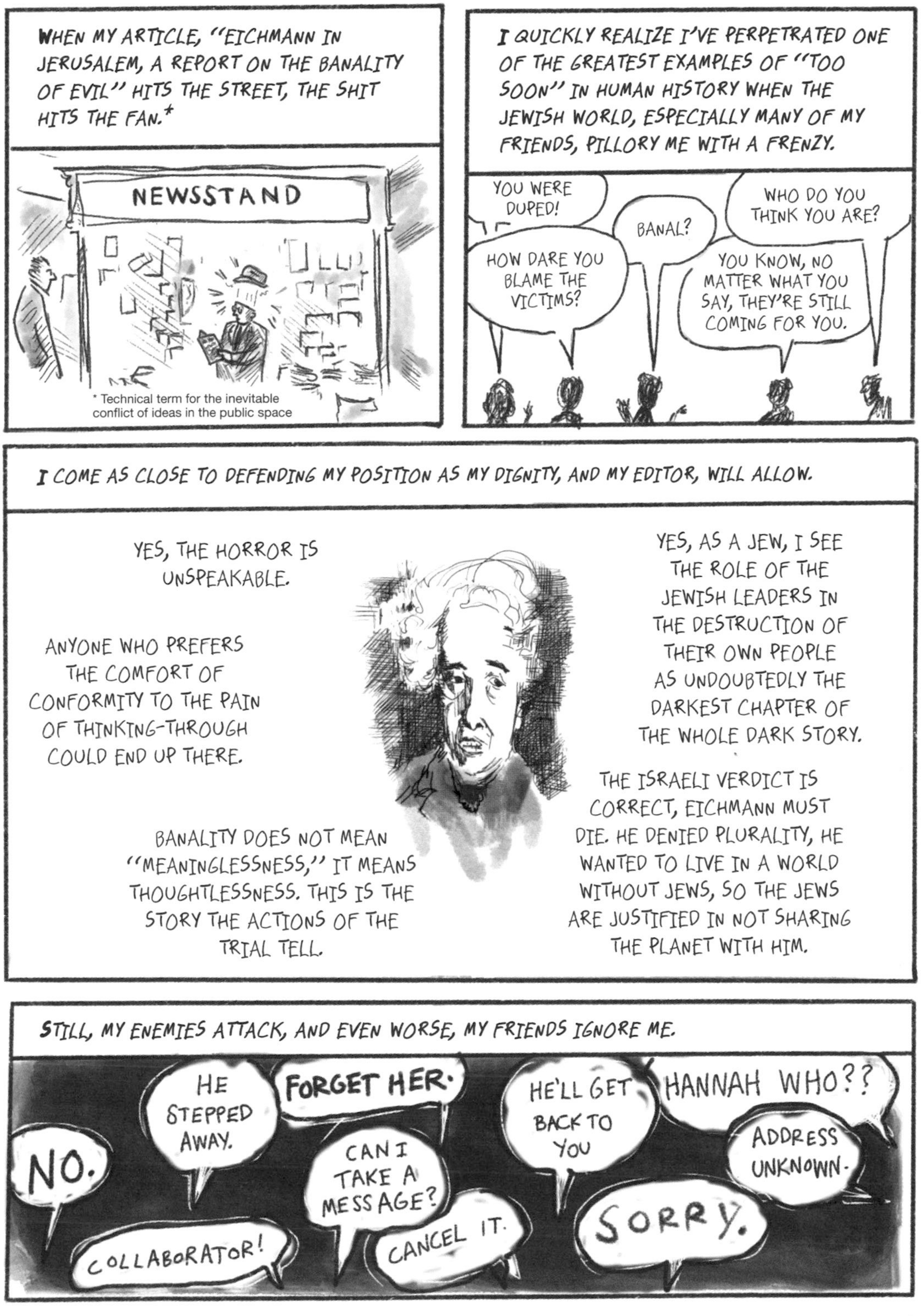
WHEN MY ARTICLE, "EICHMANN IN JERUSALEM, A REPORT ON THE BANALITY OF EVIL" HITS THE STREET, THE SHIT HITS THE FAN.*
NEWSSTAND
* Technical term for the inevitable conflict of ideas in the public space
I QUICKLY REALIZE I'VE PERPETRATED ONE OF THE GREATEST EXAMPLES OF "TOO SOON" IN HUMAN HISTORY WHEN THE JEWISH WORLD, ESPECIALLY MANY OF MY FRIENDS, PILLORY ME WITH A FRENZY.
YOU WERE DUPED!
HOW DARE YOU BLAME THE VICTIMS?
BANAL?
WHO DO YOU THINK YOU ARE?
YOU KNOW, NO MATTER WHAT YOU SAY, THEY'RE STILL COMING FOR YOU.
I COME AS CLOSE TO DEFENDING MY POSITION AS MY DIGNITY, AND MY EDITOR, WILL ALLOW.
YES, THE HORROR IS UNSPEAKABLE.
ANYONE WHO PREFERS THE COMFORT OF CONFORMITY TO THE PAIN OF THINKING-THROUGH COULD END UP THERE.
BANALITY DOES NOT MEAN "MEANINGLESSNESS," IT MEANS THOUGHTLESSNESS. THIS IS THE STORY THE ACTIONS OF THE TRIAL TELL.
YES, AS A JEW, I SEE THE ROLE OF THE JEWISH LEADERS IN THE DESTRUCTION OF THEIR OWN PEOPLE AS UNDOUBTEDLY THE DARKEST CHAPTER OF THE WHOLE DARK STORY.
THE ISRAELI VERDICT IS CORRECT, EICHMANN MUST DIE. HE DENIED PLURALITY, HE WANTED TO LIVE IN A WORLD WITHOUT JEWS, SO THE JEWS ARE JUSTIFIED IN NOT SHARING THE PLANET WITH HIM.
STILL, MY ENEMIES ATTACK, AND EVEN WORSE, MY FRIENDS IGNORE ME.
NO.
HE STEPPED AWAY.
FORGET HER.
CAN I TAKE A MESSAGE?
COLLABORATOR!
CANCEL IT.
HE'LL GET BACK TO YOU
HANNAH WHO??
ADDRESS UNKNOWN.
SORRY.

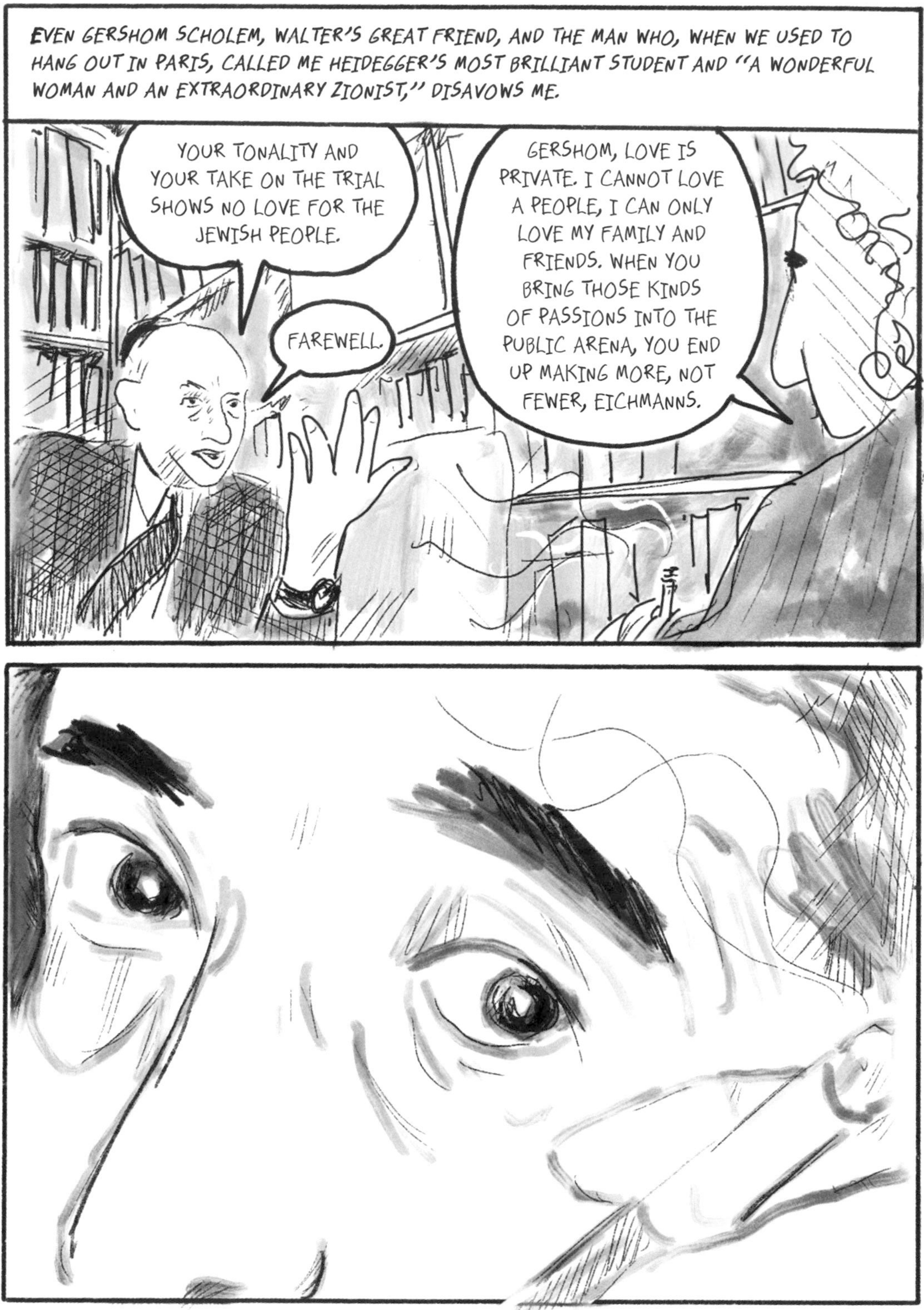
EVEN GERSHOM SCHOLEM, WALTER'S GREAT FRIEND, AND THE MAN WHO, WHEN WE USED TO HANG OUT IN PARIS, CALLED ME HEIDEGGER'S MOST BRILLIANT STUDENT AND "A WONDERFUL WOMAN AND AN EXTRAORDINARY ZIONIST," DISAVOWS ME.
YOUR TONALITY AND YOUR TAKE ON THE TRIAL SHOWS NO LOVE FOR THE JEWISH PEOPLE.
GERSHOM, LOVE IS PRIVATE. I CANNOT LOVE A PEOPLE, I CAN ONLY LOVE MY FAMILY AND FRIENDS. WHEN YOU BRING THOSE KINDS OF PASSIONS INTO THE PUBLIC ARENA, YOU END UP MAKING MORE, NOT FEWER, EICHMANNS.
FAREWELL.

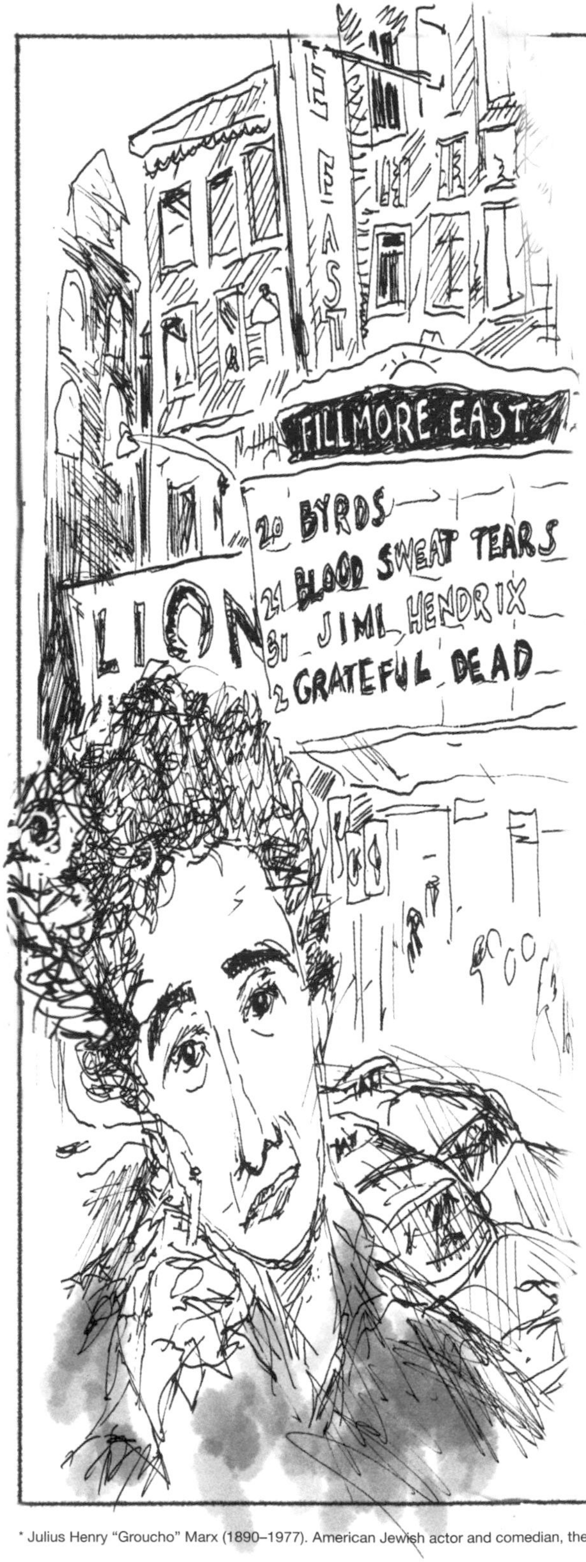
FILLMORE EAST
20 BYRDS
21 BLOOD SWEAT TEARS
31 JIMI HENDRIX
2 GRATEFUL DEAD
LION
EAST

NEVERTHELESS, IN THE WAKE OF THE ARTICLE, I HAVE NO CHOICE BUT TO CONTINUE TO STARE UNBLINKINGLY AT REALITY, STRUGGLING TO KEEP THE PRIVATE AND THE PUBLIC PARTS OF MY BEING HEALTHY, AND SEPARATE. AS SOON AS SOMEONE TRIES TO PEG ME OR LABEL ME, I SURPRISE. SO FEMINISTS LOVE ME AND LOATHE ME. LIBERTARIANS APPLAUD ME AND DECRY ME. I SUPPORT ISRAEL AND THE ARABS AND EVERY OTHER INDIVIDUAL. WHILE I PROCLAIM THAT THE RATIONALE FOR HUMAN RIGHTS DISAPPEARED AT THE GATES OF TREBLINKA, I VICIOUSLY SUPPORT EVERY HUMAN BEING'S RIGHT TO HAVE RIGHTS. WHEN MAN REACHES THE MOON, I QUESTION HUMANITY'S PROSPECTS ONCE WE LOOSE THE BONDS OF EARTH, THE VERY CONDITION THAT DEFINES OUR HUMANITY. SKIRTS GROW SHORTER, HAIR GROWS LONGER, MUSIC GROWS LOUDER, AND POLITICIANS REMAIN AS MENDACIOUS AS EVER. TIME MOVES ON, UNFLINCHINGLY, AS I NOTICED SO MANY YEARS AGO THAT IT HAS A HABIT OF DOING. AND THE LOSS OF EACH BELOVED FRIEND IS AN OPEN WOUND THAT NEVER HEALS. I TAKE COLD COMFORT IN GROUCHO MARX'S* WORDS, "I WOULDN'T WANT TO BE THE MEMBER OF ANY CLUB THAT WOULD HAVE ME AS A MEMBER."

* Julius Henry "Groucho" Marx (1890–1977). American Jewish actor and comedian, the one with the moustache, the eyebrows, and the big cigar.

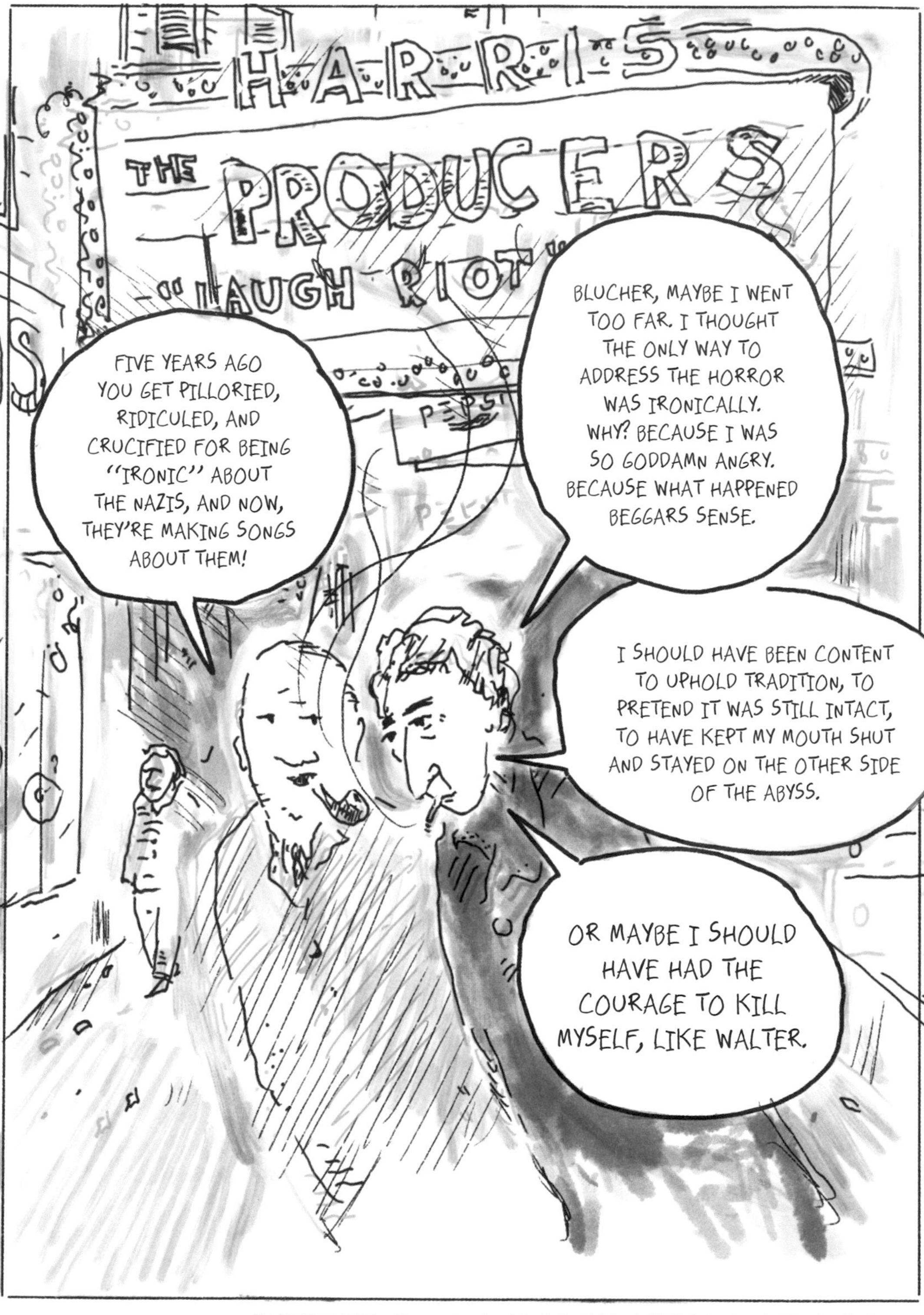
HARRIS
THE PRODUCERS
LAUGH RIOT
FIVE YEARS AGO YOU GET PILLORIED, RIDICULED, AND CRUCIFIED FOR BEING "IRONIC" ABOUT THE NAZIS, AND NOW, THEY'RE MAKING SONGS ABOUT THEM!
BLUCHER, MAYBE I WENT TOO FAR. I THOUGHT THE ONLY WAY TO ADDRESS THE HORROR WAS IRONICALLY. WHY? BECAUSE I WAS SO GODDAMN ANGRY. BECAUSE WHAT HAPPENED BEGGARS SENSE.
I SHOULD HAVE BEEN CONTENT TO UPHOLD TRADITION, TO PRETEND IT WAS STILL INTACT, TO HAVE KEPT MY MOUTH SHUT AND STAYED ON THE OTHER SIDE OF THE ABYSS.
OR MAYBE I SHOULD HAVE HAD THE COURAGE TO KILL MYSELF, LIKE WALTER.

The Producers (1967), written, produced, and directed by Mel Brooks (1926–). American Jewish writer, director, composer, actor, and funny person. Fought the Nazis with the American army in World War II. (Born Melvin Kaminsky.)

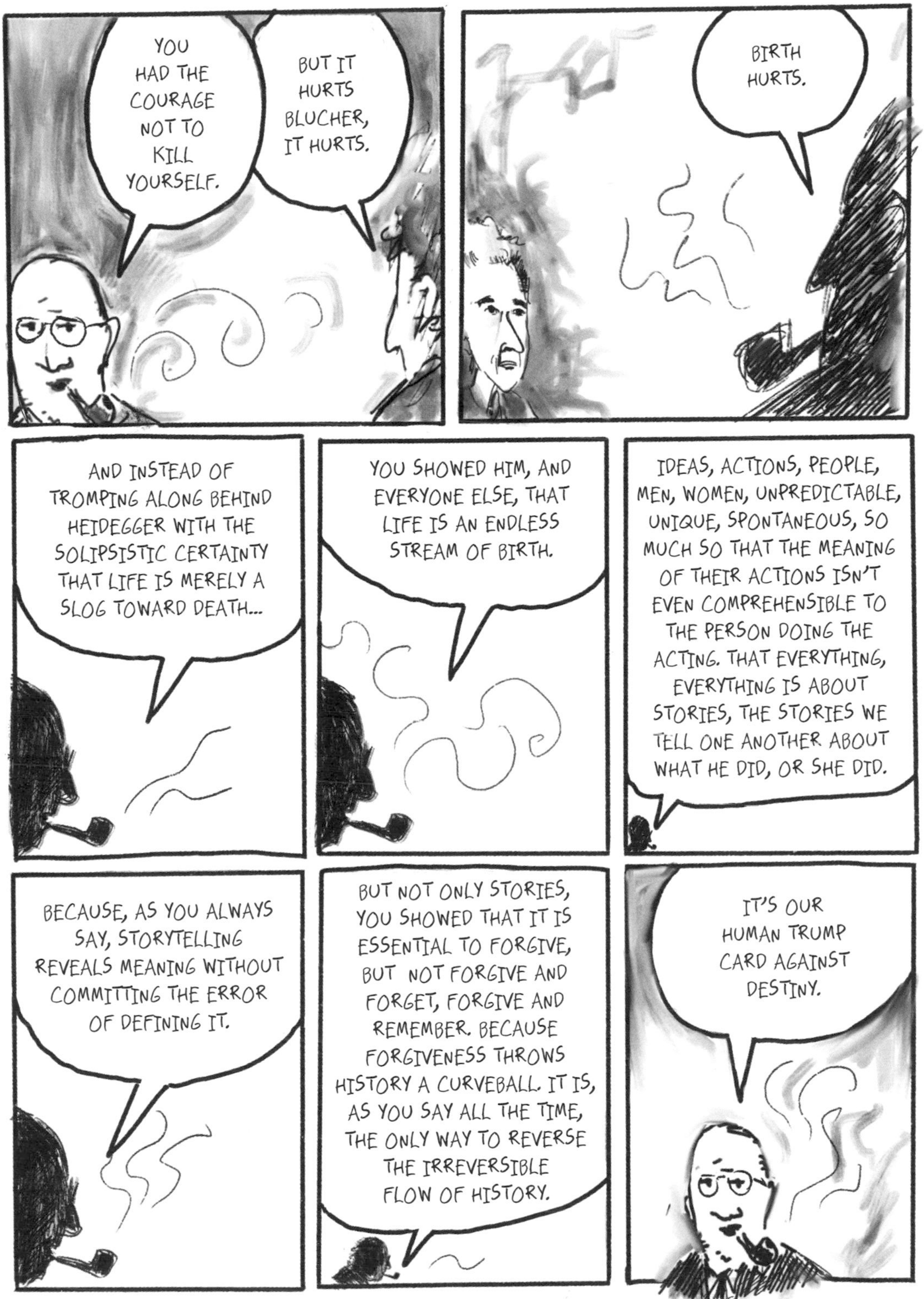
YOU HAD THE COURAGE NOT TO KILL YOURSELF.
BUT IT HURTS BLUCHER, IT HURTS.
BIRTH HURTS.
AND INSTEAD OF TROMPING ALONG BEHIND HEIDEGGER WITH THE SOLIPSISTIC CERTAINTY THAT LIFE IS MERELY A SLOG TOWARD DEATH...
YOU SHOWED HIM, AND EVERYONE ELSE, THAT LIFE IS AN ENDLESS STREAM OF BIRTH.
IDEAS, ACTIONS, PEOPLE, MEN, WOMEN, UNPREDICTABLE, UNIQUE, SPONTANEOUS, SO MUCH SO THAT THE MEANING OF THEIR ACTIONS ISN'T EVEN COMPREHENSIBLE TO THE PERSON DOING THE ACTING. THAT EVERYTHING, EVERYTHING IS ABOUT STORIES, THE STORIES WE TELL ONE ANOTHER ABOUT WHAT HE DID, OR SHE DID.
BECAUSE, AS YOU ALWAYS SAY, STORYTELLING REVEALS MEANING WITHOUT COMMITTING THE ERROR OF DEFINING IT.
BUT NOT ONLY STORIES, YOU SHOWED THAT IT IS ESSENTIAL TO FORGIVE, BUT NOT FORGIVE AND FORGET, FORGIVE AND REMEMBER. BECAUSE FORGIVENESS THROWS HISTORY A CURVEBALL. IT IS, AS YOU SAY ALL THE TIME, THE ONLY WAY TO REVERSE THE IRREVERSIBLE FLOW OF HISTORY.
IT'S OUR HUMAN TRUMP CARD AGAINST DESTINY.

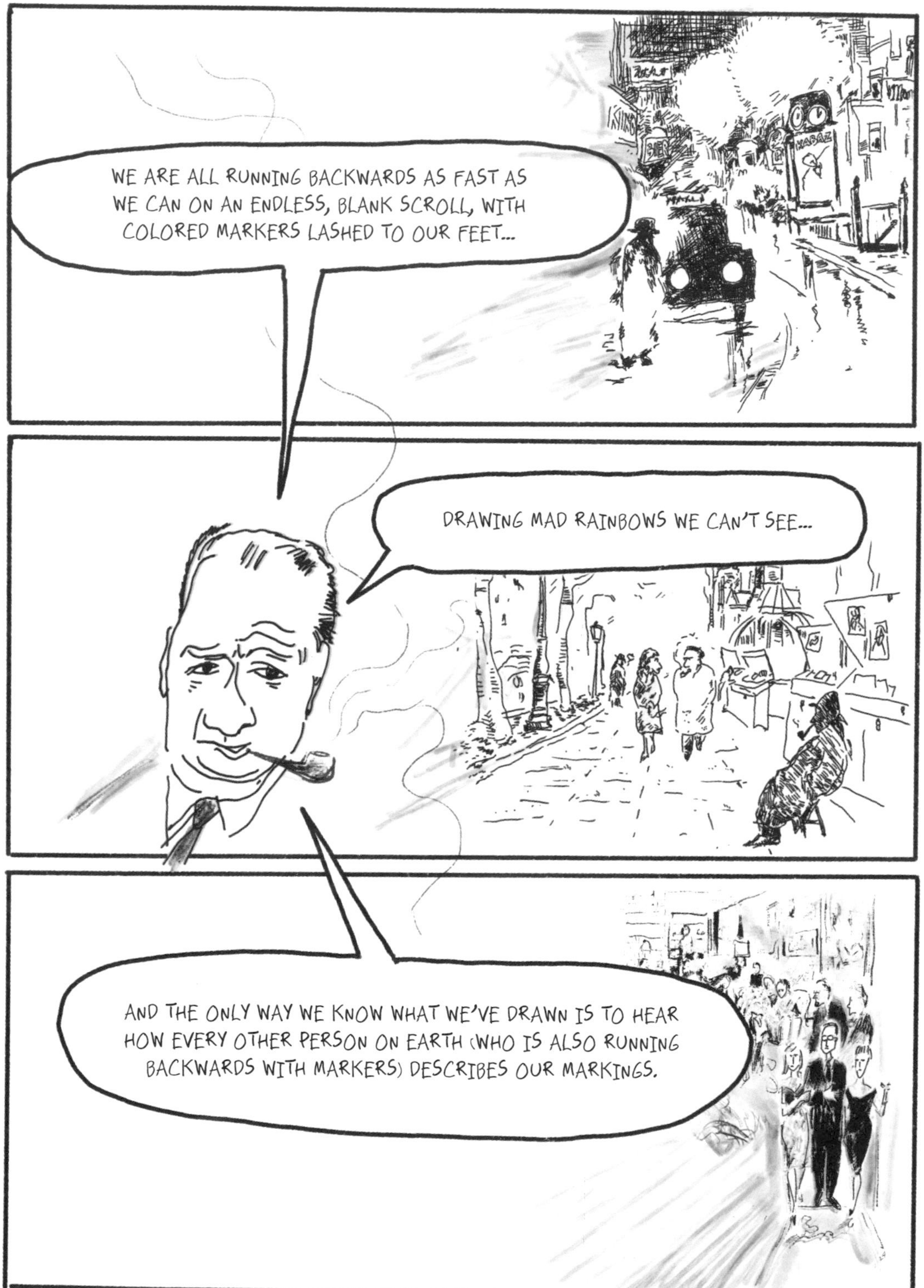
WE ARE ALL RUNNING BACKWARDS AS FAST AS WE CAN ON AN ENDLESS, BLANK SCROLL, WITH COLORED MARKERS LASHED TO OUR FEET...
DRAWING MAD RAINBOWS WE CAN'T SEE...
AND THE ONLY WAY WE KNOW WHAT WE'VE DRAWN IS TO HEAR HOW EVERY OTHER PERSON ON EARTH (WHO IS ALSO RUNNING BACKWARDS WITH MARKERS) DESCRIBES OUR MARKINGS.

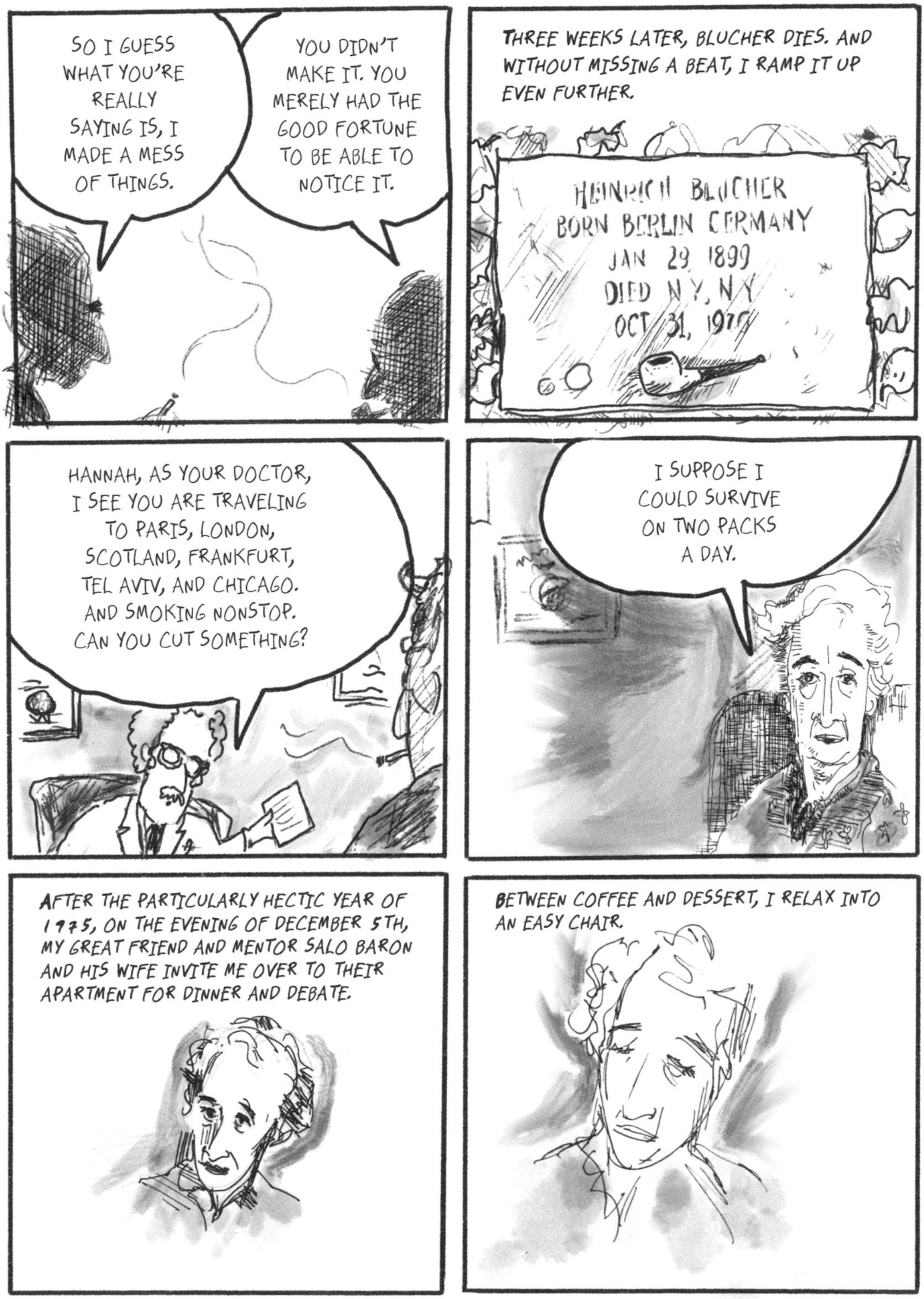
SO I GUESS WHAT YOU'RE REALLY SAYING IS, I MADE A MESS OF THINGS.
YOU DIDN'T MAKE IT. YOU MERELY HAD THE GOOD FORTUNE TO BE ABLE TO NOTICE IT.
THREE WEEKS LATER, BLUCHER DIES. AND WITHOUT MISSING A BEAT, I RAMP IT UP EVEN FURTHER.
HEINRICH BLUCHER
BORN BERLIN GERMANY
JAN 29 1899
DIED N.Y. N.Y.
HANNAH, AS YOUR DOCTOR, I SEE YOU ARE TRAVELING TO PARIS, LONDON, SCOTLAND, FRANKFURT, TEL AVIV, AND CHICAGO. AND SMOKING NONSTOP. CAN YOU CUT SOMETHING?
I SUPPOSE I COULD SURVIVE ON TWO PACKS A DAY.
AFTER THE PARTICULARLY HECTIC YEAR OF 1975, ON THE EVENING OF DECEMBER 5TH, MY GREAT FRIEND AND MENTOR SALO BARON AND HIS WIFE INVITE ME OVER TO THEIR APARTMENT FOR DINNER AND DEBATE.
BETWEEN COFFEE AND DESSERT, I RELAX INTO AN EASY CHAIR.

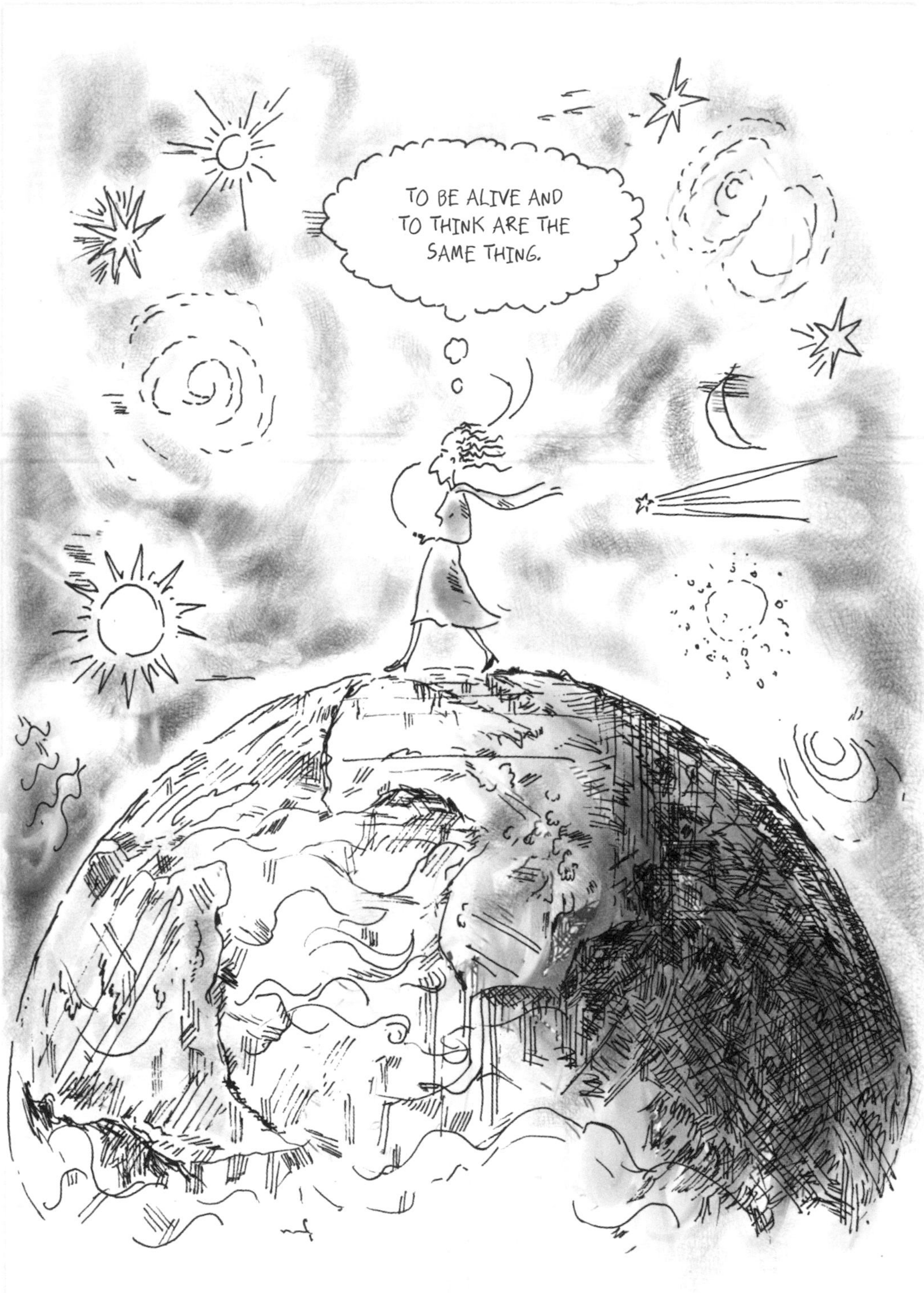
TO BE ALIVE AND
TO THINK ARE THE
SAME THING.

EPILOGUE

THE MORNING AFTER HANNAH DIES, THE FIRST SENTENCE OF "ON JUDGMENT," HER RETURN TO PHILOSOPHY, IS FOUND IN HER TYPEWRITER.

MARY MCCARTHY COLLECTS, EDITS, AND PUBLISHES THE DRAFTS OF HANNAH'S FINAL WORKS, CALLING THEM THE LIFE OF THE MIND.

THE TWO VOLUMES CONSTITUTE A FIELD GUIDE TO THE PROCESS OF THINKING-THROUGH IN THE PLURALITY-GUIDED PUBLIC WORLD.

FROM BEYOND THE GRAVE, HANNAH SAYS THAT ALTHOUGH LIVING IN THE WORLD OF PLURALITY AND NATALITY IS NO PICNIC, IF WE WANT TO AVOID AUSCHWITZ OR THE GULAG OR STONEWALL OR POL POT OR ATTICA OR ISIS, WE AS A SPECIES HAVE NO CHOICE BUT TO EMBRACE IT AND ENDURE IT.

IN OTHER WORDS, THERE IS NO SINGLE TRUTH, NO SILVER BULLET OF UNDERSTANDING TO GUIDE US, JUST A GLORIOUS, NEVERENDING MESS. THE NEVERENDING MESS OF TRUE HUMAN FREEDOM.

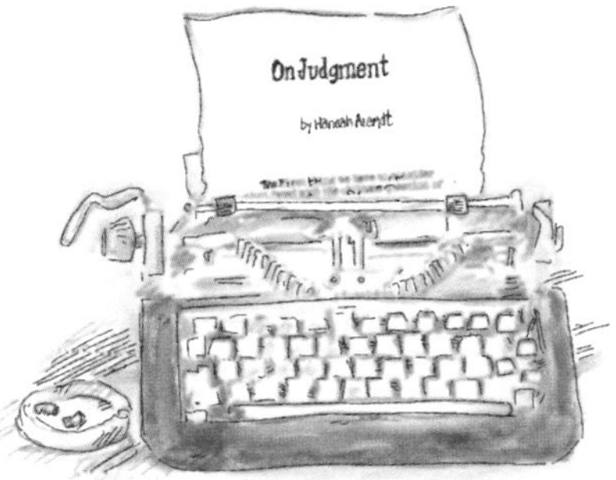
On Judgment
by Hannah Arendt

SUGGESTED READING

Aside from the lived moments of her life, Hannah Arendt lived in language. The web of words, both those that she herself wrote, and those that have been written about her, are an ever-expanding universe. While her masterwork, *The Origins of Totalitarianism*, is magisterial, as an introduction to Arendt it may prove to be too dense at first, which is why I recommend balancing writings from her own hand with critical interpretations. Back and forth.

Arendt was a conscious pariah, an ironist, bound by no rigid rules — ever — and a lightning rod for controversy. Which means that often, when one reads other people, often very smart people, writing about Arendt, one ends up learning a lot more about the writer than Arendt. So, back to Arendt. And then back to the critics, and so on.

Since Arendt's life and work are so vibrant, current, and fascinating, there is a wealth of online material available on her, much of it good, all of it passionate. From a rare movie of her speaking in German about her close friend Walter Benjamin at the Goethe Institute in New York in the mid-1960s, to a wonderful 2014 dramatic reading of her "We Refugees" essay from the Chicago Humanities Festival, to Jean-Luc Godard's (yes, that Jean-Luc Godard) strange and captivating staged reading on film, to the weekly *Amor Mundi* newsletter from Bard College's Hannah Arendt Center, to podcasts galore, Arendt is very much alive in the rapidly morphing pseudo-public space of cyberspace.

Enough throat-clearing. Here are some of the most notable sources I relied on in making this book, listed in order of salience, how much they stick.

The place to start for biography is Elizabeth Young-Bruehl's *Hannah Arendt: For the Love of the World*. A student and colleague of Hannah Arendt's, it came out just seven years after Arendt's death and is considered the standard biography. But very quickly, one can dive into dissenting opinions. Anne C. Heller's more recent *Hannah Arendt: A Life in Dark Times*, raised more than a few eyebrows by portraying Arendt as a gullible victim of the evil Heidegger, complete with scurrilous details that had stuffy philosophy departments all shook up. A fascinating contrast, or more accurately, counterpoint, is the sui generis *Unlearning with Hannah Arendt* by Marie Luise Knott, translated from German. This is a poetical, almost mystical, take on Arendt's primacy of story as the only thing we humans make, the stories others tell about our actions, to be precise. Spellbinding.

Then, it is great to dive into Arendt herself, usually, and thankfully, accompanied by sensible, even brilliant introductions. The collection of her essays, *Between Past and Future*, with an introduction by Jerome Kohn, shows how Arendt's passionate commitment to phenomenology and truth-telling guides her understanding of what it means to live. Each essay by Arendt is more thrilling than the one before as she talks about time and truth and love. Then there is what many consider Arendt's philosophical masterpiece, *The Human Condition*, the book she was considering dedicating to Heidegger, but thought better of. Here, her tripartite mind is in full flower, as she shows why things happen, what we do in life, how we know what we're doing, and the essential task of separating the public from the private in order to achieve freedom. Her *Eichmann in Jerusalem: A Report on the Banality of Evil*, is, whatever you think of her actual conclusions, a masterpiece of political journalism, a hybrid socio-intellectual screed agitprop that shows her "toosoonness" in all its fierce, possibly misguided glory.

A more recent addition to the canon of fascinating Arendt interpreters is Deborah Nelson's *Tough Enough*, a study of six virulently unsentimental woman thinkers of the past hundred or so years, which places Arendt as a linchpin, along with McCarthy.

And then, tapping into the world of Weimar thought, especially regarding revelation, religion, redemption, and all the things that were so central to that lost, last generation, *The Dialectics of Seeing: Walter Benjamin and the Arcades Project*, by Susan Buck-Morss opens a world, as does Eric Jacobsen's *Metaphysics of the Profane: The Political Theology of Walter Benjamin and Gershom Scholem*. (I know these are heavy-sounding books, but Benjamin is hard to do lite.) Which takes one to *Zohar: The Book of Splendor, Basic Readings from the Kabbalah*, edited by Scholem. And along the way, some of Arendt's American, or British-American, fans deserve a look, as Randall Jarrell's *Poetry and the Age* and just about anything by W. H. Auden factor into so much of Arendt's love of the irrational, or suprarational, power of poetic narrative. Then, to dip back into the philosophical wars, it is interesting to look at *History of Political Philosophy*, edited by Leo Strauss and Joseph Cropsey. Interestingly, Arendt doesn't even merit a mention, nor does she in Ernst Breisach's early 1960s overview, *Introduction to Modern Existentialism*, which seems to have everyone spouting Hannah Arendt's ideas, as long as they're men. The Hannah-Martin wars have been addressed directly in a few books that come to mind: *Stranger from Abroad: Hannah Arendt, Martin Heidegger, Friendship and Forgiveness*, Antonia Grunenberg's *Hannah Arendt and*

Martin Heidegger: History of a Love; for a rigorous philosophical take from a former student and philosopher, a man and a woman, there's the short but powerful *Heidegger, His Life and His Philosophy* by Alain Badiou and Barbara Cassin, translated by Susan Spitzer, introduction by Kenneth Reinhard. And that's just for starters.

I haven't even touched on Arendt's literary and critical writing, her biographical writings, her biography of her self-acknowledged "best friend who had been dead for two hundred years," Rahel Varnhagen, or her massive and wonderful correspondence with everyone from McCarthy and Blucher, to her other mentor figure German existential philosopher Karl Jaspers, as well as her political writings, journalism, and, well, you get the idea. A mind that wrestled with the world, and thanks to her passion and fury (and typing skills), still battles away.

Hannah
1925

ACKNOWLEDGMENTS

I've been supported on this journey by countless people who have contributed in so many different ways—providing wisdom, lodging, inspiration, suggestions, questions, answers, and much more—that has brought a wonderful community to this project, for which I am so thankful. Unfortunately I can only name a few names. Above all, my wife, Alex Sinclair, my first and possibly toughest editor, who endured my frequent disappearances into parallel universes (and my studio). Next, in no particular order: my agent, Jennifer Lyons; my editor, Nancy Miller, art director Patti Ratchford, Laura Phillips, and the whole team at Bloomsbury; Michael Garcia for invaluable enthusiasm, care, and production help—I literally could not have done this without you; Art Shay; Richard Shay; Jerome Kohn; Sam and Isabel Gross; Roger Berkowitz; Melvin Bukiet; Aron Packer and Lisa Zschunke; Gary Galindo-Guzman; Kathy Roeder and Stanleigh Morris; Lori Rotenberk; Robert Sabat; Roz Chast; Michael Maslin; Bob Eckstein, Pat Byrnes; Robert Mankoff; Jim Horowitz; Michael Tisserand; Jeremy Banx; Jay Boninsinga; Lorna Sinclair; Diana and David Ventura; my mom, Joan; my kids, Noah, Milo, and Ruby; Joel Freiberger; Nathan Tarcov; Bill Martin; Don Smith; Morris Parslow; Don Schultz; and, finally, of course, Hannah Arendt herself.

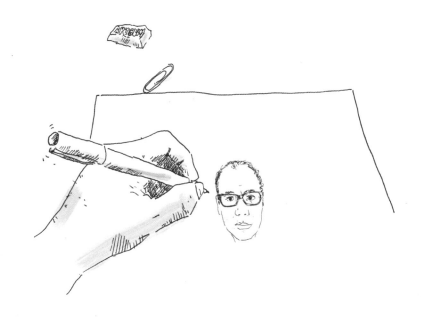

A Note on the Author

Ken Krimstein has published cartoons in the *New Yorker*, *Punch*, the *Wall Street Journal*, and more. He has written for New York *Observer*'s New Yorker's Diary and has published pieces on websites including McSweeney's Internet Tendency, Yankee Pot Roast, and Mr. Beller's Neighborhood. He is the author of *Kvetch as Kvetch Can*, and teaches at DePaul University and the School of the Art Institute of Chicago. He lives in Evanston, Illinois.